Pharmaceutical Calculations
13th Edition

$$= \sqrt{\dfrac{Ht\,(cm) \times Wt\,(kg)}{3600}}$$

$$0.693$$

$$\dfrac{165\,(cm) \times 65\,(kg)}{3600}$$

$$i = 0.097 \; MEq$$

$$= 1.7$$

$$\dfrac{1}{2}$$

80 mg%

40 mg/dL

Pharmaceutical Calculations

13th Edition

Howard C. Ansel, PhD
Professor and Dean Emeritus
College of Pharmacy
University of Georgia
Athens, Georgia

 Wolters Kluwer | Lippincott
Health | Williams & Wilkins

New Delhi · Philadelphia · Baltimore · New York · London
Buenos Aires · Hong Kong · Sydney · Tokyo

13th Edition
© 2010 Wolters Kluwer Health Lippincott Williams & Wilkins.
© 2006, 2001, 1996, 1991, 1986 by Lippincott Williams & Wilkins.

530 Walnut Street,
Philadelphia PA 19106
LWW.com

This textbook is intended to provide the *underpinnings of the methods* used in pharmaceutical calculations. The drugs, drug products, formulas, equations, uses, and doses are included in this textbook for the sole purpose of providing examples in the types of calculations described. The information *is not intended* for use in any practice or clinical application, nor should it be considered or construed as specific for any individual patient nor as a substitute for current drug package inserts. The author, editors, and publisher make no warranty, express or implied, with regard to the contents and use of this publication and are not responsible, as a matter of product liability, negligence, or otherwise, for any injury resulting from any material contained herein.

Care has been taken to confirm the accuracy of the information presented and to describe generally accepted practices. However, the authors, editors, and publisher are not responsible for errors or omissions or for any consequences from application of the information in this book and make no warranty, expressed or implied, with respect to the currency, completeness, or accuracy of the contents of the publication. Application of this information in a particular situation remains the professional responsibility of the practitioner; the clinical treatments described and recommended may not be considered absolute and universal recommendations.

The authors, editors, and publisher have exerted every effort to ensure that drug selection and dosage set forth in this text are in accordance with the current recommendations and practice at the time of publication. However, in view of ongoing research, changes in government regulations, and the constant flow of information relating to drug therapy and drug reactions, the reader is urged to check the package insert for each drug for any change in indications and dosage and for added warnings and precautions. This is particularly important when the recommended agent is a new or frequently employed drug.

Some drugs and medical devices presented in this publication have Food and Drug Administration (FDA) clearance for limited use in restricted research settings. It is the responsibility of the health care provider to ascertain the FDA status of each drug or device planned for use in his or her clinical practice.

First Indian Reprint, 2009
Second Indian Reprint, 2010
Third Indian Reprint, 2011

Indian Reprint ISBN-13: 978-81-8473-218-4
Original ISBN-13: 978-1-58255-837-0

This edition is for sale and distribution in India, Pakistan, Sri Lanka, Bangladesh, Nepal, Bhutan and the Maldives. Circulation outside this territory is illegal.

Published by Wolters Kluwer (India) Pvt. Ltd., New Delhi.

Printed and bound at Gopsons Papers Ltd.

Preface

The thirteenth edition of *Pharmaceutical Calculations* represents a thorough update of this textbook, which for more than six decades has met the needs of students in this important subject area. One of the most apparent changes in this edition is the inclusion of learning objectives for each chapter. The intent is not only to define the purpose and direct the student's focus but also to provide a basis for self-assessment following completion. Another important addition, appearing in the *Introduction*, presents a step-wise approach in solving calculations problems that should prove beneficial to students toward understanding and building confidence.

Throughout its history, one of the distinguishing characteristics of this textbook has been the inclusion of relevant background information to explain the pharmaceutical and/or clinical purpose underpinning each type of calculation. This practice has been continued, with new content in such areas as e-prescriptions; medication orders in nursing homes; hospice-care; patient self-administration of analgesia; intravenous infusion rate calculations for the critical care patient; patient conversions to alternative treatment plans; and other new and expanded areas.

Another traditional feature of this textbook has been the substantial use of examples and practice problems. New problems have been added to reflect current drugs in use, including products of biotechnology. For the first time, several problems are presented in multiple-choice format to reflect the method of testing used in some academic programs and employed on standardized examinations.

Several features that were introduced in the previous edition have been expanded, namely "Special Considerations," used to point out the specific relevance of a type of calculation to a pharmaceutics or clinical application; "Calculations Capsules," which present boxed summaries of the principle calculations in a chapter; and, "Case in Point," which present practical case studies requiring pharmaceutical calculations.

The author acknowledges the difficulty in arranging the sequence of chapters to suit the order used within each academic program. However, an attempt has been made to present a logical approach by placing the fundamentals of pharmaceutical calculations in the initial chapters, followed by chapters having a clinical- or patient-care context, then chapters that address formulation and compounding calculations, and, finally, chapters described by some reviewers as meeting a "special interest."

The concluding section of review problems contains all of the types of problems presented in the chapters and may be used both for review and for competency assessment. A new set of problems titled "Physicians' Medication Orders" is introduced.

Appendices include the common systems of measurement and intersystem conversion, select graphical methods, and a glossary of pharmaceutical dosage forms and associated routes of administration.

New Companion Website

Pharmaceutical Calculations, 13th edition, includes additional resources for both instructors and students, available on the book's companion website at http://thePoint.lww.com/Ansel13e.

Resources for Students and Instructors

- Interactive math calculations Quiz Bank, with more than 400 review problems and detailed solutions.
- Searchable Full Text Online

See the inside front cover for more details, including the passcode you will need to gain access to the website.

Acknowledgments

The author gratefully acknowledges the professional contributions to his revision of pharmacy practitioner-educators Warren Beach, Ted Chaffin, Ken Duke, Elaine Lust, and Flynn Warren for lending their expertise and time. Gratitude also is extended to Loyd V. Allen Jr. and Shelly J. Prince for their continued courtesy in allowing liberal use of their work published in the *International Journal of Pharmaceutical Compounding* and in *Pharmaceutical Calculations: The Pharmacist's Handbook*. The author thanks Barabara E. Lacher for the idea of incorporating learning objectives into the textbook and for other instructional materials. The assistance of James T. Stewart in providing access to current information from the *United States Pharmacopeia 31 – National Formulary 26* is acknowledged with appreciation.

Special tribute is paid to the memory of Mitchell J. Stoklosa who for more than 50 years co-authored and sustained this textbook. He was a scholar, dedicated educator, valued colleague, delightful human being, and treasured friend.

Gratitude is expressed to the reviewers for this revision whose experience was drawn upon during the planning process. The author appreciates their thoughtful analysis and constructive comments, which have enhanced this work. Finally, appreciation is extended to the exceptional people at Lippincott Williams & Wilkins for their masterful job in the design, preparation, and production of this revision.

Howard C. Ansel
Athens, Georgia

Contents

Introduction

Scope of Pharmaceutical Calculations

The use of calculations in pharmacy is varied and broad-based. It encompasses calculations performed by pharmacists in traditional as well as in specialized practice settings and within operational and research areas in industry, academia, and government. In the broad context, the scope of pharmaceutical calculations includes computations related to:

- chemical and physical properties of drug substances and pharmaceutical ingredients;
- biological activity and rates of drug absorption, bodily distribution, metabolism and excretion (pharmacokinetics);
- statistical data from basic research and clinical drug studies;
- pharmaceutical product development and formulation;
- prescriptions and medication orders including drug dosage, dosage regimens, and patient compliance;
- pharmacoeconomics; and other areas.

For each of these areas, there is a unique body of knowledge. Some areas are foundational whereas others are more specialized, constituting a distinct field of study. This textbook is foundational, providing the basic underpinnings of calculations applicable to pharmacy practice in community, institutional, and industrial settings.

In community pharmacies, pharmacists receive, fill, and dispense *prescriptions,* and provide relevant drug information to ensure their safe and effective use. Prescriptions may call for *prefabricated* pharmaceutical products manufactured in industry, or, they may call for individual components to be weighed or measured by the pharmacist and *compounded* into a finished product. In hospitals and other institutional settings, *medication orders* are entered on patients' charts. Prescriptions and medication orders may be handwritten by authorized health professionals or transmitted electronically.

In the preparation of pharmaceuticals, both medicinal and nonmedicinal materials are used. The medicinal components (*active therapeutic ingredients or ATIs*) provide the benefit desired.

The nonmedicinal (*pharmaceutical ingredients*) are included in a formulation to produce the desired pharmaceutical qualities, as physical form, chemical and physical stability, rate of drug release, appearance, and taste.

Whether a pharmaceutical product is produced in the industrial setting or prepared in a community or institutional pharmacy, pharmacists engage in calculations to achieve standards of quality. The difference is one of scale. In pharmacies, relatively small quantities of medications are prepared and dispensed for specific patients. In industry, *large-scale* production is designed to meet the requirements of pharmacies and their patients on a national and even international basis. The latter may involve the production of hundreds of thousands or even millions of dosage units of a specific drug product during a single production cycle. The preparation of the various dosage forms and drug delivery systems (defined in Appendix C), containing carefully calculated, measured, verified, and labeled quantities of ingredients enables accurate dosage administration.

A Step-Wise Approach Toward Pharmaceutical Calculations

Success in performing pharmaceutical calculations is based on:

*   an understanding of the purpose or goal of the problem;
*   an assessment of the arithmetic process required to reach the goal; and,
*   implementation of the correct arithmetic manipulations.

For many pharmacy students, particularly those without pharmacy experience, difficulty arises when the purpose or goal of a problem is not completely understood. The background information provided in each chapter is intended to assist the student in understanding the purpose of each area of calculations. Additionally, the following steps are suggested in addressing the calculations problems in this textbook as well as those encountered in pharmacy practice.

Step 1. Take the time necessary to carefully read and thoughtfully consider the problem *prior to* engaging in computations. An understanding of the purpose or goal of the problem and the types of calculations that are required will provide the needed direction and confidence.

Step 2. Estimate the dimension of the answer in both quantity and units of measure (e.g., milligrams) to satisfy the requirements of the problem. A section in Chapter 1 provides techniques for *estimation*.

Step 3. Perform the necessary calculations using the appropriate method both for efficiency and understanding. For some, this might require a step-wise approach whereas others may be capable of combining several arithmetic steps into one. Mathematical equations should be used only after the underlying principles of the equation are understood.

Step 4. Before assuming that an answer is correct, the problem should be read again and all calculations checked. In pharmacy practice, pharmacists are encouraged to have a professional colleague check all calculations prior to completing and dispensing a prescription or medication order. Further, if the process involves components to be weighed or measured, these procedures should be double-checked as well.

Step 5. Consider the *reasonableness* of the answer in terms of the numerical value, including the proper position of a decimal point, and the units of measure.

Fundamentals of Pharmaceutical Calculations

Objectives

Upon successful completion of this chapter, the student will be able to:

- Convert common fractions, decimal fractions, and percentages to their corresponding equivalent expressions and apply each in calculations.
- Utilize exponential notations in calculations.
- Apply the method of ratio and proportion in problem-solving.
- Apply the method of dimensional analysis in problem-solving.
- Demonstrate an understanding of significant figures.

Pharmaceutical calculations is the area of study that applies the basic principles of mathematics to the preparation and safe and effective use of pharmaceuticals. Mathematically, pharmacy students beginning use of this textbook are well prepared. It is the *application* of the mathematics that requires study.

This initial chapter is intended to remind students of some previously learned mathematics. Most students likely will progress rapidly through this chapter. A student's performance on the practice problems following each section can serve as the guide to the degree of refreshment required.

Common and Decimal Fractions

Common fractions are portions of a whole, expressed at $\frac{1}{3}$, $\frac{7}{8}$, and so forth. They are used only rarely in pharmacy calculations nowadays. It is recalled, that when adding or subtracting fractions, the use of a *common denominator* is required. The process of multiplying and dividing with fractions is recalled by the following examples.

Examples:

If the adult dose of a medication is 2 teaspoonsful (tsp.), calculate the dose for a child if it is $\frac{1}{4}$ of the adult dose.

$$\frac{1}{4} \times \frac{2 \text{ tsp.}}{1} = \frac{2}{4} = \frac{1}{2} \text{ tsp., } answer$$

If a child's dose of a cough syrup is $\frac{3}{4}$ teaspoonful and represents $\frac{1}{4}$ of the adult dose, calculate the corresponding adult dose.

$$\frac{3}{4} \text{ tsp.} \div \frac{1}{4} = \frac{3}{4} \text{ tsp.} \times \frac{4}{1} = \frac{3 \times 4}{4 \times 1} \text{ tsp.} = \frac{12}{4} \text{ tsp.} = 3 \text{ tsp., } answer$$

NOTE: When common fractions appear in a calculations problem, it is often best to convert them to decimal fractions before solving.

A *decimal fraction* is a fraction with a denominator of 10 or any power of 10 and is expressed decimally rather than as a common fraction. Thus, $\frac{1}{10}$ is expressed as 0.10 and $\frac{45}{100}$ as 0.45. It is important to include the zero before the decimal point. This draws attention to the decimal point and helps eliminate potential errors. Decimal fractions often are used in pharmaceutical calculations.

To convert a common fraction to a decimal fraction, divide the denominator into the numerator. Thus, $\frac{1}{8} = 1 \div 8 = 0.125$.

To convert a decimal fraction to a common fraction, express the decimal fraction as a ratio and reduce.

Thus, $0.25 = \frac{25}{100} = \frac{1}{4}$ or $\frac{1}{4}$.

Arithmetic Symbols

Table 1.1 presents common arithmetic symbols used in pharmaceutical calculations.

Percent

The term *percent* and its corresponding sign, %, mean "in a hundred." So, *50 percent (50%)* means 50 parts in each one hundred of the same item.

TABLE 1.1 SOME ARITHMETIC SYMBOLS USED IN PHARMACY[a]

SYMBOL	MEANING
%	percent; parts per hundred
‰	per mil; parts per thousand
+	plus; add; or positive
−	minus; subtract; or negative
±	add or subtract; plus or minus; positive or negative; expression of range, error, or tolerance
÷	divided by
/	divided by
×	times; multiply by
<	value on left is less than value on right (e.g., 5<6)
=	is equal to; equals
>	value on left is greater than value on right (e.g., 6>5)
≠	is not equal to; does not equal
≈	is approximately equal to
≡	is equivalent to
≤	value on left is less than or equal to value on right
≥	value on left is greater than or equal to value on right
.	decimal point
,	decimal marker (comma)
:	ratio symbol (e.g., *a:b*)
::	proportion symbol (e.g., *a:b::c:d*)
∝	varies as; is proportional to

[a] Table adapted from *Barron's Mathematics Study Dictionary* (Barron's Educational Series, Inc. Hauppauge, NY: 1998.) by Frank Tapson with the permission of the author. Many other symbols (either letters or signs) are used in pharmacy, as in the metric and apothecaries' systems of weights and measures, in statistics, in pharmacokinetics, in prescription writing, in physical pharmacy, and in other areas. Many of these symbols are included and defined elsewhere in this text.

TABLE 1.2 EQUIVALENCIES OF COMMON FRACTIONS, DECIMAL FRACTIONS, AND PERCENT

COMMON FRACTION	DECIMAL FRACTION	PERCENT (%)	COMMON FRACTION	DECIMAL FRACTION	PERCENT (%)
$\frac{1}{1000}$	0.001	0.1	$\frac{1}{5}$	0.2	20
$\frac{1}{500}$	0.002	0.2	$\frac{1}{4}$	0.25	25
$\frac{1}{100}$	0.01	1	$\frac{1}{3}$	0.333	33.3
$\frac{1}{50}$	0.02	2	$\frac{3}{8}$	0.375	37.5
$\frac{1}{40}$	0.025	2.5	$\frac{2}{5}$	0.4	40
$\frac{1}{30}$	0.033	3.3	$\frac{1}{2}$	0.5	50
$\frac{1}{25}$	0.04	4	$\frac{3}{5}$	0.6	60
$\frac{1}{15}$	0.067	6.7	$\frac{5}{8}$	0.625	62.5
$\frac{1}{10}$	0.1	10	$\frac{2}{3}$	0.667	66.7
$\frac{1}{9}$	0.111	11.1	$\frac{3}{4}$	0.75	75
$\frac{1}{8}$	0.125	12.5	$\frac{4}{5}$	0.8	80
$\frac{1}{7}$	0.143	14.3	$\frac{7}{8}$	0.875	87.5
$\frac{1}{6}$	0.167	16.7	$\frac{8}{9}$	0.889	88.9

Common fractions may be converted to percent by dividing the numerator by the denominator and multiplying by 100.

Example:

Convert $\frac{3}{8}$ to percent.

$$\frac{3}{8} \times 100 = 37.5\%, answer.$$

Decimal fractions may be converted to percent by multiplying by 100.

Example:

Convert 0.125 to percent.

$$0.125 \times 100 = 12.5\%, answer.$$

Examples of equivalent expressions of common fractions, decimal fractions, and percent are shown in Table 1.2. A useful exercise is to add to the content of this table by working with common fractions that are not listed (e.g., $\frac{1}{400}$, $\frac{1}{60}$, etc.).

PRACTICE PROBLEMS

1. How many 0.000065-gram doses can be made from 0.130 gram of a drug?

2. Give the decimal fraction and percent equivalents for each of the following common fractions:
   (a) $\frac{1}{35}$
   (b) $\frac{3}{7}$
   (c) $\frac{1}{250}$
   (d) $\frac{1}{400}$

3. If a clinical study of a new drug demonstrated that the drug met the effectiveness criteria in 646 patients of the 942 patients enrolled in the study, express these results as a decimal fraction and as a percent.

4. A pharmacist had 3 ounces of hydromorphone hydrochloride. He used the following:
   $\frac{1}{8}$ ounce
   $\frac{1}{4}$ ounce
   $1\frac{1}{2}$ ounces

   How many ounces of hydromorphone hydrochloride were left?

5. A pharmacist had 5 grams of codeine sulfate. He used it in preparing the following:

8 capsules each containing 0.0325 gram
12 capsules each containing 0.015 gram
18 capsules each containing 0.008 gram

How many grams of codeine sulfate were left after he had prepared the capsules?

6. The literature for a pharmaceutical product states that 26 patients of the 2,103 enrolled in a clinical study reported headache after taking the product. Calculate (a) the decimal fraction and (b) the percentage of patients reporting this adverse response.

Exponential Notation

Many physical and chemical measurements deal with either very large or very small numbers. Because it often is difficult to handle numbers of such magnitude in performing even the simplest arithmetic operations, it is best to use exponential notation or *powers of 10* to express them. Thus, we may express *121* as *1.21×10^2*, *1210* as *1.21×10^3*, and *1,210,000* as *1.21×10^6*. Likewise, we may express *0.0121* as *1.21×10^{-2}*, *0.00121* as *1.21×10^{-3}*, and *0.00000121* as *1.21×10^{-6}*.

When numbers are written in this manner, the first part is called the **coefficient**, customarily written with one figure to the left of the decimal point. The second part is the **exponential factor** or *power of 10*.

The exponent represents the number of places that the decimal point has been moved—positive to the left and negative to the right—to form the exponential. Thus, when we convert *19,000* to *1.9×10^4*, we move the decimal point 4 places to the left; hence the exponent 4. And when we convert *0.0000019* to *1.9×10^{-6}*, we move the decimal point 6 places to the right; hence the *negative* exponent $^{-6}$.

In the *multiplication* of exponentials, the exponents are *added*. For example, $10^2 \times 10^4 = 10^6$. In the multiplication of numbers that are expressed in exponential form, the *coefficients* are multiplied in the usual manner, and then this product is multiplied by the power of *10* found by algebraically *adding* the exponents.

Examples:

$$(2.5 \times 10^2) \times (2.5 \times 10^4) \quad = 6.25 \times 10^6, \text{ or } 6.3 \times 10^6$$
$$(2.5 \times 10^2) \times (2.5 \times 10^{-4}) = 6.25 \times 10^{-2}, \text{ or } 6.3 \times 10^{-2}$$
$$(5.4 \times 10^2) \times (4.5 \times 10^3) \quad = 24.3 \times 10^5 = 2.4 \times 10^6$$

In the *division* of exponentials, the exponents are *subtracted*. For example, $10^2 \div 10^5 = 10^{-3}$. In the division of numbers that are expressed in exponential form, the *coefficients* are divided in the usual way, and the result is multiplied by the power of *10* found by algebraically *subtracting* the exponents.

Examples:

$$(7.5 \times 10^5) \quad \div (2.5 \times 10^3) \quad = \quad 3.0 \times 10^2$$
$$(7.5 \times 10^{-4}) \div (2.5 \times 10^6) \quad = \quad 3.0 \times 10^{-10}$$
$$(2.8 \times 10^{-2}) \div (8.0 \times 10^{-6}) = 0.35 \times 10^4 = 3.5 \times 10^3$$

Note that in each of these examples, the result is rounded off to the number of *significant figures* contained in the *least* accurate factor, and it is expressed with only one figure to the left of the decimal point.

In the *addition* and *subtraction* of exponentials, the expressions must be changed (by moving the decimal points) to forms having any common power of 10, and then the coefficients only are added or subtracted. The result should be rounded off to the number of *decimal places* contained in the *least* precise component, and it should be expressed with only one figure to the left of the decimal point.

Examples:

$$(1.4 \times 10^4) + (5.1 \times 10^3)$$

$$
\begin{array}{rcl}
& 1.4 & \times \; 10^4 \\
5.1 \times 10^3 = & 0.51 & \times \; 10^4 \\
\hline
\text{Total:} & 1.91 & \times \; 10^4, \text{ or } 1.9 \times 10^4, \textit{answer.}
\end{array}
$$

$$(1.4 \times 10^4) - (5.1 \times 10^3)$$

$$
\begin{array}{rcl}
1.4 \times 10^4 = & 14.0 & \times \; 10^3 \\
& -5.1 & \times \; 10^3 \\
\hline
\text{Difference:} & 8.9 & \times \; 10^3, \textit{answer.}
\end{array}
$$

$$(9.83 \times 10^3) + (4.1 \times 10^1) + (2.6 \times 10^3)$$

$$
\begin{array}{rcl}
& 9.83 & \times \; 10^3 \\
4.1 \times 10^1 = & 0.041 & \times \; 10^3 \\
& 2.6 & \times \; 10^3 \\
\hline
\text{Total: } 12.471 & \times \; 10^3, \text{ or} \\
12.5 & \times \; 10^3 = 1.25 \times 10^4, \textit{answer.}
\end{array}
$$

PRACTICE PROBLEMS

1. Write each of the following in exponential form:
    (a) 12,650
    (b) 0.0000000055
    (c) 451
    (d) 0.065
    (e) 625,000,000

2. Write each of the following in the usual numeric form:
    (a) 4.1×10^6
    (b) 3.65×10^{-2}
    (c) 5.13×10^{-6}
    (d) 2.5×10^5
    (e) 8.6956×10^3

3. Find the product:
    (a) $(3.5 \times 10^3) \times (5.0 \times 10^4)$
    (b) $(8.2 \times 10^2) \times (2.0 \times 10^{-6})$
    (c) $(1.5 \times 10^{-6}) \times (4.0 \times 10^6)$
    (d) $(1.5 \times 10^3) \times (8.0 \times 10^4)$
    (e) $(7.2 \times 10^5) \times (5.0 \times 10^{-3})$

4. Find the quotient:
    (a) $(9.3 \times 10^5) \div (3.1 \times 10^2)$
    (b) $(3.6 \times 10^{-4}) \div (1.2 \times 10^6)$
    (c) $(3.3 \times 10^7) \div (1.1 \times 10^{-2})$

5. Find the sum:
    (a) $(9.2 \times 10^3) + (7.6 \times 10^4)$
    (b) $(1.8 \times 10^{-6}) + (3.4 \times 10^{-5})$
    (c) $(4.9 \times 10^2) + (2.5 \times 10^3)$

6. Find the difference:
    (a) $(6.5 \times 10^6) - (5.9 \times 10^4)$
    (b) $(8.2 \times 10^{-3}) - (1.6 \times 10^{-3})$
    (c) $(7.4 \times 10^3) - (4.6 \times 10^2)$

Ratio, Proportion, and Variation

Ratio

The relative magnitude of two quantities is called their **ratio**. Since a ratio relates the relative value of two numbers, it resembles a common fraction except in the way in which it is presented. Whereas a fraction is presented as, for example, $\frac{1}{2}$, a ratio is presented as 1:2 and is not read as "one half," but rather as "one is to two."

All the rules governing common fractions equally apply to a ratio. Of particular importance is the principle that *if the two terms of a ratio are multiplied or are divided by the same number, the value is unchanged,* the *value* being the quotient of the first term divided by the second. For example, the ratio *20 :4* or $^{20}\!/_{4}$ has a value of 5; if both terms are divided by 2, the ratio becomes *10 :2* or $^{10}\!/_{2}$, again the value of 5.

The terms of a ratio must be of the same kind, for the *value* of a ratio is an abstract number expressing how many *times* greater or smaller the first term (or numerator) is than the second term (or denominator).[a] The terms may themselves be abstract numbers, or they may be concrete numbers of the same denomination. Thus, we can have a ratio of *20 to 4* ($^{20}\!/_{4}$) or *20 grams to 4 grams* (20 grams/4 grams).

When two ratios have the same value, they are *equivalent*. An interesting fact about equivalent ratios is that the *product of the numerator of the one and the denominator of the other always equals the product of the denominator of the one and the numerator of the other; that is, the cross products are equal:*

Because $^{2}\!/_{4} = {}^{4}\!/_{8}$,

2×8 (or 16) $= 4 \times 4$ (or 16).

It is also true that *if two ratios are equal, their reciprocals are equal:*

Because $^{2}\!/_{4} = {}^{4}\!/_{8}$, then $^{4}\!/_{2} = {}^{8}\!/_{4}$.

We discover further that the *numerator of the one fraction equals the product of its denominator and the other fraction:*

If $^{6}\!/_{15} = {}^{2}\!/_{5}$,

then $6 = 15 \times {}^{2}\!/_{5}$ $\left(\text{or } \dfrac{15 \times 2}{5}\right) = 6,$

and $2 = 5 \times {}^{6}\!/_{15}$ $\left(\text{or } \dfrac{5 \times 6}{15}\right) = 2.$

And the denominator of the one equals the quotient of its numerator divided by the other fraction:

$15 = 6 \div {}^{2}\!/_{5}$ (or $6 \times {}^{5}\!/_{2}$) $= 15,$

and $5 = 2 \div {}^{6}\!/_{15}$ (or $2 \times {}^{15}\!/_{6}$) $= 5.$

An extremely useful practical application of these facts is found in *proportion.*

Proportion

A **proportion** is the expression of the equality of two ratios. It may be written in any one of three standard forms:

(1) $a:b = c:d$

(2) $a:b :: c:d$

(3) $\dfrac{a}{b} = \dfrac{c}{d}$

---

[a] The ratio of *1 gallon to 3 pints* is not *1 :3,* for the gallon contains 8 pints, and the ratio therefore is *8 :3*.

Each of these expressions is read: *a is to b as c is to d*, and *a* and *d* are called the *extremes* (meaning "outer members") and *b* and *c* the *means* ("middle members").

In any proportion, *the product of the extremes is equal to the product of the means*. This principle allows us to find the missing term of any proportion when the other three terms are known. If the missing term is a *mean*, it will be *the product of the extremes divided by the given mean*, and if it is an *extreme*, it will be *the product of the means divided by the given extreme*. Using this information, we may derive the following fractional equations:

$$\text{If } \frac{a}{b} = \frac{c}{d}, \text{ then}$$

$$a = \frac{bc}{d}, b = \frac{ad}{c}, c = \frac{ad}{b}, \text{ and } d = \frac{bc}{a}.$$

In a proportion that is properly set up, the position of the unknown term does not matter. However, some persons prefer to place the unknown term in the fourth position—that is, in the denominator of the second ratio. *It important to label the units in each position (e.g., mL, mg) to ensure the proper relationship between the ratios of a proportion.*

The application of ratio and proportion enables the solution to many of the pharmaceutical calculation problems in this text and in pharmacy practice.

Examples:

If 3 tablets contain 975 milligrams of aspirin, how many milligrams should be contained in 12 tablets?

$$\frac{3 \text{ (tablets)}}{12 \text{ (tablets)}} = \frac{975 \text{ (milligrams)}}{x \text{ (milligrams)}}$$

$$x = \frac{12 \times 975}{3} \text{ milligrams} = 3900 \text{ milligrams, } \textit{answer.}$$

If 3 tablets contain 975 milligrams of aspirin, how many tablets should contain 3900 milligrams?

$$\frac{3 \text{ (tablets)}}{x \text{ (tablets)}} = \frac{975 \text{ (milligrams)}}{3900 \text{ (milligrams)}}$$

$$x = 3 \times \frac{3900}{975} \text{ tablets} = 12 \text{ tablets, } \textit{answer.}$$

If 12 tablets contain 3900 milligrams of aspirin, how many milligrams should 3 tablets contain?

$$\frac{12 \text{ (tablets)}}{3 \text{ (tablets)}} = \frac{3900 \text{ (milligrams)}}{x \text{ (milligrams)}}$$

$$x = 3 \times \frac{3900}{12} \text{ milligrams} = 975 \text{ milligrams, } \textit{answer.}$$

If 12 tablets contain 3900 milligrams of aspirin, how many tablets should contain 975 milligrams?

$$\frac{12 \text{ (tablets)}}{x \text{ (tablets)}} = \frac{3900 \text{ (milligrams)}}{975 \text{ (milligrams)}}$$

$$x = \frac{12 \times 975}{3900} \text{ tablets} = 3 \text{ tablets, } \textit{answer.}$$

Proportions need not contain whole numbers. If common or decimal fractions are supplied in the data, they may be included in the proportion without changing the method. For ease of calculation, it is recommended that common fractions be converted to decimal fractions prior to setting up the proportion.

Example:

If 30 milliliters (mL) represent $\frac{1}{6}$ of the volume of a prescription, how many milliliters will represent $\frac{1}{4}$ of the volume?

$$\frac{1}{6} = 0.167 \text{ and } \frac{1}{4} = 0.25$$
$$\frac{0.167 \text{ (volume)}}{0.25 \text{ (volume)}} = \frac{30 \text{ (mL)}}{x \text{ (mL)}}$$
$$x = 44.91 \text{ or} \approx 45 \text{ mL}, \text{ answer.}$$

Variation

In the preceding examples, the relationships were clearly *proportional*. Most pharmaceutical calculations deal with simple, *direct* relationships: twice the cause, double the effect, and so on. Occasionally, they deal with *inverse* relationships: twice the cause, half the effect, and so on, as when you *decrease* the strength of a solution by *increasing* the amount of diluent.[b]
Here is a typical problem involving inverse proportion:

If 10 pints of a 5% solution are diluted to 40 pints, what is the percentage strength of the dilution?

$$\frac{10 \text{ (pints)}}{40 \text{ (pints)}} = \frac{x \text{ (%)}}{5 \text{ (%)}}$$
$$x = \frac{10 \times 5}{40}\% = 1.25\%, \text{ answer.}$$

Dimensional Analysis

When performing pharmaceutical calculations, some students prefer to use a method termed **dimensional analysis** (also known as **factor analysis, factor-label method,** or **unit-factor method**). This method involves the logical sequencing and placement of a series of ratios (termed *factors*) into an equation. The ratios are prepared from the given data as well as from selected conversion factors and contain both arithmetic quantities and their units of measurement. Some terms are inverted (to their reciprocals) to permit the cancellation of like units in the numerator(s) and denominator(s) and leave only the desired terms of the answer. One advantage of using dimensional analysis is the consolidation of several arithmetic steps into a single equation.
In solving problems by dimensional analysis, the student unfamiliar with the process should consider the following steps:[1,2]

Step 1. Identify the given quantity and its unit of measurement.
Step 2. Identify the wanted unit of the answer.
Step 3. Establish the *unit path* (to go from the given quantity and unit to the arithmetic answer in the wanted unit), and identify the conversion factors needed. This might include:
   (a) a conversion factor for the given quantity and unit, and/or
   (b) a conversion factor to arrive at the wanted unit of the answer.
Step 4. Set up the ratios in the unit path such that cancellation of units of measurement in the numerators and denominators will retain only the desired unit of the answer.
Step 5. Perform the computation by multiplying the numerators, multiplying the denominators, and dividing the product of the numerators by the product of the denominators.

---

[b] In expressing an inverse proportion, we must not forget that *every* proportion asserts the equivalence of two ratios; therefore, the numerators must both be smaller or both larger than their respective denominators.

CALCULATIONS CAPSULE

Ratio and Proportion

- A *ratio* expresses the relative magnitude of two like quantities (e.g., 1:2, expressed as "1 to 2.")
- A *proportion* expresses the equality of two ratios (e.g., 1:2 = 2:4).
- The four terms of a proportion are stated as:

$$a{:}b = c{:}d, \text{ or, } a{:}b :: c{:}d, \text{ or } \frac{a}{b} = \frac{c}{d}$$

  and expressed as "*a* is to *b* as *c* is to *d*."
- Given three of the four terms of a proportion, the value of the fourth, or missing, term may be calculated.
- The ratio-and-proportion method is a useful tool in solving many pharmaceutical calculation problems.

The general scheme shown here and in the "Calculations Capsule: Dimensional Analysis" may be helpful in using the method.

Unit Path

Given Quantity	Conversion Factor for Given Quantity	Conversion Factor for Wanted Quantity	Conversion Computation	Wanted Quantity
				=

Example Calculations Using Dimensional Analysis

How many fluidounces (fl. oz.) are there in 2.5 liters (L)?

Step 1. The given quantity is *2.5 L.*
Step 2. The wanted unit for the answer is *fluidounces.*
Step 3. The conversion factors needed are those that will take us from liters to fluidounces. As the student will later learn, these conversion factors are:
   1 liter = 1000 mL (to convert the given 2.5 L to milliliters), and
   1 fluidounce = 29.57 mL (to convert milliliters to fluidounces)
Step 4. The unit path setup:

Unit Path

Given Quantity	Conversion Factor for Given Quantity	Conversion Factor for Wanted Quantity	Conversion Computation	Wanted Quantity
2.5 L	1000 mL / 1 L	1 fl. oz. / 29.57 mL		=

Note: The unit path is set up such that all units of measurement will cancel out except for the unit wanted in the answer, *fluidounces,* which is placed in the numerator.

Step 5. Perform the computation:

Unit Path

Given Quantity	Conversion Factor for Given Quantity	Conversion Factor for Wanted Quantity	Conversion Computation	Wanted Quantity

$$\frac{2.5\ \cancel{L}}{} \left|\ \frac{1000\ \cancel{mL}}{1\ \cancel{L}}\ \right|\ \frac{1\ \text{fl. oz.}}{29.57\ \cancel{mL}}\ \left|\ \frac{2.5 \times 1000 \times 1}{1 \times 29.57} = \frac{2500}{29.57}\ \right| = 84.55\ \text{fl. oz.}$$

or

$$2.5\ \cancel{L} \times \frac{1000\ \cancel{mL}}{1\ \text{L}} \times \frac{1\ \text{fl. oz.}}{29.57\ \cancel{mL}} = \frac{2.5 \times 1000 \times 1}{1 \times 29.57} = \frac{2500}{29.57} = 84.55\ \text{fl. oz.}$$

Note: The student may wish to see the problem solved by ratio and proportion:

Step 1.

$$\frac{1\ (\text{L})}{2.5\ (\text{L})} = \frac{1000\ (\text{mL})}{x\ (\text{mL})}; x = 2500\ \text{mL}$$

Step 2.

$$\frac{29.57\ (\text{mL})}{2500\ (\text{mL})} = \frac{1\ (\text{fl. oz.})}{x\ (\text{fl. oz.})}$$
$$x = 84.55\ \text{fl. oz.,}\ \textit{answer.}$$

A medication order calls for 1000 milliliters of a dextrose intravenous infusion to be administered over an 8-hour period. Using an intravenous administration set that delivers 10 drops/milliliter, how many drops per minute should be delivered to the patient?

Solving by dimensional analysis:

$$8\ \text{hours} = 480\ \text{minutes (min.)}$$

CALCULATIONS CAPSULE

Dimensional Analysis

- An alternative method to ratio and proportion in solving pharmaceutical calculation problems.
- The method involves the logical sequencing and placement of a series of ratios to consolidate multiple arithmetic steps into a single equation.
- By applying select conversion factors in the equation—some as reciprocals—unwanted units of measure cancel out, leaving the arithmetic result and desired unit.
- Dimensional analysis scheme:

Unit Path

Given Quantity	Conversion Factor for Given Quantity	Conversion Factor for Wanted Quantity	Conversion Computation	Wanted Quantity

$$\frac{}{}\ \left|\ \frac{}{}\ \right|\ \frac{}{}\ \left|\ \frac{}{}\ \right| =$$

$$1000 \; \cancel{mL} \times \frac{10 \; drops}{1 \; \cancel{mL}} \times \frac{1}{480 \; min.} = 20.8 \; or \; 21 \; drops \; per \; minute, \; answer.$$

Note: "Drops" was placed in the numerator and "minutes" in the denominator to arrive at the answer in the desired term, *drops per minute*.

The student may wish to see this problem solved by ratio and proportion:

Step 1.

$$\frac{480 \; (min.)}{1 \; (min.)} = \frac{1000 \; (mL)}{x \; (mL)}; x = 2.08 \; mL$$

Step 2.

$$\frac{1 \; (mL)}{2.08 \; (mL)} = \frac{10 \; (drops)}{x \; (drops)}; x = 20.8 \; mL \; or \; 21 \; drops \; per \; minute, \; answer.$$

PRACTICE PROBLEMS

1. If an insulin injection contains 100 units of insulin in each milliliter, how many milliliters should be injected to receive 40 units of insulin?

2. Digoxin (LANOXIN) pediatric elixir contains 0.05 mg of digoxin in each milliliter of elixir. How many milligrams of digoxin would be administered with a dose of 0.6 mL?

3. In a clinical study, a drug produced drowsiness in 30 of the 1500 patients studied. How many patients of a certain pharmacy could expect similar effects, based on a patient count of 100?

4. A formula for 1250 tablets contains 6.25 grams (g) of diazepam. How many grams of diazepam should be used in preparing 350 tablets?

5. If 100 capsules contain 500 mg of an active ingredient, how many milligrams of the ingredient will 48 capsules contain?

6. Each tablet of TYLENOL WITH CO-DEINE contains 30 mg of codeine phosphate and 300 mg of acetaminophen. By taking two tablets daily for a week, how many milligrams of each drug would the patient take?

7. A cough syrup contains 10 mg of dextromethorphan hydrobromide per 5 mL. How many milligrams of the drug are contained in a 120-mL container of the syrup?

8. If an intravenous fluid is adjusted to deliver 15 mg of medication to a patient per hour, how many milligrams of medication are delivered per minute?

9. The biotechnology drug filgrastim (NEUPOGEN) is available in vials containing 480 micrograms (mcg) of filgrastim per 0.8 mL. How many micrograms of the drug would be administered by each 0.5 mL injection?

10. A prescription drug cost the pharmacist $42.00 for a bottle of 100 tablets. What would be the cost for 24 tablets?

11. How many 0.1-mg tablets will contain the same amount of drug as 50 tablets, each of which contains 0.025 mg of the identical drug?

12. Acyclovir (ZOVIRAX) suspension contains 200 mg of acyclovir in each 5 mL. How many milligrams of acyclovir are contained in a pint (473 mL) of suspension?

13. A metered dose inhaler contains 225 mg of metaproterenol sulfate, which is sufficient for 300 inhalations. How many milligrams of metaproterenol

sulfate would be administered in each inhalation?

14. A pediatric vitamin drug product contains the equivalent of 0.5 mg of fluoride ion in each milliliter. How many milligrams of fluoride ion would be provided by a dropper that delivers 0.6 mL?

15. If a pediatric vitamin contains 1500 units of vitamin A per milliliter of solution, how many units of vitamin A would be administered to a child given 2 drops of the solution from a dropper calibrated to deliver 20 drops per milliliter of solution?

16. An elixir contains 40 mg of drug in each 5 mL. How many milligrams of the drug would be used in preparing 4000 mL of the elixir?

17. An elixir of ferrous sulfate contains 220 mg of ferrous sulfate in each 5 mL. If each milligram of ferrous sulfate contains the equivalent of 0.2 mg of elemental iron, how many milligrams of elemental iron would be represented in each 5 mL of the elixir?

18. At a constant temperature, the volume of a gas varies inversely with the pressure. If a gas occupies a volume of 1000 mL at a pressure of 760 mm, what is its volume at a pressure of 570 mm?

19. If an ophthalmic solution contains 1 mg of dexamethasone phosphate in each milliliter of solution, how many milligrams of dexamethasone phosphate would be contained in 2 drops if the eyedropper used delivered 20 drops per milliliter?

20. A 15-mL package of nasal spray delivers 20 sprays per milliliter of solution, with each spray containing 1.5 mg of drug. (a) How many total sprays will the package deliver? (b) How many milligrams of drug are contained in the 15-mL package of the spray?

21. A penicillin V potassium preparation provides 400,000 units of activity in each 250-mg tablet. How many total units of activity would a patient receive from taking four tablets a day for 10 days?

22. If a 5-g packet of a potassium supplement provides 20 milliequivalents of potassium ion and 3.34 milliequivalents of chloride ion, (a) how many grams of the powder would provide 6 milliequivalents of potassium ion, and (b) how many milliequivalents of chloride ion would be provided by this amount of powder?

23. If a potassium chloride elixir contains 20 milliequivalents of potassium ion in each 15 mL of elixir, how many milliliters will provide 25 milliequivalents of potassium ion to the patient?

24. The blood serum concentration of the antibacterial drug ciprofloxacin increases proportionately with the dose of drug administered. If a 250-mg dose of the drug results in a serum concentration of 1.2 micrograms of drug per milliliter of serum, how many micrograms of drug would be expected per milliliter of serum following a dose of 500 mg of drug?

25. The dosage of the drug thiabendazole (MINTEZOL) is determined in direct proportion to a patient's weight. If the dose of the drug for a patient weighing 150 pounds is 1.5 grams, what would be the dose for a patient weighing 110 pounds?

26. If 0.5 mL of a mumps virus vaccine contains 5000 units of antigen, how many units would be present in each milliliter if the 0.5 mL of vaccine was diluted to 2 mL with water for injection?

27. A sample of Oriental ginseng contains 0.4 mg of active constituents in each 100 mg of powdered plant. How many milligrams of active constituents would be present in 15 mg of powdered plant?

Alligation

Alligation is an arithmetic method of solving problems relating mixtures of components of different strengths. There are two types of alligation: *alligation medial* and *alligation alternate*.

Alligation medial may be used to determine the strength of a common ingredient in a mixture of two or more preparations. For example, if a pharmacist mixed together known volumes of two or more solutions containing known amounts of a common ingredient, the strength of that ingredient in the resulting mixture can be determined by alligation medial.

Alligation alternate may be used to determine the proportion or quantities of two or more components to combine in order to prepare a mixture of a desired strength. For example, if a pharmacist wished to prepare a solution of a specified strength by combining two or more other solutions of differing concentrations of the same ingredient, the proportion or volumes of each solution to use may be determined by alligation alternate.

Alligation medial and alligation alternate may be used as options in solving a number of pharmaceutical calculations problems. The methods and problem examples are presented in Chapter 15.

Significant Figures

When we *count* objects accurately, *every* figure in the numeral expressing the total number of objects must be taken at its face value. Such figures may be said to be *absolute*. When we record a *measurement,* the last figure to the right must be taken to be an *approximation,* an admission that the limit of possible precision or of necessary accuracy has been reached and that any further figures to the right would not be significant—that is, either meaningless or, for a given purpose, needless.

A denominate number, like 325 *grams,* is interpreted as follows: The 3 means *300 grams,* neither more nor less, and the 2 means *exactly 20 grams more;* but the final 5 means *approximately 5 grams more,* i.e., *5 grams plus or minus some fraction of a gram.* Whether this fraction is, for a given purpose, negligible depends on how precisely the quantity was (or is to be) weighed.

Significant figures, then, are consecutive figures that express the value of a denominate number accurately enough for a given purpose. The accuracy varies with the number of significant figures, which are all absolute in value except the last, and this is properly called *uncertain.*

Any of the digits in a valid denominate number must be regarded as significant. Whether *zero* is significant, however, depends on its position or on known facts about a given number. The interpretation of *zero* may be summed up as follows:

CALCULATIONS CAPSULE

Significant Figures

- Digits other than zero are significant.
- A zero between digits is significant.
- Final zeros after a decimal point are significant.
- Zeros used only to show the location of the decimal point are not significant.

1. Any zero between digits is significant.
2. Initial zeros to the left of the first digit are never significant; they are included merely to show the location of the decimal point and thus give place value to the digits that follow.
3. One or more final zeros to the right of the decimal point may be taken to be significant.

Examples:

Assuming that the following numbers are all denominate:

1. In *12.5*, there are *three* significant figures; in *1.256*, *four* significant figures; and in *102.56*, *five* significant figures.
2. In *0.5*, there is *one* significant figure. The digit 5 tells us how many *tenths* we have. The nonsignificant *0* simply calls attention to the decimal point.
3. In *0.05*, there is still only *one* significant figure, as there is in *0.005*.
4. In *0.65*, there are *two* significant figures, and likewise *two* in *0.065* and *0.0065*.
5. In *0.0605*, there are *three* significant figures. The first *0* calls attention to the decimal point, the second *0* shows the number of places to the right of the decimal point occupied by the remaining figures, and the third *0* significantly contributes to the value of the number. In *0.06050*, there are *four* significant figures, because the final *0* also contributes to the value of the number.

One of the factors determining the degree of approximation to perfect measurement is the precision of the instrument used. It would be incorrect to claim that *7.76 milliliters* had been measured in a graduate calibrated in units of *1 milliliter*, or that *25.562 grams* had been weighed on a balance sensitive to 0.01 gram.

We must clearly distinguish *significant figures* from *decimal places*. When recording a measurement, the number of decimal places we include indicates *the degree of precision with which the measurement has been made*, whereas the number of significant figures retained indicates *the degree of accuracy* that is sufficient for a given purpose.

Sometimes we are asked to record a value "correct to (so many) decimal places." We should never confuse this familiar expression with the expression "correct to (so many) significant figures." For example, if the value 27.625918 is rounded to *five decimal places*, it is written 27.62592; but when this value is rounded to *five significant figures*, it is written 27.626.

Rules for Rounding

1. When rounding a measurement, retain as many figures as will give only one *uncertain* figure. For example, in using a ruler calibrated only in full centimeter units, it would be correct to record a measurement of 11.3 centimeters but not 11.32 centimeters, because the 3 (tenths) is uncertain and no figure should follow it.
2. When eliminating superfluous figures following a calculation, add 1 to the last figure retained in a calculation if it is 5 or more. For example, 2.43 may be rounded off to 2.4, but 2.46 should be rounded off to 2.5.
3. When adding or subtracting *approximate* numbers, include only as many decimal places as are in the number with the *fewest* decimal places. For example, when adding 162.4 grams + 0.489 grams + 0.1875 grams + 120.78 grams, the sum is 283.8565 grams, but the rounded sum is 283.9 grams. However, when an instrument has the capability to weigh precisely all the quantities in such a calculation, rounding may be deemed inappropriate.

    In this regard, *there is an assumption made in pharmaceutical calculations that all measurements in the filling of a prescription or in compounding a formula are performed with equal precision by the pharmacist.* Thus, for example, if the quantities 5.5 grams, 0.01 gram, and 0.005 gram are specified in a formula, they may be added as if they are precise weights, with a sum of 5.515 grams.

4. When multiplying or dividing two approximate numbers, retain no more significant figures than the number having the fewest significant figures. For example, if multiplying 1.6437 grams by 0.26, the answer may be rounded from the calculated 0.427362 grams to 0.43 grams.

5. When multiplying or dividing an approximate number by an absolute number, the result should be rounded to the same number of significant figures as in the approximate number. Thus, if 1.54 milligrams is multiplied by 96, the product, 243.84 milligrams, may be rounded to 244 milligrams, or to three significant figures.

PRACTICE PROBLEMS

1. State the number of significant figures in each of the *italicized* quantities:
   (a) One fluidounce equals *29.57* milliliters.
   (b) One liter equals *1000* milliliters.
   (c) One inch equals *2.54* centimeters.
   (d) The chemical costs *$1.05* per pound.
   (e) One gram equals *1,000,000* micrograms.
   (f) One microgram equals *0.001* milligram.

2. Round each of the following to three significant figures:
   (a) 32.75
   (b) 200.39
   (c) 0.03629
   (d) 21.635
   (e) 0.00944

3. Round each of the following to three decimal places:
   (a) 0.00083
   (b) 34.79502
   (c) 0.00494
   (d) 6.12963

4. If a mixture of seven ingredients contains the following approximate weights, what can you validly record as the approximate total combined weight of the ingredients?
   26.83 grams, 275.3 grams, 2.752 grams, 4.04 grams, 5.197 grams, 16.64 grams, and 0.085 gram.

5. Perform the following computations, and retain only significant figures in the results:
   (a) $6.39 - 0.008$
   (b) $7.01 - 6.0$
   (c) 5.0×48.3 grams
   (d) 24×0.25 gram
   (e) $56.824 \div 0.0905$
   (f) $250 \div 1.109$

Estimation

One of the best checks of the *reasonableness* of a numeric computation is an estimation of the answer. If we arrive at a wrong answer by using a wrong method, a mechanical repetition of the calculation may not reveal the error. But an absurd result, such as occurs when the decimal point is put in the wrong place, will not likely slip past if we check it against a preliminary estimation of what the result should be.

Because it is imperative that pharmacists ensure the accuracy of their calculations by every possible means, pharmacy students are urged to adopt *estimation* as one of those means. Proficiency in estimating comes only from constant practice. Therefore, pharmacy students are urged to acquire the habit of estimating the answer to every problem encountered before attempting to solve it. Estimation serves as a means for judging the reasonableness of the final result.

The estimating process is basically simple. First, the numbers given in a problem are *mentally* rounded off to slightly larger or smaller numbers containing fewer significant figures; for example,

59 would be rounded off to *60*, and 732 to *700*. Then, the required computations are performed, as far as possible *mentally*, and the result, although known to be somewhat greater or smaller than the exact answer, is close enough to serve as an estimate.

In *addition*, we can obtain a reasonable estimate of the total by first adding the figures in the leftmost column. The neglected remaining figures of each number are equally likely to express more or less than one-half the value of a unit of the order we have just added, and hence to the sum of the leftmost column we add half for every number in the column.

Example:

Add the following numbers: 7428, 3652, 1327, 4605, 2791, and 4490.
Estimation:
The figures in the thousands column add up to 21,000, and with each number on the average contributing 500 more, or every pair 1000 more, we get 21,000 + 3000 = 24,000, *estimated answer* (actual answer, 24,293).

In *multiplication,* the product of the two leftmost digits plus a sufficient number of *zeros* to give the right place value serves as a fair estimate. The number of *zeros* supplied must equal the total number of all discarded figures to the left of the decimal point. Approximation to the correct answer is closer if the discarded figures are used to round the value of those retained.

Example:

Multiply 612 by 413.
Estimation:
4 × 6 = 24, and because we discarded four figures, we must supply four zeros, giving 240,000, *estimated answer* (actual answer, 252,756).

In *division,* the given numbers may be rounded off to convenient approximations, but again, care is needed to preserve the correct place values.

Example:

Divide 2456 by 5.91.
Estimation:
The numbers may be rounded off to 2400 and 6. We may divide 24 by 6 mentally, but we must remember the two zeros substituted for the given 56 in 2456. The estimated answer is 400 (actual answer, 416).

PRACTICE PROBLEMS

1. Estimate the sums:

	(a)	(b)	(c)
	5641	3298	$75.82
	2177	368	37.92
	294	5192	14.69
	8266	627	45.98
	3503	4835	28.91
			49.87

2. Estimate the products:
   (a) 42 × 39 =
   (b) 365 × 98 =
   (c) 596 × 204 =
   (d) 6549 × 830 =
   (e) 8431 × 9760 =

(f) 2.04 × 705.3 =
(g) 0.0726 × 6951 =
(h) 6.1 × 67.39 =

3. Estimate the quotients:
   (a) 171 ÷ 19 =
   (b) 184 ÷ 2300 =
   (c) 160 ÷ 3200 =
   (d) 86,450 ÷ 72 =
   (e) 98,000 ÷ 49 =
   (f) 1.0745 ÷ 500 =
   (g) 1.9214 ÷ 0.026 =
   (h) 458.4 ÷ 8 =

ANSWERS TO PRACTICE PROBLEMS

Common Fractions, Decimal Fractions, and Percent

1. 2000 doses

2. (a) 0.029 or 2.9%
   (b) 0.43 or 43%
   (c) 0.004 or 0.4%
   (d) 0.0025 or 0.25%

3. 0.69 or 69%

4. 1⅛ or 1.25 ounces hydromorphone hydrochloride

5. 4.416 grams codeine sulfate

6. 0.012 or 1.2%

Exponential Notations

1. (a) 1.265×10^4
   (b) 5.5×10^{-9}
   (c) 4.51×10^2
   (d) 6.5×10^{-2}
   (e) 6.25×10^8

2. (a) 4,100,000
   (b) 0.0365
   (c) 0.00000513
   (d) 250,000
   (e) 8,695.6

3. (a) $17.5 \times 10^7 = 1.75 \times 10^8$
   (b) $16.4 \times 10^{-4} = 1.64 \times 10^{-3}$
   (c) $6.0 \times 10^0 = 6.0$
   (d) $12 \times 10^7 = 1.2 \times 10^8$
   (e) $36 \times 10^2 = 3.6 \times 10^3$

4. (a) 3.0×10^3
   (b) 3.0×10^{-10}
   (c) 3.0×10^9

5. (a) 8.52×10^4, or 8.5×10^4
   (b) 3.58×10^{-5}, or 3.6×10^{-5}
   (c) 2.99×10^3, or 3.0×10^3

6. (a) 6.441×10^6, or 6.4×10^6
   (b) 6.6×10^{-3}
   (c) 6.94×10^3, or 6.9×10^3

Ratio, Proportion, Variation, and Dimensional Analysis

1. 0.4 mL insulin injection

2. 0.03 mg digoxin

3. 2 patients

4. 1.75 g diazepam

5. 240 mg

6. 420 mg codeine phosphate
   4200 mg acetaminophen

7. 240 mg dextromethorphan hydrobromide

8. 0.25 mg

9. 300 mcg filgrastim

10. $10.08

11. 12½ tablets

12. 18,920 mg acyclovir

13. 0.75 mg metaproterenol sulfate

14. 0.3 mg fluoride ion

15. 150 units vitamin A

16. 32,000 mg

17. 44 mg elemental iron

18. 1333 mL

19. 0.1 mg dexamethasone phosphate

20. (a) 300 sprays
    (b) 450 mg

21. 16,000,000 units

22. (a) 1.5 g
    (b) 1 milliequivalent chloride ion

23. 18.75 mL

24. 2.4 mc grams ciprofloxacin

25. 1.1 g thiabendazole

26. 2500 units antigen

27. 0.06 mg

Significant Figures

1. (a) four
   (b) four
   (c) three
   (d) three
   (e) seven
   (f) one

2. (a) 32.8
   (b) 200
   (c) 0.0363
   (d) 21.6
   (e) 0.00944

3. (a) 0.001
   (b) 34.795
   (c) 0.005
   (d) 6.130

4. 330.8 g

5. (a) 6.38
   (b) 1.0
   (c) 240 g
   (d) 6.0 g
   (e) 628
   (f) 225

Estimation

1. (a) 20,500 (*19,881*)
   (b) 14,500 (*14,320*)
   (c) $240.00 (*$253.19*)

2. (a) 40 × 40 = 1600 (*1638*)
   (b) 360 × 100 = 36,000 (*35,700*)
   (c) 600 × 200 = 120,000 (*121,584*)
   (d) 7000 × 800 = 5,600,000
       (*5,435,670*)
   (e) 8000 × 10,000 = 80,000,000
       (*82,286,560*)
   (f) 2 × 700 = 1400 (*1438.812*)
   (g) (7 × 70) = 490 (*504.6426*)
   (h) 6 × 70 = 420 (*411.079*)

3. (a) 170 ÷ 20 = 8.5 (*9.0*)
   (b) 180 ÷ 2000 = 0.09 (*0.08*)
   (c) 16 ÷ 320 = 1/20 or 0.05 (*0.05*)
   (d) 8400 ÷ 7 = 1200 (*1200.7*)
   (e) 9800 ÷ 5 = 1960 (*2000*)
   (f) 0.01 ÷ 5 = 0.002 (*0.002149*)
   (g) 19 ÷ 0.25 = 19 × 4 = 76 (*73.9*)
   (h) 460 ÷ 8 = 57.5 (*57.3*)

REFERENCES

1. Available at: http://www.members.tripod.com/susanp3/snurse/id28_analysis.htm. Accessed September 3, 2008.
2. Craig GP. *Clinical Calculations Made Easy*. 4th Ed. Baltimore: Lippincott Williams & Wilkins, 2008.

International System of Units

Objectives

Upon successful completion of this chapter, the student will be able to:

- Demonstrate an understanding of the International System of Units.
- Convert measures within the International System of Units.
- State equivalent measures between the International System of Units and other systems of measure used in pharmacy practice.
- Convert measures between the International System of Units and other systems of measure used in pharmacy.
- Apply the International System of Units correctly in calculations.

The **International System of Units (SI)**, formerly called the **metric system**, is the internationally recognized decimal system of weights and measures. The system was formulated in France in the late eighteenth century. In 1866, the use of the metric system in the United States was legalized but not made mandatory. In 1875, the United States signed an international agreement, known as the *Treaty of the Meter*, which established the *International Bureau of Weights and Measures* in Sèvres, France, to provide standards of measurement for worldwide use. In 1960, the International System of Units (*Le Système International d'Unites*), a modernized version of the metric system, was developed by the General Conference of Weights and Measures (*Conference Generale des Poids et Mesures*). In an effort to encourage conversion to the international system, the U.S. Congress passed the Metric Conversion Act of 1975 and the Omnibus Trade and Competitiveness Act of 1988. The process of changing from the common systems and units of measurement (e.g., pounds, feet, gallons) to the SI metric system is termed **metric transition** or **metrification**. Today, the pharmaceutical research and manufacturing industry, the official compendia, the *United States Pharmacopeia—National Formulary*, and the practice of pharmacy reflect conversion to the SI system. The reasons for the transition include the simplicity of the decimal system, the clarity provided by the base units and prefixes of the SI, and the ease of scientific and professional communications through the use of a standardized and internationally accepted system of weights and measures.

The base units of the SI are the *meter* and the *kilogram*. Originally, the meter was defined as $\frac{1}{40,000,000}$ of the Earth's polar circumference. Modern science has refined the definition to be more precise: the distance light travels in a vacuum in $\frac{1}{299,792,458}$ of a second. In common-system terms, the meter is 39.37 inches, or slightly longer than the familiar 36-inch yard stick. The mass (weight) of a kilogram, originally defined as the mass of a liter of water, is now represented by a standard mass of platinum-iridium preserved in a vault in France. For comparison to the common system, a kilogram is approximately equivalent to 2.2 pounds. Although

TABLE 2.1 PREFIXES AND RELATIVE VALUES OF THE INTERNATIONAL SYSTEM (SI)

PREFIX	MEANING
Subdivisions	
atto-	one quintillionth (10^{-18}) of the basic unit
femto-	one quadrillionth (10^{-15}) of the basic unit
pico-	one trillionth (10^{-12}) of the basic unit
nano-	one billionth (10^{-9}) of the basic unit
micro-	one millionth (10^{-6}) of the basic unit
milli-	one thousandth (10^{-3}) of the basic unit
centi-	one hundredth (10^{-2}) of the basic unit
deci-	one tenth (10^{-1}) of the basic unit
Multiples	
deka-	10 times the basic unit
hecto-	100 times (10^2) the basic unit
kilo-	1000 times (10^3) the basic unit
myria-	10,000 times (10^4) the basic unit
mega-	1 million times (10^6) the basic unit
giga-	1 billion times (10^9) the basic unit
tera-	1 trillion times (10^{12}) the basic unit
peta-	1 quadrillion times (10^{15}) the basic unit
exa-	1 quintillion times (10^{18}) the basic unit

not included in this text, other areas of measurement addressed by the SI include force, viscosity, electricity, illuminance, sound, and more.[1]

Each table of the SI contains a definitive, or primary, unit. For length, the primary unit is the *meter*; for volume, the *liter*; and for weight, the *gram* (although technically the *kilogram* is considered the historic base unit). Subdivisions and multiples of these primary units, their relative values, and their corresponding prefixes are shown in Table 2.1.

The standard subdivisions and multiples of the primary units are termed **denominations**, and the number used in conjunction with a denomination is termed a **denominate number**. For example, in *5 milligrams*, 5 is the denominate number and milligrams is the denomination. The short forms for SI units (such as *cm*, for centimeter) are termed **symbols**, not abbreviations.[1]

Guidelines for the Correct Use of the SI

The following are select guidelines for the correct use of the SI from the U.S. Metric Association, with additional considerations relevant to the practice of pharmacy:[1,2]

- Unit names and symbols generally are not capitalized except when used at the beginning of a sentence or in headings. However, the symbol for liter (L) may be capitalized or not. *Examples:* 4 L or 4 l, 4 mm, and 4 g; *not* 4 Mm and 4 G.
- In the United States, the decimal marker (or decimal point) is placed on the line with the denomination and denominate number; however, in some countries, a comma or a raised dot is used. *Examples:* 4.5 mL (U.S.); 4,5 mL or 4·5 mL (non-U.S.).
- Periods are not used following SI symbols except at the end of a sentence. *Examples:* 4 mL and 4 g, *not* 4 mL. and 4 g.
- A compound unit that is a ratio or quotient of two units is indicated by a solidus (/) or a negative exponent. *Examples:* 5 mL/h or 5 mL·h^{-1}, *not* 5 mL per hour.
- Symbols should not be combined with spelled-out terms in the same expression. *Examples:* 3 mg/mL, *not* 3 mg/milliliter.

- Plurals of unit names, when spelled out, have an added *s*. Symbols for units, however, are the same in singular and plural. *Examples:* 5 milliliters or 5 mL, *not* 5 mLs.
- Two symbols exist for microgram: *mcg* (often used in pharmacy practice) and μg (SI).
- The symbol for square meter is m^2; for cubic centimeter, cm^3; and so forth. In pharmacy practice, cm^3 is considered equivalent to milliliter.[2] The symbol cc, for cubic centimeter, is *not* an accepted SI symbol.
- Decimal fractions are used, not common fractions. *Examples:* 5.25 g, *not* $5\frac{1}{4}$ g.
- A zero should be placed in front of a leading decimal point to prevent medication errors caused by *uncertain* decimal points. *Example:* 0.5 g, *not* .5 g.
  It is critically important for pharmacists to recognize that a misplaced or misread decimal point can lead to an error in calculation or in dispensing of a minimum of one tenth or ten times the desired quantity.
- To prevent misreadings and medication errors, "trailing" zeros *should not* be placed following a whole number on prescriptions and medication orders. *Example:* 5 mg, *not* 5.0 mg. However, in some tables (such as those of the SI in this chapter), pharmaceutical formulas, and quantitative results, trailing zeros often are used to indicate exactness to a specific number of decimal places.
- In selecting symbols of unit dimensions, the choice generally is based on selecting the unit that will result in a numeric value between 1 and 1000. *Examples:* 500 g, *rather than* 0.5 kg; 1.96 kg, *rather than* 1960 g; and 750 mL, *rather than* 0.75 L.

Special Considerations of the SI in Pharmacy

Although some remnants of the common systems of measurement (see Appendix A) in pharmacy remain, the use of the SI is nearly total. The system is used to manufacture and label pharmaceutical products (Fig. 2.1); write, fill, and compound prescriptions and institutional medication orders; dose patients; express clinical laboratory test results; and communicate both verbally and through scientific and professional literature.

In the large-scale manufacture of dosage forms, pharmaceutical ingredients are measured in kilogram and kiloliter quantities. In the community and institutional pharmacy, compounding

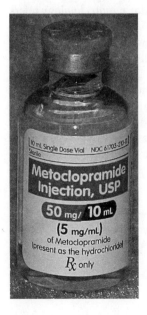

FIGURE 2.1 Example of a pharmaceutical product with the label indicating the quantity (10 mL) and strength (5 mg/mL) in SI or metric units. *(Reprinted with permission from Lacher BE. Pharmaceutical Calculations for the Pharmacy Technician. Philadelphia: Lippincott Williams & Wilkins, 2007.)*

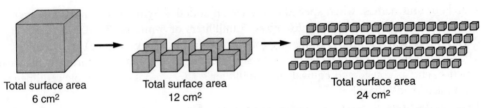

FIGURE 2.2 Depiction of increased surface area by particle size reduction. *(Adapted from company literature, Nanocrystal, Elan Drug Delivery, Inc.)*

and dispensing in milligram, gram, and milliliter quantities are more common. Drug doses are typically administered in milligram or microgram amounts and prepared in solid dosage forms, such as tablets or capsules, or in a stated volume of a liquid preparation, such as an oral solution (e.g., 30 mg/5 mL) or injection (e.g., 2 mg/mL). Doses for certain drugs are calculated on the basis of body weight and expressed as mg/kg, meaning a certain number of *milligrams of drug per kilogram of body weight*. Clinical laboratory values are in metric units and expressed, for example, as mg/dL, meaning *milligrams of drug per deciliter of body fluid* (such as blood).

Particle Size and Nanotechnology

Drug particle size has long been an important consideration in pharmaceutical technology. Through the milling and reduction of drug materials to micron and nano size, the surface area of particles is increased (Fig. 2.2), and pharmaceutical and clinical benefits often accrue. These benefits may include:[3]

- increased aqueous dissolution rates for poorly soluble substances;
- improved bioavailability, with increased rates of absorption of orally administered drugs;
- lower oral dosage possibilities with enhanced drug absorption; and
- expanded formulation options in the preparation of stable and predictable pharmaceutical suspensions and colloidal dispersions for all routes of administration, including oral, parenteral, respiratory, ophthalmic, and nasal.

An area of technology with great potential is nanotechnology. **Nanotechnology** may be defined as the development and use of materials on the nano-size scale. **Molecular nanotechnology** refers to the method of building organic and inorganic structures atom by atom or molecule by molecule. With nanotechnology, scientists and engineers generally work with materials between 1 and 1000 nanometers (nm). For perspective, a nanometer is one billionth of a meter; about 25,400,000 nm equals 1 in.; the helix of DNA has a diameter of about 2 nm; and a typical bond between two atoms is about 0.15 nm.[4] Nanotechnology has applications for many potential products, including those that integrate chemistry, the biological sciences, medicine, and computer technology. The term **nanomedicine** refers to the application of nanotechnology to the prevention and treatment of disease. It may further be defined as "the monitoring, repair, construction and control of human biological systems at the molecular level, using engineered nanodevices and nanostructures."[5]

Measure of Length

The meter is the primary unit of length in the SI
The **table of metric length**:

1 kilometer (km)	= 1000.000 meters	
1 hectometer (hm)	= 100.000 meters	1 meter (m)
1 dekameter (dam)	= 10.000 meters	

FIGURE 2.3 Ruler calibrated in millimeter, centimeter, and inch units. *(Courtesy of Schlenker Enterprise, Ltd.)*

1 decimeter (dm)	= 0.100 meter
1 centimeter (cm)	= 0.010 meter
1 millimeter (mm)	= 0.001 meter
1 micrometer (μm)	= 0.000,001 meter
1 nanometer (nm)	= 0.000,000,001 meter

The table may also be written:

1 meter	= 0.001 kilometer
	= 0.01 hectometer
	= 0.1 dekameter
	= 10 decimeters
	= 100 centimeters
	= 1000 millimeters
	= 1,000,000 micrometers
	= 1,000,000,000 nanometers

Equivalencies of the most common length denominations:

1000 millimeters (mm)	= 100 centimeters (cm)
100 centimeters (cm)	= 1 meter (m)

A ruler calibrated in millimeter and centimeter units is shown in Figure 2.3.

Distance exercise is undertaken by many people as a component of maintaining good health status and is usually measured by a combination of time and miles or meters. It is useful to understand the relationships shown in Table 2.2.

Measure of Volume

The *liter* is the primary unit of volume. It represents the volume of the cube of one tenth of a meter, that is, of 1 dm^3.

The **table of metric volume**:

1 kiloliter (kL)	= 1000.000 liters
1 hectoliter (hL)	= 100.000 liters
1 dekaliter (daL)	= 10.000 liters
1 liter (L)	= 1.000 liter
1 deciliter (dL)	= 0.100 liter
1 centiliter (cL)	= 0.010 liter
1 milliliter (mL)	= 0.001 liter
1 microliter (μL)	= 0.000,001 liter

TABLE 2.2 DEMONSTRATIONS OF LINEAR RELATIONSHIPS

	FEET	YARDS	MILES	METERS	KILOMETERS
1 mile	5280	1760	1	1609.3	1.6093
1 kilometer	3280.8	1093.6	0.62137	1000	1

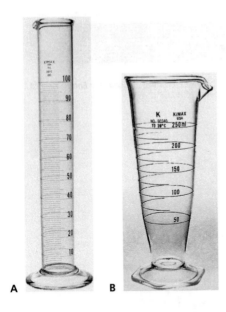

FIGURE 2.4 Examples of metric-scale cylindrical **(A)** and conical pharmaceutical graduates **(B)**. *(Courtesy of Kimble/Kontes Glass.)*

This table may also be written:

1 liter	= 0.001 kiloliter
	= 0.010 hectoliter
	= 0.100 dekaliter
	= 10 deciliters
	= 100 centiliters
	= 1000 milliliters
	= 1,000,000 microliters

Although in theory the liter was meant to have the volume of $1\ dm^3$ or $1000\ cm^3$, precise modern measurement has discovered that the standard liter contains slightly less than this volume. The discrepancy is insignificant for most practical purposes, however, and because the milliliter has so nearly the volume of $1\ cm^3$, *The United States Pharmacopeia—National Formulary*[2] states: "One milliliter (mL) is used herein as the equivalent of 1 cubic centimeter (cc)."

Equivalencies of the most common volume denominations:

$$1000 \text{ milliliters (mL)} = 1 \text{ liter (L)}$$

Examples of metric graduates for measuring volume are shown in Figure 2.4.

Measure of Weight

The primary unit of weight in the SI is the *gram*, which is the weight of $1\ cm^3$ of water at 4°C, its temperature of greatest density.

The **table of metric weight**:

1 kilogram (kg)	= 1000.000 grams
1 hectogram (hg)	= 100.000 grams
1 dekagram (dag)	= 10.000 grams
1 gram (g)	= 1.000 gram
1 decigram (dg)	= 0.1000 gram
1 centigram (cg)	= 0.010 gram
1 milligram (mg)	= 0.001 gram
1 microgram (μg or mcg)	= 0.000,001 gram

1 nanogram (ng)   = 0.000,000,001 gram
1 picogram (pg)   = 0.000,000,000,001 gram
1 femtogram (fg)   = 0.000,000,000,000,001 gram

This table may also be written:

1 gram   = 0.001 kilogram
           = 0.010 hectogram
           = 0.100 dekagram
           = 10 decigrams
           = 100 centigrams
           = 1000 milligrams
           = 1,000,000 micrograms
           = 1,000,000,000 nanograms
           = 1,000,000,000,000 picograms
           = 1,000,000,000,000,000 femtograms

Equivalencies of the most common weight denominations:

1000 micrograms (μg or mcg)   = 1 milligram (mg)
1000 milligrams (mg)   = 1 gram (g)
1000 grams (g)   = 1 kilogram (kg)

An example of a metric set of weights is shown in Chapter 3.

It should be noted that for *micrograms*, the abbreviation *mcg* and the symbol μg are both used in this text. Although the symbol μg is used at present in *The United States Pharmacopeia—National Formulary,*[2] the abbreviation *mcg* is widely used in pharmaceutical package labeling and in prescription writing. The term *gamma*, symbolized by γ, is customarily used for microgram in biochemical literature.

Prescription Writing Style Using the SI

Prescriptions written in the SI use Arabic numerals *before* the abbreviations for the denominations (e.g., 6 g). Quantities of weight are usually written as grams and *decimals* of a gram, and volumes as milliliters and *decimals* of a milliliter.

Example:

R	Dextromethorphan HBr	320 mg
	Guiafenesin	3.2 g
	Cherry Syrup, to make	240 mL

Fundamental Computations

Reducing SI Units to Lower or Higher Denominations by Using a Unit-Position Scale

The metric system is based on the decimal system; therefore, conversion from one denomination to another can be done simply by moving the decimal point as demonstrated in Figure 2.5.

To change a metric denomination to the next smaller denomination, move the decimal point one place to the right.

To change a metric denomination to the next larger denomination, move the decimal point one place to the left.

Examples:

Reduce 1.23 kilograms to grams.

1.23 kg = 1230 g, *answer.*

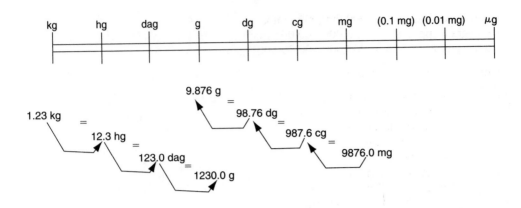

Decimal Movement

⊙→ To Convert From Larger to Smaller Units

←⊙ To Convert From Smaller to Larger Units

FIGURE 2.5 Position scale of units of weight.

Reduce 9876 milligrams to grams.
$$9876 \text{ mg} = 9.876 \text{ g, } answer.$$

In the first example, 1.23 kg are to be converted to grams. On the scale, the gram position is three decimal positions from the kilogram position. Thus, the decimal point is moved three places toward the right. In the second example, the conversion from milligrams also requires the movement of the decimal point three places, but this time to the left.

Examples:

Reduce 85 micrometers to centimeters.
$$85 \ \mu m = 0.085 \text{ mm} = 0.0085 \text{ cm, } answer.$$

Reduce 2.525 liters to microliters.
$$2.525 \text{ L} = 2525 \text{ mL} = 2,525,000 \ \mu L, \ answer.$$

The 3-Decimal Point Shift

In pharmacy practice, and health care in general, the denominations most used differ by 1000 or by a factor of 3 decimal places. Thus, on the decimal scale (Fig. 2.5), a 3-place decimal point shift, left to right or right to left, will yield most commonly used denominations.

3-Place Shift for Common Weight Denominations:
    kilograms (kg) _ _ _ grams (g) _ _ _ milligrams (mg) _ _ _ micrograms (mcg)

3-Place Shift for Common Volume Denominations:
    liters (L) _ _ _ milliliters (mL)

Reducing SI Units to Lower or Higher Denominations by Ratio and Proportion or by Dimensional Analysis

Examples:

Reduce 1.23 kilograms to grams.
From the table: 1 kg = 1000 g

CALCULATIONS CAPSULE

International System of Units (SI)

- The SI or decimal system of measurement is used in the practice of pharmacy and throughout the pharmaceutical industry.
- The primary SI units for calculating mass or weight (gram), volume (liter), and length (meter) are used along with prefixes to indicate multiples or subdivisions of the primary units.
- To change an SI denomination to the next *smaller* denomination, the decimal point is moved one place to the right:

    gram (g) > decigram (dg) > centigram (cg) > milligram (mg)
    5.555 g = 55.55 dg = 555.5 cg = 5555 mg

Each value is equivalent.
- To change an SI denomination to the next *larger* denomination, the decimal point is moved one place to the left:

    kilogram (kg) > hectogram (hg) > dekagram (dg) > gram (g)
    5.555 kg = 55.55 hg = 555.5 dg = 5555 mg

Each value is equivalent.
- A unit position scale (e.g., see Fig 2.5), ratio and proportion, or dimensional analysis may be used to change denominations.
- Only numbers of the same denomination may be added to or subtracted from one another.

By ratio and proportion:

$$\frac{1 \text{ kg}}{1000 \text{ g}} = \frac{1.23 \text{ kg}}{x \text{ g}}; \ x = 1230 \text{ g, } \textit{answer.}$$

By dimensional analysis:

$$1.23 \text{ kg} \times \frac{1000 \text{ g}}{1 \text{ kg}} = 1230 \text{ g, } \textit{answer.}$$

Reduce 62,500 mcg to g.
From the table: 1 g = 1,000,000 mcg
By ratio and proportion:

$$\frac{1,000,000 \text{ mcg}}{1 \text{ g}} = \frac{62,500 \text{ mcg}}{x \text{ g}}; \ x = 0.0625 \text{ g, } \textit{answer.}$$

By dimensional analysis:

$$62,500 \text{ mcg} \times \frac{1 \text{ g}}{1,000,000 \text{ mcg}} = 0.0625 \text{ g, } \textit{answer.}$$

Recognizing Equivalent Expressions

On occasion, it may be necessary to recognize, or prove by calculation, equivalent expressions. For example, a given quantity expressed in terms of "mg/100 mL" is equivalent to "mg/dL."

Practice problems (# 47 to 50) at the conclusion of this chapter provide exercises to determine equivalent expressions.

Addition and Subtraction

To add or subtract quantities in the SI, reduce them to a *common denomination*, preferably a base unit, and arrange their denominate numbers for addition or subtraction as ordinary decimals.

Examples:

Add 1 kg, 250 mg, and 7.5 g. Express the total in grams.

$$
\begin{array}{lll}
1 \text{ kg} & = 1000. & \text{g} \\
250 \text{ mg} & = 0.25 & \text{g} \\
7.5 \text{ g} & = 7.5 & \text{g} \\
\hline
& 1007.75 & \text{g or 1008 g, } answer.
\end{array}
$$

Add 4 L, 375 mL, and 0.75 L. Express the total in milliliters.

$$
\begin{array}{lll}
4 \text{ L} & = 4000 \text{ mL} \\
375 \text{ mL} & = 375 \text{ mL} \\
0.75 \text{ L} & = 750 \text{ mL} \\
\hline
& 5125 \text{ mL, } answer.
\end{array}
$$

A capsule contains the following amounts of medicinal substances: 0.075 g, 20 mg, 0.0005 g, 4 mg, and 500 µg. What is the total weight of the substances in the capsule?

$$
\begin{array}{lll}
0.075 \text{ g} & = 0.075 & \text{g} \\
20 \text{ mg} & = 0.02 & \text{g} \\
0.0005 \text{ g} & = 0.0005 & \text{g} \\
4 \text{ mg} & = 0.004 & \text{g} \\
500 \text{ µg} & = 0.0005 & \text{g} \\
\hline
& 0.1000 & \text{g or 100 mg, } answer.
\end{array}
$$

Subtract 2.5 mg from 4.85 g.

$$
\begin{array}{lll}
4.85 \text{ g} & = & 4.85 \text{g} \\
2.5 \text{ mg} & = & -\ 0.0025 \text{ g} \\
\hline
& & 4.8475 \text{ g or 4.848 g, } answer.
\end{array}
$$

A prescription calls for 0.06 g of one ingredient, 2.5 mg of another, and enough of a third to make 0.5 g. How many milligrams of the third ingredient should be used?

Interpreting all quantities as accurate to the nearest tenth of a milligram:

$$
\begin{array}{lll}
\text{1st ingredient:} & 0.06 \text{ g} & = 0.0600 \text{ g} \\
\text{2nd ingredient:} & 2.5 \text{ mg} & = 0.0025 \text{ g} \\
\hline
& & 0.0625 \text{ g}
\end{array}
$$

$$
\begin{array}{ll}
\text{Total weight:} & 0.5000 \text{ g} \\
\text{Weight of 1st and 2nd:} & -\ 0.0625 \text{ g} \\
\hline
\text{Weight of 3rd:} & 0.4375 \text{ g or 437.5 mg, } answer.
\end{array}
$$

Multiplication and Division

Because every measurement in the SI is expressed in a single given denomination, problems involving multiplication and division are solved by the methods used for any decimal numbers.

Examples:

Multiply 820 mL by 12.5 and express the result in liters.

$$820 \text{ mL} \times 12.5 = 10250 \text{ mL} = 10.25 \text{ L}, \textit{answer.}$$

Divide 0.465 g by 15 and express the result in milligrams.

$$0.465 \text{ g} \div 15 = 0.031 \text{ g} = 31 \text{ mg}, \textit{answer.}$$

CASE IN POINT 2.1: A nurse telephones a pharmacy regarding the proper quantity of an injection to administer to a pediatric patient from a 1-mL vial containing 0.1 mg of digoxin. The attending physician has quantity of an injection to administer to a pediatric patient from a 1-mL vial containing 0.1 mg of digoxin. The attending physician had prescribed a dose of 25 mcg. How many milliliters should be the pharmacist's response? many milliliters should be the pharmacist's response?

Relation of the SI to Other Systems of Measurement

In addition to the International System of Units, the pharmacy student should be aware of two other systems of measurement: the *avoirdupois* and *apothecaries'* systems. The avoirdupois system, widely used in the United States in measuring body weight and in selling goods by the ounce or pound, is slowly giving way to the international system. The apothecaries' system, once the predominant pharmacist's system of volumetric and weight measure, has also largely been replaced by the SI. The pharmacist must still appreciate the relationship between the various systems of measurement, however, and deal effectively with them as the need arises.

The avoirdupois and apothecaries' systems of measurement, including all necessary equivalents and methods for intersystem conversion, are presented in Appendix A. The example equivalents presented in Table 2.3 are useful in gaining perspective and in solving certain problems in the text—for example, when there is need to convert fluidounces to milliliters or kilograms to pounds. These equivalents should be committed to memory.

> When quantities in units of the apothecaries' or avoirdupois systems of measurement (see Appendix A) are encountered, it is suggested that they be converted to equivalent quantities in SI units and the required calculation then solved in the usual manner.

TABLE 2.3 SOME USEFUL EQUIVALENTS

Equivalents of Length

1 inch	=	2.54 cm
1 meter (m)	=	39.37 in

Equivalents of Volume

1 fluidounce (fl. oz.)	=	29.57 mL
1 pint (16 fl. oz.)	=	473 mL
1 quart (32 fl. oz.)	=	946 mL
1 gallon, US (128 fl. oz.)	=	3785 mL
1 gallon, UK	=	4545 mL

Equivalents of Weight

1 pound (lb, Avoirdupois)	=	454 g
1 kilogram (kg)	=	2.2 lb

CASE IN POINT 2.2: A hospital pharmacist is asked to prepare an intravenous infusion of dopamine. Based on the patient's weight, the pharmacist calculates a dose of 500 mcg/min for continuous infusion. The concentration of a premixed dopamine infusion is 400 mg/250 mL. What is the concentration of the infusion on a mcg/mL basis? How many milligrams of dopamine is the patient to receive in the first hour of treatment? How long will the infusion last?

PRACTICE PROBLEMS

1. Add 0.5 kg, 50 mg, and 2.5 dg. Reduce the result to grams.

2. Add 7.25 L and 875 cL. Reduce the result to milliliters.

3. Add 0.0025 kg, 1750 mg, 2.25 g, and 825,000 μg, and express the answer in grams.

4. Reduce 1.256 g to micrograms, to milligrams, and to kilograms.

5. Are the terms mcg/mL and mg/L equivalent or not equivalent?

6. A low-strength children's/adult chewable aspirin tablet contains 81 mg of aspirin per tablet. How many tablets may be prepared from 1 kg of aspirin?

7. Adhesive tape made from fabric has a tensile strength of not less than 20.41 kg/2.54 cm of width. Reduce these quantities to grams and millimeters.

8. A liquid contains 0.25 mg of a substance per milliliter. How many grams of the substance will 3.5 L contain?

9. An inhalation aerosol contains 225 mg of metaproterenol sulfate, which is sufficient for 300 inhalations. How many micrograms of metaproterenol sulfate would be contained in each inhalation?

10. TRIPHASIL-28 birth control tablets are taken sequentially, 1 tablet per day for 28 days, with the tablets containing the following:

Phase 1 – 6 tablets, each containing 0.050 mg levonorgestrel and 0.030 mg ethinyl estradiol;
Phase 2 – 5 tablets, each containing 0.075 mg levonorgestrel and 0.040 mg ethinyl estradiol;
Phase 3 – 10 tablets, each containing 0.125 mg levonorgestrel and 0.030 mg ethinyl estradiol; then, 7 inert tablets (no drug).
How many total milligrams each of levonorgestrel and ethinyl estradiol are taken during the 28-day period?

11. How many colchicine tablets, each containing 600 mcg, may be prepared from 30 g of colchicine?

12. The following clinical laboratory data are within normal values for an adult. Convert each value to mcg/mL:
   (a) ammonia, 30 mcg/dL
   (b) folate, 18 pg/mL
   (c) serum creatinine, 1.0 mg/dL
   (d) prostate specific antigen (PSA), 3 ng/mL
   (e) cholesterol, total, 150 mg/dL

13. Aspirin tablets generally contain 325 mg of aspirin. How many such tablets may be prepared from 5 kg of aspirin?

14. A cold tablet contains the following amounts of active ingredients:
   Acetaminophen   325 mg
   Chlorpheniramine Maleate   2 mg
   Dextromethorphan
   Hydrobromide   15 mg
      How many tablets may be prepared if a manufacturing pharmacist has 1

kg of acetaminophen, 125 g of chlorpheniramine maleate, and unlimited quantities of dextromethorphan hydrobromide?

15. Norgestrel and ethinyl estradiol tablets are available containing 0.5 mg of norgestrel and 50 μg of ethinyl estradiol. How many grams of each ingredient would be used in making 10,000 tablets?

16. Approximately 0.02% of a 100-mg dose of the drug miglitol (GLYSET) has been shown to appear in human breast milk. Calculate the quantity of drug detected, in milligrams, following a single dose.

17. How many grams of digoxin (LANOXIN) would be required to make 25,000 tablets each containing 250 mcg of digoxin?

18. Adalimumab (HUMIRA), a recombinant human monoclonal antibody, is available in a prefilled syringe containing 40 mg/0.8 mL of injection. Calculate the concentration of drug on a mg/mL basis.

19. If an injectable solution contains 25 μg of a drug substance in each 0.5 mL, how many milliliters would be required to provide a patient with 0.25 mg of the drug substance?

20. A patient is instructed to take three 50-mcg tablets of pergolide mesylate (PERMAX) daily. How many milligrams of the drug would the patient receive weekly?

21. An oral liquid concentrate of sertraline hydrochloride (ZOLOFT) contains 20 mg/mL of the drug. How many grams of sertraline hydrochloride are in each 60-mL container of the concentrate?

22. Digoxin (LANOXIN) is available for parenteral pediatric use in a concentration of 0.1 mg/mL. How many milliliters would provide a dose of 40 μg?

23. A liquid oral concentrate of morphine sulfate contains 2.4 g of morphine sulfate in a 120-mL bottle. Calculate the concentration of morphine sulfate on a mg/mL basis.

24. If one 20-mL ampul contains 0.5 g of aminophylline, how many milliliters should be administered to provide a 25-mg dose of aminophylline?

25. An intravenous solution contains 500 μg of a drug substance in each milliliter. How many milligrams of the drug would a patient receive from the intravenous infusion of a liter of the solution?

26. If an intravenous solution containing 123 mg of a drug substance in each 250-mL bottle is to be administered at the rate of 200 μg of drug per minute, how many milliliters of the solution would be given per hour?

27. The prophylactic dose of riboflavin is 2 mg. How many micrograms of riboflavin are in a multiple vitamin capsule containing $\frac{1}{5}$ the prophylactic dose?

28. One milligram of streptomycin sulfate contains the antibiotic activity of 650 μg of streptomycin base. How many grams of streptomycin sulfate would be the equivalent of 1 g of streptomycin base?

29. A commercial package contains thirty-six 200-mg tablets of ibuprofen. How many kilograms of ibuprofen were used in the manufacture of 1000 packages of the product?

30. A gas chromatographic column measures 1.8 m in length and 3 mm in internal diameter. Convert these measurements to inches.

31. A prefilled syringe contains 20 mg of drug in 2 mL of solution. How many micrograms of drug would be administered by an injection of 0.5 mL of the solution?

32. A vial contains 80 mg of drug in 2 mL of injection. How many milliliters of the injection should be administered to obtain 0.02 g of drug?

33. One-half liter of solution for intravenous infusion contains 2 g of drug. How many milliliters of the solution would contain 0.5 mg of drug?

34. A 125-mL container of amoxicillin contains 600 mg/5 mL. How many milliliters would be used to administer 400 mg of amoxicillin?

35. An effervescent tablet has the following formula:

Acetaminophen	325 mg
Calcium Carbonate	280 mg
Citric Acid	900 mg
Potassium Bicarbonate	300 mg
Sodium Bicarbonate	465 mg

    (a) Calculate the total weight, in grams, of the ingredients in each tablet.

    (b) How many tablets could be made with a supply of 5 kg of acetaminophen?

36. A new analytic instrument is capable of detecting picogram quantities of a chemical substance. How many times more capable is this instrument than one that can detect nanogram quantities of the same chemical?

37. The dimensions of a nicotine transdermal patch system are 4.7 cm by 4.8 cm. Express these dimensions in corresponding inches if 1 inch is equivalent to 25.4 mm.

38. If an albuterol inhaler contains 18 mg of albuterol, how many inhalation-doses can be delivered if each inhalation-dose contains 90 μg?

39. Acetaminophen, in amounts greater than 4 g per day, has been associated with liver toxicity. What is the maximum number of 500-mg tablets of acetaminophen that a person may take daily and not reach the toxic level?

40. Prochlorperazine (COMPAZINE) for injection is available in 10-mL multiple dose vials containing 5 mg/mL. How many 2-mg doses can be withdrawn from the vial?

41. The recommended dose for a brand of nicotine patch is one 21-mg dose per day for 6 weeks, followed by 14 mg per day for 2 weeks, and then 7 mg per day for 2 more weeks. What total quantity, in grams, would a patient receive during this course of treatment?

42. A medical device is sterilized by gamma radiation at 2.5 megarads (Mrad). Express the equivalent quantity in rads.

43. A VIVELLE estradiol transdermal system is a round patch measuring about 4.3 cm in diameter. Convert this dimension to inches and millimeters.

44. A solution for direct IV bolus injection contains 125 mg of drug in each 25 mL of injection. What is the concentration of drug in terms of μg/μL?

45. The total number of human genomic characters is 3.5 billion. Express this quantity numerically without using a decimal point.

46. Conjugated estrogens tablets (PREMARIN) are available in strengths of 0.3 mg, 0.45 mg, 0.625 mg, 0.9 mg, and 1.25 mg. If patient "A" took one tablet daily of the lowest dose and patient "B" took one tablet daily of the highest dose, what is the difference in the total quantities taken between patients "A" and "B" over a period of 30 days?

    (a) 2.85 mg
    (b) 2850 mcg
    (c) 2.85 cg
    (d) 2.85 dg

47. Teratogenic studies of insulin glargine were undertaken in rats at doses up to 0.36 mg/kg/day. This is equivalent to which of the following?

(a) 360 cg/lb/day
(b) 792 mcg/lb/day
(c) 360 mg/lb/day
(d) 163.6 mcg/lb/day

48. Pharmacy students, traveling to attend a national pharmacy meeting, were on an airplane with an average air speed of 414 miles per hour. Which is the closest equivalent air speed?
(a) 6 mi/min
(b) 257 km/h
(c) 666 km/h
(d) 180 m/sec

49. The product of biotechnology, filgrastim (NEUPOGEN), is available in vials containing 0.3 mg of drug in each milliliter. Which choice is equivalent in concentration?
(a) 0.03 mg/0.1 dL
(b) 300 mcg/0.01 dL
(c) 3 mcg/0.01 cL
(d) 300 mcg/10 cL

50. In a clinical study of finasteride (PROSCAR), a single oral dose of 5 mg resulted in an average blood concentration of 37 ng of drug per milliliter (37 ng/mL) of blood plasma. This is equivalent to which of the following?
(a) 37,000 mcg/mL
(b) 0.037 mcg/mL
(c) 0.000037 mg/cL
(d) 0.0037 mcg/dL

ANSWERS TO "CASE IN POINT" AND PRACTICE PROBLEMS

Case in Point 2.1

0.1 mg/mL = 100 mcg/mL

$$25 \text{ mcg} \times \frac{1 \text{ mL}}{100 \text{ mcg}} = \frac{1}{4} \text{ mL or } 0.25 \text{ mL,}$$

answer.

Case in Point 2.2

Concentration of infusion, mcg/mL:

$$\frac{400 \text{ mg}}{250 \text{ mL}} = \frac{400,000 \text{ mcg}}{250 \text{ mL}}$$

$$= 1600 \text{ mcg/mL, } answer.$$

mg, dopamine, first hour:

$$\frac{500 \text{ mcg}}{1 \text{ min}} \times \frac{60 \text{ min}}{1 \text{ h}} \times \frac{1 \text{ mg}}{1000 \text{ mcg}}$$

$$= 30 \text{ mg/h, } answer.$$

Infusion duration:

$$400 \text{ mg} \times \frac{1 \text{ min}}{500 \text{ mcg}} \times \frac{1000 \text{ mcg}}{1 \text{ mg}}$$

$$= 800 \text{ min} = 13 \text{ h, } 20 \text{ min, } answer.$$

Practice Problems

1. 500.3 g

2. 16,000 mL

3. 7.325 g

4. 1,256,000 mcg
   1256 mg
   0.001256 kg

5. equivalent

6. 12,345 tablets

7. 20,410 g/25.4 mm

8. 0.875 g

9. 750 mcg metaproterenol sulfate

10. 1.925 mg levonorgestrel
    0.68 mg ethinyl estradiol

11. 50,000 tablets

12. (a) ammonia, 0.3 mcg/mL
    (b) folate, 0.000018 mcg/mL
    (c) serum creatinine, 10 mcg/mL
    (d) prostate specific antigen (PSA), 0.003 mcg/mL
    (e) cholesterol, 1500 mcg/mL

13. 15,384 tablets

14. 3076 tablets

15. 5 g norgestrel
    0.5 g ethinyl estradiol

16. 0.02 mg miglitol

17. 6.25 g digoxin

18. 50 mg/mL

19. 5 mL

20. 1.05 mg pergolide mesylate

21. 1.2 g sertraline hydrochloride

22. 0.4 mL

23. 20 mg/mL morphine sulfate

24. 1 mL

25. 500 mg

26. 24.39 mL

27. 400 mcg riboflavin

28. 1.538 g streptomycin sulfate

29. 7.2 kg

30. 70.866 or 70.9 inches
    0.118 or 0.12 inches

31. 5000 mcg

32. 0.5 mL

33. 0.125 mL

34. 3.33 mL

35. (a) 2.27 g
    (b) 15,384 tablets

36. 1000 times

37. 1.85 inches × 1.89 inches

38. 200 doses

39. 8 tablets

40. 25 doses

41. 1.176 g nicotine

42. 2,500,000 rads

43. 1.69 inches and 43 mm

44. 5 µg/µL

45. 3,500,000,000 or 35×10^8

46. (c) 2.85 cg

47. (d) 163.6 mcg/lb/day

48. (c) 666 km/h

49. (b) 300 mcg/0.01 dL

50. (b) 0.037 mcg/mL

REFERENCES

1. U.S. Metric Association. Correct SI-metric usage. Available at: http://lamar.colostate.edu/~hillger/correct.htm. Accessed September 4, 2008.
2. United States Pharmacopeia 31st Rev. National Formulary 26. Rockville, MD: United States Pharmacopeial Convention, 2008;1:13.
3. Available at: http//:www.Nanocrystal.com.html. Accessed September 4, 2008.
4. Seeman NC. Nanotechnology and the double helix. *Scientific American* 2004;290:64–75.
5. Freitas RA Jr. Nanomedicine. Available at: http://www.foresight.org/Nanomedicine/. Accessed January 23, 2008.

Pharmaceutical Measurement

Objectives

Upon successful completion of this chapter, the student will be able to:

- Describe instruments for volumetric measurement and characterize their differences in application and accuracy.
- Describe the correct procedure when using a pharmaceutical balance.
- Define *sensitivity requirement* and apply it in calculations.
- Perform calculations by the aliquot method.
- Demonstrate an understanding of *percentage of error* in pharmaceutical measurement.

Pharmaceutical measurement is an important part of pharmacy practice. It is employed in community and institutional pharmacies, in pharmaceutical research, in the development and manufacture of pharmaceuticals, in chemical and product analysis, and in quality control. This chapter focuses on the equipment and methods used in the accurate measurement of therapeutic and pharmaceutical materials in the community and institutional practice of pharmacy.

The expertise of pharmacists in accurately weighing and measuring materials is a historical and unique skill, acquired through professional education and training. Moreover, this capability is an *expectation* of other health professionals and the patient community being served. It is not an overstatement to say that *patients' lives depend on it.*

The role of the pharmacist in providing pharmaceutical care includes the ability and responsibility to **compound**—that is, to accurately weigh, measure volume, and combine individual therapeutic and pharmaceutical components in the formulation and preparation of prescriptions and medication orders.

Measurement of Volume

Common instruments for the pharmaceutical measurement of volume range from micropipets and burettes used in analytic procedures to large, industrial-size calibrated vessels. The selection of measuring instrument should be based on the level of precision required. In pharmacy practice, the most common instruments for measuring volume are cylindric and conical (cone-shaped) graduates (Fig. 3.1). For the measurement of small volumes, however, the pharmacist often uses a calibrated syringe or, when required, a pipette.

Whereas cylindric graduates are calibrated in SI or metric units, conical graduates are usually dual-scale, that is, calibrated in both metric and apothecary units of volume. (*Note*: metric units of volume are described in Chapter 2, and apothecaries' units are described in Appendix A.) Both glass and plastic graduates are commercially available in a number of capacities, ranging from 5 to 1000 milliliters and greater.

As a general rule, it is best to select the graduate with a capacity equal to or just exceeding the volume to be measured. Measurement of small volumes in large graduates tends to increase

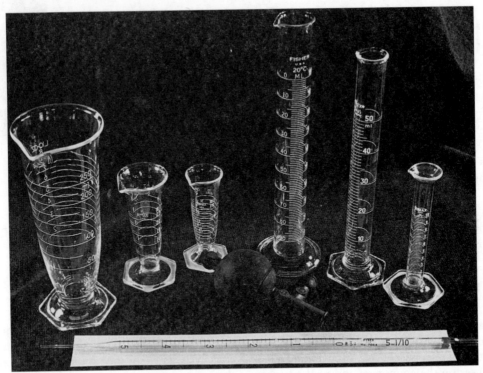

FIGURE 3.1 Examples of conical and cylindric graduates, a pipet, and a pipet-filling bulb for volumetric measurement.

the size of the error. The design of a volumetric apparatus is an important factor in measurement accuracy; the narrower the bore or chamber, the lesser the error in reading the meniscus and the more accurate the measurement (Fig. 3.2). According to the *United States Pharmacopeia*, a deviation of ± 1 mm in the meniscus reading causes an error of approximately 0.5 milliliter when a 100-milliliter cylindric graduate is used and an error of 1.8 milliliters at the 100-milliliter mark in a comparable conical graduate.[1] The *National Institute of Standards and Technology (NIST)* in its publication *Handbook 44* lists design details for graduates, including specifications for capacity (volume) and graduations.[2] Among the requirements are that graduates shall have an initial interval that is not subdivided, equal to not less than one-fifth and not more than one-fourth of the capacity of the graduate.[2] Conical graduates of less than 25-milliliter capacities are not recommended for use in pharmaceutical compounding.

It is essential for the pharmacist to select the proper type and capacity of instrument for volumetric measure and to carefully observe the meniscus at eye level to achieve the desired measurement.

Measurement of Weight

The selection of implements from the wide range of available weights, balances, and scales for pharmaceutical measurement depends on the task at hand, from highly sensitive electronic analytic balances and prescription balances in extemporaneous compounding procedures to large-capacity scales in the industrial manufacturing and production of pharmaceutical products. Each instrument used must meet established standards for sensitivity, accuracy, and capacity.

Class A prescription balances (Fig. 3.3) are designed for the weighing of medicinal or pharmaceutical substances required in the filling of prescriptions or in small-scale compound-

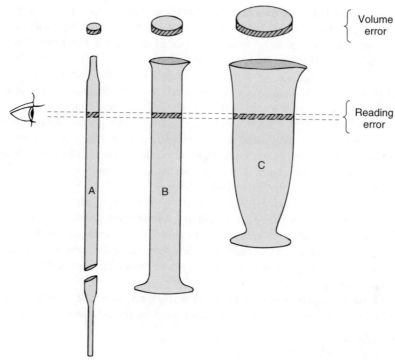

FIGURE 3.2 Volume error differentials due to instrument diameters. **(A)**, volumetric pipet; **(B)**, cylindric graduate; and **(C)**, conical graduate.

FIGURE 3.3 Torbal torsion balance and Ohaus electronic balance. *(Courtesy of Total Pharmacy Supply, Inc.)*

ing. Some prescription balances have a weighbeam and rider, and others a dial, to add up to 1 gram of weight. As required, additional external weights may be added to the right-hand balance pan. The material to be weighed is placed on the left-hand pan. Powder papers are added to each pan before any additions, and the balance is leveled by leveling feet or balancing screws. Weighings are performed through the careful portion-wise (by spatula) addition and removal of the material being weighed, with the balance being *arrested* (pans locked in place by the control knob) during each addition and removal of material, and unarrested with the lid closed for determinations of balance rest points. When the unarrested pans neither ascend nor descend, and the index plate shows the needle is in the center, the material and balance weights are considered equivalent. The student may wish to refer to other sources, such as the *United States Pharmacopeia*, for more detailed information on the proper use and testing of the prescription balance.[1]

Minimally, a Class A prescription balance should be used in all prescription compounding procedures. Balances of this type have a **sensitivity requirement (SR)** of 6 milligrams or less with no load and with a load of 10 grams in each pan. *To avoid errors of greater than 5% when using this balance, the pharmacist should not weigh less than 120 milligrams of material (i.e., a 5% error in a weighing of 120 milligrams = 6 milligrams).* Most commercially available Class A balances have a maximum capacity of 120 grams.

The term **sensitivity requirement** is defined as the load that will cause a change of one division on the index plate of the balance. It may be determined by the following procedure:

1. Level the balance.
2. Determine the rest point of the balance.
3. Determine the smallest weight that causes the rest point to shift one division on the index plate.

For greater accuracy than a Class A prescription balance allows, many pharmacies utilize high-precision electronic analytical balances to weigh very small quantities (Fig. 3.4). Many of

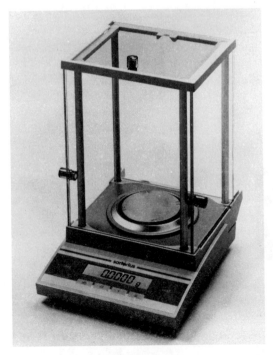

FIGURE 3.4 Sartorious BasicLite analytical balance. *(Courtesy of Sartorius Corporation.)*

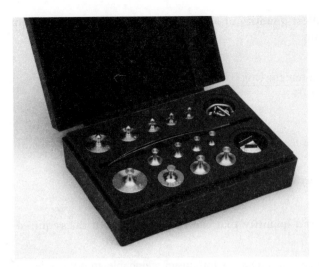

FIGURE 3.5 Set of metric weights. *(Courtesy of Mettler-Toledo, Inc.)*

these balances are capable of weighing accurately 0.1 milligram, are self-calibrating, and are equipped with convenient digital readout features. The usual maximum capacities for balances of this precision range from about 60 grams to 210 grams depending upon the model. A set of metric weights that may be used to weigh materials on a prescription balance and/or used to calibrate an analytical balance is shown in Figure 3.5.

Aliquot Method of Weighing and Measuring

When a degree of precision in measurement that is beyond the capacity of the instrument at hand is required, the pharmacist may achieve the desired precision by calculating and measuring in terms of aliquot parts. An **aliquot** is a fraction, portion, or part that is contained an exact number of times in another.

Weighing by the Aliquot Method

The *aliquot method of weighing* is a method by which small quantities of a substance may be obtained within the desired degree of accuracy by weighing a larger-than-needed portion of the substance, diluting it with an inert material, and then weighing a portion (aliquot) of the mixture calculated to contain the desired amount of the needed substance. A stepwise description of the procedure is depicted in Figure 3.6 and is described as follows:

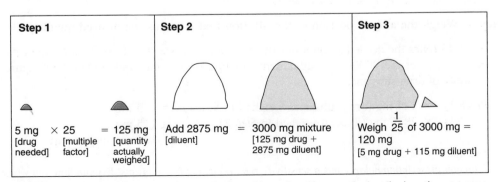

Step 1	Step 2	Step 3
5 mg × 25 = 125 mg [drug needed] [multiple factor] [quantity actually weighed]	Add 2875 mg = 3000 mg mixture [diluent] [125 mg drug + 2875 mg diluent]	Weigh $\frac{1}{25}$ of 3000 mg = 120 mg [5 mg drug + 115 mg diluent]

FIGURE 3.6 Depiction of the aliquot method of weighing using the example described on the next page.

Preliminary Step. **Calculate the smallest quantity of a substance that can be weighed on the balance with the desired precision.**

The equation used:

$$\frac{100\% \times \text{Sensitivity Requirement (mg)}}{\text{Acceptable Error (\%)}} = \text{Smallest Quantity (mg)}$$

Example:

On a balance with an SR of 6 mg, and with an acceptable error of no greater than 5%, a quantity of not less than 120 mg must be weighed.

$$\frac{100\% \times 6 \text{ mg}}{5\%} = 120 \text{ mg}$$

Step 1. **Select a multiple of the desired quantity that can be weighed with the required precision.**

- If the quantity of a required substance is *less than* the minimum weighable amount, select a "multiple" of the required quantity that will yield an amount equal to or greater than the minimum weighable amount. (A larger-than-necessary multiple may be used to exceed the minimum accuracy desired.)
- *Example:*
  *If the balance in the example in the preliminary step is used, and if 5 mg of a drug substance is required on a prescription, then a quantity at least **25 times** (the multiple) the desired amount, or 125 mg (5 mg × 25), must be weighed for the desired accuracy. (If a larger multiple is used, say 30, and 150 mg of the substance is weighed [5 mg × 30], then a weighing error of only 4% would result.)*

Step 2. **Dilute the multiple quantity with an inert substance.**

- *The amount of inert diluent* to use is determined by the fact that the aliquot portion of the drug-diluent mixture weighed in *Step 3* must be equal to or greater than the minimum weighable quantity previously determined.
- By multiplying the amount of the aliquot portion to weigh in *Step 3* by the multiple selected in *Step 1*, the total quantity of the mixture to prepare is determined.
- *Example:*
  According to the preliminary step, 120 milligrams or more must be weighed for the desired accuracy. If we decide on 120 mg for the aliquot portion in Step 3, and multiply it by the multiple selected in Step 1 (i.e., 25), we arrive at 3000 mg for the total quantity of the drug-diluent mixture to prepare. Subtracting the 125 mg of drug weighed in Step 1, we must add 2875 mg of diluent to prepare the 3000 mg of drug-diluent mixture.

Step 3. **Weigh the aliquot portion of the dilution that contains the desired quantity.**

- Since **25 times** the needed amount of drug substance was weighed (*Step 1*), an aliquot part equal to $\frac{1}{25}$ of the 3000-mg drug-diluent mixture, or 120 mg, will contain the required quantity of drug substance.

- *Proof:* $\frac{1}{25}$ × 125 mg (drug substance weighed in *Step 1*) =   5 mg
  $\frac{1}{25}$ × 2875 mg (diluent weighed in *Step 2*)   = <u>115 mg</u>
  120 mg aliquot part

- *Example:*
  A torsion prescription balance has a sensitivity requirement of 6 milligrams. Explain how you would weigh 4 milligrams of atropine sulfate with an accuracy of ± 5%, using lactose as the diluent.

Because 6 milligrams is the potential balance error, 120 milligrams is the smallest amount that should be weighed to achieve the required precision.

If 120 milligrams, or 30 times the desired amount of atropine sulfate, is chosen as the multiple quantity to be weighed in Step 1, and if 150 milligrams is set as the aliquot to be weighed in Step 3, then:

1. Weigh 30 × 4 mg, or   120 mg of atropine sulfate
2. Dilute with   <u>4380</u> mg of lactose
   to make   4500 mg of dilution
3. Weigh $\frac{1}{30}$ of dilution, or 150 mg of dilution, which will contain 4 mg of atropine sulfate, *answer*.

Proof: $\dfrac{4500 \text{ mg (dilution)}}{150 \text{ mg (dilution)}} = \dfrac{120 \text{ mg (atropine sulfate)}}{x \text{ mg (atropine sulfate)}}$

     = 4 mg, *answer*.

In this example, the weight of the aliquot was arbitrarily set as 150 mg, which exceeds the weight of the multiple quantity, as it preferably should. If 120 mg had been set as the aliquot, the multiple quantity should have been diluted with 3480 mg of lactose to get 3600 mg of dilution, and the aliquot of 120 mg would have contained 4 mg of atropine sulfate. On the other hand, if 200 mg had been set as the aliquot, the multiple quantity of atropine sulfate should have been diluted with 5880 mg of lactose to get 6000 mg of dilution.

Another Example:

A torsion prescription balance has a sensitivity requirement of 6.5 milligrams. Explain how you would weigh 15 milligrams of atropine sulfate with an accuracy of ± 5%, using lactose as the diluent.

Because 6.5 milligrams is the potential balance error, 130 milligrams (20 × 6.5 milligrams) is the smallest amount that should be weighed to achieve the required accuracy.

If 10 is chosen as the multiple, and if 130 milligrams is set as the weight of the aliquot, then:

1. Weigh 10 × 15 mg or   150 mg of atropine sulfate
2. Dilute with   <u>1150</u> mg of lactose
   to make   1300 mg of dilution
3. Weigh $\frac{1}{10}$ of dilution, or 130 mg, which will contain 15 mg of atropine sulfate, *answer*.

> **NOTE: It is important for the student to recognize that answers to aliquot calculations may vary, but still be correct, depending on the multiple factors arbitrarily chosen for use.**

Measuring Volume by the Aliquot Method

The aliquot method of measuring volume, which is identical in principle to the aliquot method of weighing, may be used when relatively small volumes must be measured with great precision:

     Step 1. Select a multiple of the desired quantity that can be measured with the required precision.
     Step 2. Dilute the multiple quantity with a compatible diluent (usually a solvent for the liquid to be measured) to an amount evenly divisible by the multiple selected.
     Step 3. Measure the aliquot of the dilution that contains the quantity originally desired.

Examples:

A formula calls for 0.5 milliliter of hydrochloric acid. Using a 10-milliliter graduate calibrated from 2 to 10 milliliters in 1-milliliter divisions, explain how you would obtain the desired quantity of hydrochloric acid by the aliquot method.

If 4 is chosen as the multiple, and if 2 milliliters is set as the volume of the aliquot, then:

1. Measure 4 × 0.5 mL, or   2 mL of the acid
2. Dilute with   <u>6 mL</u> of water
   to make   8 mL of dilution
3. Measure ¼ of dilution, or 2 mL of dilution, which will contain 0.5 mL of hydrochloric acid, *answer.*

A prescription calls for 0.2 mL of clove oil. Using a 5-mL graduate calibrated in units of 0.5 mL, how would you obtain the required amount of clove oil using the aliquot method and alcohol as the diluent?

If 5 is chosen as the multiple, then:

1. Measure 5 × 0.2 mL, or   1 mL of clove oil
2. Dilute with   <u>4 mL</u> of alcohol
   to make   5 mL of dilution
3. Measure ⅕ of the dilution, or 1 mL, which contains 0.2 mL of clove oil, *answer.*

Least Weighable Quantity Method of Weighing

This method may be used as an alternative to the aliquot method of weighing to obtain small quantities of a drug substance.

After determining the quantity of drug substance that is desired and the smallest quantity that can be weighed on the balance with the desired degree of accuracy, the procedure is as follows:

Step 1. Weigh an amount of the drug substance that is *equal to or greater than* the least weighable quantity.

CALCULATIONS CAPSULE

Weighing Accuracy

- The sensitivity requirement (SR) of a balance must be known or determined. An SR of 6 mg is usual.
- An error in weighing of ± 5% or less is acceptable.
- The smallest quantity that should be weighed on a prescription balance is determined by the equation:

$$\frac{100\% \times Sensitivity\ Requirement\ (mg)}{Acceptable\ Error\ (\%)} = Smallest\ Quantity\ (mg)$$

That quantity is usually about 120 mg.

- To weigh smaller quantities, an electronic balance or the aliquot method of weighing should be used.

Step 2. Dilute the drug substance with a calculated quantity of inert diluent such that a predetermined quantity of the drug-diluent mixture will contain the desired quantity of drug.

Example:

If 20 milligrams of a drug substance are needed to fill a prescription, explain how you would obtain this amount of drug with an accuracy of ± 5% using a balance with an SR of 6 milligrams. Use lactose as the diluent.

In the example, 20 milligrams is the amount of drug substance needed. The least weighable quantity would be 120 milligrams. The amount of drug substance to be weighed, therefore, must be equal to or greater than 120 milligrams. In solving the problem, 120 milligrams of drug substance is weighed. In calculating the amount of diluent to use, a predetermined quantity of drug-diluent mixture must be selected to contain the desired 20 milligrams of drug substance. The quantity selected must be greater than 120 milligrams because the drug-diluent mixture must be obtained accurately through weighing on the balance. An amount of 150 milligrams may be arbitrarily selected. The total amount of diluent to use may then be determined through the calculation of the following proportion:

$$\frac{20 \text{ mg (drug needed for } \text{R})}{150 \text{ mg (drug-diluent mixture to use in } \text{R})} = \frac{120 \text{ mg (total drug substance weighed)}}{x \text{ mg (total amount of drug-diluent mixture prepared)}}$$

x = 900 mg of the drug-diluent mixture to prepare
Hence, 900 mg − 120 mg = 780 mg of diluent (lactose) to use, *answer.*

It should be noted that in this procedure, each weighing, including that of the drug substance, the diluent, and the drug-diluent mixture, must be determined to be equal to or greater than the least weighable quantity as determined for the balance used and accuracy desired.

Percentage of Error

Because measurements in the community pharmacy are never *absolutely* accurate, it is important for the pharmacist to recognize the limitations of the instruments used and the magnitude of the errors that may be incurred. When a pharmacist measures a volume of liquid or weighs a material, two quantities become important: (1) the *apparent* weight or volume measured, and (2) the possible excess or deficiency in the actual quantity obtained.

Percentage of error may be defined as *the maximum potential error multiplied by 100 and divided by the quantity desired.* The calculation may be formulated as follows:

$$\frac{\text{Error} \times 100\%}{\text{Quantity desired}} = \text{Percentage of error}$$

Calculating Percentage of Error in Volumetric Measurement

As described earlier, the precision obtained in a given measurement depends on the selection of the measuring device used, the volume of liquid being measured, and the skill and care of the pharmacist.

The percentage of error in a measurement of volume may be calculated from the above equation, relating the volume in error (determined through devices of greater precision) to the volume desired (or apparently measured).

Example:

Using a graduated cylinder, a pharmacist measured 30 milliliters of a liquid. On subsequent examination, using a narrow-gauge burette, it was determined that the pharmacist had actually measured 32 milliliters. What was the percentage of error in the original measurement?

32 milliliters − 30 milliliters = 2 milliliters, the volume of error

$$\frac{2 \text{ mL} \times 100\%}{30 \text{ mL}} = 6.7\%, \textit{answer.}$$

Calculating Percentage of Error in Weighing

The various scales and balances used in pharmaceutical weighing have ascribed to them different degrees of precision. As described previously in this chapter, knowledge of the *sensitivity requirement* of the balance being used is critical in weighing to a specified degree of accuracy. The sensitivity requirement of a balance may be used to determine the percentage of error in a given weighing.

Examples:

When the maximum potential error is ± 4 milligrams in a total of 100 milligrams, what is the percentage of error?

$$\frac{4 \text{ mg} \times 100\%}{100 \text{ mg}} = 4\%, \textit{answer.}$$

A prescription calls for 800 milligrams of a substance. After weighing this amount on a balance, the pharmacist decides to check by weighing it again on a more sensitive balance, which registers only 750 milligrams. Because the first weighing was 50 milligrams short of the desired amount, what was the percentage of error?

$$\frac{50 \text{ mg} \times 100\%}{800 \text{ mg}} = 6.25\%, \textit{answer.}$$

CASE IN POINT 3.1: **A pharmacist is asked to compound the following formula for the preparation of 100 capsules:[3]**

Estriol	200 mg
Estrone	25 mg
Estradiol	25 mg
Methocel E4M	10 g
Lactose	23.75 g

Using a balance that has an SR of 6 mg, the aliquot method of weighing, lactose as the diluent, and an error in weighing of 4%, show, by calculations, how the correct quantity of estrone can be obtained to accurately compound the formula.

CASE IN POINT 3.2: A physician prescribed 25 4-mg capsules of a drug for a special needs patient, knowing that the dose prescribed was considered "subtherapeutic." The lowest strength commercially available tablets contain 25 mg.

The pharmacist decided to select the minimum required number of 25-mg tablets (4 tablets); reduce them to a powder with a mortar and pestle; weigh the powder (280 mg); and continue the process using the aliquot method. She called upon her pharmacy student intern to calculate (a) the minimum quantity of lactose (diluent) to use in preparing the crushed tablet-diluent mixture and (b) the quantity of the mixture to use to fill each capsule.

The prescription balance had a SR of 6 mg and a weighing error of 5% was acceptable. Show your calculations for (a) and (b), and (c) prove that your answer to (b) is correct by demonstrating that each capsule would indeed contain 4 mg of drug.

PRACTICE PROBLEMS

Calculations of Aliquot Parts by Weighing

1. A prescription calls for 50 milligrams of chlorpheniramine maleate. Using a prescription balance with a sensitivity requirement of 6 milligrams, explain how you would obtain the required amount of chlorpheniramine maleate with an error not greater than 5%.

2. A prescription balance has a sensitivity requirement of 0.006 gram. Explain how you would weigh 0.012 gram of atropine sulfate with an error not greater than 5%, using lactose as the diluent.

3. A torsion prescription balance has a sensitivity requirement of 4 milligrams. Explain how you would weigh 5 milligrams of hydromorphone hydrochloride with an error not greater than 5%. Use lactose as the diluent.

4. A torsion prescription balance has a sensitivity requirement of 0.004 gram. Explain how you would weigh 0.008 gram of a substance with an error not greater than 5%.

5. A prescription balance has a sensitivity requirement of 6.5 milligrams. Explain how you would weigh 20 milligrams of a substance with an error not greater than 2%.

Calculations of Aliquot Parts by Measuring Volume

6. ℞ Sodium Citrate   5 g
    Tartar Emetic   0.015 g
    Cherry Syrup ad   120 mL

   Using a balance with a sensitivity of 4 mg, an acceptable weighing error of 5% and cherry syrup as the solvent for tartar emetic, how could you obtain the correct quantity of tartar emetic to fill the prescription?

7. A formula calls for 0.6 milliliter of a coloring solution. Using a 10-milliliter graduate calibrated from 2 to 10 milliliters in 1-milliliter units, how could you obtain the desired quantity of the coloring solution by the aliquot method? Use water as the diluent.

8. Using a 10-milliliter graduate calibrated in 1-milliliter units, explain how you would measure 1.25 milliliters of a dye solution by the aliquot method. Use water as the diluent.

9. The formula for 100 milliliters of pentobarbital sodium elixir calls for 0.75 milliliter of orange oil. Using alcohol as a diluent and a 10-milliliter graduate calibrated in 1-milliliter units, how could you obtain the desired quantity of orange oil?

Calculations of Percentage of Error

10. A pharmacist attempts to weigh 120 milligrams of codeine sulfate on a balance with a sensitivity requirement of 6 milligrams. Calculate the maximum potential error in terms of percentage.

11. In compounding a prescription, a pharmacist weighed 0.050 gram of a substance on a balance insensitive to quantities smaller than 0.004 gram. What was the maximum potential error in terms of percentage?

12. A pharmacist weighed 475 milligrams of a substance on a balance of dubious accuracy. When checked on a balance of high accuracy, the weight was found to be 445 milligrams. Calculate the percentage of error in the first weighing.

13. A 10-milliliter graduate weighs 42.745 grams. When 5 milliliters of distilled water are measured in it, the combined weight of graduate and water is 47.675 grams. By definition, 5 milliliters of water should weigh 5 grams. Calculate the weight of the measured water and express any deviation from 5 grams as percentage of error.

14. A graduate weighs 35.825 grams. When 10 milliliters of water are measured in it, the weight of the graduate and water is 45.835 grams. Calculate the weight of the water and express any deviation from 10 grams as percentage of error.

15. In preparing a certain ointment, a pharmacist used 28.35 grams of zinc oxide instead of the 31.1 grams called for. Calculate the percentage of error on the basis of the desired quantity.

16. A pharmacist attempts to weigh 0.375 gram of morphine sulfate on a balance of dubious accuracy. When checked on a highly accurate balance, the weight is found to be 0.400 gram. Calculate the percentage of error in the first weighing.

ANSWERS TO "CASE IN POINT" AND PRACTICE PROBLEMS

Case in Point 3.1

The smallest quantity that should be weighed on the balance:

$$\frac{100\% \times 6 \text{ mg}}{4\%} = 150 \text{ mg}$$

Quantity desired (estrone): 25 mg
Multiple factor selected: 6
Aliquot portion selected: 150 mg

Estrone (25 × 6)	150 mg
Lactose	750 mg
Aliquot mixture	900 mg
Aliquot portion (900 mg ÷ 6)	150 mg of mixture will provide 25 mg estrone, *answer*

Case in Point 3.2

The smallest quantity that should be weighed on the balance:

$$\frac{100\% \times 6 \text{ mg}}{5\%} = 120 \text{ mg}$$

(a) Quantity of mixture required to prepare 25 capsules each containing the weighable quantity of 120 mg:

120 mg × 25 (capsules) = 3000 mg

Quantity of lactose required equals the quantity of mixture required less the weight of the crushed tablets:

3000 mg − 280 mg = 2720 mg or 2.72 g of lactose required, *answer*.

(b) Quantity of mixture to fill each capsule:

3000 mg ÷ 25 (capsules) = 120 mg, *answer*.

(c) Proof of 4 mg of drug per capsule:
    Amount of drug in mixture:

4 mg (per tablet) $\times$ 25 (tablets) = 100 mg

Amount of drug per capsule:

100 mg $\div$ 25 (capsules) = 4 mg, *answer.*

or,

$$\frac{100 \text{ mg } (drug)}{3000 \text{ mg } (mixture)} = \frac{x}{120 \text{ mg } (mixture)}$$
= 4 mg, *answer.*

Practice Problems

Aliquot Parts by Weighing

1. Weigh   150 mg chlorpheniramine
               maleate
   Dilute with 450 mg
   to make   600 mg
   Weigh   200 mg

2. Weigh   120 mg atropine sulfate
   Dilute with 1380 mg
   to make   1500 mg
   Weigh   150 mg

3. Weigh   80 mg hydromorphone
               hydrochloride
   Dilute with 1520 mg
   to make   1600 mg
   Weigh   100 mg

4. Weigh   160 mg
   Dilute with 3840 mg
   to make   4000 mg
   Weigh   200 mg

5. Weigh   400 mg
   Dilute with 7600 mg
   to make   8000 mg
   Weigh   400 mg

Aliquot Parts by Measuring Volume

6. Weigh   90 mg
   Dilute to   12 mL
   Measure   2 mL

7. Measure   3 mL
   Dilute to   10 mL
   Measure   2 mL

8. Measure   5 mL
   Dilute to   8 mL
   Measure   2 mL

9. Measure   3 mL orange oil
   Dilute to   8 mL
   Measure   2 mL

Percentage of Error

10. 5%

11. 8%

12. 6.32%

13. 1.4%

14. 0.1%

15. 8.84%

16. 6.67%

REFERENCES

1. Weights and balances and prescription balances and volumetric apparatus. United States Pharmacopeia 31st Rev. National Formulary 26. Rockville, MD: United States Pharmacopeial Convention, 2008;1:66,642–643.
2. Handbook 44–2007 Ed. Gaithersburg, MD: National Institute of Standards and Technology, Weights and Measures Division. Available at: http://www.nist.gov. Accessed September 4, 2008.
3. *International Journal of Pharmaceutical Compounding* 1993;3:401.

Interpretation of Prescriptions and Medication Orders

4

Objectives

Upon successful completion of this chapter, the student will be able to:

- Demonstrate an understanding of the format and components of a typical prescription.
- Demonstrate an understanding of the format and components of a typical institutional medication order.
- Interpret correctly standard abbreviations and symbols used on prescriptions and medication orders.
- Differentiate between *patient compliance* and *noncompliance* and apply calculations to determine compliancy.

By definition, a **prescription** is an order for medication issued by a physician, dentist, or other properly licensed medical practitioner. A prescription designates a specific medication and dosage to be prepared by a pharmacist and administered to a particular patient.

A prescription is usually written on preprinted forms containing the traditional symbol ℞ (meaning "recipe," "take thou," or "you take"), name, address, telephone number, and other pertinent information regarding the physician or other prescriber. In addition, blank spaces are used by the prescriber to provide information about the patient, the medication desired, and the directions for use. The information generally found on a completed prescription is shown in Figure 4.1. A prescription written by a veterinarian generally includes the animal species and/or pet's name and the name of the owner.

A written prescription may be presented at the pharmacy by the patient or caregiver, or it may be transmitted from the prescriber by telephone or by other electronic means. In the latter instances, the pharmacist immediately reduces the order to a properly written form or computer entry.

In hospitals and other institutions, the forms are somewhat different and are referred to as **medication orders.** A typical medication order sheet is shown in Figure 4.2. The orders shown in this example are typed; typically, these instructions are written by the physician in ink.

A prescription or medication order for an infant, child, or an elderly person may also include the age, weight, and/or body surface area (BSA) of the patient (as discussed in Chapter 8). An example of a prescription written for a pediatric patient is shown in Figure 4.3. This information is sometimes necessary in calculating the appropriate medication dosage.

It is important to recognize two broad categories of prescriptions: (1) those written for a single component or prefabricated product and *not requiring compounding* or admixture by the pharmacist, and (2) those written for more than a single component and *requiring*

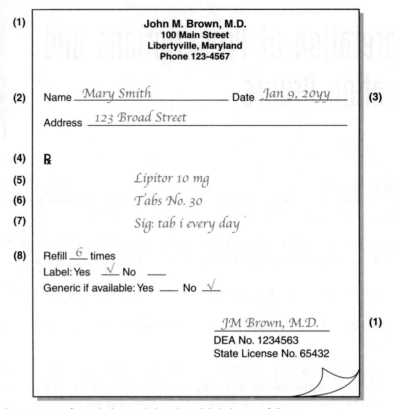

(1)

John M. Brown, M.D.
100 Main Street
Libertyville, Maryland
Phone 123-4567

(2) Name _Mary Smith_ _____ Date _Jan 9, 20yy_ ___ **(3)**

Address __123 Broad Street_____

(4) ℞

(5)   _Lipitor 10 mg_

(6)   _Tabs No. 30_

(7)   _Sig: tab i every day_

(8) Refill __6__ times
Label: Yes __✓__ No _____
Generic if available: Yes ____ No _✓_

JM Brown, M.D. **(1)**
DEA No. 1234563
State License No. 65432

FIGURE 4.1 Components of a typical prescription. Parts labeled are as follows:

(1) Prescriber information and signature
(2) Patient information
(3) Date prescription was written
(4) ℞ symbol (the Superscription), meaning "take thou,"
    "you take," or "recipe"
(5) Medication prescribed (the Inscription)
(6) Dispensing instructions to the pharmacist (the Subscription)
(7) Directions to the patient (the Signa)
(8) Special instructions. It is important to note that for any Medicaid or Medicare prescription and according to
    individual state laws, a handwritten language by the prescriber, such as "Brand necessary," may be required
    to disallow generic substitution.

compounding.[a] A prescription may include the chemical or nonproprietary (generic) name of
the substance or the manufacturer's brand or trademark name (shown in all capital letters
in this text). Prescriptions requiring compounding contain the quantities of each ingredient
required. Medications are prepared into various types of _dosage forms_ (e.g., _tablets, syrups,
injections_) and _drug delivery systems_ (e.g., _transdermal patches_) to ensure that the medication

---

[a] The extemporaneous compounding of prescriptions is an activity for which pharmacists are uniquely qualified by virtue of their
education, training, and experience. By definition, **pharmacy compounding** involves the mixing, assembling, packaging, and labeling of
a medication on receipt of a prescription order for a specific patient. In addition to the compounding of individual prescriptions as
received, guidelines of the Food and Drug Administration permit the advance preparation of very limited quantities of compounded
products _in anticipation_ of prescriptions for specific patients, based on regularly observed prescribing patterns. Unless licensed as a
manufacturer, however, pharmacies may not engage in the large-scale production or _manufacturing_ of drugs for other pharmacies or for
other entities for distribution or resale.[1]

CITY HOSPITAL
Athens, GA 30600

PATIENT NAME:	Thompson, Linda
ADDRESS:	2345 Oak Circle
CITY, STATE:	Athens, GA
AGE/SEX:	35 Female
PHYSICIAN:	J. Hardmer
HOSP.NO:	900612345
SERVICE:	Medicine
ROOM:	220 East

PHYSICIAN'S ORDER

DATE	TIME	ORDERS
02/01/yy	1200	1. Propranolol 40 mg po QID
		2. Furosemide 20 mg po q AM
		3. Flurazepam 30 mg at HS prn sleep
		4. D-5-W + 20 mEq kcl/L at 84 mL/hr
		Hardmer, MD

Unless "No substitution permitted" is clearly written after the order, a generic or therapeutic equivalent drug may be dispensed according to the Formulary policies of this hospital.

FIGURE 4.2 Typical hospital medication order sheet.

Mary M. Brown, M.D.
Pediatric Clinic
110 Main Street
Libertyville, Maryland
Phone 456-1234

Name _Suzie Smith_____ Age _5__ Weight _39.4__ lb

Address _123 Broad Street____ Date _Jan 9, 20yy___

R

Omnicef Oral Suspension
125 mg/5 mL
Disp. 100 mL
Give 14 mg/kg/day x 10 days

Sig: _____ tsp q 12 h

Refill _0_ times
Label: Yes _√_ No ___
Generic if available: Yes ___ No _√_

Mary Brown, M.D.
DEA No. MB5555555
State License No. 23456

FIGURE 4.3 Example of a prescription for a pediatric patient.

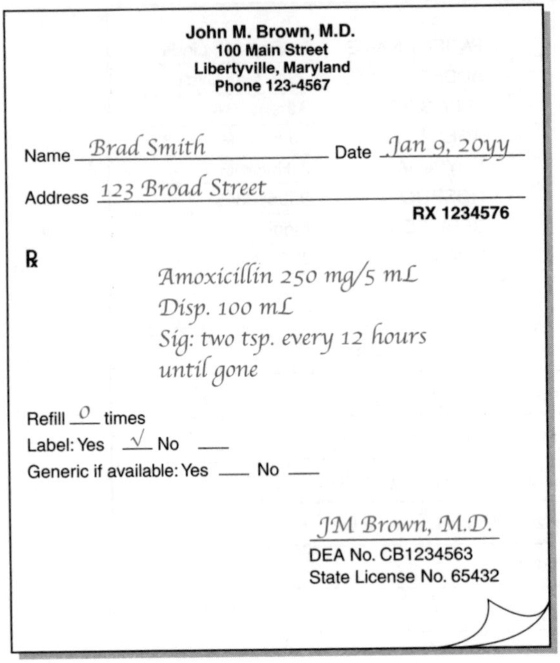

John M. Brown, M.D.
100 Main Street
Libertyville, Maryland
Phone 123-4567

Name _Brad Smith_   Date _Jan 9, 20yy_

Address _123 Broad Street_

RX 1234576

℞

        Amoxicillin 250 mg/5 mL
        Disp. 100 mL
        Sig: two tsp. every 12 hours
        until gone

Refill _0_ times
Label: Yes _√_ No _____
Generic if available: Yes _____ No _____

            JM Brown, M.D.
            DEA No. CB1234563
            State License No. 65432

FIGURE 4.4 Example of a prescription written for a generic drug.

is administered accurately and appropriately. Examples are shown for prescriptions calling for trade-name products (Fig. 4.1 and Fig. 4.3), a generic drug (Fig. 4.4), and compounding (Fig. 4.5). Definitions and descriptions of dosage forms and drug delivery systems are presented in Appendix C.

Tamper-Resistant Prescription Pads

To prevent the unauthorized copying, modification, or counterfeiting of prescriptions, *tamper-resistant prescription pads* have been developed. Their use is mandated for hand-written prescriptions for outpatient drugs covered by Medicaid.[2,3] The tamper-resistant qualities of these prescription forms is accomplished through the use of security paper, erase-resistant paper, thermochromatic ink (which results in the appearance of the word "VOID" on photocopies), and/or imbedded holograms.

e-prescribing/e-prescriptions

The use of electronic means for the generation and transmission of prescriptions is accepted throughout the United States. In the inpatient or outpatient setting, a medication order, for a patient is entered into an automated data entry system as a personal computer (PC) or a handheld device loaded with *e-prescribing* software and sent to a pharmacy as an *e-prescription*. When received, a pharmacist immediately reduces the order to a hard copy and/or stores it as a computer file.

    Among the advantages cited for *e-prescriptions* over traditional paper prescriptions are: reduced errors due to prescription legibility; concurrent software screens for drug interactions; reduced incidence of altered or forged prescriptions; efficiency for both prescriber and pharmacist; and, convenience to the patient, whose prescription would likely be ready for pick-up upon arrival at the pharmacy.[4,5]

John M. Brown, M.D.
100 Main Street
Libertyville, Maryland
Phone 123-4567

Name _Neil Smith_____ Date _Jan 9, 20yy_____

Address _123 Broad Street_____

R   Metoclopramide HCL   10 g
       Methylparaben   50 mg
       Propylparaben   20 mg
       Sodium Chloride   800 mg
       Purified Water, qs ad   100 mL

       M. ft. nasal spray

       Sig: Nasal spray for chemotherapy-
       induced emesis. Use as directed.
       Discard after 60 days.

Refill _0_ times
Label: Yes _✓_ No ___
Generic if available: Yes ___ No ___

             JM Brown, M.D.
             DEA No. CB1234563
             State License No. 65432

FIGURE 4.5 Example of a prescription requiring compounding.

States have established appropriate requirements for prescription drug orders sent by computer, facsimile, or other electronic devices. In addition to the requirements in effect for traditionally written prescriptions, they include an added assurance of authenticity through verified encrypted electronic signature, digital identification, or other authentication procedure.

Hospital and Other Institutional Medication Order Forms

As noted previously, a typical *medication order form* used in the hospital setting is shown in Figure 4.2. In addition, other forms may be used within a hospital by specialized units such as infectious disease, cardiac care, pediatrics, obstetrics, orthopedics, and others.[6] Drug-specific forms also may be used, as for heparin dosing, electrolyte infusions, and morphine sulfate in patient-controlled anesthesia. An example of the latter is shown in Figure 4.6.

Many different types of health care institutions, as acute care facilities, outpatient clinics, intermediate- and long-term care facilities (Fig. 4.7), cancer treatment centers, and a host of others utilize medication order forms designed to meet their specific requirements. Clinical drug investigators likewise may use specific medication order forms for their study protocols.[7]

Military Time

Military time is used not only in the military but in civilian life as well, such as in hospitals, other patient-care institutions, emergency services (e.g., paramedics, law enforcement, fire fight-

City Hospital

Patient Controlled Anesthesia (PCA) Orders

<u>MORPHINE SULFATE INJECTION, 1 mg/mL</u>

Patient Information (Label)

Physician:

Date: Time:

1. Mode (check)	☐PCA	☐Continuous	☐PCA & Continuous
			DOSING GUIDELINES
2. PCA Dose = _____ mL (mg)			1 mL (1 mg)
3. Period between Injections = _____ minutes			10 minutes
4. Basal (Continuous) Rate = _____ mL (mg)/hr			1 mL (1 mg)/hr
5. One-Hour Limit = _____ mL (mg)			7 mL (7 mg)
6. Initial Loading Dose = _____ mL (mg)			2-5 mL (2-5 mg)

7. Additional Instructions:

Physician's Signature _____

FIGURE 4.6 Example of a hospital form for prescribing a specific drug treatment: Patient-Controlled Anesthesia. *(Adapted with permission from www.hospital-forms.com.[6])*

ing), and in other entities. Its use provides an unambiguous expression of time. In health care institutions, military time may be used to record the time of a patient's admission, when a medication was administered, the time of surgery, and so forth.

Table 4.1 compares the expressions of military time and regular time. Military time is verbalized, as for example "twenty-three hundred hours." Colons may be used to separate hours and minutes, as 1331 or 13:31 hours (31 minutes past 1 o'clock in the afternoon) and when desired seconds, as 1331:42 or 13:31:42.

Range of Prescription and Medication Order Calculations

This chapter introduces the form, content, and interpretation of prescriptions and institutional medication orders and, as such, *provides the framework for the majority of the calculations that follow in this text, including calculations of the following:*

- *Doses:* including the quantity of a prescribed dose, the total number of doses prescribed, and the number of days the prescribed medication will last.
- *Compliance:* the patient's or caregiver's compliance in meeting the prescribed directions for dosing.

MEDICATION ORDER FORM CITY NURSING HOME *Physician's Orders*					
Attending Physician:			Order Number: (preprinted)		
Resident's Name:				Room Number:	
DRUG	QUANTITY	DOSE AND ROUTE	FREQUENCY	DIAGNOSIS	ADMINISTRATION TIMES
1.					____AM ____PM ____AM ____PM
2.					____AM ___PM ____AM ____PM
3.					____AM ___PM ____AM ___PM
4.					____AM ___PM ____AM ___PM
Physician's Signature:				Time/Date Ordered:	
Signature of Nurse Receiving Order:				Time/Date Ordered:	
Ordered from Pharmacy, Time/Date:				Received from Pharmacy, Time/Date:	

FIGURE 4.7 Example of a nursing home medication order form.

- *Drug concentration:* the quantity of an active therapeutic ingredient to use to achieve the desired drug concentration.
- *Rate of drug administration:* the quantity of drug administered per unit of time to meet prescribed dosing schedule (e.g., mg/min, drops/minute, or mL/hr for the administration of an intravenous fluid).
- *Compounding:* the quantities of active and inactive components to use in the extemporaneous preparation of a pharmaceutical product, including the use of stock solutions and/or prefabricated dosage units in the process.

TABLE 4.1 COMPARATIVE EXPRESSIONS OF REGULAR AND MILITARY TIME

REGULAR TIME	MILITARY TIME	REGULAR TIME	MILITARY TIME
Midnight	0000	Noon	1200
1:00 A.M.	0100	1:00 P.M.	1300
2:00 A.M.	0200	2:00 P.M.	1400
3:00 A.M.	0300	3:00 P.M.	1500
4:00 A.M.	0400	4:00 P.M.	1600
5:00 A.M.	0500	5:00 P.M.	1700
6:00 A.M.	0600	6:00 P.M.	1800
7:00 A.M.	0700	7:00 P.M.	1900
8:00 A.M.	0800	8:00 P.M.	2000
9:00 A.M.	0900	9:00 P.M.	2100
10:00 A.M.	1000	10:00 P.M.	2200
11:00 A.M.	1100	11:00 P.M.	2300

- *Chemical-physical factors:* including calculations to make solutions isotonic, iso-osmotic, equimolar, or buffered.
- *Pharmacoeconomics:* including medication costs, cost-benefit analysis, cost-effectiveness analysis, alternative treatment plans, and medication pricing.

The quantities of ingredients to be used almost always are expressed in SI metric units of weight and measurement. This system is described in detail in Chapter 2. In rare instances, units of the apothecaries' system may be used. This system is described in Appendix A. In the use of the SI (metric system), the decimal point may be replaced by a vertical line that is imprinted on the prescription blank or hand drawn by the prescriber. In these instances, whole or subunits of grams of weight and milliliters of volume are separated by the vertical line. Sometimes the abbreviations g (for gram) and mL (for milliliter) are absent and must be presumed.

Examples of prescriptions written in SI metric units:

℞	Acetylsalicylic Acid	4 g
	Phenacetin	0.8 g
	Codeine Sulfate	0.5 g
	Mix and make capsules no. 20	
	Sig. One capsule every 4 hours.	
℞	Dextromethorphan	0 | 18
	Guaifenesin Syrup	1 | 2
	Alcohol	2 | 1
	Flavored Syrup ad	60
	Sig. 5 mL as needed for cough.	

Prescription and Medication Order Accuracy

It is the responsibility of the pharmacist to ensure that each prescription and medication order received is correct in its form and content; is appropriate for the patient being treated; and is subsequently filled, labeled, dispensed, and administered accurately. In essence, each medication should be:

- therapeutically appropriate for the patient;
- prescribed at the correct dose;
- dispensed in the correct strength and dosage form;
- correctly labeled with complete instructions for the patient or caregiver; and
- for the patient in a hospital or other health care facility, each medication must be administered to the correct patient, at the correct time, and by the correct rate and route of administration.

Errors and Omissions

To ensure such accuracy, the pharmacist is obliged to review each prescription and medication order in a step-by-step manner to detect errors of omission and commission. This is termed a search for **errors and omissions**.

A review of the completeness and correctness of a prescription or medication order is an important *initial step* in the process of ensuring accuracy. It is important to note that other subsequent and related parameters to ensure the accuracy of medication use—such as the application of pharmacotherapeutics, medication therapy management (MTM), and the legal and regulatory aspects of drugs and prescribing authority—although essential to pharmacy practice and patient care, are not a part of this text.

Among the items that the pharmacist should check for the correct reading and interpretation of a prescription or medication order are:

- prescriber information, including address and telephone number, Drug Enforcement Administration (DEA) number (for authority to prescribe schedule drugs including narcotics), state license number and/or the National Provider Identifier (NPI), an identification number for participating health care providers, and signature;
- date of the order and its currency to the request for filling;
- patient information, including dose-relevant information, such as the age and/or weight of the patient if the dose of the drug is so based;
- drug prescribed, including dose, preparation strength, dosage form, and quantity;
- clarity of any abbreviations, symbols, and/or units of measure;
- clarity and completeness of directions for use by the patient or caregiver;
- refill and/or generic substitution authorization;
- need for special labeling, such as expiration date, conditions for storage, and foods and/or other medications not to take concomitantly; and
- a listing of the ingredients and quantities for orders to be compounded; calculations performed should be checked and double-checked, as should the positive identification of all ingredients used along with their measurements.

Once the prescription or medication order is filled and the label prepared, before dispensing, the pharmacist should make certain of the following:

- The filled prescription or medication order contains the correct drug, strength, dosage form, and quantity. Placing a medication's indication (use) on the prescription label has been shown to be of benefit in understanding of the use of their medication for some patients, particularly older patients and those taking multiple medications.[8] The bar-coding of pharmaceutical products used in hospital settings is required by the federal Food and Drug Administration (FDA) as an added protection to ensure accurate product dispensing and administration (see Fig. 4.8).
- The pharmacy-imprinted serial number on the label matches that on the order.
- The label has the name of the correct patient and physician; the correct drug name, quantity, and strength; the name or initials of the pharmacist who filled the order; and the number of refills remaining. Additional label information and/or auxiliary labels may be required according to good pharmacy practice and by federal and state law depending on the drug dispensed. A repeat comparison should be made of the drug and drug strength called for on the prescription against the labeling of the product used to fill the prescription to assure that the proper drug was used.

Example:

Refer to the prescription shown in Figure 4.4 to identify any errors and/or omissions in the following prescription label.

Main Street Pharmacy	
150 Main Street	
Libertyville, Maryland	
Phone 456-1432	
℞ 1234576	Jan 10, 20yy
Brad Smith	Dr. J. M. Brown
Take 2 teaspoonfuls every 12 hours.	
Ampicillin 250 mg/5 mL	100 mL
Refills: 0	Pharmacist: AB

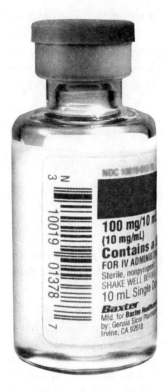

FIGURE 4.8 Example of a Pharmaceutical Bar Code used in hospitals and other health-care settings for positive drug identification to reduce medication errors. (*Courtesy of Baxter Healthcare Corporation.*)

Error: Drug name incorrect.
Omission: Directions incomplete.

Note: There would be a serious question of whether the patient received the correct medication.

Additional examples of errors and omissions are presented in the practice problems at the end of the chapter.

Use of Roman Numerals on Prescriptions

Roman numerals commonly are used in prescription writing to designate *quantities*, as the: (1) quantity of medication to be dispensed and/or (2) quantity of medication to be taken by the patient per dose.

The student may recall the eight letters of fixed values used in the Roman system:

ss	=	½	L or l	=	50
I, i, or j	=	1	C or c	=	100
V or v	=	5	D or d	=	500
X or x	=	10	M or m	=	1000

The student also may recall that the following rules apply in the use of Roman numerals:

1. A letter repeated once or more, repeats its value (e.g., xx = 20; xxx = 30).
2. One or more letters placed *after* a letter of greater value *increases* the value of the greater letter (e.g., vi = 6; xij = 12; lx = 60).
3. A letter placed *before* a letter of greater value *decreases* the value of the greater letter (e.g., iv = 4; xl = 40).

Capital or lower case letters may be used. Dotting the lowercase "i" and/or placement of a horizontal line above the "i" with the dot atop serves to avoid misinterpretation. A "j" may be used as the final "i" in a sequence (e.g., viij).

When Roman numerals are used, the tradition of placing the numerals after the term or symbol generally is followed (e.g., capsules no. xxiv; fluidounces xij).

Use of Abbreviations and Symbols

The use of abbreviations is common on prescriptions and medication orders. Some are derived from the Latin through its historical use in medicine and pharmacy, whereas others have evolved through prescribers' use of writing shortcuts. A list of some of these abbreviations is presented in Table 4.2. Unfortunately, medication errors can result from the misuse, misinterpretation, and illegible writing of abbreviations, and through the use of *ad hoc*, or made-up, abbreviations. The use of a controlled vocabulary, a reduction in the use of abbreviations, care in the writing of decimal points, and the proper use of leading and terminal zeros have been urged to help reduce medication errors.[9–11] It should be emphasized that a misplaced or misread decimal point represents a minimum of a 10-fold error.

Among the specific recommendations to help reduce medication errors arising from poorly written, illegible, or misinterpreted prescriptions and medication orders are the following:[9–12]

- *A whole number should be shown without a decimal point and without a terminal zero (e.g., express 4 milligrams as 4 mg and not as 4.0 mg).*
- *A quantity smaller than one should be shown with a zero preceding the decimal point (e.g., express two tenths of a milligram as 0.2 mg and not as .2 mg).*
- *Leave a space between a number and the unit (e.g., 10 mg and not 10mg).*
- *Use whole numbers when possible and not equivalent decimal fractions (e.g., use 100 mg and not 0.1 g).*
- *Use the full names of drugs and not abbreviations (e.g., use phenobarbital and not PB).*
- *Use USP designations for units of measure (e.g., for grams, use g and not Gm or gms; for milligrams, use mg and not mgs or mgm).*
- *Spell out "units" (e.g., use 100 units and not 100 u or 100 U since an illegible U may be misread as a zero, resulting in a 10-fold error, i.e., 1000). The abbreviation I.U., which stands for "International Units," should also be spelled out so it is not interpreted as I.V., meaning "intravenous."*
- *Certain abbreviations that could be mistaken for other abbreviations should be written out (e.g., write "right eye" or "left eye" rather than use o.d. or o.l., and spell out "right ear" and "left ear" rather than use a.d. or a.l.).*
- *Spell out "every day" rather than use q.d.; "every other day," rather than q.o.d; and "four times a day," rather than q.i.d to avoid misinterpretation.*
- *Avoid using d for "day" or "dose" because of the profound difference between terms, as in mg/kg/day versus mg/kg/dose.*
- *Integrate capital or "tall man" letters to distinguish between "look alike" drug names, such as AggreSTAT and AggreNOX; hydrOXYZINE and hydrALAZINE; and DIGoxin and DESoxyn.*
- *Amplify the prescriber's directions on the prescription label when needed for clarity (e.g., use "Swallow one (1) capsule with water in the morning" rather than "one cap in a.m.").*

The Institute for Safe Medication Practices (ISMP) regularly publishes a list of abbreviations, symbols, and dose designations that it recommends for consideration for discontinuance of use.[9]

The portions of the prescription presenting directions to the pharmacist (the Subscription) and the directions to the patient (the Signa) commonly contain abbreviated forms of English or Latin terms as well as Arabic and Roman numerals. The correct interpretation of these abbrevia-

TABLE 4.2 SELECTED ABBREVIATIONS, ACRONYMS, AND SYMBOLS USED IN PRESCRIPTIONS AND MEDICATION ORDERS[a,b]

ABBREVIATION (LATIN ORIGIN[c])	MEANING	ABBREVIATION (LATIN ORIGIN[c])	MEANING
Prescription Filling Directions		pt.	pint
		qt.	quart
aa. or (*ana*)	of each	ss or $\overline{ss}$ (*semissem*	one half
ad (*ad*)	up to; to make	**tbsp.**	tablespoonful
disp. (dispensatur)	*dispense*	**tsp.**	*teaspoonful*
div. (*dividatur*)	divide		
d.t.d. (*dentur tales doses*)	give of such doses	**Signa/Patient Instructions**	
ft (*fiat*)	make	**a.c.** (ante cibos)	*before meals*
M. (*mice*)	mix	ad lib. (*ad libitum*)	at pleasure, freely
No. (*numero*)	number	admin	administer
non rep. or NR (non repatatur)	*do not repeat*	A.M. (*ante meridiem*)	morning
q.s. (quantum sufficit)	a sufficient quantity	aq. (*aqua*)	water
		ATC	around the clock
q.s. ad (quantum sufficiat ad)	*a sufficient quantity to make*	**b.i.d.** (bis in die)	*twice a day*
		c or c̄ (*cum*)	*with*
Sig. (Signa)	write (directions on label)	**d** (die)	day
		dil. (*dilutus*)	dilute
Quantities and Measurement		et	and
		h. or **hr.** (hora)	*hour*
BSA	body surface area	**h.s.** (hora somni)	*at bedtime*
cm³	cubic centimeter or milliliter (mL)	i.c. (*inter cibos*)	between meals
		min. (*minutum*)	minute
f or *fl* (fluidus)	fluid	m&n	morning and night
fl℥ or f℥	fluid dram (≅ teaspoonful, 5 mL)	N&V	nausea and vomiting
		noct. (*nocte*)	night
fl℥ss or f℥ss	half-fluidounce (≅ tablespoonful, 15mL)	NPO (*non per os*)	nothing by mouth
		p.c. (post cibos)	*after meals*
g	gram	P.M. (post meridiem)	afternoon; evening
gal	gallon		
gtt (*gutta*)	drop	**p.o.** (per os)	*by mouth (orally)*
lb (*libra*)	pound	**p.r.n.** (pro re nata)	*as needed*
kg	kilogram	q (*quaque*)	every
L	liter	qAM	every morning
m² or M²	square meter	**q4h, q8h,** etc.	*every __ hours*
mcg	microgram	**q.i.d.** (quarter in die)	*four times a day*
mEq	milliequivalent		
mg	*milligram*	rep. (*repetatur*)	repeat
mg/kg	milligrams (of drug) per kilogram (of body weight)	s (*sine*)	without
		s.i.d. (*semel in die*)	once a day
		s.o.s. (si opus sit)	if there is need; as needed
mg/m²	milligrams (of drug) per square meter (of body surface area)		
		stat. (statim)	*immediately*
		t.i.d. (ter in die)	*three times a day*
mL	*milliliter*	ut dict. (*ut dictum*)	as directed
mL/h	milliliters (of drug administered) per hour (as through intravenous administration)	wk.	week
		Medications	
		APAP	acetaminophen
mOsm or mOsmol	milliosmoles	ASA	aspirin
oz.	*ounce*	AZT	zidovudine

(continued)

TABLE 4.2 *Continued*

ABBREVIATION (LATIN ORIGIN[c])	MEANING	ABBREVIATION (LATIN ORIGIN[c])	MEANING
EES	erythromycin ethylsuccinate	D5NS	dextrose 5% in normal saline (0.9% sodium chloride)
HC	hydrocortisone		
HCTZ	hydrochlorothiazide	D5W	dextrose 5% in water
MTX	methotrexate	D10W	dextrose 10% in water
NTG	nitroglycerin	elix.	elixir
Clinical		inj.	injection
BM	bowel movement	NS	normal saline
BP	blood preasure	½NS	half-strength normal saline
BS	blood sugar		
CHD	coronary heart disease	*oint* or *ungt.* (*unguentum*)	*ointment*
CHF	congestive heart failure		
GERD	gastrointestinal reflux disease	pulv. (*pulvis*)	powder
		RL, R/L or LR	Ringer's Lactate or Lactated Ringer's
GI	gastrointestinal		
GFR	glomerular filtration rate	*sol.* (solutio)	*solution*
GU	genitourinary	*supp.* (suppositorium)	*suppository*
HA	headache		
HBP	high blood pressure	*susp.*	*suspension*
HRT	hormone replacement therapy	*syr.* (syrupus)	*syrup*
		tab. (tabletta)	*tablet*
HT or HTN	hypertension	**Routes of Administration**	
IOP	intraocular pressure		
MI	myocardial ischemia/ infarction	CIVI	continuous (24 hour) intravenous infusion
OA	osteoarthritis	ID	intradermal
Pt	patient	IM	intramuscular
SOB	shortness of breath	IT	intrathecal
TPN	total parenteral nutrition	IV	intravenous
URI	upper respiratory infection	IVB	intravenous bolus
		IV Drip	intravenous infusion
UTI	urinary tract infection	IVP	intravenous push
Dosage Forms/Vehicles		IVPB	intravenous piggy back
		NGT	nasogastric tube
amp.	ampul	**p.o.** or PO (*per os*)	by mouth
cap.	*capsule*	rect.	rectal or rectum
D5LR	dextrose 5% in lactated Ringer's	SL	sublingual
		SubQ	subcutaneously
		Top.	topically
		V or PV	vaginally

[a] The abbreviations set in **boldface type** are considered most likely to appear on prescriptions. It is suggested that these be learned first.

[b] In practice, periods and/or capital letters may or may not be used with the abbreviations. Some abbreviations, acronyms, and symbols have medication-error risks associated with their use. Therefore, the Institute for Safe Medication Practices (ISMP) and the Joint Commission on Accreditation of Healthcare Organizations (JCAHO) have issued a list of items prohibited from use and others considered for prohibition (see text).[9] These designated items are not included in Table 4.2, with the exception of *hs*, *subQ*, *AZT*, and *HCTZ*, which *are* included for instructional purpose due to their remaining use in practice.

[c] Muldoon HC. *Pharmaceutical Latin.* 4th Ed. New York: John Wiley & Sons, 1952.

tions and prescription notations plays an important part in pharmaceutical calculations and thus in the accurate filling and dispensing of medication.

Although described fully in Chapter 7, it should be noted here that when appearing in the Signa, the symbol ʒi, 5 mL, and the abbreviation *tsp.* are each taken to mean "one teaspoonful," and the symbol ʒ ss, 15 mL, and the abbreviation *tbsp.* are each taken to mean "one tablespoonful."

Examples of prescription directions to the pharmacist:
(a) *M. ft. ung.*
    Mix and make an ointment.
(b) *Ft. sup. no xii*
    Make 12 suppositories.
(c) *M. ft. cap. d.t.d. no. xxiv*
    Mix and make capsules. Give 24 such doses.

Examples of prescription directions to the patient:
(a) *Caps. i. q.i.d. p.c. et h.s.*
    Take one (1) capsule four (4) times a day after each meal and at bedtime.
(b) *gtt. ii rt.eye every a.m.*
    Instill two (2) drops in the right eye every morning.
(c) *tab. ii stat tab. 1 q. 6 h. × 7 d.*
    Take two (2) tablets immediately, then take one (1) tablet every 6 hours for 7 days.

CASE IN POINT 4.1: A pharmacist received the following prescription, which requires the correct interpretation of abbreviations prior to engaging in calculations, compounding, labeling, and dispensing.

℞

Lisinopril	
Hydrochlorothiazide aa.	10 mg
Calcium Phosphate	40 mg
Lactose q.s. ad	300 mg
M.ft. cap. i D.T.D. # 30	
Sig: cap. i AM a.c.	

(a) How many milligrams each of lisinopril and hydrochlorothiazide are required to fill the prescription?
(b) What is the weight of lactose required?
(c) Translate the label directions to the patient.

Medication Scheduling and Patient Compliance

Medication scheduling may be defined as the frequency (i.e., times per day) and duration (i.e., length of treatment) of a drug's prescribed or recommended use. Some medications, because of their physical, chemical, or biological characteristics or their dosage formulations, may be taken just once daily for optimum benefit, whereas other drug products must be taken two, three, four, or more times daily for the desired effect. Frequency of medication scheduling is also influenced by the patient's physical condition and the nature and severity of the illness or condition being treated. Some conditions, such as indigestion, may require a single dose of medication for correction. Other conditions, such as a systemic infection, may require multiple daily, around-the-clock dosing for 10 days or more. Long-term maintenance therapy for conditions such as diabetes and high blood pressure may require daily dosing for life.

For optimum benefit from prescribed therapy or from the use of over-the-counter (nonprescription) medications, it is incumbent on the patient to adhere to the recommended medication schedule.

Patient compliance with prescribed and nonprescribed medications is defined as patient understanding and adherence to the directions for use. The compliant patient follows the label directions for taking the medication properly and adheres to any special instructions provided by the prescriber and/or pharmacist. Compliance includes taking medication at the desired strength, in the proper dosage form, at the appropriate time of day and night, at the proper interval for the duration of the treatment, and with proper regard to food and drink and consideration of other concomitant medications (both prescribed or nonprescribed) and herbal remedies.

Patient noncompliance is the failure to comply with a practitioner's or labeled direction in the self-administration of any medication. Noncompliance may involve underdosage or overdosage, inconsistent or sporadic dosing, incorrect duration of treatment, and drug abuse or misadventuring with medications.

Patient noncompliance may result from a number of factors, including unclear or misunderstood directions, undesired side effects of the drug that discourage use, lack of patient confidence in the drug and/or prescriber, discontinued use because the patient feels better or worse, economic reasons based on the cost of the medication, absence of patient counseling and understanding of the need for and means of compliance, confusion over taking multiple medications, and other factors. Frequently, patients forget whether they have taken their medications. This situation is particularly common for patients who are easily confused, who have memory failure, or who are taking multiple medications scheduled to be taken at different times during the day or night. Special compliance aids are available to assist patients in their proper scheduling of medications. These devices include medication calendars, reminder charts, and special containers.

Patient noncompliance is not entirely the problem of ambulatory or noninstitutionalized patients. Patients in hospitals, nursing homes, and other inpatient settings are generally more compliant because of the efforts of health care personnel who are assigned the responsibility of issuing and administering medication on a prescribed schedule. Even in these settings, however, a scheduled dose of medication may be omitted or administered incorrectly or in an untimely fashion because of human error or oversight.

The consequences of patient noncompliance may include worsening of the condition, the requirement of additional and perhaps more expensive and extensive treatment methods or surgical procedures, otherwise unnecessary hospitalization, and increased total health care cost. Students interested in additional information on patient compliance are referred to other sources of information.[12,13]

Some of the different types of problems relating to patient compliance with medication are exemplified by the following examples.

Examples:

R Hydrochlorothiazide   50 mg
 No. XC
 Sig. i q AM for HBP

If the prescription was filled initially on April 15, on about what date should the patient return to have the prescription refilled?

Answer: 90 tablets, taken 1 per day, should last 90 days, or approximately 3 months, and the patient should return to the pharmacy on or shortly before July 15 of the same year.

R̸   Penicillin V Potassium Oral Solution   125 mg/5 mL
     Disp._____mL
     Sig. 5 mL q 6h ATC × 10 d

How many milliliters of medicine should be dispensed?

Answer: 5 mL times 4 (doses per day) equals 20 mL times 10 (days) equals 200 mL.

A pharmacist may calculate a patient's percent compliance rate as follows:

$$\% \text{ Compliance rate} = \frac{\text{Number of days supply of medication}}{\text{Number of days since last Rx refill}} \times 100$$

Example:

What is the percent compliance rate if a patient received a 30-day supply of medicine and returned in 45 days for a refill?

$$\% \text{ Compliance rate} = \frac{30 \text{ days}}{45 \text{ days}} \times 100 = 66.6\%, \text{ answer.}$$

In determining the patient's actual (rather than apparent) compliance rate, it is important to determine if the patient had available and used extra days' dosage from some previous filling of the prescription.

PRACTICE PROBLEMS

1. Interpret each of the following *Subscriptions* (directions to the pharmacist) taken from prescriptions:
   (a) Disp. supp. rect. no. xii
   (b) M. ft. iso. sol. Disp. 120 mL.
   (c) M. et div. in pulv. no. xl
   (d) DTD vi. Non rep.
   (e) M. et ft. ung. Disp. 10 g
   (f) M. et ft. caps. DTD xlviii
   (g) M. et ft. susp. 1 g/tbsp. Disp. 60 mL.
   (h) Ft. cap. #1. DTD no.xxxvi N.R.
   (i) M. et ft. pulv. DTD #C
   (j) M. et ft. I.V. inj.
   (k) Label: hydrocortisone, 20 mg tabs.

2. Interpret each of the following *Signas* (directions to the patient) taken from prescriptions:
   (a) Gtt. ii each eye q. 4 h. p.r.n. pain.
   (b) Tbsp. i in ⅓ gl. aq. q. 6 h.
   (c) Appl. a.m. & p.m. for pain prn.
   (d) Gtt. iv right ear m. & n.
   (e) Tsp. i ex aq. q. 4 or 5 h. p.r.n. pain.
   (f) Appl. ung. left eye ad lib.

   (g) Caps i c̄ aq. h.s. N.R.
   (h) Gtt. v each ear 3× d. s.o.s.
   (i) Tab. i sublingually, rep. p.r.n.
   (j) Instill gtt. ii each eye of neonate.
   (k) Dil. c̄ = vol. aq. and use as gargle q. 5 h.
   (l) Cap. ii 1 h. prior to departure, then cap. i after 12 h.
   (m) Tab i p.r.n. SOB
   (n) Tab i qAM HBP
   (o) Tab ii q 6h ATC UTI
   (p) ℨii 4×d p.c. & h.s.
   (q) ℥ss a.c. t.i.d.
   (r) Add crushed tablet to pet's food s.i.d.

3. Interpret each of the following taken from medication orders:
   (a) AMBIEN 10 mg p.o. qhs × 5 d
   (b) 1000 mL D5W q. 8 h. IV c̄ 20 mEq KCl to every third bottle.
   (c) Admin. Prochlorperazine 10 mg IM q. 3h. prn N&V

(d) Minocycline HCl susp. 1 tsp p.o. q.i.d. DC after 5 d.

(e) Propranolol HCl 10 mg p.o. t.i.d. a.c. & h.s.

(f) NPH U-100 insulin 40 Units subc every day A.M.

(g) Cefamandole nafate 250 mg IM q. 12 h.

(h) Potassium chloride 15 mEq p.o. b.i.d. p.c.

(i) Vincristine sulfate 1 mg/m^2 pt. BSA.

(j) Flurazepam 30 mg at HS prn sleep.

(k) D5W + 20 mEq KCl/L at 84 mL/ hour.

(l) 2.5 g/kg/day amino acids TPN.

(m) PROCRIT (epoetin alpha) stat. 150 units/kg subQ. 3×wk. × 3–4 wks.

4. (a) If a 10-mL vial of insulin contains 100 units of insulin per milliliter, and a patient is to administer 20 units daily, how many days will the product last the patient? (b) If the patient returned to the pharmacy in exactly 7 weeks for another vial of insulin, was the patient compliant as indicated by the percent compliance rate?

5. A prescription is to be taken as follows: 1 tablet q.i.d. the first day; 1 tablet t.i.d. the second day; 1 tablet b.i.d. × 5 d; and 1 tablet q.d. thereafter. How many tablets should be dispensed to equal a 30-day supply?

6. In preparing the prescription in Figure 4.3, the pharmacist calculated and labeled the dose as "1 teaspoonful every 12 hours." Is this correct or in error?

7. Refer to Figure 4.1 and identify any errors or omissions in the following prescription label:

Patient: Mary Smith   Dr: JM Brown
Date: Jan 9, 20yy

Take 1 capsule every day in the morning

Refills: 5

8. Refer to Figure 4.4 and identify any errors or omissions in the following prescription label:

Patient: Brad Smith   Dr. JM Brown
Date: Jan 9, 20yy

Take two (2) teaspoonfuls every twelve (12) hours until all of the medicine is gone

Amoxicillin 250 mL/5 mL

Refills: 0

9. Refer to Figure 4.5 and identify any errors or omissions in the following prescription label:

Patient: Brad Smith   Dr. JM Brown
Date: Jan 9, 20yy

Nasal spray for chemotherapy-induced emesis. Use as directed. Discard after 60 days.

Metoclopramide HCl
10 g/100 mL Nasal Spray

Refills: 0

10. Refer to Figure 4.2 and identify any errors or omissions in a transcribed order for the first three drugs in the medication order.

(1) Propranolol, 40 mg orally every day

(2) Flutamide, 20 mg orally every morning

(3) Flurazepam, 30 mg at bedtime as needed for sleep

ANSWERS TO "CASE IN POINT" AND PRACTICE PROBLEMS

Case in Point 4.1

(a) Since aa. means "of each," 10 mg lisinopril and 10 mg hydrochlorothiazide are needed for each capsule. And since D.T.D. means "give of such doses," 30 capsules are to be prepared. Thus,

10 mg lisinopril × 30 (capsules) = 300 mg lisinopril and

10 mg hydrochlorothiazide × 30 (capsules) = 300 mg hydrochlorothiazide

are needed to fill the prescription.

(b) Since q.s. ad means "a sufficient quantity to make," the total in each capsule is 300 mg. The amount of lactose per capsule would equal 300 mg *less* the quantity of the other ingredients (10 mg + 10 mg + 40 mg), or 240 mg. Thus,

240 mg lactose/capsule × 30 (capsules) = 7200 mg = 7.2 g lactose.

(c) Take one (1) capsule in the morning before breakfast.

Practice Problems

1. (a) Dispense 12 rectal suppositories.
   (b) Mix and make an isotonic solution. Dispense 120 mL.
   (c) Mix and divide into 40 powders.
   (d) Dispense six such doses. Do not repeat.
   (e) Mix and make ointment. Dispense 10 grams.
   (f) Mix and make capsules. Dispense 48 such doses.
   (g) Mix and make a suspension containing 1 gram per tablespoon. Dispense 60 milliliters.
   (h) Make one capsule. Dispense 36 such doses. Do not repeat.
   (i) Mix and make powder. Divide into 100 such doses.
   (j) Mix and make an intravenous injection.
   (k) Label: hydrocortisone, 20 mg tabs.

2. (a) Instill 2 drops in each eye every four (4) hours as needed for pain.
   (b) Take 1 tablespoonful in one-third glass of water every 6 hours.
   (c) Apply morning and night as needed for pain.
   (d) Instill 4 drops into the right ear morning and night.
   (e) Take 1 teaspoonful in water every 4 or 5 hours as needed for pain.
   (f) Apply ointment to the left eye as needed.
   (g) Take 1 capsule with water at bedtime. Do not repeat.
   (h) Instill 5 drops into each ear 3 times a day as needed.
   (i) Place 1 tablet under the tongue, repeat if needed.
   (j) Instill 2 drops into each eye of the newborn.
   (k) Dilute with an equal volume of water and use as gargle every 5 hours.
   (l) Take 2 capsules 1 hour prior to departure, then 1 capsule after 12 hours.
   (m) Take 1 tablet as needed for shortness of breath.
   (n) Take 1 tablet every morning for high blood pressure.
   (o) Take 2 tablets every 6 hours around the clock for urinary tract infection.
   (p) Take 2 teaspoonfuls 4 times a day after meals and at bedtime.
   (q) Take 1 tablespoonful before meals 3 times a day.
   (r) Add crushed tablet to pet's food once a day.

3. (a) AMBIEN 10 milligrams by mouth at every bedtime for 5 days.
   (b) 1000 milliliters of 5% dextrose in water every 8 hours intravenously with 20 milliequivalents of potassium chloride added to every third bottle.
   (c) Administer 10 milligrams of prochlorperazine intramuscularly every 3 hours, if there is need, for nausea and vomiting.

(d) One teaspoonful of minocycline hydrochloride suspension by mouth four times a day. Discontinue after 5 days.

(e) 10 milligrams of propranolol hydrochloride by mouth three times a day before meals and at bedtime.

(f) 40 units of NPH 100-Unit insulin subcutaneously every day in the morning.

(g) 250 milligrams of cefamandole nafate intramuscularly every 12 hours.

(h) 15 milliequivalents of potassium chloride by mouth twice a day after meals.

(i) 1 milligram of vincristine sulfate per square meter of patient's body surface area.

(j) Administer 30 mg of flurazepam at bedtime as needed for sleep.

(k) Administer 20 milliequivalents of potassium chloride per liter in D5W (5% dextrose in water) at the rate of 84 milliliters per hour.

(l) Administer 2.5 grams per kilogram of body weight per day of amino acids in total parenteral nutrition.

(m) Start epoetin alpha (PROCRIT) immediately at 150 units per kilogram of body weight subcutaneously and then 3 times a week for 3 to 4 weeks.

4. (a) 50 days
   (b) yes

5. (a) 40 tablets

6. (a) correct

7. ℞ calls for *tablets* but label indicates *capsules.*
   Sig: "in the morning" has been added, which may be correct if that is the prescriber's usual directive.
   Refill "5" times is incorrect; the original filling of a prescription does not count as a refill.
   ℞ calls for drug name/strength on label; an omission.

8. The words "all of the medicine" have been added and the numbers enhanced; this clarifies the directions and thus is positive. 250 *mL* should be 250 *mg.*

9. Patient's name is incorrect.
   The active drug name *only* on the label is proper for a compounded prescription. The other ingredients are "pharmaceutic."

10. (1) "QID" means 4 times a day.
    (2) Drug name is incorrect.
    (3) Correct.

REFERENCES

1. http://www.fda.gov/cder/pharmcomp/default.htm. Accessed October 30, 2007.
2. http://www.aphanet.org. Accessed August 31, 2007.
3. Jamgochian H. *Pharmacy Today* 2007;13(9):44.
4. Kilbridge P. E-Prescribing. California HealthCare Foundation. 2001. Available at: http://www.chcf.org/documents/EPrescribing.pdf. Accessed August 20, 2007.
5. American College of Physicians. Statement, June 26, 2006. Available at: http://www.acponline.org/hpp/dea-218n.pdf. Accessed August 20, 2007.
6. http://www.hospital-forms.com. Accessed September 5, 2008.
7. Tamer H, Shehab S. Using preprinted medication order forms to improve the safety of investigational drug use. *American Journal of Health-System Pharmacy* 2006;63:1022–1028.
8. Burnside NL, Bardo JA, Bretz CJ, et al. Effects of including medication indications on prescription labels. *Journal of the American Pharmacists Association* 2007;47:756–758.
9. Institute for Safe Medication Practices. Available at: http://www.ismp.org. Accessed September 5, 2008.
10. Davis NM. A controlled vocabulary for reducing medication errors. *Hospital Pharmacy* 2000;35:227–228.
11. Davis NM. Danger in making 10-fold dosage strengths available. *Hospital Pharmacy* 1999;34:394.
12. Bond WS, Hussar DA. Detection methods and strategies for improving medication compliance. *American Journal of Hospital Pharmacy* 1991;48:1978.
13. Mackowiak JI. *Enhancing Patient Compliance*. Ridgefield, CT: Boehringer Ingelheim Pharmaceuticals, 1990.

5

Density, Specific Gravity, and Specific Volume

Objectives

Upon successful completion of this chapter, the student will be able to:

- Define *density*, *specific gravity*, and *specific volume* and determine each through appropriate calculations.
- Calculate specific gravity from data derived from the use of a pycnometer.
- Apply specific gravity correctly in converting weight to volume and volume to weight.

Density

Density (*d*) is mass per unit volume of a substance. It is *usually* expressed as *grams per cubic centimeter (g/cc)*. Because the *gram* is defined as the mass of 1 cc of water at 4°C, the density of water is *1 g/cc*. For our purposes, because the *United States Pharmacopeia*[1] states that 1 mL may be used as the equivalent of 1 cc, the density of water may be expressed as *1 g/mL*. In contrast, one milliliter of mercury weighs 13.6 g; hence, its density is *13.6 g/mL*.

Density may be calculated by dividing mass by volume, that is:

$$\text{Density} = \frac{\text{Mass}}{\text{Volume}}$$

Thus, if 10 mL of sulfuric acid weighs 18 g, its density is:

$$\text{Density} = \frac{18 \text{ (g)}}{10 \text{ (mL)}} = 1.8 \text{ grams per milliliter}$$

Specific Gravity

Specific gravity (*sp gr*) is a ratio, *expressed decimally,* of the weight of a substance to the weight of an equal volume of a substance chosen as a standard, both substances at the same temperature or the temperature of each being known.

Water is used as the standard for the specific gravities of liquids and solids; the most useful standard for gases is hydrogen.

Specific gravity may be calculated by dividing the weight of a given substance by the weight of an equal volume of water, that is:

$$\text{Specific gravity} = \frac{\text{Weight of substance}}{\text{Weight of equal volume of water}}$$

Thus, if 10 mL of sulfuric acid weighs 18 g, and 10 mL of water, under similar conditions, weighs 10 g, the specific gravity of the acid is:

TABLE 5.1 SOME REPRESENTATIVE SPECIFIC GRAVITIES AT 25°C

AGENT	SP GR
Ether (at 20°C)	0.71
Isopropyl alcohol	0.78
Acetone	0.79
Alcohol	0.81
Liquid petrolatum	0.87
Peppermint oil	0.90
Olive oil	0.91
Peanut oil	0.92
Cod liver oil	0.92
Castor oil	0.96
Water	**1.00**
Propylene glycol	1.03
Clove oil	1.04
Liquefied phenol	1.07
Polysorbate 80	1.08
Polyethylene glycol 400	1.13
Glycerin	1.25
Syrup	1.31
Hydrochloric acid	1.37
Nitric acid	1.42
Chloroform	1.47
Nitroglycerin	1.59
Phosphoric acid	1.70
Mercury	13.6

$$\text{Specific gravity} = \frac{18 \text{ (g)}}{10 \text{ (g)}} = 1.8$$

- *Substances that have a specific gravity less than 1 are lighter than water.*
- *Substances that have a specific gravity greater than 1 are heavier than water.*

Table 5.1 presents some representative specific gravities. Figure 5.1 depicts the layering of immiscible liquids due to their relative weights.

Specific gravities may be expressed decimally to as many places as the accuracy of their determination warrants. In pharmaceutical work, this expression may be to two, three, or four decimal places. Because substances expand or contract at different rates when their temperatures change, accurate work necessitates allowing carefully for variations in the specific gravity of a substance. In the *United States Pharmacopeia*, the standard temperature for specific gravities is 25°C, except for that of alcohol, which is 15.56°C by government regulation.[2]

Density Versus Specific Gravity

The density of a substance is a concrete number (*1.8 g/mL* in the example), whereas specific gravity, being a ratio of like quantities, is an abstract number (*1.8* in the example). Whereas density varies with the units of measure used, specific gravity has no dimension and is therefore a constant value for each substance (when measured under controlled conditions). Thus, whereas the density of water may be variously expressed as *1 g/mL, 1000 g/L,* or *62½ lb/cu ft,* the specific gravity of water is always 1.

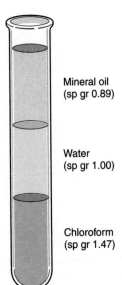

Mineral oil
(sp gr 0.89)

Water
(sp gr 1.00)

Chloroform
(sp gr 1.47)

FIGURE 5.1 Depiction of layering of immiscible liquids in a test tube, mineral oil being lighter than water and chloroform being heavier.

Calculating the Specific Gravity of Liquids

Known Weight and Volume

Calculating the specific gravity of a liquid when its weight and volume are known involves the use of the equation:

$$\text{Specific gravity} = \frac{\text{Weight of substance}}{\text{Weight of equal volume of water}}$$

Examples:

If 54.96 mL of an oil weighs 52.78 g, what is the specific gravity of the oil?

54.96 mL of water weighs 54.96 g

$$\text{Specific gravity of oil} = \frac{52.78 \text{ (g)}}{54.96 \text{ (g)}} = 0.9603, \textit{answer.}$$

If a pint of a certain liquid weighs 601 g, what is the specific gravity of the liquid?

1 pint = 16 fl. oz.
16 fl. oz. of water weighs 473 g

$$\text{Specific gravity of liquid} = \frac{601 \text{ (g)}}{473 \text{ (g)}} = 1.27, \textit{answer.}$$

Pycnometer or Specific Gravity Bottle

A **pycnometer** is a special glass bottle used to determine specific gravity (Fig. 5.2). Pycnometers are generally available for laboratory use in volumes ranging from 1 mL to 50 mL. Pycnometers have fitted glass stoppers with a capillary opening to allow trapped air and excess fluid to escape. Some pycnometers have thermometers affixed, because temperature is a factor in specific gravity determinations.

In using a pycnometer, it is first weighed empty and then weighed again when filled to capacity with water. The weight of the water is calculated by difference. Since 1 g of water equals

FIGURE 5.2 Examples of *pycnometers* used to determine the specific gravity of liquids. Shown are 1-mL and 25-mL sizes. See text for description of their use. *(Courtesy of Thomas Scientific.)*

1 mL, the exact volume of the pycnometer becomes known. Then, when any other liquid subsequently is placed in the pycnometer, it is of *equal volume* to the water, and its specific gravity may be determined.

Example:

A 50 mL pycnometer is found to weigh 120 g when empty, 171 g when filled with water, and 160 g when filled with an unknown liquid. Calculate the specific gravity of the unknown liquid.

$$\text{Weight of water: } 171 \text{ g} - 120 \text{ g} = 51 \text{ g}$$
$$\text{Weight of unknown liquid: } 160 \text{ g} - 120 \text{ g} = 40 \text{ g}$$

$$\text{Specific gravity} = \frac{\text{Weight of substance}}{\text{Weight of equal volume of water}}$$

$$\text{Specific gravity of unknown liquid} = \frac{40 \text{ (g)}}{51 \text{ (g)}} = 0.78, \text{ answer.}$$

Example:

A specific gravity bottle weighs 23.66 g. When filled with water, it weighs 72.95 g; when filled with another liquid, it weighs 73.56 g. What is the specific gravity of the liquid?

$$73.56 \text{ g} - 23.66 \text{ g} = 49.90 \text{ g of liquid}$$
$$72.95 \text{ g} - 23.66 \text{ g} = 49.29 \text{ g of water}$$

$$\text{Specific gravity of liquid} = \frac{49.90 \text{ (g)}}{49.29 \text{ (g)}} = 1.012, \text{ answer.}$$

Displacement or Plummet Method

Calculating the specific gravity of a liquid determined by the displacement or plummet method is based on *Archimedes' principle*, which states that a body immersed in a liquid displaces an amount of the liquid equal to its own volume and suffers an apparent loss in weight equal to the weight of the displaced liquid. Thus, we can weigh a plummet when suspended in water and when suspended in a liquid the specific gravity of which we want to determine; and by subtracting these weights from the weight of the plummet in air, we get the *weights of equal volumes of the liquids* needed in our calculation.

Example:

A glass plummet weighs 12.64 g in air, 8.57 g when immersed in water, and 9.12 g when immersed in an oil. Calculate the specific gravity of the oil.

$$12.64 \text{ g} - 9.12 \text{ g} = 3.52 \text{ g of displaced oil}$$
$$12.64 \text{ g} - 8.57 \text{ g} = 4.07 \text{ g of displaced water}$$

$$\text{Specific gravity of oil} = \frac{3.52 \text{ (g)}}{4.07 \text{ (g)}} = 0.865, \text{ } answer.$$

Note: The specific gravity of solid materials may also be calculated, and methods for these calculations appear in the 10th edition of this textbook. They are not included here due to their limited application.

Use of Specific Gravity in Calculations of Weight and Volume

When *specific gravity is used as a factor in a calculation, the result should contain no more significant figures than the number in the factor.*

It is important to remember that specific gravity is a *factor* that expresses how much heavier or lighter a substance is than water, the standard with a specific gravity of 1.0. For example, a liquid with a specific gravity of 1.25 is 1.25 times as heavy as water, and a liquid with a specific gravity of 0.85 is 0.85 times as heavy as water.

Thus, if we had 50 mL of a liquid with a specific gravity of 1.2, it would weigh 1.2 times as much as an equivalent volume of water. An equivalent volume of water, 50 mL, would weigh 50 g, and therefore the liquid would weigh 1.2 times that, or 60 g.

Calculating Weight, Knowing the Volume and Specific Gravity

Based on the explanation in the previous paragraphs, we can derive the following equation:

$$\text{Grams} = \text{Milliliters} \times \text{Specific gravity}$$

Although it is both obvious and true that one cannot multiply milliliters by specific gravity and have a product in grams, the equation "works" because the volume of the liquid in question is assumed to be the same volume as water for which milliliters equal grams. So, in essence, the true equation would be:

Grams (other liquid) = Grams (of equal volume of water) × Specific gravity (other liquid)

Examples:

What is the weight, in grams, of 3620 mL of alcohol with a specific gravity of 0.820?

$$3620 \text{ mL of water weigh } 3620 \text{ g}$$
$$3620 \text{ g} \times 0.820 = 2968 \text{ g}, \text{ } answer.$$

What is the weight, in grams, of 2 fl. oz. of a liquid having a specific gravity of 1.118?

In this type of problem, it is best to convert the given volume to its metric equivalent first and then solve the problem in the metric system.

$$2 \times 29.57 \text{ mL} = 59.14 \text{ mL}$$
$$59.14 \text{ mL of water weigh } 59.14 \text{ g}$$
$$59.14 \text{ g} \times 1.118 = 66.12 \text{ g}, \text{ } answer.$$

Calculating Volume, Knowing the Weight and Specific Gravity

By rearranging the previous equation, we can calculate the volume of a liquid using the equation:

$$\text{Milliliters} = \frac{\text{Grams}}{\text{Specific gravity}}$$

Examples:

What is the volume, in milliliters, of 492 g of nitric acid with a specific gravity of 1.40?

492 g of water measure 492 mL

$$\frac{492 \text{ mL}}{1.40} = 351 \text{ mL, } answer.$$

What is the volume, in milliliters, of 1 lb of methyl salicylate with a specific gravity of 1.185?

1 lb = 454 g
454 g of water measure 454 mL

$$\frac{454 \text{ mL}}{1.185} = 383.1 \text{ mL, } answer.$$

What is the volume, in pints, of 50 lb of glycerin having a specific gravity of 1.25?

50 lb = 454 g × 50 = 22,700 g
22,700 g of water measure 22,700 mL and 1 pint = 473 mL

$$\frac{22,700 \text{ mL}}{1.25} = 18,160 \text{ mL} \div 473 \text{ mL} = 38.4 \text{ pints, } answer.$$

Examples:

What is the cost of 1000 mL of glycerin, specific gravity 1.25, bought at $54.25 per pound?

1000 mL of water weigh 1000 g
Weight of 1000 mL of glycerin = 1000 g × 1.25 = 1250 g
1 lb = 454 g

$$\frac{454 \text{ (g)}}{1250 \text{ (g)}} = \frac{(\$) 54.25}{(\$) \text{ x}}$$
$$\text{x} = \$149.37, \text{ } answer.$$

What is the cost of 1 pint of chloroform, specific gravity 1.475, bought at $25.25 per pound?

1 pint = 473 mL
473 mL of water weigh 473 g
Weight of 473 mL of chloroform = 473 g × 1.475 = 697.7 g
1 lb = 454 g

$$\frac{454 \text{ (g)}}{697.7 \text{ (g)}} = \frac{(\$) 25.25}{(\$) \text{ x}}$$
$$\text{x} = \$38.80, \text{ } answer.$$

Special Considerations of Specific Gravity

Pharmaceutical Applications

As described previously, specific gravity is employed when a pharmacist wishes to convert the weight of an ingredient or preparation to volume or vice versa. In practice, liquid materials are usually the objects of the conversions. The purpose of a conversion is either to measure the volume of a material when a formula is expressed in units of weight or to weigh an equivalent amount of a material when a formula is expressed in units of volume. As presented in the next chapter, specific gravity is also used to calculate the equivalent strength of a preparation on the basis of either weight or volume.

Another application of specific gravity is in automated pharmaceutical equipment used by pharmacists to prepare total parenteral nutrition (TPN) admixtures. In these *automated compounders*, the purpose of the specific gravity of the large-volume liquids being mixed is to determine the weights of components (e.g., dextrose, amino acids, and water). The component weights are automatically calculated, based on the specific gravity, volume, and percentage concentration of the solutions used (e.g., 70% dextrose injection) in the admixture. The automatic compounder then uses the *weight* to make the correct mixture rather than the *volume* of the solution being measured.

Clinical Application

Specific gravity is an important factor in urinalysis. In normal adults, the specific gravity of urine is usually within the range of 1.010 and 1.025 with a normal fluid intake (this range may vary with the reference source).

Specific gravity is an indicator of both the concentration of particles in the urine and a patient's degree of hydration. A higher-than-normal specific gravity indicates that the urine is concentrated. This may be due to the presence of excess waste products or electrolytes in the urine, the presence of glucose (glucosuria) or protein (proteinuria), excessive water loss, decreased fluid intake, or other factors. A low specific gravity indicates that the urine is dilute, which may be a result of diabetes insipidus, renal disease (by virtue of the kidney's reduced ability to concentrate urine), increased fluid intake, intravenous hydration, or other factors.[3,4]

In the modern clinical laboratory, the specific gravity of urine is determined (using the refractive index method) as a component of a comprehensive urinalysis performed by sophisticated, fully automated equipment that determines, in seconds, urine chemistry, specific gravity, pH, color, and clarity.[5]

CASE IN POINT 5.1[6]

R̥ **Lactic Acid**

Salicylic Acid   aa.   1.5 g

Flexible Collodion qs ad   15 mL

Sig: Apply one drop to wart twice a day.

Label: Wart remover. For external use only.

Lactic acid is available as a liquid containing 85 g of the acid in 100 g of solution (sp.gr. 1.21). Calculate the quantity of this solution, in milliliters, needed to fill the prescription.

Calculating Specific Volume

Specific volume, in pharmaceutical practice, is usually defined as an abstract number representing the ratio, *expressed decimally,* of the volume of a substance to the volume of an equal weight of another substance taken as a standard, both having the same temperature. Water is the standard.

Whereas specific gravity is a comparison of weights of equal volumes, specific volume is a comparison of volumes of equal weights. Because of this relationship, specific gravity and specific

CALCULATIONS CAPSULE

Specific Gravity

The specific gravity (sp gr) of a substance or a pharmaceutical preparation may be determined by the following equation:

$$Specific\ gravity = \frac{Weight\ of\ substance\ (g)}{Weight\ of\ equal\ volume\ of\ water\ (g)}$$

The following equation may be used to convert the volume of a substance or pharmaceutical preparation to its weight:*

$$Weight\ of\ substance = Volume\ of\ substance \times Specific\ gravity$$

Or simply,

$$\mathbf{g = mL \times sp\ gr}$$

The following equation may be used to convert the weight of a substance or pharmaceutical preparation to its volume:*

$$Volume\ of\ substance = \frac{Weight\ of\ substance}{Specific\ gravity}$$

Or simply,

$$\mathbf{mL = \frac{g}{sp\ gr}}$$

* The full explanation on why these equations work may be found in the section "Use of Specific Gravity in Calculations of Weight and Volume," on page 73.

---

volume are *reciprocals*; that is, if they are multiplied together, the product is 1. Specific volume tells us how much greater (or smaller) in volume a mass is than the same weight of water. It may be calculated by dividing the volume of a given mass by the volume of an equal weight of water. Thus, if 25 g of glycerin measures 20 mL and 25 g of water measures 25 mL under the same conditions, the specific volume of the glycerin is:

$$\frac{Volume\ of\ 25\ g\ of\ glycerin}{Volume\ of\ 25\ g\ of\ water} = \frac{20\ (mL)}{25\ (mL)} = 0.8$$

Calculating the specific volume of a liquid, given the volume of a specified weight, involves the following type of calculation.

Example:

Calculate the specific volume of a syrup, 91.0 mL of which weighs 107.16 g.

107.16 g of water measures 107.16 mL

$$Specific\ volume\ of\ syrup = \frac{91.0\ (mL)}{107.16\ (mL)} = 0.849,\ answer.$$

Because specific gravity and specific volume are reciprocals, a substance that is heavier than water will have a higher specific gravity and a lower specific volume, whereas a substance that is lighter than water will have a lower specific gravity and a higher specific volume. It follows, therefore, that we may determine the specific volume of a substance by dividing 1 by its specific gravity, and we may determine the specific gravity of a substance by dividing 1 by its specific volume.

Examples:

What is the specific volume of phosphoric acid having a specific gravity of 1.71?

$$\frac{1}{1.71} = 0.585, \text{ answer.}$$

If a liquid has a specific volume of 1.396, what is its specific gravity?

$$\frac{1}{1.396} = 0.716, \text{ answer.}$$

PRACTICE PROBLEMS

Calculations of Density

1. If 250 mL of alcohol weighs 203 g, what is its density?

2. A piece of copper metal weighs 53.6 g, and has a volume of 6 mL. Calculate its density.

Calculations of Specific Gravity

3. If 150 mL of a sorbitol solution weigh 170 g, what is its specific gravity?

4. If a liter of a cough syrup weighs 1285 g, what is its specific gravity?

5. If 500 mL of ferric chloride solution weighs 650 g, what is its specific gravity?

6. If 380 g of cottonseed oil measures 415 mL, what is its specific gravity?

7. If 2 fl. oz. of glycerol weighs 74.1 g, what is its specific gravity?

8. Five pints of diluted hydrochloric acid weighs 2.79 kg. Calculate its specific gravity.

9. A pycnometer weighs 21.62 g. Filled with water, it weighs 46.71 g; filled with another liquid, it weighs 43.28 g. Calculate the specific gravity of the liquid.

10. A glass plummet weighs 14.35 g in air, 11.40 g when immersed in water, and 8.95 g when immersed in sulfuric acid. Calculate the specific gravity of the acid.

11. A modified Ringer's Irrigation has the following formula:

Sodium chloride	8.6	g
Potassium chloride	0.3	g
Calcium chloride	0.33	g
PEG 3350	60	g
Water for injection ad	1000	mL

Assuming that 980 mL of water is used in preparing the irrigation, calculate its specific gravity.

Calculations of Specific Volume

12. If 73.42 g of a liquid measures 81.5 mL, what is its specific volume?

13. If 120 g of acetone measures 150 mL, what is its specific volume?

14. The specific gravity of alcohol is 0.815. What is its specific volume?

15. If chloroform has a specific gravity of 1.476, what is its specific volume?

Calculations of Weight or Volume Using Specific Gravity

Note: Use the information in Table 5.1 if necessary.

16. Calculate the weight, in grams, of 100 mL of each of the following:
    (a) acetone
    (b) liquid petrolatum
    (c) syrup
    (d) nitroglycerin
    (e) mercury

17. What is the weight, in kilograms, of 5 liters of sulfuric acid with a specific gravity of 1.84?

18. What is the weight, in pounds, of 5 pints of nitric acid?

19. What is the weight, in kilograms, of 1 gallon of sorbitol solution having a specific gravity of 1.285?

20. If 500 mL of mineral oil is used to prepare a liter of mineral oil emulsion, how many grams of the oil, having a specific gravity of 0.87, would be used in the preparation of 1 gallon of the emulsion?

21. Calculate the volume, in milliliters, of 100 g of each of the following:
    (a) peanut oil
    (b) castor oil
    (c) polysorbate 80
    (d) phosphoric acid
    (e) mercury

22. What is the volume, in milliliters, of 1 lb of benzyl benzoate having a specific gravity of 1.120?

23. What is the volume, in milliliters, of 1 kg of sulfuric acid with a specific gravity of 1.83?

24. Calculate the corresponding weights of liquefied phenol and propylene glycol needed to prepare 24 15-mL bottles of the following formula for a cold sore topical liquid:

Liquefied phenol	0.4 mL
Camphor	0.5 g
Benzocaine	2.2 g
Ethanol	65 mL
Propylene glycol	17 mL
Purified water ad	100 mL

25. Calculate the total weight of the following formula for a pediatric chewable gummy gel base for medication.[7]

Gelatin	43.4 g
Glycerin	155 mL
Purified Water	21.6 mL

26. Calculate the number of milliliters of polysorbate 80 required to prepare 48 100-g tubes of the following formula for a progesterone vaginal cream.[8]

Progesterone, micronized	3 g
Polysorbate 80	1 g
Methylcellulose 2% Gel	96 g

27. If fifty glycerin suppositories are made from the following formula, how many milliliters of glycerin, having a specific gravity of 1.25, would be used in the preparation of 96 suppositories?

Glycerin	91 g
Sodium stearate	9 g
Purified water	5 g

28. Two 10-mL samples of urine have specific gravities of 1.003 and 1.030. What is the difference in weight, in milligrams, between the two samples?

29. How many grams of dextrose are contained in a 250-mL intravenous infusion of a dextrose injection containing 60 g of dextrose per 100 mL if its specific gravity is 1.20?

30. ℞[9]

Testosterone propionate	2 g
Mineral Oil, light	10 g
Polysorbate 80	1 g
Methylcellulose 2% gel	87 g

The specific gravity of light mineral oil is 0.85 and that of polysorbate 80 is 1.08. Calculate the milliliters of each needed to fill the prescription.

31. Cocoa butter (theobroma oil), which is solid at room temperature and melts at 34°C, has a specific gravity of 0.86. If a formula calls for 48 mL of theobroma oil, what would be the corresponding weight of cocoa butter to use?

32. A transdermal patch for smoking cessation contains 30 mg of liquid nicotine per patch. If nicotine has a specific gravity of 1.01, how many milliliters of the agent are required to manufacture 1 million patches?

Calculations of Drug Costs Using Specific Gravity

33. The formula for 1000 g of polyethylene glycol ointment calls for 600 g polyethylene glycol 400. At $19.15 per pint, what is the cost of the polyethylene glycol 400, specific gravity 1.140, needed to prepare 4000 g of the ointment?

34. Glycerin, USP (specific gravity 1.25) costs $54.25 per pound. If students in a dispensing laboratory use 1 pint of glycerin in preparing compounded prescriptions, what is the cost of the glycerin used?

ANSWERS TO "CASE IN POINT" AND PRACTICE PROBLEMS

Case in Point 5.1

Quantity of lactic acid needed to fill ℞:
1.5 g
Source of lactic acid: liquid containing 85 g/100 g; or, by using specific gravity:

100 g ÷ 1.21 = 82.64 mL

Thus, 85 g of lactic acid are in 82.64 mL of the source liquid.
By proportion:

$$\frac{85\ g}{82.64\ mL} = \frac{1.5\ g}{x\ mL}; x = 1.46\ mL, answer.$$

Practice Problems

1. 0.812 g/mL
2. 8.933 g/mL
3. 1.133
4. 1.285
5. 1.300
6. 0.916
7. 1.253
8. 1.180
9. 0.863
10. 1.831
11. 1.049
12. 1.110
13. 1.250
14. 1.227
15. 0.678
16. (a) 79 g
    (b) 87 g
    (c) 131 g
    (d) 159 g
    (e) 1360 g
17. 9.2 kg
18. 7.397 or 7.4 lb
19. 4.86 kg
20. 1646.5 g
21. (a) 108.7 mL
    (b) 104.17 mL
    (c) 92.59 mL
    (d) 58.82 mL
    (e) 7.35 mL
22. 405.357 mL
23. 546.448 mL
24. 1.54 g
    63.04 g
25. 258.75 g
26. 44.44 mL

27. 139.776 mL

28. 270 mg

29. 150 g

30. 11.76 mL
    0.93 mL

31. 41.28 g

32. 29,702.97 mL

33. $85.23

34. $70.65

REFERENCES

1. United States Pharmacopeia 31st Rev. National Formulary 26. Rockville, MD: United States Pharmacopeial Convention, 2008;1:13.
2. United States Pharmacopeia 31st Rev. National Formulary 26. Rockville, MD: United States Pharmacopeial Convention, 2008;1:6,8.
3. Pagana KD, Pagana TJ. *Mosby's Diagnostic and Laboratory Test Reference*. 7th Ed. Philadelphia: Elsevier, 2005.
4. The Internet Pathology Laboratory for Medical Education. Urinalysis tutorial. Available at: http://www-medlib.med.utah.edu/WebPath/TUTORIAL/URINE/URINE.html. Accessed September 5, 2007.
5. NITEK 500 Urine Chemistry Analyzer [product information]. Tarrytown, NY: Bayer Healthcare LLC Diagnostic Division.
6. Prince SJ. Calculations. *International Journal of Pharmaceutical Compounding* 1998;2:310.
7. *International Journal of Pharmaceutical Compounding* 1997;1:106.
8. *International Journal of Pharmaceutical Compounding* 1998;2:58.
9. *International Journal of Pharmaceutical Compounding* 1998;2:67.

Percentage, Ratio Strength, and Other Expressions of Concentration

Objectives

Upon successful completion of this chapter, the student will be able to:

- Define the expressions *percent weight-in-volume, percent volume-in -volume,* and *percent weight-in-weight.*
- Define the expression *ratio strength.*
- Convert percent strength to ratio strength and ratio strength to percent strength.
- Calculate the percentage strength and ratio strength of a pharmaceutical preparation.
- Apply percent strength and ratio strength to calculate the quantity of an ingredient present in a pharmaceutical preparation.
- Apply percent strength and ratio strength to calculate the quantity of an ingredient to use in compounding a pharmaceutical preparation.

Percentage

The term **percent** and its corresponding sign (%) mean "by the hundred" or "in a hundred," and **percentage** means "rate per hundred"; so *50 percent* (or *50%*) and *a percentage of 50* are equivalent expressions. A percent may also be expressed as a *ratio,* represented as a common or decimal fraction. For example, *50%* means *50 parts in 100* of the same kind, and may be expressed as $^{50}/_{100}$ or 0.50. Percent, therefore, is simply another fraction of such frequent and familiar use that its numerator is expressed but its denominator is left understood. It should be noted that percent is always an abstract quantity and that, as such, it may be applied to anything.

For the purposes of computation, percents are usually changed to equivalent decimal fractions. This change is made by dropping the percent sign (%) and dividing the expressed numerator by 100. Thus, $12.5\% = \frac{12.5}{100}$, or 0.125; and $0.05\% = \frac{0.05}{100}$, or 0.0005. We must not forget that in the reverse process (changing a decimal to a percent), the decimal is multiplied by 100 and the percent sign (%) is affixed.

Percentage is an essential part of pharmaceutical calculations. The pharmacist encounters it frequently and uses it as a convenient means of expressing the concentration of an active or inactive material in a pharmaceutical preparation.

Percentage Preparations

The percentage concentrations of active and inactive constituents in various types of pharmaceutical preparations are defined as follows by the *United States Pharmacopeia*[1]:

Percent weight-in-volume (w/v) expresses the number of *grams* of a constituent in *100 mL* of solution or liquid preparation and is used regardless of whether water or another liquid is the solvent or vehicle. Expressed as: _____ % *w/v.*

Percent volume-in-volume (v/v) expresses the number of *milliliters* of a constituent in *100 mL* of solution or liquid preparation. Expressed as: _____ % *v/v.*

Percent weight-in-weight (w/w) expresses the number of *grams* of a constituent in *100 g* of solution or preparation. Expressed as: _____ % *w/w.*

The term *percent*, or the symbol %, when used *without qualification* means:

- for solutions or suspensions of solids in liquids, *percent weight-in-volume*;
- for solutions of liquids in liquids, *percent volume-in-volume*;
- for mixtures of solids or semisolids, *percent weight-in-weight*; and
- for solutions of gases in liquids, *percent weight-in-volume*.

Special Considerations in Percentage Calculations

In general, the nature of the ingredients in a pharmaceutical preparation determines the basis of the calculation. That is, a powdered substance dissolved or suspended in a liquid vehicle would generally be calculated on a *weight-in-volume* basis; and a powdered substance mixed with a solid or semisolid, such as an ointment base, would generally be calculated on a *weight-in-weight* basis; and, a liquid component in a liquid preparation would be calculated on a *volume-in-volume* basis. *Based on these considerations, if the designation of the term of a calculation (e.g., w/v, w/w, or v/v) is not included in a problem, the appropriate assumption must be made.* Table 6.1 presents examples of the usual basis for calculations of concentration for some dosage forms.

In most instances, use of percentage concentrations in the manufacture and labeling of pharmaceutical preparations is restricted to instances in which the dose of the active therapeutic ingredient (ATI) is not specific. For example, the ATIs in ointments, lotions, external solutions, and similar products may commonly be expressed in percent strength (e.g., a 1% hydrocortisone ointment). However, in most dosage forms, such as tablets, capsules, injections, oral solutions, and syrups, among others, the amounts of ATIs are expressed in definitive units of measure, such as milligrams per capsule, milligrams per milliliter, or other terms. On the other hand, in many pharmaceutical formulations, *pharmaceutical components* such as flavoring agents, solvents, excipients, preservatives, and so on, may be expressed in terms of their percentage concentration.

Specific gravity may be a factor in a number of calculations involving percentage concentration. Many formulations are presented on the basis of weight, even though some of the ingredients are liquids. Depending on the desired method of measurement, it may be necessary to convert

TABLE 6.1 EXAMPLES OF PHARMACEUTICAL DOSAGE FORMS IN WHICH THE ACTIVE INGREDIENT IS OFTEN CALCULATED AND EXPRESSED ON A PERCENTAGE BASIS

PERCENTAGE BASIS	EXAMPLES OF APPLICABLE DOSAGE FORMS
Weight-in-volume	Solutions (e.g., ophthalmic, nasal, otic, topical, large-volume parenterals), and lotions
Volume-in-volume	Aromatic waters, topical solutions, and emulsions
Weight-in-weight	Ointments, creams, and gels

weight to liquid or, in some instances, vice versa. Thus, the student should recall the equations from the previous chapter, namely:

$$g = mL \times sp\ gr$$

$$mL = \frac{g}{sp\ gr}$$

Percentage Weight-in-Volume

In a *true* expression of *percentage (i.e., parts per 100 parts)*, the percentage of a liquid preparation (e.g., solution, suspension, lotion) would represent the *grams* of solute or constituent in *100 g* of the liquid preparation. However, in practice, the pharmacist most frequently uses a different definition of percentage for solutions and for other liquid preparations, one in which the *parts* of the percentage represent *grams* of a solute or constituent in *100 mL* of solution or liquid preparation.

Indeed, in weight-in-volume expressions, the "correct" strength of a 1% (w/v) solution or other liquid preparation is defined as containing 1 g of constituent in 100 mL of product. This variance to the definition of *true percentage* is based on an assumption that the *solution/liquid preparation has a specific gravity of 1, as if it were water.* It is on this assumption that each 100 mL of solution/liquid preparation is presumed to weigh 100 g and thus is used as the basis for calculating percentage weight-in-volume (e.g., 1% w/v = 1% of [100 mL taken to be] 100 g = 1 g in 100 mL).

Taking water to represent any solvent or vehicle, we may prepare weight-in-volume percentage solutions or liquid preparations by the SI metric system if we use the following rule.

Multiply the required number of milliliters by the percentage strength, expressed as a decimal, to obtain the number of grams of solute or constituent in the solution or liquid preparation. *The volume, in milliliters, represents the weight in grams of the solution or liquid preparation as if it were pure water.*

Volume (mL, representing grams) × % (expressed as a decimal) = grams (g) of solute or constituent

Examples of Weight-in-Volume Calculations

How many grams of dextrose are required to prepare 4000 mL of a 5% solution?

4000 mL represents 4000 g of solution
5% = 0.05
4000 g × 0.05 = 200 g, *answer.*

Or, solving by dimensional analysis:

$$\frac{5\ g}{100\ mL} \times 4000\ mL = 200\ g,\ answer.$$

How many grams of potassium permanganate should be used in compounding the following prescription?

℞   Potassium Permanganate   0.02%
     Purified Water ad   250 mL
     Sig. as directed.
   250 mL represents 250 g of solution
        0.02% = 0.0002
   250 g × 0.0002 = 0.05 g, *answer.*

How many grams of aminobenzoic acid should be used in preparing 8 fluidounces of a 5% solution in 70% alcohol?

8 fl. oz. = 8 × 29.57 mL = 236.56 mL
236.56 mL represents 236.56 g of solution
5% = 0.05
236.56 g × 0.05 = 11.83 g, *answer.*

To calculate the percentage weight-in-volume of a solution or liquid preparation, given the weight of the solute or constituent and the volume of the solution or liquid preparation, it should be remembered that the volume, in milliliters, of the solution represents the weight, in grams, of the solution or liquid preparation as if it were pure water.

What is the percentage strength (w/v) of a solution of urea, if 80 mL contains 12 g?

80 mL of water weighs 80 g

$$\frac{80 \ (g)}{12 \ (g)} = \frac{100 \ (\%)}{x \ (\%)}$$
$$x = 15\%, \ answer.$$

Calculating the volume of a solution or liquid preparation, given its percentage strength weight-in-volume and the weight of the solute or constituent, involves the following:

How many milliliters of a 3% solution can be made from 27 g of ephedrine sulfate?

$$\frac{3 \ (\%)}{100 \ (\%)} = \frac{27 \ (g)}{x \ (g)}$$
$$x = 900 \ g, \text{ weight of the solution if it were water}$$
$$\text{Volume (in mL)} = 900 \text{ mL, } answer.$$

Percentage Volume-in-Volume

Liquids are usually measured by volume, and the percentage strength indicates the number of parts by volume of an ingredient contained in the total volume of the solution or liquid preparation considered as 100 parts by volume. If there is any possibility of misinterpretation, this kind of percentage should be specified: e.g., *10% v/v.*

Examples of Volume-in-Volume Calculations

How many milliliters of liquefied phenol should be used in compounding the following prescription?

℞   Liquefied Phenol   2.5%
       Calamine Lotion   ad   240 mL
       Sig. For external use.

Volume (mL) × % (expressed as a decimal) = milliliters of active ingredient

240 mL × 0.025 = 6 mL, *answer.*

Or, solving by dimensional analysis:

$$\frac{2.5 \text{ mL}}{100 \text{ mL}} \times 240 \text{ mL} = 6 \text{ mL, } answer.$$

In preparing 250 mL of a certain lotion, a pharmacist used 4 mL of liquefied phenol. What was the percentage (v/v) of liquefied phenol in the lotion?

$$\frac{250 \text{ (mL)}}{4 \text{ (mL)}} = \frac{100 \text{ (\%)}}{x \text{ (\%)}}$$

$$x = 1.6\%, \text{ answer.}$$

What is the percentage strength v/v of a solution of 800 g of a liquid with a specific gravity of 0.800 in enough water to make 4000 mL?

800 g of water measures 800 mL
800 mL ÷ 0.800 = 1000 mL of active ingredient

$$\frac{4000 \text{ (mL)}}{1000 \text{ (mL)}} = \frac{100 \text{ (\%)}}{x \text{ (\%)}}$$

$$x = 25\%, \text{ answer.}$$

Or, solving by dimensional analysis:

$$\frac{800 \text{ mL}}{0.800} \times \frac{1}{4000 \text{ mL}} \times 100\% = 25\%, \text{ answer.}$$

The volume of a solution or liquid preparation, given the volume of the active ingredient and its percentage strength (v/v), may require first determining the volume of the active ingredient from its weight and specific gravity.

Peppermint spirit contains 10% v/v of peppermint oil. What volume of the spirit will contain 75 mL of peppermint oil?

$$\frac{10 \text{ (\%)}}{100 \text{ (\%)}} = \frac{75 \text{ (mL)}}{x \text{ (mL)}}$$

$$x = 750 \text{ mL}, \text{ answer.}$$

If a veterinary liniment contains 30% v/v of dimethyl sulfoxide, how many milliliters of the liniment can be prepared from 1 lb of dimethyl sulfoxide (sp gr 1.10)?

1 lb = 454 g
454 g of water measures 454 mL
454 mL ÷ 1.10 = 412.7 mL of dimethyl sulfoxide

$$\frac{30 \text{ (\%)}}{100 \text{ (\%)}} = \frac{412.7 \text{ (mL)}}{x \text{ (mL)}}$$

$$x = 1375.7 \text{ or } 1376 \text{ mL}, \text{ answer.}$$

Or, solving by dimensional analysis:

$$\frac{1 \text{ lb}}{30\%} \times \frac{454 \text{ g}}{1 \text{ lb}} \times \frac{1 \text{ mL}}{1 \text{ g}} \times \frac{1}{1.10} \times 100\% = 1375.7 \text{ or } 1376 \text{ mL}, \text{ answer.}$$

Percentage Weight-in-Weight

Percentage weight-in-weight (*true percentage* or *percentage by weight*) indicates the number of parts by weight of active ingredient contained in the total weight of the solution or mixture considered as 100 parts by weight.

Examples of Weight-in-Weight Calculations

How many grams of phenol should be used to prepare 240 g of a 5% (w/w) solution in water?

Weight of solution (g) × % (expressed as a decimal) = g of solute

240 g × 0.05 = 12 g, *answer.*

How many grams of a drug substance are required to make 120 mL of a 20% (w/w) solution having a specific gravity of 1.15?

120 mL of water weighs 120 g
120 g × 1.15 = 138 g, weight of 120 mL of solution
138 g × 0.20 = 27.6 g plus enough water to make 120 mL, *answer.*

Or, solving by dimensional analysis:

$$120 \text{ mL} \times \frac{1.15 \text{ g}}{1 \text{ mL}} \times \frac{20\%}{100\%} = 27.6 \text{ g, } answer.$$

Sometimes in a weight-in-weight calculation, the weight of one component is known but *not* the total weight of the intended preparation. This type of calculation is performed as demonstrated by the following example.

How many grams of a drug substance should be added to 240 mL of water to make a 4% (w/w) solution?

100% − 4% = 96% (by weight) of water
240 mL of water weighs 240 g

$$\frac{96 \ (\%)}{4 \ (\%)} = \frac{240 \ (g)}{x \ (g)}$$
$$x = 10 \text{ g, } answer.$$

It is usually impossible to prepare a specified *volume* of a solution or liquid preparation of given weight-in-weight percentage strength because the volume displaced by the active ingredient cannot be known in advance. If an excess is acceptable, we may make a volume somewhat more than that specified by taking the given volume to refer to the solvent or vehicle and from this quantity calculating the weight of the solvent or vehicle (the specific gravity of the solvent or vehicle must be known). Using this weight, we may follow the method just described to calculate the corresponding weight of the active ingredient needed.

How should you prepare 100 mL of a 2% (w/w) solution of a drug substance in a solvent having a specific gravity of 1.25?

100 mL of water weighs 100 g
100 g × 1.25 = 125 g, weight of 100 mL of solvent
100% − 2% = 98% (by weight) of solvent

$$\frac{98 \ (\%)}{2 \ (\%)} = \frac{125 \ (g)}{x \ (g)}$$
$$x = 2.55 \text{ g}$$

Therefore, dissolve 2.55 g of drug substance in 125 g (or 100 mL) of solvent, *answer.*

Calculating Percentage Strength Weight-in-Weight

If the weight of the finished solution or liquid preparation is not given when calculating its percentage strength, other data must be supplied from which it may be calculated: the weights of both ingredients, for instance, or the volume and specific gravity of the solution or liquid preparation.

If 1500 g of a solution contains 75 g of a drug substance, what is the percentage strength (w/w) of the solution?

$$\frac{1500\ (g)}{75\ (g)} = \frac{100\ (\%)}{x\ (\%)}$$
$$x = 5\%,\ answer.$$

Or, solving by dimensional analysis:

$$\frac{75\ g}{1500\ g} \times 100\% = 5\%,\ answer.$$

If 5 g of boric acid is added to 100 mL of water, what is the percentage strength (w/w) of the solution?

100 mL of water weighs 100 g
100 g + 5 g = 105 g, weight of solution

$$\frac{105\ (g)}{5\ (g)} = \frac{100\ (\%)}{x\ (\%)}$$
$$x = 4.76\%,\ answer.$$

If 1000 mL of syrup with a specific gravity of 1.313 contains 850 g of sucrose, what is its percentage strength (w/w)?

1000 mL of water weighs 1000 g
1000 g × 1.313 = 1313 g, weight of 1000 mL of syrup

$$\frac{1313\ (g)}{850\ (g)} = \frac{100\ (\%)}{x\ (\%)}$$
$$x = 64.7\%,\ answer.$$

Weight-in-Weight Calculations in Compounding

Weight-in-weight calculations are used in the following types of manufacturing and compounding problems.

What weight of a 5% (w/w) solution can be prepared from 2 g of active ingredient?

$$\frac{5\ (\%)}{100\ (\%)} = \frac{2\ (g)}{x\ (g)}$$
$$x = 40\ g,\ answer.$$

How many milligrams of hydrocortisone should be used in compounding the following prescription?

℞　Hydrocortisone　　　　　⅛%
　　Hydrophilic Ointment ad　10 g
　　Sig. Apply.

⅛% = 0.125%
10 g × 0.00125 = 0.0125 g or 12.5 mg, *answer.*

How many grams of benzocaine should be used in compounding the following prescription?

℞　Benzocaine　　　　　　　2%
　　Polyethylene Glycol Base ad　2
　　Make 24 such suppositories
　　Sig. Insert one as directed.

2 g × 24 = 48 g, total weight of mixture
48 g × 0.02 = 0.96 g, *answer.*

Or, solving by dimensional analysis:

$$24 \text{ supp.} \times \frac{2 \text{ g}}{1 \text{ supp.}} \times \frac{2\%}{100\%} = 0.96 \text{ g, } answer.$$

Use of Percent in Compendial Standards

Percent is used in the *United States Pharmacopeia* to express the degree of tolerance permitted in the purity of single-chemical entities and in the labeled quantities of ingredients in dosage forms. For instance, according to the United States Pharmacopeia,[2] "Aspirin contains not less than 99.5% and not more than 100.5% of $C_9H_8O_4$ (pure chemical aspirin) calculated on the dried basis." Further, "Aspirin Tablets contain not less than 90.0% and not more than 110.0% of the labeled amount of $C_9H_8O_4$." Although dosage forms are formulated with the intent to provide 100% of the quantity of each ingredient declared on the label, some tolerance is permitted to allow for analytic error, unavoidable variations in manufacturing and compounding, and for deterioration to an extent considered insignificant under practical conditions.

The following problem demonstrates calculations involving percent in compendial standards.

If ibuprofen tablets are permitted to contain not less than 90% and not more than 110% of the labeled amount of ibuprofen, what would be the permissible range in content of the drug, expressed in milligrams, for ibuprofen tablets labeled 200 mg each?

$$
\begin{aligned}
90\% \text{ of } 200 \text{ mg} &= 180 \text{ mg} \\
110\% \text{ of } 200 \text{ mg} &= 220 \text{ mg} \\
\text{Range} &= 180 \text{ mg to } 220 \text{ mg, } answer.
\end{aligned}
$$

CALCULATIONS CAPSULE

Percentage Concentration

The amounts of therapeutically active and/or inactive ingredients in certain types of pharmaceutical preparations are expressed in terms of their percentage concentrations.

Unless otherwise indicated:

(a) Liquid components in liquid preparations have *volume-in-volume* relationships with calculations following the equation:

mL of preparation × % concentration[a] = mL of component

(b) Solid components in liquid preparations have *weight-in-volume* relationships with calculations following the equation:

mL of preparation × % concentration[a] = g of component

The terms of this equation are valid due to the assumption that the specific gravity of the preparation is 1, as if it were water, and thus each milliliter represents the weight of one gram.

(c) Solid or semisolid components in solid or semisolid preparations have *weight-in-weight* relationships with calculations following the equation:

g of preparation × % concentration[a] = g of component

[a] In these equations, "% concentration" is expressed decimally (e.g., 0.05, *not* 5%).

CASE IN POINT 6.1[3]: A patient with myasthenia gravis has undergone treatment to separate and remove certain abnormal antibodies and other unwanted elements from the blood (plasmapheresis). The desired red blood cell component is then returned back to the blood, but the patient has lost protein and blood volume.

The patient's physician orders 2000 mL of a 5% w/v solution of albumin in 0.9% w/v sodium chloride injection to replace lost protein and fluid.

In filling the order, the pharmacist decides to use a piece of automated equipment to compound the mixture. The equipment must be programmed with the specific gravities of the solutions being mixed. The pharmacist selects to use a 25% w/v albumin solution as the source of the albumin plus a 0.9% sodium chloride injection.

From the literature, the pharmacist finds that 0.9% sodium chloride has a specific gravity of 1.05. Using a precise 25-mL pycnometer with a tare weight of 28 g, the pharmacist fills it with the 25% w/v albumin solution and determines the weight of the flask and its content to be 58 g.

(a) What is the specific gravity of the albumin solution?
(b) How many milliliters of the 25% w/v albumin solution are needed to make 2000 mL containing 5% w/v albumin?
(c) What is the weight of the 25% albumin solution needed to fill the order?
(d) If the pharmacist mixed the required number of milliliters of the 25% albumin solution with a sufficient 0.9% w/v sodium chloride injection to make the required 2000 mL mixture, what would be the specific gravity of the resultant solution?

CASE IN POINT 6.2[3]: A pharmacist receives the following prescription but does not have hydrocortisone powder on hand. However, the pharmacist does have an injection containing 100 mg of hydrocortisone per milliliter of injection. A search of the literature indicates that the injection has a specific gravity of 1.5.

℞   Hydrocortisone   1.5%
     Cold Cream qs   30 g

(a) How many grams of hydrocortisone are needed to fill the prescription?
(b) How many milliliters of the hydrocortisone injection would provide the correct amount of hydrocortisone?
(c) How many grams of cold cream are required?

Ratio Strength

The concentrations of weak solutions are frequently expressed in terms of ratio strength. Because all percentages are a ratio of parts per hundred, ratio strength is merely another way of expressing the percentage strength of solutions or liquid preparations (and, less frequently, of mixtures of solids). For example, *5% means 5 parts per 100 or 5:100.* Although *5 parts per 100* designates a ratio strength, it is customary to translate this designation into a ratio, the first figure of which is *1;* thus, *5:100 = 1:20.*

When a ratio strength, for example, *1:1000,* is used to designate a concentration, it is to be interpreted as follows:

- For *solids in liquids* = *1 g* of solute or constituent in *1000 mL* of solution or liquid preparation.

- For *liquids in liquids* = *1 mL* of constituent in *1000 mL* of solution or liquid preparation.

- For *solids in solids* = *1 g* of constituent in *1000 g* of mixture.

The ratio and percentage strengths of any solution or mixture of solids are proportional, and either is easily converted to the other by the use of proportion.

Example Calculations Using Ratio Strength

Express 0.02% as a ratio strength.

$$\frac{0.02\ (\%)}{100\ (\%)} = \frac{1\ (part)}{x\ (parts)}$$
$$x = 5000$$
Ratio strength = 1:5000, *answer.*

Express 1:4000 as a percentage strength.

$$\frac{4000\ (parts)}{1\ (part)} = \frac{100\ (\%)}{x\ (\%)}$$
$$x = 0.025\%, \text{ } answer.$$

Note: To change ratio strength to percentage strength, it is sometimes convenient to "convert" the last two zeros in a ratio strength to a percent sign (%) and change the remaining ratio first to a common fraction and then to a decimal fraction in expressing percent:

$$1:100 = \frac{1}{1}\% \quad = 1\%$$
$$1:200 = \frac{1}{2}\% \quad = 0.5\%$$
$$3:500 = \frac{3}{5}\% \quad = 0.6\%$$
$$1:2500 = \frac{1}{25}\% \quad = 0.04\%$$
$$1:10,000 = \frac{1}{100}\% = 0.01\%$$

Calculating the ratio strength of a solution or liquid preparation, given the weight of solute or constituent in a specified volume of solution or liquid preparation involves the following.

A certain injectable contains 2 mg of a drug per milliliter of solution. What is the ratio strength (w/v) of the solution?

$$2\text{ mg} = 0.002\text{ g}$$

$$\frac{0.002\ (g)}{1\ (g)} = \frac{1\ (mL)}{x\ (mL)}$$
$$x = 500\text{ mL}$$
Ratio strength = 1:500, *answer.*

What is the ratio strength (w/v) of a solution made by dissolving five tablets, each containing 2.25 g of sodium chloride, in enough water to make 1800 mL?

$$2.25\text{ g} \times 5 = 11.25\text{ g of sodium chloride}$$

$$\frac{11.25\ (g)}{1\ (g)} = \frac{1800\ (mL)}{x\ (mL)}$$
$$x = 160\text{ mL}$$
Ratio strength = 1:160, *answer.*

In solving problems in which the calculations are based on ratio strength, it is sometimes convenient to translate the problem into one based on percentage strength and to solve it according to the rules and methods discussed under percentage preparations.

How many grams of potassium permanganate should be used in preparing 500 mL of a 1:2500 solution?

$$1{:}2500 \qquad = 0.04\%$$
$$500 \text{ (g)} \times 0.0004 \quad = 0.2 \text{ g, } answer.$$

Or,

1:2500 means 1 g in 2500 mL of solution

$$\frac{2500 \text{ (mL)}}{500 \text{ (mL)}} = \frac{1 \text{ (g)}}{x \text{ (g)}}$$
$$x = 0.2 \text{ g, } answer.$$

How many milligrams of gentian violet should be used in preparing the following solution?

> ℞   Gentian Violet Solution   500 mL
>   1:10,000
>   Sig. Instill as directed.

$$1{:}10{,}000 = 0.01\%$$
$$500 \text{ (g)} \times 0.0001 = 0.050 \text{ g or 50 mg, } answer.$$

Or,
1:10,000 means 1 g of 10,000 mL of solution

$$\frac{10{,}000 \text{ (mL)}}{500 \text{ (mL)}} = \frac{1 \text{ (g)}}{x \text{ (g)}}$$
$$x = 0.050 \text{ g or 50 mg, } answer.$$

How many milligrams of hexachlorophene should be used in compounding the following prescription?

> ℞   Hexachlorophene   1:400
>   Hydrophilic Ointment   ad   10 g
>   Sig. Apply.

1:400 = 0.25%
10 (g) × 0.0025 = 0.025 g or 25 mg, *answer.*
Or,

1:400 means 1 g in 400 g of ointment

$$\frac{400 \text{ (g)}}{10 \text{ (g)}} = \frac{1 \text{ (g)}}{x \text{ (g)}}$$
$$x = 0.025 \text{ g or 25 mg, } answer.$$

Simple Conversions of Concentration to "mg/mL"

Occasionally, pharmacists, particularly those practicing in patient care settings, need to *convert rapidly* product concentrations expressed as percentage strength, ratio strength, or as grams per liter (as in IV infusions) *to milligrams per milliliter* (mg/mL). These conversions may be made quickly by using simple techniques. Some suggestions follow.

CALCULATIONS CAPSULE

Ratio Strength

The concentrations of very weak pharmaceutical preparations (usually weight-in-volume solutions) often are expressed in terms of their ratio strengths.

Ratio strength is another way of expressing percentage strength. For example, a 1% w/v solution and a ratio strength of 1:100 w/v are equivalent.

The preferable style of a ratio strength is to have the numeric value of the solute as 1. This is accomplished when calculating a ratio strength, by setting up a proportion from the data as:

$$\frac{g\ (given\ solute)}{mL\ (given\ solution)} = \frac{1}{x};\ then,\ 1{:}value\ of\ x,\ answer.$$

In using a ratio strength in a calculations problem, there are two options: (a) convert it to a percentage strength and perform calculations in the usual manner, or (2) use the ratio strength directly in a problem-solving proportion.

(a) To convert a ratio strength to a percentage strength; for example, 1:10,000 w/v:

$$\frac{1\ g}{10,000\ mL} = \frac{x\ (g)}{100\ mL}$$

Solving for x yields percent, by definition (parts per hundred).

(b) Problem-solving proportion, for example:

$$\frac{1\ g}{10,000\ mL} = \frac{x\ g}{(given\ quality,\ mL)};\ x = g\ in\ given\ mL$$

To convert *product percentage strengths to mg/mL*, multiply the percentage strength, expressed as a whole number, by 10.

Example:

Convert 4% (w/v) to mg/mL.

$$
\begin{array}{ll}
4 \times 10 & = 40\ mg/mL,\ answer. \\
\text{Proof or alternate method: } 4\%\ (w/v) & = 4\ g/100\ mL \\
& = 4000\ mg/100\ mL \\
& = 40\ mg/mL
\end{array}
$$

To convert *product ratio strengths to mg/mL*, divide the ratio strength by 1000.

Example:

Convert 1:10,000 (w/v) to mg/mL.

$$
\begin{array}{ll}
10,000 \div 1000 & = 1\ mg/10\ mL,\ answer. \\
\text{Proof or alternate method: } 1{:}10,000\ (w/v) & = 1\ g/10,000\ mL \\
& = 1000\ mg/10,000\ mL \\
& = 1\ mg/10\ mL
\end{array}
$$

To convert *product strengths expressed as grams per liter (g/L) to mg/mL*, convert the numerator to milligrams and divide by the number of milliliters in the denominator.

Example:

Convert a product concentration of 1 g per 250 mL to mg/mL.

$1000 \div 250$ = 4 mg/mL, *answer.*

Proof or alternate method: 1 g/250 mL = 1000 mg/250 mL = 4 mg/mL

Milligrams Percent

The term *milligrams percent* (mg%) expresses the number of milligrams of substance in 100 mL of liquid. It is used frequently to denote the concentration of a drug or natural substance in a biologic fluid, as in the blood. Thus, the statement that the concentration of nonprotein nitrogen in the blood is 30 mg% means that each 100 mL of blood contains 30 mg of nonprotein nitrogen. As discussed in Chapter 10, quantities of substances present in biologic fluids also commonly are stated in terms of milligrams per deciliter (mg/dL) of fluid.

Parts per Million (PPM) and Parts per Billion (PPB)

The strengths of very dilute solutions are commonly expressed in terms of *parts per million (ppm)* or *parts per billion (ppb)*, i.e., the number of parts of the agent per 1 million or 1 billion parts of the whole. For example, we are all familiar with fluoridated drinking water in which fluoride has been added at levels of between 1 to 4 parts per million (1:1,000,000 to 4:1,000,000) for the purpose of reducing dental caries.

We also are aware of and concerned with the presence of trace amounts of *contaminants* in our drinking water and food which can pose a risk to our health and safety. Many persons have food allergies, immune system disorders, and other conditions that render them more at risk than the general population. Potential contaminants include micro-organisms, inorganic and organic chemical contaminants (some arising from the careless disposal of prescribed and over-the-counter medications, e.g., flushing), pesticides and herbicides, and radioactive compounds.

Many pharmacists serve on community committees and boards which address environmental issues. Although they may not refer to themselves as **environmental pharmacists**, their backgrounds and interest in public health make them invaluable members of such bodies. Among the concerns are the levels of contaminants found in sources of drinking water and how those levels compare with the standards set by the United States Environmental Protection Agency (EPA). The EPA has established **maximum contaminant levels** (**MCLs**) which quantify the highest level of a contaminant that is allowed in drinking water below which there is no known or expected risk to a person's health or safety. Such levels are established for copper, lead, fluoride, chlorine, total organic compounds, and other trace constituents. These levels generally are expressed either in parts per million or parts per billion.

Example Calculations of Parts per Million and Parts per Billion

Express 5 ppm of iron in water in percentage strength and ratio strength.

5 ppm = 5 parts in 1,000,000 parts = 1:200,000, ratio strength, *and*
= 0.0005%, percentage strength, *answers.*

The concentration of a drug additive in an animal feed is 12.5 ppm. How many milligrams of the drug should be used in preparing 5.2 kg of feed?

12.5 ppm = 12.5 g (drug) in 1,000,000 g (feed)

Thus,

$$\frac{1,000,000 \text{ g}}{12.5 \text{ g}} = \frac{5,200 \text{ g}}{\text{x g}}$$

$$\text{x} = 0.065 \text{ g} = 65 \text{ mg, } answer.$$

The drinking water in a community has detected lead in its drinking water at a level of 2.5 ppb. The EPA's MCL is set at 15 ppb. Express the difference between these two values as a ratio strength.

15 ppb − 2.5 ppb = 12.5 ppb = 12.5:1,000,000,000 = 1:80,000,000, *answer.*

PRACTICE PROBLEMS

Weight-in-Volume Calculations

1. ℞   Antipyrine   5%
        Glycerin ad   60
        Sig: Five drops in right ear.

   How many grams of antipyrine should be used in preparing the prescription?

2. ℞   Ofloxacin Ophthalmic
           Solution   0.3%
        Disp.   10 mL
        Sig: 2 drops into eyes q 4 hours ×
        2 days; then 2 drops q 6 hours × 4
        days.

   A pharmacist filled the prescription with OCUFLOX. How many milligrams of ofloxacin are contained in the dispensed prescription?

3.[4] ℞ Dexamethasone Sodium
           Phosphate   100 mg
        Sterile Water for Injection
           ad   100 mL
        Sig: 2 drops into eyes q 4 hours ×
        2 days; then 2 drops q 6 hours × 4
        days.

   Calculate the percent strength of dexamethasone sodium phosphate in the prescription.

4. If 100 mL of a pharmaceutical preparation contains 20 μL of a 50% w/v solution of benzalkonium chloride, what is the percentage strength of that agent in the solution?

5. A tissue plasminogen activator (TPA) ophthalmic solution is prepared to contain 25 μg/100 μL.
   (a) Calculate the percentage concentration of TPA in the solution.

   (b) What volume of a solution containing TPA, 50 mg/50 mL, should be used to prepare each 100 μL of the opthalmic solution?

6. How many milligrams of methylparaben are needed to prepare 8 fluidounces of a solution containing 0.12% (w/v) of methylparaben?

7. If a pharmacist dissolved the contents of eight capsules, each containing 300 mg of clindamycin phosphate, into a sufficient amount of an astringent liquid base to prepare 60 mL of topical solution, what would be the percentage strength (w/v) of clindamycin phosphate in the prescription?

8. ℞   ACULAR (ketorolac tromethamine)
        Ophthalmic Solution   0.5%
        Disp.   5 mL
        Sig: One drop q.i.d. prn allergic
        conjunctivitis

   How many milligrams of the active constituent would be present in each drop of the ophthalmic solution if the dropper service delivers 20 drops per milliliter?
   (a) 0.25 mg
   (b) 25 mg
   (c) 0.025 mg
   (d) 1.25 mg

9. A formula for an antifungal shampoo contains 2% w/v ketoconazole. How many grams of ketoconazole would be needed to prepare 25 liters of the shampoo?

10. The biotechnology drug interferon gamma-1b (ACTIMMUNE) contains 100 mcg/0.5 mL. Calculate the percentage strength of the solution.

11. NEUPOGEN (filgrastim) prefilled syringes contain 480 mcg of active constituent in each 0.8 mL. The equivalent concentration is:
    (a) 0.6%
    (b) 0.384 mg/mL
    (c) 0.06%
    (d) 0.6 g/mL

12. LEVAQUIN (levofloxacin) injection contains 5 mg/mL of levofloxacin and 5% of dextrose. How much of each would be delivered to a patient upon the administration of a 100-mL injection?
    (a) 5 g levofloxacin and 5 g dextrose
    (b) 50 mg levofloxacin and 5 g dextrose
    (c) 500 mg levofloxacin and 500 mg dextrose
    (d) 0.5 g levofloxacin and 5 g dextrose

13. An ear drop formula contains 54 mg of antipyrine and 14 mg of benzocaine in each milliliter of solution. Calculate the percentage strength (w/v) of each ingredient in the formula.

14. An injection of adalimumab (HUMIRA) contains 40 mg/0.8 mL. Calculate the percentage concentration of the injection.

15.[5] ℞   Erythromycin Lactobio-
             nate   500   mg
         Dexamethasone Sodium
             Phosphate   100   mg
             Glycerin   2.5   mL
         Sterile Water for Injec-
             tion ad   100   mL
         M. ft. Ophthalmic Solution

    (a) What is the percentage strength of erythromycin lactobionate in the prescription?
    (b) If glycerin has a specific gravity of 1.25, what is its concentration (w/v) in the prescription?

16. How many milliliters of a 0.9% (w/v) solution of sodium chloride can be prepared from 50 tablets, each containing 2.25 g of sodium chloride?

17. If an intravenous injection contains 20% (w/v) of mannitol, how many milliliters of the injection should be administered to provide a patient with 100 g of mannitol?

18. A prefilled syringe contains 50 mg of lidocaine hydrochloride per 5 mL of injection. Express the percentage concentration of lidocaine hydrochloride in the injection.

19. A blood volume expansion solution contains 6% (w/v) of hetastarch and 0.9% (w/v) of sodium chloride. How many grams of each agent would be present in 250 mL of the solution?

20. A pharmacist adds 10 mL of a 20% (w/v) solution of a drug to 500 mL of D5W for parenteral infusion. What is the percentage strength of the drug in the infusion solution?
    (a) 2% v/v
    (b) 2% w/v
    (c) 1.96% w/v
    (d) 0.39% w/v

21. Calculate the percentage strength of an injection that contains 2 mg of hydromorphone hydrochloride in each milliliter of injection.

22. VIRAMUNE Oral Suspension contains 1% w/v of nevirapine. Calculate the milligrams of nevirapine present in a 240 mL bottle of the suspension.

23. ℞[6]   Misoprostol 200-μg
               tablets   12 tablets
            Lidocaine Hydro-
               chloride   1 g
            Glycerin qs ad   100 mL

    Calculate the strength of misoprostol in the prescription.
    (a) 2.4% w/v misoprostol
    (b) 0.0002% w/v misoprostol
    (c) 0.024 mg/mL misoprostol
    (d) 2.4 mcg/mL misoprostol

24. ℞[7] Fentanyl Citrate   20 μg/mL
    Bupivacaine Hydro-
       chloride   0.125 %
    Sodium Chloride
       (0.9%) Injection ad 100 mL

    Calculate the percentage concentration of fentanyl citrate in the prescription.

25. ATROVENT Nasal Spray contains 0.03% of ipratropium bromide in a 30-mL metered dose container. If the container is calibrated to deliver 345 sprays, calculate the volume of each spray, in microliters, and the medication content of each spray, in micrograms.

26. If 100 mL of a solution for patient-controlled anesthesia contains 200 mg of morphine sulfate and 8 mg of droperidol, calculate the percentage strength of each of these ingredients in the solution.

27. Oxycodone hydrochloride oral concentrate solution (OXYFAST) contains 20 mg/1 mL. If a dose of 0.75 mL is added to 30 mL of juice prior to administration, calculate (a) the milligrams of oxycodone hydrochloride administered, and (b) the percentage concentration (w/v) of oxycodone hydrochloride in the drink.

28. A morphine sulfate extended-release liposome injection (DEPODUR) contains morphine sulfate 10 mg/mL of injection. Calculate the percentage strength of morphine sulfate in the injection.

29. A topical solution contains 3% w/v hydroquinone. How many liters of the solution can be prepared from 30 g of hydroquinone?

Volume-in-Volume Calculations

30. What is the percentage strength (v/v) if 225 g of a liquid having a specific gravity of 0.8 is added to enough water to make 1.5 liters of the solution?

31. How many liters of a mouthwash can be prepared from 100 mL of cinnamon flavor if its concentration is to be 0.5% (v/v)?

32. A lotion vehicle contains 15% (v/v) of glycerin. How much glycerin should be used in preparing 5 gallons of the lotion?
    (a) 2271 g glycerin
    (b) 3339.7 mL glycerin
    (c) 2671.8 g glycerin
    (d) 3548.4 g glycerin

33. The formula for 1 liter of an elixir contains 0.25 mL of a flavoring oil. What is the percentage (v/v) of the flavoring oil in the elixir?

34. A dermatologic lotion contains 1.25 mL of liquefied phenol in 500 mL. Calculate the percentage (v/v) of liquefied phenol in the lotion.

Weight-in-Weight Calculations

35. How many grams of sucrose must be added to 475 mL of water to make a 65% (w/w) solution?

36. How many grams of a drug substance should be added to 1800 mL of water to make a 10% (w/w) solution?

37. What is the percentage strength (w/w) of a solution made by dissolving 62.5 g of potassium chloride in 187.5 mL of water?

38. If 500 g of dextrose are dissolved in 600 mL of water with a resultant final volume of 1 liter, what is the percentage strength of dextrose in the solution on a w/w basis?

39. Hydromorphone hydrochloride suppositories contain 3 mg of active ingredient and weigh approximately 2 grams each. What is the equivalent percentage strength?
    (a) 1.5%
    (b) 0.15%
    (c) 0.015%
    (d) none of the above

40. A metronidazole vaginal gel contains 0.75% of drug in 70-g tubes. An applicator will hold 5 g of gel for each administration. How much drug will be contained in each application?

(a) 0.0375 mg metronidazole
(b) 3.75 mg metronidazole
(c) 37.5 mg metronidazole
(d) 375 mg metronidazole

41. ℞ ZOVIRAX (acyclovir) 5% Cream
       Lidocaine 4% Cream aa. 15g

The percent of acyclovir and quantity of lidocaine in the filled prescription are:
(a) 3.75% acyclovir, 0.3 g lidocaine
(b) 5% acyclovir, 1.2 g lidocaine
(c) 2.5% acyclovir, 0.6 g lidocaine
(d) 2.5% acyclovir, 1.2 g lidocaine

42. How many grams of hydrocortisone should be used in preparing 120 suppositories, each weighing 2 g and containing 1% of hydrocortisone?

43. If a topical cream contains 1.8% (w/w) of hydrocortisone, which of the following strengths is equivalent?
(a) 2.7 mg hydrocortisone in 15 g of cream
(b) 27 mg hydrocortisone in 15 g of cream
(c) 0.54 g hydrocortisone in 30 g of cream
(d) 54 mg hydrocortisone in 30 g of cream

44.[8] ℞ Benzoin Tincture   18 mL
         Peru Balsam   10 g
         Cold Cream   70 g
         Sig: cold sore ointment

If benzoin tincture has a specific gravity of 0.88, calculate its percentage strength (w/w) in the mixture.
(a) 1.26% w/w
(b) 25.7% w/w
(c) 22.5% w/w
(d) 16.5% w/w

45. Alclometasone dipropionate (ACLO-VATE) ointment contains 0.05% w/w of the drug in 15-g and 45-g tubes. Calculate the difference in the quantity of drug between the two tube sizes.

46. How many grams of azelaic acid (FINA-CEA) are contained in 30-g tubes of the 15% w/w ointment?

47. Tretinoin gel (RETIN-A MICRO) is available in two strengths: 0.1% w/w and 0.04% w/w. Which of these represents equivalent concentrations of the two strengths?
(a) 15 mg/15 g and 30 mg/30 g
(b) 5 mg/5 g and 0.06 g/15 g
(c) 15 mg/15 g and 60 mg/15 g
(d) 30 mg/30 g and 6 mg/15 g

Mixed Percent Calculations

48.[9] ℞ Progesterone, micronized   4 g
         Glycerin   5 mL
         Methylcellulose (1%)
           Solution   50 mL
         Cherry Syrup ad   100 mL

(a) What is the percentage concentration (w/v) of progesterone in the prescription?
(b) What is the percentage concentration (w/v) of methylcellulose in the prescription?
(c) What is the percentage concentration (v/v and w/v) of glycerin (sp gr 1.25) in the prescription?

49.[10] ℞ Lactic Acid   4 g
          Salicylic Acid   5 g
          Trichloroacetic Acid   2 g
          Flexible Collodion
            q.s. ad   100 g
          Sig: wart remover. Use as directed.

(a) Flexible collodion contains 20% w/w camphor and 30% w/w castor oil. How many grams of each would be contained in 30 g of the mixture?
(b) The specific gravity of castor oil is 0.955. How many milliliters of the oil are contained in 30 g of the mixture?
(c) If the specific gravity of the mixture is 0.781, what are the w/v concentrations of lactic acid, salicylic acid, and trichloroacetic acid in the mixture?

Ratio Strength Calculations

50. Express each of the following as a percentage strength:

    (a) 1:1500   (d) 1:400
    (b) 1:10,000   (e) 1:3300
    (c) 1:250   (f) 1:4000

51. Express each of the following as a ratio strength:

    (a) 0.125%   (d) 0.6%
    (b) 2.5%   (e) $\frac{1}{3}$%
    (c) 0.80%   (f) $\frac{1}{20}$%

52. Express each of the following concentrations as a ratio strength:
    (a) 2 mg of active ingredient in 2 mL of solution
    (b) 0.275 mg of active ingredient in 5 mL of solution
    (c) 2 g of active ingredient in 250 mL of solution
    (d) 1 mg of active ingredient in 0.5 mL of solution

53. A vaginal cream contains 0.01% (w/v) of dienestrol. Express this concentration as a ratio strength.

54. A doxycycline calcium syrup is preserved with 0.08% (w/v) of methylparaben, 0.02% (w/v) of propylparaben, and 0.10% (w/v) of sodium metabisulfite. Express these concentrations as ratio strengths.

55. An ophthalmic solution is preserved with 0.0008% (w/v) of an antibacterial. Express this concentration as a ratio strength.

56. An injection contains 0.50% (w/v) of lidocaine hydrochloride and 1:200,000 (w/v) of epinephrine. Express the concentration of lidocaine hydrochloride as a ratio strength and that of epinephrine as a percentage.

57. A sample of white petrolatum contains 10 mg of tocopherol per kilogram as a preservative. Express the amount of tocopherol as a ratio strength.

58. Calcium hydroxide topical solution contains 170 mg of calcium hydroxide per 100 mL at 15°C. Express this concentration as a ratio strength.

59. An assay for ergocalciferol calls for the dissolution of 0.5 mg of ergocalciferol with chloroform up to 5 mL, and the addition of 0.3 mL of acetic anhydride and 0.2 mL of sulfuric acid. Calculate the ratio strength of ergocalciferol in the mixture.

60. ℞   Potassium Permanganate
          Tablets   0.2 g
          Disp. #100
          Sig: two tablets in 4 pt of water and use as directed.

    Express the concentration, as a ratio strength, of the solution prepared according to the directions given in the prescription.

61. Hepatitis B virus vaccine inactivated is inactivated with 1:4000 (w/v) of formalin. Express this ratio strength as a percentage strength.

62. VERSED Injection contains 5 mg of midazolam per milliliter of injection. Calculate the ratio strength of midazolam in the injection.

63. If a liquid vitamin preparation contains 0.16 μg of vitamin B_{12} per 5 mL, what is the ratio strength of the preparation?

64. A skin test for fire ant allergy involves the intradermal skin prick of 0.05 mL of a 1:1,000,000 (w/v) dilution of fire ant extract. How many micrograms of extract would be administered in this manner?

65. In acute hypersensitivity reactions, 0.5 mL of a 1:1000 (w/v) solution of epinephrine may be administered subcutaneously or intramuscularly. Calculate the milligrams of epinephrine given.

66.[11] ℞   Tetracaine Hydro-
            chloride   0.75%
            Epinephrine Hydro-
            chloride   1:4000
            Cocaine Hydro-
            chloride   3 %
            Sodium Chloride, qs
            Sterile Water ad   30 mL

How many milligrams each of tetracaine hydrochloride, epinephrine hydrochloride, and cocaine hydrochloride are needed to fill the prescription?

Parts per Million Calculations

67. Purified water contains not more than 10 ppm of total solids. Express this concentration as a percentage.

68. How many grams of sodium fluoride should be added to 100,000 liters of drinking water containing 0.6 ppm of sodium fluoride to provide a recommended concentration of 1.75 ppm?

69. If a city water supply has a limit of 250 ppm of nitrate ion, what is the maximum amount of nitrate ion, in grams, that may be present in a 10,000-gallon reservoir?

70. If a commercially available insulin preparation contains 1 ppm of proinsulin, how many micrograms of proinsulin would be contained in a 10-mL vial of insulin?

ANSWERS TO "CASE IN POINT" AND PRACTICE PROBLEMS

Case in Point 6.1

(a) 58 g (weight of filled pycnometer) − 28 g (weight of pycnometer) = 30 g (weight of 25 mL of albumin solution);

30 g ÷ 25 mL = 1.2, specific gravity of albumin solution, *answer*.

(b) 2000 mL × 0.05 (5%) = 100 g of albumin needed;

$$\frac{25\ g}{100\ mL} = \frac{100\ g}{x\ mL}; x = 400\ mL,$$
albumin solution needed, *answer*.

(c) 400 mL × 1.2 (specific gravity) = 480 g, albumin solution needed, *answer*.

(d) 2000 mL (total solution) − 400 mL (albumin solution) = 1600 mL (0.9% sodium chloride solution);

1600 mL × 1.05 (specific gravity) = 1680 g (weight of 0.9% sodium chloride solution);
1680 g + 480 g = 2160 g (total weight of the 2000 mL);
2160 g ÷ 2000 mL = 1.08, specific gravity of the mixture, *answer*.

Case in Point 6.2

(a) 30 g × 0.015 (1.5% w/w) = 0.45 g hydrocortisone needed, *answer*.

(b) $\frac{0.1\ g}{1\ mL} = \frac{0.45\ g}{x\ mL}$; x = 4.5 mL hydrocortisone injection, *answer*.

(c) 4.5 mL × 1.5 (specific gravity) = 6.75 g (weight of hydrocortisone injection); 30 g − 6.75 g = 23.25 g cold cream needed, *answer*.

Practice Problems

1. 3 g antipyrine

2. 30 mg ofloxacin

3. 0.1% w/v dexamethasone sodium phosphate

4. 0.01% w/v benzalkonium chloride

5. (a) 0.025% w/v TPA
   (b) 0.025 mL

6. 283.9 mg methylparaben

7. 4 % w/v clindamycin phosphate

8. (a) 0.25 mg ketorolac tromethamine

9. 500 g ketoconazole

10. 0.02% w/v interferon gamma-1b

11. (c) 0.06%

12. (d) 0.5 g levofloxacin and 5 g dextrose

13. (a) 5.4% w/v antipyrine
    (b) 1.4% w/v benzocaine

14. 5% w/v adalimumab

15. (a) 0.5% w/v erythromycin lactobionate
    (b) 3.125% w/v glycerin

16. 12,500 mL

17. 500 mL

18. 1% w/v lidocaine hydrochloride

19. 15 g hetastarch
    2.25 g sodium chloride

20. (d) 0.39% w/v

21. 0.2% w/v hydromorphone

22. 2400 mg nevirapine

23. (c) 0.024 mg/mL misoprostol

24. 0.002% w/v fentanyl citrate

25. 86.96 μL /spray and 26.09 μg ipratropium

26. 0.2% w/v morphine sulfate and 0.008% w/v droperidol

27. (a) 15 mg oxycodone hydrochloride
    (b) 0.049% w/v oxycodone hydrochloride

28. 1% w/v morphine sulfate

29. 1 liter

30. 18.75% v/v

31. 20 liters

32. (d) 3548.4 g glycerin

33. 0.025% v/v flavoring oil

34. 0.25% v/v liquefied phenol

35. 882.14 g sucrose

36. 200 g

37. 25% w/w potassium chloride

38. 45.45% w/w dextrose

39. (b) 0.15%

40. (c) 37.5 mg metronidazole

41. (c) 2.5% acyclovir, 0.6 g lidocaine

42. 2.4 g hydrocortisone

43. (c) 0.54g hydrocortisone in 30g of cream

44. (d) 16.5% w/w

45. 15 mg alclometasone dipropionate

46. 4.5 g azelaic acid

47. (d) 30 mg/30 g and 6 mg/15 g

48. (a) 4% w/v progesterone
    (b) 0.5% w/v methylcellulose
    (c) 5% v/v and 6.25% w/v glycerin

49. (a) 5.34 g camphor and 8.01 g castor oil
    (b) 8.39 mL castor oil
    (c) 3.12% w/v lactic acid, 3.91% w/v salicylic acid, and 1.56% w/v trichloroacetic acid

50. (a) 0.067%
    (b) 0.01%
    (c) 0.4 %
    (d) 0.25%
    (e) 0.03%
    (f) 0.025%

51. (a) 1:800
    (b) 1:40
    (c) 1:125
    (d) 1:166.67 or 1:167
    (e) 1:300
    (f) 1:2000

52. (a) 1:1000
    (b) 1:18,182
    (c) 1:125
    (d) 1:500

53. 1:10,000 w/v

54. 1:1250 w/v methylparaben
    1:5000 w/v propylparaben
    1:1000 w/v sodium metabisulfite

55. 1:125,000 w/v

56. 1:200 w/v lidocaine hydrochloride 0.0005% w/v epinephrine

57. 1:100,000 w/w tocopherol

58. 1:588 w/v calcium hydroxide

59. 1:11,000 w/v ergocalciferol

60. 1:4730 w/v potassium permanganate

61. 0.025% w/v formalin

62. 1:200 w/v midazolam

63. 1:31,250,000 w/v vitamin B_{12}

64. 0.05 μg fire ant extract

65. 0.5 mg epinephrine

66. 225 mg tetracaine hydrochloride 7.5 mg epinephrine hydrochloride 900 mg cocaine hydrochloride

67. 0.001% w/v

68. 115 g sodium fluoride

69. 9462.5 g nitrate ion

70. 10 μg proinsulin

REFERENCES

1. United States Pharmacopeia 31st Rev. National Formulary 26. Rockville, MD: United States Pharmacopeial Convention, 2008;1:13.
2. United States Pharmacopeia 31st Rev. National Formulary 26. Rockville, MD: United States Pharmacopeial Convention, 2008;2:1447.
3. Warren F. Athens, GA: College of Pharmacy, University of Georgia. 2004.
4. *International Journal of Pharmaceutical Compounding* 1998;2:147.
5. *International Journal of Pharmaceutical Compounding* 2002;6:452.
6. Ford P. *International Journal of Pharmaceutical Compounding* 1999;3:48.
7. *International Journal of Pharmaceutical Compounding* 1997;1:178.
8. *International Journal of Pharmaceutical Compounding* 2002;6:127.
9. *International Journal of Pharmaceutical Compounding* 1998;2:57.
10. Prince S. *International Journal of Pharmaceutical Compounding* 2003;7:46.
11. Prince SJ. Calculations. *International Journal of Pharmaceutical Compounding* 2000;4:221.

Calculation of Doses: General Considerations

Objectives

Upon successful completion of this chapter, the student will be able to:

- Differentiate between the various kinds of doses.
- Describe the primary routes of drug/dose, administration and, for each, the dosage forms utilized.
- Perform calculations of doses involving household measures.
- Perform calculations pertaining to the quantity of a dose, the dosage regimen, and the supply of medication required for the prescribed period.

Dose Definitions

The **dose** of a drug is the quantitative *amount* administered or taken by a patient for the intended medicinal effect. The dose may be expressed as a **single dose,** the amount taken at one time; a **daily dose**; or a **total dose**, the amount taken during the course of therapy. A daily dose may be subdivided and taken in **divided doses**, two or more times per day depending on the characteristics of the drug and the illness. The schedule of dosing (e.g., *four times per day for 10 days*) is referred to as the **dosage regimen**.

Quantitatively, drug doses vary greatly among drug substances; some drugs have small doses, other drugs have relatively large doses. The dose of a drug is based on its biochemical and pharmacologic activity, its physical and chemical properties, the dosage form used, the route of administration, and various patient factors. The dose of a drug for a particular patient may be determined in part on the basis of the patient's age, weight, body surface area, general physical health, liver and kidney function (for drug metabolism and elimination), and the severity of the illness being treated. An introduction to **pharmacokinetic** dosing is presented in Chapter 22.

CALCULATIONS CAPSULE

Doses

Given two factors in the following equation, by rearrangement, the third may be calculated:

$$\text{Number of doses} = \frac{\text{Total quantity}}{\text{Size of dose}}$$

In using the equation, the total quantity and the size of dose must be in the same unit of measure.

Pharmacokinetic dosing takes into account a patient's ability to metabolize and eliminate drugs from the body due to impaired liver or renal function, which often necessitates a reduction in dosage.

The **usual adult dose** of a drug is the amount that ordinarily produces the medicinal effect intended in the adult patient. The **usual pediatric dose** is similarly defined for the infant or child patient. The "usual" adult and pediatric doses of a drug serve as a guide to physicians who may select to prescribe that dose initially or vary it depending on the assessed requirements of the particular patient. The **usual dosage range** for a drug indicates the quantitative range or amounts of the drug that may be prescribed within the guidelines of usual medical practice. Drug use and dose information is provided in the package labeling and inserts that accompany manufacturers' pharmaceutical products, as well as in a variety of references, such as *Drug Facts and Comparisons*,[1] *Physicians' Desk Reference*,[2] *Pediatric Dosage Handbook*,[3] *Geriatric Dosage Handbook*,[4] and *Drug Information Handbook*.[5]

The dose response of individuals varies as depicted in Figure 7.1 and may require dosage adjustment in a given patient. For certain conditions, as in the treatment of cancer patients, drug dosing is highly specialized and individualized. Frequently, combinations of drugs are used, with the doses of each adjusted according to the patient's response. Many anticancer drugs are administered *cyclically*, usually for 21 to 28 days, with a rest period between dosing cycles to allow recovery from the toxic effects of the drugs. As presented in Chapter 8, anticancer drugs are most commonly dosed on the basis of the patient's body surface area.

The **median effective dose** of a drug is the amount that produces the desired intensity of effect in 50% of the individuals tested. The **median toxic dose** of a drug is the amount that produces toxic effects in 50% of the individuals tested. Drugs intended to produce systemic effects must be absorbed or placed directly into the circulation and distributed in adequate concentrations to the body's cellular sites of action. For certain drugs, a correlation exists between drug dosage, the drug's blood serum concentration after administration, and the presentation and degree of drug effects. An average blood serum concentration of a drug can be measured,and the minimum concentration determined that can be expected to produce the drug's desired effects in a patient. This concentration is referred to as the **minimum effective concentration**

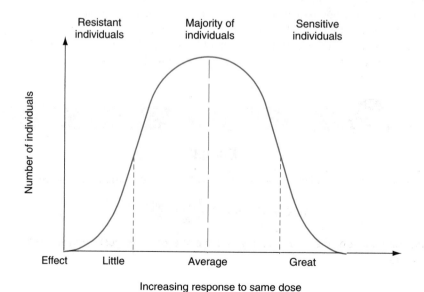

FIGURE 7.1 Drug effect in a population sample.

(MEC). The base level of blood serum concentration that produces dose-related toxic effects is referred to as the *minimum toxic concentration* (MTC) of the drug.

Optimally, appropriate drug dosage should result in blood serum drug concentrations that are above the MEC and below the MTC for the period of time that drug effects are desired. As shown in Figure 7.2 for a hypothetical drug, the serum concentration of the drug reaches the MEC 2 hours after its administration, achieves a peak concentration in 4 hours, and falls below the MEC in 10 hours. If it would be desired to maintain the drug serum concentration above the MEC for a longer period, a second dose would be required at about an 8-hour time frame.

For certain drugs, a larger-than-usual initial dose may be required to achieve the desired blood drug level. This dose is referred to as the *priming* or *loading dose*. Subsequent *maintenance* doses, similar in amount to usual doses, are then administered according to the dosage regimen to sustain the desired drug blood levels or drug effects. To achieve the desired drug blood level rapidly, the loading dose may be administered as an injection or oral liquid, whereas the subsequent maintenance doses may be administered in other forms, such as tablets or capsules.

As discussed later in this chapter, there are certain instances in which *low-dose therapy* or *high-dose therapy* is prescribed for a particular patient. And, for certain drugs there may be different doses required depending on whether the use is for *monotherapy*, that is, as the primary drug treatment, or *adjunctive therapy*, that is, additional to or supportive of a different primary treatment.

Certain biologic or immunologic products, such as vaccines, may be administered in *prophylactic doses* to protect the patient from contracting a specific disease. Other products, such as antitoxins, may be administered in *therapeutic doses* to counter a disease after exposure or contraction. The doses of some biologic products, such as insulin, are expressed in *units of activity*, derived from biologic assay methods. Calculations pertaining to these types of products are presented in Chapter 9.

Most pharmaceutical products are prepared on a large scale within the pharmaceutical manufacturing industry for distribution to institutional and community pharmacies. These *prefabricated* products and dosage units are used in filling prescriptions and medication orders in the pharmacy. On a smaller scale, many community and hospital pharmacists fill prescriptions and medication orders requiring *compounding*—that is, the fabrication of a pharmaceutical product from individual ingredients, carefully weighed, measured, and mixed. Pharmaceutical products may be prepared to contain one or more therapeutic agents. Products containing more than one therapeutic agent are termed *combination products*.

Whether a pharmaceutical product is prepared on a large or small scale or is compounded individually in the pharmacy, drug dosage is a part of the pharmacist's calculation and, along

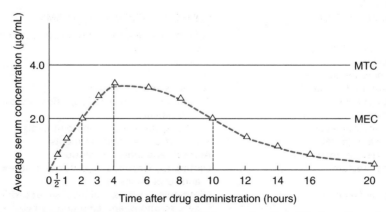

FIGURE 7.2 Example of a blood level curve for a hypothetical drug as a function of the time after oral administration. MEC, minimum effective concentration; MTC, minimum toxic concentration.

with the prescribed dosage regimen, is vital to the health and welfare of the patient. This chapter presents dosage calculations relevant to the dispensing of prefabricated dosage forms and the preparation of compounded prescriptions. Calculations encountered in the large- and small-scale manufacture of pharmaceutical products are provided in Chapters 16 and 17.

One of the primary responsibilities of the pharmacist is to check doses specified in prescriptions based on a knowledge of the usual doses, usual dose ranges, and dosage regimens of the medicines prescribed. If an unusual dose is noted, the pharmacist is ethically bound to consult the physician to make certain that the dose as written or interpreted is the dose intended and that it is suitable for the patient and condition being treated. As noted later in this chapter, certain treatments involve the use of low-dose and high-dose therapies, of which the pharmacists must be aware.

Routes of Drug/Dose Administration and Dosage Forms

Doses of drugs are administered by a variety of dosage forms and routes of administration, as shown in Table 7.1. In addition to the drug itself, dosage forms contain **pharmaceutical ingredients,** which provide the physical features, stability requirements, and aesthetic characteristics desired for optimal therapeutic effects. Included in the array of pharmaceutical ingredients are solvents, vehicles, preservatives, stabilizers, solubilizers, binders, fillers, disintegrants, flavorants, colorants, and others.

With added pharmaceutical ingredients, the quantity of an active ingredient in a dosage form represents only a portion (often a small portion) of the total weight or volume of a product. For example, a tablet with 10 mg of drug actually could weigh many times that amount because of the added pharmaceutical ingredients.

Definitions of the various dosage forms and drug delivery systems are found in Appendix C.

Dose Measurement

In the institutional setting, doses are measured and administered by professional and paraprofessional personnel. A variety of measuring devices may be used, including calibrated cups for oral liquids (Fig. 7.3) and syringes and intravenous sets for parenteral medication.

TABLE 7.1 SELECTED ROUTES OF ADMINISTRATION AND REPRESENTATIVE DOSAGE FORMS

ROUTE OF ADMINISTRATION	REPRESENTATIVE DOSAGE FORMS
Oral (mouth, GI tract)	Tablets, capsules, lozenges, solutions, drops, syrups, and suspensions
Sublinqual (under the tongue)	Tablets
Parenteral (injection)	Solutions and suspensions
Epicutaneous/ Transdermal (skin)	Ointments, creams, powders, lotions, aerosols, and patches
Conjunctival (eye)	Solutions, suspensions, and ointments
Intranasal (nose)	Solutions, sprays, and ointments
Intrarespiratory (lungs)	Aerosols and inhalant solutions
Rectal (rectum)	Ointments, creams, suppositories, solutions, and suspensions
Vaginal (vagina)	Ointments, creams, tablets, suppositories, gels, solutions, and emulsion foams
Urethral (urethra)	Solutions and suppositories

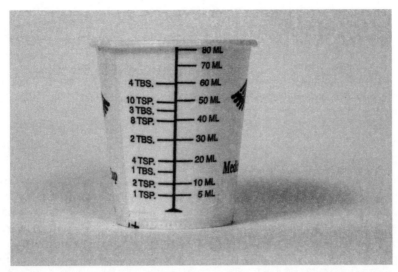

FIGURE 7.3 An example of a calibrated medication cup for administering oral liquid medication.

In the home setting, the adult patient or a child's parent generally measures and administers medication. Exceptions occur when home health care personnel are involved in a patient's care. Liquid dosage is usually measured in "household" terms, most commonly by the teaspoonful and tablespoonful. An oral dispenser (Fig. 7.4) finds use in administering calibrated quantities of liquid medication to children. For calculating dosages, useful equivalent measures are provided in Table 7.2.

Teaspoon and Tablespoon

In *calculating* doses, pharmacists and physicians accept a capacity of 5 mL for the teaspoonful and 15 mL for the tablespoonful. It should be noted that the capacities of household teaspoons may vary from 3 to 7 mL and those of tablespoons may vary from 15 to 22 mL. Such factors

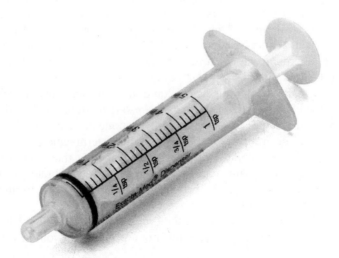

FIGURE 7.4 An example of a calibrated Exacta-Med® Oral Dispenser for administering liquid medication to pediatric patients. *(Courtesy of BAXA Corporation.)*

TABLE 7.2 USEFUL APPROXIMATE EQUIVALENT OF HOUSEHOLD MEASURE

HOUSEHOLD MEASURE (ABBREVIATION)	OUNCE	METRIC MEASURE
1 teaspoonful (tsp.)	≈ ⅙ fluidounce ≈	5 mL
1 tablespoonful (tbsp.)	≈ ½ fluidounce ≈	15 mL

as viscosity and surface tension of a given liquid, as well as the technique of the person measuring the liquid, can influence the actual volume held by a household spoon.

According to the *United States Pharmacopeia,* "For household purposes, an American Standard Teaspoon has been established by the American National Standards Institute as containing 4.93 ± 0.24 mL. In view of the almost universal practice of using teaspoons ordinarily available in the household for the administration of medicine, the teaspoon may be regarded as representing 5 mL. Preparations intended for administration by teaspoon should be formulated on the basis of dosage in 5-mL units. Any dropper, syringe, medicine cup, special spoon, or other device used to administer liquids should deliver 5 mL wherever a teaspoon calibration is indicated."[6] In general, pharmaceutical manufacturers use the 5-mL teaspoon and the 15-mL tablespoon as a basis for the formulation of oral liquid preparations.

Through habit and tradition, the f℥-symbol (fluidram) still is used by some physicians in the *Signa* portion of the prescription when indicating teaspoonful dosage. The pharmacist may interpret this symbol as a teaspoonful in dispensing prefabricated manufacturers' products called for on prescriptions and allow the patient to use the household teaspoon. Doses less than a teaspoonful (usually for children) are often indicated on the labeling as fractions of a teaspoonful, such as ¼ or ½ of a teaspoonful. Special medicinal spoons for these amounts are available, or standard household (kitchen) measuring spoons may be used.

The Drop as a Unit of Measure

Occasionally, the *drop* (abbreviated *gtt*) is used as a measure for small volumes of liquid medications. A drop does not represent a definite quantity, because drops of different liquids vary greatly. In an attempt to standardize the drop as a unit of volume, the *United States Pharmacopeia* defines the official medicine dropper as being constricted at the delivery end to a round opening with an external diameter of about 3 mm.[7] The dropper, when held vertically, delivers water in drops, each of which weighs between 45 and 55 mg. Accordingly, the official dropper is calibrated to deliver approximately 20 drops of water per milliliter (i.e., 1 mL of water = 1 gram or 1000 mg ÷ 50 mg [ave.]/drop ≅ 20 drops).

It should be kept in mind, that few medicinal liquids have the same surface and flow characteristics as water, and therefore the size of drops varies materially from one liquid to another. The drop should not be used as a measure for a specific liquid medication until the volume that the drop represents has been determined for that liquid. This determination is made by *calibrating* the dispensing dropper. The calibrated dropper is the only one that should be used for the measurement of medicine. Most manufacturers include a specially calibrated dropper along with their prepackaged medications for use by patients in measuring dosage. Examples of specially calibrated droppers are shown in Figure 7.5.

A dropper may be calibrated by counting the drops of a liquid as they fall into a graduate until a measurable volume is obtained. The number of drops per unit volume is then established (e.g., 20 drops/mL).

If a pharmacist counted 40 drops of a medication in filling a graduate cylinder to the 2.5-mL mark, how many drops per milliliter did the dropper deliver?

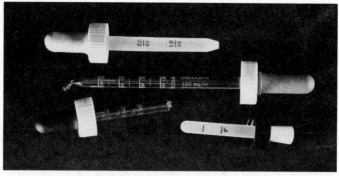

FIGURE 7.5 Examples of calibrated droppers used in the administration of pediatric medications.

$$\frac{40 \text{ (drops)}}{x \text{ (drops)}} = \frac{2.5 \text{ (mL)}}{1 \text{ (mL)}}$$

$$x = 16 \text{ drops mL, } answer.$$

Case in Point 7.1 A physician asks a pharmacist to calculate the dose of a cough syrup so that it may be safely administered dropwise to a child. The cough syrup contains the active ingredient dextromethorphan HBr, 30 mg/15 mL, in a 120-mL bottle.

Based on the child's weight and literature references, the pharmacist determines the dose of dextromethorphan HBr to be 1.5 mg for the child.

The medicine dropper to be dispensed with the medication is calibrated by the pharmacist and shown to deliver 20 drops of the cough syrup per 1 mL.

Calculate the dose, in drops, for the child.

General Dose Calculations

A pharmacist often needs to calculate the size of a dose, the number of doses, or the total quantity of medication to dispense. For these calculations the following equation is useful *with the terms rearranged depending on the answer required.* In using the equation, the units of weight or volume must be the same for the total quantity and size of the dose.

$$\textbf{Number of doses} = \frac{\textbf{Total quantity}}{\textbf{Size of dose}}$$

Example Calculations of the Number of Doses

If the dose of a drug is 200 mg, how many doses are contained in 10 g?

$$10 \text{ g} = 10,000 \text{ mg}$$

$$\text{Number of doses} = \frac{10,000 \text{ (mg)}}{200 \text{ (mg)}} = 50 \text{ doses, } answer.$$

Or, solving by dimensional analysis:

$$\frac{1 \text{ dose}}{200 \text{ mg}} \times \frac{1000 \text{ mg}}{1 \text{ g}} \times 10 \text{ g} = 50 \text{ doses, } answer.$$

If 1 tablespoon is prescribed as the dose, approximately how many doses will be contained in 1 pint of the medicine?

$$1 \text{ tablespoon} = 15 \text{ mL}$$
$$1 \text{ pint} = 473 \text{ mL}$$

$$\text{Number of doses} = \frac{473 \text{ mL}}{15 \text{ mL}} = 31.5 \text{ or } 31 \text{ doses, } answer.$$

If the dose of a drug is 50 μg, how many doses are contained in 0.020 g?

$$0.020 \text{ g} = 20 \text{ mg}$$
$$50 \text{ μg} = 0.05 \text{ mg}$$

$$\text{Number of doses} = \frac{20 \text{ (mg)}}{0.05 \text{ (mg)}} = 400 \text{ doses, } answer.$$

Example Calculations of the Size of a Dose

$$\textbf{Size of dose} = \frac{\textbf{Total quantity}}{\textbf{Number of doses}}$$

The *size of the dose* is expressed in whatever denomination is chosen for measuring the given total quantity.

How many teaspoonfuls would be prescribed in each dose of an elixir if 180 mL contained 18 doses?

$$\text{Size of dose} = \frac{180 \text{ mL}}{18} = 10 \text{ mL} = 2 \text{ teaspoonfuls, } answer.$$

How many drops would be prescribed in each dose of a liquid medicine if 15 mL contained 60 doses? The dispensing dropper calibrates 32 drops/mL.

$$15 \text{ mL} = 15 \times 32 \text{ drops} = 480 \text{ drops}$$
$$\text{Size of dose} = \frac{480 \text{ (drops)}}{60} = 8 \text{ drops, } answer.$$

Or, solving by dimensional analysis:

$$\frac{32 \text{ drops}}{1 \text{ mL}} \times \frac{1}{60 \text{ doses}} \times 15 \text{ mL} = 8 \text{ drops/dose, } answer.$$

Example Calculations of the Total Quantity of Product

$$\textbf{Total quantity = number of doses} \times \textbf{size of dose}$$

It is convenient first to convert the given dose to the denomination in which the total quantity is to be expressed.

How many milliliters of a liquid medicine would provide a patient with 2 tablespoonfuls twice a day for 8 days?

Number of doses = 16
Size of dose = 2 tablespoonfuls or 30 mL
Total quantity = 16 × 30 mL = 480 mL, *answer.*

How many milliliters of a mixture would provide a patient with a teaspoonful dose to be taken three times a day for 16 days?

Number of tsp doses $= 16 \times 3 = 48$ tsp
Total quantity $= 48 \times 5$ mL $= 240$ mL, *answer.*

How many grams of a drug will be needed to prepare 72 dosage forms if each is to contain 30 mg?

Number of doses $= 72$
Size of dose $= 30$ mg
Total quantity $= 72 \times 30$ mg $= 2160$ mg $= 2.16$ g, *answer.*

It takes approximately 4 g of ointment to cover an adult patient's leg. If a physician prescribes an ointment for a patient with total leg eczema to be applied twice a day for 1 week, which of the following product sizes should be dispensed: 15 g, 30 g, or 60 g?

Number of doses $= 2$ per day $\times 7$ days $= 14$
Size of dose $= 4$ g
Total quantity $= 14 \times 4$ g $= 56$ g; thus, 60 g product size, *answer.*

Additional Examples of Calculations of Dose

If 0.050 g of a substance is used in preparing 125 tablets, how many micrograms are represented in each tablet?

$$0.050 \text{ g} = 50 \text{ mg} = 50{,}000 \ \mu\text{g}$$
$$\frac{50{,}000 \ (\mu\text{g})}{125} = 400 \ \mu\text{g}, \text{ answer.}$$

Or, solving by dimensional analysis:

$$\frac{1{,}000{,}000 \ \mu\text{g}}{1 \text{ g}} \times \frac{1}{125 \text{ tablets}} \times 0.050 \text{ g} = 400 \ \mu\text{g/tablet, answer.}$$

If a preparation contains 5 g of a drug in 500 mL, how many grams are contained in each tablespoonful dose?

$$1 \text{ tablespoonful} = 15 \text{ mL}$$
$$\frac{500 \ (\text{mL})}{15 \ (\text{mL})} = \frac{5 \ (\text{g})}{x}$$
$$x = 0.15 \text{ g, answer.}$$

A cough mixture contains 48 mg of hydromorphone hydrochloride in 8 fl. oz. How many milligrams of hydromorphone hydrochloride are in each 2-teaspoonful dose?

1 fl. oz. $= 6$ tsp.
8 fl. oz. $= 48$ tsp.
48 tsp $\div 2$ $= 24$ doses
48 mg $\div 24$ $= 2$ mg, *answer.*

Or,

$$\frac{48 \ (\text{tsp.})}{2 \ (\text{tsp.})} = \frac{48 \ (\text{mg})}{x \ (\text{mg})}$$
$$x = 2 \text{ mg, answer.}$$

How many milligrams each of hydrocodone bitartrate and guaifenesin will be contained in each dose of the following prescription?

℞   Hydrocodone Bitartrate   0.12 g
      Guaifenesin   2.4 g
      Cherry Syrup ad   120 mL
      Sig. Teaspoonful for cough.
      1 teaspoonful = 5 mL
      120 ÷ 5 = 24 doses
      0.12 g ÷ 24 = 0.005 g = 5 mg hydrocodone bitartrate, *and*
      2.4 g ÷ 24 = 0.1 g = 100 mg guaifenesin, *answers.*

How many grams of a drug substance are required to make 120 mL of a solution each teaspoonful of which contains 3 mg of the drug substance?

$$1 \text{ teaspoonful} = 5 \text{ mL}$$

$$\frac{5 \text{ (mL)}}{120 \text{ (mL)}} = \frac{3 \text{ (mg)}}{x \text{ (mg)}}$$

$$x = 72 \text{ mg or } 0.072 \text{ g, } answer.$$

Or, solving by dimensional analysis:

$$\frac{1 \text{ g}}{1000 \text{ mg}} \times \frac{3 \text{ mg}}{5 \text{ mL}} \times 120 \text{ mL} = 0.072 \text{ g, } answer.$$

A physician ordered 500-mg capsules of tetracycline to be taken twice a day for 10 days. How many total grams of tetracycline would be prescribed?

Size of dose   = 500 mg
Total number of doses = 2 (a day) × 10 (days) = 20 doses
Total quantity   = 500 mg × 20 (doses) = 10,000 mg = 10 g, *answer.*

Dosing Options

Low-Dose and High-Dose Therapies

The administration of doses that are much smaller or much larger than the *usual dose* of a drug is referred to as *low-dose* or *high-dose* therapy, respectively. This terminology is different in intent from the normal variation in a standard dose based on a patient's age, weight, renal function, or other specific parameter (see Chapter 8).

The most common example of low-dose therapy is the use of aspirin in 81-mg amounts (rather than the usual dose of 325 mg) to lower the risk of heart attack and clot-related stroke. Another example is the use of low-dose postmenopausal hormone therapy, in which doses often 50% smaller than standard doses are administered.[8]

High-dose therapy is commonly associated with the chemotherapeutic treatment of cancer, in which there is an attempt, through increased dose intensity, to kill tumor cells.[9] Another example is the specialized use of high-dose progestin in the treatment of endometriosis.[10]

Pharmacists must be aware of the use of high-dose therapies while remaining vigilant in protecting patients against unintended high doses and consequent drug overdose. A related and important concern both for patients and for pharmacists is the *inadvertent* taking of an excessive quantity of a particular drug substance. This circumstance most often occurs when a patient takes multiple medications (prescription and nonprescription) containing a common ingredient which, in total, may exceed a safe level. The drug acetaminophen, which is a component of a great number of products, is an example of such a drug.

Example Calculations of Low-Dose and High-Dose Therapies

If a patient is changed from a daily standard-dose postmenopausal product containing 0.625 mg of conjugated estrogens (CE) to a low-dose formulation containing 0.35 mg CE, how many milligrams less of CE would the patient take per week?

0.625 mg − 0.35 mg = 0.275 mg × 7 (days) = 1.925 mg conjugated estrogens, *answer.*

To reduce the inflammation of an optic nerve, a patient is administered high-dose prednisone, 900 mg/day for 5 days by intravenous infusion. The usual daily dose of prednisone is 5 to 60 mg/day, depending on the condition being treated. Calculate the dose that the patient received, as a multiple of the highest usual daily dose.

$$\frac{900 \text{ mg}}{60 \text{ mg}} = 15, \text{ multiple of the highest usual dose, } answer.$$

Fixed-Dose Combination Products

A variety of prescription and nonprescription products are available containing two or more therapeutic agents in fixed-dose combinations. An advantage of combination products is that two or more needed drugs may be taken in a single dose, which may be more convenient, enhance compliance, and be less expensive for the patient than taking the same drugs individually. A disadvantage is the relative inflexibility in dosing compared with individual drug dosing.

Whether the fixed-dose combination is a liquid (e.g., a syrup) or a solid (e.g., a tablet) dosage form, when a dose is taken, the component drugs are taken in a fixed-dose ratio. To provide some options in dosing, many combinations of prescription drugs are formulated into different strengths. For example, capsules containing amlodipine and benazepril HCl (LOTREL), two drugs used in the treatment of hypertension, are available in strengths of 2.5 mg/10 mg, 5 mg/ 10 mg, 5 mg/20 mg, and 10 mg/20 mg. The prescriber can select the desired combination.

Example Calculation Based on Fixed-Dose Combination Products

Valsartan and hydrochlorothiazide tablets are available separately or in combination in strengths of 80 mg/12.5 mg, 160 mg/12.5 mg, and 160 mg/25 mg. If a patient was receiving the lowest-dose combination product and the physician wished to double the dose of hydrochlorothiazide, what is the option?

An additional prescription for 12.5 mg of hydrochlorothiazide or individual prescriptions for 80 mg of valsartan and 25 mg of hydrochlorothiazide may be written, *answer.*

Splitting Tablets

A number of tablets are **scored**, or grooved, to allow breaking into approximately equal pieces (usually halves). This allows dosage flexibility, particularly when a patient is started at a half dose and then is titrated up to a full dosage level. It also enables a patient to take a product at a strength that is not otherwise available.

Some patients use tablet-splitting devices to cut scored or unscored tablets for economic reasons. For some medications, the price of tablets of twice the strength required is similar to the lower-strength tablets, and the patient can double his or her supply by tablet splitting. Unfortunately, this practice often results in unequal portions of tablets and thus in uneven doses.[11] Additionally, patients may not be aware that many solid dosage forms should not be cut or crushed but must remain intact for proper drug absorption.[12] However, for tablets that *can* be crushed without destroying desired absorption characteristics, *tablet crushing* is a commonly employed practice for home- or institutional-patients who are unable to swallow intact solid dosage forms. In these instances, mortars and pestles or specially designed tablet crushers are used. After crushing, the resulting particles may be suspended in a beverage or mixed with a foodstuff as applesauce or yogurt prior to administration.

Example Calculation Based on Tablet Splitting

A patient attempted to split in half 20-mg unscored tablets of a drug, resulting in "half-tablets" differing by 1.5 mg in drug content. Assuming a whole tablet was uniform in drug content, calculate the amount of drug in each "half tablet."

If L = larger "half" and S = smaller "half,"
then L + S = 20   mg
$$\underline{L - S = 1.5 \text{ mg}}$$
2 L = 21.5 mg

L = 10.75 mg and
S = 20 mg − 10.75 mg = 9.25 mg, *answers.*

Proof: 10.75 mg − 9.25 mg = 1.5 mg difference in drug content and
10.75 mg + 9.25 mg = 20 mg total drug content

Special Dosing Regimens

Certain drugs have unique dosing regimens. Among them are chemotherapeutic agents (discussed in Chapter 8) and oral contraceptives. In the case of the latter, the prescribed regimen is based on a 28-day dosing cycle of 21 consecutive days of tablets containing a combination of estrogenic and progestational drugs followed by 7 consecutive days of tablets containing nondrug material. One tablet is taken daily, preferably at approximately the same time. The tablets generally are color coded and packaged in special dispensers to facilitate compliance.

Example Calculation Based on Special Dosing Regimen

The ORTHO TRI-CYCLEN LO 28-day regimen consists of norgestimate (N), ethinyl estradiol (EE), and nonmedicated tablets as follows:

7 white tablets containing 0.18 mg (N) + 0.025 mg (EE);
7 light blue tablets containing 0.215 mg (N) + 0.025 mg (EE);
7 dark blue tablets containing 0.25 mg (N) + 0.025 mg (EE);
7 green tablets containing 0 mg (N) + 0 mg (EE).

How many milligrams each of norgestimate and ethinyl estradiol are taken during each 28-day cycle?

Norgestimate: 0.18   mg × 7 = 1.26   mg
0.215 mg × 7 = 1.505 mg
$$\underline{0.25 \text{ mg} \times 7 = 1.75 \text{ mg}}$$
4.515 mg norgestimate and

Ethinyl estradiol: 0.025 mg × 7 = 0.175 mg
0.025 mg × 7 = 0.175 mg
$$\underline{0.025 \text{ mg} \times 7 = 0.175 \text{ mg}}$$
0.525 mg ethinyl estradiol, *answers.*

Doses: Solid Dosage Forms

1. How many capsules, each containing a 150-mcg dose of a drug may be prepared from 0.12 g of the drug?

2. The following regimen for oral prednisone is prescribed for a patient: 50 mg/day × 10 days; 25 mg/day × 10 days; 12.5 mg/day × 10 days; 5 mg/day × 10 weeks. How many scored 25-mg tablets and how many 5-mg tablets should be dispensed to meet the dosing requirements?

3. A physician reduces a patient's once-daily dose of conjugated estrogen (PREMARIN) from tablets containing 0.625 mg to tablets containing 0.45 mg. What is the total reduction in conjugated estrogens taken, in milligrams, during a 30-day month?

4. A fixed-dose combination product contains amlodipine besylate and atorvastatin calcium (CADUET) for the treatment of both hypertension and hypercholesterolemia. If a physician starts a patient on a 5-mg/10-mg dose for 14 days and then raises the dose to 10 mg/20 mg, how many milligrams of each drug will the patient take during the first 30 days?

5. A patient cuts 100-mg scored tablets to take his 50-mg prescribed daily dose. A prescription for thirty 100-mg tablets costs $45, and a prescription for thirty 50-mg tablets costs $40. The patient asked the pharmacist to weigh an uncut tablet on an electronic balance into two "halves." The uncut tablet was found to weigh 240 mg, and the cut "halves" weighed 125 mg and 115 mg, respectively. (a) How much money did the patient save on a monthly basis by dosing with half tablets? (b) What was the percentage error in the weight of the cut tablets compared with "exact halves"?

6. The recommended dose of memantine HCl (NAMENDA) is:

Week 1, 5 mg/day
Week 2, 10 mg/day (5 mg, b.i.d.)
Week 3, 15 mg/day (10 mg a.m., 5 mg p.m.)
Week 4, 20 mg/day (10 mg b.i.d.)

How many 5-mg tablets must be dispensed for a 4-week supply of the medication?

7. Prior to a colonoscopy, a patient is instructed to take OSMOPREP tablets each of which contains 1.102 g sodium phosphate monobasic monohydrate and 0.398 g sodium phosphate dibasic anhydrous. The dose is:
   • *The evening before the procedure:* 4 tablets with 8 ounces of clear liquids every 15 minutes for 5 cycles, and
   • *Starting 3 to 5 hours before the procedure:* 4 tablets with 8 ounces of clear liquids every 15 minutes for 3 cycles.
   How many tablets, how much liquid, and how much total sodium phosphates are taken?
   (a) 8 tablets, 16 ounces liquid, 2 g sodium phosphates
   (b) 16 tablets, 1000 mL liquid, 32g sodium phosphates
   (c) 32 tablets, 1 quart liquid, 40 g sodium phosphates
   (d) 32 tablets, 0.5 gallon liquid, 48 g sodium phosphates

8. CHANTIX (varenicline tartrate), a smoking cessation, is available in two strengths, 0.5-mg and 1-mg tablets. The dose is:
   • *Days 1 to 3*: 0.5 mg once daily;
   • *Days 4 to 7*: 0.5 mg twice daily; and
   • Days 8 to end of treatment: 1 mg twice daily.

   The treatment period is 12 weeks. How many 0.5-mg tablets and 1-mg tablets should be dispensed?
   (a) 7 0.5-mg tablets and 11 1-mg tablets
   (b) 8 0.5-mg tablets and 84 1-mg tablets
   (c) 10 0.5-mg tablets and 84 1-mg tablets
   (d) 11 0.5-mg tablets and 154 1-mg tablets

Doses: Drops

9. The formula for AURALGAN, an otic solution, is:

Antipyrine	54 mg
Benzocaine	14 mg
Glycerin, dehydrated ad	1 mL

If a dropper delivers 20 drops/mL, how many milligrams of benzocaine would be delivered by a 3-drop dose of the solution?

10. ℞ Acetaminophen Drops
Disp. 15 mL
Sig. 0.5 mL t.i.d.
(a) If acetaminophen drops contain 1.5 g of acetaminophen per 15-mL container, how many milligrams are there in each prescribed dose?
(b) If the dropper is calibrated to deliver 22 drops/mL, how many drops should be administered per dose?

11. RESTASIS Ophthalmic Emulsion contains 0.05% w/v cyclosporin. If a dose of one drop measures 28 μL, how many micrograms of cyclosporin are present?

12.[13] The oral dose of a drug is 2.5 mg. If a solution contains 0.5% w/v of the drug in a dropper bottle that delivers 12 drops/mL, how many drops would supply the dose?

13. MYLICON drops contain 2 g of simethicone in a 30-mL container. How many milligrams of the drug are contained in each 0.6-mL dose?

Doses: Oral Liquids

14. Rimantadine HCl syrup contains 2.4 g of rimantadine HCl in each 240 mL of syrup. How many milligrams of rimantadine HCl would there be in 2.5 mL delivered by oral dispenser?

15. If a liquid medicine is to be taken three times daily, and if 180 mL are to be taken in 4 days, how many tablespoonfuls should be prescribed for each dose?

16. If a cough syrup contains 0.18 g of dextromethorphan HBr in 120 mL, how many milligrams of the drug are contained in each teaspoonful dose?

17. A cough syrup contains 0.09 g of dextromethorphan HBr in each fluidounce. How many milligrams of this agent would be present in each teaspoonful dose?

18. A physician prescribes tetracycline HCl syrup for a patient who is to take 2 teaspoonfuls four times per day for 4 days, and then 1 teaspoonful four times per day for 2 days. How many milliliters of the syrup should be dispensed to provide the quantity for the prescribed dosage regimen?

19. Ipecac oral solution has the following formula:

Powdered Ipecac	70 g
Glycerin	100 mL
Syrup ad	1000 mL

Powdered ipecac contains 2 grams of the combined alkaloids emetine and cephaeline in each 100 grams of powder. Calculate the quantity of these alkaloids, in milligrams, in each 5-mL dose of ipecac oral solution.

20. A dose of digoxin for rapid digitalization is a total of 1 mg, divided into two or more portions at intervals of 6 to 8 hours. How many milliliters of digoxin elixir containing 50 μg/mL would provide the 1 mg dose?

21. Ciprofloxacin (CIPRO) oral suspension contains 250 mg of ciprofloxacin per 5 mL. A physician prescribed 125 mg of ciprofloxacin q.i.d. × 10 days. (a) How many doses are needed? (b) How many milliliters should be given per dose? (c) How many milliliters of ciprofloxacin oral suspension containing 250 mg per 5 mL should be dispensed?

22. A patient has been instructed to take 15 mL of alumina and magnesium oral suspension every other hour for four doses daily. How many days will two 12-fl.-oz. bottles of the suspension last?

23. ℞ Dextromethorphan HBr 50 mg/tsp.
    Guaifenesin Syrup ad   120 mL
    Sig. ℥i q.i.d. a.c. & h.s.

    How many grams of dextromethorphan HBr would be needed to fill the prescription?

Doses: Injections

24. How many milliliters of an injection containing 20 mg of gentamicin in each 2 mL should be used in filling a medication order calling for 2.5 mg of gentamicin to be administered intramuscularly?

25. A physician ordered 20 mg of MEPERGAN and 0.3 mg of atropine sulfate to be administered preoperatively to a patient. MEPERGAN is available in a syringe containing 25 mg/mL, and atropine sulfate is in an ampul containing 0.4 mg per 0.5 mL. How many milliliters of each should be used in filling the medication order?

26. How many milliliters of an injection containing 250 mg of aminophylline in each 10 mL should be used in filling a medication order calling for 15 mg of aminophylline?

27.[14] Pediatric LANOXIN injection contains digoxin, 100 mcg/mL. What volume must be administered to provide a dose of 0.04 mg?

Doses: Other Dosage Forms

28. The recommended maintenance dose of BECLOVENT (beclomethasone dipropionate), an aerosolized inhalant, is 100 mcg administered twice daily. The commercial inhaler delivers 50 mcg per metered inhalation and contains 200 inhalations. How many inhalers should be dispensed to a patient if a 60-day supply is prescribed?

29. A 16-week regimen for a brand of a nicotine patch calls for a patient to wear a 21-mg patch each day for the first 6 weeks, followed by a 14-mg patch each day for the next 2 weeks, and then a 7-mg patch for the next 2 weeks to conclude the treatment regimen. In all,

how many milligrams of nicotine are administered?

30. A transdermal patch contains 5 mg of fentanyl and has a drug-release rate of 50 mcg/hour. The patch is worn for 72 hours. Calculate (a) the milligrams of fentanyl delivered daily, (b) the milligrams of fentanyl remaining in the patch when it is removed, and (c) the percentage of drug remaining in the patch when it is removed.

31. If a VENTOLIN inhaler contains 20 mg of albuterol, how many inhalation-doses can be delivered if each inhalation-dose contains 90 mcg?

32. FLONASE Nasal Spray contains 50 mcg of fluticasone propionate per actuation spray in each 100 mg of formulation. Each container provides 120 metered sprays. How many milligrams of fluticasone propionate are contained in each container?

33. The dose of VOLTAREN (diclofenac sodium) GEL, when applied to the hands in the treatment of arthritic pain, is 2 g four times a day. The gel contains diclofenac sodium 1% and is available in 100-g tubes. How many grams of the drug diclofenac sodium would be administered per day and how many days of treatment would be available per tube of gel?
    (a) 8 g diclofenac sodium per day for 8 days
    (b) 8 g diclofenac sodium per day for 12.5 days
    (c) 80 mg diclofenac sodium per day for 8 days
    (d) 0.08 g diclofenac sodium per day for 12.5 days

34. SYMBICORT 80/4.5 is an oral inhalation product containing 80 mcg of budesonide and 4.5 mcg of formoterol fumarate per inhalation. The dose is stated as "two inhalations twice daily." How much of *each drug* would be administered daily?
    (a) 160 mcg budesonide and 9 mcg formoterol fumarate
    (b) 0.32 mg budesonide and 0.18 mg formoterol fumarate
    (c) 320 mcg budesonide and 0.18 mg formoterol fumarate
    (d) 0.32 mg budesonide and 0.018 mg formoterol fumarate

ANSWERS TO "CASE IN POINT" AND PRACTICE PROBLEMS

Case in Point 7.1

First calculate the volume of cough syrup containing the child's dose of 1.5 mg of dextromethorphan HBr:

$$\frac{30 \text{ mg}}{15 \text{ mL}} = \frac{1.5 \text{ mg}}{x \text{ mL}}; x = 0.75 \text{ mL}$$

Then determine the number of drops of cough syrup that will provide the 0.75-mL dose:

$$\frac{1 \text{ mL}}{20 \text{ drops}} = \frac{0.75 \text{ mL}}{x \text{ drops}};$$
$$x = 15 \text{ drops of cough syrup, answer.}$$

Practice Problems

1. 800 capsules

2. thirty-five 25-mg tablets and seventy 5-mg tablets

3. 5.25 mg conjugated estrogen

4. 230 mg amlodipine besylate and 460 mg atorvastatin calcium

5. (a) $17.50
   (b) 4.2%

6. 70 tablets

7. (d) 32 tablets, 0.5 gallon liquid, 48 g sodium phosphates

8. (d) 11 0.5-mg tablets and 154 1-mg tablets

9. 2.1 mg benzocaine

10. (a) 50 mg acetaminophen
    (b) 11 drops

11. 14 mcg cyclosporin

12. 6 drops

13. 40 mg simethicone

14. 25 mg rimantadine HCl

15. 1 tablespoonful

16. 7.5 mg dextromethorphan HBr

17. 15.2 mg dextromethorphan HBr

18. 200 mL tetracycline HCl syrup

19. 7 mg alkaloids

20. 20 mL digoxin elixir

21. (a) 40 doses
    (b) 2.5 mL/dose
    (c) 100 mL ciprofloxacin oral suspension

22. 11[+] days

23. 1.2 g dextromethorphan HBr

24. 0.25 mL gentamicin injection

25. 0.8 mL MEPERGAN and 0.375 mL atropine sulfate injections

26. 0.6 mL aminophylline injection

27. 0.4 mL LANOXIN injection

28. 2 inhalers

29. 1176 mg nicotine

30. (a) 1.2 mg fentanyl
    (b) 1.4 mg fentanyl
    (c) 28%

31. 222 doses

32. 6 mg fluticasone propionate

33. (d) 0.08 g diclofenac sodium per day for 12.5 days

34. (d) 0.32 mg budesonide and 0.018 mg formoterol fumarate

REFERENCES

1. *Drug Facts and Comparisons.* St. Louis, MO: Wolters Kluwer, 2008.
2. *Physicians' Desk Reference.* Montvale, NJ: Medical Economics, 2008.
3. Taketomo CK, Hodding JH, Kraus DM. *Pediatric Dosage Handbook.* 14th Ed. Hudson, OH: Lexi-Comp, 2007.
4. Semla TP, Beizer JL, Higbee MD. *Geriatric Dosage Handbook.* 13th Ed. Hudson, OH: Lexi-Comp, 2008.
5. Lacy CF, Armstrong LL, Goldman MP, Lance LL. *Drug Information Handbook.* 15th Ed. Hudson, OH: Lexi-Comp, 2007.
6. United States Pharmacopeia 31st Rev. National Formulary 26. Rockville, MD: United States Pharmacopeial Convention, 2008;(1221)1:678.

7. United States Pharmacopeia 31st Rev. National Formulary 26. Rockville, MD: United States Pharmacopeial Convention, 2008;(1101)1:578.
8. Maddox RW. The efficacy and safety of low-dose hormone therapy. *U.S. Pharmacist* 2004;29:103–109.
9. Hernández-Bronchud M, Molife R. Pharmacology and principles of high-dose chemotherapy. In: P Lorigan and E Vanderberghe, eds. *High-Dose Chemotherapy: Principles and Practice.* London: Martin Dunitz, 2002.
10. http://www.women.webmd.com/endometriosis/high-dose-progestin-for-endometriosis. Accessed September 5, 2008.
11. Rashed SM, Nolly RJ, Robinson L, et al. Weight variability of scored and unscored split psychotropic drug tablets. *Hospital Pharmacy* 2003;38:930–934.
12. Mitchell JF, Leady MA. Oral dosage forms that should not be crushed. *Hospital Pharmacy* 2002;37:213–214.
13. Prince S. *International Journal of Pharmaceutical Compounding* 2003;7:212.
14. Beach W. College of Pharmacy. Athens, GA: University of Georgia, 2004.

8

Calculation of Doses: Patient Parameters

Objectives

Upon successful completion of this chapter, the student will be able to:

- Describe factors to consider in determining doses for pediatric and elderly patients.
- Calculate doses based on factors of age, body weight, and body surface area.
- Utilize dosing tables and nomograms in calculations.
- Calculate doses for single and combination chemotherapy regimens.

As noted in the previous chapter, the **usual dose** of a drug is the amount that ordinarily produces the desired therapeutic response in the majority of patients in a general, or otherwise defined, population group. The drug's **usual dosage range** is the range of dosage determined to be safe and effective in that same population group. This provides the prescriber with dosing guidelines in initially selecting a drug dose for a particular patient and the flexibility to change that dose as the patient's clinical response warrants. Usual doses and dosage regimens are based on the results of clinical studies conducted during the drug development process as well as on clinical information gathered following the initial approval and marketing of the drug (*postmarketing surveillance/postmarketing studies*).

For certain drugs and for certain patients, drug dosage is determined on the basis of specific patient parameters. These parameters include the patient's age, weight, body surface area, and nutritional and functional status. Among patients requiring individualized dosage are neonates and other pediatric patients, elderly patients with diminished biologic functions, individuals of all age groups with compromised liver and/or kidney function (and thus reduced ability to metabolize and eliminate drug substances), critically ill patients, and patients being treated with highly toxic chemotherapeutic agents. Certain drugs with a narrow therapeutic window often require individualized dosing based on blood level determinations and therapeutic monitoring. Digoxin, for example, at a blood level of 0.9 to 2 ng/mL is considered therapeutic, but above 2 ng/mL it is toxic.[1]

Since age, body weight, and body surface area are often-used factors in determining the doses of drugs for pediatric and elderly patients, these parameters represent the majority of the calculations presented in this chapter. The dosing of chemotherapeutic agents also is included because it represents a unique dosing regimen compared with most other categories of drugs.

Pediatric Patients

Pediatrics is the branch of medicine that deals with disease in children from birth through adolescence. Because of the range in age and bodily development in this patient population, the inclusive groups are defined further as follows: **neonate** (newborn), from birth to 1 month;

infant, 1 month to 1 year; *early childhood*, 1 year through 5 years; *late childhood*, 6 years through 12 years; and *adolescence*, 13 years through 17 years of age.[2] A neonate is considered *premature* if born at less than 37 weeks' gestation.

Proper drug dosing of the pediatric patient depends on a number of factors, including the patient's age and weight, overall health status, the condition of such biologic functions as respiration and circulation, and the stage of development of body systems for drug metabolism (e.g., liver enzymes) and drug elimination (e.g., renal system). In the neonate, these biologic functions and systems are underdeveloped. Renal function, for example, develops over the span of the first 2 years of life. This fact is particularly important because the most commonly used drugs in neonates, infants, and young children are antimicrobial agents, which are eliminated primarily through the kidneys. If the rate of drug elimination is not properly considered, drug accumulation in the body could occur, leading to drug overdosage and toxicity. Thus, the use of *pharmacokinetic* data (i.e., the rates and extent of drug absorption, distribution, metabolism, and elimination; see Chapter 22), together with individual patient drug-handling characteristics and therapeutic response, provides a rational approach to pediatric drug dosage calculations.[2]

Doses of drugs used in pediatrics, including neonatology, may be found in individual drug product literature as well as in references, such as those listed at the conclusion of this chapter.[3–5] In addition to the calculations presented in this chapter, calculations associated with pediatric dosing by intravenous infusion are discussed in Chapter 13, and those related to pediatric parenteral and enteral nutrition appear in Chapter 14.

Case in Point 8.1: A hospital pharmacist is asked to determine the dose of clindamycin for a 3-day-old neonate weighing 3 lb. 7 oz. In checking the literature, the pharmacist determines that the dose is listed as follows:[4]

>   <1200 g: 10 mg/kg/day divided q12h.
>   <2000 g and 0–7 days old: 10 mg/kg/day divided q12h
>   <2000 g and >7 days old: 15 mg/kg/day divided q8h
>   >2000 g and 0–7 days old: 15 mg/kg/day divided q8h
>   >2000 g and >7 days old: 20 mg/kg/day divided q6h

Each divided dose is to be added to an intravenous infusion at the scheduled hour and infused over a period of 20 minutes.

Clindamycin is available in an IV bag containing 600 mg/50 mL of injectable solution. How many milliliters of this solution should be given for each divided dose?

Case in Point 8.2: A pediatric patient is being administered enalaprilat (VASOTEC IV) every 12 hours by intravenous injection to manage hypertension and possible heart failure.[4] Based on a dose of 5 mcg/kg, the patient is receiving 55 mcg of enalaprilat per dose. The physician wishes to convert the patient to oral enalapril at a dosage of 100 mcg/kg as a single daily dose. The standard procedure is to crush a 2.5-mg tablet of enalapril, mix with sterile water to make 12.5 mL, and administer the appropriate dose using a calibrated oral dispenser. Calculate the dose, in milliliters, to be administered to this patient.

Geriatric Patients

Although the term *elderly* is subject to varying definitions with regard to chronologic age, it is clear that the functional capacities of most organ systems decline throughout adulthood, and important changes in drug response occur with advancing age. *Geriatric medicine* or *geriatrics* is the field that encompasses the management of illness in the elderly.

Pharmacotherapy—that is, the use of pharmacologically active substances in the treatment of disease and illness—is of much greater use in the elderly compared with other age groups. In addition to medical conditions affecting all age groups, some conditions are particularly common in the elderly, including degenerative osteoarthritis, congestive heart failure, venous and arterial insufficiency, stroke, urinary incontinence, prostatic carcinoma, parkinsonism, and Alzheimer disease. Many elderly patients have coexisting pathologies that require multiple-drug therapies. Medications in the elderly are prescribed not only to relieve symptoms and manage diseases but also to improve bodily function, enhance the quality of life, and prolong survival.[6]

Most age-related physiologic functions peak before age 30 years, with subsequent gradual linear decline.[2] Reductions in physiologic capacity and function are cumulative, becoming more profound with age. Kidney function is a major consideration in drug dosing in the elderly because reduced function results in reduced drug elimination. Renal blood flow diminishes nearly 1% per year after age 30, making the cumulative decline in most persons 60 to 70 years of age, about 30% to 40%, a value that is even greater in older persons.[2]

Because reduced kidney function increases the possibility of toxic drug levels in the body and adverse drug effects, initial drug dosing in the elderly patient often reflects a downward variance from the usual adult dose. There is also a frequent need for dosage adjustment or medication change due to adverse effects or otherwise unsatisfactory therapeutic outcomes. Pharmacokinetic parameters are important in the dosing of certain drugs in the elderly patient.

There are a number of other common features of medication use in the elderly, including the long-term use of maintenance drugs; the need for multidrug therapy, with the attendant increased possibility of drug interactions and adverse drug effects; and difficulties in patient compliance. The latter is often due to impaired cognition, confusion over the various dosing schedules of multiple medications, depression or apathy, and economic reasons in not being able to afford the prescribed medication.[6]

Special Considerations in Dose Determinations for Elderly Patients

Dose determinations for elderly patients frequently require consideration of some or all of the following:

- Therapy is often initiated with a lower-than-usual adult dose.
- Dose adjustment may be required based on the therapeutic response.
- The patient's physical condition may determine the drug dose and the route of administration employed.
- The dose may be determined, in part, on the patient's weight, body surface area, health and disease status, and pharmacokinetic factors.
- Concomitant drug therapy may affect drug/dose effectiveness.
- A drug's dose may produce undesired adverse effects and may affect patient compliance.
- Complex dosage regimens of multiple drug therapy may affect patient compliance.

Dosage Forms Applicable to Pediatric and Geriatric Patients

In the general population, solid dosage forms, such as tablets and capsules, are preferred for the oral administration of drugs because of their convenience, ease of administration, ready identification, transportation, and lower cost per dose relative to other dosage forms. However, solid dosage forms are often difficult or impossible for the pediatric, geriatric, or infirm patient to swallow. In these instances, liquid forms are preferred, such as oral solutions, syrups, suspensions, and drops. An advantage of liquid forms is that the dose can easily be adjusted by changing the volume of liquid administered. When necessary, liquid forms of medication may be administered by oral feeding tube. Pharmacists are often asked to compound an oral liquid from a counterpart solid dosage form when a liquid product is not available. Chewable tablets and solid gel forms (medicated "gummy bears") that disintegrate or dissolve in the mouth are also often used for pediatric and geriatric patients. In addition, and as noted in the previous chapter, *tablet splitting* and *tablet crushing* are options for individuals unable or unwilling to swallow whole tablets.

For systemic effects, injections may be used rather than the oral route of administration when needed for pediatric and elderly patients, with the dose or strength of the preparation adjusted to meet the requirements of the individual patient.

Drug Dosage Based on Age

The age of the patient is a consideration in the determination of drug dosage. As stated previously, neonates have immature hepatic and renal functions that affect drug response. The elderly, in addition to diminished organ function, frequently have issues of concomitant pathologies and increased sensitivities to drugs.

Before the physiologic differences between adult and pediatric patients were clarified, the latter were treated with drugs as if they were merely miniature adults. Various rules of dosage in which the pediatric dose was a fraction of the adult dose, based on relative age, were created for youngsters (e.g., Young's rule). *Today these rules are not in general use because age alone is no longer considered a singularly valid criterion in the determination of accurate dosage for a child, especially when calculated from the usual adult dose, which itself provides wide clinical variations in response. Some of these rules are presented in the footnote for perspective and historical purposes.*[a]

Currently, when age is considered in determining dosage of a *potent* therapeutic agent, it is used generally in conjunction with another factor, such as weight. This is exemplified in Table 8.1, in which the dose of the drug digoxin is determined by a combination of the patient's age and weight.

Example Calculations of Dose Based on Age

An over-the-counter cough remedy contains 120 mg of dextromethorphan in a 60-mL bottle of product. The label states the dose as 1½ teaspoonfuls for a child 6 years of age. How many milligrams of dextromethorphan are contained in the child's dose?

---

[a] Young's rule, based on age:

$$\frac{Age}{Age + 12} \times Adult\ dose = Dose\ for\ child$$

Cowling's rule:

$$\frac{Age\ at\ next\ birthday\ (in\ years) \times Adult\ dose}{24} = Dose\ for\ child$$

Fried's rule for infants:

$$\frac{Age\ (in\ months) \times Adult\ dose}{150} = Dose\ for\ infant$$

Clark's rule, based on weight:

$$\frac{Weight\ (in\ lb) \times Adult\ dose}{150\ (average\ weight\ of\ adult\ in\ lb.)} = Dose\ for\ child$$

Note: The value of 150 in Fried's rule was an estimate of the age (12.5 years or 150 months) of an individual who would normally receive an adult dose, and the number 150 in Clark's rule was an estimate of the weight of an individual who likewise would receive an adult dose.

TABLE 8.1 CALCULATION OF PEDIATRIC DOSAGES OF DIGOXIN BASED ON AGE AND WEIGHT

AGE	DIGOXIN DOSE (μg/kg)
Premature	15 to 25
Full term	20 to 30
1 to 24 months	30 to 50
2 to 5 years	25 to 35
5 to 10 years	15 to 30
Over 10 years	8 to 12

$$1\tfrac{1}{2} \text{ teaspoonfuls } = 7.5 \text{ mL}$$

$$\frac{60 \text{ mL}}{120 \text{ mg}} = \frac{7.5 \text{ ml}}{x \text{ mg}}$$

$$x = 15 \text{ mg dextromethorphan}, \textit{answer}.$$

From the data in Table 8.1, calculate the dosage range for digoxin for a 20-month-old infant weighing 6.8 kg.

$$\frac{30 \ \mu g}{x \ \mu g} = \frac{1 \text{ kg}}{6.8 \text{ kg}} \qquad \frac{50 \ \mu g}{x \ \mu g} = \frac{1 \text{ kg}}{6.8 \text{ kg}}$$

$$x = 204 \ \mu g; \qquad x = 340 \ \mu g$$

Dose range, 204 to 340 μg, *answer*.

In contrast to the preceding example of dose determination for a potent prescription drug, over-the-counter medications purchased for self-medication include labeling instructions that provide guidelines for safe and effective dosing. For pediatric use, doses generally are based on age groupings; for example, 2 to 6 years old, 6 to 12 years old, and over 12 years of age. For children 2 years of age or younger, the label recommendation generally states "consult your physician."

Drug Dosage Based on Body Weight

The *usual doses* of drugs are considered generally suitable for the majority of individuals likely to take the medication. In some cases, the *usual dose* is expressed as a specific quantity of drug per unit of patient weight, such as *milligrams of drug per kilogram of body weight* (abbreviated *mg/kg*). Dosing in this manner makes the quantity of drug administered specific to the weight of the patient being treated.

CALCULATIONS CAPSULE

Dose Based on Body Weight

A useful equation for the calculation of dose based on body weight is:

$$\textit{Patient's dose (mg)} = \textit{Patient's weight (kg)} \times \frac{\textit{Drug dose (mg)}}{\textit{1 (kg)}}$$

This equation is based on a drug dose in mg/kg and the patient's weight in kilograms. When different units are given or desired, other units may be substituted in the equation as long as the terms used are consistently applied.

The patient's weight is an important factor in dosing since the size of the body influences the drug's concentration in the body fluids and at its site of action. Dose calculations based on body weight have become standard for certain drugs in dosing both adult and pediatric patients.

Example Calculations of Dose Based on Body Weight

The doses of the majority of drugs based on body weight are conveniently expressed in terms of *mg/kg*, since the doses of most drugs are administered in milligram amounts. However, this is not always the case. Depending on the drug, dosage form, and/or route of administration, the doses of some drugs are expressed in other units of measure, such as micrograms or milliliters per pound or kilogram of body weight.

A useful equation for the calculation of dose based on body weight is:

$$\text{Patient's dose (mg)} = \text{Patient's weight (kg)} \times \frac{\text{Drug dose (mg)}}{1 \text{ (kg)}}$$

This equation is based on a drug dose in mg/kg and the patient's weight in kilograms. When different units are given or desired, other units may be substituted in the equation as long as the terms used are consistently applied.

The usual initial dose of chlorambucil is 150 mcg/kg of body weight. How many milligrams should be administered to a person weighing 154 lb.?

Solving by the equation:
150 mcg = 0.15 mg

$$\text{Patient's dose (mg)} = 154 \text{ lb.} \times \frac{0.15 \text{ mg}}{2.2 \text{ lb.}} = 10.5 \text{ mg chlorambucil, } answer.$$

Or, solving by ratio and proportion:

150 mcg = 0.15 mg   1 kg = 2.2 lb.

$$\frac{2.2 \text{ lb}}{154 \text{ lb}} = \frac{0.15 \text{ mg}}{x \text{ mg}}; x = 10.5 \text{ mg chlorambucil, } answer.$$

Or, solving by dimensional analysis:

$$\frac{1 \text{ mg}}{1000 \text{ mcg}} \times \frac{150 \text{ mcg}}{1 \text{ kg}} \times \frac{1 \text{ kg}}{2.2 \text{ lb}} \times \frac{154 \text{ lb.}}{1} = 10.5 \text{ mg chlorambucil, } answer.$$

The usual dose of sulfisoxazole for infants over 2 months of age and children is 60 to 75 mg/kg of body weight. What would be the usual range for a child weighing 44 lb.?

1 kg	= 2.2 lb
20 kg	= 44 lb
60 mg/kg × 20 kg	= 1200 mg
75 mg/kg × 20 kg	= 1500 mg

Thus, the dosage range would be 1200 to 1500 mg, *answer*.

CASE IN POINT 8.3: A hospital pharmacist is called to a pediatric nursing station to calculate the quantity of an injection to administer to a pediatric patient. The daily dose of the injection for the child's weight is stated as 15 mg/kg/day, divided into three equal portions. The child weighs 10 kg. The injection contains 5 mg/mL of the prescribed drug.

How many milliliters of injection should be administered?

TABLE 8.2 DOSING BY BODY WEIGHT FOR A HYPOTHETICAL DRUG

BODY WEIGHT		TOTAL mg/DAY		
KILOGRAMS	POUNDS	0.5 mg/kg	1 mg/kg	2 mg/kg
40	88	20	40	80
50	110	25	50	100
60	132	30	60	120
70	154	35	70	140
80	176	40	80	160
90	198	45	90	180
100	220	50	100	200

Dosing Tables

For some drugs dosed according to body weight or body surface area, dosing tables appear in product literature to assist the physician and pharmacist. An example is presented in Table 8.2.

Using Table 8.2 and a daily dose of 0.5 mg/kg, how many 20-mg capsules of the drug product should be dispensed to a patient weighing 176 lb. if the dosage regimen calls for 15 weeks of therapy?

2 capsules/day × 7 days/week × 15 weeks = 210 capsules, *answer.*

Drug Dosage Based on Body Surface Area

The *body surface area (BSA)* method of calculating drug doses is widely used for two types of patient groups: cancer patients receiving chemotherapy and pediatric patients, with the general exception of neonates, who are usually dosed on a weight basis with consideration of age and a variety of biochemical, physiologic, functional, pathologic, and immunologic factors.

Table 8.3 shows the *approximate* relation between body weight and body surface area, in square meters (m^2), based on average body dimensions. The average adult is considered to have a BSA of 1.73 m^2. Thus, in reading Table 8.3, a person with a BSA of 1.30 (or about 75% of that of the average adult) would receive about 75% of the adult dose.

Example Calculations of Dose Based on Body Surface Area

A useful equation for the calculation of dose based on BSA is:

$$\text{Patient's dose} = \frac{\text{Patient's BSA (m}^2)}{1.73 \text{ m}^2} \times \text{Drug dose (mg)}$$

If the adult dose of a drug is 100 mg, calculate the approximate dose for a child with a BSA of 0.83 m^2, using (a) the equation and (b) Table 8.3.

(a) Child's dose $= \dfrac{0.83 \text{ m}^2}{1.73 \text{ m}^2} \times 100 \text{ mg} = 47.97$ or 48 mg, *answer.*

(b) According to Table 8.3, a BSA of 0.83 m^2 represents 48% of the average adult BSA of 1.73 m^2; thus, the child dose would be 48% of the usual adult dose:

100 mg × 0.48 = 48-mg dose for child, *answer.*

Dosing Tables

For certain drugs, dosing tables may be provided to determine the approximate dose based on a patient's body surface area. Table 8.4 presents an example for a hypothetical drug.

TABLE 8.3 APPROXIMATE RELATION OF SURFACE AREA AND WEIGHTS OF INDIVIDUALS OF AVERAGE BODY DIMENSION

KILOGRAMS	POUNDS	SURFACE AREA IN SQUARE METERS	PERCENTAGE OF ADULT DOSE*
2	4.4	0.15	9
3	6.6	0.20	11.5
4	8.8	0.25	14
5	11.0	0.29	16.5
6	13.2	0.33	19
7	15.4	0.37	21
8	17.6	0.40	23
9	19.8	0.43	25
10	22.0	0.46	27
15	33.0	0.63	36
20	44.0	0.83	48
25	55.0	0.95	55
30	66.0	1.08	62
35	77.0	1.20	69
40	88.0	1.30	75
45	99.0	1.40	81
50	110.0	1.51	87
55	121.0	1.58	91

* Based on average adult surface area of 1.73 square meters.
Adapted from Martin EW et al., *Techniques of Medication*, J. B. Lippincott, 1969:31, who adapted it from *Modell's Drugs of Choice* (Mosby).

Using Table 8.4, find the dose of the hypothetical drug at a dose level of 300 mg/m² for a child determined to have a BSA of 1.25 m². Calculate to verify.

From Table 8.4, the dose = 375 mg, *answer*.
From calculations: 300 mg/m² × 1.25 m² = 375 mg dose, *answer*.

Nomograms

Most BSA calculations use a standard *nomogram*, which includes both weight and height. Nomograms for children and adults are shown in Figures 8.1 and 8.2. The BSA of an individual is determined by drawing a straight line connecting the person's height and weight. The point at which the line intersects the center column indicates the person's BSA in square meters. In the

TABLE 8.4 PEDIATRIC DOSING GUIDELINE FOR A HYPOTHETICAL DRUG BASED ON BSA

PATIENT'S BSA (m²)	DOSE LEVEL			
	250 mg/m² DOSE	300 mg/m² DOSE	350 mg/m² DOSE	400 mg/m² DOSE
0.25	62.5 mg	75 mg	87.5 mg	100 mg
0.50	125 mg	150 mg	175 mg	200 mg
1.00	250 mg	300 mg	350 mg	400 mg
1.25	312.5 mg	375 mg	437.5 mg	500 mg
1.50	375 mg	450 mg	525 mg	600 mg

Nomogram for Determination of Body Surface Area from Height and Weight

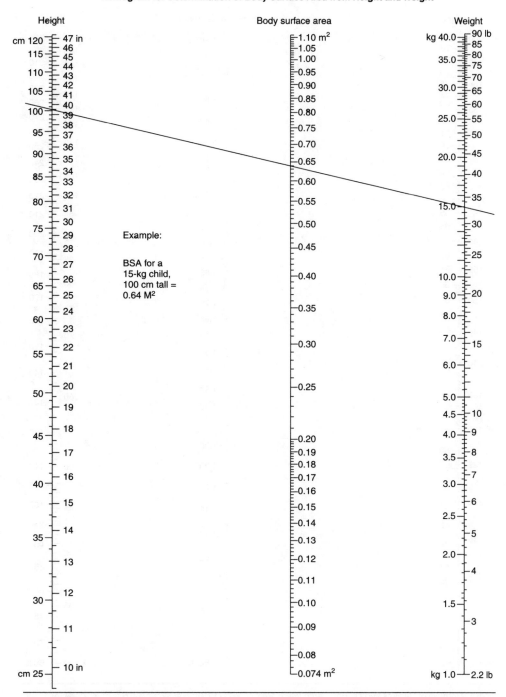

From the formula of Du Bots and Du Bots, *Arch Intern Med* 17, 863 (1916): $S = W^{0.425} \times H^{0.725} \times 71.84$, or log S = log $W \times 0.425$ + log $H \times 0.725$ + 1.8564 (S = body surface in cm², W = weight in kg, H = height in cm).

FIGURE 8.1 Body surface area of children. *(From Diem K, Lentner C, Geigy JR. Scientific Tables. 7th Ed. Basel, Switzerland: JR Geigy, 1970:538.)*

Nomogram for Determination of Body Surface Area from Height and Weight

Height	Body surface area	Weight

```
Height                      Body surface area              Weight

cm 200 ┬ 79 in                   ╡ 2.80 m²            kg 150 ═╤═ 330 lb
       ├ 78                      ╡ 2.70                  145 ═╪═ 320
   195 ┼ 77                                              140 ═╪═ 310
       ├ 76                      ╡ 2.60                   135 ═╪═ 300
   190 ┼ 75                                              130 ═╪═ 290
       ├ 74                      ╡ 2.50                        ═╪═ 280
   185 ┼ 73                                              125 ═╪═ 270
       ├ 72                      ╡ 2.40                   120 ═╪═
   180 ┼ 71                                                  ═╪═ 260
       ├ 70                      ╡ 2.30                   115 ═╪═ 250
   175 ┼ 69                      ╡ 2.20                   110 ═╪═ 240
       ├ 68                                              105 ═╪═ 230
   170 ┼ 67                      ╡ 2.10                   100 ═╪═ 220
       ├ 66
   165 ┼ 65                      ╡ 2.00                    95 ═╪═ 210
       ├ 64                      ╡ 1.95                    90 ═╪═ 200
   160 ┼ 63                      ╡ 1.90
       ├ 62                      ╡ 1.85                    85 ═╪═ 190
   155 ┼ 61                      ╡ 1.80                        ═╪═ 180
       ├ 60                      ╡ 1.75                    80 ═╪═
   150 ┼ 59                      ╡ 1.70                        ═╪═ 170
       ├ 58                      ╡ 1.65                    75 ═╪═ 160
   145 ┼ 57                      ╡ 1.60                    70 ═╪═
       ├ 56                      ╡ 1.55                        ═╪═ 150
   140 ┼ 55                      ╡ 1.50                    65 ═╪═ 140
       ├ 54                      ╡ 1.45
   135 ┼ 53                      ╡ 1.40                    60 ═╪═ 130
       ├ 52                      ╡ 1.35
   130 ┼ 51                      ╡ 1.30                    55 ═╪═ 120
       ├ 50
   125 ┼ 49                      ╡ 1.25                    50 ═╪═ 110
       ├ 48                      ╡ 1.20                        ═╪═ 105
   120 ┼ 47                      ╡ 1.15                    45 ═╪═ 100
       ├ 46                      ╡ 1.10                        ═╪═ 95
   115 ┼ 45                      ╡ 1.05                    40 ═╪═ 90
       ├ 44                                                   ═╪═ 85
   110 ┼ 43                      ╡ 1.00                        ═╪═ 80
       ├ 42                      ╡ 0.95                    35 ═╪═ 75
   105 ┼ 41
       ├ 40                      ╡ 0.90                        ═╪═ 70
cm 100 ┴ 39 in                   ╧ 0.86 m²           kg 30 ═╧═ 66 lb
```

From the formula of Du Bots and Du Bots, *Arch Intern Med* 17, 863 (1916): $S = W^{0.425} \times H^{0.725} \times 71.84$, or $\log S = \log W \times 0.425 + \log H \times 0.725 + 1.8564$ (S = body surface in cm², W = weight in kg, H = height in cm).

FIGURE 8.2 Body surface area of adults. *(From Diem K, Lentner C, Geigy JR.* Scientific Tables. *7th Ed. Basel, Switzerland: JR Geigy, 1970:538.)*

CALCULATIONS CAPSULE

Dose Based on Body Surface Area

A useful equation for the calculation of dose based on body surface area is:

$$Patient's\ dose = \frac{Patient's\ BSA\ (m^2)}{1.73\ m^2} \times Drug\ dose\ (mg)$$

If there is need to determine a patient's BSA, a nomogram, or the following equation may be used:

$$Patient's\ BSA\ (m^2) = \sqrt{\frac{Patient's\ height\ (cm) \times Patient's\ weight\ (kg)}{3600}}$$

example shown in Figure 8.1, a child weighing 15 kg and measuring 100 cm in height has a BSA of 0.64 m².

If the adult dose of a drug is 75 mg, what would be the dose for a child weighing 40 lb. and measuring 32 in. in height using the BSA nomogram?

From the nomogram, the BSA = 0.60 m²

$$\frac{0.60\ m^2}{1.73\ m^2} \times 75\ mg = 26\ mg,\ answer.$$

The usual pediatric dose of a drug is stated as 25 mg/m². Using the nomogram, calculate the dose for a child weighing 18 kg and measuring 82 cm in height.

From the nomogram, the BSA = 0.60 m²
25 mg × 0.60 = 15 mg, *answer.*

The nomogram in Figure 8.2 designed specifically for determining the BSA of *adults* may be used in the same manner as the one previously described. The adult dose is then calculated as follows:

$$\frac{BSA\ of\ adult\ (m^2)}{1.73\ m^2} \times Usual\ adult\ dose = Dose\ for\ adult$$

If the usual adult dose of a drug is 120 mg, what would be the dose based on BSA for a person measuring 6 ft tall and weighing 200 lb.?

BSA (from the nomogram) = 2.13 m²

$$\frac{2.13\ m^2}{1.73\ m^2} \times 120\ mg = 147.75\ mg\ or\ 148\ mg,\ answer.$$

If the dose of a drug is 5 mg/m², what would be the dose for a patient with a BSA of 1.9 m²?

5 mg × 1.9 = 9.5 mg, *answer.*

BSA Equation

In addition to the use of the nomogram, BSA may be determined through use of the following formula:

$$\text{BSA, m}^2 = \sqrt{\frac{\text{Ht (cm)} \times \text{Wt (kg)}}{3600}}$$

Calculate the BSA for a patient measuring 165 cm in height and weighing 65 kg.

$$\text{BSA, m}^2 = \sqrt{\frac{165 \text{ (cm)} \times 65 \text{ (kg)}}{3600}}$$

$$\text{BSA} = 1.73 \text{ m}^2, \text{ answer.}$$

Note: For the sake of comparison, check Figure 8.2 to derive the BSA for the same patient using the nomogram.

Dosage Based on the Medical Condition to be Treated

In addition to the factors previously discussed that might be used to determine a drug's dose, the medical condition to be treated and the severity of that condition must also be considered.

Table 8.5 presents an example of a dosage schedule for a drug based both on a patient's age and the medical condition to be treated.

Example:

By using Table 8.5, calculate the IV drug dose for a 3-pound 3-ounce neonate.

$$3 \text{ pounds} = 3 \times 454 \text{ g} = 1362 \text{ g}$$
$$3 \text{ ounces} = 3 \times 28.35 \text{ g} = 85 \text{ g}$$
$$\text{Weight of neonate} = 1362 \text{ g} + 85 \text{ g} = 1447 \text{ g}$$
$$1447 \text{ g}/1000 = 1.447 \text{ kg}$$
$$30 \text{ mg/kg} \times 1.447 \text{ kg} = 43.4 \text{ mg every 12 hours, } answer.$$

Special Dosing Considerations in Cancer Chemotherapy

The term *chemotherapy* applies to the treatment of disease with chemical drugs or *chemotherapeutic agents*. Chemotherapy is primarily associated with the treatment of cancer patients and is considered the mainstay of such treatment in that it is effective in widespread or metastatic

TABLE 8.5 PARENTERAL DOSAGE SCHEDULE FOR A HYPOTHETICAL DRUG BASED ON PATIENT AGE AND CONDITION BEING TREATED

	DOSE	ROUTE	FREQUENCY
Adults			
Urinary tract infection	250 mg	IV or IM	q12h
Bone and joint infections	2 g	IV	q12h
Pneumonia	500 mg–1 g	IV or IM	q8h
Mild skin infections	500 mg–1 g	IV or IM	q8h
Life-threatening infections	2 g	IV	q8h
Lung infections (normal kidney function)	30–50 mg/kg (NMT 6 g/day)	IV	q8h
Neonates (up to 1 month)	30 mg/kg	IV	q12h
Infants and Children (1 month to 12 years)	30–50 mg/kg (NMT 6g/day)	IV	q8h

cancer, whereas treatments such as surgery and radiation therapy are limited to specific body sites. Often **combination therapy** is used, with more than a single treatment modality included in a patient's treatment plan (e.g., radiation *and* chemotherapy).[7]

Almost all chemotherapeutic agents act by destroying cancer cells through their effect on DNA synthesis or function.[8] The major categories of chemotherapeutic agents include alkylating agents, antimetabolites, plant alkaloids, antitumor antibiotics, and steroid hormones. Chemotherapeutic agents most often are administered orally, by intravenous injection, or by continuous intravenous infusion; however, other routes of administration are used as required, including intraarterial (artery), intrathecal (spinal column), or intramuscular injection, or administration to a specific site, such as the lung (intrapleural), the abdomen (intraperitoneal), the skin (topical), or others.

Although a single anticancer drug may be used in a patient's treatment plan, *combination chemotherapy* perhaps is more usual. By using combinations of drugs having different mechanisms of action against the target cancer cells, the effectiveness of treatment may be enhanced, lower doses used, and side effects reduced. The combination chemotherapy plans often include *two-agent regimens, three-agent regimens,* and *four-agent regimens.*[9]

Cancer chemotherapy is unique in the following ways:

- It may involve single or multiple drugs of well-established drug therapy regimens or protocols, or it may involve the use of investigational drugs as a part of a clinical trial.
- Combinations of drugs may be given by the same or different routes of administration, most often oral and/or intravenous.
- The drugs may be administered concomitantly or alternately on the same or different days during a prescribed treatment cycle (e.g., 28 days). The days of treatment generally follow a prescribed format of written instructions, with D for "day," followed by the day(s) of treatment during a cycle, with a dash (–) meaning "to" and a comma (,) meaning "and." Thus, *D 1–4* means "days 1 to 4," and *D1,4* means "days 1 and 4."[10]
- The drugs used in combination chemotherapy often fit into a standard drug/dosage regimen identified by abbreviations or *acronyms*. For example, a treatment for bladder cancer referred to as MVAC consists of methotrexate + vinblastine + doxorubicin (or actinomycin) + cisplatin; a treatment for colorectal cancer called FU/LU consists of fluorouracil + leucovorin; a treatment for lung cancer called PC consists of paclitaxel + carboplatin; and one for ovarian cancer called CHAD consists of cyclophosphamide + hexamethylmelamine + adriamycin + diamminedichloroplatinum (cisplatin).
- In addition to the use of abbreviations for the drug therapy regimens, the drugs themselves are commonly abbreviated in medication orders, such as MTX for "methotrexate," DOX, for "doxirubicin," VLB, for "vinblastine," and CDDP for "cisplatin." Tables of standard chemotherapy treatments, dosing regimens, and abbreviations of the drugs and treatment regimens may be found in the indicated references.[7–11]
- For systemic action, chemotherapeutic agents are usually dosed based either on body weight or on body surface area. Often, the drug doses stated in standard regimens must be reduced, based on a particular patient's diminished kidney or liver function and, thus, his or her ability to metabolize and eliminate the drug(s) from the body.
- For certain patients, high-dose chemotherapy is undertaken in an effort to kill tumor cells.[9]

To help prevent errors in chemotherapy, pharmacists must correctly interpret medication orders for the chemotherapeutic agents prescribed, follow the individualized dosing regimens, calculate the doses of each medication prescribed, and dispense the appropriate dosage forms and quantities/strengths required.[12]

Example Calculations of Chemotherapy Dosage Regimens

Regimen: VC[13]
Cycle: 28 d; repeat for 2–8 cycles
Vinorelbine, 25 mg/m^2, IV, D 1,8,15,22
Cisplatin, 100 mg/m^2, IV, D 1.

For each of vinorelbine and cisplatin, calculate the total intravenous dose per cycle for a patient measuring 5 ft. 11 in. in height and weighing 175 lb.

From the nomogram for determining BSA (a) find the patient's BSA and (b) calculate the quantity of each drug in the regimen.

(a) BSA = 2.00 m^2, *answer.*
(b) Vinorelbine: 25 mg × 2.00 (BSA) × 4 (days of treatment) = 200 mg,
     Cisplatin: 100 mg × 2.00 (BSA) × 1 = 200 mg, *answers.*

Regimen: CMF[10]
Cycle: 28 d
Cyclophosphamide, 100 mg/m^2/d po, D 1–14.
Methotrexate, 40 mg/m^2, IV, D 2,8.
Fluorouracil, 600 mg/m^2, IV, D 1,8.

Calculate the total cycle dose for cyclophosphamide, methotrexate, and fluorouracil for a patient having a BSA of 1.5 m^2.

Cyclophosphamide: 100 mg × 1.5 (BSA) × 14 (days) = 2100 mg = 2.1 g,
Methotrexate: 40 mg × 1.5 × 2   = 120 mg,
Fluorouracil: 600 mg × 1.5 × 2   = 1800 mg = 1.8 g, *answers.*

Case in Point 8.4[14]: In treating a 54-year-old female patient, an oncologist selects the drug temozolomide, an antitumor agent used in the treatment of refractory astrocytoma (brain tumor). The drug is used as part of a 28-day regimen, during which the first five days of treatment include temozolomide at a once-daily dose of 150 mg/m^2/day. The patient's medical chart indicates that she measures 5 ft. in height and weighs 117 lb. The physician asks the pharmacist to determine the proper combination of available capsules to use in dosing the patient. The drug is available in capsules containing 5, 20, 100, and 250 mg of temozolomide. What combination of capsules would provide the daily dose of this drug?

PRACTICE PROBLEMS

Calculations Based on Body Weight

1. The dose of a drug is 500 mcg/kg of body weight. How many milligrams should be given to a child weighing 55 lb.?

2. The dose of gentamicin for premature and full-term neonates is 2.5 mg/kg administered every 12 hours. What would be the daily dose for a newborn weighing 5.6 lb.?

3. The dose of gentamicin for patients with impaired renal function is adjusted to ensure therapeutically optimal dosage. If the normal daily dose of the drug for adults is 3 mg/kg/day, administered in three divided doses, what would be the single (8-hour) dose for a patient weighing 165 lb. and scheduled to receive only 40% of the usual dose, based on renal impairment?

4. A patient weighing 120 lb. was administered 2.1 g of a drug supposed to be dosed at 30 mg/kg. Was the dose administered *correct,* or was it an *overdose,* or was it an *underdose?*

5. In a clinical trial of ciprofloxacin (CIPRO), pediatric patients were initiated on 6 to 10 mg/kg intravenously every 8 hours and converted to oral therapy, 10 to 20 mg/kg, every 12 hours. Calculate the ranges of the total daily amounts of ciprofloxacin that would have been administered intravenously and orally to a 40-lb. child.

6. ℞   Erythromycin   400 mg/5 mL
         Ethylsuccinate
         Disp. 100 mL
         Sig. _____ tsp. q.i.d. until all
         medication is taken.

   If the dose of erythromycin ethylsuccinate is given as 40 mg/kg per day,
   (a) What would be the proper dose of the medication in the Signa if the prescription is for a 44-lb. child?
   (b) How many days will the medication last?

7. If the pediatric dosage of chlorothiazide (DIURIL) is 10 to 20 mg/kg of body weight per day in a single dose or two divided doses, not to exceed 375 mg per day, calculate the *daily dosage range* of an oral suspension containing 250 mg chlorothiazide per 5 mL that should be administered to a 48-lb child.

8. Cyclosporine is an immunosuppressive agent administered before and after organ transplantation at a single daily dose of 15 mg/kg. How many milliliters of a 50-mL bottle containing 100 mg of cyclosporine per milliliter would be administered to a 140-lb. kidney transplant patient?

9. The adult dose of a liquid medication is 0.1 mL/kg of body weight to be administered as a single dose. How many teaspoonfuls should be administered to a person weighing 220 lb.?

10. A physician orders 2 mg of ampicillin to be added to each milliliter of a 250-mL bottle of 5% dextrose in water (D5W) for intravenous infusion.
    (a) How many milligrams of ampicillin should be added?
    (b) If the 250 mL of solution represents a single dose and if the dose of ampicillin is 25 mg/kg of body weight, how many pounds does the patient weigh?

11. ℞   Fluconazole tabs   100 mg
         Disp. ___ tabs
         Sig: tab ii stat, then 3 mg/kg b.i.d. ✕
         7 d thereafter.

    Calculate the number of tablets to dispense to a patient weighing 147 lb.

12. A physician desires a dose of 40 mcg/kg of digoxin for an 8-lb. newborn child. How many milliliters of an injection containing 0.25 mg of digoxin per milliliter should be given?

13. Intravenous digitalizing doses of digoxin in children are 80% of oral digitalizing doses. Calculate the intravenous dose for a 5-year-old child weighing 40 lb. if the oral dose is determined to be 20 mcg/kg.

14. An intratracheal suspension for breathing enhancement in premature infants is dosed at 2.5 mL/kg of birth weight. How many milliliters of the suspension should be administered to a neonate weighing 3 lb.?

15. A 142-lb. patient was receiving filgrastim (NEUPOGEN) in doses of 10 mcg/kg/day when, as a result of successful blood tests, the dose was lowered to 6 mcg/kg/day. Using an injection containing 0.3 mg filgrastim per 0.5 mL, calculate the previous and new dose to be administered.
    (a) 17.7 mL and 64.6 mL
    (b) 5.23 mL and 3.14 mL
    (c) 1.08 mL and 0.65 mL
    (d) 3.87 mL and 2.3 mL

16. A 25-lb. child is to receive 4 mg of phenytoin per kilogram of body weight daily as an anticonvulsant. How many milliliters of pediatric phenytoin suspension containing 30 mg per 5 mL should the child receive?

17. The loading dose of digoxin in premature infants with a birth weight of less than 1.5 kg is 20 mcg/kg administered in three *unequally* divided doses ($\frac{1}{2}$, $\frac{1}{4}$, $\frac{1}{4}$) at 8-hour intervals. What would be the initial dose for an infant weighing 1.2 kg?

18. The pediatric dose of cefadroxil is 30 mg/kg/day. If a child was given a daily dose of 2 teaspoonfuls of a pediatric suspension containing 125 mg of cefadroxil per 5 mL, what was the weight, in pounds, of the child?

19. How many milliliters of an injection containing 1 mg of drug per milliliter of injection should be administered to a 6-month-old child weighing 16 lb. to achieve a subcutaneous dose of 0.01 mg/kg?

20. Prior to hip replacement surgery, a patient receives an injection of an anticoagulant-drug at a dose of 30 mg. Following the patient's surgery, the drug is injected at 1 mg/kg. For a 140-lb. patient, calculate the total of the pre- and postsurgical doses.

21. Using Table 8.2 and a daily dose of 2 mg/kg, how many 20-mg capsules would a 176-lb. patient be instructed to take per dose if the daily dose is to be taken in divided doses, q.i.d.?

22. For a 22-lb pediatric patient, the dose of cefdinir (OMNICEF) was determined to be 7 mg/kg. What quantity of an oral suspension containing 125 mg of cefdinir in each 5 mL should be administered?
    (a) 2.8 mL
    (b) 5.6 mL
    (c) 8.9 mL
    (d) 13.6 mL

23. How many capsules, each containing 250 mg of clarithromycin, are needed to provide 50 mg/kg/day for 10 days for a person weighing 176 lb.?

24. If the pediatric dose of dactinomycin is 15 mcg/kg/day for 5 days, how many micrograms should be administered to a 40-lb. child over the course of treatment?

25. If the administration of gentamicin at a dose of 1.75 mg/kg is determined to result in peak blood serum levels of 4 mcg/mL, calculate the dose, in milligrams, for a 120-lb. patient that may be expected to result in a blood serum gentamicin level of 4.5 mcg/mL.

26. A medication order calls for tobramycin sulfate, 1 mg/kg of body weight, to be administered by IM injection to a patient weighing 220 lb. Tobramycin sulfate is available in a vial containing 80 mg per 2 mL. How many milliliters of the injection should the patient receive?

27. The usual pediatric dose of acyclovir is 20 mg/kg administered by infusion and repeated every 8 hours. What would be the single dose, in milligrams, for a child weighing 33 lb.?

28. If the recommended dose of tobramycin for a premature infant is 4 mg/kg/day, divided into two equal doses administered every 12 hours, how many milligrams of the drug should be given every 12 hours to a 2.2-lb. infant?

29. If a 3-year-old child weighing 35 lb. accidentally ingested twenty 81-mg aspirin tablets, how much aspirin did the child ingest on a milligram per kilogram basis?

30. The recommended pediatric dose of epinephrine for allergic emergencies is 0.01 mg/kg. If a physician, utilizing this dose, administered 0.15 mg, what was the weight of the patient in pounds?

31. The initial maintenance dose of vancomycin for infants less than 1 week old is 15 mg/kg every 18 hours.
    (a) What would be the dose, in milligrams, for an infant weighing 2500 g?
    (b) How many milliliters of an injection containing 500 mg per 25 mL should be administered to obtain this dose?

32. The loading dose of indomethacin in neonates is 0.2 mg/kg of body weight by intravenous infusion.
    (a) What would be the dose for a neonate weighing 6 lb., 4 oz.?
    (b) How many milliliters of an injection containing 1 mg of indomethacin per 0.5 mL should be administered to obtain this dose?

33. ℞[14]   Jimmy Jones   Age: 8 years
    Wt: 88 pounds
    Metronidazole   Suspension
    7.5 mg/kg/day
    M.ft. dose = 5 mL
    Sig: 5 mL bid × 10 days

    (a) How many milligrams of metronidazole will the patient receive per dose?
    (b) How many milliliters of the prescription should be prepared and dispensed?
    (c) If metronidazole is available in 250-mg tablets, how many tablets will be needed to fill the prescription?

34. ℞[14]   Betty Smith   Age: 4 years
    Weight: 52.8 pounds
    Erythromycin Ethyl Succinate (EES) 200 mg/5 mL

Disp. 300 mL
Sig: _____ mL qid until gone

    (a) If the dose of EES is 50 mg/kg/day, how many milliliters would provide each dose?
    (b) How many days would the prescription last the patient?

Calculations Based on Body Surface Area

Note: As needed, use nomogram method unless otherwise indicated.

35. If the daily dose of a drug is given in the literature as 8 mg/kg of body weight or 350 mg/m^2, calculate the dose on each basis for a patient weighing 150 lb. and measuring 5 ft. 8 in. in height.

36. If the dose of TAXOL (paclitaxel) in the treatment of metastatic ovarian cancer is 135 mg/m^2, what would be the dose for a patient 155 cm tall and weighing 53 kg?

37. If the adult dose of a drug is 100 mg, what would be the dose for a child with a body surface area of 0.70 m^2?

38. If the adult dose of a drug is 25 mg, what would be the dose for a child weighing 40 lb. and measuring 32 in. in height?

39. If the dose of a drug is 10 mg/m^2 per day, what would be the daily dose, in milligrams, for a child weighing 30 lb. and measuring 26 in. in height?

40. The dose of mitomycin injection is 20 mg/m^2 per day. Determine the daily dose for a patient who weighs 144 lb. and measures 68 in. in height.

41. An anticancer treatment includes methotrexate, 35 mg/m^2 of body surface area once per week for 8 weeks. How many grams of methotrexate would a 150-lb. patient, 5 ft. 8 in. tall, receive during this course of therapy?

42. The pediatric starting dose of ritonavir (NORVIR) is 250 mg/m^2 by mouth twice daily. The available oral solution contains 600 mg of ritonavir in each 7.5 mL of

solution. The correct volume and corresponding quantity of ritonavir to be administered to a child with a body surface area of 0.75 m^2 per dose is:
(a) 5.6 mL (450.4 mg)
(b) 2.8 mL (450.4 mg)
(c) 2.8 mL (225.2 mg)
(d) 2.3 mL (187.5 mg)

43. Calculate the dose for a child 4 years of age, 39 in. in height, and weighing 32 lb. for a drug with an adult dose of 100 mg, using the following: (a) Young's rule, (b) Cowling's rule, (c) Clark's rule, and (d) BSA (use the BSA equation).

44. The daily dose of diphenhydramine HCl for a child may be determined on the basis of 5 mg/kg of body weight or on the basis of 150 mg/m^2. Calculate the dose on each basis for a child weighing 55 lb. and measuring 40 in. in height.

45. The dose of TAXOL (paclitaxel) in metastatic breast cancer is 135 to 175 mg/m^2 by intravenous infusion over 3 hours. Calculate the number of milligrams of the drug infused every 15 minutes to a patient measuring 60 inches in height and weighing 120 pounds if the maximum dose in the dosing range is administered.

46. Using the equation to calculate body surface area, determine the BSA in square meters for an adolescent patient measuring 4 ft. 2 in. and weighing 90 lb.

47. The drug carboplatin for ovarian carcinoma is administered intravenously at a dose of 360 mg/m^2 except in patients with impaired kidney function, in which case the dose is reduced by 30%. How many milligrams of the drug should be administered to a renally impaired patient measuring 5 ft. 2 in. and weighing 110 lb.?

Calculations of Chemotherapeutic Regimens

48. A high-dose treatment of osteosarcoma includes the use of methotrexate at a starting dose of 12 g/m^2 as a 4-hour intravenous infusion. For a patient having a BSA of 1.7 m^2 and weighing 162 lb., calculate the dose on the basis of mg/kg/min.

49. A two-agent dosage regimen, termed MP, for the treatment of multiple myeloma is as follows:[15]

| Melphalan | 0.25 mg/kg, PO, D1–4/week × 6 weeks |
| Prednisone | 2 mg/kg, PO, D1–4/week × 6 weeks |

(a) Calculate the total milligrams each of melphalan and prednisone taken per week by a patient who weighs 165 lb.
(b) If melphalan is available in 2-mg tablets, how many tablets are required to dose this patient for the entire treatment cycle?
(c) If the patient prefers prednisone oral solution to prednisone tablets, how many milliliters of the solution (5 mg/mL) should be dispensed weekly?

50. A three-agent dosage regimen, termed VAD, for the treatment of multiple myeloma includes the following drugs taken over a 28-day cycle:[16]

Vincristine	0.4 mg/d, CIVI, D 1–4
Doxorubicin	9 mg/m^2/d, CIVI, D 1–4
Dexamethasone	40 mg/d, PO, D 1–4, 9–12, 17–20

Calculate the total quantity of each drug administered over the course of the treatment cycle for a patient with a BSA of 1.65 m^2.

51. A four-agent dosage regimen, termed MOPP, for the treatment of Hodgkin lymphoma includes the following drugs taken over a 28-day cycle:[17]

Mechlorethamine	6 mg/m^2, I.V., D 1,8
Vincristine	1.4 mg/m^2, I.V., D 1,8
Procarbazine	100 mg/m^2/d, p.o., D 1–14
Prednisone	40 mg/m^2/d, p.o., D 1–14

Calculate the total number of 20-mg tablets of prednisone and 50-mg tablets of procarbazine to dispense to treat a patient with a BSA of 1.5 m² during the course of one treatment cycle.

52. The oncolytic agent lapatinib (TYKERB) is administered in the treatment of breast cancer in daily doses of 1250 mg for 21 consecutive days in combination with the drug capecitabine (XELODA), which is administered in doses of 1000 mg/m²/day during days 1 to 14 of the 21-day treatment cycle. Calculate the total quantity of *each drug* to be administered during the treatment cycle to a 5'2" woman weighing 110 pounds.

53. Among the single chemotherapy agents for breast cancer is docetaxel (TAXOTERE) which is administered 40 mg/m² IV weekly for 6 weeks followed by a 2-week rest and then repeated.[18] Calculate the total dose administered during the initial 6-week period to a patient 5'4" tall and weighing 160 pounds.

54. Based on the dose calculated in the above problem, how many milliliters of an injection containing 80 mg/2 mL docetaxel would be administered per dose?

55. The chemotherapy regimen "FAC" during a 21- to 18-day cycle is:[18]

5-Fluorouracil	500–600 mg/m², D1 & D8
Doxorubicin	50–60 mg/m², D1
Cyclophosphamide	500–600 mg/m², D1

If the lowest dose were administered to a patient determined to have a BSA of 1.9 m², calculate the quantity of each drug given per cycle.

ANSWERS TO "CASE IN POINT" AND PRACTICE PROBLEMS

Case in Point 8.1

The metric weight of a 3 lb. 7 oz. neonate is calculated:

1 lb. = 454 g; 1 oz. = 28.35 g
3 lb. × 454 g/lb. = 1362 g
7 oz. × 28.35 g/oz. = 198.45 g
1362 g + 198.45 g = 1560.45 g, weight of the neonate

According to the dosing table, the dose for a 3-day-old neonate weighing less than 2000 g is 10 mg/kg/day divided every 12 hours.
The dose, in mg, may be calculated by dimensional analysis:

$$\frac{1 \text{ kg}}{1000 \text{ g}} \times \frac{10 \text{ mg}}{1 \text{ kg/day}} \times 1560.45 \text{ g}$$
= 15.6 mg clindamycin/day

Since the daily dose is administered in two divided doses, each divided dose is:

$$\frac{15.6 \text{ mg}}{2}$$
= 7.8 mg clindamycin every 12 hours.

The volume of injectable solution is then calculated:

$$\frac{50 \text{ mL}}{600 \text{ mg}} \times 7.8 \text{ mg} = 0.65 \text{ mL}, answer.$$

Case in Point 8.2

To calculate the oral dose of enalapril for the patient, it is necessary to know the patient's weight. This may be calculated from the intravenous dose:

$$\frac{1 \text{ kg}}{5 \text{ mcg}} \times 55 \text{ mcg}$$
= 11 kg, the weight of the patient

Then the oral dose may be calculated:

$$\frac{100 \text{ mcg}}{1 \text{ kg}} \times 11 \text{ kg} = 1100 \text{ mcg} = 1.1 \text{ mg}$$

By crushing and mixing the 2.5-mg enalapril tablet with sterile water to make 12.5 mL, the oral dose may be calculated:

$$\frac{2.5 \text{ mg}}{12.5 \text{ mL}} = \frac{1.1 \text{ mg}}{x \text{ mL}}; x = 5.5 \text{ mL}, \textit{answer}.$$

Case in Point 8.3

Daily dose: 15 mg/kg × 10 kg = 150 mg
Single dose: 150 mg ÷ 3 = 50 mg

Quantity of injection: 50 mg × $\frac{1 \text{ mL}}{5 \text{ mg}}$ = 10 mL, *answer*.

Case in Point 8.4

To calculate the dose for the patient, the pharmacist must first determine the patient's body surface area. The pharmacist elects to use the following equation:

$$\text{BSA (m}^2) = \sqrt{\frac{\text{Ht(cm)xWt(kg)}}{3600}}$$

To use this equation, the patient's weight and height are converted to metric units:

Height = 5 ft. = 60 in. × 2.54 cm/in.
      = 152.4 cm

Weight = 117 lb. ÷ 2.2 lb./kg = 53.2 kg

Solving the equation:

$$\text{BSA (m}^2) = \sqrt{\frac{152.4 \times 53.2}{3600}} = 1.50 \text{ m}^2$$

The daily dose is calculated as 150 mg/m² × 1.50 m² = 225 mg
To obtain 225 mg, the patient may take two 100-mg capsules, one 20-mg capsule, and one 5-mg capsule daily, *answer*.

Practice Problems

1. 12.5 mg

2. 12.73 mg gentamicin

3. 30 mg gentamicin

4. overdose

5. I.V.: 327.3–545.5 mg ciprofloxacin
   Oral: 363.6–727.3 mg ciprofloxacin

6. (a) ½ tsp. (2.5 mL) erythromycin ethylsuccinate
   (b) 10 days

7. 4.4–7.5 mL chlorothiazide oral suspension

8. 9.55 mL cyclosporin

9. 2 tsp.

10. (a) 500 mg ampicillin
    (b) 44 lb.

11. 30 tablets

12. 0.58 mL digoxin injection

13. 290.9 or 291 mcg digoxin

14. 3.41 mL

15. (c) 1.08 mL and 0.65 mL filgrastim injection

16. 7.58 mL phenytoin suspension

17. 12 mcg digoxin

18. 18.33 lb.

19. 0.073 mL

20. 93.64 or 94 mg

21. 2 capsules

22. (a) 2.8 mL cefdinir oral suspension

23. 160 clarithromycin capsules

24. 1364 mcg dactinomycin

25. 107.39 mg gentamicin

26. 2.5 mL tobramycin injection

27. 300 mg acyclovir

28. 2 mg tobramycin

29. 101.83 mg/kg aspirin

30. 33 pounds

31. (a) 37.5 g vancomycin
    (b) 1.875 mL vancomycin injection

32. (a) 0.57 mg indomethacin
    (b) 0.28 mL indomethacin injection

33. (a) 150 mg metronidazole
    (b) 100 mL
    (c) 12 metronidazole tablets

34. (a) 7.5 mL
    (b) 10 days

35. 545.5 mg and 630 mg

36. 202.5 mg TAXOL

37. 40.46 mg

38. 8.53 mg

39. 4.5 mg

40. 35.4 mg mitomycin

41. 0.504 g methotrexate

42. 2.3 mL (187.5 mg) ritonavir

43. (a) 25 mg
    (b) 20.83 mg
    (c) 21.33 mg
    (d) 36.57 mg

44. (a) 125 mg diphenhydramine HCl
    (b) 120 mg diphenhydramine HCl

45. 21.88 mg TAXOL

46. 1.20 m^2

47. 372.96 mg carboplatin

48. 1.15 mg/kg/min methotrexate

49. (a) 75 mg melphalan and 600 mg prednisone
    (b) 225 tablets
    (c) 120 mL prednisone oral solution

50. 1.6 mg vincristine
    59.4 mg doxorubicin
    480 mg dexamethasone

51. 42 procarbazine tablets
    42 prednisone tablets

52. 26.25 g lapatinib and 20.72 g capecitabine

53. 434.9 mg docetaxel (by equation)
    424.8 mg docetaxel (by nomogram)

54. 1.8 mL docetaxel injection

55. 1900 mg 5-fluorouracil
    95 mg doxorubicin
    950 mg cyclophosphamine

REFERENCES

1. Ferri FF. *Practical Guide to the Care of the Medical Patient.* 7th ed. St. Louis, MO: Mosby, 2007.
2. Berkow R, ed. *The Merck Manual.* 16th Ed. Rahway, NJ: Merck Research Laboratories, 1992.
3. Taketomo CK, Hodding JH, Kraus DM. *Pediatric Dosage Handbook.* 14th Ed. Hudson, OH: Lexi-Comp, 2007.
4. Gomella TL, Cunningham MD, Eyal FG, et al. *Neonatology: Management, Procedures, On-Call Problems, Diseases, and Drugs.* New York: McGraw-Hill, 2004.
5. Pagliaro LA, Pagliaro AM, eds. *Problems in Pediatric Drug Therapy.* 4th Ed. Washington, DC: American Pharmacists Association, 2002.
6. Hanlon JT, Linblad C, Maher RL, et al. Problem-based geriatric medicine. In: Tallis CT and Fillit HM, eds. *Bockklehurst's Textbook of Geriatric Medicine and Gerontology.* 6th Ed. London: Churchill Livingstone, 2003.
7. American Cancer Society. Cancer Resource Center. Available at: http://www.cancer.org/docroot/CRI/CRI_0.asp. Accessed November 20, 2007.
8. OncoLink. University of Pennsylvania Cancer Center. Available at: http://www.oncolink.upenn.edu/treatment. Accessed November 20, 2007.
9. Hernandez-Bronchud M, Molife R. Pharmacology and principles of high dose chemotherapy. In: Lorigan P and Vandenberghe E, eds. *High-Dose Chemotherapy: Practice and Principles.* London: Martin Dunitz, 2002.
10. Medicine Online. Available at: http://www.meds.com/DoseCalc/dcintro.html.Accessed November 20, 2007.
11. Solimando DA Jr. Combination cancer chemotherapy regimens. *Hospital Pharmacy* 2004;39:628–633.
12. Schwarz LR. Delivering cytotoxic chemotherapy safely in a community hospital. *Hospital Pharmacy* 1996;31: 1108–1118.
13. Brueggemeyer DL, Waddell JA, Solimando DA Jr. Vinorelbine and cisplatin (VC) regimen. *Hospital Pharmacy* 2000; 35:485.
14. Beach W. College of Pharmacy. Athens, GA: University of Georgia, 2004.
15. Sano HS, Solimando Jr DA, Waddell JA. Melphalan and prednisone (MP) regimen for multiple myeloma. *Hospital Pharmacy* 2004;39:320–327.
16. Doulaveris P, Solimando DA Jr, Waddell JA. Vincristine, doxorubicin, and dexamethasone (VAD) regimen for multiple myeloma. *Hospital Pharmacy* 2004;39:418–427.
17. DeVita VT. PPO Updates. 1993;7:1B11. Available at: http://www.meds.com/DoseCalc/reg_hodgkins.html. Accessed November 20, 2007.
18. Smith J. Overview of breast cancer drug therapy. *U.S. Pharmacist Supplement* 2005:3–11.

Some Calculations Involving "Units," "µg/mg," and Other Measures of Potency

Objectives

Upon successful completion of this chapter, the student will be able to:

- Demonstrate an understanding of *units of activity* and other standardized measures of potency.
- Perform calculations of pharmaceutical products, prescriptions, and medication orders involving units of activity and other measures of potency.

The potencies of some antibiotics, endocrine products, vitamins, products derived through biotechnology, and biologics (e.g., vaccines) are based on their *activity* and are expressed in terms of *units* (of activity), in *micrograms per milligram (µg/mg)*, or in other standardized terms of measurement. These measures of potency meet standards approved by the Food and Drug Administration and are set forth in the *United States Pharmacopeia* (USP).[1] In general, they conform also to international standards defined by the World Health Organization and termed *International Units (IU)*.

Degrees of activity are determined by comparison against a suitable working standard, generally a USP Reference Standard. Reference standards are authentic specimens used as comparison standards in compendial tests and assays. The number of USP Units of an antibiotic, for example, is based on a comparison of activity of a sample of that antibiotic on a milligram basis to the corresponding USP Reference Standard. For instance, there are 1590 USP Units of penicillin G sodium per milligram of the USP Reference Standard of the antibiotic. Pharmaceutical products and preparations are allowed specific variances in potency; for example, the USP monograph for sterile penicillin G sodium specifies a potency of not less than 1500 Penicillin G Units and not more than 1750 Penicillin G Units per milligram.[2] The activity or potency of antibiotics is determined by their inhibitory effect on microorganisms. No relationship exists between the unit of potency of one drug and the unit of potency of another drug.

The potency of antibiotics may also be designated in terms of µg (micrograms) of activity. This concept originated at a time when reference standards for antibiotics were thought to consist entirely of single chemical entities and were therefore assigned potencies of 1000 µg/mg. As newer methods of antibiotic manufacture and purification were developed, however, it was determined that some highly purified antibiotics had greater than 1000 µg of activity per milligram compared with the original reference standard. Differences in potency were also found when comparing the chemical base versus the salt form. For example, ampicillin sodium has a potency equivalent to between 845 and 988 µg/mg of its parent compound ampicillin.

A comparison of units and micrograms of potency of some official drugs and their respective weight equivalents is given in Table 9.1.

Just as potencies of certain drugs are designated in units, so too the doses of these drugs and of their preparations are measured in units. Of the drugs for which potency is expressed in

CALCULATIONS CAPSULE

Units of Activity

The potency of many pharmaceutical products derived from biological sources is based on *units of activity*. Units of activity are determined against specific biologic standards and vary between products. Generally, there is an established relationship between a product's units of activity and a measurable quantity (e.g., units per milligram; units per milliliter). This relationship may be used in a ratio and proportion to determine either the number of units of activity or the weight or volume containing a specified number of units:

$$\frac{\text{Units of activity (given)}}{\text{Weight or volume (given)}} = \frac{\text{Units of activity (given or desired)}}{\text{Weight or volume (given or desired)}}$$

units, insulin is perhaps the most commonly used. In the case of insulin, although the commercially available types vary according to time of onset of action, time of peak action, and duration of action, all products are standardized to contain either 100 or 500 insulin units per milliliter of solution or suspension. These strengths are designated as U-100 and U-500 as shown in Figure 9.1. As noted earlier in this text, dispensing errors can occur when a medication order abbreviates the term *units* with a *U* and places it *after* the number of units, since a poorly written *U* can be mistaken for a zero; for example, "100U" could be mistaken for 1000 units. Thus, it is good practice to spell out the term *units* when used following the designated number; for example, 100 units or 100 Units. Special syringes are available for measuring units of insulin, and the required dosage is then measured in milliliters, or directly in units, depending on the calibration of the syringe. Figure 9.2 shows an example of an insulin syringe calibrated in units.

Blood or blood serum levels of certain drugs may be expressed in the literature as mU/mL, meaning "milliunits of the agent per milliliter of blood or blood serum."

Biologics are preparations produced from a living source. They include vaccines, toxoids, and immune sera, used for the development of *immunity,* or resistance to disease; certain antitoxins and antivenins, used as treatment against specific antigens; and, toxins and skin antigens, used as diagnostic aids. Biologics are prepared from human serum (e.g., immune globulin), horse serum (e.g., tetanus antitoxin), chick cell culture (e.g., measles virus vaccine), and other such animate media.

The strengths of the various biologic products are expressed in a number of ways. The strength of a bacterial vaccine commonly is expressed in terms of micrograms (μg) or units of antigen per milliliter. The strength of a viral vaccine is expressed most commonly in terms of the *tissue culture infectious dose (TCID$_{50}$),* which is the quantity of virus estimated to infect 50% of inoculated cultures. Viral vaccines may also be described in terms of units, micrograms of antigen, or number or organisms per milliliter. The strength of a toxoid is generally expressed in terms of *flocculating units (Lf Unit),* with 1 Lf Unit having the capacity to flocculate or precipitate one unit of standard antitoxin. Units of activity are generally used to characterize the strengths of many immune sera and diagnostic antigens.

The Food and Drug Administration (FDA) through its Center for Biologics Evaluation and Research (CBER)[a] is responsible for ensuring the safety and efficacy of blood and blood products,

---

[a] CBER is one of the major subdivisions of the FDA; the others are: The Center for Food Safety and Applied Nutrition (CFSAN), The Center for Drug Evaluation and Research (CDER), The Center for Devices and Radiological Health (CDRH), The Center for Veterinary Medicine (CVM), The National Center for Toxicological Research (NCTR), and The Office of Regulatory Affairs (ORA).

TABLE 9.1 EXAMPLES OF DRUG POTENCY EQUIVALENTS

DRUG	UNITS OR µg OF POTENCY PER WEIGHT EQUIVALENT*
Alteplase	580,000 USP Alteplase Units per mg of protein
Ampicillin Sodium	NLT (not less than) 845 µg and NMT (not more than) 988 µg of ampicillin per mg
Antihemophilic Factor	NLT 100 Antihemophilic Factor Units per g of protein
Bacitracin	NLT 40 Bacitracin Units per mg
Bacitracin Zinc	NLT 40 Bacitracin Units per mg
Cephalothin Sodium	NLT 850 µg of cephalothin per mg
Chymotrypsin	NLT 1000 USP Chymotrypsin Units per mg
Clindamycin Hydrochloride	NLT 800 µg of clindamycin per mg
Cod Liver Oil	In each gram: NLT 180 µg (600 USP Units) and NMT 750 µg (2500 USP Units) of Vitamin A and NLT 1.5 µg (60 USP Units) and NMT 6.25 µg (250 USP Units) of Vitamin D
Colistimethate Sodium	390 µg colistin per mg
Digitalis	NLT 1 USP Digitalis Unit per 100 mg
Erythromycin Estolate	NLT 600 µg of erythromycin per mg
Gentamicin Sulfate	NLT 590 µg of gentamicin per mg
Heparin Calcium	NLT 140 USP Heparin Units per mg
Heparin Sodium	NLT 140 USP Heparin Units per mg
Insulin	NLT 26.5 USP Insulin Units per mg
Insulin Human	NLT 27.5 USP Insulin Human Units per mg
Insulin Lispro	NLT 27 USP Insulin Lispro Units per mg
Kanamycin Sulfate	NLT 750 µg of kanamycin per mg
Menotropins	NLT 40 USP Follicle-Stimulating Hormone Units and NLT 40 USP Luteinizing Hormone Units per mg
Minocycline Hydrochloride	NLT 890 µg and NMT 950 µg minocycline per mg
Mitomycin	NLT 970 µg mitomycin per mg
Neomycin Sulfate	NLT 600 µg of neomycin per mg
Nystatin	NLT 4400 USP Nystatin Units per mg
Pancreatin	NLT 25 USP Units of amylase activity, NLT 2 USP Units of lipase activity, and NLT 25 USP Units of protease activity per mg
Penicillin G Benzathine	NLT 1090 and NMT 1272 Penicillin G Units per mg
Penicillin G Potassium	NLT 1440 and NMT 1680 Penicillin G Units per mg
Penicillin G Sodium	NLT 1500 and NMT 1750 Penicillin G Units per mg
Penicillin V	NLT 1525 and NMT 1780 Penicillin V Units per mg
Penicillin V Potassium	NLT 1380 and NMT 1610 Penicillin V Units per mg
Polymyxin B Sulfate	NLT 6000 Polymyxin B Units per mg
Sargramostim	5.6 million Sargramostim Units per mg of protein
Streptomycin Sulfate	NLT 650 µg and NMT 850 µg of streptomycin per mg
Thiostrepton	900 Thiostrepton Units per mg
Tobramycin	NLT 900 µg of tobramycin per mg
Trypsin, crystalized	NLT 2500 USP Trypsin Units per mg
Vancomycin	NLT 950 µg vancomycin per mg
Vasopressin	NLT 300 Vasopressin Units per mg
Vitamin A	1 USP Vitamin A Unit equals the biologic activity of 0.3 µg of the all-*trans* isomer of retinol

* Examples taken from the United States Pharmacopeia 31st Rev. National Formulary 26. Rockville, MD: United States Pharmacopeial Convention, 2008;2,3.

vaccines, allergenics, biotechnology products, somatic cell therapy, gene therapy, and cellular and tissue-based products.[3]

Vaccines are available for a large number of diseases, including cervical cancer (human papillomavirus), hepatitis A and B, influenza, measles, mumps, pneumococcal, shingles (herpes zoster), smallpox, and tuberculosis. In addition, many additional vaccines are in various

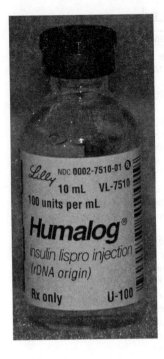

FIGURE 9.1 Example of a pharmaceutical product standardized in units of activity.

stages of development. The *Jordan Report*, a publication of the National Institute of Allergy and Infectious Diseases (NIAID) of the National Institutes of Health (NIH), lists all vaccines licensed for use in the United States as well as the status of vaccines in current research and development.[4] The Centers for Disease Control and Prevention (CDC) offers guidelines for vaccine use in different population groups, as infants, children, adults, and pregnant women.[5]

Specific examples of the *potency* of vaccines expressed in terms other than weight are:

Hepatitis A Vaccine, Inactivated, 1440 EL.U (ELISA units) per 1-mL dose
Influenza Virus Vaccine, Live (intranasal), $10^{6.5-7.5}$ FFU (fluorescent focus units per 0.2 mL dose
Measles Virus Vaccine, Live NLT 1000 $TCID_{50}$ (50% tissue culture infectious dose) in each 0.5-mL dose
Zoster Vaccine, Live, 19,400 PFU (plaque-forming units) per 0.65-mL dose

Pharmacy-Based Immunizations

The American Pharmacists Association (APhA), in coordination with other national professional organizations, has included *the administration of immunizations* among the professional activities of pharmacists.[6] Many colleges of pharmacy and pharmacy organizations have developed pharmacy immunization training programs and states permit pharmacists to administer immunizations under established guidelines and protocols.[7]

FIGURE 9.2 Example of an insulin syringe calibrated in Units. (*Courtesy of Becton, Dickinson and Company.*)

Example Calculations of Measures of Activity or Potency

Determinations of the activity or potency of a biologic material considered in this chapter may be performed through the use of ratio and proportion or dimensional analysis, as demonstrated by the following examples.

Units of Activity. Calculations involving units of activity are exemplified as follows.

How many milliliters of U-100 insulin should be used to obtain 40 units of insulin?
U-100 insulin contains 100 units/mL

$$\frac{100 \text{ (units)}}{40 \text{ (units)}} = \frac{1 \text{ (mL)}}{x \text{ (mL)}}$$

$$x = 0.4 \text{ mL, } answer$$

Or, solving by dimensional analysis:

$$40 \text{ units} \times \frac{1 \text{ mL}}{100 \text{ units}} = 0.4 \text{ mL, } answer.$$

A physician prescribed 100 units of insulin to be added to 500 mL of D5W in treating a patient with severe diabetic acidosis. How many milliliters of insulin injection concentrate, U-500, should be used?

U-500 insulin contains 500 units/mL

$$\frac{500 \text{ (units)}}{100 \text{ (units)}} = \frac{1 \text{ (mL)}}{x \text{ (mL)}}$$

$$x = 0.2 \text{ mL, } answer.$$

Or, solving by dimensional analysis:

$$100 \text{ units} \times \frac{1 \text{ mL}}{500 \text{ units}} = 0.2 \text{ mL, } answer.$$

How many milliliters of a heparin sodium injection containing 200,000 units in 10 mL should be used to obtain 5,000 Heparin Sodium Units that are to be added to an intravenous dextrose solution?

$$\frac{200,000 \text{ (units)}}{5,000 \text{ (units)}} = \frac{10 \text{ (mL)}}{x \text{ (mL)}}$$

$$x = 0.25 \text{ mL, } answer.$$

Activity Based on Weight. Calculations involving the determination of activity per unit of weight are exemplified as follows.

If neomycin sulfate has a potency of 600 μg of neomycin per milligram, how many milligrams of neomycin sulfate would be equivalent in potency to 1 mg of neomycin?

$$\frac{600 \text{ (}\mu g \text{ of neomycin)}}{1,000 \text{ (}\mu g \text{ of neomycin)}} = \frac{1 \text{ (mg of neomycin sulfate)}}{x \text{ (mg of neomycin sulfate)}}$$

$$x = 1.67 \text{ mg, } answer.$$

Dose or Antigen Content of a Biologic Based on Potency. Calculations of the dose or the antigen content of a biologic product are exemplified as follows.

A biologic contains 50 Lf Units of diphtheria toxoid in each 2.5 mL of product. If a pediatric patient is to receive 10 Lf Units, how many milliliters of product should be administered?

$$\frac{50 \text{ (Lf Units)}}{10 \text{ (Lf Units)}} = \frac{2.5 \text{ (mL)}}{x \text{ (mL)}}$$

$$x = 0.5 \text{ mL, } answer.$$

CASE IN POINT 9.1: A hospital pharmacist has been asked to calculate the dose of the biotechnology-derived drug epoetin alpha (EPOGEN, PROCRIT) for a 146.7-lb. patient. The drug is indicated in the treatment of anemia associated with chronic renal failure at a starting dose of 50 to 100 units/kg. The patient's hematocrit (HCT) is taken initially and twice weekly to avoid exceeding or reaching the target range (HCT 30% to 36%) too rapidly. Once the HCT target is reached, the dose is reduced to a titrated maintenance dose. The physician prescribes an initial dose of 75 units/kg subcutaneously, three times a week, with the dose reduced by half when the HCT approaches 33%. The patient's initial HCT is 29%.

The drug is available in 1-mL vials containing 2000, 3000, 4000, 10,000, and 40,000 units/mL. Calculate the:

(a) initial dose, in units;
(b) weekly dose, in units;
(c) maintenance dose, in units; and
(d) most convenient vial size and mL to administer for each therapeutic daily dose.

Measles Virus Vaccine Live is prepared to contain 1000 TCID$_{50}$ per 0.5-mL dose. What is the TCID$_{50}$ content of a 50-mL multiple dose vial of the vaccine?

$$\frac{1000\ (\text{TCID}_{50})}{\text{x}\ (\text{TCID}_{50})} = \frac{0.5\ (\text{mL})}{50\ (\text{mL})}$$
$$\text{x} = 100,000\ \text{TCID}_{50},\ answer.$$

PRACTICE PROBLEMS

Units of Activity Calculations

1. How many milliliters of U-100 insulin zinc suspension should be used to obtain 18 units of insulin?

2. If a diabetic patient injects 20 Units of insulin twice daily, how many days will a 10-mL vial of the U-100 product last the patient?

3. The biotechnology-derived product interferon beta-1b contains 32 million international units per milligram. Calculate the number of international units present in a vial containing 0.3 mg of interferon beta-1b.

4. ALFERON N injection contains 5 million IU of interferon alpha-n3 per milliliter. How many units will an injection of 0.05 mL deliver?

5. Insulin glargine (LANTUS) injection is available in 10-mL vials containing 100 units/mL. How many milliliters would a patient administer for (a) a starting dose of 10 units and (b) a maintenance dose of 4 units?

6. The content of a vial of penicillin G potassium weighs 600 mg and represents 1 million units. How many milligrams are needed to prepare 15 g of an ointment that is to contain 15,000 units of penicillin G potassium per gram?

7. HUMALOG contains 100 units of insulin lispro (rDNA origin) per milliliter. How many complete days will a 3-mL HUMALOG PEN last a patient whose dose is 35 units b.i.d?

8. A physician prescribes 2.5 million units of penicillin G potassium daily for 1 week. If 1 unit of penicillin G potassium equals 0.6 μg, how many tablets, each containing 250 mg, will provide the prescribed dosage regimen?

9. ℞ Penicillin G
    Potassium   5000 units
                            per mL

    Isotonic Sodium
        Chloride Solution ad   15 mL
    Sig. Nose drops.

    Using soluble penicillin tablets, each
    containing 200,000 units of crystalline
    penicillin G potassium, explain how you
    would obtain the penicillin G potassium
    needed in compounding the prescription.

10. FOSAMAX PLUS D contains 70 mg alen-
    dronate and 140 mcg of vitamin D_3, the
    latter equivalent to 5600 international
    units of vitamin D. At a once-a-week
    dose, calculate the daily intake of vitamin
    D_3 in milligrams and units.

11. A vial for preparation of 100 mL of injec-
    tion of the drug alteplase (ACTIVASE)
    contains 100 mg of drug equivalent to 58
    million international units to be adminis-
    tered by intravenous infusion. Calculate
    (a) the units administered to a 176-lb. pa-
    tient at a dose of 0.9 mg/kg and (b) the
    milliliters of injection to use.

12. Calcitonin is available as an injection con-
    taining 200 international units per millili-
    ter. Adult doses of up to 32 units per kilo-
    gram have produced no adverse effects.
    On this basis, if a 120-lb. patient were
    administered 0.75 mL of injection, would
    adverse effects be anticipated?

13. A physician's hospital medication order
    calls for a patient to receive 1 unit of insu-
    lin injection subcutaneously for every 10
    mg/dL of blood sugar over 175 mg/dL,
    with blood sugar levels and injections
    performed twice daily in the morning and
    evening. The patient's blood sugar was
    200 mg/dL in the morning and 320 mg/
    dL in the evening. How many total units
    of insulin injection were administered?

14. A physician's hospital medication order
    calls for isophane insulin suspension to
    be administered to a 136-lb. patient on
    the basis of 1 unit/kg per 24 hours. How

many units of isophane insulin suspension should be administered daily?

15. A physician's hospital medication order
    calls for 0.5 mL of U-500 insulin injection
    to be placed in a 500-mL bottle of 5%
    dextrose injection for infusion into a pa-
    tient. If the rate of infusion was set to run
    for 8 hours, how many units of insulin
    did the patient receive in the first 90 min-
    utes of infusion?

16. Somatropin (NUTROPIN) contains 5 mg
    of drug equivalent to approximately 15
    international units of drug in a vial to pre-
    pare 10 mL of injection. If the starting
    adult dose is 0.006 mg/kg, calculate the
    dose (a) in units and (b) in milliliters for
    a 132-lb. patient.

17. For children, heparin sodium is adminis-
    tered by intermittent intravenous infusion
    in a range of 50 to 100 units/kg body
    weight every 4 hours. For a 50-lb. child,
    calculate the range, in milliliters, of a hep-
    arin sodium injection containing 5000
    units/mL to be administered daily.

18. The maintenance dose of heparin sodium
    in children has been recommended as
    20,000 units/m^2/24 hr. Using the nomo-
    gram in Chapter 8 and a heparin sodium
    injection containing 1000 units/mL, cal-
    culate the daily volume to be adminis-
    tered to a child measuring 22 in. in height
    and weighing 25 lb.

19. Penicillin G potassium is available as a
    dry powder in a vial containing 1 million
    units, which when constituted with 9.6
    mL of solvent, results in a 10-mL solution
    for injection. At a potency of 1560 units/
    mg, calculate the amount, in milligrams,
    of penicillin G potassium in each milliliter
    of injection.

20. Cod liver oil is available in capsules
    containing 0.6 mL per capsule. Using
    Table 9.1, calculate the amounts, in
    units, each of vitamins A and D in each
    capsule. The specific gravity of cod liver
    oil is 0.92.

21. A hepatitis B immune globulin contains 312 international units per milliliter. If the dose is 0.06 mL/kg for certain at-risk persons, calculate the dose (a) in units and (b) in milliliters for a 132-lb. person.

22. If a 5-mL vial of HUMATROPE, a biosynthetic somatotropin of rDNA origin, contains 5 mg of somatotropin equivalent to 13 international units, how many milligrams of somatotropin and how many international units would be administered in a 0.6-mL dose?

23. EPOGEN injection is available containing in each milliliter, 2000, 3000, 4000, or 10,000 units of epoetin alfa. If the staring dose for a 160-lb. patient is prescribed at 50 units/kg, which of the following would provide that dose?
    (a) 4 mL of 2000 units/mL
    (b) 1 mL of 3000 units/mL
    (c) 0.9 mL of 4000 units/mL
    (d) 0.8 mL of 10,000 units/mL

24. The prophylactic dose of tetanus antitoxin is 1500 units for persons weighing less than 65 lb. and 3000 to 5000 units for persons weighing more than 65 lb. The antitoxin is available in dose vials of 1500 units, 3000 units, 5000 units, and 20,000 units. Which vial should a pharmacist provide for administration to a patient weighing 25 kg?

Additional Calculations of Potency

25. Using Table 9.1, calculate the clindamycin potency equivalence, in milligrams per milliliter, of a solution containing 1 g of clindamycin hydrochloride in 10 mL of solution.

26. Each 1-mL adult dose of hepatitis A vaccine contains 1440 EL.U. of viral antigen. What would be the pediatric dose of this vaccine if 360 EL.U. of viral antigen are to be administered?
    (a) 0.8 mL
    (b) 0.25 mL
    (c) 4 mL
    (d) 0.4 mL

27. Each 0.01 mL of a mumps vaccine contains 400 $TCID_{50}$ of the mumps virus. If the usual dose contains 20,000 $TCID_{50}$, how many milliliters of vaccine should be administered?

28. If a biologic product contains 7.5 Lf Units of diphtheria toxoid per 0.5 mL, how many flocculating units would be present in a 7.5-mL multiple dose vial?

29. Zoster Vaccine Live (ZOSTAVAX) contains about 29,850 plaque-forming units (PFU) of attenuated virus per 0.1 cL. Approximately how many PFUs would be contained in each 0.65-mL dose?
    (a) 45,900 PFU
    (b) 4590 PFU
    (c) 1940 PFU
    (d) 19,400 PFU

ANSWERS TO "CASE IN POINT" AND PRACTICE PROBLEMS

Case in Point 9.1

(a) 1 kg = 2.2 lb

$$\frac{75 \text{ units}}{2.2 \text{ lb.}} = \frac{x \text{ units}}{146.7 \text{ lb.}};$$
$$= x \ 5001 \text{ or } 5000 \text{ units},$$
initial dose, *answer*.

(b) 5,000 units × 3 = 15,000 units, weekly dose, *answer*.

(c) 5,000 units ÷ 2 = 2,500 units, maintenance dose, *answer*.

(d) 10,000 units/mL vial, and

$$\frac{10,000 \text{ units}}{1 \text{ mL}} = \frac{5000 \text{ units}}{x \text{ mL}};$$
$$x = 0.5 \text{ mL}, \text{ answers}.$$

Practice Problems

1. 0.18 mL U-100 insulin zinc suspension

2. 25 days

3. 9,600,000 units interferon beta 1-b

4. 250,000 international units

5. (a) 0.1 mL insulin glargine
   (b) 0.04 mL insulin glargine

6. 135 mg penicillin G potassium

7. 4 days

8. 42 penicillin G potassium tablets

9. Dissolve 1 tablet in enough isotonic sodium chloride solution to make 8 mL, and take 3 mL of the dilution.

10. 800 units and 0.02 mg/day

11. (a) 41.76 million units alteplase
    (b) 72 mL alteplase injection

12. No

13. 17 units insulin

14. 61.82 units isophane insulin

15. 46.88 units insulin

16. (a) 1.08 units somatropin
    (b) 0.72 mL somatropin injection

17. 1.36 to 2.73 mL heparin sodium injection

18. 7.44 mL heparin sodium injection

19. 64.1 mg penicillin G potassium

20. 331.2 to 1380 units of vitamin A
    33.12 to 138 units of vitamin D

21. (a) 1123.2 IU hepatitis B immune globulin
    (b) 3.6 mL hepatitis B immune globulin

22. 0.6 mg, and 1.56 or 1.6 IU somatropin

23. (c) 0.9 mL of 4000 units/mL

24. 1500-unit vial

25. 80 mg/mL clindamycin

26. (b) 0.25 mL

27. 0.5 mL mumps vaccine

28. 112.5 Lf Units dipthheria toxoid

29. (d) 19,400 PFU

REFERENCES

1. United States Pharmacopeia 31st Rev. National Formulary 26. Rockville, MD: The United States Pharmacopeial Convention, 2008;(1041)1:5402.
2. United States Pharmacopeia 31st Rev. National Formulary 26. Rockville, MD: United States Pharmacopeial Convention, 2008;3:2942–2943.
3. http://www.fda.gov.cber. Accessed September 6, 2008.
4. The Jordan Report: Accelerated development of vaccines 2007. Available at: http://www.niaid.gov. Accessed November 17, 2007.
5. http://www.cdc.gov/vaccines. Accessed September 6, 2008.
6. "Pharmacy Practice Activity Classification," American Pharmacists Association. Available at: http://www.pharmacist.com. Accessed October 9, 2007.
7. Goad JA. Collaborative practice for pharmacy-based immunization. *Pharmacy Today* 2007;13:77.

10

Selected Clinical Calculations

Objectives

Upon successful completion of this chapter, the student will be able to:

- Calculate heparin doses and infusion rates from medication orders and standardized protocols.
- Calculate ideal body weight and apply in dose determinations.
- Calculate estimated creatinine clearance rates and apply in dose determinations.
- Convert blood serum chemistry values from *mg/dL* to *mmol/L* (international system).

Heparin-Dosing Calculations

Heparin is a heterogenous group of mucopolysaccharides that have anticoagulant properties. Heparin slows clotting time. It is derived from the intestinal mucosa or other suitable tissues of domestic animals (often porcine) used for food by man. Salt forms of heparin, such as heparin sodium, are standardized to contain 140 USP Heparin Units in each milligram. Heparin salts are administered as sterile aqueous solutions by intravenous infusion, intermittent intravenous injection, or deep subcutaneous injection for the prophylaxis and treatment of venous thrombosis. The commercial preparations, available in single-use syringes and multiple-dose vials, indicate on their labeling the number of USP Heparin Units of activity contained per milliliter.

Heparin is the fundamental treatment in acute venous thromboembolism; however, its use carries with it, the risk of hemorrhage. Patients especially at risk include elderly patients, postsurgical patients, patients with a history of peptic ulcers, severe renal or hepatic failure, and patients who recently have taken other medications that affect blood clotting time.[1]

When heparin sodium is administered in therapeutic amounts, its dosage is adjusted according to the results of tests measuring the patient's level of blood coagulation, or partial thromboplastin time (PTT). These tests are performed before each intravenous injection and approximately every 4 to 6 hours when administered by intravenous infusion or subcutaneously. In general, the PTT value should be maintained at 1.5 to 2 times the patient's pretreatment PTT value or, when the whole blood-clotting time is evaluated, approximately 2 to 3 times the control value.

The dose varies depending on the circumstances. Bolus doses, given by direct intravenous injection, may be followed by intravenous infusion as a heparin drip.

Low-dose heparin administration provides effective prophylaxis (rather than therapeutic effects) in a variety of surgical procedures. Patients receive 5000 units given by deep subcutaneous injection 2 hours before surgery and an additional 5000 units every 8 to 12 hours thereafter as required.[2]

Medium-dose heparin, indicated for patients with active phlebitis, with pulmonary emboli, and in hip replacement surgery, has a dosage range of 20,000 to 60,000 units per day, generally by intravenous infusion.[2]

High-dose heparin is indicated in patients with massive pulmonary embolism. Doses of 60,000 to 120,000 units are given by continuous intravenous infusion for the first day and then decreased to medium-dose heparin after 24 hours.[2]

In pediatric use, the initial dose may be 50 mg/kg by intravenous drip, followed by maintenance doses of 100 mg/kg every 4 hours or 20,000 units/m[2]/24 hours, infused continuously.[3]

Figure 10.1 presents a hospital form for an adult weight-based heparin protocol. The form allows physicians' orders for bolus doses, as well as protocols for low-dose and high-dose intravenous heparin infusions. The values given in this figure may differ from heparin protocols at other institutions. Pharmacists must follow those used within their institutions of practice.

It is important to note that a variety of low-molecular-weight heparins are also used as antithrombotic agents: for example, enoxaparin sodium (LOVENOX) and dalteparin sodium (FRAGMIN). Heparin has a molecular weight ranging from 3000 to 30,000 daltons whereas low molecular-weight heparins are fragments of heparin with mean molecular weights of 4000 to 6000 daltons.[4] These shorter compounds may be administered subcutaneously (rather than intravenously, as is heparin), they interfere less with platelet function, and they generally have a more predictable anticoagulant response that does not require monitoring of clotting times.

Example Calculations of Heparin Dosing

An intravenous infusion contained 20,000 units of heparin sodium in 1000 mL of D5W. The rate of infusion was set at 1600 units per hour for a 160-lb. patient. Calculate (a) the concentration of heparin sodium in the infusion, in units/mL; (b) the length of time the infusion would run, in hours; and (c) the dose of heparin sodium administered to the patient, on a unit/kg/minute basis.

(a) $\dfrac{20,000 \text{ units}}{1000 \text{ mL}}$ = 20 units/mL, *and*

(b) $\dfrac{20,000 \text{ units}}{1600 \text{ units/hour}}$ = 12.5 hours, *and*

(c) 160 pounds = 72.7 kg

12.5 hours = 750 minutes

$\dfrac{20,000 \text{ units}}{750 \text{ minutes}}$ = 26.67 units/minute

$\dfrac{26.67 \text{ units/minute}}{72.7 \text{ kg}}$ = 0.37 units/kg/minute, *answers.*

A patient weighing 80 kg was given an initial bolus dose of heparin and a heparin drip for the first 6 hours. Using Figure 10.1 and the low-dose heparin protocol, what was the total amount of heparin administered in this period?[5]

Bolus dose [70 units/kg]: 70 units × 80 (kg) = 5600 units
Heparin drip [15 units/kg/hr]: 15 units × 80 (kg) × 6 (hours) = 7200 units
Thus, 5600 units + 7200 units = 12,800 units, *answer.*

Example Calculations of Low-Molecular-Weight Heparin Dosing

The recommended dose of dalteparin sodium (FRAGMIN) for patients undergoing hip replacement surgery is 2500 international units (IU) within 2 hours before surgery, 2500 IU 4 to 8

CITY HOSPITAL

ADULT WEIGHT-BASED HEPARIN PROTOCOL

Standard Heparin IV Premixed Solution is 25,000 units in 250 mL (100 units per mL)
Initial laboratory tests (draw before starting heparin): PTT, PT, CBC with platelet count
Day 2 and every 3 days thereafter. CBC with platelet count
PTT six (6) hours after heparin drip is started
PTT six (6) hours after every change in heparin administration rate or bolus dose of heparin
Once a therapeutic PTT level is reached, do a PTT six (6) hours later
After two (2) consecutive therapeutic PTT levels are obtained, do a PTT daily at 0600
Discontinue all IM medications and other IM injections

Patient _____ MAY _____ MAY NOT receive drugs containing aspirin.

Patient _____ MAY _____ MAY NOT receive drugs containing non-steroidal antiinflammatory agents.

_____ For a PTT Value of 50 to 70 seconds (LOW-DOSE HEPARIN PROTOCOL)	
_____ No Bolus Dose	Start heparin drip at a rate of
_____ Bolus with 70 units of heparin per kg (limit 10,000 units)	_____ 15 units per kg per hr
_____ Bolus with _____ units of heparin	or _____ units per kg per hr

PTT Value	Heparin Dose Adjustments
<35 seconds	Bolus with 70 units per kg and increase infusion rate by 4 units per kg per hour
35 to 49 seconds	Bolus with 40 units per kg and increase infusion rate by 2 units per kg per hour
50 to 70 seconds	No change in heparin infusion rate
71 to 99 seconds	Decrease infusion rate by 1 unit per kg per hour
100 to 120 seconds	Decrease infusion rate by 2 units per kg per hour
>120 seconds	Hold heparin infusion for 1 hour; when restarted, decrease heparin infusion rate by 3 units per kg per hour

_____ For a PTT Value of 70 to 99 seconds (HIGH-DOSE HEPARIN PROTOCOL)	
_____ No Bolus Dose	Start heparin drip at a rate of
_____ Bolus with 70 units of heparin per kg (limit 10,000 units)	_____ 18 units per kg per hr
_____ Bolus with _____ units of heparin	or _____ units per kg per hr

PTT Value	Heparin Dose Adjustments
<35 seconds	Bolus with 70 units per kg and increase infusion rate by 4 units per kg per hour
35 to 49 seconds	Bolus with 40 units per kg and increase infusion rate by 3 units per kg per hour
50 to 70 seconds	Increase infusion rate by 2 units per kg per hour
71 to 99 seconds	No change in heparin infusion rate
100 to 120 seconds	Decrease infusion rate by 1 unit per kg per hour
>120 seconds	Hold heparin infusion for 1 hour; when restarted, decrease heparin infusion rate by 2 units per kg per hour
DATE TIME	
	M.D.

FIGURE 10.1 Example of hospital form for adult weight-based heparin protocol. *(Courtesy of Flynn Warren, College of Pharmacy, The University of Georgia, Athens, GA.)*

hours after surgery, and 5000 IU daily × 5 to 10 days, starting on the postoperative day. How many milliliters from a vial containing 10,000 IU/mL should be administered (a) before surgery, (b) after surgery, and (c) the day following surgery?

(a) $\dfrac{1 \text{ ml}}{10,000 \text{ IU}} \times 2500 \text{ IU} = 0.25 \text{ mL},$

(b) same as (a) = 0.25 mL

(c) $\dfrac{1 \text{ mL}}{10,000 \text{ IU}} \times 5000 \text{ IU} = 0.5 \text{ mL},$ *answers.*

CASE IN POINT 10.1[5]: A 198-lb. hospitalized patient is placed on a high-dose heparin protocol. The patient requires a bolus injection followed by a heparin infusion. The hospital follows the protocol shown in Figure 10.1.

The hospital pharmacist has heparin available for bolus doses containing 5000 units per milliliter in 5-mL vials and heparin for intravenous infusion in 250-mL infusion bags each containing 25,000 units of heparin.

(a) How many milliliters of the 5000 units/mL injection should the pharmacist recommend as a bolus dose?

(b) How many milliliters per hour of the heparin infusion should the pharmacist instruct the nurse to deliver, based on the standard drip protocol?

(c) If the intravenous set is programmed to deliver 60 drops per milliliter, what should be the flow rate, in drops per minute, to deliver the mL/hr required in answer (b)?

(d) How long will the 250-mL infusion bag last, in hours?

Dosage Calculations Based on Creatinine Clearance

Dose of a Drug. The two major mechanisms by which drugs are eliminated from the body are through hepatic (liver) metabolism and renal (kidney) excretion. When renal excretion is the major route, a loss of kidney function will dramatically affect the rate at which the drug is cleared from the body. Polar drugs are eliminated predominantly by renal excretion and are generally affected by decreased kidney function.

With many drugs, it is important to reach and maintain a specific drug concentration in the blood to realize the proper therapeutic effect. The initial blood concentration attained from a specific dose depends, in part, on the weight of the patient and the volume of body fluids in which the drug is distributed.

The ideal body weight (IBW) provides an excellent estimation of the distribution volume, particularly for some polar drugs that are not well distributed in adipose (fat) tissue. These calculations have been used clinically with the aminoglycoside antibiotics and with digoxin to determine doses and to predict blood levels. The IBW may be calculated readily through the use of the following formulas based on the patients's height and sex.

For males:
IBW = 50 kg + 2.3 kg for each inch of patient's height over 5 feet
or, in pounds
110 lb. + 5 lb. for each inch over 5 feet

For females:
IBW = 45.5 kg + 2.3 kg for each inch of patient height over 5 feet
or, in pounds
100 lb. + 5 lb. for each inch over 5 feet

Example Calculations of Ideal Body Weight

Calculate the ideal body weight for a male patient weighing 164 lb. and measuring 5 ft. 8 in. in height.

IBW = 110 lb. + (8 × 5 lb.)
110 lb. + 40 lb. = 150 lb, *answer.*

Calculate the ideal body weight for a female patient weighing 60 kg and measuring 160 cm in height.

160 cm = 63 in. = 5 ft. 3 in.
IBW = 45.5 kg + (3 × 2.3 kg)
45.5 kg + 6.9 kg = 52.4 kg, *answer.*

Note: In instances in which the IBW is determined to be greater than the actual body weight, the latter is used in dosage calculations.

The kidneys receive about 20% of the cardiac output (blood flow) and filter approximately 125 mL per minute of plasma. As kidney function is lost, the quantity of plasma filtered per minute decreases, with an accompanying decrease in drug clearance. The filtration rate of the kidney can be estimated by a number of methods. One of the most useful, however, is the estimation of the creatinine clearance rate (CrCl) through the use of the following empiric formulas based on the patient's age, weight, and serum creatinine value. Creatine, which is a break-down product of muscle metabolism, is generally produced at a constant rate and in quantities that depend on the muscle mass of the patient. Because creatinine is eliminated from the body essentially through renal filtration, reduced kidney performance results in a reduced creatinine clearance rate. The normal adult value of serum creatinine is 0.7 to 1.5 mg/dL. The creatinine clearance rate represents the volume of blood plasma that is cleared of creatinine by kidney filtration per minute. It is expressed in milliliters per minute.

By the Jelliffe equation:[6–7]
For males:

$$CrCl = \frac{98 - 0.8 \times (\text{Patient's age in years} - 20)}{\text{Serum creatinine in mg/dL}}$$

For females:

$$CrCl = 0.9 \times CrCl \text{ determined using formula for males}$$

By the Cockcroft-Gault equation:[8]
For males:

$$CrCl = \frac{(140 - \text{Patient's age in years}) \times \text{Body weight in kg}}{72 \times \text{Serum creatinine in mg/dL}}$$

For females:

$$CrCl = 0.85 \times CrCl \text{ determined using formula for males}$$

Example Calculations of Creatinine Clearance

Determine the creatinine clearance rate for an 80-year-old male patient weighing 70 kg and having a serum creatinine of 2 mg/dL. Use both the Jelliffe and Cockcroft-Gault equations.

By the Jelliffe equation:

$$CrCl = \frac{98 - 0.8 \times (80 - 20)}{2 \text{ (mg/dL)}}$$

$$= \frac{98 - (0.8 \times 60)}{2 \text{ (mg/dL)}} = \frac{98 - 48}{2 \text{ (mg/dL)}} = \frac{50}{2 \text{ (mg/dL)}}$$

$$= 25 \text{ mL/min, } answer.$$

By the Cockcroft-Gault equation:

$$CrCl = \frac{(140 - 80) \times 70}{72 \times 2 \text{ (mg/dL)}}$$
$$= \frac{60 \times 70}{144}$$
$$= \frac{4200}{144}$$
$$= 29.2 \text{ mL/min, } answer.$$

In addition to the Jelliffe and Cockcroft-Gault equations, other equations are used to estimate creatinine clearance, including the Sanaka equation, for select patients over 60 years of age, and the Schwartz equation, for pediatric and adolescent patients from neonates to 17 years of age.[9]

Sanaka equation:
For males:

$$CrCl = \frac{\text{Patient's weight (kg)} \times [19 \times \text{Plasma albumin (g/dL)} + 32]}{100 \times \text{Serum creatinine (mg/dL)}}$$

For females:

Substitute in the equation: [13 Plasma albumin (g/dL) + 29]

Schwartz equation:

$$CrCl = \frac{k \times \text{Patient's height (cm)}}{\text{Serum creatinine (mg/dL)}}$$

where k is a proportionality constant with a value ranging from 0.33 (for neonates) to 0.70 (for adolescent males).

Adjusting Creatinine Clearance for Body Surface Area. It is sometimes desirable to adjust the calculated creatinine clearance for body surface area to account for this possible variable in determining drug dosage. This adjustment is accomplished through the use of a nomogram of body surface area (BSA), as described previously in Chapter 8, and the following formula:

$$\frac{BSA}{1.73} \times CrCl = \text{Adjusted CrCl}$$

If a patient weighing 120 lb. and measuring 60 in. in height has a calculated creatinine clearance of 40 mL per minute, adjust the CrCl based on body surface area.

Using the nomogram in Chapter 8, the patient's BSA is determined to be 1.50 m². Thus,

$$\frac{1.50 \text{ m}^2}{1.73 \text{ m}^2} \times 40 \text{ mL/min} = 34.7 \text{ mL/min, adjusted CrCl, } answer.$$

Normal creatinine clearance rate may be considered 100 mL per minute. Thus, in the preceding example, the patient would exhibit 25% to 35% of normal creatinine clearance.

The creatinine clearance rate method for determining drug dose is used with various categories of drugs in which renal function is a factor. Such dosing is routine, for example, for aminoglycoside antibiotics including gentamicin, tobramycin, and amikacin.

Once the creatinine clearance rate and the ideal body weight have been calculated, the *loading dose* (initial dose) required to reach a certain drug concentration in the patient and the *maintenance dose* needed to maintain the specified concentration can be calculated.

The loading dose is based solely on the ideal body weight of the patient (except in obese patients), whereas the maintenance dose is based on the ideal body weight *and* the renal clearance rate of the drug.

To calculate the **loading dose (LD)**, *perform the following:*

LD = IBW in kg or lb. × Drug dose per kg or lb.

To calculate the **maintenance dose (MD)**, *perform the following:*

For the "normal" patient:

$$MD = IBW (kg) \times Dose per kg per dosing interval$$

For the renally impaired patient:

$$MD = \frac{CrCl (patient)}{CrCl (normal)} \times Dose for "normal" patient$$

Determine the loading and maintenance doses of gentamicin for a 76-year-old male patient weighing 190 lb. with a height of 6 feet and having a serum creatinine of 2.4 mg/dL. The physician desires a loading dose of 1.5 mg/kg of ideal body weight and a maintenance dose of 1.0 mg/kg of ideal body weight to be administered every 8 hours after the initial dose.

$$
\begin{aligned}
IBW &= 110 \text{ lb.} + (5 \text{ lb.} \times 12) \\
&= 110 \text{ lb.} + 60 \text{ lb.} \\
&= 170 \text{ lb. or } 77.3 \text{ kg}
\end{aligned}
$$

$$
\begin{aligned}
CrCl &= \frac{98 - 0.8 \times (76 - 20)}{2.4 \text{ (mg/dL)}} \\
&= \frac{98 - 44.8}{2.4 \text{ (mg/dL)}} = \frac{53.2}{2.4 \text{ (mg/dL)}} = 22.2 \text{ mL per minute} \\
LD &= 77.3 \text{ kg} \times 1.5 \text{ mg/kg} = 116 \text{ mg, } answer.
\end{aligned}
$$

MD for "normal" patient:

$$
\begin{aligned}
&= 77.3 \text{ kg} \times 1.0 \text{ mg/kg every 8 hours} \\
&= 77.3 \text{ mg every 8 hours}
\end{aligned}
$$

MD for renally impaired patient:

$$
\begin{aligned}
&= \frac{22.2 \text{ mL per minute}}{100 \text{ mL per minute}} \times 77.3 \text{ mg} \\
&= 17.2 \text{ mg every 8 hours, } answer.
\end{aligned}
$$

Use of Creatinine Clearance Dosage Tables. For certain drugs, tables of dosage guidelines may be presented in the labeling/literature to adjust for impaired renal function. For example, the usual dose of the anti-infective drug ceftazidime is 1 g every 8 to 12 hours, with dosage adjusted based on the location and severity of the infection and the patient's renal function. For adult patients with impaired renal function, guidelines for dosage based on creatinine clearance with adjustment for body surface area are given in Table 10.1.

Using the table of dosage guidelines for ceftazidime and adjusting for body surface area, determine the dose and daily dose schedule for a patient weighing 70 kg, measuring 70 in. in height, and having a creatinine clearance (CrCl) of 48 mL per minute.

TABLE 10.1 CREATININE CLEARANCE DOSING GUIDELINES FOR CEFTAZIDIME (IV OR IM)[a]

RENAL FUNCTION	CREATININE CLEARANCE (mL/min/1.73m²)	DOSE	FREQUENCY
Normal to mild impairment	100–51	1 g	q8–12h
Moderate impairment	50–31	1 g	q12h
Severe impairment	30–16	1 g	q24h
Very severe impairment	15–6	500 mg	q24h
Essentially none	<5	500 mg	q48h

[a] Table modified from product literature for FORTAZ (ceftazidime), GlaxoSmithKline, Research Triangle Park, NC, 2007.

CALCULATIONS CAPSULE

Creatinine Clearance Equations[6-9]

Jelliffe equation

For males:

$$CrCl = \frac{98 - 0.8 \times (Patient's\ age\ in\ years\ -\ 20)}{Serum\ creatinine\ in\ mg/dL}$$

For females:

$$CrCl = 0.9 \times CrCl\ determined\ by\ equation\ for\ males$$

Cockcroft-Gault equation

For males:

$$CrCl = \frac{(140 - Patient's\ age\ in\ years) \times pt.\ wt.,\ kg}{72 \times Serum\ creatinine\ in\ mg/dL}$$

For females:

$$CrCl = 0.85 \times CrCl\ determined\ using\ formula\ for\ males$$

Adjusting CrCl for body surface area

$$\frac{BSA}{1.73} \times CrCl = Adjusted\ CrCl$$

Schwartz equation

For pediatric and adolescent patients:

$$CrCl = \frac{k \times Patient's\ height\ (cm)}{Serum\ creatinine\ (mg/dL)}$$

Where k is a proportionality constant ranging from 0.33 (for neonates) to 0.70 (for adolescent males)

Using the nomogram in Chapter 8, the patient is determined to have a BSA of 1.87 m². Applying the formula for the adjustment of CrCl based on BSA, the patient's CrCl is then determined:

$$\frac{1.87 \text{ m}^2}{1.73 \text{ m}^2} \times 48 \text{ mL/min} = 51.9 \text{ or } 52 \text{ mL/min}$$

The dosage table and the adjusted CrCl indicate a dosage of:

1 g every 8 to 12 hours, *answer*.

CASE IN POINT 10.2[5]: **A 35-year-old male patient weighing 180 lb. and standing 5 ft. 8 in. tall has been diagnosed with AIDS. His physician prescribes lamivudine (EPIVIR) as a component of his treatment program and knows that the dose of the drug must be adjusted based on the patient's renal function. Laboratory tests indicate that the patient's serum creatinine is 2.6 mg/dL and has held at the same level for 5 days.**
(a) Calculate the patient's ideal body weight (IBW) and use in subsequent calculations if the IBW is lower than the patient's actual weight.
(b) Calculate the patient's CrCl by the Cockcroft-Gault equation.
(c) Select the appropriate dose of lamivudine from the dosing schedule:

Creatinine Clearance	Initial Dose	Maintenance Dose
<5 mL/min	50 mg	25 mg once daily
5–14 mL/min	150 mg	50 mg once daily
15–29 mL/min	150 mg	100 mg once daily
30–49 mL/min	150 mg	150 mg once daily

Clinical Laboratory Tests

It is common practice in assessing health status to analyze biologic fluids, especially blood and urine, for specific chemical content. The clinical laboratory tests used, known as *chemistries*, analyze samples for such chemicals as glucose, cholesterol, total lipids, creatinine, blood urea nitrogen, bilirubin, potassium, sodium, calcium, carbon dioxide, and other substances, including drugs following their administration. Blood chemistries are performed on plasma (the fluid part of the blood) or serum (the watery portion of clotted blood). Depending on the laboratory equipment used as well as patient factors (such as age and gender), the "usual" amount of each chemical substance varies, with no single "normal" value, but rather a common range. For example, the reference range of glucose in serum is, by some laboratories, 65 to 99 mg/dL and that for creatinine is 0.5 to 1.4 mg/dL.

Table 10.2 presents examples of the normal ranges of serum chemistry values for some commonly analyzed blood components. The "conversion factors" shown are used to convert the units most often used in the United States to those of the international system.

The unit of measurement for cholesterol levels changed from a reading in milligrams per deciliter to the international system of units that uses millimoles per liter of blood plasma. For example, a cholesterol reading of 180 (mg/dL) is now recorded as 4.65 millimoles per liter (mmol/L). Low-density lipoprotein cholesterol (LDL-C), high-density lipoprotein (HDL-C), and total cholesterol (TC) are each measured in assessing a patient's risk for atherosclerosis.[10] The greatest risk comes from the non–high-density lipoprotein cholesterol (non–HDL-C), particularly in patients with high serum levels of triglycerides. In addition, certain accompanying patient factors are considered added risk factors and affect the LDL-C goal for a particular patient.

TABLE 10.2 EXAMPLES OF NORMAL RANGES OF SERUM CHEMISTRY VALUES[a]

LABORATORY TEST	*NORMAL* VALUES (RANGE, IN US UNITS)	CONVERSION FACTOR (MULTIPLY)		INTERNATIONAL SYSTEM[b]
Albumin	3.6–5.1 g/dL	10	=	36–51 g/L
Calcium	8.6–10.3 mg/dL	0.25	=	2.2–2.6 mmol/L
Cholesterol, total	125–200 mg/dL	0.026	=	3.25–5.2 mmol/L
HDL cholesterol	> or = 40 mg/dL	0.026	=	> or = 1.04 mmol/L
LDL cholesterol	<130 mg/dL	0.026	=	<3.38 mmol/L
Glucose	65–99 mg/dL	0.055	=	3.58–5.45 mmol/L
Triglycerides	<150 mg/dL	0.011	=	<1.65 mmol/L
Creatinine	0.5–1.4 mg/dL	88.4	=	44.2–123.8 μmol/L
Urea Nitrogen (BUN)	7–25 mg/dL	0.357	=	2.50–8.93 mmol/L

[a] *Normal* values shown may vary between test laboratories and may be referred to as "reference," "healthy," or "goal" values.
[b] The international system is generally expressed in mmol (or other units) per liter.

These include personal and/or familial history of coronary heart disease, atherosclerotic disease, diabetes, hypertension, and cigarette smoking.

The pharmacist needs to understand both the quantitative aspects of clinical laboratory values as well as their clinical significance. "Abnormal" levels may reflect clinical problems requiring further evaluation and treatment.

Example Calculations Involving Clinical Laboratory Tests

If a patient is determined to have a serum cholesterol level of 200 mg/dL, (a) what is the equivalent value expressed in terms of milligrams percent, and (b) how many milligrams of cholesterol would be present in a 10-mL sample of the patient's serum?

(a) 200 mg/dL = 200 mg/100 mL = 200 mg%, *answer.*

(b) $\dfrac{200 \text{ (mg)}}{x \text{ (mg)}} = \dfrac{100 \text{ (mL)}}{10 \text{ (mL)}}$

$x = 20$ mg, *answer.*

If a patient is determined to have a serum cholesterol level of 200 mg/dL, what is the equivalent value expressed in terms of millimoles (mmol) per liter?

Molecular Weight (m.w. of cholesterol) = 387
1 mmol cholesterol = 387 mg
200 mg/dL = 2000 mg/L

$\dfrac{387 \text{ (mg)}}{2000 \text{ (mg)}} = \dfrac{1 \text{ (millimole)}}{x \text{ (millimoles)}}$

$x = 5.17$ mmol/L, *answer.*

Therapeutic Drug Monitoring

Also termed **drug therapy monitoring**, this process often includes the analysis of blood serum samples to ensure optimum drug therapy. This is especially important for categories of drugs in which the margin between safe and toxic levels is narrow. Data are available indicating these levels.[11]

Drug-Specific Clinical Equations

For certain clinical conditions, there are equations that are useful for determining patient requirements. For example, the following is used in determining the amount of iron required to bring hemoglobin (Hb) values to normal levels:

$$\text{Iron required (mg)} =$$
$$\text{Body weight (lb.)} \times 0.3 \times \left[100 - \frac{\text{Hb (g/dL)} \times 100}{14.8 \text{ g/dL}} \right]$$

In the equation, 14.8 g/dL is the normal value of hemoglobin in adults and the factor 0.3 is its iron content (percent).

Example:

Using the equation for determining iron deficiency, calculate the number of milliliters of an iron dextran solution containing 50 mg/mL of iron to be administered to a 150-lb. patient with a hemoglobin value of 10 g/dL.

$$\text{Iron required (mg)} = 150 \times 0.3 \times \left[100 - \frac{10 \times 100}{14.8} \right]$$
$$= 150 \times 0.3 \times 32.4$$
$$= 1458 \text{ mg}$$
$$\text{by proportion, } \frac{50 \text{ mg}}{1458 \text{ mg}} = \frac{1 \text{ mL}}{\text{x mL}}$$
$$\text{x} = 29 \text{ mL, } \textit{answer.}$$

PRACTICE PROBLEMS

Heparin-Dosing Calculations

1. A hospital pharmacy order calls for 5000 units of heparin to be administered to a patient, twice daily, subcutaneously, for the prevention of thrombi. The pharmacist has on hand a vial containing 10,000 Heparin Units/mL. How many milliliters of the injection should be administered for each dose?

2. A physician orders 1500 units of heparin to be administered by intravenous infusion per hour. The pharmacy provides a heparin intravenous bag containing 25,000 units of heparin in 250 mL of D5W. How many milliliters should be administered per minute?

3.[12] A male patient weighing 76 kg is placed on heparin therapy for the prevention of deep vein thrombosis after surgery.

(a) How many milliliters of a heparin injection containing 5000 units/mL should be administered for a loading dose of 80 units/kg?

(b) What should be the infusion rate, in mL/hr, using a solution that contains heparin 25,000 units/500 mL, to administer 18 units/kg/hr?

(c) Six hours after heparin therapy is initiated, the patient's PTT is found to be 60 seconds. Adjust the infusion rate, in mL/hr, according to the high-dose heparin protocol (Fig. 10.1).

4.[12] A blood sample taken from a 113-lb. patient 6 hours after heparin therapy is initiated shows a PTT of 24 seconds. Calculate (a) the bolus dose and (b) the infusion rate, in mL/hr, according to the high-dose heparin protocol (Fig. 10.1).

5. Enoxaparin sodium (LOVENOX) injection, a low-molecular-weight heparin, contains 150 mg/mL in 0.8-mL prefilled syringes. The recommended dose for knee replacement surgery is 30 mg every 12 hours. How many milliliters of the injection should be administered per dose?

6.[5] When a PTT was performed on the patient described in "Case in Point 10.1," the patient's value was 40 seconds. Based on the high-dose protocol (Fig. 10.1), calculate (a) the needed bolus dose, in units, and (b) the new infusion rate, in mL/hr, using the heparin solution with 25,000 units/250 mL.

Creatinine Clearance Calculations

7. Determine the loading and maintenance doses of tobramycin for a 72-year-old female patient weighing 187 lb. and measuring 5 ft. 3 in. in height with a serum creatinine of 2.8 mg/dL. The loading dose desired is 1.0 mg/kg of ideal body weight and 1.66 mg/kg of ideal body weight every 8 hours as the maintenance dose (adjusted for renal impairment).

8. Determine the loading and maintenance doses of amikacin for a 42-year-old female patient weighing 210 lb. and measuring 5 ft. in height with a serum creatinine of 1.8 mg/dL. The physician requests a loading dose of 7.5 mg/kg of ideal body weight and a maintenance dose of 5 mg/kg of ideal body weight (adjusted for renal impairment) to be administered continually at intervals of 8 hours.

9. Calculate the creatinine clearance rate for a 20-year-old male patient weighing 70 kg with a serum creatinine of 1 mg/dL. If a patient is 5 ft. 8 in. tall, adjust the creatinine clearance based on body surface area.

10. Using the creatinine clearance dosing table in this chapter and the nomogram for body surface area in Chapter 8, what would be the dose and dosage schedule of ceftazidime for a patient weighing 50 kg, measuring 66 in. in height, and having a creatinine clearance (unadjusted for BSA) of 31 mL per minute?

Clinical Laboratory Test Calculations

11. If a serum sample is determined to contain 270 mg/dL of cholesterol, what is the concentration of cholesterol (m.w. 386) in terms of millimoles per liter?

12. Cholesterol readings of 190 mg/dL are considered in the "good" range. Express this value of cholesterol (m.w. 386) in terms of millimoles per liter.

13. If a patient has a serum cholesterol (m.w. 386) of 4.40 mmol/L, what is the corresponding value in milligrams per deciliter?

14. Complete the following table, comparing serum cholesterol (m.w. 386) levels expressed equivalently in milligrams per deciliter and in millimoles per liter:

mg/dL	mmol/L
Good:	Good:
170	(a)
(b)	4.91
Borderline:	Borderline:
(c)	5.69
240	(d)
High:	High:
(e)	6.46

15. A glucose meter shows that a patient's blood contains 125 mg% of glucose. Express this value as mg/mL.

16. Total serum cholesterol includes LDL-C and HDL-C. If a patient has a HDL-C level of 65 mg/dL and a total cholesterol of 5.43 mmol/L, what is the LDL-C value in milligrams per deciliter?

17. Federal rules prohibit transportation workers from performing safety-sensitive functions when breath alcohol is 0.04% or greater. Express this value on a milligram-per-deciliter basis.

18. A blood alcohol level of 80 mg/dL is considered to diminish driving performance. Express this value in terms of percentage.

19. The average blood alcohol concentration in fatal intoxication is about 400 mg/dL. Express this concentration in terms of percentage.

20. On the basis of the information in Table 10.2, calculate the mmol/L of glucose equivalent to a value of 140 mg/dL.

    (a) 7.7 mmol/L
    (b) 2.5 mmol/L
    (c) 5.4 mmol/L
    (d) 6.2 mmol/L

21. Among clinical recommendations to prevent cardiovascular disease in women is the maintenance of lipid levels as follows: low-density lipoproteins (LDL) <100 mg/dL; high-density lipoproteins (HDL) >50 mg/dL; and triglycerides (TG) <150 mg/dL.[13] Which of the following meet these criteria?
    (a) LDL <2.6 mmol/L
    (b) HDL >1.3 mmol/L
    (c) TG <1.65 mmol/L
    (d) all of the above

ANSWERS TO "CASE IN POINT" AND PRACTICE PROBLEMS

Case in Point 10.1

(a) Patient's weight in kg:

$$198 \text{ lb.} \times \frac{1 \text{ kg}}{2.2 \text{ lb.}} = 90 \text{ kg}$$

High-dose protocol, bolus dose: 70 units heparin/kg

$$70 \text{ units} \times 90 \text{ (kg)} = 6300 \text{ units}$$

$$6300 \text{ units} \times \frac{1 \text{mL}}{500 \text{ units}}$$

$$= 1.26 \text{ mL, } answer$$

(b) High-dose protocol, infusion rate: 18 units/kg/hr

$$18 \text{ units/kg/hr} \times 90 \text{ (kg)} = 1620 \text{ units/hr}$$

$$\frac{250 \text{ mL}}{25,000 \text{ units}} \times \frac{1620 \text{ units}}{1 \text{ hr}}$$

$$= 16.2 \text{ mL/hr, } answer.$$

(c) $$\frac{16.2 \text{ mL}}{1 \text{ hr}} \times \frac{60 \text{ drops}}{1 \text{ mL}} \times \frac{1 \text{ hr}}{60 \text{ min}}$$

$$= 16.2 \text{ or } 16 \text{ drops/min, } answer.$$

(d) $$250 \text{ mL} \times \frac{1 \text{ hr}}{16.2 \text{ mL}} = 15.43 \text{ hr,}$$

answer.

Case in Point 10.2

(a) IBW = 50 kg + (2.3 × 8 in) = 68.4 kg, *answer.*

Patient's actual weight = 180 lb. ÷ 2.2 lb./kg = 81.8 kg

(b) $$\text{CrCl} = \frac{[(140 - 35) \times 68.4 \text{ kg]}}{72 \times 2.6 \text{ mg/dL}}$$

$$= \frac{7182}{187.2} = 38.37 \text{ mL/min,}$$

answer.

(c) Dose = 150 mg initially and 150 mg maintenance dose once daily, *answer.*

Practice Problems

1. 0.5 mL heparin injection

2. 0.25 mL/min

3. (a) 1.2 mL heparin injection
   (b) 27.36 or 27 mL/hr
   (c) 30.4 or 30 mL/hr

4. (a) 3595 units
   (b) 11.3 mL/hr

5. 0.2 mL enoxaparin sodium injection

6. (a) 3,600 units
   (b) 18.9 mL/hr

7. 52.3 mg tobramycin (loading dose)
   15.7 mg tobramycin (maintenance dose)

8. 340.9 mg amikacin (loading dose)
   91.3 mg amikacin (maintenance dose)

9. 117 mL/min
   123.8 mL/min

10. 1 g ceftazidime every 24 hours

11. 6.99 mmol/L

12. 4.92 mmol/L

13. 169.84 mg/dL

14. (a) 4.40 mmol/L
    (b) 189.53 mg/dL

(c) 219.63 mg/dL
(d) 6.22 mmol/L
(e) 249.36 mg/dL

15. 1.25 mg/mL

16. 144.6 mg/dL

17. 40 mg/dL

18. 0.08%

19. 0.4%

20. (a) 7.7 mmol/L

21. (d) all of the above

REFERENCES

1. http://www.rxkinetics.com/heparin.html. Accessed November 28, 2007.
2. Berkow R, ed. *The Merck Manual.* 14th Ed. Rahway, NJ: Merck Sharpe & Dohme Research Laboratories, 1982: 2404–2405.
3. Heparin Sodium Injection [product literature]. Indianapolis, IN: Eli Lilly & Company, 1998.
4. Bontempo FA, Hassett AC. Low-molecular-weight heparin. Transfusion Medicine Update. June 1996. Available at: http://www.itxm.org/TMU1996/tmu6-96.htm. Accessed November 28, 2007.
5. Warren F. Problem set. Athens, GA: College of Pharmacy, University of Georgia, 2004.
6. Jelliffe RW. Estimations of creatinine clearance when urine cannot be collected. *Lancet* 1971;1:975.
7. Jelliffe RW. Creatinine clearance bedside estimate. *Annals of Internal Medicine* 1973;79:604.
8. Cockcroft DW, Gault MH. Prediction of creatinine clearance from serum creatinine. *Nephron* 1976;16:31.
9. Anaizi N. Estimation of creatinine clearance. Drug Monitor. Available at: http://www.thedrugmonitor.com/clcreqs.html. Accessed November 29, 2007.
10. National Cholesterol Education program report. *Circulation* 2004:227–239. Available at: http://www.circulationaha.org. Accessed November 30, 2007.
11. Pagana KD, Pagana TJ. *Mosby's Diagnostic and Laboratory Test Reference.* 6th Ed. Philadelphia: Mosby, 2003.
12. Ansel HC, Prince SJ. Pharmaceutical calculations. In: *The Pharmacist's Handbook.* Baltimore, MD: Lippincott Williams & Wilkins, 2004:236–240.
13. Women's health: What's hot. *Pharmacy Today* 2007;13(9):28.

Isotonic and Buffer Solutions

Objectives

Upon successful completion of this chapter, the student will be able to:

- Differentiate between the terms *isosmotic, isotonic, hypertonic,* and *hypotonic.*
- Apply physical chemical principles in the calculation of isotonic solutions.
- Perform the calculations required to prepare isotonic compounded prescriptions.
- State the buffer equation and apply it in calculations.

When a solvent passes through a semipermeable membrane from a dilute solution into a more concentrated one, the concentrations become equalized and the phenomenon is known as *osmosis*. The pressure responsible for this phenomenon is termed *osmotic pressure* and varies with the nature of the solute.

If the solute is a nonelectrolyte, its solution contains only molecules and the osmotic pressure varies with the concentration of the solute. If the solute is an electrolyte, its solution contains ions and the osmotic pressure varies with both the concentration of the solute and its degree of dissociation. Thus, solutes that dissociate present a greater number of particles in solution and exert a greater osmotic pressure than *un*dissociated molecules.

Like osmotic pressure, the other *colligative properties* of solutions, *vapor pressure, boiling point*, and *freezing point*, depend on the number of particles in solution. Therefore, these properties are interrelated and a change in any one of them will result in a corresponding change in the others.

Two solutions that have the same osmotic pressure are termed *isosmotic*. Many solutions intended to be mixed with body fluids are designed to have the same osmotic pressure for greater patient comfort, efficacy, and safety. A solution having the same osmotic pressure as a *specific* body fluid is termed *isotonic* (meaning of equal tone) with *that* specific body fluid.

Solutions of *lower* osmotic pressure than that of a body fluid are termed **hypotonic**, whereas those having a *higher* osmotic pressure are termed **hypertonic**. Pharmaceutical dosage forms intended to be added directly to the blood or mixed with biological fluids of the eye, nose, and bowel are of principal concern to the pharmacist in their preparation and clinical application.

Special Clinical Considerations of Tonicity

It is generally accepted that for ophthalmic and parenteral administration, isotonic solutions are better tolerated by the patient than those at the extremes of hypo- and hypertonicity. With the administration of an isotonic solution, there is a homeostasis with the body's intracellular fluids. Thus, *in most instances,* preparations that are isotonic, or nearly so, are preferred. However, there are exceptions, as in instances in which hypertonic solutions are used to "draw" fluids out of edematous tissues and into the administered solution.

Most ophthalmic preparations are formulated to be isotonic, or approximately isotonic, to duplicate ophthalmic tears for the comfort of the patient. These solutions are also prepared and buffered at an appropriate pH, both to reduce the likelihood of irritation to the eye's tissues and to maintain the stability of the preparations.

Injections that are not isotonic should be administered slowly and in small quantities to minimize tissue irritation, pain, and cell fluid imbalance. The tonicity of small-volume injections is generally inconsequential when added to large-volume parenteral infusions because of the presence of tonic substances, such as sodium chloride or dextrose in the large-volume infusion, which serve to adjust the tonicity of the smaller added volume.[1]

Intravenous infusions, which are hypotonic or hypertonic, can have profound adverse effects because they generally are administered in large volumes.[1] Large volumes of *hypertonic* infusions containing dextrose, for example, can result in hyperglycemia, osmotic diuresis, and excessive loss of electrolytes. Excess infusions of *hypotonic* fluids can result in the osmotic hemolysis of red blood cells and surpass the upper limits of the body's capacity to safely absorb excessive fluids. Even isotonic fluids, when infused intravenously in excessive volumes or at excessive rates, can be deleterious due to an overload of fluids placed into the body's circulatory system.

Physical/Chemical Considerations in the Preparation of Isotonic Solutions

The calculations involved in preparing isotonic solutions may be made in terms of data relating to the colligative properties of solutions. Theoretically, any one of these properties may be used as a basis for determining tonicity. Practically and most conveniently, a comparison of freezing points is used for this purpose. It is generally accepted that $-0.52°C$ is the freezing point of both blood serum and lacrimal fluid.

When one gram molecular weight of any nonelectrolyte, that is, a substance with negligible dissociation, such as boric acid, is dissolved in 1000 g of water, the freezing point of the solution is about 1.86°C below the freezing point of pure water. By simple proportion, therefore, we can calculate the weight of any nonelectrolyte that should be dissolved in each 1000 g of water if the solution is to be isotonic with body fluids.

Boric acid, for example, has a molecular weight of 61.8; thus (in theory), 61.8 g in 1000 g of water should produce a freezing point of $-1.86°C$. Therefore:

$$\frac{1.86 \ (°C)}{0.52 \ (°C)} = \frac{61.8 \ (g)}{x \ (g)}$$
$$x = 17.3 \ g$$

In short, 17.3 g of boric acid in 1000 g of water, having a weight-in-volume strength of approximately 1.73%, should make a solution isotonic with lacrimal fluid.

With electrolytes, the problem is not so simple. Because osmotic pressure depends more on the number than on the kind of particles, substances that dissociate have a tonic effect that increases with the degree of dissociation; the greater the dissociation, the smaller the quantity required to produce any given osmotic pressure. If we assume that sodium chloride in weak solutions is about 80% dissociated, then each 100 molecules yields 180 particles, or 1.8 times as many particles as are yielded by 100 molecules of a nonelectrolyte. This dissociation factor, commonly symbolized by the letter *i*, must be included in the proportion when we seek to determine the strength of an isotonic solution of sodium chloride (m.w. 58.5):

$$\frac{1.86 \ (°C) \times 1.8}{0.52 \ (°C)} = \frac{58.5 \ (g)}{x \ (g)}$$
$$x = 9.09 \ g$$

Hence, 9.09 g of sodium chloride in 1000 g of water should make a solution isotonic with blood or lacrimal fluid. In practice, a 0.90% w/v sodium chloride solution is considered isotonic with body fluids.

Simple isotonic solutions may then be calculated by using this formula:

$$\frac{0.52 \times \text{molecular weight}}{1.86 \times \text{dissociation (i)}} = \text{g of solute per 1000 g of water}$$

The value of i for many a medicinal salt has not been experimentally determined. Some salts (such as zinc sulfate, with only some 40% dissociation and an i value therefore of 1.4) are exceptional, but most medicinal salts approximate the dissociation of sodium chloride in weak solutions. If the number of ions is known, we may use the following values, lacking better information:

Nonelectrolytes and substances of slight dissociation: 1.0
Substances that dissociate into 2 ions: 1.8
Substances that dissociate into 3 ions: 2.6
Substances that dissociate into 4 ions: 3.4
Substances that dissociate into 5 ions: 4.2

A special problem arises when a prescription directs us to make a solution isotonic by adding the proper amount of some substance other than the active ingredient or ingredients. Given a 0.5% w/v solution of sodium chloride, we may easily calculate that 0.9 g − 0.5 g = 0.4 g of additional sodium chloride that should be contained in each 100 mL if the solution is to be made isotonic with a body fluid. But how much sodium chloride should be used in preparing 100 mL of a 1% w/v solution of atropine sulfate, which is to be made isotonic with lacrimal fluid? The answer depends on *how much sodium chloride is in effect represented by the atropine sulfate.*

The relative tonic effect of two substances—that is, the quantity of one that is the equivalent in tonic effects to a given quantity of the other—may be calculated if the quantity of one having a certain effect in a specified quantity of solvent is divided by the quantity of the other having the same effect in the same quantity of solvent. For example, we calculated that 17.3 g of boric acid per 1000 g of water and 9.09 g of sodium chloride per 1000 g of water are both instrumental in making an aqueous solution isotonic with lacrimal fluid. If, however, 17.3 g of boric acid are equivalent in tonicity to 9.09 g of sodium chloride, then 1 g of boric acid must be the equivalent of 9.09 g ÷ 17.3 g or 0.52 g of sodium chloride. Similarly, 1 g of sodium chloride must be the "tonicic equivalent" of 17.3 g ÷ 9.09 g or 1.90 g of boric acid.

We have seen that one quantity of any substance should in theory have a constant tonic effect if dissolved in 1000 g of water: 1 g molecular weight of the substance divided by its i or dissociation value. Hence, the relative quantity of sodium chloride that is the tonicic equivalent of a quantity of boric acid may be calculated by these ratios:

$$\frac{58.5 \div 1.8}{61.8 \div 1.0} \text{ or } \frac{58.5 \times 1.0}{61.8 \times 1.8}$$

and we can formulate a convenient rule: *quantities of two substances that are tonicic equivalents are proportional to the molecular weights of each multiplied by the i value of the other.*

To return to the problem involving 1 g of atropine sulfate in 100 mL of solution:

Molecular weight of sodium chloride   = 58.5; i = 1.8
Molecular weight of atropine sulfate   = 695; i = 2.6

$$\frac{695 \times 1.8}{58.5 \times 2.6} = \frac{1 \text{ (g)}}{x \text{ (g)}}$$

x = 0.12 g of sodium chloride represented by
1 g of atropine sulfate

Because a solution isotonic with lacrimal fluid should contain the equivalent of 0.90 g of sodium chloride in each 100 mL of solution, the difference to be added must be 0.90 g − 0.12 g = 0.78 g of sodium chloride.

Table 11.1 gives the *sodium chloride equivalents* (E values) of each of the substances listed. These values were calculated according to the rule stated previously. *If the number of grams of a substance included in a prescription is multiplied by its sodium chloride equivalent, the amount of sodium chloride represented by that substance is determined*.

The procedure for the *calculation of isotonic solutions with sodium chloride equivalents* may be outlined as follows:

Step 1. Calculate the amount (in grams) of sodium chloride represented by the ingredients in the prescription. Multiply the amount (in grams) of each substance by its sodium chloride equivalent.

Step 2. Calculate the amount (in grams) of sodium chloride, alone, that would be contained in an isotonic solution of the volume specified in the prescription, namely, *the amount of sodium chloride in a 0.9% solution of the specified volume.* (Such a solution would contain 0.009 g/mL.)

Step 3. Subtract the amount of sodium chloride represented by the ingredients in the prescription (Step 1) from the amount of sodium chloride, alone, that would be represented in the specific volume of an isotonic solution (Step 2). The answer represents the amount (in grams) of sodium chloride to be added to make the solution isotonic.

Step 4. If an agent other than sodium chloride, such as boric acid, dextrose, or potassium nitrate, is to be used to make a solution isotonic, divide the amount of sodium chloride (Step 3) by the sodium chloride equivalent of the other substance.

Example Calculations of the *i* Factor

Zinc sulfate is a 2-ion electrolyte, dissociating 40% in a certain concentration. Calculate its dissociation (i) factor.

On the basis of 40% dissociation, 100 particles of zinc sulfate will yield:

> 40 zinc ions
> 40 sulfate ions
> 60 undissociated particles
> or 140 particles

Because 140 particles represent 1.4 times as many particles as were present before dissociation, the dissociation (*i*) factor is 1.4, *answer.*

Zinc chloride is a 3-ion electrolyte, dissociating 80% in a certain concentration. Calculate its dissociation (i) factor.

On the basis of 80% dissociation, 100 particles of zinc chloride will yield:

> 80 zinc ions
> 80 chloride ions
> 80 chloride ions
> 20 undissociated particles
> or 260 particles

Because 260 particles represents 2.6 times as many particles as were present before dissociation, the dissociation (*i*) factor is 2.6, *answer.*

TABLE 11.1 SODIUM CHLORIDE EQUIVALENTS (*E* VALUES)

SUBSTANCE	MOLECULAR WEIGHT	IONS	*i*	SODIUM CHLORIDE EQUIVALENT (E VALUE)
Antazoline phosphate	363	2	1.8	0.16
Antipyrine	188	1	1.0	0.17
Atropine sulfate·H_2O	695	3	2.6	0.12
Benoxinate hydrochloride	345	2	1.8	0.17
Benzalkonium chloride	360	2	1.8	0.16
Benzyl alcohol	108	1	1.0	0.30
Boric acid	61.8	1	1.0	0.52
Chloramphenicol	323	1	1.0	0.10
Chlorobutanol	177	1	1.0	0.24
Chlortetracycline hydrochloride	515	2	1.8	0.11
Cocaine hydrochloride	340	2	1.8	0.16
Cromolyn sodium	512	2	1.8	0.11
Cyclopentolate hydrochloride	328	2	1.8	0.18
Demecarium bromide	717	3	2.6	0.12
Dextrose (anhydrous)	180	1	1.0	0.18
Dextrose·H_2O	198	1	1.0	0.16
Dipivefrin hydrochloride	388	2	1.8	0.15
Ephedrine hydrochloride	202	2	1.8	0.29
Ephedrine sulfate	429	3	2.6	0.23
Epinephrine bitartrate	333	2	1.8	0.18
Epinephryl borate	209	1	1.0	0.16
Eucatropine hydrochloride	328	2	1.8	0.18
Fluorescein sodium	376	3	2.6	0.31
Glycerin	92	1	1.0	0.34
Homatropine hydrobromide	356	2	1.8	0.17
Hydroxyamphetamine hydrobromide	232	2	1.8	0.25
Idoxuridine	354	1	1.0	0.09
Lidocaine hydrochloride	289	2	1.8	0.22
Mannitol	182	1	1.0	0.18
Morphine sulfate·5H_2O	759	3	2.6	0.11
Naphazoline hydrochloride	247	2	1.8	0.27
Oxymetazoline hydrochloride	297	2	1.8	0.20
Oxytetracycline hydrochloride	497	2	1.8	0.12
Phenacaine hydrochloride	353	2	1.8	0.20
Phenobarbital sodium	254	2	1.8	0.24
Phenylephrine hydrochloride	204	2	1.8	0.32
Physostigmine salicylate	413	2	1.8	0.16
Physostigmine sulfate	649	3	2.6	0.13
Pilocarpine hydrochloride	245	2	1.8	0.24
Pilocarpine nitrate	271	2	1.8	0.23
Potassium biphosphate	136	2	1.8	0.43
Potassium chloride	74.5	2	1.8	0.76
Potassium iodide	166	2	1.8	0.34
Potassium nitrate	101	2	1.8	0.58
Potassium penicillin G	372	2	1.8	0.18
Procaine hydrochloride	273	2	1.8	0.21
Proparacaine hydrochloride	331	2	1.8	0.18
Scopolamine hydrobromide·3H_2O	438	2	1.8	0.12
Silver nitrate	170	2	1.8	0.33
Sodium bicarbonate	84	2	1.8	0.65
Sodium borate·10H_2O	381	5	4.2	0.42

(continued)

TABLE 11.1 *continued*

SUBSTANCE	MOLECULAR WEIGHT	IONS	*i*	SODIUM CHLORIDE EQUIVALENT (E VALUE)
Sodium carbonate	106	3	2.6	0.80
Sodium carbonate·H_2O	124	3	2.6	0.68
Sodium chloride	58	2	1.8	1.00
Sodium citrate·$2H_2O$	294	4	3.4	0.38
Sodium iodide	150	2	1.8	0.39
Sodium lactate	112	2	1.8	0.52
Sodium phosphate, dibasic, anhydrous	142	3	2.6	0.53
Sodium phosphate, dibasic·$7H_2O$	268	3	2.6	0.29
Sodium phosphate, monobasic, anhydrous	120	2	1.8	0.49
Sodium phosphate, monobasic·H_2O	138	2	1.8	0.42
Tetracaine hydrochloride	301	2	1.8	0.18
Tetracycline hydrochloride	481	2	1.8	0.12
Tetrahydrozoline hydrochloride	237	2	1.8	0.25
Timolol maleate	432	2	1.8	0.14
Tobramycin	468	1	1.0	0.07
Tropicamide	284	1	1.0	0.11
Urea	60	1	1.0	0.59
Zinc chloride	136	3	2.6	0.62
Zinc sulfate·$7H_2O$	288	2	1.4	0.15

Example Calculations of the Sodium Chloride Equivalent

The sodium chloride equivalent of a substance may be calculated as follows:

$$\frac{\text{Molecular weight of sodium chloride}}{i \text{ Factor of sodium chloride}} \times \frac{i \text{ factor of the substance}}{\text{Molecular weight of the substance}} = \frac{\text{Sodium chloride}}{\text{equivalent}}$$

Papaverine hydrochloride (m.w. 376) is a 2-ion electrolyte, dissociating 80% in a given concentration. Calculate its sodium chloride equivalent.

Because papaverine hydrochloride is a 2-ion electrolyte, dissociating 80%, its i factor is 1.8.

$$\frac{58.5}{1.8} \times \frac{1.8}{376} = 0.156, \text{ or } 0.16, \text{ answer.}$$

Calculate the sodium chloride equivalent for glycerin, a nonelectrolyte with a molecular weight of 92.[2]

Glycerin, i factor = 1.0

$$\frac{58.5}{1.8} \times \frac{1.0}{92} = 0.35, \text{ answer.}$$

Calculate the sodium chloride equivalent for timolol maleate, which dissociates into two ions and has a molecular weight of 432.[2]

Timolol maleate, i factor = 1.8

$$\frac{58.5}{1.8} \times \frac{1.8}{432} = 0.14, \text{ answer.}$$

Calculate the sodium chloride equivalent for fluorescein sodium, which dissociates into three ions and has a molecular weight of 376.[2]

Fluorescein sodium, *i* factor = 2.6

$$\frac{58.5}{1.8} \times \frac{2.6}{367} = 0.23, \text{ answer.}$$

Example Calculations of Tonicic Agent Required

How many grams of sodium chloride should be used in compounding the following prescription?

℞	Pilocarpine Nitrate	0.3 g
	Sodium Chloride	q.s.
	Purified Water ad	30 mL
	Make isoton. sol.	
	Sig. For the eye.	

Step 1. 0.23 × 0.3 g = 0.069 g of sodium chloride represented by the pilocarpine nitrate

Step 2. 30 × 0.009 = 0.270 g of sodium chloride in 30 mL of an isotonic sodium chloride solution

Step 3. 0.270 g (from Step 2)
  − 0.069 g (from Step 1)
  0.201 g of sodium chloride to be used, *answer.*

How many grams of boric acid should be used in compounding the following prescription?

℞	Phenacaine Hydrochloride	1%
	Chlorobutanol	½%
	Boric Acid	q.s.
	Purified Water ad	60
	Make isoton. sol.	
	Sig. One drop in each eye.	

The prescription calls for 0.6 g of phenacaine hydrochloride and 0.3 g of chlorobutanol.

Step 1. 0.20 × 0.6 g = 0.120 g of sodium chloride represented by phenacaine hydrochloride
  0.24 × 0.3 g = 0.072 g of sodium chloride represented by chlorobutanol
  Total: 0.192 g of sodium chloride represented by both ingredients

Step 2. 60 × 0.009 = 0.540 g of sodium chloride in 60 mL of an isotonic sodium chloride solution

Step 3. 0.540 g (from Step 2)
  − 0.192 g (from Step 1)
  0.348 g of sodium chloride required to make the solution isotonic

But because the prescription calls for boric acid:

Step 4. 0.348 g ÷ 0.52 (sodium chloride equivalent of boric acid) = 0.669 g of boric acid to be used, *answer.*

How many grams of potassium nitrate could be used to make the following prescription isotonic?

℞	Sol. Silver Nitrate	60
	1:500 w/v	
	Make isoton. sol.	
	Sig. For eye use.	

The prescription contains 0.12 g of silver nitrate.

Step 1. 0.33 × 0.12 g = 0.04 g of sodium chloride represented by silver nitrate
Step 2.   60 × 0.009   = 0.54 g of sodium chloride in 60 mL of an isotonic sodium chloride
solution
Step 3. 0.54 g (from step 2)
  − 0.04 g (from step 1)
  0.50 g of sodium chloride required to make solution isotonic
Because, in this solution, sodium chloride is incompatible with silver nitrate, the tonic agent
of choice is potassium nitrate. Therefore,
Step 4. 0.50 g ÷ 0.58 (sodium chloride equivalent of potassium nitrate) = 0.86 g of potassium
nitrate to be used, *answer.*

How many grams of sodium chloride should be used in compounding the following prescription?

R̥   Ingredient X   0.5
      Sodium Chloride   q.s.
      Purified Water   ad   50
      Make isoton. sol.
      Sig. Eye drops.

Let us assume that ingredient X is a new substance for which no sodium chloride equivalent
is to be found in Table 11.1, and that its molecular weight is 295 and its *i* factor is 2.4. The
sodium chloride equivalent of ingredient X may be calculated as follows:

$$\frac{58.5}{1.8} \times \frac{2.4}{295} = 0.26, \text{ the sodium chloride equivalent for ingredient X}$$

Then,
Step 1. 0.26 × 0.5 g = 0.13 g of sodium chloride represented by ingredient X
Step 2. 50 × 0.009 = 0.45 g of sodium chloride in 50 mL of an isotonic sodium chloride
solution
Step 3. 0.45 g (from Step 2)
  − 0.13 g (from Step 1)
  0.32 g of sodium chloride to be used, *answer.*

Using an Isotonic Sodium Chloride Solution to Prepare Other Isotonic Solutions

A 0.9% w/v sodium chloride solution may be used to compound isotonic solutions of other
drug substances as follows:

Step 1. Calculate the quantity of the drug substance needed to fill the prescription or medication
order.
Step 2. Use the following equation to calculate the volume of water needed to render a solution
of the drug substance isotonic:

$$\frac{\text{g of drug} \times \text{drug's } E \text{ value}}{0.009} = \text{mL of water needed to make an isotonic solution of the drug}$$

(the volume of the drug substance is considered negligible)

Step 3. Add 0.9% w/v sodium chloride solution to complete the required volume of the prescription or medication order.

*Using this method, determine the volume of purified water and 0.9% w/v sodium chloride solution
needed to prepare 20 mL of a 1% w/v solution of hydromorphone hydrochloride (E = 0.22).*

Step 1. 20 mL × 1% w/v = 0.2 g hydromorphone needed

Step 2. $\dfrac{0.2 \text{ g} \times 0.22}{0.009}$ = 4.89 mL purified water required to make an isotonic solution of hydromorphone hydrochloride, *answer.*

Step 3. 20 mL − 4.89 mL = 15.11 mL 0.9% w/v sodium chloride solution required, *answer.*

Proof: 20 mL × 0.9% = 0.18 g sodium chloride or equivalent required

0.2 × 0.22 = 0.044 g (sodium chloride represented by 0.2 g hydromorphone hydrochloride)

15.11 mL × 0.9 % = 0.136 g sodium chloride present

0.044 g + 0.136 g = 0.18 g sodium chloride required for isotonicity

Use of Freezing Point Data in Isotonicity Calculations

Freezing point data (ΔT_f) can be used in isotonicity calculations when the agent has a tonicic effect and does not penetrate the biologic membranes in question (e.g., red blood cells). As stated previously, the freezing point of both blood and lacrimal fluid is −0.52°C. Thus, a pharmaceutical solution that has a freezing point of −0.52°C is considered isotonic.

Representative data on freezing point depression by medicinal and pharmaceutical substances are presented in Table 11.2. Although these data are for solution strengths of 1% ($\Delta T_f^{1\%}$), data for other solution strengths and for many additional agents may be found in physical pharmacy textbooks and in the literature.

Freezing point depression data may be used in isotonicity calculations as shown by the following.

TABLE 11.2 FREEZING POINT DATA FOR SELECT AGENTS

AGENT	FREEZING POINT DEPRESSION, 1% SOLUTIONS ($\Delta T_f^{1\%}$)
Atropine sulfate	0.07
Boric acid	0.29
Butacaine sulfate	0.12
Chloramphenicol	0.06
Chlorobutanol	0.14
Dextrose	0.09
Dibucaine hydrochloride	0.08
Ephedrine sulfate	0.13
Epinephrine bitartrate	0.10
Ethylmorphine hydrochloride	0.09
Glycerin	0.20
Homatropine hydrobromide	0.11
Lidocaine hydrochloride	0.063
Lincomycin	0.09
Morphine sulfate	0.08
Naphazoline hydrochloride	0.16
Physostigmine salicylate	0.09
Pilocarpine nitrate	0.14
Sodium bisulfite	0.36
Sodium chloride	0.58
Sulfacetamide sodium	0.14
Zinc sulfate	0.09

Example Calculations Using Freezing Point Data

How many milligrams each of sodium chloride and dibucaine hydrochloride are required to prepare 30 mL of a 1% solution of dibucaine hydrochloride isotonic with tears?

To make this solution isotonic, the freezing point must be lowered to -0.52. From Table 11.2, it is determined that a 1% solution of dibucaine hydrochloride has a freezing point lowering of 0.08°. Thus, sufficient sodium chloride must be added to lower the freezing point an additional 0.44° (0.52° $-$ 0.08°).

Also from Table 11.2, it is determined that a 1% solution of sodium chloride lowers the freezing point by 0.58°. By proportion:

$$\frac{1\% \ (NaCl)}{x\% \ (NaCl)} = \frac{0.58°}{0.44°}$$

$$x = 0.76\% \text{ (the concentration of sodium chloride}$$
$$\text{needed to lower the freezing point by 0.44°,}$$
$$\text{required to make the solution isotonic)}$$

Thus, to make 30 mL of solution,

30 mL $\times$ 1% = 0.3 g = 300 mg dibucaine hydrochloride, and

30 mL $\times$ 0.76% = 0.228 g = 228 mg sodium chloride, *answers.*

Note: Should a prescription call for more than one medicinal and/or pharmaceutic ingredient, the sum of the freezing points is subtracted from the required value in determining the additional lowering required by the agent used to provide isotonicity.

 CALCULATIONS CAPSULE

Isotonicity

To calculate the "equivalent tonic effect" to sodium chloride represented by an ingredient in a preparation, multiply its weight by its *E* value:

g $\times$ E *value* = *g, equivalent tonic effect to sodium chloride*

To make a solution isotonic, calculate and ensure the quantity of sodium chloride and/or the equivalent tonic effect of all other ingredients to total 0.9% w/v in the preparation:

$$\frac{g \ (NaCl) + g \ (NaCl \ tonic \ equivalents)}{mL \ (preparation)} \times 100 = 0.9\% \ w/v$$

To make an isotonic solution from a drug substance, add sufficient water by the equation:

$$\frac{g \ (drug \ substance) \times E \ value \ (drug \ substance)}{0.009} = mL \ water$$

This solution may then be made to any volume with isotonic sodium chloride solution to maintain its isotonicity.

The *E* value can be derived from the same equation, given the grams of drug substance and the milliliters of water required to make an isotonic solution.

CASE IN POINT 11.1[3]: A local ophthalmologist is treating one of his patients for a post-LASIK eye infection that is not responding to topical ciprofloxacin. These infections, although rare, can occur after laser in situ keratomileusis (LASIK) surgery for vision correction.

Topical amikacin sulfate has been shown to be effective for the treatment of eye infections due to ciprofloxacin-resistant *Pseudomonas*,[4-5] *Burkholderia ambifaria*,[6] Mycobacterium chelonae, and *Mycobacterium* fortuitum.[7-9]

The ophthalmologist prescribes 60 mL of a 2.5% amikacin sulfate isotonic solution, 2 drops in the affected eye every 2 hours.
Amikacin sulfate USP ($C_{22}H_{43}N_5O_{13} \cdot 2H_2SO_2$), m.w., 781.76, is an aminoglycoside-type antibiotic containing 3 ions.

(a) Determine the weight in grams of amikacin sulfate needed to prepare the solution.
(b) Calculate the sodium chloride equivalent (*E* value) for amikacin sulfate.
(c) Calculate the amount of sodium chloride needed to make the prepared solution isotonic.
(d) How many milliliters of 23.5 % sodium chloride injection should be used to obtain the needed sodium chloride?

Buffers and Buffer Solutions

When a minute trace of hydrochloric acid is added to pure water, a significant increase in *hydrogen-ion* concentration occurs immediately. In a similar manner, when a minute trace of sodium hydroxide is added to pure water, it causes a correspondingly large increase in the *hydroxyl-ion* concentration. These changes take place because water alone cannot neutralize even traces of acid or base, that is, it has no ability to resist changes in hydrogen-ion concentration or pH. A solution of a neutral salt, such as sodium chloride, also lacks this ability. Therefore, it is said to be *unbuffered*.

The presence of certain substances or combinations of substances in aqueous solution imparts to the system the ability to maintain a desired pH at a relatively constant level, even with the addition of materials that may be expected to change the hydrogen–ion concentration. These substances or combinations of substances are called *buffers*; their ability to resist changes in pH is referred to as *buffer action*; their efficiency is measured by the function known as *buffer capacity*; and solutions of them are called *buffer solutions*. By definition, then, a *buffer solution* is a system, usually an aqueous solution, that possesses the property of resisting changes in pH with the addition of small amounts of a strong acid or base.

Buffers are used to establish and maintain an ion activity within rather narrow limits. In pharmacy, the most common buffer systems are used in (i) the preparation of such dosage forms as injections and ophthalmic solutions, which are placed directly into pH-sensitive body fluids; (ii) the manufacture of formulations in which the pH must be maintained at a relatively constant level to ensure maximum product stability; and (iii) pharmaceutical tests and assays requiring adjustment to or maintenance of a specific pH for analytic purposes.

A buffer solution is usually composed of a weak acid and a salt of the acid, such as acetic acid and sodium acetate, or a weak base and a salt of the base, such as ammonium hydroxide and ammonium chloride. Typical buffer systems that may be used in pharmaceutical formulations include the following pairs: acetic acid and sodium acetate, boric acid and sodium borate, and disodium phosphate and sodium acid phosphate. Formulas for standard buffer solutions for pharmaceutical analysis are given in the *United States Pharmacopeia*.[10]

TABLE 11.3 DISSOCIATION CONSTANTS OF SOME WEAK ACIDS AT 25°C

ACID	K_a
Acetic	1.75×10^{-5}
Barbituric	1.05×10^{-4}
Benzoic	6.30×10^{-5}
Boric	6.4×10^{-10}
Formic	1.76×10^{-4}
Lactic	1.38×10^{-4}
Mandelic	4.29×10^{-4}
Salicylic	1.06×10^{-3}

In the selection of a buffer system, due consideration must be given to the dissociation constant of the weak acid or base to ensure maximum buffer capacity. This dissociation constant, in the case of an acid, is a measure of the strength of the acid; the more readily the acid dissociates, the higher its dissociation constant and the stronger the acid. Selected dissociation constants, or K_a values, are given in Table 11.3.

The dissociation constant, or K_a value, of a weak acid is given by the equation:

$$K_a = \frac{(H^+)\,(A^-)}{(HA)} \qquad \text{where } A^- = \text{salt} \\ HA = \text{acid}$$

Because the numeric values of most dissociation constants are small numbers and may vary over many powers of 10, it is more convenient to express them as negative logarithms:

$$pK_a = -\log K_a$$

When equation $K_a = \dfrac{(H^+)\,(A^-)}{(HA)}$ is expressed in logarithmic form, it is written:

$$pK_a = -\log (H^+) - \log \frac{\text{salt}}{\text{acid}}$$

and because $pH = -\log (H^+)$:

then

$$pK_a = pH - \log \frac{\text{salt}}{\text{acid}}$$

and

$$pH = pK_a + \log \frac{\text{salt}}{\text{acid}}$$

Buffer Equation

The equation just derived is the Henderson-Hasselbalch equation for weak acids, commonly known as the *buffer equation*.

Similarly, the dissociation constant, or K_b value, of a weak base is given by the equation:

$$K_b = \frac{(B^+)\,(OH^-)}{(BOH)} \qquad \text{in which } B^+ = \text{salt} \\ \text{and } BOH = \text{base}$$

and the buffer equation for weak bases, which is derived from this relationship, may be expressed as:

$$pH = pK_w - pK_b + \log \frac{\text{base}}{\text{salt}}$$

The buffer equation is useful for calculating (1) the pH of a buffer system if its composition is known and (2) the molar ratio of the components of a buffer system required to give a solution of a desired pH. The equation can also be used to calculate the change in pH of a buffered solution with the addition of a given amount of acid or base.

pK$_a$ Value of a Weak Acid with Known Dissociation Constant

Calculating the pK$_a$ value of a weak acid, given its dissociation constant, K$_a$:

The dissociation constant of acetic acid is 1.75 $\times$ 10^{-5} at 25°C. Calculate its pK$_a$ value.

$$K_a = 1.75 \times 10^{-5}$$

and
$$\log K_a = \log 1.75 + \log 10^{-5}$$
$$= 0.2430 - 5 = -4.757 \text{ or } -4.76$$

Because
$$pK_a = -\log K_a$$
$$pK_a = -(-4.76) = 4.76, \text{ answer.}$$

pH Value of a Salt/Acid Buffer System

Calculating the pH value:

What is the pH of a buffer solution prepared with 0.05 M sodium borate and 0.005 M boric acid? The pK$_a$ value of boric acid is 9.24 at 25°C.

Note that the ratio of the components of the buffer solution is given in molar concentrations. Using the buffer equation for weak acids:

$$pH = pK_a + \log \frac{\text{salt}}{\text{acid}}$$
$$= 9.24 + \log \frac{0.05}{0.005}$$
$$= 9.24 + \log 10$$
$$= 9.24 + 1$$
$$= 10.24, \text{ answer.}$$

pH Value of a Base/Salt Buffer System

Calculating the pH value:

What is the pH of a buffer solution prepared with 0.05 M ammonia and 0.05 M ammonium chloride? The K$_b$ value of ammonia is 1.80 $\times$ 10^{-5} at 25°C.

Using the buffer equation for weak bases:

$$pH = pK_w - pK_b + \log \frac{\text{base}}{\text{salt}}$$

Because the K$_w$ value for water is 10^{-14} at 25°C, pK$_w$ = 14.

and
$$K_b = 1.80 \times 10^{-5}$$
$$\log K_b = \log 1.8 + \log 10^{-5}$$
$$= 0.2553 - 5 = -4.7447 \text{ or } -4.74$$
$$pK_b = -\log K_b$$
$$= -(-4.74) = 4.74$$

and
$$pH = 14 - 4.74 + \log \frac{0.05}{0.05}$$
$$= 9.26 + \log 1$$
$$= 9.26, \textit{answer.}$$

Molar Ratio of Salt/Acid for a Buffer System of Desired pH

Calculating the molar ratio of salt/acid required to prepare a buffer system with a desired pH value:

What molar ratio of salt/acid is required to prepare a sodium acetate-acetic acid buffer solution with a pH of 5.76? The pK_a value of acetic acid is 4.76 at 25°C.

Using the buffer equation:

$$pH = pK_a + \log \frac{salt}{acid}$$

$$\log \frac{salt}{acid} = pH - pK_a$$

$$= 5.76 - 4.76 = 1$$

antilog of 1 $= 10$
ratio $= 10/1$ or $10:1$, *answer.*

Quantity of Components in a Buffer Solution to Yield a Specific Volume

Calculating the amounts of the components of a buffer solution required to prepare a desired volume, given the molar ratio of the components and the total buffer concentration:

The molar ratio of sodium acetate to acetic acid in a buffer solution with a pH of 5.76 is 10:1. Assuming the total buffer concentration is 2.2×10^{-2} mol/L, how many grams of sodium acetate (m.w. 82) and how many grams of acetic acid (m.w. 60) should be used in preparing a liter of the solution?

Because the molar ratio of sodium acetate to acetic acid is $10:1$,

$$\text{the mole fraction of sodium acetate} = \frac{10}{1 + 10} \text{ or } \frac{10}{11}$$

$$\text{and the mole fraction of acetic acid} = \frac{1}{1 + 10} \text{ or } \frac{1}{11}$$

If the total buffer concentration $= 2.2 \times 10^{-2}$ mol/L,

$$\text{the concentration of sodium acetate} = \frac{10}{11} \times (2.2 \times 10^{-2})$$

$$= 2.0 \times 10^{-2} \text{ mol/L}$$

$$\text{and the concentration of acetic acid} = \frac{1}{11} \times (2.2 \times 10^{-2})$$

$$= 0.2 \times 10^{-2} \text{ mol/L}$$

then 2.0×10^{-2} or $0.02 \times 82 = 1.64$ g of sodium acetate per liter of solution, *and* 0.2×10^{-2} or $0.002 \times 60 = 0.120$ g of acetic acid per liter of solution, *answers.*

The efficiency of buffer solutions—that is, their specific ability to resist changes in pH—is measured in terms of *buffer capacity*; the *smaller* the pH change with the addition of a given amount of acid or base, the *greater* the buffer capacity of the system. Among other factors, the buffer capacity of a system depends on (1) the relative concentration of the buffer components and (2) the ratio of the components. For example, a 0.5 M-acetate buffer at a pH of 4.76 would have a higher buffer capacity than a 0.05 M-buffer.

If a strong base such as sodium hydroxide is added to a buffer system consisting of equimolar concentrations of sodium acetate and acetic acid, the base is neutralized by the acetic acid forming more sodium acetate, and the resulting *increase* in pH is slight. Actually, the addition of the base increases the concentration of sodium acetate and decreases *by an equal amount* the concentration of acetic acid. In a similar manner, the addition of a strong acid to a buffer system consisting of a weak base and its salt would produce only a small *decrease* in pH.

Change in pH with Addition of an Acid or Base

Calculating the change in pH of a buffer solution with the addition of a given amount of acid or base:

Calculate the change in pH after adding 0.04 mol of sodium hydroxide to a liter of a buffer solution containing 0.2 M concentrations of sodium acetate and acetic acid. The pK_a value of acetic acid is 4.76 at 25°C.

The pH of the buffer solution is calculated by using the buffer equation as follows:

$$pH = pK_a + \log \frac{salt}{acid}$$
$$= 4.76 + \log \frac{0.2}{0.2}$$
$$= 4.76 + \log 1$$
$$= 4.76$$

The addition of 0.04 mol of sodium hydroxide converts 0.04 mol of acetic acid to 0.04 mol of sodium acetate. Consequently, the concentration of acetic acid is *decreased* and the concentration of sodium acetate is *increased* by equal amounts, according to the following equation:

$$pH = pK_a + \log \frac{salt + base}{acid - base}$$
$$\text{and} \qquad pH = pK_a + \log \frac{0.2 + 0.04}{0.2 - 0.04}$$
$$= pK_a + \log \frac{0.24}{0.16}$$
$$= 4.76 + 0.1761 = 4.9361 \text{ or } 4.94$$

Because the pH before the addition of the sodium hydroxide was 4.76, the change in pH = 4.94 − 4.76 = 0.18 unit, *answer.*

PRACTICE PROBLEMS

Calculations of Tonicity

1. Isotonic sodium chloride solution contains 0.9% w/v sodium chloride. If the E value of boric acid is 0.52, calculate the percentage strength (w/v) of an isotonic solution of boric acid.

2. Sodium chloride is a 2-ion electrolyte, dissociating 90% in a certain concentration. Calculate (a) its dissociation factor, and (b) the freezing point of a molal solution.

3. A solution of anhydrous dextrose (m.w. 180) contains 25 g in 500 mL of water. Calculate the freezing point of the solution.

4. Procaine hydrochloride (m.w. 273) is a 2-ion electrolyte, dissociating 80% in a certain concentration.
   (a) Calculate its dissociation factor.
   (b) Calculate its sodium chloride equivalent.
   (c) Calculate the freezing point of a molal solution of procaine hydrochloride.

5. The freezing point of a molal solution of a nonelectrolyte is −1.86°C. What is the freezing point of a 0.1% solution of zinc chloride (m.w. 136), dissociating 80%? (For lack of more definite information, assume that the volume of the molal solution is approximately 1 liter.)

6. The freezing point of a 5% solution of boric acid is −1.55°C. How many grams of boric acid should be used in preparing 1000 mL of an isotonic solution?

7. ℞ Ephedrine Sulfate   0.3 g
   Sodium Chloride   q.s.
   Purified Water ad   30 mL
   Make isoton. sol.
   Sig. Use as directed.

   How many milligrams of sodium chloride should be used in compounding the prescription?

8. ℞ Dipivefrin Hydrochloride ½%
   Scopolamine Hydrobro-
      mide   ⅓%
   Sodium Chloride   q.s.
   Purified Water ad   30
   Make isoton. sol.
   Sig. Use in the eye.

   How many grams of sodium chloride should be used in compounding the prescription?

9. ℞ Zinc Sulfate   0.06
   Boric Acid   q.s.
   Purified Water ad   30
   Make isoton. sol.
   Sig. Drop in eyes.

   How many grams of boric acid should be used in compounding the prescription?

10. ℞ Cromolyn Sodium   4% (w/v)
    Benzalkonium Chloride   1:10,000
                            (w/v)
    Buffer Solution (pH 5.6) q.s.
    Water for Injection ad 10 mL
    Sig. One (1) drop in each eye b.i.d.

    How many milliliters of the buffer solution (E = 0.30) should be used to render the solution isotonic?

11. Dextrose, anhydrous 2.5%
    Sodium Chloride q.s.
    Sterile Water for Injection ad 1000 mL
    Label: Isotonic Dextrose and Saline Solution.

    How many grams of sodium chloride should be used in preparing the solution?

12. ℞ Sol. Silver Nitrate 0.5%   15
    Make isoton. sol.
    Sig. For the eyes.

    How many grams of potassium nitrate should be used to make the prescription isotonic?

13. ℞ Cocaine Hydrochloride   0.15
    Sodium Chloride   q.s.
    Purified Water ad   15
    Make isoton. sol.
    Sig. One drop in left eye.

    How many grams of sodium chloride should be used in compounding the prescription?

14. ℞   Cocaine Hydrochloride   0.6
     Eucatropine Hydro-
          chloride   0.6
     Chlorobutanol   0.1
     Sodium Chloride   q.s.
     Purified Water   ad   30
     Make isoton. sol.
     Sig. For the eye.

How many grams of sodium chloride should be used in compounding the prescription?

15. ℞   Tetracaine Hydrochloride 0.1
     Zinc Sulfate   0.05
     Boric Acid   q.s.
     Purified Water   ad   30
     Make isoton. sol.
     Sig. Drop in eye.

How many grams of boric acid should be used in compounding the prescription?

16. ℞   Sol. Homatropine Hydro-
          bromide 1%   15
     Make isoton. sol. with boric acid.
     Sig. For the eye.

How many grams of boric acid should be used in compounding the prescription?

17. ℞   Procaine Hydrochloride   1%
     Sodium Chloride   q.s.
     Sterile Water for
          Injection   ad   100
     Make isoton. sol.
     Sig. For injection.

How many grams of sodium chloride should be used in compounding the prescription?

18. ℞   Phenylephrine Hydro-
          chloride   1%
     Chlorobutanol   0.5%
     Sodium Chloride   q.s.
     Purified Water   ad   15
     Make isoton. sol.
     Sig. Use as directed.

How many milliliters of an 0.9% solution of sodium chloride should be used in compounding the prescription?

19. ℞   Oxymetazoline Hydro-
          chloride   ½%
     Boric Acid Solution   q.s.
     Purified Water   ad   15
     Make isoton. sol.
     Sig. For the nose, as decongestant.

How many milliliters of a 5% solution of boric acid should be used in compounding the prescription?

20. ℞   Ephedrine Hydrochloride 0.5
     Chlorobutanol   0.25
     Dextrose, monohydrate   q.s.
     Rose Water   ad   50
     Make isoton. sol.
     Sig. Nose drops.

How many grams of dextrose monohydrate should be used in compounding the prescription?

21. ℞   Naphazoline Hydro-
          chloride   1%
     Sodium Chloride   q.s.
     Purified Water   ad   30 mL
     Make isoton. sol.
     Sig. Use as directed in the eye.

How many grams of sodium chloride should be used in compounding the prescription? Use the freezing point depression method.

22. ℞   Oxytetracycline Hydro-
          chloride   0.05
     Chlorobutanol   0.1
     Sodium Chloride   q.s.
     Purified Water   ad   30
     Make isoton. sol.
     Sig. Eye drops.

How many milligrams of sodium chloride should be used in compounding the prescription?

23. ℞ Tetracaine Hydrochloride 0.5%
    Sol. Epinephrine Bitar-
       trate 1:1000   10
    Boric Acid   q.s.
    Purified Water   ad   30
    Make isoton. sol.
    Sig. Eye drops.

The solution of epinephrine bitartrate (1:1000) is already isotonic. How many grams of boric acid should be used in compounding the prescription?

24.   Monobasic Sodium
          Phosphate, anhydrous 5.6 g
       Dibasic Sodium Phos-
          phate, anhydrous   2.84 g
       Sodium Chloride   q.s.
       Purified Water   ad   1000 mL
       Label: Isotonic Buffer
          Solution, pH 6.5.

How many grams of sodium chloride should be used in preparing the solution?

25. How many grams of anhydrous dextrose should be used in preparing 1 liter of a ½% isotonic ephedrine sulfate nasal spray?

26. ℞ Ephedrine Sulfate   1%
    Chlorobutanol   ½%
    Purified Water   ad   100
    Make isoton. sol. and buffer to pH 6.5
    Sig. Nose drops.

You have on hand an isotonic buffered solution, pH 6.5. How many milliliters of purified water and how many milliliters of the buffered solution should be used in compounding the prescription?

27. ℞ Oxytetracycline Hydro-
          chloride   0.5%
       Tetracaine Hydrochloride
          Sol. 2%   15 mL
       Sodium Chloride   q.s.
       Purified Water   ad   30 mL
       Make isoton. sol.
       Sig. For the eye.

The 2% solution of tetracaine hydrochloride is already isotonic. How many milliliters of an 0.9% solution of sodium chloride should be used in compounding the prescription?

28. Determine if the following commercial products are hypotonic, isotonic, or hypertonic:
    (a) An ophthalmic solution containing 40 mg/mL of cromolyn sodium and 0.01% of benzalkonium chloride in purified water.
    (b) A parenteral infusion containing 20% (w/v) of mannitol.
    (c) A 500-mL large volume parenteral containing D5W (5% w/v of anhydrous dextrose in sterile water for injection).
    (d) A FLEET saline enema containing 19 g of monobasic sodium phosphate (monohydrate) and 7 g of dibasic sodium phosphate (heptahydrate) in 118 mL of aqueous solution.

29. For agents having the following sodium chloride equivalents, calculate the percentage concentration of an isotonic solution:
    (a) 0.20
    (b) 0.32
    (c) 0.61

30. How many milliliters each of purified water and an isotonic sodium chloride solution should be used to prepare 30 mL of a 1% w/v isotonic solution of fentanyl citrate ($E = 0.11$)?

31. Using the E values in Table 11.1, calculate the number of milliliters of water required to make an isotonic solution from 0.3 g of each of the following:
    (a) antipyrine
    (b) chlorobutanol
    (c) ephedrine sulfate
    (d) silver nitrate
    (e) zinc sulfate

32. Calculate the E values for each of the following, given that the number of milliliters of water shown will produce an isotonic solution from 0.3 g of drug substance.
    (a) apomorphine hydrochloride, 4.7 mL water
    (b) ethylmorphine hydrochloride, 5.3 mL water
    (c) holocaine hydrochloride, 6.7 mL water
    (d) procainamide hydrochloride, 7.3 mL water
    (e) viomycin sulfate, 2.7 mL water

Calculations of Buffer Solutions

33. The dissociation constant of ethanolamine is 2.77×10^{-5} at 25°C. Calculate its pK_b value.

34. What is the pH of a buffer solution prepared with 0.055 M sodium acetate and 0.01 M acetic acid? The pK_a value of acetic acid is 4.76 at 25°C.

35. What is the pH of a buffer solution prepared with 0.5 M disodium phosphate and 1 M sodium acid phosphate? The pK_a value of sodium acid phosphate is 7.21 at 25°C.

36. What molar ratio of salt to acid would be required to prepare a buffer solution with a pH of 4.5? The pK_a value of the acid is 4.05 at 25°C.

37. What is the change in pH on adding 0.02 mol of sodium hydroxide to a liter of a buffer solution containing 0.5 M of sodium acetate and 0.5 M acetic acid? The pK_a value of acetic acid is 4.76 at 25°C.

38. The molar ratio of salt to acid needed to prepare a sodium acetate-acetic acid buffer solution is 1:1. Assuming that the total buffer concentration is 0.1 mol/L, how many grams of sodium acetate (m.w. 60) should be used in preparing 2 liters of the solution?

39. What is the change in pH with the addition of 0.01 moL hydrochloric acid to a liter of a buffer solution containing 0.05 M of ammonia and 0.05 M of ammonium chloride? The K_b value of ammonia is 1.80×10^{-5} at 25°C.

ANSWERS TO "CASE IN POINT" AND PRACTICE PROBLEMS

Case in Point 11.1

(a) 60 mL × 2.5% w/v = 1.5 g amikacin sulfate, *answer.*
(b) sodium chloride m.w. = 58.5
    amikacin m.w. = 781.76

    $i = 2.6$

    $$\frac{58.5}{1.8} \times \frac{2.6}{781.76} = E$$

    $E = 0.108$, *answer.*

(c) 60 mL × 0.9% w/v = 0.54 g sodium chloride, *answer.*
(d) 1.5 g (amikacin sulfate) × 0.108 (NaCl equivalent) = 0.162 g
    0.54 g − 0.162g = 0.378 g sodium chloride required for isotonicity

    $$\frac{23.5 \text{ g}}{100 \text{ mL}} = \frac{0.378 \text{ g}}{x \text{ mL}},$$

    $x = 1.61$ mL sodium chloride injection, *answer.*

Practice Problems

1. 1.73% w/v

2. (a) 1.9
   (b) −3.53°C

3. −0.52°C

4. (a) 1.8
   (b) 0.21
   (c) −3.35°C

5. −0.036°C

6. 16.8 g

7. 201 mg sodium chloride

8. 0.236 g sodium chloride

9. 0.502 g boric acid

10. 0.153 mL buffer solution

11. 4.5 g sodium chloride

12. 0.19 g potassium nitrate

13. 0.111 g sodium chloride

14. 0.042 g sodium chloride

15. 0.47 g boric acid

16. 0.211 g boric acid

17. 0.69 g sodium chloride

18. 7.667 mL sodium chloride solution

19. 4.62 mL boric acid solution

20. 1.531 g dextrose monohydrate

21. 0.189 g sodium chloride

22. 240 mg sodium chloride

23. 0.294 g boric acid

24. 4.751 g sodium chloride

25. 43.61 g anhydrous dextrose

26. 38.89 mL purified water
    61.11 mL buffered solution

27. 13 mL sodium chloride solution

28. (a) hypotonic
    (b) hypertonic
    (c) isotonic
    (d) hypertonic

29. (a) 4.5%
    (b) 2.81%
    (c) 1.48%

30. 3.67 mL purified water
    26.33 mL sodium chloride solution

31. (a) 5.7 mL water
    (b) 8.0 mL water
    (c) 7.7 mL water
    (d) 11.0 mL water
    (e) 5.0 mL water

32. (a) 0.14
    (b) 0.16
    (c) 0.20
    (d) 0.22
    (e) 0.08

33. 4.56

34. 5.5

35. 6.91

36. 2.82:1

37. 0.03 unit

38. 8.2 g
    6.0 g

39. 0.18 unit

REFERENCES

1. Reich I, Poon CY, Sugita ET. Tonicity, osmoticity, osmolality, and osmolarity. In: Gennaro AR, ed. *Remington: The Science and Practice of Pharmacy*. 20th Ed. Baltimore: Lippincott Williams & Wilkins, 2000:246–250.
2. Ansel HC, Prince SJ. Pharmaceutical calculations. In: *The Pharmacist's Handbook*. Baltimore: Lippincott Williams & Wilkins, 2004:111.
3. Beach W, Athens, GA: College of Pharmacy, University of Georgia, 2004.
4. Titcomb LC. *Pharmaceutical Journal* 2000;264:441–445.
5. Garg P, et al. *Ophthalmology* 1999;106:1319–1323.
6. Matoba AY. *American Journal of Ophthalmology* 2003;136:748–749.
7. Chung MS, et al. *American Journal of Ophthalmology* 2000;129:382–384.
8. Chandra NS, et al. *American Journal of Ophthalmology* 2001;132:819–830.
9. Ford JG, et al. *Ophthalmology* 1998;105:1652–1658.
10. United States Pharmacopeia 31st Rev. National Formulary 26. Rockville, MD: United States Pharmacopeial Convention, 2008;1:813–814.

12

Electrolyte Solutions: Milliequivalents, Millimoles, and Milliosmoles

Objectives

Upon successful completion of this chapter, the student will be able to:

- Calculate the milliequivalent weight from an atomic or formula weight.
- Convert between milligrams and milliequivalents.
- Calculate problems involving milliequivalents.
- Calculate problems involving millimoles and milliosmoles.

As noted in Chapter 11, the molecules of chemical compounds in solution may remain intact, or they may dissociate into particles known as **ions,** which carry an electric charge. Substances that are not dissociated in solution are called **nonelectrolytes**, and those with varying degrees of dissociation are called **electrolytes**. Urea and dextrose are examples of nonelectrolytes in body water; sodium chloride in body fluids is an example of an electrolyte.

Sodium chloride in solution provides Na^+ and Cl^- ions, which carry electric charges. If electrodes carrying a weak current are placed in the solution, the ions move in a direction opposite to the charges. Na^+ ions move to the negative electrode (*cathode*) and are called *cations*. Cl^- ions move to the positive electrode (*anode*) and are called *anions*.

Electrolyte ions in the blood plasma include the cations Na^+, K^+, Ca^{++}, and Mg^{++} and the anions Cl^-, HCO_3^-, HPO_4^{--}, SO_4^{--}, organic acids$^-$, and protein$^-$. Electrolytes in body fluids play an important role in maintaining the acid-base balance in the body. They play a part in controlling body water volumes and help to regulate body metabolism.

Applicable Dosage Forms

Electrolyte preparations are used in the treatment of disturbances of the electrolyte and fluid balance in the body. In clinical practice, they are provided in the form of oral solutions and syrups, as dry granules intended to be dissolved in water or juice to make an oral solution, as oral tablets and capsules and, when necessary, as intravenous infusions.

Milliequivalents

A *chemical unit*, the **milliequivalent (mEq),** is now used almost exclusively in the United States by clinicians, physicians, pharmacists, and manufacturers to express the concentration of electrolytes in solution. This unit of measure is related to the total number of ionic charges in solution, and it takes note of the valence of the ions. In other words, it is a unit of measurement of the amount of *chemical activity* of an electrolyte. In the International System (SI), which is used in European countries and in many others throughout the world, molar concentrations [as milli-

TABLE 12.1 BLOOD PLASMA ELECTROLYTES IN MILLIEQUIVALENTS PER LITER (mEq/L)

CATIONS	mEq/L	ANIONS	mEq/L
Na^+	142	HCO_3^-	24
K^+	5	Cl^-	105
Ca^{++}	5	HPO_4^{--}	2
Mg^{++}	2	SO_4^{--}	1
		Org. Ac.$^-$	6
		Proteinate$^-$	16
	154		154

moles per liter (mmol/L) and micromoles per liter (μmol/L)] are used to express most clinical laboratory values, including those of electrolytes.

Under normal conditions, blood plasma contains 154 mEq of cations and an equal number of anions (Table 12.1). However, it should be understood that normal laboratory values of electrolytes vary, albeit within a rather narrow range, as shown in Table 12.2. The total concentration of cations always equals the total concentration of anions. Any number of milliequivalents of Na^+, K^+, or any cation$^+$ always reacts with precisely the same number of milliequivalents of Cl^-, HCO_3^-, or any anion$^-$. *For a given chemical compound, the milliequivalents of cation equals the milliequivalents of anion equals the milliequivalents of the chemical compound.*

In preparing a solution of K^+ ions, a potassium salt is dissolved in water. In addition to the K^+ ions, the solution will also contain ions of opposite negative charge. These two components will be chemically equal in that the milliequivalents of one are equal to the milliequivalents of the other. The interesting point is that if we dissolve enough potassium chloride in water to give us 40 mEq of K^+ per liter, we also have exactly 40 mEq of Cl^-, but the solution will *not* contain the *same weight* of each ion.

A milliequivalent represents the amount, in milligrams, of a solute equal to $\frac{1}{1000}$ of its gram equivalent weight, taking into account the valence of the ions. The milliequivalent expresses the chemical activity or combining power of a substance relative to the activity of 1 mg of hydrogen. Thus, based on the atomic weight and valence of the species, 1 mEq is represented by 1 mg of hydrogen, 20 mg of calcium, 23 mg of sodium, 35.5 mg of chlorine, 39 mg of potassium, and

TABLE 12.2 USUAL REFERENCE RANGE OF BLOOD SERUM VALUES FOR SOME ELECTROLYTES[a]

CATION/ANION	mEq/L	SI UNITS (mmol/L)
Sodium	135–145	135–145
Potassium	3.5–5.5	3.5–5.5
Calcium	4.6–5.5	2.3–2.75
Magnesium	1.5–2.5	0.75–1.25
Chloride	96–106	96–106
Carbon Dioxide	24–30	24–30
Phosphorus	2.5–4.5	0.8–1.5

[a] Reference ranges may vary slightly between clinical laboratories based, in part, on the analytical methods and equipment used.

TABLE 12.3 VALUES FOR SOME IMPORTANT IONS

ION	FORMULA	VALENCE	ATOMIC OR FORMULA WEIGHT	EQUIVALENT WEIGHT[a]
Aluminum	Al^{+++}	3	27	9
Ammonium	NH_4^+	1	18	18
Calcium	Ca^{++}	2	40	20
Ferric	Fe^{+++}	3	56	18.7
Ferrous	Fe^{++}	2	56	28
Lithium	Li^+	1	7	7
Magnesium	Mg^{++}	2	24	12
Potassium	K^+	1	39	39
Sodium	Na^+	1	23	23
Acetate	$C_2H_3O_2^-$	1	59	59
Bicarbonate	HCO_3^-	1	61	61
Carbonate	CO_3^{--}	2	60	30
Chloride	Cl^-	1	35.5	35.5
Citrate	$C_6H_5O_7^{---}$	3	189	63
Gluconate	$C_6H_{11}O_7^-$	1	195	195
Lactate	$C_3H_5O_3^-$	1	89	89
Phosphate	$H_2PO_4^-$	1	97	97
	HPO_4^{--}	2	96	48
Sulfate	SO_4^{--}	2	96	48

[a] Equivalent weight $= \dfrac{Atomic\ or\ formula\ weight}{Valence}$

so forth. Important values for some ions are presented in Table 12.3, and a complete listing of atomic weights is provided on the back inside cover of this text.

The concentration of electrolytes in intravenous infusion fluids is most often stated in mEq/L.

Example Calculations of Milliequivalents

To convert the concentration of electrolytes in solution expressed as milliequivalents per unit volume to weight per unit volume and vice versa, use the following:

CALCULATIONS CAPSULE

Milliequivalents

To convert milligrams (mg) to milliequivalents (mEq):

$$mEq = \frac{mg \times Valence}{Atomic,\ formular,\ or\ molecular\ weight}$$

To convert milliequivalents (mEq) to milligrams (mg):

$$mg = \frac{mEq \times Atomic,\ formula,\ or\ molecular\ weight}{Valence}$$

To convert milliequivalents per milliliter (mEq/mL) to milligrams per milliliter (mg/mL):

$$mg/mL = \frac{mEq/mL \times Atomic,\ formula,\ or\ molecular\ weight}{Valence}$$

$$mEq = \frac{mg \times Valence}{Atomic,\ formula,\ or\ molecular\ weight}$$

$$mg = \frac{mEq \times Atomic,\ formula,\ or\ molecular\ weight}{Valence}$$

$$mg/mL = \frac{mEq\ /\ mL \times Atomic,\ formula,\ or\ molecular\ weight}{Valence}$$

What is the concentration, in milligrams per milliliter, of a solution containing 2 mEq of potassium chloride (KCl) per milliliter?

Molecular weight of KCl = 74.5
Equivalent weight of KCl = 74.5
1 mEq of KCl = $\frac{1}{1000} \times 74.5$ g = 0.0745 g = 74.5 mg
2 mEq of KCl = 74.5 mg × 2 = 149 mg/mL, *answer.*

Or, by using the preceding equation:

$$mg/mL = \frac{2\ (mEq/mL) \times 74.5}{1}$$
$$= 149\ mg/mL,\ answer.$$

What is the concentration, in grams per milliliter, of a solution containing 4 mEq of calcium chloride ($CaCl_2 \cdot 2H_2O$) *per milliliter?*

Recall that the equivalent weight of a binary compound may be found by dividing the formula weight by the *total valence* of the positive or negative radical.

Formula weight of $CaCl_2 \cdot 2H_2O$ = 147
Equivalent weight of $CaCl_2 \cdot 2H_2O$ = $^{147}\!/_2$ = 73.5
1 mEq of $CaCl_2 \cdot 2H_2O$ = $\frac{1}{1000} \times 73.5$ g = 0.0735 g
4 mEq of $CaCl_2 \cdot 2H_2O$ = 0.0735 g × 4 = 0.294 g/mL, *answer.*

Or, solving by dimensional analysis:

$$\frac{1\ g\ CaCl_2 \cdot 2H_2O}{1000\ mg\ CaCl_2 \cdot 2H_2O} \times \frac{147\ mg}{1\ mmole} \times \frac{1\ mmole}{2\ mEq} \times \frac{4\ mEq}{1\ mL} = 0.294\ g/mL,\ answer.$$

Note: The water of hydration molecules does not interfere in the calculations as long as the correct molecular weight is used.

What is the percent (w/v) concentration of a solution containing 100 mEq of ammonium chloride per liter?

Molecular weight of NH_4Cl = 53.5
Equivalent weight of NH_4Cl = 53.5
1 mEq of NH_4Cl = $\frac{1}{1000} \times 53.5$ = 0.0535 g
100 mEq of NH_4Cl = 0.0535 g × 100 = 5.35 g/L or
0.535 g per 100 mL, or 0.535%, *answer.*

A solution contains 10 mg/100 mL of K^+ *ions. Express this concentration in terms of milliequivalents per liter.*

Atomic weight of K^+ = 39
Equivalent weight of K^+ = 39
1 mEq of K^+ = $\frac{1}{1000} \times 39$ g = 0.039 g = 39 mg
10 mg/100 mL of K^+ = 100 mg of K^+ per liter
100 mg ÷ 39 = 2.56 mEq/L, *answer.*

Or, by the equation detailed previously:

$$mEq/L = \frac{100 \ (mg/L) \times 1}{39}$$
$$= 2.56 \ mEq/L, \ answer.$$

A solution contains 10 mg/100 mL of Ca⁺⁺ ions. Express this concentration in terms of milliequivalents per liter.

Atomic weight of Ca^{++} = 40
Equivalent weight of Ca^{++} = $^{40}\!/_2$ = 20
1 mEq of Ca^{++} = $^1\!/_{1000}$ × 20 g = 0.020 g = 20 mg
10 mg/100 mL of Ca^{++} = 100 mg of Ca^{++} per liter
100 mg ÷ 20 = 5 mEq/L, *answer.*

A magnesium (Mg⁺⁺) level in blood plasma is determined to be 2.5 mEq/L. Express this concentration in terms of milligrams.

Atomic weight of Mg^{++} = 24
Equivalent weight of Mg^{++} = $^{24}\!/_2$ = 12
1 mEq of Mg^{++} = $^1\!/_{1000}$ × 12 g = 0.012 g = 12 mg
2.5 mEq of Mg^{++} = 30 mg
30 mg/L, *answer.*

How many milliequivalents of potassium chloride are represented in a 15-mL dose of a 10% (w/v) potassium chloride elixir?

Molecular weight of KCl = 74.5
Equivalent weight of KCl = 74.5
1 mEq of KCl = $^1\!/_{1000}$ × 74.5 g = 0.0745 g = 74.5 mg
15-mL dose of 10% (w/v) elixir = 1.5 g or 1500 mg of KCl
$$\frac{74.5 \ (mg)}{1500 \ (mg)} = \frac{1 \ (mEq)}{x \ (mEq)}$$
x = 20.1 mEq, *answer.*

How many milliequivalents of magnesium sulfate are represented in 1 g of anhydrous magnesium sulfate (MgSO₄)?

Molecular weight of $MgSO_4$ = 120
Equivalent weight of $MgSO_4$ = 60
1 mEq of $MgSO_4$ = $^1\!/_{1000}$ × 60 g = 0.06 g = 60 mg
1.0 g of $MgSO_4$ = 1000 mg
$$\frac{60 \ (mg)}{1000 \ (mg)} = \frac{1 \ (mEq)}{x \ (mEq)}$$
x = 16.7 mEq, *answer.*

How many milliequivalents of Na⁺ would be contained in a 30-mL dose of the following solution?

Disodium hydrogen phosphate	18 g
Sodium biphosphate	48 g
Purified water ad	100 mL

Each salt is considered separately in solving the problem.

Disodium hydrogen phosphate

$$\text{Formula} = Na_2HPO_4.7H_2O$$
$$\text{Molecular weight} = 268 \text{ and the equivalent weight} = 134$$
$$\frac{18 \text{ (g)}}{x \text{ (g)}} = \frac{100 \text{ (mL)}}{30 \text{ (mL)}}$$
$$x = 5.4 \text{ g of disodium hydrogen phosphate per 30 mL}$$
$$1 \text{ mEq} = \frac{1}{1000} \times 134 \text{ g} = 0.134 \text{ g} = 134 \text{ mg}$$
$$\frac{134 \text{ (mg)}}{5400 \text{ (mg)}} = \frac{1 \text{ (mEq)}}{x \text{ (mEq)}}$$
$$x = 40.3 \text{ mEq of disodium hydrogen phosphate}$$

Because the milliequivalent value of Na^+ ion equals the milliequivalent value of disodium hydrogen phosphate, then

$$x = 40.3 \text{ mEq of } Na^+$$

Sodium biphosphate

$$\text{Formula} = NaH_2PO_4.H_2O$$
$$\text{Molecular weight} = 138 \text{ and the equivalent weight} = 138$$
$$\frac{48 \text{ (g)}}{x \text{ (g)}} = \frac{100 \text{ (mL)}}{30 \text{ (mL)}}$$
$$x = 14.4 \text{ g of sodium biphosphate per 30 mL}$$
$$1 \text{ mEq} = \frac{1}{1000} \times 138 \text{ g} = 0.138 \text{ g} = 138 \text{ mg}$$
$$\frac{138 \text{ (mg)}}{14,400 \text{ (mg)}} = \frac{1 \text{ (mEq)}}{x \text{ (mEq)}}$$
$$x = 104.3 \text{ mEq of sodium biphosphate}$$
$$\text{and also,} = 104.3 \text{ mEq of } Na^+$$

Adding the two milliequivalent values for Na^+ = 40.3 mEq + 104.3 mEq = 144.6 mEq, *answer*.

A person is to receive 2 mEq of sodium chloride per kilogram of body weight. If the person weighs 132 lb., how many milliliters of a 0.9% sterile solution of sodium chloride should be administered?

$$\text{Molecular weight of NaCl} = 58.5$$
$$\text{Equivalent weight of NaCl} = 58.5$$
$$1 \text{ mEq of NaCl} = \frac{1}{1000} \times 58.5 \text{ g} = 0.0585 \text{ g}$$
$$2 \text{ mEq of NaCl} = 0.0585 \text{ g} \times 2 = 0.117 \text{ g}$$
$$1 \text{ kg} = 2.2 \text{ lb.} \qquad \text{Weight of person in kg} = \frac{132 \text{ lb.}}{2.2 \text{ lb.}} = 60 \text{ kg}$$

Because the person is to receive 2 mEq/kg, then 2 mEq or 0.117 g × 60 = 7.02 g of NaCl needed and because 0.9% sterile solution of sodium chloride contains

9 g of NaCl per liter,

then

$$\frac{9 \text{ (g)}}{7.02 \text{ (g)}} = \frac{1000 \text{ (mL)}}{x \text{ (mL)}}$$
$$x = 780 \text{ mL, } answer.$$

Millimoles and Micromoles

As noted previously, the SI expresses electrolyte concentrations in *millimoles per liter (mmol/L)* in representing the combining power of a chemical species. For monovalent species, the numeric values of the milliequivalent and millimole are identical.

A *mole* is the molecular weight of a substance in grams. A *millimole* is one thousandth of a mole and a *micromole* is one millionth of a mole.

Example Calculations of Millimoles and Micromoles

How many millimoles of monobasic sodium phosphate (m.w. 138) are present in 100 g of the substance?

$$m.w. = 138$$
$$1 \text{ mole} = 138 \text{ g}$$
$$\frac{1 \text{ (mole)}}{x \text{ (mole)}} = \frac{138 \text{ (g)}}{100 \text{ (g)}}$$
$$x = 0.725 \text{ moles} = 725 \text{ mmol, } answer.$$

How many milligrams would 1 mmol of monobasic sodium phosphate weigh?

$$1 \text{ mole } = 138 \text{ g}$$
$$1 \text{ mmol } = 0.138 \text{ g} = 138 \text{ mg, } answer.$$

What is the weight, in milligrams, of 1 mmol of $HPO_4^=$?

$$\text{Atomic weight of } HPO_4^= = 95.98$$
$$1 \text{ mole of } HPO_4^= = 95.98 \text{ g}$$
$$1 \text{ mmol of } HPO_4^= = 95.98 \text{ g} \times \frac{1}{1000} = 0.09598 \text{ g}$$
$$= 95.98 \text{ mg, } answer.$$

Convert blood plasma levels of 0.5 µg/mL and 2µg/mL of tobramycin (mw = 467.52) to µmol/L.[1]

By dimensional analysis:

$$\frac{0.5 \text{ } \mu g}{1 \text{ mL}} \times \frac{1 \text{ } \mu mol}{467.52 \text{ } \mu g} \times \frac{1000 \text{ mL}}{1 \text{ L}} = 1.07 \text{ } \mu mol/L$$

and,

$$\frac{2 \text{ } \mu g}{1 \text{ mL}} \times \frac{1 \text{ } \mu mol}{467.52 \text{ } \mu g} \times \frac{1000 \text{ mL}}{1 \text{ L}} = 4.28 \text{ } \mu mol/L, \text{ } answers.$$

Osmolarity

As indicated in Chapter 11, osmotic pressure is important to biologic processes that involve the diffusion of solutes or the transfer of fluids through semipermeable membranes. The *United States Pharmacopeia*[2] states that knowledge of the osmolar concentrations of parenteral fluids is important. The labels of pharmacopeial solutions that provide intravenous replenishment of fluid, nutrients, or electrolytes, and the osmotic diuretic mannitol are required to state the osmolar concentration. This information indicates to the practitioner whether the solution is hypo-osmotic, iso-osmotic, or hyperosmotic with regard to biologic fluids and membranes.

Osmotic pressure is proportional to the *total number* of particles in solution. The unit used to measure osmotic concentration is the *milliosmole* (mOsmol). For dextrose, a nonelectrolyte, 1 mmol (1 formula weight in milligrams) represents 1 mOsmol. This relationship is not the same with electrolytes, however, because the total number of particles in solution depends on the degree of dissociation of the substance in question. Assuming complete dissociation, 1 mmol of NaCl represents 2 mOsmol ($Na^+ + Cl^-$) of total particles, 1 mmol of $CaCl_2$ represents 3 mOsmol (Ca^{++} + $2Cl^-$) of total particles, and 1 mmol of sodium citrate ($Na_3C_6H_5O_7$) represents 4 mOsmol ($3Na^+$ + $C_6H_5O_7^-$) of total particles.

The milliosmolar value of *separate* ions of an electrolyte may be obtained by dividing the concentration, in milligrams per liter, of the ion by its atomic weight. The milliosmolar value of the *whole* electrolyte in solution is equal to the sum of the milliosmolar values of the separate ions. According to the *United States Pharmacopeia*, the ideal osmolar concentration may be calculated according to the equation[2]:

$$mOsmol/L = \frac{\text{Weight of substance (g/L)}}{\text{Molecular weight (g)}} \times \text{Number of species} \times 1000$$

In practice, as the concentration of the solute increases, physicochemical interaction among solute particles increases, and actual osmolar values decrease when compared to ideal values. Deviation from ideal conditions is usually slight in solution within the physiologic range and for more dilute solutions, but for highly concentrated solutions, the actual osmolarities may be appreciably lower than ideal values. For example, the ideal osmolarity of 0.9% sodium chloride injection is:

$$mOsmol/L = \frac{9 \text{ g/L}}{58.5 \text{ g}} \times 2 \times 1000 = 308 \text{ mOsmol/L}$$

Because of bonding forces, however, n is slightly less than 2 for solutions of sodium chloride at this concentration, and the actual measured osmolarity of the solution is about 286 mOsmol/L.

Some pharmaceutical manufacturers label electrolyte solutions with ideal or stoichiometric osmolarities calculated by the equation just provided, whereas others list experimental or actual osmolarities. The pharmacist should appreciate this distinction.

A distinction also should be made between the terms *osmolarity* and *osmolality*. Whereas **osmolarity** *is the milliosmoles of solute per liter of solution,* **osmolality** *is the milliosmoles of solute per kilogram of solvent.* For dilute aqueous solutions, osmolarity and osmolality are nearly identical. For more concentrated solutions, however, the two values may be quite dissimilar. The pharmacist should pay particular attention to a product's label statement regarding molarity versus molality.

Normal serum osmolality is considered to be within the range of 275 to 300 mOsmol/kg. The contribution of various constituents to the osmolality of normal serum is shown in Table 12.4. *Osmometers* are commercially available for use in the laboratory to measure osmolality.[3] Abnormal blood osmolality that deviates from the normal range can occur in association with shock, trauma, burns, water intoxication (overload), electrolyte imbalance, hyperglycemia, or renal failure.[3]

Example Calculations of Milliosmoles

A solution contains 5% of anhydrous dextrose in water for injection. How many milliosmoles per liter are represented by this concentration?

Formula weight of anhydrous dextrose = 180
1 mmol of anhydrous dextrose (180 mg) = 1 mOsmol
5% solution contains 50 g or 50,000 mg/L
50,000 mg ÷ 180 = 278 mOsmol/L, *answer.*

Or, solving by dimensional analysis:

$$\frac{50,000 \text{ mg}}{1 \text{ L}} \times \frac{1 \text{ mOsmol}}{180 \text{ mg}} = 278 \text{ mOsmol/L, } answer.$$

TABLE 12.4 THE CONTRIBUTION OF VARIOUS CONSTITUENTS OF NORMAL HUMAN SERUM TO THE TOTAL SERUM OSMOTIC PRESSURE[a]

CONSTITUENT	MEAN CONCENTRATION (mEq/L)	OSMOTIC PRESSURE (mOsmol/kg of water)[b]	PERCENTAGE OF TOTAL OSMOTIC PRESSURE
Sodium	142.0	139.0	48.3%
Potassium	5.0	4.9	1.7
Calcium	2.5	1.2	0.4
Magnesium	2.0	1.0	0.3
Chloride	102.0	99.8	34.7
Bicarbonate	27.0	26.4	9.2
Proteinate	16.0	1.0	0.3
Phosphate	2.0	1.1	0.4
Sulfate	1.0	0.5	0.2
Organic Anions	3.5	3.4	1.2
Urea	30 (mg/100 mL)	5.3	1.8
Glucose	70 (mg/100 mL)	4.1	1.4
TOTALS		287.7 mOsmol/kg	99.9%
OBSERVED NORMAL MEAN		289.0 mOsmol/kg	

[a] From Chughtai MA, Hendry EB. Serum electrolytes, urea, and osmolality in cases of chloride depletion. *Clinical Biochemistry* 1967;1:91. Adapted from Fluid and Electrolytes. Chicago: Abbott Laboratories, 1970.
[b] Water content of normal serum taken as 94 g/100 mL.

A solution contains 156 mg of K^+ ions per 100 mL. How many milliosmoles are represented in a liter of the solution?

$$\text{Atomic weight of } K^+ = 39$$
$$1 \text{ mmol of } K^+ \text{ (39 mg)} = 1 \text{ mOsmol}$$
$$156 \text{ mg of } K^+ \text{ per 100 mL} = 1560 \text{ mg of } K^+ \text{ per liter}$$
$$1560 \text{ mg} \div 39 = 40 \text{ mOsmol, } answer.$$

A solution contains 10 mg% of Ca^{++} ions. How many milliosmoles are represented in 1 liter of the solution?

$$\text{Atomic weight of } Ca^{++} = 40$$
$$1 \text{ mmol of } Ca^{++} \text{ (40 mg)} = 1 \text{ mOsmol}$$
$$10 \text{ mg\% of } Ca^{++} = 10 \text{ mg of } Ca^{++} \text{ per 100 mL or}$$
$$100 \text{ mg of } Ca^{++} \text{ per liter}$$
$$100 \text{ mg} \div 40 = 2.5 \text{ mOsmol, } answer.$$

How many milliosmoles are represented in a liter of a 0.9% sodium chloride solution?

Osmotic concentration (in terms of milliosmoles) is a function of the total number of particles present. Assuming complete dissociation, 1 mmol of sodium chloride (NaCl) represents 2 mOsmol of total particles ($Na^+ + Cl^-$).

$$\text{Formula weight of NaCl} = 58.5$$
$$1 \text{ mmol of NaCl (58.5 mg)} = 2 \text{ mOsmol}$$
$$1000 \times 0.009 = 9 \text{ g or } 9000 \text{ mg of NaCl per liter}$$
$$\frac{58.5 \text{ (mg)}}{9000 \text{ (mg)}} = \frac{2 \text{ (mOsmol)}}{x \text{ (mOsmol)}}$$
$$x = 307.7, \text{ or } 308 \text{ mOsmol, } answer.$$

Clinical Considerations of Water and Electrolyte Balance

Maintaining body water and electrolyte balance is an essential component of good health. Water provides the environment in which cells live and is the primary medium for the ingestion of nutrients and the excretion of metabolic waste products. Normally, the osmolality of body fluid is maintained within narrow limits through dietary input, the regulatory endocrine processes, and balanced output via the kidneys, lungs, skin, and the gastrointestinal system.

In clinical practice, fluid and electrolyte therapy is undertaken either to provide maintenance requirements or to replace serious losses or deficits. Body losses of water and/or electrolytes can result from a number of causes, including vomiting, diarrhea, profuse sweating, fever, chronic renal failure, diuretic therapy, surgery, and others. The type of therapy undertaken (i.e., oral or parenteral) and the content of the fluid administered depend on a patient's specific requirements.

For example, a patient taking diuretics may simply require a daily oral potassium supplement along with adequate intake of water. An athlete may require rehydration with or without added electrolytes. Hospitalized patients commonly receive parenteral maintenance therapy of fluids and electrolytes to support ordinary metabolic function. In severe cases of deficit, a patient may require the prompt and substantial intravenous replacement of fluids and electrolytes to restore acute volume losses resulting from surgery, trauma, burns, or shock.

Total body water in adult males normally ranges between 55% and 65% of body weight depending on the proportion of body fat. The greater the proportion of fat, the lesser the proportion of water. Values for adult women are about 10% less than those for men. Newborn infants have approximately 75% body water, which decreases with growth and increases in body fat. Of the adult body's water content, up to two thirds is intracellular and one third is extracellular. The proportion of extracellular body water, as a fraction of total body weight, decreases in infants in the first year from approximately 45% to 30% while the intracellular portion increases.[4] For an adult, approximately 2500 mL of daily water intake (from ingested liquids and foods and from oxidative metabolism) are needed to balance the daily water output.

In general terms, 1500 mL of water per square meter of body surface area may be used to calculate the daily requirement for adults. On a weight basis, estimates of 32 mL/kg for adults and 100 to 150 mL/kg for infants have been cited as average daily requirements of water intake for healthy individuals.[5] These estimated requirements differ greatly in persons with clinical disorders affecting water and electrolyte homeostasis and in conditions of acute deficit.

The composition of body fluids generally is described with regard to body compartments: *intracellular* (within cells), *intravascular* (blood plasma), or *interstitial* (between cells in the tissue). Intravascular and interstitial fluids commonly are grouped together and termed *extracellular* fluid.

The usual reference ranges of electrolytes in blood plasma are shown in Table 12.2. Although all electrolytes and nonelectrolytes in body fluids contribute to osmotic activity, sodium and chloride exert the principal effect in *extra*cellular fluid, and potassium and phosphate predominate in *intra*cellular fluid.

Since cell membranes generally are freely permeable to water, the osmolality of the extracellular fluid (about 290 mOsm/kg water) is about equal to that of the intracellular fluid. Therefore, the plasma osmolality is a convenient and accurate guide to intracellular osmolality and may be approximated by the formula[4]:

$$\text{Plasma osmolality (mOsm/kg)} = 2\,([\text{Na}] + [\text{K}])\,\text{plasma} + \frac{[\text{BUN}]}{2.8} + \frac{[\text{Glucose}]}{18}$$

where: sodium (Na) and potassium (K) are in mEq/L, and blood urea nitrogen (BUN) and glucose concentrations are in mg/100 mL (mg/dL).

Representative clinical calculations in this section include the determination of body water requirement, estimation of plasma osmolality, and calculation of the osmolality and milliequivalent content of physiologic electrolyte solutions. Calculations pertaining to parenteral nutrition are included in Chapter 14.

Example Calculations of Water Requirements and Electrolytes in Parenteral Fluids

Calculate the estimated daily water requirement for a healthy adult with a body surface area of 1.8 m².

$$\text{Water Requirement} = 1500 \text{ mL/m}^2$$
$$\frac{1 \text{m}^2}{1.8 \text{ m}^2} = \frac{1500 \text{ mL}}{\text{x mL}}$$
$$\text{x} = 2700 \text{ mL, } answer.$$

Estimate the plasma osmolality from the following data: sodium, 135 mEq/L; potassium, 4.5 mEq/L; blood urea nitrogen, 14 mg/dL; and glucose, 90 mg/dL.
Equation from text:

$$\text{mOsm/kg} = 2 \left([\text{Na}] + [\text{K}] \right) + \frac{[\text{BUN}]}{2.8} + \frac{[\text{Glucose}]}{18}$$

$$\text{mOsm/kg} = 2 \left(135 \text{ mEq/L} + 4.5 \text{ mEq/L} \right) + \frac{14 \text{ mg/dL}}{2.8} + \frac{90 \text{ mg/dL}}{18}$$

$$= 2 (139.5) + 5 + 5$$
$$= 289, answer.$$

Calculate the milliequivalents of sodium, potassium and chloride, the millimoles of anhydrous dextrose, and the osmolarity of the following parenteral fluid.

Dextrose, anhydrous	50 g
Sodium Chloride	4.5 g
Potassium Chloride	1.49 g
Water for Injection, ad	1000 mL

Molecular weight of NaCl = 58.5
Equivalent weight of NaCl = 58.5
1 mEq of NaCl = $^1/_{1000} \times 58.5 = 0.0585$ g $= 58.5$ mg
4.5 g of NaCl = 4500 mg
$$\frac{58.5 \text{ mg}}{4500 \text{ mg}} = \frac{1 \text{ mEq}}{\text{x mEq}}$$
$$\text{x} = 76.9 \text{ or } 77 \text{ mEq of Na}^+ \text{ and}$$
$$76.9 \text{ or } 77 \text{ mEq of Cl}^-$$

Molecular weight of KCl = 74.5
Equivalent weight of KCl = 74.5
1 mEq of KCl = $^1/_{1000} \times 74.5 = 0.0745$ g $= 74.5$ mg
1.49 g of KCl = 1490 mg
$$\frac{74.5 \text{ mg}}{1490} = \frac{1 \text{ mEq}}{\text{x mEq}}$$
$$\text{x} = 20 \text{ mEq of K}^+ \text{ and}$$
$$20 \text{ mEq of Cl}^-$$

Total: Na$^+$ = 77 mEq
K$^+$ = 20 mEq
Cl$^-$ = 77 mEq + 20 mEq = 97 mEq, *answers.*

CALCULATIONS CAPSULE

Millimoles and Milliosmoles

To calculate millimoles (mmol):

A *millimole* is $^1/_{1000}$ of the gram molecular weight of a substance.

$$1 \; millimole = \frac{Molecular \; weight, \; grams}{1000}$$

To calculate milliosmoles (mOsmol):

A *milliosmole* is $^1/_{1000}$ of an osmol. When substances do not dissociate, the numbers of millimoles and milliosmoles are the same. There are 2 milliosmoles per millimole for substances that dissociate into two particles and 3 milliosmoles per millimole for substances that dissociate into three particles.

$$mOsmol = mg \; of \; drug \times \frac{1 \; mmol \; of \; drug}{Molecular \; weight \; (mg)}$$

Molecular weight of anhydrous dextrose = 180
1 mmol of anhydrous dextrose = 180 mg
50 g of anhydrous dextrose = 50,000 mg

$$\frac{180 \; mg}{50,000 \; mg} = \frac{1 \; mmol}{x \; mmol}$$

x = 277.7 or 278 mmol, *answer.*

Osmolarity:

Dextrose, anhyd.: 278 mmol × 1 particle per mmol = 278 mOsmol
NaCl: 77 mEq × 2 particles per mEq (or mmol) = 154 mOsmol
KCl: 20 mEq × 2 particles per mEq (or mmol) = 40 mOsmol
Total = 472 mOsmol, *answer.*

CASE IN POINT 12.1[6]: A hospital pharmacist fills a medication order calling for an intravenous fluid of dextrose 5% in a 0.9% sodium chloride injection and 40 mEq of potassium chloride in a total volume of 1000 mL. The intravenous infusion is administered through an IV set that delivers 15 drops per milliliter. The infusion has been running at a rate of 12 drops per minute for 15 hours.

During the 15-hour period:

(a) How many mEq of KCl have been administered?

(b) How many grams of KCl have been administered?

(c) How many millimoles of KCl have been administered?

(d) What is the total osmolarity of the intravenous fluid?

Express the answer in millimoles (rounded to the nearest whole number) per 1000 mL.

PRACTICE PROBLEMS

Calculations Based on Millimoles, Micromoles, and Milliequivalents

1. Convert a blood plasma level range of 5 to 20 µg/mL of tobramycin (mw = 467.52) to µmol/L.[1]

2. A preparation contains in each milliliter, 236 mg of dibasic potassium phosphate (mw = 174.18) and 224 mg of monobasic potassium phosphate (mw = 136.09). Calculate the total concentration of phosphorus, in mmol/mL, in the preparation.[7]

3. A 10-mL ampul of potassium chloride contains 2.98 g of potassium chloride (KCl). What is the concentration of the solution in terms of milliequivalents per milliliter?

4. A person is to receive 36 mg of ammonium chloride per kilogram of body weight. If the person weighs 154 lb., how many milliliters of a sterile solution of ammonium chloride (NH_4Cl—m.w. 53.5) containing 0.4 mEq/mL should be administered?

5. A sterile solution of potassium chloride (KCl) contains 2 mEq/mL. If a 20-mL ampul of the solution is diluted to 1 liter with sterile distilled water, what is the percentage strength of the resulting solution?

6. A certain electrolyte solution contains, as one of the ingredients, the equivalent of 4.6 mEq of calcium per liter. How many grams of calcium chloride ($CaCl_2 \cdot H_2O$—m.w. 147) should be used in preparing 20 liters of the solution?

7. Sterile solutions of ammonium chloride containing 21.4 mg/mL are available commercially in 500- and 1000-mL intravenous infusion containers. Calculate the amount, in terms of milliequivalents, of ammonium chloride (NH_4Cl—m.w. 53.5) in the 500-mL container.

8. A solution contains, in each 5 mL, 0.5 g of potassium acetate ($C_2H_3KO_2$—m.w. 98), 0.5 g of potassium bicarbonate ($KHCO_3$—m.w. 100), and 0.5 g of potassium citrate ($C_6H_5K_3O_7 \cdot H_2O$— m.w. 324). How many milliequivalents of potassium (K^+) are represented in each 5 mL of the solution?

9. How many grams of sodium chloride (NaCl) should be used in preparing 20 liters of a solution containing 154 mEq/L?

10. Sterile solutions of potassium chloride (KCl) containing 5 mEq/mL are available in 20-mL containers. Calculate the amount, in grams, of potassium chloride in the container.

11. How many milliliters of a solution containing 2 mEq of potassium chloride (KCl) per milliliter should be used to obtain 2.98 g of potassium chloride?

12. A patient is given 125 mg of phenytoin sodium ($C_{15}H_{11}N_2NaO_2$—m.w. 274) three times a day. How many milliequivalents of sodium are represented in the daily dose?

13. A 40-mL vial of sodium chloride solution was diluted to 1 liter with sterile distilled water. The concentration (w/v) of sodium chloride (NaCl) in the finished product was 0.585%. What was the concentration, in milliequivalents per milliliter, of the original solution?

14. How many grams of sodium bicarbonate ($NaHCO_3$—m.w. 84) should be used in preparing a liter of a solution to contain 44.6 mEq per 50 mL?

15. A solution contains 20 mg% (20 mg/100 mL) of Ca^{++} ions. Express this concentration in terms of milliequivalents per liter.

16. Sterile sodium lactate solution is available commercially as a $\frac{1}{6}$-molar solution of sodium lactate in water for injection. How many milliequivalents of sodium lactate ($C_3H_5NaO_3$—m.w. 112) would be provided by a liter of the solution?

17. A certain electrolyte solution contains 0.9% of sodium chloride in 10% dextrose solution. Express the concentration of sodium chloride (NaCl) in terms of milliequivalents per liter.

18. ℞ Potassium Chloride   10%
       Cherry Syrup q.s. ad   480 mL
       Sig. Tablespoonful b.i.d.

    How many milliequivalents of potassium chloride are represented in each prescribed dose?

19. How many milliequivalents of potassium are in 5 million units of Penicillin V Potassium ($C_{16}H_{17}KN_2O_6S$—m.w. 388)? One milligram of penicillin V potassium represents 1380 Penicillin V Units.

20. The normal potassium level in the blood plasma is 17 mg% (17 mg/100 mL). Express this concentration in terms of milliequivalents per liter.

21. How many grams of potassium citrate ($C_6H_5K_3O_7 \cdot H_2O$—m.w. 324) should be used in preparing 500 mL of a potassium ion elixir so as to supply 15 mEq of K^+ in each 5-mL dose?

22. A potassium supplement tablet contains 2.5 g of potassium bicarbonate ($KHCO_3$—m.w. 100). How many milliequivalents of potassium (K^+) are supplied by the tablet?

23. Ringer's injection contains 0.86% of sodium chloride, 0.03% of potassium chloride, and 0.033% of calcium chloride. How many milliequivalents of each chloride are contained in 1 liter of the injection?

24. Calculate the sodium (Na^+) content, in terms of milliequivalents, of 1 g of ampicillin sodium ($C_{16}H_{18}N_3NaO_4S$—m.w. 371).

25. A 20-mL vial of concentrated ammonium chloride solution containing 5 mEq/mL is diluted to 1 liter with sterile distilled water. Calculate (a) the total milliequivalent value of the ammonium ion in the dilution and (b) the percentage strength of the dilution.

26. Ringer's solution contains 0.33 g of calcium chloride per liter. Express the concentration in terms of milliequivalents of calcium chloride ($CaCl_2 \cdot 2H_2O$—m.w. 147) per liter.

27. How many milliequivalents of potassium would be supplied daily by the usual dose (0.3 mL three times a day) of saturated potassium iodide solution? Saturated potassium iodide solution contains 100 g of potassium iodide per 100 mL.

28. An intravenous solution calls for the addition of 25 mEq of sodium bicarbonate. How many milliliters of 8.4% w/v sodium bicarbonate injection should be added to the formula?

29. Calcium gluconate ($C_{12}H_{22}CaO_{14}$—m.w. 430) injection 10% is available in a 10-mL ampul. How many milliequivalents of Ca^{++} does the ampul contain?

30. A flavored potassium chloride packet contains 1.5 g of potassium chloride. How many milliequivalents of potassium chloride are represented in each packet?

31. How many milliequivalents of Li^+ are provided by a daily dose of four 300-mg tablets of lithium carbonate (Li_2CO_3—m.w. 74)?

32. How many milliequivalents of ammonium (NH_4^+) ion are contained in 1 liter of a 4.2% w/v solution of ammonium chloride?

33. A patient is to receive 10 mEq of potassium gluconate ($C_6H_{11}KO_7$—m.w. 234) four times a day for 3 days. If the dose is to be 1 teaspoonful in a cherry syrup vehicle, (a) how many grams of potassium gluconate should be used, and (b)

what volume, in milliliters, should be dispensed to provide the prescribed dosage regimen?

34. A physician wishes to administer 1,200,000 units of penicillin G potassium every 4 hours. If 1 unit of penicillin G potassium ($C_{16}H_{17}KN_2O_4S$—m.w. 372) equals 0.6 μg, how many milliequivalents of K^+ will the patient receive in a 24-hour period?

35. Five milliliters of lithium citrate syrup contain the equivalent of 8 mEq of Li^+. Calculate the equivalent, in milligrams, of lithium carbonate (Li_2CO_3—m.w. 74) in each 5-mL dose of the syrup.

36. How many milligrams of magnesium sulfate ($MgSO_4$—m.w. 120) should be added to an intravenous solution to provide 5 mEq of Mg^{++} per liter?

37. K-TAB, a slow-release potassium chloride tablet, contains 750 mg of potassium chloride in a wax/polymer matrix. How many milliequivalents of potassium chloride are supplied by a dosage of one tablet three times a day?

38. An electrolyte solution contains 222 mg of sodium acetate ($C_2H_3NaO_2$—m.w. 82) and 15 mg of magnesium chloride ($MgCl_2$—m.w. 95) in each 100 mL. Express these concentrations in milliequivalents of Na^+ and Mg^{++} per liter.

39. Ammonium chloride (NH_4Cl—m.w. 53.5) is to be used as a urinary acidifier with a dose of 150 mEq. How many 500-mg tablets should be administered?

40. A patient has a sodium deficit of 168 mEq. How many milliliters of isotonic sodium chloride solution (0.9% w/v) should be administered to replace the deficit?

41. A normal 70 kg (154 lb) adult has 80 to 100 g of sodium. It is primarily distributed in the extracellular fluid. Body retention of 1 g additional of sodium results in excess body water accumulation of approximately 310 mL. If a person retains 100 mEq of extra sodium, how many milliliters of additional water could be expected to be retained?

42. A patient receives 3 liters of an electrolyte fluid containing 234 mg of sodium chloride (NaCl—m.w. 58.5), 125 mg of potassium acetate ($C_2H_3KO_2$—m.w. 98), and 21 mg of magnesium acetate ($C_4H_6MgO_4$—m.w. 142) per 100 mL. How many milliequivalents each of Na^+, K^+, and Mg^{++} does the patient receive?

43. How many milliliters of a 2% w/v solution of ammonium chloride (NH_4Cl—m.w. 53.5) should be administered intravenously to a patient to provide 75 mEq?

44. The usual adult dose of calcium for elevating serum calcium is 7 to 14 mEq. How many milliliters of a calcium gluceptate injection, each milliliter of which provides 18 mg of elemental calcium, would provide the recommended dosage range?

45. The oral pediatric maintenance solution PEDIALYTE liquid has the following electrolyte content per liter: sodium, 45 mEq; potassium, 20 mEq; chloride, 35 mEq; and citrate, 30 mEq. Calculate the equivalent quantities of each in terms of milligrams.

46. Calculate the milliequivalents of chloride per liter of the following parenteral fluid:

Sodium Chloride	516 mg
Potassium Chloride	89.4 mg
Calcium Chloride, anhyd.	27.8 mg
Magnesium Chloride, anhyd.	14.2 mg
Sodium Lactate, anhyd.	560 mg
Water for Injection ad	100 mL

47. The pediatric infusion rate for potassium is 5 mEq/hour. If 9 mL of a 39.2% solution of potassium acetate ($KC_2H_3O_2$) is diluted to 1 L of infusion solution, calculate the proper infusion rate in mL/hr.[6]

48. COLYTE, a colon lavage preparation contains the following mixture of dry powder to prepare 4 liters of solution:

Sodium Chloride	5.84 g
Potassium Chloride	2.98 g
Sodium Bicarbonate	6.72 g
Sodium Sulfate, anhyd.	22.72 g
Polyethylene Glycol (3350)	240 g

Calculate the milliequivalents each of sodium and chloride present per liter of prepared solution.

Calculations Based on Milliosmoles

49. At 3:00 P.M., a pharmacist received an order to add 30 mEq/L of potassium chloride to the already running intravenous fluid for a patient. After checking the medication order, the pharmacist found that the patient is receiving a 5% dextrose/0.9% sodium chloride infusion at a rate of 85 mL/hour, and that the patient's liter of fluid was started at 1:30 PM.[8]

   (a) Assuming that it took 30 minutes to provide the needed potassium chloride to the floor nurse, how many milliequivalents of potassium chloride should have been added to the patient's running IV fluid to achieve the ordered concentration?
   (b) How many milliliters of an injection containing 2 mEq of potassium chloride/mL should have been used to supply the amount of potassium chloride needed?
   (c) What was the osmolality of the infusion with the potassium chloride added? Assume complete dissociation of the sodium chloride and potassium chloride.

50. A solution contains 322 mg of Na^+ ions per liter. How many milliosmoles are represented in the solution?

51. How many milliosmoles of sodium are represented in 1 liter of 3% hypertonic sodium chloride solution? Assume complete dissociation.

52. A solution of sodium chloride contains 77 mEq/L. Calculate its osmolar strength in terms of milliosmoles per liter. Assume complete dissociation.

53. Calculate the osmolar concentration, in terms of milliosmoles, represented by 1 liter of a 10% w/v solution of anhydrous dextrose (m.w. 180) in water.

54. Calculate the osmolarity, in milliosmoles per milliliter, of a parenteral solution containing 2 mEq/mL of potassium acetate ($KC_2H_3O_2$—m.w. 98).

55. Calculate (a) the milliequivalents per milliliter, (b) the total milliequivalents, and (c) the osmolarity of a 500-mL parenteral fluid containing 5% w/v of sodium bicarbonate.

56. What is the osmolarity of an 8.4% w/v solution of sodium bicarbonate?

57. A hospital medication order calls for the administration of 100 g of mannitol to a patient as an osmotic diuretic over a 24-hour period. Calculate (a) how many milliliters of a 15% w/v mannitol injection should be administered per hour, and (b) how many milliosmoles of mannitol (m.w. 182) would be represented in the prescribed dosage.

58. How many (a) millimoles, (b) milliequivalents, and (c) milliosmoles of calcium chloride ($CaCl_2 \cdot 2H_2O$—m.w. 147) are represented in 147 mL of a 10% w/v calcium chloride solution?

59. From the information in this chapter, calculate the daily water requirement for a healthy adult weighing 165 lb.

60. Estimate the plasma osmolality, in milliosmoles per kilogram, from the following data: sodium, 136 mEq/L; potassium, 5 mEq/L; blood urea nitrogen, 26 mg/100 mL; and glucose, 90 mg/dL.

ANSWERS TO "CASE IN POINT" AND PRACTICE PROBLEMS

Case in Point 12.1

(a) $\dfrac{15 \text{ drops}}{1 \text{ mL}} = \dfrac{12 \text{ drops}}{x \text{ mL}}$

   $= 0.8$ mL administered per minute

   0.8 mL/min × 60 min/hr × 15 hr
   = 720 mL infused in 15 hr

   $\dfrac{40 \text{ mEq KCl}}{1000 \text{ mL}} = \dfrac{x \text{ mEq}}{720 \text{ mL}} = 28.8$ mEq KCl, *answer.*

(b) 39 (K) + 35.5 (Cl) = 74.5 molecular weight of KCl; monovalent salt, so 74.5 mg = 1 mEq

   74.5 mg/mEq × 28.8 mEq = 2145.6 mg ÷ 1000 mg/g = 2.1456 g, *answer.*

(c) 74.5 mg KCl = 1 mmol KCl = 1 mEq KCl

   74.5 mg KCl/mEq × 40 mEq KCl/1000 mL = 2980 mg KCl in 1000 mL

   720 mL infused in 15 hr [from (a)]
   $\dfrac{2980 \text{ mg KCl}}{1000 \text{ mL}} = \dfrac{x \text{ mg KCl}}{720 \text{ mL}}$,
   x = 2145.6 mg KCl
   $\dfrac{1 \text{ mmol KCl}}{74.5 \text{ mg}} = \dfrac{x \text{ mmol KCl}}{2145.6 \text{ mg}}$,
   x = 28.8 mmol KCl, *answer.*

(d) *For the NaCl*
   23 (Na) + 35.5 (Cl) = 58.5 mg, milli-molecular weight of NaCl

   NaCl → Na^+ and Cl^- or 2 mOsmol/mmol of 58.8 mg

   0.9% sodium chloride = 9 mg NaCl/mL × 1000 mL = 9000 mg NaCl in the IV fluid

   $\dfrac{2 \text{ mOsmol}}{58.5 \text{ mg}} = \dfrac{x \text{ mOsmol}}{9000 \text{ mg}}$,
   x = 307.6923 ≈ 308 mOsmol NaCl per 1000 mL

   For the KCl
   39 (K) + 35.5 (Cl) = 74.5 mg = milli-molecular weight of KCl

   KCl → K^+ and Cl^- or 2 mOsmol/mmol of 74.5 mg
   2980 mg KCl in 1000 mL of infusion [from (c)]
   $\dfrac{2 \text{ mOsmol}}{74.5 \text{ mg}} = \dfrac{x \text{ mOsmol}}{2980 \text{ mg}}$,
   x = 80 mOsmol KCl per 1000 mL

   For the dextrose
   dextrose = 180 mg/mmol and does not hydrolyze, so 180 mg = 1 mOsmol

   Dextrose 5% = 50 mg/mL × 1000 mL = 50,000 mg per 1000 mL of IV fluid

   $\dfrac{1 \text{ mOsmol}}{180 \text{ mg}} = \dfrac{x \text{ mOsmol}}{50,000 \text{ mg}}$,
   x = 277.7778 ≈ 278 mOsmol dextrose per 1000 mL

   Total osmolarity
   mOsmol NaCl =   308
   mOsmol KCl =   80
   mOsmol dextrose = <u>278</u>
   total =   666 mOsmol/1000 mL of IV fluid, *answer.*

   Note: The osmolarity of serum is about 300 mOsmol/L, so this solution is *hyperosmotic.*

Practice Problems

1. 10.69 to 42.78 μmol/L
2. 3.001 mmol/mL
3. 4 mEq
4. 117.76 mL
5. 0.298%
6. 6.762 g
7. 200 mEq
8. 14.73 mEq
9. 180.18 g
10. 7.45 g
11. 20 mL
12. 1.37 mEq

13. 2.5 mEq/mL

14. 74.928 g

15. 10 mEq/L

16. 166.67 mEq

17. 153.85 mEq/mL

18. 20.13 mEq

19. 9.34 mEq

20. 4.36 mEq/L

21. 162 g

22. 25 mEq

23. 147 mEq sodium chloride
    4.03 mEq potassium chloride
    5.95 mEq calcium chloride

24. 2.7 mEq

25. (a) 100 mEq
    (b) 0.54%

26. 4.5 mEq/L

27. 5.42 mEq

28. 25 mL

29. 4.65 mEq

30. 20.13 mEq

31. 32.43 mEq

32. 785.05 mEq

33. (a) 28.08 g
    (b) 60 mL

34. 11.61 mEq

35. 296 mg

36. 300 mg

37. 30.2 or 30 mEq

38. 27.07 mEq Na
    3.16 mEq Mg

39. 16 tablets

40. 1092 mL

41. 713 mL

42. 120 mEq Na
    38.27 mEq K
    8.87 mEq Mg

43. 200.63 mL

44. 7.78 to 15.56 mL

45. 1035 mg Na
    1242.5 mg Cl
    780 mg K
    1890 mg citrate

46. 108.2 mEq

47. 138.89 mL/hr

48. 124.96 mEq/L Na
    34.96 mEq/L Cl

49. (a) 24.9 mEq
    (b) 12.45 mL
    (c) 645.47 mOsmol

50. 14 mOsmol

51. 512.82 mOsmol

52. 154 mOsmol/L

53. 555.56 mOsmol

54. 4000 mOsmol/mL

55. (a) 0.595 mEq/mL
    (b) 297.6 mEq
    (c) 1190.48 mOsmol/L

56. 2000 mOsmo/L

57. (a) 27.78 mL/hr
    (b) 549.49 mOsmol

58. (a) 100 mmol
    (b) 200 mEq
    (c) 300 mOsmol

59. 2400 mL

60. 296.29 mOsmol/kg

REFERENCES

1. Prince SJ. Calculations. *International Journal of Pharmaceutical Compounding* 2001;5:485.
2. United States Pharmacopeia 31st Rev. National Formulary 26. Rockville, MD: United States Pharmacopeial Convention, 2008;(785)1:307–308.
3. VAPRO Vapor Pressure Osmometer [product literature]. Logan, UT: Wescor, Inc., 1997.
4. Berkow R, ed. *The Merck Manual.* 14th Ed. Rahway, NJ: Merck Sharpe & Dohme Research Laboratories, 1982: 922–952, 1833–1850.
5. The Fundamentals of Body Water and Electrolytes. Deerfield, IL: Travenol Laboratories, 1967.
6. Warren F. Athens, GA: College of Pharmacy, University of Georgia, 2004.
7. Prince SJ. *International Journal of Pharmaceutical Compounding* 1998;2:378.
8. Prince SJ. Calculations. *International Journal of Pharmaceutical Compounding* 1999;3:311.

Intravenous Infusions, Parenteral Admixtures, and Rate-of-Flow Calculations

13

Objectives

Upon successful completion of this chapter, the student will be able to:

- Perform calculations for adult and pediatric intravenous infusions.
- Perform calculations for intravenous additives.
- Perform rate-of-flow calculations for intravenous fluids.
- Utilize correctly rate-of-flow tables and nomograms

Injections

Injections are sterile pharmaceutical solutions or suspensions of a drug substance in an aqueous or nonaqueous vehicle. They are administered by needle into almost any part of the body, including the joints (*intra-articular*), joint fluid (*intrasynovial*), spinal column (*intraspinal*), spinal fluid (*intrathecal*), arteries (*intra-arterial*), and in an emergency, even the heart (*intracardiac*). However, most injections are administered into a vein (*intravenous, I.V., IV*), muscle (*intramuscular, I.M., IM*), skin (*intradermal, I.D., ID, intracutaneous*), or under the skin (*subcutaneous, sub-Q, SQ, hypodermic*).

Depending upon their use, injections are packaged in small volumes in ***ampuls*** or in prefilled disposable syringes for single-dose use; in ***vials*** and pen-injectors for single- or multiple-dose use; or in large volume plastic bags or glass containers for administration by slow intravenous *infusion*.

Some injections are available as *prepared* solutions or suspensions with their drug content labeled as, for example, "10 mg/mL." Others contain dry powder for reconstitution *to form* a solution or suspension by adding a specified volume of diluent prior to use and are labeled as, for example, "10 mg/vial." The calculations required to determine the correct volume of diluent needed to prepare an injection of a certain concentration are provided in Chapter 17.

Small-volume injections may be administered as such or they may be used as *additives* to large-volume parenteral fluids for intravenous infusion. The term ***parenteral*** is defined as *any medication route other than the alimentary canal* and thus includes all routes of injection.

Intravenous Infusions

Intravenous (IV) infusions are sterile, aqueous preparations administered intravenously in relatively large volumes. They are used to extend blood volume and/or provide electrolytes, nutrients, or medications. Most intravenous infusions are administered to critical care, infirm, dehydrated, or malnourished patients, or to patients prior to, during, and/or following surgery. Intravenous infusions are widely employed in emergency care units, in hospitals and other patient care

205

TABLE 13.1 SOME COMMON INTRAVENOUS INFUSION SOLUTIONS

SOLUTION[a]	ABBREVIATION
0.9% Sodium Chloride	NS (Normal Saline)
0.45% Sodium Chloride	½NS
5% Dextrose in Water	D5W or D_5W
10% Dextrose in Water	D10W or $D_{10}W$
5% Dextrose in 0.9% Sodium Chloride	D5NS or D_5NS
5% Dextrose in 0.45% Sodium Chloride	D5½NS or $D_5$1/2NS
Lactated Ringer's (0.86% Sodium Chloride, 0.03% Potassium Chloride, 0.033% Calcium Chloride)	LR
5% Dextrose in Lactated Ringer's	D5LR or D_5LR

[a] All solutions are prepared in Water for Injection, USP. In addition to the solutions listed, other concentrations of dextrose and sodium chloride are commercially available. These solutions may be administered as such or used as vehicles for therapeutic agents, nutrients, or other additives.

institutions, and in home care. Pharmacists participate in the preparation and administration of institutional as well as home intravenous infusion therapy. The *United States Pharmacopeia* has established requirements for the compounding of sterile preparations.[1]

Most intravenous infusions are solutions; however, some are very fine dispersions of nutrients or therapeutic agents, or blood and blood products. Although some intravenous solutions are isotonic or nearly isotonic with blood, isotonicity is not absolutely necessary because the volumes of fluid usually administered are rapidly diluted by the circulating blood.[2]

Commercially prepared infusions are available in glass or plastic bottles or collapsible plastic "bags" in volumes of 50 mL (a *minibag*), 100 mL, 250 mL, 500 mL, and 1000 mL. The smaller volumes find particular application in treating pediatric patients and adults who require relatively small volumes to be infused. When a smaller IV bag is attached to the tubing of a larger IV being administered, it is referred to as an IV piggyback (IVPB). The abbreviation LVP is commonly used to indicate a *large-volume parenteral,* and SVP indicates a *small-volume parenteral.*

Some common solutions for intravenous infusion are listed in Table 13.1. In practice, additional components or **additives** frequently are added to these basic solutions. Drugs and other additives administered by infusion are rapidly distributed throughout the circulation.

An **administration set** is attached to an intravenous bottle or bag to deliver the fluid into a patient's vein. The sets may be standard (macrodrip) or pediatric (microdrip). Depending on the particular set used, the drip rate can vary from 10 to 15 drops/mL for standard sets to 60 drops/mL for microdrip sets. The drip rate for blood transfusion sets is usually 10 to 15 drops/mL with infusions of 250 to 500 mL administered over a 2- to 4-hour period.

The passage of an infusion solution into a patient's vein of entry may be assisted by gravity (the solution is hung on a stand well above the portal of entry) or by electronic volumetric infusion pumps. Some infusion pumps can be calibrated to deliver microinfusion volumes, such as 0.1 mL per hour, to as much as 2000 mL per hour, depending on the drug being administered and the requirements of the patient. Electronic controllers can be used to maintain the desired flow rate.

In the administration of infusions, special needles or catheters provide intravenous entry for the intravenous fluid. Large-, intermediate-, and small-gauge (bore) needles or catheters are used, with the portal of entry selected based on the patient's age (i.e., adult, child, infant, or neonate) and the clinical circumstances. The narrower the gauge, the slower the flow rate and thus the longer period required to infuse a specified volume. Veins of the back of the hand, forearm, subclavian, jugular, and scalp (e.g., in premature neonates) may be used. Figure 13.1 depicts

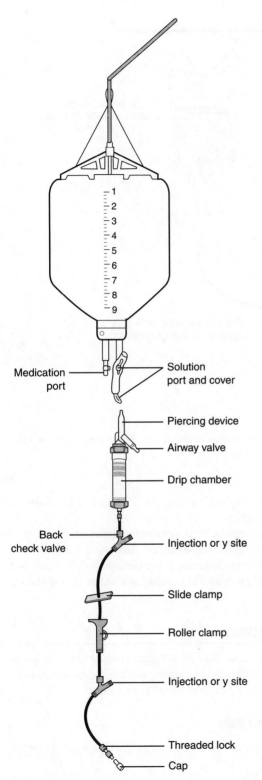

Medication port

Solution port and cover

Piercing device

Airway valve

Drip chamber

Back check valve

Injection or y site

Slide clamp

Roller clamp

Injection or y site

Threaded lock

Cap

FIGURE 13.1 A depiction of an intravenous fluid with an administration set.

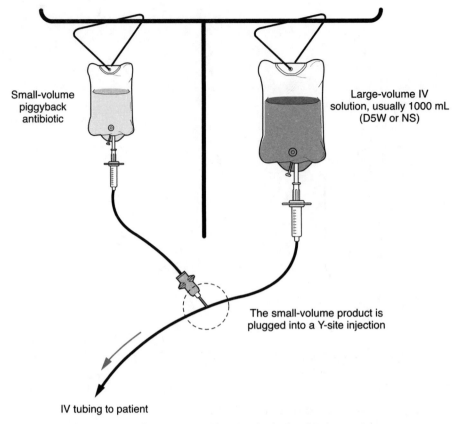

Small-volume
piggyback
antibiotic

Large-volume IV
solution, usually 1000 mL
(D5W or NS)

The small-volume product is
plugged into a Y-site injection

IV tubing to patient

FIGURE 13.2 A typical intravenous infusion set-up with a piggybacked antibiotic. *(Courtesy of Lacher B.* Pharmaceutical Calculations for the Pharmacy Technician. *Baltimore: Lippincott Williams & Wilkins, 2008.)*

an intravenous fluid and attached administration set (see also Fig. 14.1). Figure 13.2 shows a typical intravenous set-up with a piggyback attachment.

Intravenous infusions may be continuous or intermittent. In **continuous infusions**, large volumes of fluid (i.e., 250 to 1000 mL), with or without added drug, are run into a vein uninterrupted, whereas **intermittent infusions** are administered during scheduled periods.[2] The rapid infusion of a medication into a vein is termed **IV push** and is usually conducted in less than a minute.

Common Intravenous Infusion Solutions

Aqueous solutions of dextrose, sodium chloride, and lactated Ringer's solution are the most commonly used intravenous fluids. Table 13.1 describes the content of these solutions, which may be administered as such, or with additional drug or nutritional components.

Example Calculations of Basic Intravenous Infusions

How many grams each of dextrose and sodium chloride are used to prepare a 250-mL bag of D5½NS *for intravenous infusion?*

> 250 mL × 0.05 (5% w/v) = 12.5 g dextrose, and
> 250 mL × 0.0045 (0.45% w/v) = 1.125 g sodium chloride, *answers.*

Compare (a) the number of drops and (b) the length of time, in minutes, required to deliver 50-mL of intravenous solutions when using a microdrip set, at 60 drops/mL, and a standard administration set, at 15 drops/mL, if in each case one drop is to be administered per second.

Microdrip set:
(a) 60 drops/mL × 50 mL = 3000 drops
(b) 3000 drops ÷ 60 drops/minute = 50 minutes, *answers.*

Standard set:
(a) 15 drops/mL × 50 mL = 750 drops
(b) 750 drops ÷ 60 drops/minute = 12.5 minutes, *answers.*

Or, by dimensional analysis:

$$50 \text{ mL} \times \frac{60 \text{ drops}}{1 \text{ mL}} \times \frac{1 \text{ min}}{60 \text{ drops}} = 50 \text{ minutes, } answer.$$

Or, by dimensional analysis:

$$50 \text{ mL} \times \frac{15 \text{ drops}}{1 \text{ mL}} \times \frac{1 \text{ min}}{60 \text{ drops}} = 12.5 \text{ minutes, } answer.$$

Intravenous Push (IVP) Drug Administration

The rapid injection of intravenous medications, as in emergency or critical care situations, is termed **IV push**, **IVP**, **IV Stat**, or sometimes a ***bolus*** dose. For the most part, drugs administered by IV push are intended to quickly control heart rate, blood pressure, cardiac output, respiration, or other life-threatening conditions. Intravenous push medications frequently are administered in less than one minute. The safe administration of a drug by IV push depends on precise calculations of dose and rate of administration. When feasible, a diluted injection rather than a highly concentrated one (e.g., 1 mg/mL versus 5 mg/mL) may be administered as an added safety precaution.[3] An example of an intravenous flush syringe is shown in Fig. 13.3.

Example Calculations of IV Push Drug Administration

A physician orders enalaprilat (VASOTEC IV) 2 mg IVP for a hypertensive patient. A pharmacist delivers several 1-mL injections, each containing 1.25 mg of enalaprilat. How many milliliters of the injection should be administered?

$$\frac{1.25 \text{ mg}}{1 \text{ mL}} = \frac{2 \text{ mg}}{x \text{ mL}}; \text{ x} = 1.6 \text{ mL (1 mL from one syringe and 0.6 mL from another), } answer.$$

Or, by dimensional analysis:

$$2 \text{ mg} \times \frac{1 \text{ mL}}{1.25 \text{ mg}} = 1.6 \text{ mL, } answer.$$

A physician orders midazolam hydrochloride (VERSED) 2 mg IV Stat. A pharmacist delivers a vial containing midazolam hydrochloride 5 mg/mL. How many milliliters should be administered?

$$\frac{5 \text{ mg}}{1 \text{ mL}} = \frac{2 \text{ mg}}{x \text{ mL}}; \text{ x} = 0.4 \text{ mL, } answer.$$

Or, by dimensional analysis:

$$2 \text{ mg} \times \frac{1 \text{ mL}}{5 \text{ mg}} = 0.4 \text{ mL, } answer.$$

FIGURE 13.3 An intravenous flush syringe for the administration of heparin. *(Courtesy of Becton Dickinson.)*

General guidelines in the treatment of severe diabetic ketoacidosis include an initial bolus dose of 0.1 to 0.4 unit of insulin/kg IVP, followed by an insulin drip. Calculate the bolus dosage range for a 200-lb patient.

$$200 \text{ lb} \div 2.2 \text{ lb/kg} = 90.9 \text{ kg,}$$
$$90.9 \text{ kg} \times 0.1 \text{ unit/kg} = 9.09 \text{ units, and}$$
$$90.9 \text{ kg} \times 0.4 \text{ unit/kg} = 36.36 \text{ units, } \textit{answers.}$$

Special Considerations in Pediatric IV Infusion Delivery

Depending on the institutional protocol, a medication order for an intravenous infusion for a 10-kg child may be stated as, for example, "dopamine 60 mg/100 mL, IV to run at 5 mL/hr to give 5 mcg/kg/min." At some institutions in which *standardized drug products and established protocols* have been developed, the same medication order may be written simply as "dopamine 5 mcg/kg/min IV" to provide equivalently accurate drug dosing of the patient.[4] This is because the standard solution of dopamine used in the institution (as described in the previous example), containing 60 mg of dopamine in each 100 mL and run at 5 mL/hr, *would deliver the same dose of 5 mcg/kg/min* to the 10-kg patient. Calculate it:

$$\frac{60 \text{ mg}}{100 \text{ mL}} = \frac{x \text{ mg}}{5 \text{ mL}}; x = 3 \text{ mg or } 3000 \text{ mcg dopamine administered per hour}$$

$$3000 \text{ mcg} \div 60 \text{ min/hr} = 50 \text{ mcg dopamine administered per minute}$$

Since the 50 mcg/min are administered to a 10-kg child, the dose, per kg per minute, is:

$$\frac{50 \text{ mcg}}{10 \text{ kg}} = \frac{x \text{ mcg}}{1 \text{ kg}}; x = 5 \text{ mcg dopamine/kg/min, } answer.$$

Or, by dimensional analysis:

$$\frac{60 \text{ mg}}{100 \text{ mL}} \times \frac{1000 \text{ mcg}}{1 \text{ mg}} \times \frac{5 \text{ mL}}{1 \text{ hr}} \times \frac{1 \text{ hr}}{60 \text{ min}} =$$

50 mcg/min (dose for 10-kg child) = 5 mcg/kg/min

All medication doses for pediatric patients, including those administered intravenously, must be carefully determined from available literature and reference sources.

In addition to medications administered by intravenous infusion to pediatric patients, fluid and electrolyte therapy is especially important in the clinical management of preterm and term neonates, particularly those with extremely low birth weights who tend to have greater loss of water through the skin, especially when they are maintained in a warm incubator.[5]

Example Calculations of Pediatric Infusions

Calculate the daily infusion volume of D10W to be administered to a neonate weighing 3 lb. 8 oz. on the basis of 60 mL/kg/day.

3 lb. 8 oz. = 3.5 lb. ÷ 2.2 lb./kg = 1.59 kg or 1.6 kg
1.6 kg × 60 mL = 96 mL, *answer.*

Using an administration set that delivers 60 drops/mL at 20 drops per minute, calculate the total time for the above infusion.

$$96 \text{ mL} \times \frac{60 \text{ drops}}{1 \text{ mL}} \times \frac{1 \text{ minute}}{20 \text{ drops}} = 288 \text{ minutes, or 4 hours 48 minutes, } answer.$$

Gentamicin sulfate, 2.5 mg/kg, is prescribed for a 1.5-kg neonate. Calculate (a) the dose of the drug, and (b) when the drug is placed in a 50-mL IV bag, the flow rate, in mL/minute, if the infusion is to run for 30 minutes.

(a) 2.5 mg/kg × 1.5 kg = 3.75 mg gentamicin sulfate
(b) 50 mL ÷ 30 minutes = 1.67 mL/minute, *answers.*

Intravenous Admixtures

The preparation of intravenous admixtures involves the addition of one or more drugs to large-volume sterile fluids such as sodium chloride injection, dextrose injection, lactated Ringer's injection, and others. The additives are generally in the form of small-volume sterile solutions packaged in ampuls, vials, small-volume minibags for use as piggybacks, or sterile solids, some requiring constitution with a sterile solvent before transfer.

Although a wide variety of drugs and drug combinations are used in preparing dilute infusions for intravenous therapy, some of the more common additives include electrolytes, antibiotics, vitamins, trace minerals, heparin, and, in some instances, insulin. Figure 13.4 shows the aseptic addition of an additive to a large-volume solution.

In any properly administered intravenous admixture program, all basic fluids (large-volume solutions), additives (already in solution or extemporaneously constituted), and *calculations* must be carefully checked against the medication orders.

FIGURE 13.4 Aseptic addition of an additive to a large-volume parenteral solution. *(Courtesy of Millipore Corporation.)*

Patient care facilities often adopt *standard concentrations* of intravenous solutions of commonly used drugs to provide uniformity within the institution. Common examples are dopamine 400 mg in 250 mL of D5W, insulin 25 units in 250 mL of NS, and nitroglycerin 50 mg in 250 mL D5W. In preparing these standard concentrations, the pharmacist withdraws the determined volume from an ampul or vial containing the concentrated drug solution and transfers it to the specified volume of D5W, NS, or other intravenous fluid. Table 13.2 shows various infusion concentrations that may be conveniently prepared from 40 mg/mL and 80 mg/mL concentrations of dopamine injection.

TABLE 13.2 OPTIONS TO PREPARE INFUSIONS OF DIFFERENT CONCENTRATIONS

VOLUME USED			CONCENTRATION OF DOPAMINE HCl[a]	
IV FLUID	INJECTION	INJECTION:	40 mg/mL	80 mg/mL
250 mL	5 mL		800 mcg/mL	1.6 mg/mL
	10 mL		1.6 mg/mL	3.2 mg/mL
500 mL	5 mL		400 mcg/mL	800 mcg/mL
	10 mL		800 mcg/mL	1.6 mg/mL
1000 mL	5 mL		200 mcg/mL	400 mcg/mL
	10 mL		400 mcg/mL	800 mcg/mL

[a] Note: In practice, the volume of the added injection is generally disregarded in expressing the drug concentration of the resultant infusion solution.

It is important to recognize that drug dosing by infusion is varied by the drug concentration in the infusion, the volume of infusion administered, the infusion set used, and the rate of flow of the infusion (e.g., mL/min, mg/min). Rate of infusion calculations are presented in the next section.

Example Calculations of Additives to Intravenous Infusion Solutions

A medication order for a patient weighing 154 lb. calls for 0.25 mg of amphotericin B per kilogram of body weight to be added to 500 mL of 5% dextrose injection. If the amphotericin B is to be obtained from a constituted injection that contains 50 mg/10 mL, how many milliliters should be added to the dextrose injection?

$$1 \text{ kg} = 2.2 \text{ lb.}$$

$$\frac{154 \text{ (lb.)}}{2.2 \text{ (lb.)}} = 70 \text{ kg}$$

$$0.25 \text{ mg} \times 70 = 17.5 \text{ mg}$$

Constituted solution contains 50 mg/10 mL:

$$\frac{50 \text{ (mg)}}{17.5 \text{ (mg)}} = \frac{10 \text{ (mL)}}{x \text{ (mL)}}$$

$$x = 3.5 \text{ mL, } answer.$$

Or, solving by dimensional analysis:

$$154 \text{ lb.} \times \frac{1 \text{ kg}}{2.2 \text{ lb.}} \times \frac{0.25 \text{ mg}}{1 \text{ kg}} \times \frac{10 \text{ mL}}{50 \text{ mg}} = 3.5 \text{ mL, } answer.$$

An intravenous infusion is to contain 15 mEq of potassium ion and 20 mEq of sodium ion in 500 mL of 5% dextrose injection. Using potassium chloride injection containing 6 g/30 mL and 0.9% sodium chloride injection, how many milliliters of each should be used to supply the required ions?

15 mEq of K^+ ion will be supplied by 15 mEq of KCl, and 20 mEq of Na^+ ion will be supplied by 20 mEq of NaCl

$$1 \text{ mEq of KCl} = 74.5 \text{ mg}$$

$$15 \text{ mEq of KCl} = 1117.5 \text{ mg or } 1.118 \text{ g}$$

$$\frac{6 \text{ (g)}}{1.118 \text{ (g)}} = \frac{30 \text{ (mL)}}{x \text{ (mL)}}$$

$$x = 5.59 \text{ or } 5.6 \text{ mL, } and$$

$$1 \text{ mEq of NaCl} = 58.5 \text{ mg}$$

$$20 \text{ mEq of NaCl} = 1170 \text{ mg or } 1.170 \text{ g}$$

$$\frac{0.9 \text{ (g)}}{1.17 \text{ (g)}} = \frac{100 \text{ (mL)}}{x \text{ (mL)}}$$

$$x = 130 \text{ mL, } answers.$$

Or, solving by dimensional analysis:

$$15 \text{ mEq} \times \frac{74.5 \text{ mg}}{1 \text{ mEq}} \times \frac{1 \text{ g}}{1000 \text{ mg}} \times \frac{30 \text{ mL}}{6 \text{ g}} = 5.59 \text{ or } 5.6 \text{ mL, and}$$

$$20 \text{ mEq} \times \frac{58.5 \text{ mg}}{1 \text{ mEq}} \times \frac{1 \text{ g}}{1000 \text{ mg}} \times \frac{100 \text{ mL}}{0.9 \text{ g}} = 130 \text{ mL, } answers.$$

A medication order for a child weighing 44 lb. calls for polymyxin B sulfate to be administered by the intravenous drip method in a dosage of 7500 units/kg of body weight in 500 mL of 5% dextrose injection. Using a vial containing 500,000 units of polymyxin B sulfate and sodium chloride injection as the solvent, explain how you would obtain the polymyxin B sulfate needed in preparing the infusion.

$$1 \text{ kg} = 2.2 \text{ lb.}$$
$$\frac{44}{2.2} = 20 \text{ kg}$$
$$7500 \text{ units} \times 20 = 150,000 \text{ units}$$

Step 1. Dissolve contents of vial (500,000 units) in 10 mL of sodium chloride injection.
Step 2. Add 3 mL of constituted solution to 500 mL of 5% dextrose injection, *answer.*

Rate of Flow of Intravenous Fluids

On medication orders, the physician specifies the rate of flow of intravenous fluids in milliliters per minute, drops per minute, amount of drug (as milligrams per hour), or, more frequently, as the approximate duration of time of administration of the total volume of the infusion. Pharmacists may be called on to perform or check rate-of-flow calculations as those described in the following example problems in this section.

Oftentimes, the following equation finds use in rate-of-flow calculations:

$$\text{Rate of flow (drops/minute)} = \frac{\text{Volume infusion (mL)} \times \text{Drip set (drops/mL)}}{\text{Time (minutes)}}$$

In common usage are *macro sets* that deliver 10, 15, or 20 drops per milliliter and m*icrodrip* or *minidrip sets* that deliver 60 drops per milliliter.

Examples of Rate-of-Flow Calculations

A medication order calls for 1000 mL of D5W to be administered over an 8-hour period. Using an IV administration set that delivers 10 drops/mL, how many drops per minute should be delivered to the patient?

$$\text{Volume of fluid} = 1000 \text{ mL}$$
$$8 \text{ hours} = 480 \text{ minutes}$$

$$\frac{1000 \text{ (mL)}}{480 \text{ (minutes)}} = 2.08 \text{ mL per minute}$$

$$2.08 \text{ mL/min} \times 10 \text{ (drops/mL)} = 20.8 \text{ or } 21 \text{ drops per minute, } answer.$$

Or, solving by dimensional analysis:

$$\frac{10 \text{ drops}}{1 \text{ mL}} \times \frac{1000 \text{ mL}}{8 \text{ hr}} \times \frac{1 \text{ hr}}{60 \text{ min}} = 20.8, \text{ or } 21 \text{ drops per minute, } answer.$$

Or, solving by the equation:

$$\text{Rate of flow (drops/minute)} = \frac{\text{Volume infused (mL)} \times \text{Drip set (drops/mL)}}{\text{Time (minutes)}}$$
$$= \frac{1000 \text{ mL} \times 10 \text{ drops/mL}}{480 \text{ minutes}}$$
$$= 20.8 \text{ or } 21 \text{ drops per minute, } answer.$$

Ten (10) milliliters of 10% calcium gluconate injection and 10 mL of multivitamin infusion are mixed with 500 mL of a 5% dextrose injection. The infusion is to be administered over 5 hours. If the dropper in the venoclysis set calibrates 15 drops/mL, at what rate, in drops per minute, should the flow be adjusted to administer the infusion over the desired time interval?

Total volume of infusion =
10 mL + 10 mL + 500 ml = 520 mL
Dropper calibrates 15 drops/mL
520 × 15 drops = 7800 drops
$$\frac{7800 \text{ (drops)}}{300 \text{ (minutes)}} = 26 \text{ drops per minute, } answer.$$

Or, solving by dimensional analysis:

$$\frac{15 \text{ drops}}{1 \text{ mL}} \times \frac{520 \text{ mL}}{5 \text{ hours}} \times \frac{1 \text{ hr}}{60 \text{ min}} = 26 \text{ drops per minute, } answer.$$

Or, solving by the equation:

$$\text{Rate of flow (drops/minute)} = \frac{\text{Volume infused (mL)} \times \text{Drip set (drops/mL)}}{\text{Time (minutes)}}$$
$$= \frac{520 \text{ mL} \times 15 \text{ drops/mL}}{300 \text{ minutes}}$$
$$= 26 \text{ drops per minute, } answer.$$

An intravenous infusion contains 10 mL of a 1:5000 solution of isoproterenol hydrochloride and 500 mL of a 5% dextrose injection. At what flow rate should the infusion be administered to provide 5 μg of isoproterenol hydrochloride per minute, and what time interval will be necessary for the administration of the entire infusion?

10 mL of a 1:5000 solution contain 2 mg
2 mg or 2000 μg are contained in a volume of 510 mL

$$\frac{2000 \text{ } (\mu g)}{5 \text{ } (\mu g)} = \frac{510 \text{ (mL)}}{x \text{ (mL)}}$$
$$x = 1.275 \text{ or } 1.28 \text{ mL per minute, } and$$
$$\frac{1.28 \text{ (mL)}}{510 \text{ (mL)}} = \frac{1 \text{ (minute)}}{x \text{ (minutes)}}$$
$$x = 398 \text{ minutes or approx. } 6\frac{1}{2} \text{ hours, } answers.$$

Or, solving by dimensional analysis:

$$\frac{1 \text{ min}}{5 \text{ } \mu g} \times \frac{0.002 \text{ g}}{510 \text{ mL}} \times \frac{1,000,000 \text{ } \mu g}{1 \text{ g}} \times 510 \text{ mL} = 400 \text{ minutes} \approx 6\frac{1}{2} \text{ hours, } answer.$$

If 10 mg of a drug are added to a 500-mL large-volume parenteral fluid:

(a) what should be the rate of flow, in milliliters per hour, to deliver 1 mg of drug per hour?

$$\frac{10 \text{ (mg)}}{1 \text{ (mg)}} = \frac{500 \text{ (mL)}}{x \text{ (mL)}}$$
$$x = 50 \text{ mL per hour, } answer.$$

(b) If the infusion set delivers 15 drops/mL, what should be the rate of flow in drops per minute?

15 drops/mL × 50 mL/hr = 750 drops per hour
$$\frac{750 \text{ (drops)}}{x \text{ (drops)}} = \frac{60 \text{ (minutes)}}{1 \text{ (minute)}}$$
$$x = 12.5 \text{ drops/minute, } answer.$$

Or, solving by dimensional analysis:

$$\frac{15 \text{ drops}}{1 \text{ mL}} \times \frac{50 \text{ mL}}{1 \text{ hr}} \times \frac{1 \text{ hr}}{60 \text{ min}} = 12.5 \text{ drops per minute, } answer.$$

(c) How many hours should the total infusion last?

$$\frac{50 \text{ (mL)}}{500 \text{ (mL)}} = \frac{1 \text{ (hour)}}{x \text{ (hour)}}$$
$$x = 10 \text{ hours, } answer.$$

IV Infusion Rate Calculations for the Critical Care Patient

Many patients, including those in critical care, require both a maintenance fluid, as D5W, and a therapeutic drug additive, as an antibiotic (see Fig. 13.2). However, many critical care patients have fluid restrictions and must be maintained and treated within a stated maximum volume of fluid intake per day. Thus, consideration must be given to the rate and volumes of any infusions administered including intravenous piggybacked (IVPB) additives.

Example:

An order for a patient, with a 3-liter daily IV fluid limit, calls for 3 L of D5W with a 100-mL IVPB antibiotic to be run-in alone over a 1-hour period and administered every 6 hours. The administration set is calibrated to deliver 10 drops per milliliter. Calculate:

(a) The flow rate of the IVPB antibiotic;
(b) The total flow time for the IV antibiotic;
(c) The total volume for the IV antibiotic;
(d) The total flow time for the D5W;
(e) The total volume for the D5W;
(f) The flow rate for the D5W.

(a) $\dfrac{100 \text{ mL} \times 10 \text{ drops/mL}}{60 \text{ min}} = 16.6$ or 17 drops per minute;

(b) 1 hour × 4 times a day = 4 hours or 240 minutes;
(c) 100 mL × 4 times a day = 400 mL;
(d) 24 hours − 4 hours (run time for the antibiotic) = 20 hours or 1200 minutes;
(e) 3000 mL − 400 mL (the IVPB antibiotic) = 2600 mL;

(f) $\dfrac{2600 \text{ mL} \times 10 \text{ drops/mL}}{1200 \text{ min}} = 21.6$ or 22 drops per minute, *answers.*

Using a Nomogram

A nomogram, like that shown in Figure 13.5, may be used in determining the rate of flow of a parenteral fluid. Given the volume to be administered, the infusion time (duration), and the drops per milliliter delivered by the infusion set, the rate of flow, in drops per minute, may be determined directly.

If 1 liter of a parenteral fluid is to be infused over a 12-hour period using an infusion set that delivers 20 drops/mL, what should be the rate of flow in drops per minute?

First, locate the intercept of the diagonal line representing an infusion time of 12 hours with the horizontal line representing 1 liter of fluid. Next, follow the point of the intercept down to the drop counter scale representing "20 drops/mL" to determine the answer. In the example, the horizontal line would be crossed between 20 and 30 drops per minute—closer to the 30, or approximately 28 drops per minute, *answer.*

Nomogram for number of drops per minute

The number of drops per minute required to administer a particular quantity of infusion solution in a certain time can be read off directly from this nomogram. The nomogram allows for the increase in drop size as the dropping rate increases and is based on the normal drop defined by the relationship: 20 drops distilled water at 15° C = 1 g (±0.05 g) when falling at the rate of 60/min. The dependence of drop size on dropping rate is allowed for by the increasing width of the scale units of the three abscissae as the dropping rate. increases.

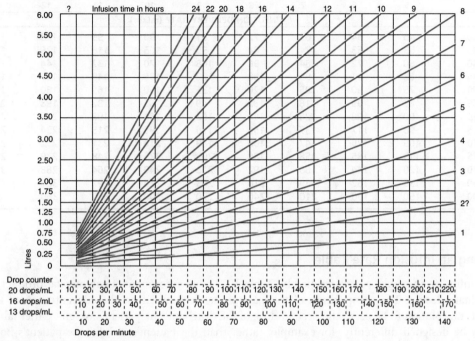

FIGURE 13.5 Rate of flow versus quantity of infusion solution versus time nomogram. *(From Documenta Geigy Scientific Tables, 7th Ed., 1970. With permission of Ciba-Geigy Limited, Basel, Switzerland.)*

As a check to the proper use of the nomogram, the preceding example may be calculated as follows:

$$\text{Infusion time} = 12 \text{ hours} = 720 \text{ minutes}$$
$$\text{Infusion fluid} = 1 \text{ liter} = 1000 \text{ mL}$$
$$\text{Drops per milliliter} = 20$$
$$\text{Total drops in infusion liquid} = 20 \text{ drops/mL} \times 1000 \text{ mL} = 20{,}000$$
$$\frac{20{,}000 \text{ (drops)}}{720 \text{ (minutes)}} = 27.7 \text{ or } 28 \text{ drops per minute}, \textit{answer.}$$

Or, solving by dimensional analysis:

$$\frac{20 \text{ drops}}{1 \text{ mL}} \times \frac{1000 \text{ mL}}{12 \text{ hrs}} \times \frac{1 \text{ hr}}{60 \text{ min}} = 27.7 \text{ or } 28 \text{ drops per minute}, \textit{answer.}$$

Or, solving by the equation:

$$\text{Rate of flow (drops/minute)} = \frac{\text{Volume infused (mL)} \times \text{Drip set (drops/mL)}}{\text{Time (minutes)}}$$
$$= \frac{1000 \text{ mL} \times 20 \text{ drops/mL}}{720 \text{ minutes}}$$
$$= 27.7 \text{ or } 28 \text{ drops per minute}, \textit{answer.}$$

TABLE 13.3 INFUSION RATE OF A HYPOTHETICAL DRUG FOR A CONCENTRATION OF 0.2 mg/mL

PATIENT WEIGHT (kg)	DRUG DELIVERY RATE (mcg/kg per minute)								
	5	6	7	8	9	10	11	12	13
	INFUSION DELIVERY RATE (mL/hr)								
30	45	54	63	72	81	90	99	108	117
35	53	63	74	84	95	105	116	126	137
40	60	72	84	96	108	120	132	144	156
45	68	81	95	108	122	135	149	162	176
50	75	90	105	120	135	150	165	180	195
55	83	99	116	132	149	165	182	198	215
60	90	108	126	144	162	180	198	216	234
65	98	117	137	156	176	195	215	234	254
70	105	126	147	168	189	210	231	252	273
75	113	135	158	180	203	225	248	270	293
80	120	144	168	192	216	240	264	288	312
90	135	162	189	216	243	270	297	324	351
100	150	180	210	240	270	300	330	360	390

Using an Infusion Rate Table

An infusion rate table, as exemplified by Table 13.3, may accompany a commercial product to facilitate dosing. The composition of the example table is based on the concentration of the infusion solution to be used, the desired dose of the drug, and the patient's weight. Other tables may be designed differently; for example, rather than the patient's weight, the patient's body

CALCULATIONS CAPSULE

Intravenous Infusions

In certain calculations, the following equations find application.

To calculate infusion time:

$$Infusion\ time = \frac{Volume\ of\ infusion\ in\ mL}{Flow\ rate\ in\ mL/hr\ or\ mL/min}$$

To calculate flow rate in drops/minute:

$$Rate\ of\ flow\ (drops/minute) = \frac{Volume\ infused\ (mL) \times Drip\ set\ (drops/mL)}{Time\ (minutes)}$$

To calculate flow rate in mL/hour when based on dose[4]:

$$Infusion\ rate\ (mL/hr) = \frac{Patient's\ weight\ (kg) \times Dose\ (mcg,\ mg,\ or\ units/kg/min) \times 60}{Drug\ concentration,\ infusion\ (mcg,\ mg,\ or\ units/mL)}$$

In using this equation, the denominations for the dose and drug concentration must be the same (e.g., mcg, mg, or units). Also, if the dosage rate is stated in hours (e.g., mcg/kg/hr), the 60 is not needed in the equation to arrive at flow rate per hour.

CASE IN POINT 13.1: A physician prescribes amiodarone HCl IV (CORDARONE) for a patient with ventricular fibrillation. The prescribing information is:

Loading infusions:

Rapid infusion over first 10 minutes:	15 mg/min
Slow infusion over the next 6 hours:	1 mg/min

Maintenance infusion:

Slow infusion over the remaining 18 hours:	0.5 mg/min

Amiodarone HCl IV is available in 3-mL ampuls containing 50 mg/mL. The pharmacist uses a 100-mL bag of D5W for the rapid infusion and 250-mL bottles of D5W for the slow infusions.

(a) How many milliliters from an amiodarone HCl IV ampul should be placed in the 100-mL bag for the rapid infusion?

(b) What is the drug concentration in the rapid infusion, in mg/mL?

(c) If the pharmacist added the contents of 3 ampuls to each 250-mL bottle of D5W needed for the slow infusions, calculate the drug concentration in mg/mL.

(d) What rate of administration, in mL/hr, should the pharmacist have recommend during the 6-hour infusion segment?

(e) Calculate the rate of administration in (d) in drops/minute with an administration set that delivers 15 drops/mL.

(f) Calculate the milligrams of drug administered by slow infusion over the 6-hour segment.

(g) Make the same calculation as that in (f) but over the 18-hour segment.

surface area, in square meters, may be used. In each case, however, the table provides guidelines for the delivery rate of an infusion. Table 13.3 is used by matching the column of the desired drug delivery rate against the patient's weight to yield the infusion delivery rate in mL/hr. The pharmacist is quite capable of developing such a dosing table, as demonstrated in the final example problem below.

Using Table 13.3, determine the delivery rate, in mL/hr, for a drug to be administered at 10 mcg/ kg/minute to a patient weighing 65 kg.

$$\text{Drug delivery rate} = 10 \text{ mcg/kg/minute}$$
$$\text{Patient weight} = 65 \text{ kg}$$
$$\text{Table intercept} = 195 \text{ mL/hr, } answer.$$

If the infusion pump used in the previous example delivers 60 microdrops per milliliter, how many microdrops would be administered to the patient per minute?

$$195 \text{ (mL/hr)} \times 60 \text{ (microdrops/mL)} = 11,700 \text{ (microdrops/hr)}$$
$$11,700 \text{ (microdrops/hr)} \div 60 \text{ (minutes/hr)} = 195 \text{ microdrops per minute, } answer.$$

Calculate the entry shown in Table 13.3 for the infusion delivery rate as determined in the first example problem (i.e., 195 mL/hr).

$$\text{Drug concentration: } 0.2 \text{ mg/mL} = 200 \text{ mcg/mL}$$
$$\text{Desired delivery rate: } 10 \text{ mcg/kg/min}$$
$$\text{Patient weight: } 65 \text{ kg}$$

Drug to be delivered = 10 (mcg/kg/min) × 65 (kg) = 650 mcg/min

650 (mcg/min) × 60 (min) = 3900 mcg/hr

Infusion delivery rate = 3900 (mcg/hr) ÷ 200 (mcg/mL) = 195 mL/hr, *answer*.

Note: For data such as these, when the patient's weight, the dose of the drug, and the drug concentration in the infusion are given or may be calculated, the infusion rate may be calculated by the following equation[4]:

$$\text{Infusion rate (mL/hr)} = \frac{\text{Patient's weight (kg)} \times \text{Dose (mcg, mg, or units/kg/min)} \times 60}{\text{Drug concentration, infusion (mcg, mg, or units/mL)}}$$

$$= \frac{65 \text{ (kg)} \times 10 \text{ (mcg/kg/min)} \times 60}{200 \text{ (mcg/mL)}}$$

$$= \textbf{195 mL/hr}, \text{ answer}.$$

In using this equation, the denominations for the dose and drug concentration must be the same (e.g., mcg, mg, or units). Also, if the dosage rate is stated in hours (e.g., mcg/kg/hr), the 60 is not needed in the equation to arrive at flow rate per hour.

PRACTICE PROBLEMS

Calculations of Basic Intravenous Infusion Solutions

1. How many grams each of sodium chloride and dextrose are present in a 1000-mL IV bag of 0.18% sodium chloride and 4% dextrose?

2. How many grams each of sodium chloride, potassium chloride, calcium chloride, and dextrose are contained in a 500-mL IV bag of D$_5$LR?

Calculations of Infusion Time

3. A patient received 250 mL of an infusion at a rate of 40 mL/hr. What was the infusion time in hours, minutes?

4. A patient was administered 150 mL of D$_5$W at a rate of 25 mL/hr. If the infusion was begun at 8 AM, at what time was it completed?

5. A patient received 500 mL of D$_5$W½NS at a rate of 15 drops/minute. If the administration set used delivered 15 drops/mL, calculate the infusion time in hours, minutes.

6. A pediatric patient received 50 mL of an infusion at 10 drops/minute with an administration set that delivered 60 drops/

mL. Calculate the duration of the infusion in minutes.

7. A patient received a 500-mL whole blood transfusion at 9:13 PM at a rate of 30 drops per minute via an administration set that delivers 10 drops/mL. At what time was the transfusion completed?

Calculations of Intravenous Infusions with Additives

8. Daptomycin (CUBICIN), 4 mg/kg, is recommended for administration over a 30-minute period by intravenous infusion in 0.9% sodium chloride. How many milliliters of a vial containing 500 mg of daptomycin in 5 mL should be added to a 100-mL bag of normal saline in treating a 165-lb. patient?

9. An emergency syringe contains lidocaine, 1 g/5 mL. How many milliliters should be used in preparing 250 mL of an infusion to contain 4 mg/mL of lidocaine in D5W?

10. A fluconazole injection contains 400 mg of fluconazole in 200 mL of normal saline injection for infusion. Calculate the concentration of fluconazole in mg/mL.

11.[6] Intravenous immunoglobulin (IVIG) has been administered in the pretransplantation of organs at a rate of 0.08 mL/kg/min. Calculate the number of milliliters administered to a 70-kg patient if a 10% w/v solution is infused over a period of 4 hours.

12. A pharmacist prepared a "standard concentration" of a dopamine HCl solution to contain 400 mg/250 mL D5W. Calculate (a) the concentration of dopamine HCl in the infusion, in mg/mL, and (b) the infusion flow rate, in mL/hr, for a 150-lb. patient, based on a dose of 5 mcg/kg/minute.

13. A pharmacist receives a medication order for 300,000 units of penicillin G potassium to be added to 500 mL of D5W. The directions on the 1,000,000-unit vial state that if 1.6 mL of solvent are added, the solution will measure 2 mL. How many milliliters of the solution must be withdrawn and added to the D5W?

14. A physician orders 2 g of an antibiotic to be placed in 1000 mL of D5W. Using an injection that contains 300 mg of the antibiotic per 2 mL, how many milliliters should be added to the dextrose injection in preparing the medication order?

15. An intravenous infusion for a patient weighing 132 lb. calls for 7.5 mg of amikacin sulfate per kilogram of body weight to be added to 250 mL of 5% dextrose injection. How many milliliters of an amikacin sulfate injection containing 500 mg per 2 mL should be used in preparing the infusion?

16. In preparing an intravenous solution of lidocaine in D5W, a pharmacist added a concentrated solution of lidocaine (1 g per 5 mL) to 250 mL of D5W. What was the final concentration of lidocaine on a milligrams-per-milliliter basis?

17. In preparing an intravenous infusion containing sodium bicarbonate, 50 mL of a 7.5% sodium bicarbonate injection were added to 500 mL of 5% dextrose injection. How many milliequivalents of sodium were represented in the total volume of the infusion?

18. A potassium phosphate solution contains 0.9 g of potassium dihydrogen phosphate and 4.7 g of potassium monohydrogen phosphate in 30 mL. If 15 mL of this solution are added to a liter of D5W, how many milliequivalents of potassium phosphate will be represented in the infusion?

19. A physician orders 20 mg of ampicillin per kilogram of body weight to be administered intravenously in 500 mL of sodium chloride injection. How many milliliters of a solution containing the equivalent of 250 mg of ampicillin per milliliter should be used in filling the medication order for a 110-lb. patient?

Various Calculations of Infusions Including Drip Rates

20. The biotechnology drug cetuximab (ERBITUX), used in the treatment of colorectal cancer, has a loading dose of 400 mg/m² administered as an intravenous infusion over a 120-minute period. Using an IV set that delivers 15 drops/mL, calculate (a) the dose for a patient with a BSA of 1.6 m², and (b) the rate of delivery, in drops/min, for 250 mL of an IV fluid containing the dose.

21. How many milliliters of an injection containing 1 g of drug in 4 mL should be used in filling a medication order requiring 275 mg of the drug to be added to 500 mL of D5W solution? If the solution is administered at the rate of 1.6 mL per minute, how many milligrams of the drug will the patient receive in 1 hour?

22. A physician orders a 2-g vial of a drug to be added to 500 mL of D5W. If the administration rate is 125 mL per hour, how many milligrams of the drug will a patient receive per minute?

23. A certain fluid measures 1 liter. If the solution is to be administered over a period of 6 hours and if the administration set is calibrated at 25 drops/mL, at what rate, in drops per minute, should the set be adjusted to administer the solution during the designated interval?

24. A physician orders 35 mg of amphotericin B and 25 units of heparin to be administered intravenously in 1000 mL of D5W over an 8-hour period to a hospitalized patient. In filling the medication order, the available sources of the additives are a vial containing 50 mg of amphotericin B in 10 mL and a syringe containing 10 units of heparin per milliliter.

    (a) How many milliliters of each additive should be used in filling the medication order?
    (b) How many milliliters of the intravenous fluid per minute should the patient receive to administer the fluid over the designated interval?

25. A solution containing 500,000 units of polymyxin B sulfate in 10 mL of sterile water for injection is added to 250 mL of 5% dextrose injection. The infusion is to be administered over 2 hours. If the administration set calibrates 15 drops/mL, at what rate, in drops per minute, should the flow be adjusted to administer the infusion over the designated time interval?

26. Five hundred (500) milliliters of a 2% sterile solution of a drug are to be administered by intravenous infusion over a period of 4 hours. If the administration set calibrates 20 drops/mL, at what rate, in drops per minute, should the flow be adjusted to administer the infusion over the desired time interval? Solve the problem by calculation *and* by using the nomogram in this chapter.

27. An 8-kg infant requires a continuous infusion of a drug to run at 1 mL/hour to deliver 4 mcg of drug/kg per minute. Calculate the milligrams of drug that must be added to a 100-mL intravenous infusion solution.

28. Five hundred (500) milliliters of an intravenous solution contain 0.2% of succinylcholine chloride in sodium chloride injection. At what flow rate should the infusion be administered to provide 2.5 mg of succinylcholine chloride per minute?

29. A hospital pharmacist prepared thirty 100-mL epidural bags containing 0.125% of bupivacaine hydrochloride and 1 μg/mL of fentanyl citrate in 0.9% sodium chloride injection. How many (a) 30-mL vials of 0.5% bupivacaine hydrochloride, (b) 20-mL vials of 50 μg/mL of fentanyl citrate, and (c) 1-L bags of 0.9% sodium chloride were required?

30. An intravenous fluid of 1000 mL of lactated Ringer's injection was started in a patient at 8 AM and was scheduled to run for 12 hours. At 3 PM, 800 mL of the fluid remained in the bottle. At what rate of flow should the remaining fluid be regulated using an IV set that delivers 15 drops/mL to complete the administration of the fluid in the scheduled time?

31. If a physician orders 5 units of insulin to be added to a 1-liter intravenous solution of D5W to be administered over 8 hours, (a) how many drops per minute should be administered using an IV set that delivers 15 drops/mL, and (b) how many units of insulin would be administered in each 30-minute period?

32. A patient is to receive 3 μg/kg/min of nitroglycerin from a solution containing 100 mg of the drug in 500 mL of D5W. If the patient weighs 176 lb. and the infusion set delivers 60 drops/mL, (a) how many milligrams of nitroglycerin would be delivered per hour, and (b) how many drops per minute would be delivered?

33. Using the nomogram in Figure 13.5, determine the approximate rate of infusion delivery, in drops per minute, based on 1.5 liters of fluid to be used over a period of 8 hours with an infusion set calibrated to deliver 16 drops/mL.

34. The drug alfentanil hydrochloride is administered by infusion at the rate of 2 μg/kg/min for anesthesia induction. If a total of 0.35 mg of the drug is to be administered to a 110-lb. patient, how long should be the duration of the infusion?

35. The recommended maintenance dose of aminophylline for children is 1.0 mg/kg/hr by injection. If 10 mL of a 25 mg/mL solution of aminophylline is added to a 100-mL bottle of dextrose injection, what should be the rate of delivery, in milliliters per hour, for a 40-lb. child?

36. A patient is to receive an infusion of a drug at the rate of 5 mg/hr for 8 hours. The drug is available in 10-mL vials containing 8 mg of drug per milliliter. If a 250-mL bottle of D5W is used as the vehicle, (a) how many milliliters of the drug solution should be added, and (b) what should be the flow rate in milliliters per minute?

37. A patient is receiving an IV drip of the following:

    Sodium heparin 25,000 units
    Sodium chloride injection (0.45%) 500 mL

    (a) How many milliliters per hour must be administered to achieve a rate of 1200 units of sodium heparin per hour?
    (b) If the IV set delivers 15 drops/mL, how many drops per minute should be administered?

38. A 50-mL vial containing 1 mg/mL of the drug alteplase is added to 100 mL of D5W and administered intravenously with an infusion set that delivers 15 drops/mL. How many drops per minute should be given to administer 25 mg of the drug per hour?

39. If the loading dose of phenytoin in children is 20 mg/kg of body weight to be infused at a rate of 0.5 mg/kg/min, over how many minutes should the dose be administered to a 32-lb. child?

40.[7] The following was ordered for a critical care patient: 2 L of D5/0.45% NS to run over 24 hours with a 2000 mL IV fluid daily limit. An IVPB antibiotic is ordered to run every 6 hours separately in 50 mL of D5W over 30 minutes. The drop factor is 60 drops per milliliter. Calculate the flow rate of the IVPB and the D5/0.45% NS.

41. If a medication order calls for a dobutamine drip, 5 μg/kg/min, for a patient weighing 232 lb. what should be the drip rate, in drops per minute, if the 125-mL infusion bag contains 250 mg of dobutamine and a microdrip chamber is used that delivers 60 drops/mL?

42. At what rate, in drops per minute, should a dose of 20 μg/kg/min of dopamine be administered to a 65-kg patient using a solution containing dopamine, 1200 μg/mL, and a drip set that delivers 60 drops/mL?

43. A pharmacist places 5 mg/mL of acyclovir sodium in 250 mL of D5W for parenteral infusion into a pediatric patient. If the infusion is to run for 1 hour and the patient is to receive 500 mg/m^2 BSA, what would be the rate of flow in milliliters per minute for a patient measuring 55 cm in height and weighing 10 kg?

44. Aminophylline is not to be administered in pediatric patients at a rate greater than 25 mg per minute to avoid excessive peak serum concentrations and possible circulatory failure. What should be the maximum infusion rate, in milliliters per minute, for a solution containing 10 mg/mL of aminophylline in 100 mL of D5W?

45. An intravenous infusion contains 5 mg of RECLAST (zoledronic acid) in 100 mL. If the infusion is to be administered in 15 minutes, how many (a) milligrams of zoledronic acid, and (b) milliliters of infusion must be administered per minute? And (c), using a drip-set that delivers 20 drops/milliliter, how many drops per minute must be infused?

46. ORENCIA (abatacept), used to treat rheumatoid arthritis, is available in vials, each containing 250 mg of powdered drug, intended to be reconstituted to10 mL with sterile water for injection. The dose of abatacept depends on a patient's body weight: <60 kg, 500 mg; 60 to 100 kg, 750 mg; and >100 kg, 1 g. The contents of the appropriate number of vials are aseptically added to a 100-mL infusion bag or bottle of sodium chloride injection *after* the corresponding volume of sodium chloride injection has been removed. The concentration of abatacept in an infusion for a 200-lb. patient would be:
    (a) 5.8 mg/mL
    (b) 6.25 mg/mL
    (c) 6.8 mg/mL
    (d) 7.5 mg/mL

47. TORISEL (temsirolimus), for use in advanced renal cell carcinoma, is prepared for infusion by adding 1.8 mL of special diluent to the drug vial resulting in 3 mL of injection containing 10 mg/mL of temsirolimus. The required quantity is then added to a 250-mL container of sodium chloride injection for infusion. The recommended dose of temsirolimus is 25 mg infused over 30 to 60 minutes. The quantity of drug delivered, in mg/mL, and the rate of infusion, in mL/min, for a 30-minute infusion are:
    (a) 0.099 mg/mL and 8.42 mL/min
    (b) 0.099 mg/mL and 8.33 mL/min
    (c) 1 mg/mL and 8.42 mL/min
    (d) 1 mg/mL and 8.33 mL/min

48. CARDENE IV (nicardipine hydrochloride) is administered in the short-term treatment of hypertension by slow intravenous infusion at a concentration of 0.1 mg/mL. A 10-mL ampule containing 25 mg of nicardipine hydrochloride should be added to what volume of D5W to achieve the desired concentration of infusion?
    (a) 80 mL
    (b) 100 mL
    (c) 240 mL
    (d) 250 mL

ANSWERS TO "CASE IN POINT" AND PRACTICE PROBLEMS

Case in Point 13.1

(a) 15 mg/min × 10 min = 150 mg amiodarone HCl needed for the rapid infusion. Ampul contains 50 mg/mL, so 3 mL are needed = one 3-mL ampul, *answer*.

(b) 150 mg amiodarone in 103 mL; 150 mg ÷ 103 mL = 1.46 mg/mL, *answer*.

(c) 3 (ampuls) × 3 mL = 9 mL × 50 mg/mL = 450 mg amiodarone HCl
450 mg ÷ 259 mL = 1.74 mg/mL amiodarone HCl, *answer*.

(d) 60 minutes × 1 mg/min = 60 mg amio-darone HCl
60 mg ÷ 1.74 mg/mL = 34.5 mL/hr, *answer.*

(e) 34.5 mL × 15 drops/mL = 517.5 drops in 1 hour
517.5 drops ÷ 60 = 8.625 or about 9 drops per minute, *answer.*

(f) 1 mg/min × 60 min/hr × 6 hr = 360 mg, *answer.*

(g) 0.5 mg/min × 60 min/hr × 18 hr = 540 mg, *answer.*

Practice Problems

1. 1.8 g sodium chloride
   40 g dextrose

2. 4.3 g sodium chloride
   0.15 g potassium chloride
   0.165 g calcium chloride
   25 g dextrose

3. 6 hours, 15 minutes

4. 2:00 PM

5. 8 hours, 20 minutes

6. 300 minutes

7. 12 midnight

8. 3 mL daptomycin injection

9. 5 mL lidocaine injection

10. 2 mg/mL fluconazole

11. 1344 mL IVIG

12. (a) 1.6 mg/mL dopamine
    (b) 12.78 mL/hr

13. 0.6 mL

14. 13.33 mL

15. 1.8 mL amikacin sulfate injection

16. 3.92 mg/mL lidocaine

17. 44.6 mEq sodium

18. 30.32 mEq potassium phosphate

19. 4 mL

20. (a) 640 mg cetuximab
    (b) 31.25 or 31 drops/min

21. 1.1 mL
    52.8 mg

22. 8.33 mg

23. 69.4 or 69 drops/min

24. (a) 7 mL amphotericin B
    2.5 mL heparin
    (b) 2.08 mL/min

25. 32.6 or 33 drops/min

26. 41.7 or 42 drops/min

27. 192 mg

28. 1.25 mL/min

29. (a) 25
    (b) 3
    (c) 3

30. 40 drops/min

31. (a) 31.25 or 31 drops/min
    (b) 0.3 unit

32. (a) 14.4 mg/hr
    (b) 72 drops/min

33. approximately 50 drops/min

34. 3.5 minutes

35. 8 mL/hr

36. (a) 5 mL
    (b) 0.53 mL/min

37. (a) 24 mL/hr
    (b) 6 drops/min

38. 18.75 or 19 drops/min

39. 40 minutes

40. IVPB, 100 drops/minute
    D5/0.45NS, 82 drops/minute

41. 15.82 or 16 drops/min

42. 66 drops/min

43. 0.58 mL/min

44. 2.5 mL/min

45. (a) 0.33 mg zoledronic acid
    (b) 6.67 mL
    (c) 133 drops/minute

46. (d) 7.5 mg/mL

47. (a) 0.099 mg/mL and 8.42 mL/min

48. (c) 240 mL

REFERENCES

1. http://www.usp.org/pdf/EN/USPNF/generalChapter797.pdf. Accessed December 3, 2007; United States Pharmacopeia 31st Rev. National Formulary 26. Rockville, MD: United States Pharmacopeial Convention, 2008;(797)1: 319–336.
2. Boh L. *Pharmacy Practice Manual: A Guide to the Clinical Experience.* Baltimore: Lippincott Williams & Wilkins, 2001: 418.
3. Institute for Safe Medication Practices. ISMP medication safety alert: how fast is too fast of IV push medications. May 15, 2003. Available at: http://www.ismp.org/MSAarticles/HowPrint.htm. Accessed November 16, 2004.
4. Mitchell A, Sommo P, Mocerine T, et al. A standardized approach to pediatric parenteral medication delivery. *Hospital Pharmacy* 2004;39:433–459.
5. Gomella TL, Cunningham MD, Eyal FG, et al. *Neonatology: Management Procedures, On-Call Problems, Diseases, and Drugs* New York: Lange Medical Books, 2004:69–73.
6. Vo A and Jordan SC. IVIG therapy: an emerging role in organ transplantation. *U.S. Pharmacist* March 2004:HS 36–40.
7. Lacher B. *Pharmaceutical Calculations for the Pharmacy Technician.* Baltimore: Lippincott Williams & Wilkins, 2008: 287.

Enteral and Parenteral Nutrition, Body Mass Index, and the Food Nutrition Label

14

Objectives

Upon successful completion of this chapter, the student will be able to:

- Perform basic calculations for enteral feeding and parenteral nutrition.
- Calculate body mass index (BMI) from a standard formula.
- Apply the food nutrition label in related calculations.

Today's pharmacists are increasingly involved in the provision of enteral and parenteral nutrition services in institutional and home care settings. In this capacity, pharmacists often provide the calculations needed and participate in the selection, preparation, and administration of nutritional formulas.

In community practice, pharmacists routinely are involved in counseling patients on matters of nutrition. It is well recognized that poor dietary choices contribute to obesity and many chronic conditions, including hypertension, coronary heart disease, sleep apnea, and type 2 diabetes mellitus (the term *diabesity* has been coined to describe the relationship between type 2 diabetes and obesity).[1–4] Community pharmacists frequently advise patients on general dietary requirements for the maintenance of good health, provide counseling with regard to weight control, help patients understand the nutritional labeling on food products, and explain the use and composition of various dietary supplements.

Figure 14.1 depicts the three routes of nutrition: oral, enteral, and parenteral.

Enteral Nutrition

Enteral nutrition is a method of providing nutritional support via tubes inserted into the stomach or small intestine. It finds application in patients who have an inability or decreased ability to ingest nutrients by mouth. As shown in Figure 14.1, nasogastric tubes may be used, or tubes may be inserted through surgical openings into the stomach, duodenum, or jejunum.[5] Surgical insertions generally are reserved for the relatively long-term feeding requirements of patients (e.g., more than 4 weeks). Enteral nutrition may be used for total nutrition, for supplemental nutrition, or as a transitional phase for patients coming off parenteral nutrition. Tube feedings may be intermittent or continuous, and in addition to nutritional requirements, they address the need to replace water lost daily through urination, bowel function, respiration, and perspiration.

Enteral nutrition takes into account a patient's caloric requirements and his or her need for protein, carbohydrate and fat, vitamins and minerals, dietary fiber, electrolytes, and fluids. Commercial formulas for enteral feeding are multiple and varied. Some are designed specifically for pediatric or adult patients. Some provide a balanced or general requirement; others are high in calories, protein, amino acids, fat, and/or fiber; and still others are low in carbohydrate, sodium, or cholesterol. Some commercial formulas are designed to meet the disease-specific

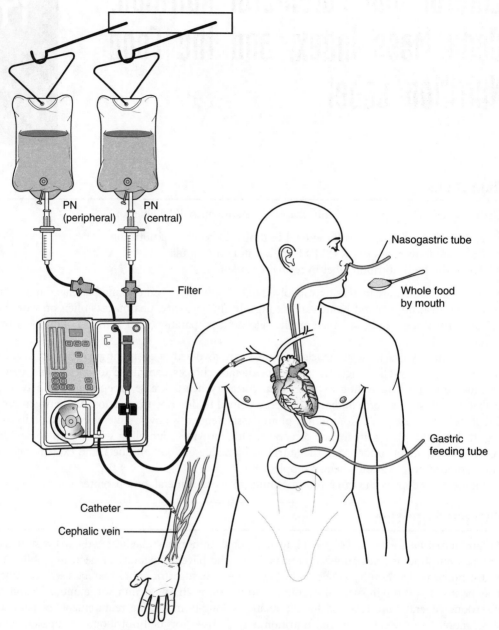

FIGURE 14.1 Routes of nutrition: oral, enteral, and parenteral.

requirements of certain patients, such as those with renal or hepatic disease or those who are diabetic, lactose intolerant, or allergic to specific foods. As required, additions may be made to commercial formulas to meet the needs of a specific patient.

The osmolality of an enteral formula is an important consideration. Some patients exhibit intolerance to a hyperosmolar formula, resulting in vomiting, osmotic diarrhea, abdominal distention, and other symptoms.[6] Most infant formulas have osmolalities between 150 and 380 mOsmol/kg, and adult formulas from about 270 to 700 mOsmol/kg. It should be recalled that the osmolality of extracellular fluid is considered to be 285 to 295 mOsmol/kg.

When necessary, medications can be administered through the enteral feeding tubes, preferably with liquid dosage forms. As required, well-diluted slurries can be prepared and administered from the solid contents of tablets or capsules. Liquid medications with high osmolalities (some are greater than 1000 mOsmol/kg) can be diluted with 10 to 30 mL of sterile water prior to administration.[5,7]

Medications generally are administered separately from the nutrient formulas, with care taken not to conflict with the feeding schedule, to avoid drug incompatibilities with other medications and nutritional components, to consider a medication's possible gastrointestinal effects (e.g., diarrhea or constipation), and to make certain that no residual medication remains in the feeding tubes after medication delivery.[5,7]

Parenteral Nutrition

Parenteral nutrition (PN) or *intravenous hyperalimentation (IVH or HAL)* is the feeding of a patient by the intravenous infusion of fluids and basic nutrients. *Partial parenteral nutrition (PPN)* is nutritional support that *supplements* oral intake and provides only part of daily nutritional requirements. *Total parenteral nutrition (TPN)* provides *all* the patient's daily nutritional requirements.

Parenteral nutrition is used for patients who cannot obtain adequate nutrition by oral means. This includes patients who are severely malnourished, those whose critical illness temporarily precludes their receiving oral or enteral nutrition and there is need to *prevent* starvation-induced complications, those whose gastrointestinal tracts are unavailable or malfunctioning, those with a demonstrated or assessed probability of ineffective nourishment by enteral feeding, and patients in renal or hepatic failure, among others.[8,9]

Figure 14.2 is an example of a hospital adult parenteral nutrition form. Note that the prescribing physician may select the standard formulas or modifications for central or peripheral administration. Central administration lines are inserted into the superior vena cava, whereas peripheral lines are inserted into veins of the arm or hand (see Fig. 14.1). Because concentrated dextrose solutions are hypertonic and may be damaging to veins, central lines are preferred over peripheral lines for higher concentrations of dextrose (e.g., 25%). Nutritional formulas for peripheral parenteral nutrition generally are isotonic or near isotonic.

Typically, parenteral nutrition formulas contain the following:

- *Macronutrients*:
  Carbohydrate (e.g., dextrose)
  Protein (e.g., amino acids)
  Fat (e.g., lipid emulsions)
- *Micronutrients*:
  Electrolytes
  Vitamins
  Trace elements
- *Sterile water for injection*

Parenteral nutrition formulas can be obtained commercially or they may be prepared in the pharmacy, often through the use of automated mixing devices. Nutritional requirements and thus formulations differ based on age groups (e.g., neonates, general pediatrics, adults) as well as patient-specific diseases (e.g., renal, liver, pulmonary). In preparing formulas for parenteral nutrition, pharmacists use calculated quantities of small-volume parenterals (ampuls and vials) as the source of electrolytes, vitamins, and minerals, and large-volume parenterals (LVPs) as the source of amino acids, dextrose, and sterile water for injection.

Typically, infusion rates are begun at about 25 to 50 mL per hour and adjusted every 8 to 12 hours as dictated by the patient's condition and fluid and nutritional status.[9] TPN solutions

STANDARD CENTRAL LINE FORMULA	STANDARD PERIPHERAL LINE FORMULA	STANDARD RENAL CENTRAL LINE FORMULA
Standard ☐ Modified ☐	Standard ☐ Modified ☐	Standard ☐ Modified ☐
Amino Acid 4.25% _____%	Amino Acid 2.75% _____%	Amino Acid 1.95% _____%
Dextrose 25% _____%	Dextrose 10% _____%	Dextrose 44% _____%
Rate _____mL/hr	Rate _____mL/hr	Rate _____mL/hr
Electrolytes (per liter)	**Electrolytes (per liter)**	**Electrolytes (per liter)**
Standard ☐ Modified ☐	Standard ☐ Modified ☐	Standard ☐ Modified ☐
Na 35 mEq _____mEq	Na 35 mEq _____mEq	Na 0 mEq _____mEq
K 30 mEq _____mEq	K 30 mEq _____mEq	K 0 mEq _____mEq
Mg 5 mEq _____mEq	Mg 5 mEq _____mEq	Mg 0 mEq _____mEq
Ca 3 mEq _____mEq	Ca 3 mEq _____mEq	Ca 0 mEq _____mEq
P 15 mM _____mM	P 15 mM _____mM	P 0 mM _____mM
Acetate: Cl = 1:1 _____	Acetate: Cl = 1:1 _____	
Each bag contains the standard amount of multi-vitamins and trace elements.	Each bag contains the standard amount of multi-vitamins and trace elements.	Check if you wish to add the standard amount of trace elements and multivitamins. Trace Elements _____ Multivitamins _____
Additional Ingredients (per liter)	**Additional Ingredients (per liter)**	**Additional Ingredients (per liter)**
Standard ☐ Modified ☐	_____	_____
___Cimetidine 900 mg/24 hr OR:_____ mg/24 hr	_____	_____
___Ranitidine 150 mg/24 hr OR:_____ mg/24 hr	_____	_____
___Reg Insulin _____units/L Other: _____ _____ _____	_____	_____

Intravenous Fat 10% 500 mL (1.1 kcal/mL):_____(rate)

Intravenous Fat 20% 500 mL (2 kcal/mL):_____(rate)

Date:_____ MD _____

NOTE:
Standing physician's orders for line management and patient monitoring of parenteral hyperalimentation will be followed unless initialed here:_____

FIGURE 14.2 Example of part of an order form for adult parenteral nutrition. *(Published with the permission of Wake Medical Center, Raleigh, NC.)*

may be administered continuously over a 24-hour period or cyclically, depending on a patient's requirements. Infusions may be administered by gravity flow or through the use of automated, high-speed multichannel pumping devices.

In many instances, parenteral nutrition begun in an institutional setting is continued on an outpatient basis at home. Many pharmacists participate in the administration of home parenteral nutrition.

Nutritional Requirements

Nutritional requirements are the quantities of macronutrients and micronutrients needed for a patient to obtain or maintain the desired nutritional status. The quantitative amounts of fluid and specific nutrients required vary with an individual's age, gender, physical parameters, disease state, and current nutritional status. The purpose of this section is to provide only *general* considerations. More detailed and patient-specific considerations are presented in other resources, including those referenced.[7-14]

Fluid Requirements

A factor of 30 mL/kg of body weight, 1500 mL per square meter of body surface area, or 1 mL/kcal of nutrition required are among the methods used to estimate a patient's daily fluid or water requirement. On a case-by-case basis, these values may be increased (e.g., for patients who are dehydrated) or decreased (e.g., for patients with renal failure or congestive heart failure). A daily requirement of between 2 and 3 liters per day is usual for adults. For neonates, infants, children, and adolescents without abnormal water losses, the approximate daily water requirement may be calculated by:

Parameter	*Water Requirement*
Based on age:	
Neonates	120 to 180 mL/kg/day
1 to 12 months	150 mL/kg/day (maximum, 200 mL)
Based on Weight:	
<10 kg	100 mL/kg/day
10 to 20 kg	1000 mL + 50 mL/kg/day over 10 kg
>20 kg	1500 mL + 20 mL/kg/day over 20 kg
Based on Body Surface Area:	
m² × 1500 mL/day/m²	__mL/day
Based on Caloric Requirement:	
1.2 mL/kcal × kcal/day	__mL/day

Caloric Requirements

The **kilocalorie (kcal)** is the unit used in metabolism studies. By definition, the kilocalorie (or large Calorie, C, or Cal.) is the amount of heat required to raise the temperature of 1 kg of water 1°C. The caloric requirements for patients vary, depending on their physical state and medical condition. The Harris-Benedict equations, which follow, are commonly used to estimate the *basal energy expenditure (BEE)* requirements for nonprotein calories. The BEE is also referred to as the *resting metabolic energy (RME)* or the *resting energy expenditure (REE)*.

For males:

BEE = 66.67 + [13.75 × Weight (kg)] + [5 × Height (cm)] − [6.76 × Age (yr)]

For females:

BEE = 655.1 + [9.56 × Weight (kg)] + [1.86 × Height (cm)] − [4.68 × Age (yr)]

The *total daily expenditure (TDE)* of energy, as calculated, may be adjusted for activity and stress factors[8,14]:

BEE × activity factors × stress factors = TDE

Activity factors: Confined to bed: 1.2
Ambulatory: 1.3

Stress factors: Surgery: 1.2
                           Infection: 1.4 to 1.6
                           Trauma: 1.3 to 1.5
                           Burns: 1.5 to 2.1

As an alternative to the use of the Harris-Benedict equations, clinicians can estimate the BEE for adults as 25 kcal/kg/day for mildly stressed hospitalized patients, up to 35 kcal/kg/day for moderately stressed patients, up to 45 kcal/kg/day for postoperative patients, and up to 60 kcal/kg/day for hypercatabolic patients. Energy requirements for infants, children, and teenagers are different than those for adults and vary according to age, growth rate, and clinical/metabolic status. The caloric requirements are about 100 kcal/kg/day for infants, 80 to 100 kcal/kg/day for children, and 35 to 60 kcal/kg/day for teenagers.

Carbohydrate Requirements

Carbohydrates are the primary source of cellular energy. In formulas for parenteral nutrition, dextrose provides 3.4 kcal of energy per gram; for example, each 100 mL of a 25% dextrose injection provides 85 kcal of energy. For enteral nutrition, the factor used is 4 kcal/g.[11]

Protein Requirements

In TPN, protein is provided as protein hydrolysate or amino acids. The purpose of the protein support is not to produce energy, although energy is produced by proteins by a factor of 4 kcal/g, but rather to build tissues and body strength.[14] A patient's caloric needs should be provided by *nonprotein calories*. The daily quantity of protein required in adults is generally estimated to be about:

- 0.8 g/kg/day in an unstressed patient;
- 0.8 to 1 g/kg of body weight for a mildly stressed patient;
- 1.2 g/kg for a renal dialysis patient;
- 1.1 to 1.5 g/kg for a moderately stressed patient;
- 1.5 to 2 g/kg for a severely stressed patient and those with a critical illness or trauma; and
- 3 g/kg for a severely burned patient.

Infants may require 2 to 3 g/kg/day, children 1.5 to 2 g/kg/day, and teenagers 1 to 1.5 g/kg/day of protein.[8,14]

Lipid (Fat) Requirements

Lipids may be used to provide energy when the body cannot obtain all the necessary energy requirement from carbohydrates. The proportion of calories provided by lipids is usually restricted to 30% to 40% of the total daily calories. Lipids provide 9 kcal of energy per gram. Lipids are generally administered in the form of an emulsion containing carbohydrate-based emulsifying agents, which also contribute to the caloric content. It has been determined that a 10% lipid emulsion provides 11 kcal/g of total energy, and a 20% to 30% lipid emulsion provides 10 kcal/g of total energy.[11,12]

Fiber Requirements

Dietary guidelines generally recommend a daily intake of 14 g of fiber for each 1000 calories consumed. This translates to approximately 21 to 25 grams of daily fiber for women and between 30 to 38 g for men. *Insoluble* fiber reaches the large intestine after ingestion and is associated with good bowel function whereas *soluble* fiber partially dissolves in the upper gastrointestinal tract and is associated with reduced absorption of dietary fat and cholesterol.[15]

Micronutrients

As shown in Figure 14.2, the *standard* quantities of electrolytes may be used as parenteral nutrition or modified as required.

Enteral and Parenteral Nutrition Calculations

Example Calculations of Enteral Nutrition[11]

The nutritional requirements for a 76-year-old male who is 6 ft. 2 in. tall and weighs 201 lb. have been determined to be as follows:

  Protein: 73.09 g/day
  Lipids: 81.23 g/day
  Carbohydrates: 266.34 g/day
  Water: 2088.82 to 2740.91 mL/day
  Total calories: 2088.82 kcal/day

ENSURE liquid is chosen for enteral nutrition for this patient. A quart container provides 37 g protein, 143 g carbohydrates, 37 g lipids, and 1.06 kcal/mL.

(a) *How many milliliters of ENSURE should this patient receive daily to meet his caloric requirements?*

$$\frac{2088.82 \text{ kcal}}{1 \text{ day}} \times \frac{1 \text{ mL}}{1.06 \text{ kcal}} = 1970.58 \text{ mL/day, } \textit{answer.}$$

(b) *How many grams each of protein, carbohydrates, and lipids would this volume provide?*

$$\text{Protein: } \frac{1970.58 \text{ mL}}{1 \text{ day}} \times \frac{1 \text{ qt}}{946 \text{ mL}} \times \frac{37 \text{ g}}{1 \text{ qt}} = 77.07 \text{ g/day;}$$

$$\text{Carbohydrates: } \frac{1970.58 \text{ mL}}{1 \text{ day}} \times \frac{1 \text{ qt}}{946 \text{ mL}} \times \frac{143 \text{ g}}{1 \text{ qt}} = 297.88 \text{ g/day; } \textit{and}$$

$$\text{Lipids: } \frac{1970.58 \text{ mL}}{1 \text{ day}} \times \frac{1 \text{ qt}}{946 \text{ mL}} \times \frac{37 \text{ g}}{1 \text{ qt}} = 77.07 \text{ g/day, } \textit{answers.}$$

(c) *If the product contains 85% free water, does it meet the patient's daily water requirement?*

$$1970.58 \text{ mL/day} \times 85\% = 1675 \text{ mL/day}$$

Therefore, the amount of water provided by 1970.58 mL of the formula would *not* fully meet the patient's daily water requirement, *answer.*

(d) *If the formula is to be delivered continuously over a 24-hour period, what would be the flow rate in mL/hr?*

$$\frac{1970.58 \text{ mL}}{1 \text{ day}} \times \frac{1 \text{ day}}{24 \text{ hrs}} = 82.11 \text{ mL/hr} \approx 82 \text{ mL/hr, } \textit{answer}$$

(e) *If the patient is to continue receiving this formula at home by intermittent feedings over 40 minutes every 4 hours, what volume would be administered with each feeding, and what would be the flow rate in mL/hr?*

$$\frac{1970.58 \text{ mL}}{1 \text{ day}} \times \frac{1 \text{ day}}{24 \text{ hrs}} \times \frac{4 \text{ hrs}}{1 \text{ dose}} = 328.43 \text{ mL/dose, } and$$

$$\frac{328.43 \text{ mL}}{40 \text{ min}} \times \frac{60 \text{ min}}{1 \text{ hr}} = 492.65 \text{ mL/hr} \approx 493 \text{ mL/hr, } answers.$$

Example Calculations of Parenteral Nutrition

The following basic steps may be used as a guide in TPN calculations.[11]

Step 1. Calculate the total daily calories required using the Harris-Benedict equations, and apply the appropriate stress or activity factors.

Step 2. Calculate the daily quantity (g) of amino acids (protein) required based on 0.8 g/kg of body weight, and adjust as needed for stress factors and certain disease states.

Step 3. Calculate the number of calories supplied by the amino acids (from Step 2) at 4 kcal/g.

Step 4. Calculate the kcal of lipids required at 30% to 40% of the total daily calories.

Step 5. Calculate the grams of lipids required (from Step 4) based on 9 kcal/g or based on the lipid emulsion used [as discussed in the section titled "Lipid (Fat) Requirements" earlier in the text].

Step 6. Calculate the quantity of carbohydrate required based on 3.4 kcal/g after accounting for the contribution of the lipids.

Step 7. Calculate the daily fluid requirement using 30 mL/kg/day or one of the other methods described earlier in the text.

Notes: In some clinical practices (a) a patient's actual body weight, the ideal body weight, or some middle ground may be used in the calculations (in Step 1), and (b) in Step 6, the energy provided by the protein, in addition to that from lipids, may or may not be taken into account. In addition to Steps 1 through 7, TPN calculations also can include:

• determination of the quantities of the pharmaceutical sources of the macronutrients (e.g., vials) and micronutrients (e.g., LVPs) to use to obtain the required components; and
• determination of the total TPN volume, the number of TPN bags to be prepared, and the rate of flow.

Calculate the parenteral nutrition and fluid requirements for a 58-year-old woman who is 5 ft. 3 in. tall and weighs 140 lb., assuming that she has no disease states that would alter her nutritional requirements.[11]

Step 1. Total daily kcal required by Harris-Benedict equation:

$$655.1 + (9.56 \times 63.63 \text{ kg}) + (1.86 \times 160 \text{ cm}) - (4.68 \times 58 \text{ yr}) = 1289.62 \text{ kcal}$$

Step 2. Protein required (grams):

$$140 \text{ lb.} \times \frac{1 \text{ kg}}{2.2 \text{ lb.}} \times \frac{0.8 \text{ g}}{1 \text{ kg/day}} = 50.91 \text{ g/day}$$

Step 3. Protein (kcal):

$$\frac{50.91 \text{ g}}{1 \text{ day}} \times \frac{4 \text{ kcal}}{1 \text{ g}} = 203.64 \text{ kcal/day}$$

Step 4. Lipids required (kcal), using 35% of total daily calories:

$$1289.62 \text{ kcal/day (total)} \times 35\% = 451.37 \text{ kcal/day}$$

Step 5. Lipids required (grams), using a 10% lipid emulsion:

$$\frac{451.37 \text{ kcal}}{1 \text{ day}} \times \frac{1 \text{ g}}{11 \text{ kcal}} = 41.03 \text{ g/day}$$

Step 6. Carbohydrates (dextrose) required (grams), accounting for kcal from both protein and lipids:

$$1289.62 \text{ kcal/day} - 203.64 \text{ kcal/day (protein)} - 451.37 \text{ kcal/day (lipids)}$$
$$= 634.61 \text{ kcal/day}$$

$$\frac{634.61 \text{ kcal}}{1 \text{ day}} \times \frac{1 \text{ g}}{3.4 \text{ kcal}} = 186.65 \text{ g/day}$$

Step 7. Fluid required (milliliters):

Based on 30 mL/kg/day:

$$140 \text{ lb.} \times \frac{1 \text{ kg}}{2.2 \text{ lb.}} \times \frac{30 \text{ mL}}{1 \text{ kg/day}} = 1909.09 \text{ mL/day}$$

Based on 1 mL/kcal required/day:

$$\frac{1289.62 \text{ kcal}}{1 \text{ day}} \times \frac{1 \text{ mL}}{1 \text{ kcal}} = 1289.62 \text{ mL/day}$$

The patient should receive 50.91 g of protein, 41.03 g of lipids, 186.65 g of dextrose, and between 1289.62 and 1909.09 mL of fluid per day, *answer.*

Using the Harris-Benedict equation, calculate the caloric requirement for a mildly stressed 56-year-old hospitalized female patient weighing 121 lb. and measuring 5 ft 3 in. in height.

$$\begin{aligned}
121 \text{ lb.} \quad &= 55 \text{ kg} \\
5 \text{ ft. 3 in.} \quad &= 63 \text{ in.} = 160 \text{ cm} \\
\text{BEE} \quad &= 655.1 + (9.56 \times 55) + (1.86 \times 160) - (4.68 \times 56) \\
&= 655.1 + (525.8) + (297.6) - (262) \\
&= 1216.5 \text{ kcal}
\end{aligned}$$

Using the average factor of 1.3 for a mildly stressed patient:

$$1216.5 \times 1.3 = 1581.45 \text{ kcal, } answer.$$

Calculate the daily quantity of protein required for the 55-kg-patient based on 0.8 g/kg and the caloric value based on 4 kcal/g for proteins.

$$\begin{aligned}
55 \text{ kg} \times 0.8 \text{ g/kg} \quad &= 44 \text{ g protein, } and \\
44 \text{ g} \times 4 \text{ kcal/g} \quad &= 176 \text{ kcal, } answers.
\end{aligned}$$

From the previous two example problems, calculate the number of milliliters of 50% dextrose solution (170 kcal/dL) that may be used to provide the additional kilocalories required.

$$\begin{aligned}
\text{Total kcal required} \quad &= 1581.45 \\
\text{kcal provided by proteins} \quad &= 176 \\
\text{Additional kcal required} \quad &= 1405.45 \ (1581.45 - 176)
\end{aligned}$$

Thus,

$$\frac{1405 \text{ kcal}}{170 \text{ kcal}} = \frac{x \text{ mL}}{100 \text{ mL}}$$
$$x = 826.7 \text{ mL, } answer$$

The following is a formula for a desired parenteral nutrition solution. Using the source of each drug as indicated, calculate the amount of each component required in preparing the solution.

Formula	Component Source
(a) Sodium Chloride 35 mEq	Vial, 5 mEq per 2 mL
(b) Potassium Acetate 35 mEq	Vial, 10 mEq per 5 mL
(c) Magnesium Sulfate 8 mEq	Vial, 4 mEq per mL
(d) Calcium Gluconate 9.6 mEq	Vial, 4.7 mEq per 10 mL
(e) Potassium Chloride 5 mEq	Vial, 40 mEq per 20 mL
(f) Folic Acid 1.7 mg	Ampul, 5 mg per mL
(g) Multiple Vitamin Infusion 10 mL	Ampul, 10 mL

To be added to:

Amino Acids Infusion (8.5%) 500 mL
Dextrose Injection (50%) 500 mL

(a)
$$\frac{5 \text{ (mEq)}}{35 \text{ (mEq)}} = \frac{2 \text{ (mL)}}{x \text{ (mL)}}$$
$$x = 14 \text{ mL};$$

(b)
$$\frac{10 \text{ (mEq)}}{35 \text{ (mEq)}} = \frac{5 \text{ (mL)}}{x \text{ (mL)}}$$
$$x = 17.5 \text{ mL};$$

(c)
$$\frac{4 \text{ (mEq)}}{8 \text{ (mEq)}} = \frac{1 \text{ (mL)}}{x \text{ (mL)}}$$
$$x = 2 \text{ mL};$$

(d)
$$\frac{4.7 \text{ (mEq)}}{9.6 \text{ (mEq)}} = \frac{10 \text{ (mL)}}{x \text{ (mL)}}$$
$$x = 20.4 \text{ mL};$$

(e)
$$\frac{40 \text{ (mEq)}}{5 \text{ (mEq)}} = \frac{20 \text{ (mL)}}{x \text{ (mL)}}$$
$$x = 2.5 \text{ mL};$$

(f)
$$\frac{5 \text{ (mg)}}{1.7 \text{ (mg)}} = \frac{1 \text{ (mL)}}{x \text{ (mL)}}$$
$$x = 0.34 \text{ mL}; \text{ and}$$

(g) 10 mL, *answers.*

The formula for a TPN solution calls for the addition of 2.7 mEq of Ca^{++} and 20 mEq of K^+ per liter. How many milliliters of an injection containing 20 mg of calcium chloride per milliliter and how many milliliters of a 15% (w/v) potassium chloride injection should be used to provide the desired additives?

$$\begin{aligned}
\text{Formula weight of } CaCl_2 \cdot 2\,H_2O &= 147 \\
\text{Formula weight of KCl} &= 74.5 \\
1 \text{ mEq of } Ca^{++} &= 20 \text{ mg} \\
2.7 \text{ mEq of } Ca^{++} &= 20 \text{ mg} \times 2.7 = 54 \text{ mg}
\end{aligned}$$

54 mg of Ca^{++} are furnished by 198.45 or 198 mg of calcium chloride

Because the injection contains 20 mg of calcium chloride per mL, then $198 \div 20 = 9.9$ mL, and

$$1 \text{ mEq of } K^+ = 39 \text{ mg}$$
$$20 \text{ mEq of } K^+ = 39 \text{ mg} \times 20 = 780 \text{ mg}$$

780 mg of K^+ are furnished by 1.49 g of potassium chloride
15% (w/v) solution contains 15 g of potassium chloride per 100 mL, then

$$\frac{15 \text{ (g)}}{1.49 \text{ (g)}} = \frac{100 \text{ (mL)}}{x \text{ (mL)}}$$
$$x = 9.9 \text{ mL}, \textit{answers.}$$

A potassium phosphate injection contains a mixture of 224 mg of monobasic potassium phosphate (KH_2PO_4) and 236 mg of dibasic potassium phosphate (K_2HPO_4) per milliliter. If 10 mL of the injection are added to 500 mL of D5W (5% dextrose in water for injection), (a) how many milliequivalents of K^+ and (b) how many millimoles of total phosphate are represented in the prepared solution?

$$\text{Formula weight of } KH_2PO_4 = 136$$
$$1 \text{ mmol of } KH_2PO_4 = 136 \text{ mg}$$

10 mL of injection contains 2240 mg of KH_2PO_4

and thus provide $2240 \div 136 = 16.4$ or 16 mmol of KH_2PO_4
or 16 mmol of K^+ and 16 mmol of $H_2PO_4^=$

$$\text{Formula weight of } K_2HPO_4 = 174$$
$$1 \text{ mmol of } K_2HPO_4 = 174 \text{ mg}$$

10 mL of injection contain 2360 mg of K_2HPO_4
and thus provide $2360 \div 174 = 13.6$ or 14 mmol of K_2HPO_4
or 14 (mmol) $\times$ 2 (K^+) = 28 mmol of K^+, and 14 mmol of $HPO_4^=$
thus 10 mL of injection provide a total of :
44 mmol of K^+ or (because the valence of K^+ is 1) 44 mEq of K^+, *and*
30 mmol of total phosphate, *answers.*

Body Mass Index (BMI)

As previously stated, being overweight carries an increased risk for a number of health consequences. However, being *grossly* overweight, or *obese*, predisposes one to an even greater risk of disease, disease complications, and mortality.[3] In addition to diet, other factors that can result in obesity include behavioral, cultural, metabolic, and genetic disposition.

The initial phase in managing the overweight or obese patient is an assessment of the degree of excessive weight. Today, **body mass index (BMI)** is accepted as the clinical standard for judging excessive weight and obesity. BMI is defined as body weight in kilograms divided by the square of height measured in meters. According to the National Institutes of Health (NIH),[3] individuals with a BMI:

- less than 18.5 may be considered underweight;
- between 18.5 and 24.9 may be considered normal weight;
- between 25 and 29.9 are considered overweight;
- 30 and above are considered obese;
- over 40 are considered extremely obese.

For an elderly person, a BMI of less than 21 can be a sign of malnutrition.[16] BMI in *most people* is an indicator of high body fat (this may not be the case for persons who are especially muscular). In addition to BMI, the NIH also considers waist circumference an important factor in obesity-related disease.[3] A waist circumference of more than 40 inches in men and more than 35 inches in women indicates an increased risk of obesity-related diseases in persons who have a BMI of 25 to 35. Strategies for treating overweight and obese patients include dietary therapy, physical activity, behavioral therapy, pharmacotherapy, and, in extreme cases of obesity, weight loss surgery.[3]

Calculations Involving Body Mass Index

Determining BMI from a Standardized Table

BMI may be determined by using a standardized table like that shown in Table 14.1, in which the intercept of a person's height and weight indicates the body mass index. Many of the standardized tables available are in units of the common systems of measurement (i.e., feet/inches and pounds) to facilitate ease of use by the general public. Others are available in metric or dual scale.

Using Table 14.1, determine the BMI for a person measuring 5 ft. 8 in. and weighing 160 lb.
The intercept of 5 ft. 8 in. and 160 lb. shows a BMI of 24, *answer.*

Using Table 14.1, determine the BMI for a person 183 cm in height and weighing 82 kg.

TABLE 14.1 DETERMINING BODY MASS INDEX (BMI)

WEIGHT

HEIGHT	100	110	120	130	140	150	160	170	180	190	200	210	220	230	240	250
5'0"	20	21	23	25	27	29	31	33	35	37	39	41	43	45	47	49
5'1"	19	21	23	25	26	28	30	32	34	36	38	40	42	43	45	47
5'2"	18	20	22	24	26	27	29	31	33	35	37	38	40	42	44	46
5'3"	18	19	21	23	25	27	28	30	32	34	35	37	39	41	43	44
5'4"	17	19	21	22	24	26	27	29	31	33	34	36	38	39	41	43
5'5"	17	18	20	22	23	25	27	28	30	32	33	35	37	38	40	42
5'6"	16	18	19	21	23	24	26 ·	27	29	31	32	34	36	37	39	40
5'7"	16	17	19	20	22	23	25	27	28	30	31	33	34	36	38	39
5'8"	15	17	18	20	21	23	24	26	27	29	30	32	33	35	36	38
5'9"	15	16	18	19	21	22	24	25	27	28	30	31	32	34	35	37
5'10"	14	16	17	19	20	22	23	24	26	27	29	30	32	33	34	36
5'11"	14	15	17	18	20	21	22	24	25	26	27	28	30	32	33	35
6'0"	14	15	16	18	19	20	22	23	24	26	27	28	30	31	33	34
6'1"	13	15	16	17	18	20	21	22	24	25	26	28	29	30	32	33
6'2"	13	14	15	17	18	19	21	22	23	24	26	27	28	30	31	32
6'3"	12	14	15	16	17	19	20	21	22	24	25	26	27	29	30	31
6'4"	12	13	15	16	17	18	19	21	22	23	24	26	27	28	29	30

BMI interpretation

Underweight: under 18.5

Normal: 18.5–24.9

Overweight: 25–29.9

Obese: 30 and over

$$\frac{2.54\ cm}{183\ cm} = \frac{1\ in.}{x\ in.}; \quad x = 72\ in.$$

$$\frac{1\ kg}{82\ kg} = \frac{2.2\ lb.}{x\ lb.}; \quad x = 180\ lb.$$

Then, in Table 14.1, the intercept of 72 in, or 6 ft. 0 in. in height and 180 lb., shows a BMI of 24, *answer*.

Determining BMI by Calculation

If a person's height and weight are outside the range of a BMI table, or if a BMI table is unavailable, BMI may be determined by the formula:

$$BMI = \frac{Weight\ (kg)}{Height\ (m^2)}$$

Calculate the BMI of a person 4 ft. 11 in. in height and weighing 98 lb.

$$\frac{2.2\ lb.}{98\ lb.} = \frac{1\ kg}{x\ kg}; \quad x = 44.5\ kg$$

$$\frac{39.37\ in.}{59\ in.} = \frac{1\ meter}{x\ meter}; \quad x = 1.5\ meters$$

$$\frac{44.5\ kg}{1.5\ m \times 1.5\ m} = \frac{44.5\ kg}{2.25\ m^2} = 19.8\ BMI,\ answer.$$

Calculate the BMI of a person 6 ft. 0 in. in height weighing 182 lb.

$$\frac{2.2\ lb.}{182\ lb.} = \frac{1\ kg}{x\ kg} \quad x = 82.7\ kg,\ and$$

$$\frac{39.37\ in.}{72\ in.} = \frac{1\ meter}{x\ meter}; \quad x = 1.83\ meters,\ thus$$

$$\frac{82.7\ kg}{1.83\ m \times 1.83\ m} = \frac{82.7\ kg}{3.35\ m^2} = 24.7\ BMI,\ answer.$$

Note: In these calculations, pounds may be multiplied by 0.454 to get kilograms, and inches may be multiplied by 0.0254 to get meters.

An Alternative Formula for the Calculation of BMI

BMI may be calculated by the formula:

$$\frac{Weight\ (lb.)}{Height\ (in.)^2} \times 704.5 = BMI$$

Note: The factor 704.5, used by the National Institutes of Health, is derived by dividing the square of 39.37 (in./m) by 2.2 (lb./kg).

Calculate the BMI for a person weighing 182 lb. and standing 72 in. in height.

$$\frac{182\ lb.}{(72\ in.)^2} = \frac{182\ lb.}{5184\ in.} \times 704.5 = 24.7\ BMI,\ answer.$$

A layperson may be instructed to determine BMI by multiplying weight in pounds by 704.5 (or for ease, rounded off to 700), dividing the result by height, in inches, and then dividing the result again by height in inches. Using the example problem above:

$$182 \text{ lb.} \times 700 \div 72 \text{ in.} \div 72 \text{ in.} = 24.6, \text{ approximate BMI}$$

The Nutrition Label

The passage of the Nutrition Labeling and Education Act in 1990 gave the Food and Drug Administration (FDA) authority to develop a mandatory program for the inclusion of standardized nutrition information on the labeling of processed foods and nutritional supplements. Then, under the 1994 Dietary Supplement Health and Education Act, product ingredients and certain "Nutrition Facts" were required to be shown on a product's label (Fig. 14.3). Today's mandatory requirements include the listing of serving sizes, the number of servings per package or container, and the quantitative amounts of total calories, calories derived from fat, total fat, saturated fat, *trans* fat, cholesterol, total carbohydrate, sugars, dietary fiber, protein, sodium, vitamins A and C, calcium, and iron.[17-18] The listing of other components, such as polyunsaturated fat, is voluntary.

Nutrition Facts

Serving Size 1 cup (228g)
Servings Per Container 2

Amount Per Serving	
Calories 260	Calories from Fat 120

	% Daily Value*
Total Fat 13g	20%
Saturated Fat 5g	25%
Trans Fat 2g	
Cholesterol 30mg	10%
Sodium 660mg	28%
Total Carbohydrate 31g	10%
Dietary Fiber 0g	0%
Sugars 5g	
Protein 5g	

Vitamin A	4%
Vitamin C	2%
Calcium	15%
Iron	4%

* Percent Daily Values are based on a 2,000 calorie diet. Your Daily Values may be higher or lower depending on your calorie needs:

	Calories:	2,000	2,500
Total Fat	Less than	65g	80g
Sat Fat	Less than	20g	25g
Cholesterol	Less than	300mg	300mg
Sodium	Less than	2,400mg	2,400mg
Total Carbohydrate		300g	375g
Dietary Fiber		25g	30g

Calories per gram:
Fat 9 • Carbohydrate 4 • Protein 4

FIGURE 14.3 Example of a nutrition label.

Serving Size and Servings per Container

The labeled *serving size* reflects the amount that people generally eat at one time and is indicated in common household units (e.g., 1 cup) and approximate corresponding metric measure (e.g., 240 g). Items of discrete size, such as cookies, are listed in both units and metric equivalent, e.g., "2 cookies (26 g)." The *servings per container* indicates the number of servings in the package.

Calories

On the nutrition label, *calories per serving* and the number of *calories derived from fat* are of special importance to many consumers. High-calorie and high-fat diets are linked to overweight and obesity and the consequent illnesses.

A *calorie* (spelled with a small *c*) is the amount of energy needed to raise the temperature of 1 g of water 1°C. A *kilocalorie (kcal)* equals 1000 calories. The kilocalorie, or Calorie (spelled with a capital *C*), is the unit used in metabolism studies and in nutrition to describe the energy provided by various foods. Although *Calorie* is the appropriate term for energy intake and expenditure, the term *calorie* is most often used.

According to the United States Department of Agriculture, the caloric requirements as stated in Table 14.2 generally are suitable for most persons.

For the calculations in this section, it is important to note that:

> **carbohydrates yield 4 kcal/g;**
> **protein, 4 kcal/g; and**
> **fat, 9 kcal/g.**

Fats and Cholesterol

The most recent addition to the required nutrition label is *trans* fat. As saturated fat, *trans* fat helps raise the level of low-density lipoprotein (LDL), the so-called bad cholesterol. The most common source of *trans* fat is hydrogenated or partially hydrogenated vegetable oil, found in many vegetable shortenings and hard margarines. *Trans* fats are formed when hydrogen is added to a vegetable oil through *hydrogenation*, resulting in the solidification of the product to increase shelf life and flavor stability. *Trans* fats also are found naturally in meat and dairy products.

TABLE 14.2 ESTIMATED DAILY CALORIE REQUIREMENTS[a]

	SEDENTARY[b]		MODERATELY ACTIVE[c]		ACTIVE[d]	
AGES	FEMALE	MALE	FEMALE	MALE	FEMALE	MALE
2–3	1000	1000	1000–1400	1000–1400	1000–1400	1000–1400
4–8	1200	1400	1400–1600	1400–1600	1400–1800	1600–2000
9–13	1600	1800	1600–2000	1800–2200	1800–2200	2000–2600
14–18	1800	2200	2000	2400–2800	2400	2800–3200
19–30	2000	2400	2000–2200	2600–2800	2400	3000
31–50	1800	2200	2000	2400–2600	2200	2800–3000
51+	1600	2000	1800	2200–2400	2000–2200	2400–2800

[a] Adapted from Dietary Guidelines for Americans, 2005. Available at: http://www.health.gov/dietaryguidelines/. Accessed January 3, 2008.
[b] Sedentary includes only light physical activity associated with daily life.
[c] Moderately active includes walking 1.5 to 3 miles per day at 3 to 4 miles per hour or equivalent other activity.
[d] Active includes walking more than 3 miles per day at 3 to 4 miles per hour or equivalent other activity.

Presently, a percent daily value has not been scientifically established for *trans* fat and thus a quantitative amount is not a part of the nutrition label.[19]

Consuming too much fat, saturated fat, *trans* fat, and cholesterol may increase the risk of certain chronic diseases, as heart disease. Good health guidelines suggest that total daily fat consumed should be less than 65g, saturated fat less than 20 g, and cholesterol less than 300 mg.

Sodium and Potassium

Sodium is the electrolyte that is essential for maintaining body water balance, osmotic equilibrium, acid-base balance, regulation of plasma volume, nerve impulses, and muscle contractions. The minimum physiological requirement for sodium is approximately 500 mg daily. Excessive sodium in the diet is associated with certain chronic conditions as edema, congestive heart failure, and hypertension. Whereas the nutritional label indicates an acceptable daily intake of 2400 mg of sodium, the recommended amount for persons on sodium-restricted diets may be 1500 mg or less.

Potassium is essential for the proper function of all body cells, tissues and organs and is listed on some nutrition labels. A deficiency of potassium may occur during the throes of severe vomiting, prolonged diarrhea, with some metabolic disorders, or as a result of taking diuretics or certain other medications. An increased level of potassium may result from reduced kidney function or from certain medications, as potassium sparing diuretics. For adults, the recommended daily allowance of potassium is 4.7 g/day. The requirement is less for infants (0.4–0.7 g/day) and children (3–4.5 g/day).

Total Carbohydrate

Carbohydrates provide the body with the fuel needed for physical activity and for proper organ function. The digestive system breaks carbohydrates down into sugar molecules used by the body's cells as an energy source. Diabetics must control their carbohydrate intake. A system, called the glycemic index, classifies carbohydrates based on how quickly and how high they boost blood sugar compared to pure glucose. Carbohydrate-restricted patients may employ information on the glycemic index in concert with the nutrition label.

As noted earlier, dietary fiber, which is a carbohydrate, is an important component of a healthy diet. The sugars in dietary fiber are structured in such a way that the body has difficulty converting them to simple sugars. Thus, the more fiber a food has, the less digestible is its carbohydrate and the less sugar it can provide for absorption.

Protein

Protein is a major component of the skin, muscles, organs, and glands. However, a diet high in protein derived from meat can contribute to elevated cholesterol levels, cardiovascular disease, and may adversely affect kidney function. General health guidelines suggest that the healthy body requires about 0.8 g of protein daily per 2.2 pounds of body weight.

Vitamins and Minerals

Vitamins A and C, and calcium and iron are listed on nutrition labels for information to consumers regarding the quantities of these essential vitamins and minerals.

% Daily Value

The *percent daily values* are based on referenced amounts (daily reference values, or DRVs) for each nutrient based on a 2000-calorie diet. The 2000-calorie diet was selected as the label standard largely because it approximates the maintenance caloric requirements of postmenopausal women, the group most often seeking weight reduction, and because the rounded number makes it easier for consumers to calculate their individual nutrient requirements. Some package labels also include values based on a 2500-calorie diet, and *all* labels include a footnote stating that "Your daily values may be higher or lower, depending on your calorie needs."

Daily reference values have been established for nutrients that are sources of energy (i.e., fat, saturated fat, total carbohydrate [including fiber], and protein). DRVs also have been established for cholesterol, sodium, and potassium, which do not contribute calories.

DRVs for the energy-producing nutrients are calculated as follows:

- Total fat based on 20 to 35 percent of calories
- Saturated fat based on less than 10 percent of calories
- Carbohydrate based on 45 to 65 percent of calories
- Protein based on 10 to 35 percent of calories (applicable only to adults and children over 4 years of age)
- Fiber based on 11.5 g of fiber per 1000 calories

The following quantities of nutrients are considered the upper limit for the maintenance of good health:

- Total fat: less than 65 g
- Saturated fat: less than 20 g
- Cholesterol: less than 300 mg
- Sodium: less than 2300 mg (persons with hypertension, less than 1500 mg).

The daily values of sodium and cholesterol are the same regardless of the calorie diet.

Use of Special Terms on Nutrition Labels

The FDA has developed standardized definitions for some commonly used terms on nutrition labels.[18]

"Free" foods: contain no amount or an amount that is nutritionally trivial or physiologically inconsequential. For example:

Calorie free: fewer than 5 calories per serving.
Sugar free: less than 0.5 g of sugar per serving.
Fat free: less than 0.5 g of fat per serving.
Sodium free: less than 5 mg of sodium per serving.
Cholesterol free: less than 2 mg of cholesterol per serving and 2 g or less of saturated fat per serving.

"Low" foods: may be eaten frequently without exceeding dietary guidelines. For example:

Low calorie: 40 calories or less per serving
Low sodium: 140 mg of sodium or less per serving
Very low sodium: 35 mg of sodium or less per serving
Low fat: 3 g of fat or less per serving
Low saturated fat: 1 g of fat or less per serving
Low cholesterol: 20 mg of cholesterol or less and 2 g or less of saturated fat per serving

Definitions of terms such as *light*, *reduced*, *high fiber*, *lean*, and others may be found in the reference indicated.[17]

It should be noted that labels on foods for children under 2 years of age may not carry information about fat or calories from fat to prevent parents from *wrongly* assuming that infants and toddlers should restrict their fat intake when, in fact, they should not. Also, the labels on foods for children under 4 years of age *may not* include the %DVs for components other than protein, vitamins, and minerals, because these are the only nutrients for which the FDA has set daily values for this age group. Infant formulas have special labeling rules under the Infant Formula Act of 1980.

Example Calculations Involving the Nutrition Label

Note: In calculations of the labeled "% Daily Values," the FDA allows latitude in rounding.

For a diet of 3000 calories, calculate the dietary grams of fat based on the daily reference values (DRVs) for this substance. Is the calculated amount of fat "acceptable" according to the standards of upper limits for a healthy diet?

$$\text{DRV for fat} = 30\% \text{ of calories}$$
$$\text{Thus, for fat, } 30\% \text{ of } 3000 \text{ calories} = 900 \text{ calories}$$

Since fat provides 9 calories/g:

$$\frac{9 \text{ calories}}{900 \text{ calories}} = \frac{1 \text{ g fat}}{x \text{ g fat}}; \quad x = 100 \text{ g fat}$$

Since the "upper limit" of fat for a healthy diet is "less than 65 g," 100 g of fat is not acceptable, *answers.*

How many calories from fat and how many grams of fat should be the limit per day for a person on a 2000-calorie diet?

$$2000 \times 35\% = 700 \text{ calories from fat, and}$$
$$\frac{9 \text{ calories}}{700 \text{ calories}} = \frac{1 \text{ g}}{x \text{ g}}; \quad x = 78 \text{ grams of fat, } answers$$

How many food calories would be provided by a diet of 65 grams of fat, 500 grams of carbohydrate, and 180 grams of protein?

$$
\begin{array}{lcl}
65 \text{ g fat} \times 9 \text{ calories/g} & = & 585 \text{ calories} \\
500 \text{ g carbohydrate} \times 4 \text{ calories/g} & = & 2000 \text{ calories} \\
180 \text{ g protein} \times 4 \text{ calories/g} & = & \underline{720 \text{ calories}} \\
& & 3305 \text{ calories, } answer.
\end{array}
$$

If a food item contains 100 calories per serving with 10 calories coming from fat, is it considered both "low calorie" and "low fat"?

By definition, *low calorie* is less than 40 calories per serving. Thus, the food item is not "low calorie," and on the basis of 9 calories per gram of fat:

$$\frac{9 \text{ calories}}{10 \text{ calories}} = \frac{1 \text{ g}}{x \text{ g}}; \quad x = 1.1 \text{ g}$$

Thus the product is "low fat" (less than 3 g/serving), *answer.*

Minimum daily amounts of certain dietary supplements, such as vitamins and minerals, have been established as necessary for the maintenance of good health. The labels of vitamin and mineral products contain the quantity of each component present, as well as the %DV that each represents.

A multiple vitamin tablet contains 7500 international units (IU) of vitamin A. If this amount represents a %DV of 150%, what is the 100% daily requirement of vitamin A?

$$\frac{150\% \text{ DV}}{100\% \text{ DV}} = \frac{7500 \text{ I.U.}}{x \text{ I.U.}}; \quad x = 5000 \text{ I.U., } answer.$$

A multiple vitamin contains 10 mcg of biotin, representing 3% of the minimum daily requirement. What amount of biotin would represent 100% of the minimum daily requirement?

$$\frac{3\% \text{ MDR}}{100\% \text{ MDR}} = \frac{10 \text{ mcg}}{x \text{ mcg}}; \quad x = 333.3 \text{ mcg, } answer.$$

A multiple vitamin and mineral tablet contains 162 mg of calcium. If the minimum daily value for calcium is 1000 mg, what percentage of the minimum daily value of calcium is contained in each tablet?

$$\frac{162 \text{ mg}}{1000 \text{ mg}} \times 100 = 16.2\%, \ answer$$

CALCULATIONS CAPSULE

Adult Nutrition

Basal energy expenditure (BEE):

The Harris-Benedict equations may be used to approximate the BEE, in kcal:

$BEE_{males} = 66.67 + [13.75 \times Weight \ (kg)] + [5 \times Height \ (cm)] - [6.76 \times Age \ (yr)]$

$BEE_{females} = 655.1 + [9.56 \times Weight \ (kg)] + [1.86 \times Height \ (cm)] - [4.68 \times Age \ (yr)]$

The BEE is adjusted by activity and stress factors to yield the estimated total daily energy expenditure (TDE).

Kcal/g values:
  Carbohydrates @ 4 kcal/g (enteral), 3.4 kcal/g (parenteral)
  Proteins @ 4 kcal/g
  Fats (lipids) @ 9 kcal/g

Fluid requirement:

  30 mL/kg patient weight, or
  1 mL/kcal, nutrition provided, or
  1500 mL/m² BSA

CASE IN POINT 14.1: A mother asks a pharmacist to help her understand the nutritional content of PEDIASURE Enteral Formula, which has been recommended for her 12-year-old child. The label indicates that 1500 mL of the product, taken daily, provides complete nutrition for children ages 9 to 13 years. The product comes in cans containing 237 mL. If each liter of the product provides 1000 kcal, 30 g of protein, 132.5 g of carbohydrate, and 39.7 g of lipid, along with 852 mL of water, calculate the following provided in the recommended dose:

(a) Kilocalories
(b) Grams of protein
(c) Grams of carbohydrate
(d) Percentage of calories derived from fat
(e) Daily water

PRACTICE PROBLEMS

Calculations of Nutritional Requirements

1. Calculate the daily protein requirement, in g/day, for a 141-lb. severely stressed postsurgical patient.

2. A nutritional formula calls for 500 g of dextrose in a total volume of 2000 mL. How many milliliters of a 70% w/v dextrose injection are needed to provide the required amount of dextrose?

3. A patient requires 1800 kcal/day, including 60 g of protein. How many kilocalories would be provided by the protein?

4. If the source of the protein in problem 3 is a 5% amino acid solution, how many milliliters of the solution would be needed to provide the requirement?

5. Calculate the following for enteral nutrition:

   (a) Grams of dextrose needed to supply 1400 kcal
   (b) grams of protein needed to supply 800 kcal
   (c) grams of lipid needed to supply 1000 kcal (111.1 g lipid)

6. Calculate the approximate daily water requirement for a/an:

   (a) 165-lb. patient
   (b) adult patient with a BSA of 1.6 m^2
   (c) patient receiving 1500 kcal by TPN
   (d) 2.2-kg neonate
   (e) 19-kg child
   (f) child with a BSA of 0.65

7.[11] The daily caloric requirement for a 201-lb. 76-year-old male has been determined to be 2088.82 kcal/day. Calculate the protein, carbohydrate, lipid (35% TDC), and fluid requirements for enteral nutrition, assuming no stress or disease factors.

8. A medication order calls for a liter of hyperalimentation solution to contain 2.125% of amino acids and 20% of dextrose. How many milliliters each of 8.5% amino acid injection, 50% dextrose injection, and sterile water for injection should be used to prepare the solution?

9. If a 50% dextrose injection provides 170 kcal in each 100 mL, how many milliliters of a 70% dextrose injection would provide the same caloric value?

10. Using the Harris-Benedict equation and assuming no stress factor, calculate (a) the daily calories required, and (b) the daily protein needed for a 58-year-old woman who is 5 ft. 3 in. tall and weighs 152 lb.

11. Using the Harris-Benedict equation, calculate the TPN caloric requirement for a severely stressed (use average factor) 160-lb. 60-year-old male patient measuring 5 ft. 8 in. in height.

12. If amino acids have a caloric value of 4 kcal/g and the daily protein requirement is 0.8g/kg, calculate the kilocalories administered to a patient weighing 180 lb.

13. A medication order for a TPN solution calls for additives as indicated in the following formula. Using the sources designated below, calculate the amount of each component required in filling the medication order.

TPN Solution Formula	Component Source
Sodium Chloride 40 mEq	10-mL vial of 30% solution
Potassium Acetate 15 mEq	20-mL vial containing 40 mEq
Vitamin B_{12} 10 μg	Vial containing 1 mg in 10 mL
Insulin 8 units	Vial of Insulin U-100

To be added to:
500 mL of 50% dextrose injection
500 mL of 7% protein hydrolysate injection

14. A solution of potassium phosphate contains a mixture of 164 mg of monobasic potassium phosphate and 158 mg of dibasic potassium phosphate per milliliter.

   (a) If a hyperalimentation fluid calls for the addition of 45 mEq of K^+, how many milliliters of the solution should be used to provide this level of potassium?

   (b) How many millimoles of total phosphate will be represented in the calculated volume of potassium phosphate solution?

15. Using the component sources as indicated, calculate the amount of each component required in preparing 1000 mL of the following parenteral nutrition solution:

Parenteral Nutrition Solution Formula	Component Source
(a) Amino Acids 2.125%	500 mL of 8.5% amino acids injection
(b) Dextrose 20%	500 mL of 50% dextrose injection
(c) Sodium Chloride 30 mEq	20-mL vial of 15% solution
(d) Calcium Gluconate 2.5 mEq	10-mL vial containing 4.6 mEq
(e) Insulin 15 units	Vial of U-100 insulin
(f) Heparin 2500 units	5-mL vial containing 1000 units/mL
(g) Sterile Water for Injection to make 1000 mL	500 mL of sterile water for injection

Calculations of Body Mass Index

16. Using Table 14.1, determine the body mass index for a person measuring 62 in. in height and weighing 150 lb.

17. Calculate the body mass index for a person measuring 1.7 meters in height and weighing 87 kilograms (round answer).

18. An investigational drug for obesity is being dosed at either of two protocols: (a) 7.6 mg/0.5 BMI for persons with a BMI over 25 but less than 30, or (b) 9.6 mg/0.5 BMI for persons with a BMI greater than 30. In each protocol, the dose is equally divided and administered "t.i.d. a.c." What would be the divided dose for a male standing 5 ft. 8 in. and weighing 230 pounds?

Calculations of Nutrition Label Information

19. If a person consumes 3000 calories per day, calculate the intake of fat in grams based on dietary fat being 30 percent of caloric intake.

20. A high-fiber cereal contains 13 g of dietary fiber in each 30 g of cereal. Calculate the %DV of dietary fiber, based on a 2000-calorie diet.

21. A sweetened cereal contains 14 g of sugar (carbohydrate) per 30 g serving size of cereal. Calculate the %DV based on a 2000-calorie diet.

22. How many grams of fat are contained in a 2500-calorie diet if 450 of those calories are derived from fat?

23. If an 8-oz. container of yogurt contains 300 mg of calcium, calculate the percent daily requirement for a young adult met by consuming half the contents of the container. The daily requirement of calcium is listed as 1000 mg.

24. If a food serving contains 240 mg of potassium, listed as 7 percent of the daily value, calculate 100% of the daily value of potassium in milligrams.

25. Using the information in Figure 14.3, calculate the %DV for sodium if a different product contained 140 mg of sodium.

ANSWERS TO "CASE IN POINT" AND PRACTICE PROBLEMS

Case in Point 14.1

With a dose of 1500 mL, the child would take 1.5 times the nutritional content provided in each liter $\left(\dfrac{1500 \text{ mL}}{1000 \text{ mL}} = 1.5\right)$, thus:

(a) 1000 kcal × 1.5 = 1500 kcal
(b) 30 g × 1.5 = 45 g protein
(c) 132.5 g × 1.5 = 198.75 g carbohydrate
(d) 39.7 g × 1.5 = 59.55 g fat × 9 kcal/g = 535.95 kcal from fat
   535.95 kcal ÷ 1500 kcal × 100 = 35.73% kcal derived from fat
(e) 852 mL × 1.5 = 1278 mL water, *answers.*

Practice Problems

1. 96.14 g to 128.18 g

2. 714.29 mL

3. 240 kcal

4. 1200 mL

5. (a) 350 g dextrose
   (b) 200 g protein
   (c) 111.1 g lipid

6. (a) 2250 mL
   (b) 2400 mL
   (c) 1500 mL
   (d) 264 mL to 396 mL
   (e) 1450 mL
   (f) 975 mL

7. 73.09 g protein
   266.34 g carbohydrate
   81.23 g lipid
   2088.82 to 2740.91 mL fluid

8. 250 mL amino acids injection
   400 mL dextrose injection
   350 mL sterile water for injection

9. 71.43 mL dextrose injection

10. (a) 1341.76 kcal
    (b) 55.27 g protein

11. 2668 kcal

12. 261.8 kcal

13. 7.8 mL sodium chloride solution
    7.5 mL potassium acetate solution
    0.1 mL vitamin B_{12}
    0.08 mL insulin

14. (a) 14.89 mL
    (b) 31.48 mmol

15. (a) 250 mL amino acids injection
    (b) 400 mL dextrose injection
    (c) 11.7 mL sodium chloride solution
    (d) 5.43 mL calcium gluconate solution
    (e) 0.15 mL insulin
    (f) 2.5 mL heparin
    (g) sterile water for injection to make 1 L

16. 27 BMI

17. 30 BMI

18. 224 mg

19. 100 g fat

20. 52% DV

21. 4.7% DV

22. 50 g fat

23. 15%

24. 3429 mg potassium

25. 5.8% DV

REFERENCES

1. Dombrowski SR. Pharmacist counseling on nutrition and physical activity—part 1 of 2: understanding current guidelines. *Journal of the American Pharmacists Association* 1999;39:479–491.
2. Diabesity®. Shape Up America. Available at: http://www.shapeup.org/prof/diabesity.php. Accessed December 23, 2007.
3. National Heart Lung and Blood Institute, National Institutes of Health. Clinical guidelines on the identification, evaluation, and treatment of overweight and obesity in adults. Available at: http://www.nhlbi.nih.gov/guidelines/obesity/ob__gdlns.pdf. Accessed December 24, 2007.
4. Continuing Education Monograph: Managing Obesity as a Chronic Disease. Washington, DC: American Pharmacists Association, 2001.
5. Beckwith MC, Feddema SS, Barton RG, et al. A guide to drug therapy in patients with enteral feeding tubes: dosage form selection and administration methods. *Hospital Pharmacy* 2004;39:225–237.
6. Davis A. Indications and techniques for enteral feeds. In: Baker SB, Baker RD Jr, Davis A, eds. *Pediatric Enteral Nutrition*. New York: Chapman Hall, 1994;67–94.
7. Wolf TD. Enteral nutrition. In: Boh LE, ed. *Pharmacy Practice Manual: A Guide to the Clinical Experience*. Baltimore: Lippincott Williams & Wilkins, 2001:431–459.
8. Whitney J. Parenteral nutrition. In: Boh LE, ed. *Pharmacy Practice Manual: A Guide to the Clinical Experience*. Baltimore: Lippincott Williams & Wilkins, 2001:460–506.
9. Wallace JI. Malnutrition and enteral/parenteral alimentation. In: Hazzard WR, Blass JP, Halter JB, et al, eds. *Principles of Geriatric Medicine and Gerontology*. New York: McGraw-Hill, 2003:1179–1192.
10. DiPiro JT, Talbert RL, Yee GC, et al. *Pharmacotherapy: A Pathophysiologic Approach*. 5th Ed. New York: McGraw-Hill, 2002:2456–2457, 2523.
11. Ansel HC, Prince SJ. *Pharmaceutical Calculations: The Pharmacist's Handbook*. Baltimore: Lippincott Williams & Wilkins, 2004:193–212.
12. DiPiro JT, Talbert RL, Yee GC, et al. *Pharmacotherapy: A Pathophysiologic Approach*. 5th Ed. New York: McGraw-Hill, 2002:2480.
13. Craig SB, Dietz WH. Nutritional requirements. In: Baker SB, Baker RD Jr, Davis A, eds. *Pediatric Enteral Nutrition*. New York: Chapman Hall, 1994:67–94.
14. O'Sullivan TA. Parenteral nutrition calculations. In: *Understanding Pharmacy Calculations*. Washington, DC: American Pharmacists' Association, 2002:143–237.
15. Newton GD. A Pharmacist's guide to fiber and fiber supplements. *Pharmacy Today* 2007;13:13–14.
16. Zagaria MAE. Nutrition in the elderly. *U.S. Pharmacist* 2000;25:42–44.
17. U.S. Department of Agriculture, U.S. Department of Health and Human Services. Using the food guide pyramid: a resource for nutrition educators. Available at: http://www/.cnpp.usda.gov/pyramid.html. Accessed January 14, 2005.
18. U.S. Food and Drug Administration, U.S. Department of Health and Human Services. FDA backgrounder: the food label. Available at: http://vm.cfsan.fda.gov/label.html. Accessed November 1, 2000.
19. Federal Register, November 17, 1999 (64 FR 62746).

Altering Product Strength, Use of Stock Solutions, and Problem-Solving by Alligation

Objectives

Upon successful completion of this chapter, the student will be able to:

- Perform calculations for altering product strength by dilution, concentration, or fortification.
- Perform calculations for the preparation and use of stock solutions.
- Apply *alligation medial* and *alligation alternate* in problem-solving.

The strength of a pharmaceutical preparation may be increased or decreased by changing the proportion of active ingredient to the whole. A preparation may be *strengthened* or made more *concentrated* by the addition of active ingredient, by admixture with a like preparation of greater strength, or through the evaporation of its vehicle, if liquid. The strength of a preparation may be decreased or *diluted* by the addition of diluent or by admixture with a like preparation of lesser strength.

Alternative methods of calculation for the alteration of the strength of pharmaceutical preparations are presented in this chapter.

Special Considerations of Altering Product Strength in Pharmaceutical Compounding

In the course of pharmacy practice, there are occasions in which the alteration of the strength of a pharmaceutical preparation is either desirable or required.

CALCULATIONS CAPSULE

Concentration/Quantity Relationship

The percentage or ratio strength (concentration) of a component in a pharmaceutical preparation is based on its quantity relative to the total quantity of the preparation. If the quantity of the component remains constant, any change in the total quantity of the preparation, through dilution or concentration, changes the concentration of the component in the preparation inversely.

An equation useful in these calculations is:

(1st quantity) $\times$ *(1st concentration)* = *(2nd quantity)* $\times$ *(2nd concentration)*

The *dilution* of a liquid dosage form, as a solution or suspension, may be desired to provide a product strength more suitable for use by a particular patient (e.g., pediatric, elderly, those in disease states). The diluent is selected based on its compatibility with the vehicle of the original product; that is, aqueous, alcoholic, hydroalcoholic, or other. The dilution of a solid dosage form (as a powder or the contents of a capsule) or a semisolid dosage form (as an ointment or cream) also may be performed to alter the dose or strength of a product. Again, the diluent is selected based on its compatibility with the original formulation. Pharmacists also may find occasion to dilute concentrated acids, alcohol preparations, or very potent therapeutic agents, as discussed in this chapter, to meet special compounding requirements.

The *concentration* of a liquid preparation, as through the evaporation of a portion of its solvent or vehicle, rarely is performed nowadays. However, the *fortification* of a liquid, solid, or semisolid dosage form, by the addition of a calculated quantity of additional therapeutic agent, remains a viable practice in pharmacy compounding.

Relationship Between Strength and Total Quantity

If a mixture of a given percentage or ratio strength is diluted to twice its original quantity, its active ingredient will be contained in twice as many parts of the whole, and its strength therefore will be reduced by one half. By contrast, if a mixture is concentrated by evaporation to one-half its original quantity, the active ingredient (assuming that none was lost by evaporation) will be contained in one half as many parts of the whole, and the strength will be doubled. So, if 50 mL of a solution containing 10 g of active ingredient with a strength of 20% or 1:5 w/v are diluted to 100 mL, the original volume is doubled, but the original strength is now reduced by one half to 10% or 1:10 w/v. If, by evaporation of the solvent, the volume of the solution is reduced to 25 mL or one half the original quantity, the 10 g of the active ingredient will indicate a strength of 40% or 1:2.5 w/v.

If, then, *the amount of active ingredient remains constant, any change in the quantity of a solution or mixture of solids is inversely proportional to the percentage or ratio strength;* that is, the percentage or ratio strength decreases as the quantity increases, and conversely.

This relationship is generally true for all mixtures except solutions containing components that contract when mixed together.

Problems in this section generally may be solved by any of the following methods:

1. Inverse proportion.
2. The equation: **(1st quantity) × (1st concentration) = (2nd quantity) × (2nd concentration)**, or Q1 × C1 = Q2 × C2.
3. By determining the quantity of active ingredient (solute) present or required and relating that quantity to the known or desired quantity of the preparation.
   Note: This will become clear as the chapter proceeds.

Dilution and Concentration of Liquids

Example Calculations of the Dilution and Concentration of Liquids

If 500 mL of a 15% v/v solution are diluted to 1500 mL, what will be the percentage strength (v/v)?

$$\frac{1500 \text{ (mL)}}{500 \text{ (mL)}} = \frac{15 \text{ (\%)}}{x \text{ (\%)}}$$
$$x = 5\%, \textit{answer.}$$

Or,

$$Q1 \text{ (quantity)} \times C1 \text{ (concentration)} = Q2 \text{ (quantity)} \times C2 \text{ (concentration)}$$
$$500 \text{ (mL)} \times 15 \text{ (\%)} = 1500 \text{ (mL)} \times x \text{ (\%)}$$
$$x = 5\%, \textit{answer.}$$

Or,

500 mL of 15% v/v solution contains 75 mL of solute

$$\frac{1500 \text{ (mL)}}{75 \text{ (mL)}} = \frac{100 \text{ (\%)}}{x \text{ (\%)}}$$

$$x = 5\%, \text{ answer.}$$

If 50 mL of a 1:20 w/v solution are diluted to 1000 mL, what is the ratio strength (w/v)?
Note: A student may find it simpler in solving certain problems to convert a given ratio strength to its equivalent percentage strength.

$$1:20 = 5\%$$
$$\frac{1000 \text{ (mL)}}{50 \text{ (mL)}} = \frac{5 \text{ (\%)}}{x \text{ (\%)}}$$

$$x = 0.25\% = 1:400, \text{ answer.}$$

Or,

$$\frac{1000 \text{ (mL)}}{50 \text{ (mL)}} = \frac{\frac{1}{20}}{x}$$

$$x = \frac{1}{400} = 1:400, \quad \text{answer.}$$

Or,

$$Q1 \text{ (quantity)} \times C1 \text{ (concentration)} = Q2 \text{ (quantity)} \times C2 \text{ (concentration)}$$
$$50 \text{ (mL)} \times 5 \text{ (\%)} = 1000 \text{ (mL)} \times \text{ (\%)}$$
$$x = 0.25\% = 1:400, \text{ answer.}$$

Or,

50 mL of a 1:20 solution contains 2.5 g of solute

$$\frac{2.5 \text{ (g)}}{1 \text{ (g)}} = \frac{1000 \text{ (mL)}}{x \text{ (mL)}}$$
$$x = 400 \text{ mL}$$
$$\text{Ratio strength} = 1:400, \text{ answer.}$$

If a syrup containing 65% w/v of sucrose is evaporated to 85% of its volume, what percentage (w/v) of sucrose will it contain?

Any convenient amount of the syrup, for example, 100 mL, may be used in the calculation. If we evaporate 100 mL of the syrup to 85% of its volume, we will have 85 mL.

$$\frac{85 \text{ (mL)}}{100 \text{ (mL)}} = \frac{65 \text{ (\%)}}{x \text{ (\%)}}$$
$$x = 76.47\% \text{ or } 76\%, \text{ answer.}$$

How many grams of 10% w/w ammonia solution can be made from 1800 g of 28% w/w strong ammonia solution?

$$\frac{10 \text{ (\%)}}{28 \text{ (\%)}} = \frac{1800 \text{ (g)}}{x \text{ (g)}}$$
$$x = 5040 \text{ g, answer.}$$

Or,

$$Q1 \times C1 = Q2 \times C2$$
$$1800 \text{ (g)} \times 28 \text{ (\%)} = x \text{ (g)} \times 10\%$$
$$x = 5040 \text{ g, } answer.$$

Or,

1800 g of 28% ammonia water contains 504 g of ammonia (100%)

$$\frac{10 \text{ (\%)}}{100 \text{ (\%)}} = \frac{504 \text{ (g)}}{x \text{ (g)}}$$
$$x = 5040 \text{ g, } answer.$$

How many milliliters of a 1:5000 w/v solution of the preservative lauralkonium chloride can be made from 125 mL of a 0.2% solution?

$$1:5000 = 0.02\%$$
$$\frac{0.02 \text{ (\%)}}{0.2 \text{ (\%)}} = \frac{125 \text{ (mL)}}{x \text{ (mL)}}$$
$$x = 1250 \text{ mL, } answer.$$

Or,

$$0.2\% = 1:500$$
$$\frac{1/5000}{1/500} = \frac{125 \text{ (mL)}}{x \text{ (mL)}}$$
$$x = 1250 \text{ mL, } answer.$$

Or,

125 mL of a 0.2% solution contains 0.25 g of lauralkonium chloride

$$\frac{1 \text{ (g)}}{0.25 \text{ (g)}} = \frac{5000 \text{ (mL)}}{x \text{ (mL)}}$$
$$x = 1250 \text{ mL, } answer.$$

Or,

$$125 \text{ (mL)} \times 0.2 \text{ (\%)} = x \text{ (mL)} \times 0.02 \text{ (\%)}$$
$$x = 1250 \text{ mL, } answer.$$

If 1 gallon of a 30% w/v solution is to be evaporated so that the solution will have a strength of 50% w/v, what will be its volume in milliliters?

$$1 \text{ gallon} = 3785 \text{ mL}$$
$$\frac{50 \text{ (\%)}}{30 \text{ (\%)}} = \frac{3785 \text{ (mL)}}{x \text{ (mL)}}$$
$$x = 2271 \text{ mL, } answer.$$

Strengthening of a Pharmaceutical Product

As noted previously, there is occasion in which a pharmacist may be called upon to strengthen an existing pharmaceutical product. This may be accomplished by the addition of active ingredient or by the admixture with a calculated quantity of a like-product of greater concentration. The latter type of calculation is presented later in this chapter under the discussion of *alligation alternate*.

The following problem and Case in Point 15.1 offer example calculations of product strengthening.

Example:

If a cough syrup contains in each teaspoonful, 1 mg of chlorpheniramine maleate and if a pharmacist desired to double the strength, how many milligrams of that ingredient would need to be added to a 60-mL container of the syrup. Assume no increase in volume.

$$\frac{1 \text{ mg}}{5 \text{ mL}} \times 60 \text{ mL} = 12 \text{ mg chlorpheniramine maleate in original syrup}$$

To double the strength, 12 mg of additional chlorpheniramine maleate would be required, *answer.*

CASE IN POINT 15.1: **A pharmacist received a prescription for 100 mL of a cefuroxime axetil suspension to contain 300 mg of drug in each 5 mL. The pharmacist has 100 mL of a suspension containing 250 mg/5 mL and also has 250-mg scored tablets of the drug. How many tablets should be pulverized and added to the suspension to achieve the desired strength? Assume no increase in the volume of the suspension.**

<u>**A Second Look**</u>

The pharmacist observed that after adding the pulverized tablets, the suspension measured 102 mL in volume. Calculations revealed that rather than the prescribed drug strength of 300 mg/5 mL, there were 294.1 mg/5 mL. What should the pharmacist do to bring the suspension to the desired strength?

Stock Solutions

Stock solutions are concentrated solutions of active (e.g., drug) or inactive (e.g., colorant) substances and are used by pharmacists as a convenience to prepare solutions of lesser concentration.

Example Calculations of Stock Solutions

How many milliliters of a 1:400 w/v stock solution should be used to make 4 liters of a 1:2000 w/v solution?

$$4 \text{ liters} = 4000 \text{ mL}$$
$$1:400 = 0.25\%$$
$$1:2000 = 0.05\%$$
$$\frac{0.25 \ (\%)}{0.05 \ (\%)} = \frac{4000 \ (\text{mL})}{x \ (\text{mL})}$$
$$x = 800 \text{ mL, } answer.$$

Or,

$$\frac{\frac{1}{400}}{\frac{1}{2000}} = \frac{4000 \ (\text{mL})}{x \ (\text{mL})}$$
$$x = 800 \text{ mL, } answer.$$

Or,

4000 mL of a 1:2000 w/v solution requires 2 g of active constituent (solute); thus:

$$\frac{1 \ (g)}{2 \ (g)} = \frac{400 \ (\text{mL})}{x \ (\text{mL})}$$
$$x = 800 \text{ mL, } answer.$$

Or,

$$Q1 \times C1 = Q2 \times C2$$
$$4000 \text{ (mL)} \times 0.25 \text{ (\%)} = x \times 0.05 \text{ (\%)}$$
$$x = 800 \text{ mL, } \textit{answer.}$$

How many milliliters of a 1:400 w/v stock solution should be used in preparing 1 gallon of a 1:2000 w/v solution?

$$1 \text{ gallon} = 3785 \text{ mL}$$
$$1:400 = 0.25\%$$
$$1:2000 = 0.05\%$$
$$\frac{0.25 \text{ (\%)}}{0.05 \text{ (\%)}} = \frac{3785 \text{ (mL)}}{x \text{ (mL)}}$$
$$x = 757 \text{ mL, } \textit{answer.}$$

Or,

1 gallon of a 1:2000 w/v solution requires 1.89 g of active constituent; thus:

$$\frac{1.89 \text{ (g)}}{1 \text{ (g)}} = \frac{x \text{ (mL)}}{400 \text{ (mL)}}$$
$$x = 756 \text{ mL, } \textit{answer.}$$

How many milliliters of a 1% stock solution of a certified red dye should be used in preparing 4000 mL of a mouthwash that is to contain 1:20,000 w/v of the certified red dye as a coloring agent?

$$1:20,000 = 0.005\%$$
$$\frac{1 \text{ (\%)}}{0.005 \text{ (\%)}} = \frac{4000 \text{ (mL)}}{x \text{ (mL)}}$$
$$x = 20 \text{ mL, } \textit{answer.}$$

Check:

1% stock solution	1:20,000 solution
contains	contains
20 (mL) × 0.01 → 0.2 g	← 4000 (mL) × 0.00005
certified red dye	

Or,

4000 mL of a 1:20,000 w/v solution requires 0.2 g of certified red dye; thus:

$$\frac{1 \text{ (g)}}{0.2 \text{ (g)}} = \frac{100 \text{ (mL)}}{x \text{ (mL)}}$$
$$x = 20 \text{ mL, } \textit{answer.}$$

How many milliliters of a 1:16 solution of sodium hypochlorite should be used in preparing 5000 mL of a 0.5% solution of sodium hypochlorite for irrigation?

$$1:16 = 6.25\%$$
$$\frac{6.25 \text{ (\%)}}{0.5 \text{ (\%)}} = \frac{5000 \text{ (mL)}}{x \text{ (mL)}}$$
$$x = 400 \text{ mL, } \textit{answer.}$$

Or,

5000 mL of a 0.5% w/v solution requires 25 g of sodium hypochlorite; thus:

$$\frac{25\ (g)}{1\ (g)} = \frac{x\ (mL)}{16\ (mL)}$$
$$x = 400\ mL,\ answer.$$

How many milliliters of a 1:50 stock solution of phenylephrine hydrochloride should be used in compounding the following prescription?

℞   Phenylephrine HCl 0.25%
    Rose Water ad 30 mL
    Sig. For the nose.

$$1:50 = 2\%$$
$$\frac{2\ (\%)}{0.25\ (\%)} = \frac{30\ (mL)}{x\ (mL)}$$
$$x = 3.75\ mL,\ answer.$$

Or,

30 (g) × 0.0025 = 0.075 g of phenylephrine hydrochloride needed

1:50 means 1 g in 50 mL of stock solution

$$\frac{1\ (g)}{0.075\ (g)} = \frac{50\ (mL)}{x\ (mL)}$$
$$x = 3.75\ mL,\ answer.$$

Some interesting calculations are used in pharmacy practice in *which the strength of a diluted portion of a solution is defined, but the strength of the concentrated stock solution used to prepare it must be determined.* The relevance to pharmacy practice may be explained, for example, by the need of a pharmacist to prepare and dispense a concentrated solution of a drug and direct the patient to use a specific household measure of a solution (e.g., 1 teaspoonful) in a specified volume of water (e.g., a pint) to make of solution of the desired concentration (e.g., for irrigation or soaking). This permits the dispensing of a relatively small volume of liquid, enabling a patient to prepare relatively large volumes as needed, rather than carrying home gallons of a diluted solution from a pharmacy.

How much drug should be used in preparing 50 mL of a solution such that 5 mL diluted to 500 mL will yield a 1:1000 solution?

1:1000 means 1 g of drug in 1000 mL of solution

$$\frac{1000\ (mL)}{500\ (mL)} = \frac{1\ (g)}{x\ (g)}$$

$$x = 0.5\ g\ of\ drug\ in\ 500\ mL\ of$$
diluted solution (1:1000), which
is *also* the amount in 5 mL of the
stronger (stock) solution

And,

$$\frac{5\ (mL)}{50\ (mL)} = \frac{0.5\ (g)}{y\ (g)}$$
$$y = 5\ g,\ answer.$$

The accompanying diagrammatic sketch should prove helpful in solving the problem.

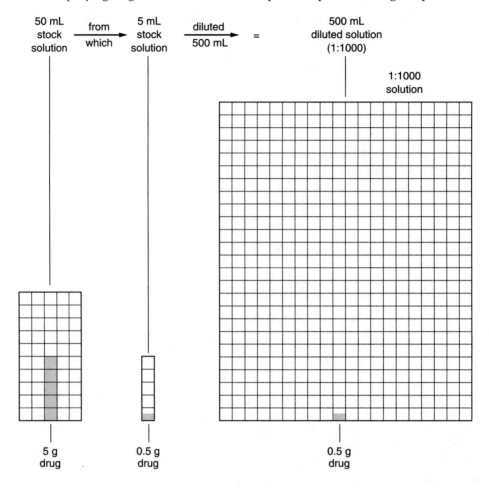

How many grams of sodium chloride should be used in preparing 500 mL of a stock solution such that 50 mL diluted to 1000 mL will yield a "⅓ normal saline" (0.3% w/v) for irrigation?

1000 (mL) × 0.003 = 3 g of sodium chloride in 1000 mL of "⅓ normal saline" (0.3% w/v), which is *also* the amount in 50 mL of the *stronger* (stock) solution to be prepared.

And,

$$\frac{50 \text{ (mL)}}{500 \text{ (mL)}} = \frac{3 \text{ (g)}}{x \text{ (g)}}$$
$$x = 30 \text{ g, } answer.$$

How many milliliters of a 17% w/v concentrate of benzalkonium chloride should be used in preparing 300 mL of a stock solution such that 15 mL diluted to 1 liter will yield a 1:5000 solution?

1 liter = 1000 mL
1:5000 means 1 g of benzalkonium chloride in 5000 mL of solution

$$\frac{5000 \text{ (mL)}}{1000 \text{ (mL)}} = \frac{1 \text{ (g)}}{x \text{ (g)}}$$

x = 0.2 g of benzalkonium chloride in 1000 mL of *diluted* solution (1:5000), which is *also* the amount in 15 mL of the *stronger* (stock) solution to be prepared, and:

$$\frac{15 \ (mL)}{300 \ (mL)} = \frac{0.2 \ (g)}{y \ (g)}$$

$$y = 4 \text{ g of benzalkonium chloride needed,}$$

because a 17% w/v concentrate contains 17 g per 100 mL, then:

$$\frac{17 \ (g)}{4 \ (g)} = \frac{100 \ (mL)}{z \ (mL)}$$

$$z = 23.5 \text{ mL, } answer.$$

A solution of known volume and strength may be diluted with water to prepare a solution of lesser strength. In such calculations, first calculate the quantity of diluted solution that may be prepared from the concentrated solution. Then, subtract the volume of the concentrated solution from the total quantity that may be prepared to determine the volume of water needed.

How many milliliters of water should be added to 300 mL of a 1:750 w/v solution of benzalkonium chloride to make a 1:2500 w/v solution?

$$1:2500 = 0.04\%$$
$$1:750 = 0.133\%$$
$$\frac{0.04 \ (\%)}{0.133 \ (\%)} = \frac{300 \ (mL)}{x \ (mL)}$$

$$x = 997.5 \text{ or } 1000 \text{ mL of } 0.04\%$$
w/v solution to be prepared

The difference between the volume of *diluted* (weaker) solution prepared and the volume of *stronger* solution used represents the volume of water (diluent) to be used.

1000 mL − 300 mL = 700 mL, *answer.*

Or,

300 mL of a 1:750 (w/v) solution contains 0.4 g of benzalkonium chloride

$$\frac{1 \ (g)}{0.4 \ (g)} = \frac{2500 \ (mL)}{x \ (mL)}$$

$$x = 1000 \text{ mL}$$
1000 mL − 300 mL = 700 mL, *answer.*

How many milliliters of water should be added to a pint of a 5% w/v solution to make a 2% w/v solution?

$$1 \text{ pint} = 473 \text{ mL}$$

$$\frac{2 \ (\%)}{5 \ (\%)} = \frac{473 \ (mL)}{x \ (mL)}$$

$$x = 1182.5 \text{ mL}$$

And,

1182.5 mL − 473 mL = 709.5 mL, *answer.*

If the *quantity of a component* is given rather than the *strength of a solution*, the solution may be diluted to a desired strength as shown by the following example.

How many milliliters of water should be added to 375 mL of a solution containing 0.5 g of benzalkonium chloride to make a 1:5000 solution?

1:5000 means 1 g in 5000 mL of solution

$$\frac{1\ (g)}{0.5\ (g)} = \frac{5000\ (mL)}{x\ (mL)}$$
$$x = 2500\ mL\ of\ 1:5000\ (w/v)$$
solution containing 0.5 g
of benzalkonium chloride

And,

$$2500\ mL - 375\ mL = 2125\ mL,\ answer.$$

If 15 mL of a 0.06% ATROVENT (ipratropium bromide) nasal spray were diluted with 6 mL of normal saline solution, what would be the final drug concentration?

$$15\ mL \times 0.06\% = 0.009\ g\ of\ ipratropium\ bromide$$
$$15\ mL + 6\ mL = 21\ mL,\ new\ total\ volume$$
$$\frac{0.009\ g}{21\ mL} \times 100 = 0.043\ \%,\ answer.$$

Or,

$$15\ (mL) \times 0.06\ (\%) = 21\ (mL) \times x\ (\%)$$
$$x = 0.043\ \%,\ answer.$$

Dilution of Alcohol

Example Calculations of Alcohol Dilutions

When water and alcohol are mixed, there is a physical contraction such that the resultant volume is less than the total of the individual volumes of the two liquids. Thus, to prepare a *volume-in-volume* strength of an alcohol dilution, the alcohol "solute" may be determined and water used to "q.s." to the appropriate volume. Because the contraction of the liquids does not affect the *weights* of the components, the *weight of water* (and from this, the *volume*) needed to dilute alcohol to a desired *weight-in-weight* strength may be calculated.

How much water should be mixed with 5000 mL of 85% v/v alcohol to make 50% v/v alcohol?

$$\frac{50\ (\%)}{85\ (\%)} = \frac{5000\ (mL)}{x\ (mL)}$$
$$x = 8500\ mL$$

Or,

$$5000\ (mL) \times 85\ (\%) = x\ (mL) \times 50\ (\%)$$
$$x = 8500\ mL$$

Therefore, use 5000 mL of 85% v/v alcohol and enough water to make 8500 mL, *answer.*

How many milliliters of 95% v/v alcohol and how much water should be used in compounding the following prescription?

℞	Xcaine	1 g
	Alcohol 70%	30 mL
	Sig. Ear drops.	

$$\frac{95\ (\%)}{70\ (\%)} = \frac{30\ (mL)}{x\ (mL)}$$
$$x = 22.1\ mL$$

Therefore, use 22.1 mL of 95% v/v alcohol and enough water to make 30 mL, *answer.*

How much water should be added to 4000 g of 90% w/w alcohol to make 40% w/w alcohol?

$$\frac{40\ (\%)}{90\ (\%)} = \frac{4000\ (g)}{x\ (g)}$$

x = 9000 g, weight of 40% w/w alcohol equivalent to 4000 g of 90% w/w alcohol

9000 g − 4000 g = 5000 g or 5000 mL, *answer.*

Dilution of Acids

The strength of an official undiluted (*concentrated*) acid is expressed as percentage weight-in-weight. For example, Hydrochloric Acid, NF, contains not less than 36.5% and not more than 38.0%, by weight, of HCl. However, the strength of an official *diluted* acid is expressed as percentage weight-in-volume. For example, Diluted Hydrochloric Acid, NF, contains, in each 100 mL, not less than 9.5 g and not more than 10.5 g of HCl.[1]

It is necessary, therefore, to consider the specific gravity of concentrated acids in calculating the volume to be used in preparing a desired quantity of a diluted acid.

Example Calculations of Acid Dilutions

How many milliliters of 37% w/w hydrochloric acid having a specific gravity of 1.20 are required to make 1000 mL of diluted hydrochloric acid 10% w/v?

1000 g × 0.10 = 100 g of HCl (100%) in 1000 mL of 10% w/v acid

$$\frac{37\ (\%)}{100\ (\%)} = \frac{100\ (g)}{x\ (g)}$$
$$x = 270\ g\ of\ 37\%\ acid$$

270 g of water measure 270 mL

$$270\ (mL) \div 1.20 = 225\ mL,\ \textit{answer.}$$

How many milliliters of 85% w/w phosphoric acid having a specific gravity of 1.71 should be used in preparing 1 gallon of ¼% w/v phosphoric acid solution to be used for bladder irrigation?

1 gallon = 3785 mL
3785 (g) × 0.0025 = 9.46 g of H_3PO_4 (100%) in 3785 mL (1 gallon) of ¼% w/v solution

$$\frac{85\ (\%)}{100\ (\%)} = \frac{9.46\ (g)}{x\ (g)}$$
$$x = 11.13\ g\ of\ 85\%\ phosphoric\ acid$$

11.13 g of water measures 11.13 mL

$$11.13\ (mL) \div 1.71 = 6.5\ mL,\ \textit{answer.}$$

Dilution and Fortification of Solids and Semisolids

The dilution of solids in pharmacy occurs when there is need to achieve a lower concentration of an active component in a more concentrated preparation (e.g., a powdered vegetable drug). There also is a type of diluted pharmaceutical preparation, termed a *trituration* (as discussed in the next section) that represents a useful means of preparing and administering very potent therapeutic substances.

Reducing or enhancing the strengths of creams and ointments is a usual part of a compounding pharmacist's practice to meet the special needs of patients. The dilution of semisolids is a usual part of a compounding pharmacist's practice in reducing the strengths of creams and ointments to meet the special needs of patients.

Example Calculations of Solid and Semisolid Dilutions

If 30 g of a 1% hydrocortisone ointment were diluted with 12 g of Vaseline, what would be the concentration of hydrocortisone in the mixture?

$$30 \text{ g} \times 1\% = 0.3 \text{ g hydrocortisone}$$
$$30 \text{ g} + 12 \text{ g} = 42 \text{ g, weight of mixture}$$
$$\frac{0.3 \text{ g}}{42 \text{ g}} \times 100 = 0.71\% \text{ (w/w), } answer.$$

Or,

$$30 \text{ (g)} \times 1 \text{ (\%)} = 42 \text{ (g)} \times \text{x (\%)}$$
$$\text{x} = 0.71\% \text{ (w/w), } answer.$$

How many grams of 20% benzocaine ointment and how many grams of ointment base (diluent) should be used in preparing 5 lb. of 2.5% benzocaine ointment?

5 lb. = 454 g × 5 = 2270 g

$$\frac{20 \text{ (\%)}}{2.5 \text{ (\%)}} = \frac{2270 \text{ (g)}}{\text{x (g)}}$$
$$\text{x} = 283.75 \text{ or } 284 \text{ g of 20\% ointment, } and$$
$$2270 \text{ g} - 284 \text{ g} = 1986 \text{ g of ointment base, } answers.$$

Or,

$$5 \text{ lb.} = 454 \text{ g} \times 5 = 2270 \text{ g}$$
$$2270 \text{ g} \times 2.5\% = 56.75 \text{ g of benzocaine needed}$$
$$\frac{20 \text{ (g)}}{56.75 \text{ (g)}} = \frac{100 \text{ (g)}}{\text{x (g)}}$$
$$\text{x} = 283.75 \text{ or } 284 \text{ g of 20\% ointment, } and$$
$$2270 \text{ g} - 284 \text{ g} = 1986 \text{ g of ointment base, } answers.$$

How many grams of zinc oxide should be added to 3200 g of 5% zinc oxide ointment to prepare an ointment containing 20% of zinc oxide?

$$3200 \text{ g} \times 0.05 \quad = 160 \text{ g of zinc oxide in 3200 g of 5\% ointment}$$
$$3200 \text{ g} - 160 \text{ g} \quad = 3040 \text{ g of base (diluent) in 3200 g of 5\% ointment}$$

In the 20% ointment, the diluent will represent 80% of the total weight

$$\frac{80 \text{ (\%)}}{20 \text{ (\%)}} = \frac{3040 \text{ (g)}}{\text{x (g)}}$$
$$\text{x} = 760 \text{ g of zinc oxide in the 20\% ointment}$$

Because the 5% ointment already contains 160 g of zinc oxide,

760 g − 160 g = 600 g, *answer.*

A simpler method of solving this problem can be used if we mentally translate it to read:

How many grams of zinc oxide should be added to 3200 g of zinc oxide ointment containing 95% diluent to prepare an ointment containing 80% diluent?

$$\frac{80\ (\%)}{95\ (\%)} = \frac{3200\ (g)}{x\ (g)}$$

x = 3800 g of ointment containing 80% diluent and 20% zinc oxide

3800 g − 3200 g = 600 g, *answer.*

Note: For another simple method, using alligation alternate (see subsequent section in this chapter).

Triturations

Triturations are dilutions of potent medicinal substances. They were at one time official and were prepared by *diluting one part by weight of the drug with nine parts of finely powdered lactose.* They are, therefore, 10% or 1:10 *w/w* mixtures.

These dilutions offer a means of obtaining conveniently and accurately small quantities of potent drugs for compounding purposes. Although no longer official as such, triturations exemplify a method for the calculation and use of dilutions of solid medicinal substances in compounding and manufacturing procedures.

A modern-day example of a trituration is the product Trituration of MUSTARGEN (mechlorethamine hydrochloride for injection), in which 10 mg of the highly toxic drug is triturated with 90 mg of sodium chloride. The trituration is dissolved in sterile water for injection or in sodium chloride injection prior to administration.

Note: The term *trituration* as used in this context should not be confused with the like term *trituration*, which is the pharmaceutical *process* of reducing substances to fine particles through grinding in a mortar and pestle.

Example Calculations of Triturations

How many grams of a 1:10 trituration are required to obtain 25 mg of drug?

$$10\ \text{g of trituration contain 1 g of drug}$$
$$25\ \text{mg} = 0.025\ \text{g}$$
$$\frac{1\ (g)}{0.025\ (g)} = \frac{10\ (g)}{x\ (g)}$$
$$x = 0.25\ \text{g, } answer.$$

How many milliliters of an injection prepared by dissolving 100 mg of a 1:10 trituration of mechlorethamine hydrochloride in sufficient water for injection to prepare 10 mL of injection is required to obtain 5 mg of drug?

$$100\ \text{mg of trituration} = 10\ \text{mg of drug}$$
$$10\ \text{mg of drug in 10 mL of injection}$$
$$\frac{10\ (mg)}{5\ (mg)} = \frac{10\ (mL)}{x\ (mL)}$$
$$x = 5\ \text{mL, } answer.$$

How many milligrams of a 1:10 dilution of colchicine should be used by a manufacturing pharmacist in preparing 100 capsules for a clinical drug study if each capsule is to contain 0.5 mg of colchicine?

$$0.5 \text{ mg} \times 100 = 50 \text{ mg of colchicine needed}$$
10 mg of dilution contain 1 mg of colchicine
$$\frac{1 \text{ (mg)}}{50 \text{ (mg)}} = \frac{10 \text{ (mg)}}{x \text{ (mg)}}$$
$$x = 500 \text{ mg, } answer.$$

Alligation

Alligation is an arithmetical method of solving problems that involves the mixing of solutions or mixtures of solids possessing different percentage strengths.

Alligation Medial. *Alligation medial* is a method by which the "weighted average" percentage strength of a mixture of two or more substances of known quantity and concentration may be easily calculated. By this method, the percentage strength of each component, expressed as a decimal fraction, is multiplied by its corresponding quantity; then the sum of the products is divided by the total quantity of the mixture; and the resultant decimal fraction is multiplied by 100 to give the percentage strength of the mixture. Of course, the quantities must be expressed in a common denomination, whether of weight or volume.

Example Calculations Using Alligation Medial

What is the percentage strength (v/v) of alcohol in a mixture of 3000 mL of 40% v/v alcohol, 1000 mL of 60% v/v alcohol, and 1000 mL of 70% v/v alcohol? Assume no contraction of volume after mixing.

$$0.40 \times 3000 \text{ mL } = 1200 \text{ mL}$$
$$0.60 \times 1000 \text{ mL } = 600 \text{ mL}$$
$$0.70 \times \underline{1000 \text{ mL}} = \underline{700 \text{ mL}}$$

Totals: 5000 mL   2500 mL
$$2500 \text{ (mL)} \div 5000 \text{ (mL)} = 0.50 \times 100 = 50\%, answer.$$

What is the percentage of zinc oxide in an ointment prepared by mixing 200 g of 10% ointment, 50 g of 20% ointment, and 100 g of 5% ointment?

$$0.10 \times 200 \text{ g } = 20 \text{ g}$$
$$0.20 \times 50 \text{ g } = 10 \text{ g}$$
$$0.05 \times \underline{100 \text{ g}} = \underline{5 \text{ g}}$$

Totals: 350 g   35 g
$$35 \text{ (g)} \div 350 \text{ (g)} = 0.10 \times 100 = 10\%, answer.$$

In some problems, the addition of a solvent or vehicle must be considered. It is generally best to consider the diluent as of zero percentage strength, as in the following problem.

What is the percentage strength of alcohol in a mixture of 500 mL of a solution containing 40% v/v alcohol, 400 mL of a second solution containing 21% v/v alcohol, and a sufficient quantity of a nonalcoholic third solution to make a total of 1000 mL?

$$0.40 \times 500 \text{ mL } = 200 \text{ mL}$$
$$0.21 \times 400 \text{ mL } = 84 \text{ mL}$$
$$0 \times \underline{100 \text{ mL}} = \underline{0 \text{ mL}}$$

Totals: 1000 mL   284 mL
$$284 \text{ (mL)} \div 1000 \text{ (mL)} = 0.284 \times 100 = 28.4\%, answer.$$

Alligation Alternate. *Alligation alternate* is a method by which we may calculate the number of parts of two or more components of a given strength when they are to be mixed to prepare a mixture of desired strength. A final proportion permits us to translate relative parts to any specific denomination.

The strength of a mixture must lie somewhere between the strengths of its components; that is, the mixture must be somewhat stronger than its weakest component and somewhat weaker than its strongest. As indicated previously, the strength of the mixture is always a "weighted" average; that is, it lies nearer to that of its weaker or stronger components depending on the relative amounts involved.

This "weighted" average can be found by means of an extremely simple scheme, as illustrated in the subsequent diagram.

Example Calculations Using Alligation Alternate

In what proportion should alcohols of 95% and 50% strengths be mixed to make 70% alcohol?

Note that the difference between the *strength of the stronger component* (95%) and the *desired strength* (70%) indicates the *number of parts of the weaker* to be used (25 parts), and the difference between the *desired strength* (70%) and the *strength of the weaker component* (50%) indicates the *number of parts of the stronger* to be used (20 parts).

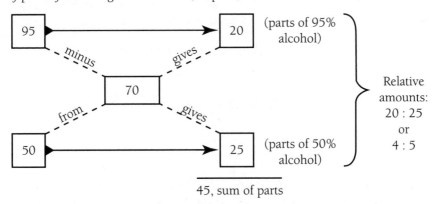

45, sum of parts

The mathematical validity of this relationship can be demonstrated.

Percent given	Percent desired	Proportional parts required
a		x
	c	
b		y

Given these data, the ratio of x to y may be derived algebraically as follows:

$$ax + by = c(x + y)$$
$$ax + by = cx + cy$$
$$ax - cx = cy - by$$
$$x(a - c) = y(c - b)$$

$$\frac{x}{y} = \frac{c - b}{a - c}$$

Given a = 95%, b = 50%, and c = 70%, we may therefore solve the problems as follows:

$$0.95x + 0.50y = 0.70(x + y)$$

Or,

$$95x + 50y = 70x + 70y$$
$$95x - 70x = 70y - 50y$$
$$x(95 - 70) = y(70 - 50)$$

$$\frac{x}{y} = \frac{70 - 50}{95 - 70} = \frac{20}{25} = \frac{4 \text{ (parts)}}{5 \text{ (parts)}}, \text{ answer.}$$

The result can be shown to be correct by *alligation medial*:

$$95 \times 4 = 380$$
$$50 \times \underline{5} = \underline{250}$$
$$\text{Totals: 9} \qquad 630$$

$$630 \div 9 = 70\%$$

The customary layout of *alligation alternate*, used in the subsequent examples, is a convenient simplification of the preceding diagram.

In what proportion should 20% benzocaine ointment be mixed with an ointment base to produce a 2.5% benzocaine ointment?

20% | | 2.5 parts of 20% ointment
              2.5%
0% | | 17.5 parts of ointment base

Relative amounts: 2.5:17.5, or 1:7, *answer.*

$$\text{Check: } 20 \times 1 = 20$$
$$0 \times \underline{7} = \underline{0}$$
$$\text{Totals: 8} \qquad 20$$
$$20 \div 8 = 2.5\%$$

A hospital pharmacist wants to use three lots of zinc oxide ointment containing, respectively, 50%, 20%, and 5% of zinc oxide. In what proportion should they be mixed to prepare a 10% zinc oxide ointment?

The two lots containing *more* (50% and 20%) than the desired percentage may be separately linked to the lot containing *less* (5%) than the desired percentage:

50% | | 5 parts of 50% ointment

20% | | 5 parts of 20% ointment
         10%
5% | | 10 + 40 = 50 parts of 5% ointment

Relative amounts: 5:5:50, or 1:1:10, *answer.*

$$\textit{Check: } 50 \times 1 = 50$$
$$20 \times 1 = 20$$
$$5 \times \underline{10} = \underline{50}$$
$$\text{Totals: 12} \qquad 120$$
$$120 \div 12 = 10\%$$

Other answers are possible, of course, because the two stronger lots may be mixed first in any proportions desired, yielding a mixture that may then be mixed with the weakest lot in a proportion giving the desired strength.

In what proportions may a manufacturing pharmacist mix 20%, 15%, 5%, and 3% zinc oxide ointments to produce a 10% ointment?

Each of the weaker lots is paired with one of the stronger to give the desired strength, and because we may pair them in two ways, we may get two sets of correct answers.

20%		7 parts of 20% ointment
15%	10%	5 parts of 15% ointment
5%		5 parts of 5% ointment
3%		10 parts of 3% ointment

Relative amounts: 7:5:5:10, *answer.*

$$\text{Check: } 20 \times 7 = 140$$
$$15 \times 5 = 75$$
$$5 \times 5 = 25$$
$$3 \times \underline{10} = \underline{30}$$
$$\text{Totals: } 27 \quad 270$$
$$270 \div 27 = 10\%$$

Or,

20%		5 parts of 20% ointment
15%	10%	7 parts of 15% ointment
5%		10 parts of 5% ointment
3%		5 parts of 3% ointment

Relative amounts: 5:7:10:5, *answer.*

$$\text{Check: } 20 \times 5 = 100$$
$$15 \times 7 = 105$$
$$5 \times 10 = 50$$
$$3 \times \underline{5} = \underline{15}$$
$$\text{Totals: } 27 \quad 270$$
$$270 \div 27 = 10\%$$

How many milliliters of 50% w/v dextrose solution and how many milliliters of 5% w/v dextrose solution are required to prepare 4500 mL of a 10% w/v solution?

50%		5 parts of 50% solution
5%	10%	40 parts of 5% solution

Relative amounts 5:40, or 1:8, with a total of 9 parts

$$\frac{9 \text{ (parts)}}{1 \text{ (part)}} = \frac{4500 \text{ (mL)}}{x \text{ (mL)}}$$

$$x = 500 \text{ mL of 50\% solution, } and$$

$$\frac{9 \text{ (parts)}}{8 \text{ (parts)}} = \frac{4500 \text{ (mL)}}{y \text{ (mL)}}$$

$$y = 4000 \text{ mL of 5\% solution, } answers.$$

How many milliliters each of a 2% w/v solution and a 7% w/v solution should be used in preparing 1 gallon of a 3.5% w/v solution?

1 gallon = 3785 mL

2%		3.5 parts of 2% solution
	3.5%	
7%		1.5 parts of 7% solution

Relative amounts: 3.5:1.5, or 7:3, with a total of 10 parts

$$\frac{10 \text{ (parts)}}{7 \text{ (parts)}} = \frac{3785 \text{ (mL)}}{x \text{ (mL)}}$$

$$x = 2650 \text{ mL of 2\% solution, } and$$

$$\frac{10 \text{ (parts)}}{3 \text{ (parts)}} = \frac{3785 \text{ (mL)}}{y \text{ (mL)}}$$

$$y = 1135 \text{ mL of 7\% solution, } answers.$$

How many grams of 2.5% hydrocortisone cream should be mixed with 360 g of 0.25% cream to make a 1% hydrocortisone cream?

2.5%		0.75 part of 2.5% cream
	1%	
0.25%		1.5 parts of 0.25% cream

Relative amounts: 0.75:1.5, or 1:2

$$\frac{2 \text{ (parts)}}{1 \text{ (part)}} = \frac{360 \text{ (g)}}{x \text{ (g)}}$$

$$x = 180 \text{ g, } answer.$$

Alternate (algebraic) solution of the same problem:

$$2.5(x) + 0.25(360) = 1(360 + x)$$
$$2.5x + 90 = 360 + x$$
$$1.5x = 270$$
$$x = 180 \text{ g, } answer.$$

How many grams of white petrolatum should be mixed with 250 g of 5% and 750 g of 15% zinc oxide ointments to prepare a 10% ointment?

$$
\begin{array}{llll}
5 \times & 250 & = & 1250 \\
15 \times & \underline{750} & = & \underline{11,250} \\
\text{Totals:} & 1000 & & 12,500
\end{array}
$$

12,500 ÷ 1000 = 12.5% of zinc oxide in 1000 g of a mixture of 5% and 15% ointments

$$
\begin{array}{c|c|c}
12.5\% & & \text{10 parts of 12.5\% mixture} \\
& 10\% & \\
0\% & & \text{2.5 parts of white petrolatum}
\end{array}
$$

Relative amounts: 10:2.5, or 4:1

$$
\frac{4 \ (\text{parts})}{1 \ (\text{part})} = \frac{1000 \ (\text{g})}{x \ (\text{g})}
$$

$$
x = 250 \text{ g, } \textit{answer.}
$$

Check: 12.5 × 1000 = 12,500
          0 × 250 =   0
Totals: 1250   12,500
          12500 ÷ 1250 = 10%

How many grams of zinc oxide should be added to 3200 g of 5% zinc oxide ointment to prepare an ointment containing 20% of zinc oxide?

Zinc oxide (active ingredient) = 100%

$$
\begin{array}{c|c|c}
100\% & & \text{15 parts of 100\% zinc oxide} \\
& 20\% & \\
5\% & & \text{80 parts of 5\% ointment}
\end{array}
$$

Relative amounts: 15:80, or 3:16

$$
\frac{16 \ (\text{parts})}{3 \ (\text{parts})} = \frac{3200 \ (\text{g})}{x \ (\text{g})}
$$

$$
x = 600 \text{ g, } \textit{answer.}
$$

Check: 100 ×   600 = 60,000
          5 × 3200 = 16,000
Totals: 3800   76,000
          76,000 ÷ 3800 = 20%

Compare the solution of this problem by use of alligation alternate with other methods shown for the identical problem earlier in this chapter on page 262.

Specific Gravity of Mixtures

The methods of alligation medial and alligation alternate may be used in solving problems involving the specific gravities of different quantities of liquids of known specific gravities, provided no change in volume occurs when the liquids are mixed and that they are measured in a common denomination of *volume*.

CASE IN POINT 15.2[2]: **A pharmacist received the following prescription:**

℞

Clindamycin Phosphate	1.5%
Alcohol (52% v/v) q.s. ad	120 mL
Sig: Apply daily for acne	

The pharmacist has no clindamycin phosphate powder but does have clindamycin phosphate sterile solution, 150 mg/mL, in vials. From the label, the pharmacist learns that the solution is aqueous.

(a) **How many milliliters of the clindamycin phosphate sterile solution should the pharmacist use in filling the prescription?**

(b) **How many milliliters of 95% v/v of alcohol are required?**

(c) **How many milliliters of water should be added to make 120 mL?**

Example Calculations of Specific Gravity Using Alligation

What is the specific gravity of a mixture of 1000 mL of syrup with a specific gravity of 1.300, 400 mL of glycerin with a specific gravity of 1.250, and 1000 mL of an elixir with a specific gravity of 0.950?

$$1.300 \times 1000 = 1300$$
$$1.250 \times 400 = 500$$
$$0.950 \times \underline{1000} = \underline{950}$$

Totals: 2400 2750

$$2750 \div 2400 = 1.146, \textit{answer.}$$

In what proportion must glycerin with a specific gravity of 1.25 and water be mixed to prepare a liquid having a specific gravity of 1.10?

$$
\begin{array}{c|c|l}
1.25 & & 0.10 \text{ parts of glycerin} \\
& 1.10 & \\
1.00 & & 0.15 \text{ parts of water}
\end{array}
$$

Relative amounts: 0.10:0.15, or 2:3, *answer.*

How many milliliters of each of two liquids with specific gravities of 0.950 and 0.875 should be used to prepare 1500 mL of a liquid having a specific gravity of 0.925?

$$
\begin{array}{c|c|l}
0.950 & & 0.050, \text{ or 50 parts of liquid with specific} \\
& & \qquad \text{gravity of } 0.950 \\
& 0.925 & \\
0.875 & & 0.025, \text{ or 25 parts of liquid with specific} \\
& & \qquad \text{gravity of } 0.875
\end{array}
$$

Relative amounts: 50:25, or 2:1, with a total of 3 parts

$$\frac{3 \text{ (parts)}}{2 \text{ (parts)}} = \frac{1500 \text{ (mL)}}{x \text{ (mL)}}$$

$$x = 1000 \text{ mL of liquid with specific gravity of } 0.950,$$
and

$$\frac{3 \text{ (parts)}}{1 \text{ (part)}} = \frac{1500 \text{ (mL)}}{y \text{ (mL)}}$$

$$y = 500 \text{ mL of liquid with specific gravity of } 0.875,$$
answers

CASE IN POINT 15.3: A pharmacist received the following prescription:

℞

Hydrocortisone	0.6%
AQUAPHOR q.s. ad	15 g

Sig. Apply to child's affected area t.i.d.

The pharmacist has no hydrocortisone powder but does have a hydrocortisone cream, 1%. How many grams each of hydrocortisone cream and Aquaphor should be used in filling the prescription?

PRACTICE PROBLEMS

Altering Strength, Stock Solutions, and Alligation Calculations

1. If 250 mL of a 1:800 (v/v) solution were diluted to 1000 mL, what would be the ratio strength (v/v)?

2. If a pharmacist added 12 g of azelaic acid to 50 g of an ointment containing 15% azelaic acid, what would be the final concentration of azelaic acid in the ointment?

3. If 400 mL of a 20% w/v solution were diluted to 2 liters, what would be the percentage strength (w/v)?

4. BACTROBAN ointment contains 2% mupirocin. How many grams of a polyethylene glycol ointment base must be mixed with the contents of a 22-g tube of the BACTROBAN ointment to prepare one having a concentration of 5mg/g?

5. How many grams of an 8% w/w progesterone gel must be mixed with 1.45 g of a single-use 4% w/w progesterone gel to achieve a gel of 5.5% w/w strength?

6. If 150 mL of a 17% (w/v) concentrate of benzalkonium chloride are diluted to 5 gallons, what will be the ratio strength (w/v) of the dilution?

7. AGENERASE oral solution contains 1.5% amprenavir. A pharmacist wished to change the drug concentration to 5 mg/mL by using a diluent of polyethylene glycols. How many milliliters of the oral solution and how many milliliters of the diluent should be used to prepare 8 fluid-ounces of the mixture?

8. ℞³ Tetracaine
   Hydrochloride   0.75% w/v
   Epinephrine
   Hydrochloride   1:4000 w/v
   Cocaine
   Hydrochloride   3% wv
   Sodium
   Chloride
   Solution ad   30 mL
   Sig. Use in eye as directed.

   How many milliliters each of a 2% w/v solution of tetracaine hydrochloride and a 1:1000 w/v solution of epinephrine hydrochloride should be used in preparing the prescription?

9. If two tablespoonfuls of povidone iodine solution (10% w/v) were diluted to 1 quart with purified water, what would be the ratio strength (w/v) of the dilution?

10. How many milliliters of a 1:50 w/v boric acid solution can be prepared from 500 mL of a 5% w/v boric acid solution?

11. How many milliliters of water must be added to 250 mL of a 25% w/v stock solution of sodium chloride to prepare a 0.9% w/v sodium chloride solution?

12. How many milliliters of undecylenic acid would need to be added to 30 mL of a 20% undecylenic acid topical solution to change its concentration to 25%?

13. A certain product contains benzalkonium chloride in a concentration of 1:5000 w/v. How many milliliters of a 17% stock solution of benzalkonium chloride should be used in preparing 4 liters of the product?

14. How many milliliters of a 10% stock solution of a chemical are needed to prepare 120 mL of a solution containing 10 mg of the chemical per milliliter?

15. How many milliliters of water should be added to 1 gallon of 70% isopropyl alcohol to prepare a 30% solution for soaking sponges?

16. NEORAL oral solution contains 100 mg/mL of cyclosporine. If, on prescription, a pharmacist desired to prepare 30 mL of an oral solution containing 10% cyclosporine, how many milliliters of diluent should be used?

17. The formula for a buffer solution contains 1.24% w/v of boric acid. How many milliliters of a 5% w/v boric acid solution should be used to obtain the boric acid needed in preparing 1 liter of the buffer solution?

18. Menthol   0.1%
    Hexachlorophene   0.1%
    Glycerin   10.0%
    Alcohol 70%, to make   500 mL
    Label: Menthol and Hexachlorophene Lotion.

    How many milliliters of a 5% w/v stock solution of menthol in alcohol should be used to obtain the amount of menthol needed in preparing the lotion?

19. ℞   Gentian Violet Solution   500 mL
         1:100,000
         Sig. Mouthwash

    How many milliliters of ½% stock solution of gentian violet should be used in preparing the prescription?

20. How many milliliters of Burow's solution (containing 5% w/v of aluminum acetate) should be used in preparing 2 liters of a 1:800 (w/v) solution to be used as a wet dressing?

21. ℞[4]   Rhus Toxicodendron
            Extract   10 μg/mL
            Sterile Water for
              Injection qs   100 mL
            Sig. As directed.

    How many milliliters of a 100 mg/mL concentrate of Rhus toxicodendron extract should be used in preparing the prescription?

22. If a pharmacist fortified 10 g of a 0.1% w/w tacrolimus (PROTOPIC) ointment by adding 12.5 g of an ointment containing 0.03% w/w of the same drug, what would be the percentage strength (w/v) of the mixture?

23. A physician prescribes an ophthalmic suspension to contain 100 mg of cortisone acetate in 8 mL of normal saline solution. The pharmacist has on hand a 2.5% suspension of cortisone acetate in normal saline solution. How many milliliters of this and how many milliliters of normal saline solution should be used in preparing the prescribed suspension?

24. ℞   Benzalkonium Chloride
         Solution   240 mL
         Make a solution such that
           10 mL diluted to a liter
           equals a 1:5000 solution.
         Sig. 10 mL diluted to a
           liter for external use.

How many milliliters of a 17% stock solution of benzalkonium chloride should be used in preparing the prescription?

25. How many milliliters of water should be added to 100 mL of a 1:125 w/v solution to make a solution such that 25 mL diluted to 100 mL will yield a 1:4000 dilution?

26. How many milliliters of a lotion base must be added to 30 mL of oxiconazole nitrate (OXISTAT) lotion 1% w/v, to reduce its concentration to 6 mg/mL?

27. $\mathbf{R}^5$ Lactic Acid   10% w/v
    Salicylic Acid   10% w/v
    Flexible Collodion q.s.   15   mL
    Sig. For wart removal. Use externally as directed.

    How many milliliters of an 85% w/w solution of lactic acid with a specific gravity of 1.21 should be used in preparing the prescription?

28. How many milliliters of water should be mixed with 1200 g of 65% w/w alcohol to make 45% w/w alcohol?

29. How many milliliters of a syrup containing 85% w/v of sucrose should be mixed with 150 mL of a syrup containing 60% w/v of sucrose to make a syrup containing 80% w/v of sucrose?

30. $\mathbf{R}$ Castor Oil   5 mL
    Resorcinol Monoacetate   15 mL
    Alcohol 85%   ad   240 mL
    Sig. For the scalp.

    How many milliliters each of 95% v/v alcohol and water should be used in preparing the prescription?

31. How many milliliters of 95% w/w sulfuric acid having a specific gravity of 1.820 should be used in preparing 2 liters of 10% w/v acid?

32. A pharmacist mixes 100 mL of 38% w/w hydrochloric acid with enough purified water to make 360 mL. If the specific gravity of hydrochloric acid is 1.20, calculate the percentage strength (w/v) of the resulting dilution.

33. How many milliliters of 28% w/w strong ammonia solution having a specific gravity of 0.89 should be used in preparing 2000 mL of 10% w/w ammonia solution with a specific gravity of 0.96?

34. In using isoproterenol hydrochloride solution (1:5000 w/v), 1 mL of the solution is diluted to 10 mL with sodium chloride injection before intravenous administration. What is the percentage concentration of the diluted solution?

35. A 1:750 w/v solution of benzalkonium chloride diluted with purified water in a ratio of 3 parts of the benzalkonium solution and 77 parts of purified water is recommended for bladder and urethral irrigation. What is the ratio strength of benzalkonium chloride in the final dilution?

36. How many milliliters of a suspension base must be mixed with 250 mL of a paroxitine (PAXIL) oral suspension, 10 mg/5 mL, to change its concentration to 0.1% w/v?

37. An insect venom concentrate for immunotherapy contains 100 μg/mL. How many milliliters of water should be added to 1.2 mL of the venom concentrate to yield a 1:100,000 dilution?

38. How many grams of a 2.5% w/w benzocaine ointment can be prepared by diluting 1 lb. of a 20% w/w benzocaine ointment with white petrolatum?

39. How many grams of salicylic acid should be added to 75 g of a polyethylene glycol ointment to prepare an ointment containing 6% w/w of salicylic acid?

40. How many grams of an ointment base must be added to 45 g of clobestasol (TEMOVATE) ointment, 0.05% w/w, to change its strength to 0.03% w/w?

41. **℞**   Hydrocortisone Acetate
       Ointment 0.25%   10 g
       Sig. Apply to the eye.

    How many grams of 2.5% ophthalmic hydrocortisone acetate ointment and how many grams of ophthalmic base (diluent) should be used in preparing the prescription?

42. How many grams of zinc oxide should be added to 3400 g of a 10% zinc oxide ointment to prepare a product containing 15% of zinc oxide?

43. How many milliliters of a nonmedicated, flavored syrup base must be added to 1 pint of ranitidine (ZANTAC) syrup, 15 mg/mL, to change its concentration to 5 mg/mL?

44. **℞**   Zinc Oxide   1.5
       Hydrophilic Petrolatum   2.5
       Purified Water   5
       Hydrophilic Ointment   ad   30
       Sig. Apply to affected areas.

    How much zinc oxide should be added to the product to make an ointment containing 10% of zinc oxide?

45. If equal portions of tretinoin gel (RETIN-A MICRO), 0.1% w/w and 0.04% w/w, are combined, what would be the resultant percentage strength?

46. A vaginal douche powder concentrate contains 2% w/w of active ingredient. What would be the percentage concentration (w/v) of the resultant solution after a 5-g packet of powder is dissolved in enough water to make 1 quart of solution?

47.[6] How many milliliters of a 0.2% solution of a skin-test antigen must be used to prepare 4 mL of a solution containing 0.04 mg/mL of the antigen?

48. How many milligrams of sodium fluoride are needed to prepare 100 mL of a sodium fluoride stock solution such that a solution containing 2 ppm of sodium fluoride results when 0.5 mL is diluted to 250 mL with water?

49. **℞**[7]   Cyclosporine   2%
       Corn Oil   qs
       Sig. Use as directed.

    (a) How many milliliters each of corn oil and a 10% solution of cyclosporine would be needed to prepare 30 mL of the prescription? (b) If you then wished to dilute the prescription to a concentration of 1.5% cyclosporine, how many additional milliliters of corn oil would be required?

50. A prescription calls for 0.005 g of morphine sulfate. How many milligrams of a 1:10 trituration may be used to obtain the morphine sulfate?

51. If 100 mg of a 1:10 trituration of mechlorethamine hydrochloride (MUSTARGEN) are diluted to 10 mL with water for injection, how many milliliters of the injection should be administered to a 132-lb. patient if the dose of mechlorethamine hydrochloride is 0.1 mg/kg?

52. A hospital worker combined 2 fluidounces of a povidone-iodine cleaner, 7.5% w/v, with 4 fluidounces of a povidone-iodine topical solution, 10 % w/v. Calculate the resulting strength of the povidone-iodine mixture.

53. If 60 mL of a combination gel of hydrocortisone acetate, 1% w/w, and pramoxide, 1% w/w, are mixed with 12.5 mL of a gel containing hydrocortisone acetate, 2.5% w/w, and pramoxide, 1% w/w, calculate the percentage strength of each of the two drugs in the mixture.

54. A drug is commercially available in capsules each containing 12.5 mg of drug and 37.5 mg of diluent. How many milligrams of additional diluent must be added to the contents of one capsule to make a dilution containing 0.5 mg of drug in each 100 mg of powder?

55. Calculate the percentage of alcohol in a lotion containing 2 liters of witch hazel (14% of alcohol), 1 liter of alcohol (95%), and enough boric acid solution to make 5 liters.

56. In what proportion should 5% and 1% hydrocortisone ointments be mixed to prepare a 2.5% ointment?

57. In what proportion should a 20% zinc oxide ointment be mixed with white petrolatum (diluent) to produce a 3% zinc oxide ointment?

58. In what proportion should 30% and 1.5% hydrogen peroxide solutions be mixed to prepare a 3% hydrogen peroxide solution?

59. The solvent for the extraction of a vegetable drug is 70% alcohol. In what proportion may 95%, 60%, and 50% alcohol be mixed to prepare a solvent of the desired concentration?

60. A parent diluted 1 mL ibuprofen oral drops (Infant's MOTRIN Concentrated Drops) with 15 mL of water prior to administering the medication. The concentrated drops contain ibuprofen, 50 mg/1.25 mL. Calculate the concentration of ibuprofen in the dilution in (a) mg/mL, and (b) as a percentage strength.

61. How many milliliters of a 2.5% w/v chlorpromazine hydrochloride injection and how many milliliters of 0.9% w/v sodium chloride injection should be used to prepare 500 mL of a 0.3% w/v chlorpromazine hydrochloride injection?

62. How many milliliters of a 2% w/v solution of lidocaine hydrochloride should be used in preparing 500 mL of a solution containing 4 mg of lidocaine hydrochloride per milliliter of solution?

63. Dopamine hydrochloride injection is available in 5-mL ampuls containing 40 mg of dopamine hydrochloride per milliliter. The injection must be diluted before administration. If a physician wishes to use sodium chloride injection as the diluent and wants a dilution containing 0.04% w/v of dopamine hydrochloride, how many milliliters of sodium chloride injection should be added to 5 mL of the injection?

64. A solution of benzalkonium chloride is available in a concentration of 1:750 w/v. How many milliliters of purified water should be added to 30 mL of the solution to prepare a 1:5000 benzalkonium chloride solution for use as a wet dressing to the skin?

65. If an antibiotic injection contains 5% w/v of the drug, how many milliliters of diluent should be added to 5 mL of the injection to prepare a concentration of 5 mg of the antibiotic per milliliter?

66.[8] How many milliliters of sterile water for injection should be added to a vial containing 5 μg/mL of a drug to prepare a solution containing 1.5 μg/mL of the drug?

67. ℞   Zephiran Chloride
            Solution (17% w/v)   q.s.
        Purified Water, to make   480 mL
        Sig. One tbsp. diluted
            to 1 gallon with water
            to make a 1:10,000
            dilution.

    How many milliliters of zephiran chloride solution should be used in preparing the prescription?

Specific Gravity Calculations of Mixtures

68. What is the specific gravity of a mixture containing 1000 mL of water, 500 mL of glycerin having a specific gravity of 1.25, and 1500 mL of alcohol having a specific gravity of 0.81? (Assume no contraction occurs when the liquids are mixed.)

69. If a pharmacist mixed 1 pint of propylene glycol having a specific gravity of 1.20 with 500 mL of water, how many milliliters additional of propylene glycol should be added to change the specific gravity to 1.15?

70. How many milliliters of a syrup having a specific gravity of 1.350 should be mixed with 3000 mL of a syrup having a specific gravity of 1.250 to obtain a product having a specific gravity of 1.310?

71. How many grams of sorbitol solution having a specific gravity of 1.285 and how many grams (milliliters) of water should be used in preparing 500 g of a sorbitol solution having a specific gravity of 1.225?

ANSWERS TO "CASE IN POINT" AND PRACTICE PROBLEMS

Case in Point 15.1

Cefuroxime axetil present in original suspension:

$$100 \text{ mL} \times \frac{250 \text{ mg}}{5 \text{ mL}} = 5000 \text{ mg}$$

Cefuroxime axetil required in strengthened suspension:

$$100 \text{ mL} \times \frac{300 \text{ mg}}{5 \text{ mL}} = 6000 \text{ mg}$$

Cefuroxime axetil to add:

$$6000 \text{ mg} - 5000 \text{ mg} = 1000 \text{ mg}$$

Tablets required:

$$1000 \text{ mg} \times \frac{1 \text{ tablet}}{250 \text{ mg}} = 4 \text{ tablets, } answer.$$

A Second Look

There are a number of ways in which this problem could be addressed. One way would be to add another 250-mg pulverized tablet, calculate the volume of suspension that could be prepared at a concentration of 300 mg/5 mL, dispense 100 mL of that and discard the remaining volume.

Cefuroxime axetil in strengthened suspension plus another tablet:

$$6000 \text{ mg} + 250 \text{ mg} = 6250 \text{ mg cefuroxime axetil}$$

Volume of suspension that could be prepared at a concentration of 300 mg/5 mL:

$$\frac{5 \text{ mL}}{300 \text{ mg}} \times 6250 \text{ mg} = 104.17 \text{ mL}$$

Volume to dispense:

100 mL, and

Volume to discard:

4.17 mL, *answers.*

Proof: "If there are 6250 mg of cefuroxime axetil in 104.17 mL, how many milligrams would be present in each 5 mL?"

$$6250 \text{ mg} \times \frac{5 \text{ mL}}{104.17 \text{ mL}} = 299.99 \text{ or } 300$$

mg, *answer.*

Case in Point 15.2

(a) 120 mL × 0.15 (1.5%) = 1.8 g
1.8 g = 1800 mg

$$1800 \text{ mg} \times \frac{1 \text{ mL}}{150 \text{ mg}} = 12 \text{ mL, clinda-}$$

mycin phosphate sterile solution, *answer.*

(b) *If* the pharmacist had had clindamycin phosphate powder with which to fill the prescription, 1.8 g would have been used, and that quantity would have taken up a negligible volume on solution in the 52% v/v alcohol. Thus, the interpretation of the prescription is that the 120 mL (not 120 mL − 12 mL) of 52% v/v alcohol should be used.

120 mL × 0.52 (52% v/v) = 62.4 mL of solute (100% v/v alcohol)

$$\frac{62.4 \text{ mL}}{x \text{ mL}} = \frac{95 \text{ mL}}{100 \text{ mL}}; x = 65.68 \text{ mL of}$$

95% v/v alcohol, *answer*.

(c)   Due to contraction when alcohol and water are mixed, the volume of water cannot be determined by subtracting 65.68 mL from 120 mL; thus, a sufficient volume of water is used (q.s.) to make 120 mL, *answer*.

Case in Point 15.3

15 g × 0.006 (0.6% w/w) = 0.09 g hydrocortisone
1% hydrocortisone cream = 1 g hydrocortisone/100 g

Thus, $\frac{0.09 \text{ g}}{x \text{ g}} = \frac{1 \text{ g}}{100 \text{ g}}; x =$

9 g hydrocortisone cream, *and*
15 g − 9 g = 6 g AQUAPHOR, *answers*.

Note: The problem also may be solved by alligation alternate.

Practice Problems

1. 1:3200 v/v

2. 31.5% w/w

3. 4% w/v

4. 66 g polyethylene glycol ointment base

5. 0.87 g progesterone gel, 8%

6. 1:742 w/v

7. 78.9 mL AGENERASE oral solution
    157.7 mL polyethylene glycols

8. 11.25 mL tetracaine hydrochloride solution
    7.5 mL epinephrine hydrochloride solution

9. 1:315 w/v

10. 1250 mL boric acid solution

11. 6694.4 mL water

12. 2 mL undecylenic acid

13. 4.7 mL stock solution

14. 12 mL stock solution

15. 5046.67 mL water

16. 0 mL diluent

17. 248 mL boric acid solution

18. 10 mL stock solution

19. 1 mL stock solution

20. 50 mL Burow's solution

21. 0.01 mL concentrate

22. 0.06% w/w

23. 4 mL cortisone acetate suspension
    4 mL normal saline solution

24. 28.2 mL stock solution

25. 700 mL water

26. 20 mL lotion base

27. 1.46 mL lactic acid solution

28. 533.33 mL water

29. 600 mL syrup

30. 196.84 mL alcohol
    q.s. with water to 240 mL

31. 115.67 mL sulfuric acid, 95%

32. 12.67% w/v

33. 770.47 mL strong ammonia solution

34. 0.002% w/v

35. 1:20,000 w/v

36. 250 mL suspension base

37. 10.8 mL water

38. 3632 g benzocaine ointment, 2.5%

39. 4.787 g salicylic acid

40. 30 g ointment base

41. 1 g hydrocortisone acetate ointment, 2.5%
    9 g ophthalmic base

42. 200 g zinc oxide

43. 946 mL syrup base

44. 1.667 g zinc oxide

45. 0.07% w/w

46. 0.011% w/v

47. 0.08 mL antigen, 0.2%

48. 100 mg sodium fluoride

49. (a) 24 mL corn oil
        6 mL cyclosporin solution
    (b) 10 mL corn oil

50. 50 mg trituration

51. 6 mL MUSTARGEN injection

52. 9.17% w/v

53. 1% pramoxide
    1.26% hydrocortisone

54. 2450 mg diluent

55. 24.6% v/v

56. 3:5

57. 3:17

58. 1.5:27 or 3:54 or 1:18

59. 6:5:5

60. (a) 2.5 mg/mL ibuprofen
    (b) 2.5% ibuprofen

61. 60 mL chlorpromazine hydrochloride injection
    440 mL sodium chloride injection

62. 100 mL lidocaine hydrochloride injection

63. 495 mL sodium chloride injection

64. 170 mL purified water

65. 45 mL diluent

66. 2.33 mL sterile water for injection

67. 71.2 mL zephiran chloride solution

68. 0.947

69. 1031.38 mL propylene glycol

70. 4500 mL syrup

71. 394.737 g sorbitol solution
    105.263 mL water

REFERENCES

1. United States Pharmacopeia 31st Rev. National Formulary 26. Rockville, MD: United States Pharmacopeial Convention, 2008;1:1147.
2. Beach W. Athens, GA: College of Pharmacy, University of Georgia, 2005.
3. Prince SJ. Calculations. *International Journal of Pharmaceutical Compounding* 2000;4:221.
4. Karolchyk S. Treating patients allergic to poison ivy. *International Journal of Pharmaceutical Compounding* 1998. 2: 421.
5. Prince SJ. Calculations. *International Journal of Pharmaceutical Compounding* 1998;2:310.
6. Prince SJ. Calculations. *International Journal of Pharmaceutical Compounding* 1998;2:453.
7. Prince SJ. Calculations. *International Journal of Pharmaceutical Compounding* 2000;4:393.
8. Prince SJ. Calculations. *International Journal of Pharmaceutical Compounding* 1999;3:145.

Reducing and Enlarging Formulas

Objectives

Upon successful completion of this chapter, the student will be able to:

- Perform calculations to reduce or enlarge formulas for pharmaceutical preparations stated in metric quantities.
- Perform calculations to reduce or enlarge formulas for pharmaceutical preparations stated in proportional parts.

Pharmacists may have to reduce or enlarge formulas for pharmaceutical preparations in the course of their professional practice or manufacturing activities. Official (United States Pharmacopeia—National Formulary) formulas generally are based on the preparation of 1000 mL or 1000 g. Other formulas, as those found in the literature, may be based on the preparation of a dosage unit (e.g., 5 mL, 1 capsule) or another quantity (e.g., 100 mL). Industrial formulas may be scaled up to quantities of ingredients sufficient to prepare hundreds of thousands of dosage units in a production batch. In each of these instances, a pharmacist may calculate the quantities of each ingredient required for a smaller or greater quantity by *reducing or enlarging* the specified formula, while maintaining the correct proportion of one ingredient to the other.

Calculations to reduce or enlarge formulas may be performed by a *two-step* process:

Step 1. Using the following equation, determine the *factor* that defines the multiple or the decimal fraction of the amount of formula to be prepared:

$$\frac{\text{Quantity of formula desired}}{\text{Quantity of formula given}} = \text{Factor}$$

A factor greater than 1 represents the multiple of the formula, and a factor less than 1 indicates the fraction of the formula to be prepared.

Step 2. Multiply the quantity of each ingredient in the formula by the factor to determine the amount of each ingredient required in the reduced or enlarged formula.

Applying the equation and factor:

If a formula for 1000 mL contains 6 g of a drug, how many grams of drug are needed to prepare 60 mL of the formula?

Step 1. $\dfrac{60 \text{ mL}}{1000 \text{ mL}} = 0.06$ (factor)

Step 2. 6 g × 0.06 = 0.36 g, *answer.*

Example Calculations of Reducing and Enlarging Formulas

From the following formula, calculate the quantity of each ingredient required to make 240 mL of calamine lotion.

Calamine	80	g
Zinc Oxide	80	g
Glycerin	20	g
Bentonite Magma	250	mL
Calcium Hydroxide Topical Solution, to make	1000	mL

$$\frac{240 \text{ mL}}{1000 \text{ mL}} = 0.24 \text{ (factor)}$$

Using the factor 0.24, the quantity of each ingredient is calculated as follows:

Calamine	=	80 g × 0.24 = 19.2 g	
Zinc Oxide	=	80 g × 0.24 = 19.2 g	
Glycerin	=	20 g × 0.24 =	4.8 mL
Bentonite Magma	=	250 g × 0.24 = 60	mL

Calcium Hydroxide Topical Solution, to make 240 mL, *answers.*

Or, solving by dimensional analysis:

$$\text{Calamine } \frac{80 \text{ g}}{1000 \text{ mL}} \times \frac{240 \text{ mL}}{1} = 19.2 \text{ g}$$

$$\text{Zinc Oxide } \frac{80 \text{ g}}{1000 \text{ mL}} \times \frac{240 \text{ mL}}{1} = 19.2 \text{ g}$$

$$\text{Glycerin } \frac{20 \text{ mL}}{1000 \text{ mL}} \times \frac{240 \text{ mL}}{1} = 4.8 \text{ mL}$$

$$\text{Bentonite Magma } \frac{250 \text{ mL}}{1000 \text{ mL}} \times \frac{240 \text{ mL}}{1} = 60 \text{ mL}$$

Calcium Hydroxide Topical Solution, to make 240 mL, *answers.*

From the following formula for artificial tears,[1] calculate the quantity of each ingredient required to prepare a dozen 30-mL containers.

Polyvinyl Alcohol	1.4 g
Povidone	0.6 g
Chlorobutanol	0.5 g
Sterile Sodium Chloride Solution, 9% ad 100 mL	

$$30 \text{ mL} \times 12 = 360 \text{ mL}$$

$$\frac{360 \text{ mL}}{100 \text{ mL}} = 3.6 \text{ (factor)}$$

Using the factor 3.6, the quantity of each ingredient is calculated as follows:

Polyvinyl Alcohol	= 1.4 g × 3.6 = 5.04 g
Povidone	= 0.6 g × 3.6 = 2.16 g
Chlorobutanol	= 0.5 g × 3.6 = 1.8 g

Sterile Sodium Chloride Solution, 9% ad 360 mL, *answers.*

From the following formula for an estradiol vaginal gel,[2] calculate the quantity of each ingredient required to prepare 1 lb. of gel.

Estradiol	200 g
Polysorbate 80	1 g
Methylcellulose Gel, 2%	95 g

$$1 \text{ lb.} = 454 \text{ g}$$

$$\text{Formula weight} = 200 \text{ g} + 1 \text{ g} + 95 \text{ g} = 296 \text{ g}$$

$$\frac{454 \text{ g}}{296 \text{ g}} = 1.534 \text{ (factor)}$$

Using the factor 1.534, the quantity of each ingredient is calculated as follows:

Estradiol	$= 200 \text{ g} \times 1.534 = 306.8 \text{ g}$
Polysorbate 80	$= 1 \text{ g} \times 1.534 = 1.534 \text{ g}$
Methylcellulose Gel, 2%	$= 95 \text{ g} \times 1.534 = 145.73 \text{ g, } answers.$

From the following formula for a dexamethasone ophthalmic ointment,[3] calculate the quantity of each ingredient needed to prepare 7.5 g of ointment.

Dexamethasone Sodium Phosphate	55 mg
Lanolin, Anhydrous	5 g
Mineral Oil	10 g
White Petrolatum ad	100 g

$$\frac{7.5 \text{ g}}{100 \text{ g}} = 0.075 \text{ (factor)}$$

Using the factor 0.075, the quantity of each ingredient is calculated as follows:

Dexamethasone Sodium Phosphate	$= 55 \text{ mg} \times 0.075 = 4.125 \text{ mg}$
Lanolin, Anhydrous	$= 5 \text{ g} \times 0.075 = 0.375 \text{ g}$
Mineral Oil	$= 10 \text{ g} \times 0.075 = 0.75 \text{ g}$
White Petrolatum ad	$= 100 \text{ g ad } 7.5 \text{ g, } answers.$

Formulas That Specify Proportional Parts

On a rare occasion, a pharmacist may encounter an old formula that indicates the ingredients in "parts" rather than in measures of weight or volume. The parts indicate the relative proportion of each of the ingredients in the formula by *either* weight or volume, but not both. A formula for solid or semisolid ingredients, therefore, may be considered in terms of *grams*, whereas a formula of liquids may be considered in terms of *milliliters*.

Example Calculation of a Formula Expressed in Parts

From the following formula, calculate the quantity of each ingredient required to make 1000 g of the ointment.

Coal Tar	5 parts
Zinc Oxide	10 parts
Hydrophilic Ointment	50 parts

Total number of parts (by weight) = 65
1000 g will contain 65 parts

$$\frac{65 \text{ (parts)}}{5 \text{ (parts)}} = \frac{1000 \text{ (g)}}{\text{x (g)}}$$

$$x = 76.92 \text{ g of Coal Tar,}$$

and

$$\frac{65 \text{ (parts)}}{10 \text{ (parts)}} = \frac{1000 \text{ (g)}}{y \text{ (g)}}$$
$$y = 153.85 \text{ g of Zinc Oxide,}$$

and

$$\frac{65 \text{ (parts)}}{50 \text{ (parts)}} = \frac{1000 \text{ (g)}}{z \text{ (g)}}$$

$$z = 769.23 \text{ g of hydrophilic ointment, } answers.$$
(Check total: 1000 g)

CALCULATIONS CAPSULE

Reducing and Enlarging Formulas

Pharmaceutical formulas are combinations of ingredients, each present in a specified amount. The quantitative relationship between ingredients is fixed; that is, irrespective of the total quantity of formula prepared, the relative amount of one ingredient to another remains the same.

Formulas may be reduced or enlarged through the use of a *factor* generated by the following equation and applied consistently to each ingredient.

$$\frac{Quantity \text{ of formula desired}}{Quantity \text{ of formula given}} = Factor$$

The quantity of each ingredient in a formula is multiplied by the *factor* to determine the quantity needed in a reduced or enlarged formula.

PRACTICE PROBLEMS

1. From the following formula for 40 sertraline capsules,[4] calculate the factor that would be used if a pharmacist wished to prepare 250 capsules.

Sertraline Hydrochloride	300 mg
Silica Gel	6 g
Calcium Citrate	4 g

2. From the following formula for a progesterone nasal spray,[5] calculate the factor that would be used if a pharmacist wished to prepare 24 15-mL containers of the product.

Progesterone	20 mg
Dimethyl-β-cyclodextrin	62 mg
Purified Water ad	1 mL

3. From the following formula, calculate the quantities required to make 5 lb. of hydrophilic ointment.

Methylparaben	0.25	g
Propylparaben	0.15	g
Sodium Lauryl Sulfate	10	g
Propylene Glycol	120	g
Stearyl Alcohol	250	g
White Petrolatum	250	g
Purified Water, to make	1000	g

4. The formula for an ophthalmic ointment is as follows:

Sulfacetamide Sodium	10% w/w
Prednisolone Acetate	0.2% w/w

Phenylmercuric
Acetate   0.0008% w/w
Mineral Oil   1% w/w
White Petrolatum, qs ad   3.5 g

How much of each ingredient would be needed to manufacture 2000 such tubes of ointment?

5. Calculate the quantity of each ingredient needed to prepare 15-mL of the following ophthalmic solution.[6]

Erythromycin Lactobionate   500 mg
Dexamethasone Sodium
Phosphate   100 mg
Glycerin   2.5 mL
Sterile Water for Injection
ad   100 mL

6. According to the literature, the biotechnology product NEULASTA (pegfilgrastim) contains the following in 0.6 mL pre-filled syringes[7]:

Pegfilgrastim   6   mg
Sorbitol   30   mg
Polysorbate 20   0.02 mg
Water for Injection, ad   0.6 mL

How much of the first three ingredients would be needed to manufacture 100,000 such syringes?

7. From the following formula, calculate the quantity of each ingredient required to make 1500 g of the powder.

Calcium Carbonate   5 parts
Magnesium Oxide   1 part
Sodium Bicarbonate   4 parts
Bismuth Subcarbonate   3 parts

8. Calculate the quantity of benzocaine needed to prepare 240 g of the following formula for a topical anesthetic.

Benzocaine   14%   w/w
Butylaminobenzoate   2%   w/w
Tetracaine Hydrochloride 2%   w/w
Benzalkonium Chloride   1.5%   w/w
Cetyl Dimethyl Ethyl
Ammonium Bromide   0.005% w/w
Aquagel q.s. ad   30 g

9. The following is a formula for 100 triple estrogen capsules.[8] Calculate the quantities of the first three ingredients, in grams, and the last two ingredients, in kilograms, required to prepare 5000 such capsules.

Estriol   200 mg
Estrone   25 mg
Estradiol   25 mg
Polyethylene Glycol 1450   20 g
Polyethylene Glycol 3350   20 g

10. According to the literature, when the product AMEVIVE (alefacept) is reconstituted with sterile water for injection to prepare 0.6 mL of injection, it contains the following in each 0.5 mL.[9]

Alefacept   7.5 mg
Sucrose   12.5 mg
Glycine   5   mg
Sodium Citrate, Dihydrate 3.6 mg
Citric Acid, Monohydrate   0.06 mg

How much alefacept would be needed to manufacture a 5000 batch of vials for reconstitution?
(a) 12.5 mg
(b) 31.25 g
(c) 37.5 g
(d) 45 g

11. The formula for a ciprofloxacin otic drop is given in the literature as follows[10]:

Ciprofloxacin   1 g
Propylene Glycol   50 mL
Glycerin qs ad   100 mL

How many grams of ciprofloxacin would be required to prepare 200 15-mL bottles of the ear drop?

12. From the following formula for a progesterone vaginal suppository, calculate the amount of each ingredient needed to prepare 36 suppositories.

Progesterone   75 mg
Polyethylene Glycol 3350   1 g
Polyethylene Glycol 1000   3 g

13. The formula for a sports rub cream is given in the literature as follows[11]:

Methyl Salicylate	15 mL
Menthol	10 g
Eucalyptus Oil	1 g
Hydrophilic Ointment, qs ad	100 g

If the specific gravity of methyl salicylate is 1.18, how many grams of each ingredient would be needed to prepare a dozen 30-g tubes of ointment?

14. From the following formula for one rectal suppository, calculate the quantity of each ingredient required to prepare 24 such suppositories.

Promethazine Hydrochloride	25 mg
Ascorbyl Palmitate	1%
White Wax	5%
Cocoa Butter ad	2 g

15. From the following formula for a synthetic elastoviscous fluid for injection into the knee to treat osteoarthritis, calculate the quantities, in grams, of each of the first four ingredients needed to prepare 5000 2-mL prefilled syringes.

Hylan Polymers	16 mg
Sodium Chloride	17 mg
Disodium Hydrogen Phosphate	0.32 mg
Sodium Dihydrogen Phosphate	0.08 mg
Water for Injection ad 2	mL

16. From the following formula for gastric lavage prior to colonoscopy, calculate the quantity of sodium bicarbonate needed to prepare 100 liters of the formula.

Polyethylene Glycol 3350	60	mL
Sodium Chloride	1.46	g
Potassium Chloride	0.745	g
Sodium Bicarbonate	1.68	g
Sodium Sulfate	5.68	g
Water q.s. ad	4	L

17. The following is a formula for the preparation of a suppository for the treatment of migraine headaches.[12] Calculate the quantities of each ingredient needed to prepare 250 suppositories.

Ergotamine Tartrate	2	mg
Caffeine	100	mg
Hyoscyamine Sulfate	0.25	mg
Pentobarbital Sodium	60	mg
FATTIBASE ad	2	g

18. Each milliliter of an otic solution contains the following ingredients. Calculate the amount of each ingredient needed to manufacture 1000 10-mL containers of the product.

Antipyrine	54 mg
Benzocaine	14 mg
Dehydrated Glycerin, to make	1 mL

19. From the following formula for an oral electrolyte solution, calculate the amount of each ingredient required to prepare 240 mL of the solution.

Sodium	45 mEq
Potassium	20 mEq
Chloride	35 mEq
Citrate	30 mEq
Dextrose	25 g
Water ad	1000 mL

ANSWERS TO PRACTICE PROBLEMS

1. 6.25

2. 360

3. 0.568 g methylparaben
   0.341 g propylparaben
   22.7 g sodium lauryl sulfate
   272.4 g propylene glycol
   567.5 g stearyl alcohol
   567.5 g white petrolatum
   ad 2270 g or 5 lb. purified water

4. 700 g sulfacetamide sodium
   14 g prednisolone acetate
   56 mg phenyl mercuric acetate
   70 g mineral oil
   6215.944 g white petrolatum

5. 75 mg erythromycin lactobionate
   15 mg dexamethasone sodium phosphate
   0.375 mL glycerin
   q.s. ad 15 mL sterile water for injection

6. 600 g pegfilgrastim
   3000 g sorbitol
   2 g polysorbate 20

7. 576.923 g calcium carbonate
   115.385 g magnesium oxide
   461.539 g sodium bicarbonate
   346.154 g bismuth subcarbonate

8. 33.6 g benzocaine

9. 10 g estriol
   1.25 g estrone
   1.25 g estradiol
   1 kg polyethylene glycol 1450
   1 kg polyethylene glycol 3350

10. (d) 45 g alefacept

11. 30 g ciprofloxacin

12. 2.7 g progesterone
    36 g polyethylene glycol 3350
    108 g polyethylene glycol 1000

13. 63.72 g methyl salicylate
    36 g menthol
    3.6 g Eucalyptus oil
    256.68 g hydrophilic ointment

14. 0.6 g promethazine hydrochloride
    0.48 g ascorbyl palmitate
    2.4 g white wax
    44.52 g cocoa butter

15. 80 g hylan polymers
    85 g sodium chloride
    1.6 g disodium hydrogen phosphate
    0.4 g sodium dihydrogen phosphate
    q.s. ad 10,000 mL water for injection

16. 42 g sodium bicarbonate

17. 500 mg ergotamine tartrate
    25 g caffeine
    62.5 mg hyoscyamine sulfate
    15 g pentobarbital sodium
    459.44 g FATTIBASE

18. 540 g antipyrine
    140 g benzocaine
    ad 10 L dehydrated glycerin

19. 10.8 mEq sodium
    4.8 mEq potassium
    8.4 mEq chloride
    7.2 mEq citrate
    6 g dextrose
    ad 240 mL water

REFERENCES

1. *International Journal of Pharmaceutical Compounding* 2000;4:376.
2. *International Journal of Pharmaceutical Compounding* 1998;2:51.
3. *International Journal of Pharmaceutical Compounding* 2003;7:215.
4. *International Journal of Pharmaceutical Compounding* 1998;2:443.
5. *International Journal of Pharmaceutical Compounding* 1998;2:56.
6. *International Journal of Pharmaceutical Compounding* 2002;6:452.
7. NEULASTA, Product Literature. Thousand Oaks, CA: Amgen, Inc., 2008.
8. *International Journal of Pharmaceutical Compounding* 1997;1:187.
9. AMEVIVE, Product Literature. Deerfield, IL: Astellas Pharma US Inc., 2008.

10. Allen LV Jr. Secundum Artem 2006;13:4. Available at: http://www.paddocklabs.com/images/SecundumArten13 .1pdf. Accessed January 4, 2008.

11. Allen LV Jr. Secundum Artem 2005;12:4. Available at: http://www.paddocklabs.com/forms/secundum/14.2pdf. Accessed January 4, 2008.

12. *International Journal of Pharmaceutical Compounding* 1998;2:151

Selected Calculations in Contemporary Compounding

Objectives

Upon successful completion of this chapter, the student will be able to:

- Perform calculations for the constitution of dry powders for oral solution or suspension.
- Perform calculations for the constitution of dry powders for parenteral use.
- Perform calculations for the use of prefabricated dosage forms in compounding procedures.
- Perform calculations applied to the filling of capsules.
- Perform calculation applied to the preparation of suppositories by molding.

Pharmaceutical compounding is the process by which pharmacists combine therapeutically active ingredients with pharmaceutical materials in the preparation of prescriptions and medication orders to meet the specific needs of *individual patients*. This is in contrast to the *large-scale* production of pharmaceutical products to meet the needs of the general population that is termed *pharmaceutical manufacturing.*

Compounding is an activity for which pharmacists are uniquely qualified by virtue of their education, training, and experience. Many pharmacists have developed *specialized practices* in compounding that have contributed greatly to the medication needs of their patients.

This chapter presents calculations that apply to the preparation of oral and parenteral fluids by the *constitution* of dry powders; the use of tablets, capsules, and injections as the source of active therapeutic ingredients (ATI) in compounding; calculations specifically applicable to the extemporaneous preparation of suppositories and capsules; and calculations relevant to specialized prescriptions, medication orders, and formulas.

General Considerations in Compounding Practice

Compounded prescriptions may be desired for a number of reasons, including[1,2]:

- the need to adjust the strength or dose of a commercially available product to meet the specific requirements of a patient (e.g., a pediatric patient);
- the need to provide a product more organoleptically acceptable (e.g., taste) to a pediatric or veterinary patient;
- the need to prepare a different dosage form (e.g., a liquid) than the commercially available product (e.g., a tablet) to meet the requirements of a patient unable to swallow the existing dosage form (e.g., a pediatric or elderly patient);
- the need to prepare a dosage form free of an agent (e.g., sugar, preservatives) in the commercially available product that cannot be tolerated by a patient; and
- the need to provide a patient with a specifically designed formulation of an approved drug or drug combination, which is unavailable as a commercial product.

The *United States Pharmacopeia—National Formulary* (USP/NF) devotes a chapter to compounding nonsterile preparations that includes sections titled *Definitions*; *Ingredient Selection and Calculations*; *Checklist for Acceptable Strength, Quality, and Purity*; *Compounded Preparations*; *Compounding Process*; and *Compounding Records and Documents*.[3] Another USP/NF chapter is devoted compounding sterile preparations.[4] These chapters, along with other pharmaceutical references, should be referred to as required to ensure that standards of good pharmaceutical practice in compounding are understood and met.[5] Among the steps included in the USP/NF section titled *Compounding Process* is, "Perform necessary calculations to establish the amounts of ingredients needed."[3]

Constitution of Dry Powders

Constitution of Dry Powders for Oral Solution or Suspension

Some drugs, most notably antibiotics, lose their potency in a relatively short period when prepared in a liquid dosage form. To enhance the shelf-life of these drugs, manufacturers provide products to the pharmacy in dry powder form for *constitution* with purified water or special diluent at the time a prescription or medication order is received. Depending on the product, the dry powder may be stable for about 24 months. After constitution, the resultant solution or suspension is stable in the quantities usually dispensed, for up to 10 days at room temperature or 14 days if maintained under refrigeration.

Dry powders for constitution are packaged in self-contained bottles of sufficient size to accommodate the addition of the required volume of diluent (Figure 17.1). In addition to the quantita-

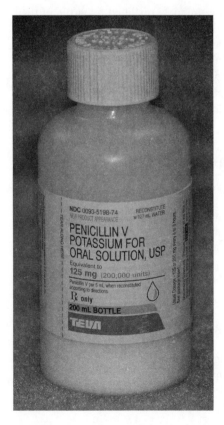

FIGURE 17.1 Example of a dry powder for reconstitution to prepare an oral solution. The label calls for the addition of 127 mL of water to prepare 200 mL of solution having a concentration of 125 mg or 200,000 units of penicillin V per 5 mL of solution.

tive amount of therapeutic agent, the powder contains such pharmaceutical ingredients as solubilizing or suspending agents, stabilizers, colorants, sweeteners, and flavorants.

On receipt of a prescription order, the pharmacist follows the label instructions for constitution,[a] adding the proper amount of purified water or other diluent to prepare the liquid form. Depending on the product's formulation, constitution results in the preparation of a clear *solution* (often called a *syrup*) or a *suspension*. The final volume of product is the sum of the volume of solvent or diluent added and the volume occupied by the dissolved or suspended powder mixture. These products generally are intended for infants and children but also can be used by adults who have difficulty swallowing the counterpart solid dosage form products, such as tablets and capsules.

For children and adults, a constituted product for oral solution or suspension generally is formulated such that the usual dose of the drug is contained in a teaspoonful amount of product. For infants, *pediatric drops*, which also require constitution, may be used. The calculations that follow demonstrate the preparation of constituted products and how the drug concentrations can be designed to meet a particular patient's requirements.

Example Calculations for the Constitution of Dry Powders for Oral Use

The label for a dry powder package of cefprozil (CEFZIL) for oral suspension directs the pharmacist to add 72 mL of purified water to prepare 100 mL of suspension. If the package contains 2.5 g of cefprozil, how many milligrams of the drug would be contained in each teaspoonful dose of the constituted suspension?

$$2.5 \text{ g} = 2500 \text{ mg}$$
$$\frac{2500 \text{ mg}}{100 \text{ ml}} = \frac{x \text{ mg}}{5 \text{ mL}}$$
$$x = 125 \text{ mg cefprozil, } answer.$$

Or, solving by dimensional analysis:

$$\frac{1000 \text{ mg}}{1 \text{ g}} \times \frac{5 \text{ mL}}{1 \text{ tsp}} \times \frac{2.5 \text{ g}}{100 \text{ mL}} = 125 \text{ mg cefprozil, } answer.$$

Label instructions for an ampicillin product call for the addition of 78 mL of water to make 100 mL of constituted suspension such that each 5 mL contains 125 mg of ampicillin. Calculate the volume of dry powder in the product and the total content of ampicillin.

Volume of dry powder: Because the addition of 78 mL of water results in the preparation of 100 mL of product, the volume occupied by the dry powder is:

100 mL − 78 mL = 22 mL, *answer*.

Total drug (ampicillin) present: If, in the constituted product, each 5 mL contains 125 mg of ampicillin, the total amount of ampicillin in the 100-mL product is:

$$\frac{5 \text{ mL}}{125 \text{ mg}} = \frac{100 \text{ mL}}{x}$$
$$x = 2500 \text{ mg, } answer.$$

---

[a] Some labeling instructions use the term "reconstitute" rather than "constitute" in describing the general process. Technically, if a dry powder is prepared from its original solution by removing the solvent (as through freeze drying), and then the solution is restored by the pharmacist, the term *reconstituted* would correctly apply. Some injectable products are prepared in this fashion.

Using the product in the previous example, if a physician desires an ampicillin concentration of 100 mg/5 mL (rather than 125 mg/5 mL), how many milliliters of water should be added to the dry powder?

Because it was determined that 2500 mg of ampicillin are in the dry product, the volume of product that can be made with a concentration of 100 mg/5 mL may be calculated by:

$$\frac{2500 \text{ mg}}{x \text{ mL}} = \frac{100 \text{ mg}}{5 \text{ mL}}$$
$$x = 125 \text{ mL, } answer.$$

Then, because it had been determined that the dry powder occupies 22 mL of volume, it is possible to determine the amount of water to add:

125 mL − 22 mL = 103 mL, *answer.*

The label of a dry powder for oral suspension states that when 111 mL of water are added to the powder, 150 mL of a suspension containing 250 mg of ampicillin per 5 mL are prepared. How many milliliters of purified water should be used to prepare, in each 5 mL of product, the correct dose of ampicillin for a 60-lb. child based on the dose of 8 mg/kg of body weight?

The dose of ampicillin may be determined by:

$$\frac{8 \text{ mg}}{2.2 \text{ lb.}} = \frac{x \text{ mg}}{60 \text{ lb.}}$$
$$x = 218 \text{ mg}$$

Then, the amount of ampicillin in the container is determined by:

$$\frac{250 \text{ mg}}{5 \text{ mL}} = \frac{x \text{ mg}}{150 \text{ mL}}$$
$$x = 7500 \text{ mg}$$

Thus, the amount of product that can be made from 7500 mg of drug such that each 5 mL contains 218 mg of drug may be found by:

$$\frac{218 \text{ mg}}{5 \text{ mL}} = \frac{7500 \text{ mg}}{x \text{ mL}}$$
$$x = 172 \text{ mL}$$

Finally, because the volume of powder occupies 39 mL (150 mL − 111 mL), the amount of water to add is determined by:

172 mL − 39 mL = 133 mL, *answer.*

The label of a dry powder for constitution into pediatric drops states that when 12 mL of purified water are added to the powder, 15 mL of a pediatric suspension containing 50 mg of amoxicillin per milliliter results. How many milliliters of water should be added to prepare the dose of amoxicillin in each 10 drops if the dropper delivers 20 drops/mL, the child has a body surface area (BSA) of 0.4 m², and the dose of the drug is based on 50 mg/m² of BSA?

The dose of amoxicillin may be determined by:

$$\frac{50 \text{ mg}}{1 \text{ m}^2 \text{ BSA}} = \frac{x \text{ mg}}{0.4 \text{ m}^2 \text{ BSA}}$$
$$x = 20 \text{ mg}$$

The volume of product to contain the 20-mg dose is determined by:

$$\frac{10 \text{ drops}}{x \text{ mL}} = \frac{20 \text{ drops}}{1 \text{ mL}}$$
$$x = 0.5 \text{ mL}$$

The amount of amoxicillin in the package is determined by:

$$\frac{50 \text{ mg}}{1 \text{ mL}} = \frac{x \text{ mg}}{15 \text{ mL}}$$
$$x = 750 \text{ mg}$$

The amount of product of the desired dose that may be prepared is determined by:

$$\frac{750 \text{ mg}}{x \text{ mL}} = \frac{20 \text{ mg}}{0.5 \text{ mL}}$$
$$x = 18.75 \text{ mL}$$

Subtracting the volume accounted for by the dry powder (15 mL − 12 mL = 3 mL), the volume of water to add is determined by:

$$18.75 \text{ mL} - 3 \text{ mL} = 15.75 \text{ mL}, \textit{ answer.}$$

CASE IN POINT 17.1[6]: A pediatrician telephones a pharmacist asking that the concentration of an antibiotic suspension be changed. The pediatrician wants the child-patient to take 200 mg of amoxicillin per teaspoonful dose. The label for amoxicillin powder for oral suspension indicates that the addition of 68 mL of purified water will result in a final volume of 100 mL with a concentration of 250 mg amoxicillin per 5 mL of suspension.

How many milliliters of water should the pharmacist add to the amoxicillin powder to produce a concentration of 200 mg/teaspoonful?

Constituion of Dry Powders for Parenteral Solution

As noted earlier, the USP/NF contains an important and often referred to chapter on the pharmaceutical compounding of sterile preparations.[4] The chapter provides the steps necessary for the safe preparation, storage, stability, and use of compounded sterile preparations. It defines the risk levels for the compounding of single-dose and multiple-dose sterile preparations.

Because of instability in liquid form, some medications (particularly antibiotics) intended for injection are provided as dry powder in vials to be constituted with sterile water for injection or other designated solvent or diluent immediately before use. Generally, these medications are small-volume products intended for use by injection or as additives to large-volume parenterals.

In contrast to the dry powders intended for oral use after constitution, injectable products may contain only limited amounts of specified added ingredients to increase the stability and effectiveness of the drug (obviously, no colorants, flavorants, or sweeteners are added). So, in effect, the bulk volume of the dry contents of a vial is largely or entirely the medication.

If the quantity of the dry drug powder is small and does not contribute significantly to the final volume of the constituted solution, the volume of solvent used will approximate the final volume of solution. For example, if 1000 units of a certain antibiotic in dry form are to be dissolved, and if the powder does not account for any significant portion of the final volume, the addition of 5 mL of solvent will produce a solution containing 200 units/mL. If the dry powder, however, because of its bulk, contributes to the final volume of the constituted solution, the increase in volume produced by the drug must be considered, and this factor must then be used in calculating the amount of solvent needed to prepare a solution of a desired concentration. For example, the package directions for making injectable solutions of piperacillin sodium specify that 4 mL of sterile solvent should be added to 2 g of the dry powder to produce 5.0 mL of a solution that is to contain 400 mg/mL. The drug, in this case, accounts for 1 mL of the final volume. Again, in dissolving 20,000,000 units of penicillin G potassium, the addition of 32 mL of sterile solvent provides a total volume of 40 mL of a solution that contains 500,000 units/mL. The dry powder now accounts for 8 mL of the final volume.

Example Calculations for the Constitution of Dry Powders for Parenteral Use

Using a vial containing 200,000 units of penicillin G potassium, how many milliliters of solvent should be added to the dry powder in preparing a solution having a concentration of 25,000 units/mL?

$$\frac{25,000 \text{ (units)}}{200,000 \text{ (units)}} = \frac{1 \text{ (mL)}}{x \text{ (mL)}}$$

$$x = 8 \text{ mL, } answer.$$

Using a vial containing 200,000 units of penicillin G sodium and sodium chloride injection as the solvent, explain how you would obtain the penicillin G sodium needed in preparing the following prescription.

℞	Penicillin G Sodium	15,000 units per mL
	Sodium Chloride Injection ad	10
	Sig. For IM Injection.	mL

15,000 units × 10 = 150,000 units of penicillin G sodium needed

Because the dry powder represents 200,000 units of penicillin G sodium or $\frac{4}{3}$ *times* the number of units desired, $\frac{3}{4}$ of the powder will contain the required number of units.

Step 1. Dissolve the dry powder in 4 mL of sodium chloride injection.
Step 2. Use 3 mL of the constituted solution, *answer.*

Or, solving by dimensional analysis:

$$10 \text{ mL} \times \frac{15,000 \text{ units}}{1 \text{ mL}} \times \frac{4 \text{ mL}}{200,000 \text{ units}} = 3 \text{ mL, } answer.$$

The package information enclosed with a vial containing 5,000,000 units of penicillin G potassium (buffered) specifies that when 23 mL of a sterile solvent are added to the dry powder, the resulting concentration is 200,000 units/mL. On the basis of this information, how many milliliters of sterile water for injection should be used in preparing the following solution?

℞	Penicillin G Potassium (buffered)	5,000,000 units
	Sterile Water for Injection	q.s.
	Make solution containing 500,000 units per mL	
	Sig. One mL = 500,000 units of Penicillin G Potassium	

The package information states that the constituted solution prepared by dissolving 5,000,000 units of the dry powder in 23 mL of sterile solvent has a final volume of 25 mL. The dry powder, then, accounts for 2 mL of this volume.

Step 1. The final volume of the prescription is determined as follows:

$$\frac{500,000\ (\text{units})}{5,000,000\ (\text{units})} = \frac{1\ (\text{mL})}{x\ (\text{mL})}$$
$$x = 10\ \text{mL}$$

Step 2. 10 mL − 2 mL (dry powder accounts for this volume) = 8 mL, *answer.*

Piperacillin sodium is available in 2-g vials, and the dry powder accounts for 1 mL of the volume of the constituted solution. Using a 2-g vial of piperacillin sodium and sodium chloride injection as the solvent, explain how you could fill the following medication order.

Piperacillin Sodium	250 mg
Sodium Chloride Injection ad	15 mL

Step 1. Dissolve the 2 g of dry powder in 9 mL of sodium chloride injection to prepare 10 mL of solution. Each milliliter will contain 200 mg of piperacillin sodium.

Step 2. Use 1.25 mL of the constituted solution and 13.75 mL of sodium chloride injection, *answer.*

CASE IN POINT 17.2: A hospital pharmacist received the following order for a patient[7]:

Medication Order: Staphcillin, 750 mg IV every 4 hours

The following product and procedures were followed:
 Product: 6-g vial Staphcillin
 Pharmacy Operations: Reconstitute vial with sterile water for injection to yield Staphcillin 500 mg/mL and further dilute in 100 mL of sodium chloride injection. Administer: 30-minute IV infusion.

(a) **How many milliliters of solution from the reconstituted vial should be used per infusion?**
(b) **What should be the infusion rate in milliliters per hour?**
(c) **With a drop factor of 10 drops per milliliter, calculate the infusion rate in drops per minute.**

Use of Prefabricated Dosage Forms in Compounding

Pharmacists frequently find that bulk supplies of certain proprietary drug substances are not available for extemporaneous compounding and that prefabricated tablets, capsules, injections, and other dosage forms provide the only available source of the medicinal agents needed. This situation occurs, for example, when an adult or pediatric patient is unable to swallow solid dosage forms, and the commercially available tablets or capsules must be used to prepare a liquid form of the same medication.

When using commercially prepared dosage forms as the source of a medicinal agent, the pharmacist selects products that are of the most simple, economic, and convenient form. For example, uncoated tablets or capsules are preferred over coated tablets or sustained-release dosage forms. For both convenience and economy, use of the fewest dosage units is preferred; for example, five 100-mg tablets rather than one hundred 5-mg tablets. An injection often provides a convenient source of medicinal agent when the volume of injection required is small and it is compatible with the physical characteristics of the dosage form being prepared (e.g., an oral liquid rather than dry-filled capsules).

Occasionally, when of the prescribed strength, small whole tablets or broken *scored* (grooved) tablets, may be placed within capsule shells when capsules are prescribed. In most instances, however, tablets are crushed in a mortar and reduced to a powder. When capsules are used as the drug source, the capsule shells are opened and their powdered contents are expelled. The correct quantity of powder is then used to fill the prescription or medication order.

It is important to understand that in addition to the medicinal agent, most solid dosage forms contain additional materials, such as fillers, binders, and disintegrants. These ingredients may need to be considered in the required calculations. For example, a tablet labeled to contain 10 mg of a drug may actually weigh 200 mg or more because of the added ingredients. Calculations involved in the use of injections generally are simplified because injections are labeled according to quantity of drug per unit volume; for example, milligrams per milliliter (mg/mL).

Example Calculations for the Use of Prefabricated Dosage Forms in Compounding

Only capsules, each containing 25 mg of indomethacin, are available. How many capsules should be used to obtain the amount of indomethacin needed in preparing the following prescription?

℞	Indomethacin	2 mg/mL
	Cherry Syrup ad	150 mL
	Sig. 5 mL b.i.d.	

Because 2 mg/mL of indomethacin are prescribed, 300 mg are needed in preparing the prescription. Given that each capsule contains 25 mg of indomethacin, then 300 (mg) ÷ 25 (mg) = 12 capsules are needed, *answer.*

The drug metoprolol tartrate (LOPRESSOR) is available as 50-mg tablets. Before preparing the following prescription, a pharmacist determined that each tablet weighed 120 mg. Explain how to obtain the proper quantity of LOPRESSOR.

℞	LOPRESSOR	15 mg
	Lactose, qs ad	300 mg
	Prepare 24 such capsules.	
	Sig. One cap. 2× a day.	

15 (mg) × 24 = 360 mg of LOPRESSOR needed
Crush 8 tablets, which contain:

400 mg (8 × 50 mg) of LOPRESSOR and
960 mg (8 × 120 mg) of total powder

$$\frac{400 \text{ mg LOPRESSOR}}{360 \text{ mg LOPRESSOR}} = \frac{960 \text{ mg total}}{x \text{ mg total}}$$

$$x = 864 \text{ mg quantity of powder to use, } answer.$$

How many milliliters of an injection containing 40 mg of triamcinolone per milliliter may be used in preparing the following prescription?

℞	Triamcinolone	0.05%
	Ointment Base ad	120 g
	Sig. Apply to affected area.	

120 g × 0.0005 = 0.06 g = 60 mg triamcinolone needed

$$\frac{40 \text{ mg}}{60 \text{ mg}} = \frac{1 \text{ mL}}{x \text{ mL}}$$

$$x = 1.5 \text{ mL, } answer.$$

The only source of sodium chloride is in the form of tablets, each containing 1 g. Explain how you would obtain the amount of sodium chloride needed for the following prescription.

R̸   Ephedrine Sulfate   0.5
     Isotonic Sodium Chloride Solution (0.9%)   50
     Sig. For the nose.

50 g × 0.009 = 0.45 g of sodium chloride needed

Because one tablet contains 1 g of sodium chloride or $^{20}/_{9}$ times the amount desired, $^{9}/_{20}$ of the tablet will contain the required quantity, or 0.45 g. The required amount of sodium chloride may be obtained as follows:

Step 1. Dissolve one tablet in enough purified water to make 20 mL of dilution.
Step 2. Take 9 mL of the dilution, *answer.*

The only source of potassium permanganate is in the form of tablets for topical solution, each containing 0.3 g. Explain how you would obtain the amount of potassium permanganate needed for the following prescription.

R̸   Potassium Permanganate Solution   250 mL
         1:5000
     Sig. Use as directed.
         1:5000 = 0.02%

250 g × 0.0002 = 0.05 g or 50 mg of potassium permanganate needed

Because one tablet for topical solution contains 300 mg of potassium permanganate or 6 times the amount needed, $^{1}/_{6}$ of the tablet will contain the required amount, or 50 mg. The required quantity of potassium permanganate may be obtained as follows:

Step 1. Dissolve one tablet for topical solution in enough purified water to make 60 mL of dilution.
Step 2. Take 10 mL of the dilution, *answer.*

Special Calculations: Capsule Filling and Suppository Molding

Capsule Filling[8]

The extemporaneous filling of capsules enables the pharmacist to prepare patient-specific doses of drugs in a conveniently administered form. Empty capsule shells, made of gelatin, are readily available in a variety of sizes, as shown in Figure 17.2, with size 000 being the largest and size 5 the smallest.

Filled capsules should be neither underfilled nor overfilled but should hold the ingredients snugly. Different drug powders have different densities, and thus different weights can be packed into a given size capsule (see Table 17.1). In filling a prescription or medication order, a pharmacist should select a capsule size that accommodates the fill and will be easy for the patient to swallow.

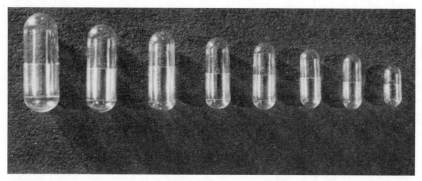

FIGURE 17.2 Hard gelatin capsule sizes, from left to right: 000, 00, 0, 1, 2, 3, 4, and 5.

Most oral drugs have relatively small doses; thus, a diluent, like lactose, commonly is added to provide the necessary bulk to completely fill the prescribed capsules.

The steps used in calculating the proper capsule fill may be described as follows:

Step 1. Select an appropriate capsule size.
Step 2. Fill the capsule shell separately with each drug and diluent, and record the weights of each.
Step 3. Calculate the *diluent displacement weight* for each drug, as demonstrated in the following example problem.
Step 4. Calculate the amount of diluent required per capsule.
Step 5. Calculate the total quantities of each drug and the diluent needed to fill all of the capsules prescribed.

Note: Some pharmacists calculate for an extra capsule or two so as not to run short of fill due to any powder residue remaining in the mortar after the mixing process; this may not be done for "accountable" drugs, such as narcotics.

Example Calculation to Determine a Capsule Fill

Determine the total quantities of each drug and lactose required to fill the following prescription.

℞ Drug A   20 mg
    Drug B   55 mg
    Lactose, q.s.
    M.ft. caps # 20

TABLE 17.1 CAPSULE SIZES AND APPROXIMATE FILL CAPACITIES

CAPSULE SIZE	APPROXIMATE VOLUME	APPROXIMATE POWDER WEIGHT
000	1.4 mL	430 mg – 1.8 g
00	0.95 mL	390 mg – 1.3 g
0	0.68 mL	325 – 900 mg
1	0.5 mL	227 – 650 mg
2	0.37 mL	200 – 520 mg
3	0.3 mL	120 – 390 mg
4	0.21 mL	100 – 260 mg
5	0.13 mL	65 – 130 mg

Step 1. For the purpose of this example, assume the pharmacist selected a size 1 capsule.

Step 2. The pharmacist filled a capsule individually with each ingredient, weighed them, and found:

    Capsule filled with drug A weighed   620 mg
    Capsule filled with drug B weighed   470 mg
    Capsule filled with lactose weighed   330 mg

Step 3. The *diluent displacement weights* for drugs A and B are calculated by ratio and proportion as follows:

For drug A:

$$\frac{620 \text{ mg (drug A in filled capsule)}}{330 \text{ mg (lactose in filled capsule)}} = \frac{20 \text{ mg (drug A per capsule)}}{x \text{ (lactose displacement)}}$$

$$x = 10.65 \text{ mg (diluent displacement by 20 mg of drug A)}$$

For drug B:

$$\frac{470 \text{ mg}}{330 \text{ mg}} = \frac{55 \text{ mg}}{x}$$

$$x = 38.62 \text{ mg (diluent displacement by 55 mg of drug B)}$$

Step 4. The diluent required per capsule:

$$330 \text{ mg} - 49.27 \text{ mg } (10.65 \text{ mg} + 38.62 \text{ mg}) = 280.73 \text{ mg lactose}$$

Step 5. The total quantities of each drug and diluent needed to fill all the capsules prescribed:

    Drug A = 20 mg × 20 (capsules) = 400 mg
    Drug B = 55 mg × 20 (capsules) = 1100 mg
    Lactose = 280.73 mg × 20 (capsules) = 5614.6 mg, *answers.*

Suppository Molding[8]

Pharmacists extemporaneously prepare suppositories by using a mold, such as that shown in Figure 17.3. The drug(s) prescribed and a suppository base are the components of any suppository.

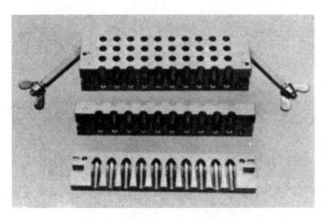

FIGURE 17.3 A partially opened 50-cell suppository mold. *(Courtesy of Chemical and Pharmaceutical Industry Co.)*

As defined in Appendix C, **suppositories** are solid dosage forms intended for insertion into body orifices where they soften, melt, or dissolve, releasing their medications to the surrounding tissues. Any of a number of suppository bases can be used as vehicles for the medication; in extemporaneous compounding, cocoa butter (also termed theobroma oil) is commonly used. Cocoa butter is a solid at room temperature but melts at body temperatures.

The calculations involved in preparing suppositories by molding are described by the following steps. Other methods are used and may be found in the cited reference.[9]

To calibrate the suppository mold:

Step 1. Fill all the cells of the suppository mold with melted base. After allowing time to cool and harden, extract the formed suppositories, weigh them, and determine the total and average suppository weights.

Step 2. Divide the total and average suppository weights by the density of the suppository base to determine the volume capacity of the suppository mold and the average volume of each cell.

To calculate and prepare medicated suppositories:

Step 1. Weigh the active ingredient for the preparation of a single suppository.

Step 2. Mix the single dose of active ingredient with a portion of melted base *insufficient* to fill one cell of the mold (based on information obtained by previously calibrating the mold).

Step 3. Pour the drug-base mixture into a cell, and add additional melted base to completely fill the cell.

Step 4. After the suppository cools and hardens, extract and weigh it.

Step 5. The weight of the base is determined by subtracting the amount of the drug from the weight of the molded suppository.

Step 6. The individual weights of the drug and base required to prepare the prescribed number of suppositories may then be determined by multiplying the amounts for a single suppository. The volume of base required may also be calculated, if desired, by the use of its known density.

Example Calculation to Prepare Suppositories by Molding

Calculate the quantities of drug A and cocoa butter needed to fill the following prescription.

> ℞ Drug A   350 mg
> Cocoa Butter q.s.
> M. ft. rectal suppos. # 12

Step 1. 350 mg of drug A is weighed.

Step 2. Since a rectal suppository mold prepares suppositories weighing approximately 2 g, the amount of cocoa butter to use that would be *insufficient* to fill one cell may be estimated by:

> 2 g − 0.35 g (drug A) = 1.65 g (cocoa butter)
> 1.65 g ÷ 0.86 g/mL (density of cocoa butter) = 1.92 mL (approximate volume of melted cocoa butter, when added to drug A, to *completely* fill the cell)

By mixing the drug with 1 mL of melted cocoa butter, the pharmacist knows that this volume is *insufficient* to fill a cell.

Step 3. The mixture of 350 mg of drug A and 1 mL of melted cocoa butter is placed in a cell, and sufficient additional melted cocoa butter is used to completely fill the cell.

Step 4. The cooled and hardened suppository is extracted and is found to weigh 1.95 g.

Step 5. The weight of the cocoa butter in one suppository is calculated:

1.95 g − 0.35 g (drug A) = 1.6 g cocoa butter

Step 6. The total quantities of drug A and cocoa butter needed to fill the prescription are:

0.35 g × 12 (suppositories) = 4.2 g drug A
1.6 g × 12 (suppositories) = 19.2 g cocoa butter, *answers.*

Note: Some pharmacists calculate for an extra suppository or two so as not to run short of fill mixture. In filling the mold, each cell should be slightly overfilled to allow for contraction on cooling.

Compounding Specialized Formulas

Not all commercially available products are suitable for every patient. Often a pharmacist must modify an existing product or prepare an original formulation to meet the requirements of a patient.

In their compounding practices, pharmacists may develop their own formulas, or they may refer to contemporary formulas developed and published by colleagues.[10] To facilitate the practice of compounding, some manufacturers make available resource materials, formulas, and a variety of compounding adjuncts, including ointment and suppository bases, oral suspending and syrup vehicles, rectal/vaginal vehicles, and other nonmedicated products to which medications may be added.[11]

Example Calculations of Specialized Formulas

Calculate the number of tablets containing the combination of spironolactone 25 mg and hydrochlorothiazide 25 mg that must be used to prepare the following formula using ORA-PLUS as the oral suspending vehicle.[12]

Spironolactone   5 mg/mL
Hydrochlorothiazide   5 mg/mL
ORA-PLUS ad   120 mL

Spironolactone/hydrochlorothiazide:
5 mg of each drug/mL × 120 mL = 600 mg of each drug
600 mg (of each drug) ÷ 25 mg (of each drug/tablet) = 24 tablets, *answer.*

Calculate the amount of FATTIBASE, a suppository base, required to prepare 200 suppositories from the following formula for one progesterone vaginal suppository.[13]

Progesterone, micronized 25 mg
Silica Gel, micronized   20 mg
FATTIBASE ad   2 g

25 mg (progesterone) + 20 mg (silica gel) = 45 mg
2 g − 0.045 g = 1.955 g
1.955 g × 200 (suppositories) = 391 g FATTIBASE, *answer.*

CASE IN POINT 17.3[14]: A pharmacist receives a telephone call from a pediatrician who has an 8.8-lb. 1-month-old patient with an acid reflux condition. The infant was started on ranitidine (ZANTAC) syrup, 15 mg/mL, at a dose of 10 mg/kg/day, and has shown improvement. However, because of the flavor (peppermint) and alcohol content (7.5%), the baby frequently rejects the medication.

The pharmacist suggests preparing a sugar-free and alcohol-free syrup/suspension with a fruity odor and taste. The physician agrees and prescribes ranitidine syrup/suspension, 60 mL, at a dose of 10 mg/kg/day, divided into two 0.5-mL doses.

The pharmacist uses finely crushed 75-mg ranitidine tablets as the source of the drug and ORA-SWEET SF as the vehicle.

How many 75-mg ranitidine tablets are required?

PRACTICE PROBLEMS

Calculations for the Constitution of Dry Powders for Oral Administration

1. After constitution of a dry powder, each 5 mL of ampicillin for oral suspension contains 250 mg of ampicillin in package sizes to prepare 100 mL, 150 mL, or 200 mL of suspension. Which package size should be dispensed for a 20-kg child who is to take 50 mg/kg/day total, q.i.d. in equally divided and spaced doses for 10 days?

2. Manufacturer's directions call for the addition of 90 mL of water to constitute a 150-mL container of cefaclor to yield a strength of 250 mg of cefaclor per 5 mL. If 60 mL of water were mistakenly added in constituting the product, calculate the resultant milligrams of cefaclor per 5 mL.

3. The label on a bottle of dry powder mix for constitution states that when 128 mL of water are added, 150 mL of an oral suspension containing 250 mg of ampicillin in each 5 mL results.
   (a) How many milliliters of water should be added to the dry powder mix if a strength of 150 mg of ampicillin per 5 mL is desired?

   (b) If the dose of ampicillin is 5 mg/kg of body weight, how many milliliters of water should be added to the dry powder mix so that a child weighing 66 lb. would receive the proper dose in each 5 mL of the suspension?

4. Amoxicillin/clavulanate potassium (AUGMENTIN) powder for oral suspension is prepared prior to dispensing by adding 134 mL of purified water to the contents of the container to prepare 150 mL of suspension. If each teaspoonful of suspension contains 125 mg of amoxicillin and 31.25 mg of clavulanate potassium, how much of each of these agents is contained in the dry powder prior to reconstitution?

5. If, in the above problem, a pharmacist wished to use the dry product to prepare an oral suspension containing 200 mg of amoxicillin and 50 mg of clavulanate potassium/5 mL of suspension, how many milliliters of purified water should be used for reconstitution?

Calculations Applied to Compounding for Parenteral Administration

6. A 7.5-g bulk pharmacy vial of cefuroxime (ZINACEF) when constituted with 77 mL of sterile water for injection, contains 375 mg of cefuroxime in each 4 mL. How many milliliters of volume were occupied by the dry powder in the vial?

7. Efalizumab (RAPTIVA) is available in vials which when reconstituted with 1.3 mL of sterile water for injection yields 1.5 mL of solution containing 100 mg/mL of drug. How much dry efalizumab is present in the vial?
   (a) 130 mg
   (b) 150 mg
   (c) 0.2 g
   (d) 15 mg

8. A hospital pharmacist constitutes a vial containing 2 g of piperacillin sodium to 10 mL with sterile water for injection. This solution is then diluted by adding it to 100 mL of 5% dextrose injection for administration by infusion. What is the concentration, in milligrams per milliliter (mg/mL), of piperacillin sodium in the infusion solution?

9. A vial of cefazolin injection contains 1 g per 3 mL. If 1.6 mL of the injection is diluted to 200 mL with sodium chloride injection, how many milliliters of the dilution should be administered daily to a child weighing 40 lb. if the daily dose is 25 mg/kg of body weight?

10.[7] Medication Order: Piperacillin, 1500 mg every 6 hours.
    Product: 3-g vial, piperacillin.
    Pharmacy operations: Reconstitute vial to 5 mL with sterile water for injection and further dilute to 50 mL with sodium chloride injection.
    Administer: 20-minute IV infusion.
    (a) How many milliliters of solution from the reconstituted vial should be used?
    (b) What should be the infusion rate in milliliters per hour?
    (c) With a drop factor of 20 drops per milliliter, calculate the infusion rate in drops per minute.

---

11. A medication order calls for 400 mg of cefazolin sodium to be administered IM to a patient every 12 hours. Vials containing 500 mg, 1 g, and 10 g of cefazolin sodium are available. According to the manufacturer's directions, dilutions may be made as follows:

Vial Size	Solvent to Be Added	Final Volume
500 mg	2 mL	2.2 mL
1 g	2.5 mL	3 mL
10 g	45 mL	51 mL

Explain how the prescribed amount of cefazolin sodium could be obtained.

12. Using the vial sizes in Problem 11 as the source of cefazolin sodium, how many milliliters of the diluted 500-mg vial should be administered to a 40-lb. child who is to receive 8 mg of cefazolin sodium per kilogram of body weight?

13. Using cefazolin sodium injection in a concentration of 125 mg/mL, complete the following table representing a *Pediatric Dosage Guide:*

Weight		Dose (25 mg/kg/day divided into 3 doses) approximate single dose (mg/q8h)	mL of dilution (125 mg/mL) needed
lb.	kg		
10	4.5	37.5 or 38 mg	0.3 mL
20	_____	_____	_____
30	_____	_____	_____
40	_____	_____	_____
50	_____	_____	_____

14. A vial contains 1 g of ceftazidime. Express the concentrations of the drug, in milligrams per milliliter, following constitution with sterile water for injection to the following volumes: (a) 2.2 mL, (b) 4.5 mL, and (c) 10 mL.

15. Acetazolamide sodium is available in 500-mg vials to be constituted to 5 mL with sterile water for injection before use. The dose of the drug for children is 5 mg/kg of body weight. How many milliliters of the injection should be administered to a child weighing 25 lb.?

16. An intravenous infusion for a child weighing 60 lb. is to contain 20 mg of vancomycin hydrochloride per kilogram of body weight in 200 mL of sodium chloride injection. Using a 10-mL vial containing 500 mg of vancomycin hydrochloride (dry powder), explain how you would obtain the amount needed in preparing the infusion.

Calculations for the Use of Prefabricated Dosage Forms in Compounding

17. ℞   Potassium Perman-
        ganate Solution   500 mL
        1:10,000
        Sig. Use as directed.

   Using tablets, each containing 0.3 g of potassium permanganate, explain how you would obtain the amount of potassium permanganate needed for the prescription.

18. ℞   Estropipate   0.0125% w/w
        Cream Base   ad   60 g
        Sig. Vaginal Cream.

   How many 0.75-mg tablets of estropipate may be used to prepare the prescription?

19. How many milliliters of a 0.9% solution of sodium chloride can be made from 10 tablets for solution each containing 2.25 g of sodium chloride?

20. ℞   Phenacaine Hydrochlo-
          ride Solution 1%   7.5 mL
        Scopolamine Hydro-
          bromide Solution
          0.2%   7.5 mL
        Sig. For the eye.

   How many tablets, each containing 600 μg of scopolamine hydrobromide, should be used in preparing the prescription?

21. ℞   Hexachlorophene
        Hydrocortisone   aa   0.25%
        Coal Tar Solution   30 mL
        Hydrophilic Ointment
          ad   120 g
        Sig. Apply.

   How many tablets, each containing 20 mg of hydrocortisone, should be used in preparing the prescription?

22. How many milliliters of an injection containing 40 mg of a drug per milliliter would provide the amount of the drug needed to prepare 120 mL of a 0.2% suspension?

23. ℞ Allopurinol   65 mg/5 mL
       Cologel   40 mL
       Syrup   ad   150 mL
       M. ft. susp.
       Sig. As directed.

    How many scored 100-mg allopurinol tablets may be used in preparing the prescription?

24. ℞ Enalapril   7.5 mg
       Lactose   ad   200 mg
       DTD Caps # 40
       Sig. Take one capsule each morning.

    How many 20-mg tablets of enalapril, each weighing 120 mg, and how many grams of lactose would be needed to prepare the prescription?

25. How many tablets for topical solution, each containing 300 mg of potassium permanganate, should be added to 1 gallon of purified water to provide a concentration of 0.012% w/v?

26. A prescription for 240 mL of a cough mixture calls for 2 mg of hydrocodone bitartrate per teaspoonful. How many tablets, each containing 5 mg of hydrocodone bitartrate, should be used in preparing the cough mixture?

27. ℞ Dantrolene Sodium   5 mg/mL
       Citric Acid   150 mg
       Purified Water   10 mL
       Syrup   ad   125 mL
       M. ft. susp.
       Sig. As directed.

    If the only source of dantrolene sodium is 100-mg capsules, each containing 200 mg of drug-diluent powder mix, (a) how many capsules must be opened, and (b) how many milligrams of the powder mix should be used in preparing the prescription?

28. ℞[15] Ketorolac Trome-
           thamine   7.5 mg/5 mL
           Suspension Vehicle
           ad   120 mL
           Sig. 1 tsp q6h

    How many 10-mg ketorolac tromethamine (TORDOL) tablets may be used to prepare this prescription?

29. How many DANTRIUM capsules, each containing 25 mg of dantrolene, are needed to prepare 100 mL of a pediatric suspension containing 5 mg of dantrolene per milliliter?

30. The following is a formula for a diazepam rectal gel.[16] How many 10-mL vials of VALIUM Injection containing 5 mg/mL of diazepam would be needed to compound the formula?

Diazepam	100 mg
Methylcellulose (1500 cps)	2.5 g
Methylparaben	100 mg
Glycerin	5 g
Purified Water ad	100 mL

31. How many tablets, each containing 25 mg of spironolactone, are needed to prepare 200 mL of a pediatric suspension to contain 5 mg of spironolactone per milliliter?

32. A physician prescribes 30 capsules, each containing 300 mg of ibuprofen, for a patient. The pharmacist has on hand 400-mg and 600-mg ibuprofen tablets. How many each of these tablets could be used to obtain the amount of ibuprofen needed in preparing the prescription?

33. ℞ Indomethacin Powder   1%
       Carbopol 941 Powder   2%
       Purified Water   10%
       Alcohol   ad   90 mL
       Sig. Use as directed.

    How many 75-mg capsules of indomethacin should be used in preparing the prescription?

34. ℞ Minoxidil   0.3%
     Vehicle/N   ad   50 mL
     Sig. Apply to affected areas of the scalp b.i.d.

    Tablets containing 2.5 mg and 10 mg of minoxidil are available. Explain how you would obtain the amount of minoxidil needed in preparing the prescription, using the available sources of the drug.

35. If a pharmacist used one 50-mg tablet of a drug to prepare 30 mL of an otic suspension in sweet oil, calculate the percentage strength of the preparation.

36. ℞ Aminophylline   500 mg
     Sodium Pentobarbital   75 mg
     Carbowax Base   ad   2 g
     Ft. suppos. no. 12
     Sig. Insert one at night.

    How many capsules, each containing 100 mg of sodium pentobarbital, should be used to provide the sodium pentobarbital needed in preparing the prescription?

37. A starting pediatric dose of phenytoin sodium (DILANTIN Sodium) is 6 mg/kg/d, administered in three equally divided doses. Using tablets containing 50 mg of phenytoin sodium, a pharmacist prepared a suspension such that each 1 mL, delivered from a calibrated dropper, contained a single dose for a 44-lb. child. How many tablets should be used to prepare 30 mL of the suspension?

38. ℞ CARAFATE   400 mg/5 mL
     Cherry Syrup   40 mL
     Sorbitol Solution   40 mL
     Flavor   q.s.
     Purified Water   ad   125 mL
     Sig. 5 mL t.i.d.

    How many 1-g CARAFATE tablets should be used in preparing the prescription?

Calculations Used in Capsule Filling and Suppository Molding

39.[8] A pharmacist needs to prepare 50 capsules, each containing 4 mg of estriol and 1 mg of estradiol. A size 3 capsule is selected for use. Capsule shells are individually filled with each drug and lactose and the weights recorded as follows:

> Estriol   250 mg
> Estradiol   190 mg
> Lactose   320 mg

(a) How many milligrams of each component will be needed to fill all the capsules?
(b) How many milligrams should the content of each capsule weigh?

40.[8] A pharmacist prepares six suppositories using a polyethylene glycol base, density 1.18 g/mL. The total weight of the suppositories is found to be 13.81 g. Calculate the volume of the mold per cell.

41.[8,17] ℞ Fluconazole   200 mg
       PEG base, q.s.
       M. ft. suppos # 20

(a) How many grams of fluconazole are needed?
(b) If a trial molded suppository weighs 2.4 g, how many grams of PEG base are needed to compound the prescription?

Calculations of Specialized Formulas

42. The following is a formula for an oral ulceration mouthwash.[18]

Hydrocortisone	55.2 mg
Lidocaine HCl	2.4 g
Erythromycin Stearate	1.5 g
Diphenhydramine HCl	150 mg
Nystatin	2,000,000 units
Xanthan Gum	240 mg
Stevia Powder Extract	280 mg
Sodium Saccharin	120 mg
Flavor	1 mL
Simple Syrup or Sorbitol Solution (70%) ad	120 mL

    (a) Calculate the percentage strength of hydrocortisone in the formula.
    (b) If nystatin is available as a powder containing 5225 units/mg, calculate the quantity required, in milligrams, to compound the formula.
    (c) Calculate the concentration of erythromycin stearate, in mg/mL, in the formula.

43. Misoprostol and Lidocaine in Glycerin Mouth Paint[19]

Misoprostol 200-mcg tablets	12 tablets
Lidocaine HCl	1 g
Glycerin qs ad	100 mL

    How many micrograms of misoprostol would be present in each milliliter of mouth paint?

44. Progesterone Liquid Fill Capsules.[20]

Progesterone, micronized	10 g
Sesame Oil qs ad	30 mL
To make 100 capsules	

    How many (a) micrograms of progesterone and (b) microliters of the formula would be contained in each capsule?

45. Tri-Est Aqueous Injection[21]

Estriol	200 mg
Estrone	25 mg
Estradiol	25 mg
Polysorbate 80	0.2 mL
Benzyl Alcohol	1 mL
Sterile Water for Injection ad	100 mL

    How many milliliters of the injection should be used to deliver 1.75 mg of total estrogens?

46. Intracavernosal Injection[22]

Prostaglandin E	5.9 μg/mL
Papaverine HCl	17.6 mg/mL
Phentolamine Mesylate	0.6 mg/mL
Sterile Water for Injection ad	1.5 mL

    How many milligrams of each ingredient should be used in preparing 12 syringes, each containing 1.5 mL of injection?

47. Progesterone Nasal Spray[23]

Progesterone	20 mg
Dimethyl-β-cyclodextrin	62 mg
Purified Water ad	1 mL

    How many milligrams each of progesterone and dimethyl-β-cyclodextrin would be delivered in each 0.05 mL spray of solution?

48. Triple Estrogen Slow-Release Capsules[24]
    For 100 capsules:

Estriol	200 mg
Estrone	25 mg
Estradiol	25 mg
Methocel E4M premium	10 g
Lactose	23.75 g

    Calculate the weight, in milligrams, of the formula in each capsule.

49. Nail Fungus Solution[25]

    NIZORAL, 200-mg
       tablets   10 tablets
    Clotrimazole   900 mg
    Ethyl Alcohol, 95%   5 mL
    Polyethylene Glycol
       300   67 mL
    Dimethyl Sulfoxide   23 mL

    If the formula prepares 98 mL, what is the percent concentration of NIZORAL in the solution?

50. Pediatric Chewable Gummy Gel Base[26]
    Gelatin   43.4 g
    Glycerin   155 mL
    Purified Water   21.6 mL

    If the specific gravity of glycerin is 1.25, what is the weight of the formula?

51. Antiemetic Injection for Cancer Chemotherapy[27]

    REGLAN (5 mg/mL)   30   mL
    ATIVAN (2 mg/mL)   0.5 mL
    Mannitol, 25%   50   mL
    COMPAZINE
       (5 mg/mL)   2   mL
    Dextrose Injection,
       5%   50 mL

    How many milligrams each of RE-GLAN, ATIVAN, and COMPAZINE are contained in each milliliter of the injection?

52. Migraine Headache Suppositories[28]
    Ergotamine Tartrate   2   mg
    Caffeine   100   mg
    Hyoscyamine Sulfate   0.25 mg
    Pentobarbital Sodium   60   mg
    FATTIBASE   ad   2   g

    The formula is for one suppository. If the specific gravity of FATTIBASE is 0.89, how many milliliters of the melted base (assuming no volume change due to heat) may be used to prepare 36 suppositories?

53. Veterinary Dexamethasone Ophthalmic Ointment[29]
    Dexamethasone
       Sodium Phosphate 39.6 mg
    Bacteriostatic Water
       for Injection   0.4 mL
    Polysorbate 80   0.3 mL
    Lacrilube   qs   30 g

    Calculate the percentage strength of dexamethasone (base) in the formula if 1 mg of dexamethasone (base) is equivalent to 1.32 mg of dexamethasone sodium phosphate.

54. The following is a formula for a captopril oral liquid.[11]

    ℞   Captopril   100-mg tablet
        ORA-SWEET ad   134 mL

    How many milliliters of the oral liquid would provide 0.75 mg of captopril?

55. The following is a formula for a rifampin oral liquid.[11]

    ℞   Rifampin   25 mg/mL
        ORA-PLUS ad   120 mL

    How many 300-mg tablets of rifampin should be used?

56. The following is a formula for fluconazole topical cream.[11]

    ℞   Fluconazole   10   g
        Glycerin   18.75 g
        DERMABASE ad   100   g

    How many milliliters of glycerin should be used (sp. gr. 1.25)?

57. The following is a formula for a clotrimazole topical preparation.[11]

    ℞   Clotrimazole, powder   1%
        DERMABASE ad   30 g

    How many grams of DERMABASE are required?

58.[30] ℞   Oseltamivir phosphate 15 mg/mL
             Cherry Syrup qs ad   60 mL
         Sig: One teasp. 2 × daily × 5 days

    How many 75-mg capsules of oseltamivir phosphate (TAMIFLU) should be used to compound this prescription?

ANSWERS TO "CASE IN POINT" AND PRACTICE PROBLEMS

Case in Point 17.1

Calculate the amount of amoxicillin in container:

$$\frac{250 \text{ mg (amoxicillin)}}{5 \text{ mL}} = \frac{x \text{ mg (amoxicillin)}}{100 \text{ mL}}$$

x = 5000 mg amoxicillin in container

Calculate volume that can be prepared from 5000 mg at 200 mg/5 mL:

$$\frac{200 \text{ mg}}{5 \text{ mL}} = \frac{5000 \text{ mg}}{x \text{ ml}},$$

x = 125 mL of oral suspension
    can be prepared

Calculate volume of amoxicillin powder in container:

100 mL − 68 mL (water added by label instructions) = 32 mL (volume of powder)

Calculate water requirement for new concentration:

125 mL − 32 mL = 93 mL of water required, *answer.*

Proof: 5000 mg amoxicillin per 125 mL = 200 mg amoxicillin per 5 mL

Case in Point 17.2

(a) $750 \text{ mg} \times \dfrac{1 \text{ mL}}{500 \text{ mL}} = 1.5 \text{ mL}$ of reconstituted solution, *answer.*

(b) Infusion time: 30 minutes
     Infusion volume: 101.5 mL
     Infusion rate per hour:

$$60 \text{ min } \frac{101.5 \text{ mL}}{30 \text{ min}} = 203 \text{ mL, infusion}$$

rate per hour, *answer.*

(c) 101.5 mL (infusion volume) ×

$$\frac{10 \text{ drops}}{1 \text{ mL}} = 1015 \text{ drops}$$

$$\frac{1015 \text{ drops}}{30 \text{ min}} = 33.8 \text{ or } 34 \text{ drops per minute, } answer.$$

Case in Point 17.3

Calculate milligrams of ranitidine required per 0.5-mL dose:

$$\frac{8.8 \text{ lb.}}{2.2 \text{ lb./kg}} = 4 \text{ kg (weight of child)}$$

4 kg × 10 mg/kg/day = 40 mg/day

40 mg ÷ 2 doses/day = 20 mg/dose; thus, 20 mg/0.5-mL dose

Calculate milligrams of ranitidine required in 60-mL prescription:

$$\frac{20 \text{ mg}}{0.5 \text{ mL}} = \frac{x \text{ mg}}{60 \text{ mL}},$$

x = 2400 mg ranitidine required

Calculate number of 75-mg ranitidine tablets needed to provide 2400 mg

2400 mg ÷ 75 mg/tablet = 32 tablets, *answer.*

Practice Problems

1. 200 mL

2. 312.5 mg cefaclor

3. (a) 228 mL water
    (b) 228 mL water

4. 3750 mg amoxicillin
    937.3 mg clavulanate potassium

5. 77.75 mL purified water

6. 3 mL

7. (b) 150 mg efalizumab

8. 18.18 mg/mL piperacillin

9. 170.5 mL

10. (a) 2.5 mL
    (b) 157.5 or 158 mL/hr
    (c) 52.5 or 53 drops/minute

11. Dilute and use 1.767 mL of the 500-mg vial, or
    dilute and use 1.2 mL of the 1-g vial, or
    dilute and use 2.04 or 2 mL of the 10-g vial

12. 0.64 mL

13. 20   9.1 kg   75.8 mg   0.61 mL
    30   13.6 kg 113.3 mg 0.91 mL
    40   18.2 kg 151.7 mg 1.21 mL
    50   22.7 kg 189.2 mg 1.51 mL

14. (a) 454.55 mg/mL
    (b) 222.22 mg/mL
    (c) 100   mg/mL

15. 0.57 mL acetazolamide sodium injection

16. 545 mg needed. Use 1 vial + 10 mL of sterile diluent to a second vial to make 10 mL, and use 0.9 mL of the dilution.

17. Dissolve 1 tablet in enough distilled water to make 60 mL, and take 10 mL of the dilution.

18. 10 tablets estropipate

19. 2500 mL sodium chloride solution

20. 25 tablets scopolamine hydrobromide

21. 15 tablets hydrocortisone

22. 6-mL injection

23. 19.5 tablets allopurinol

24. 15 tablets enalapril
    6.2 g lactose

25. 1.5 tablets potassium permanganate

26. 19.2 tablets hydrocodone bitartrate

27. (a) 7 capsules dantrolene sodium
    (b) 1250 mg powder

28. 18 tablets TORDOL

29. 20 capsules DANTRIUM

39. 2 vials VALIUM Injection

31. 40 tablets spironolactone

32. 22.5 tablets (400 mg each) ibuprofen, or 15 tablets (600 mg each) ibuprofen

33. 12 capsules indomethacin

34. 60 tablets (2.5 mg each) minoxidil, or 15 tablets (10 mg each) minoxidil

35. 0.167%

36. 9 capsules sodium pentobarbital

37. 24 tablets phenytoin sodium

38. 10 tablets CARAFATE

39. (a) 200 mg estriol
    50 mg estradiol
    15,660 mg lactose
    (b) 318.2 mg

40. 1.95 mL

41. (a) 4 g fluconazole
    (b) 44 g PEG base

42. (a) 0.046% hydrocortisone
    (b) 382.78 mg nystatin
    (c) 12.5 mg/mL erythromycin stearate

43. 24 μg misoprostol

44. (a) 100,000 μg progesterone
    (b) 300 μL

45. 0.7 mL injection

46. 0.106 mg prostaglandin E
    316.8 mg papaverine HCl
    10.8 mg phentolamine mesylate

47. 1 mg progesterone
    3.1 mg dimethyl-β-cyclodextrin

48. 340 mg

49. 2.04% NIZORAL

50. 258.75 g

51. 1.13 mg REGLAN
    0.0075 mg ATIVAN
    0.075 mg COMPAZINE

52. 74.34 mL FATTIBASE

53. 0.1% dexamethasone

54. 1 mL oral liquid

55. 10 tablets rifampin

56. 15 mL glycerin

57. 29.7 g DERMABASE

58. 12 tablets oseltamivir phosphate

REFERENCES

1. Pharmacy Compounding Accreditation Board. Available at: http://www.pcab.org/. Accessed January 4, 2008.
2. International Academy of Compounding Pharmacists. Available at: http://www.iacprx.org. Accessed January 4, 2008.
3. United States Pharmacopeia 31st Rev. National Formulary 26. Rockville, MD: United States Pharmacopeial Convention, 2008;(795)1:315–319.
4. United States Pharmacopeia 31st Rev. National Formulary 26. Rockville, MD: United States Pharmacopeial Convention, 2008;(797)1:319–336.
5. Allen JV Jr. USP Chapter <795> Pharmaceutical compounding—nonsterile preparations. Secundum Artem 2006; 13:4. Available at: http://www.paddocklabs.com/forms/secundum/volume%2013. Accessed January 4, 2008.
6. Warren F. College of Pharmacy. Athens, GA: University of Georgia, 2005.
7. Craig GP. *Clinical Calculations Made Easy.* Baltimore: Lippincott Williams & Wilkins, 2001:195–196.
8. Prince SJ. In Ansel HC, Prince SJ. *Pharmaceutical Calculations: The Pharmacist's Handbook.* Baltimore: Lippincott Williams & Wilkins, 2004:96–105.
9. Allen LV Jr, Popovich NG, Ansel HC. *Pharmaceutical Dosage Forms and Drug Delivery Systems.* 8th Ed. Baltimore: Lippincott Williams & Wilkins, 2005:325–328.
10. Allen LV Jr. *Allen's Compounded Formulations.* 2nd Ed. Washington, DC: American Pharmacist's Association, 2004.
11. Paddock Laboratories. Compounding. Available at: http://www.paddocklabs.com. Accessed January 3, 2008.
12. *International Journal of Pharmaceutical Compounding* 1997;1:183.
13. *International Journal of Pharmaceutical Compounding* 1998;2:65.
14. Beach W. College of Pharmacy. Athens, GA: University of Georgia, 2005.
15. Prince SJ. Calculations. *International Journal of Pharmaceutical Compounding* 1998;2:164.
16. Allen LV Jr. Diazepam dosed as a rectal gel. *U.S. Pharmacist* 2000;25:98.
17. Allen LV. *The Art, Science, and Technology of Pharmaceutical Compounding.* Washington, DC: American Pharmacist's Association, 1997:140.
18. *International Journal of Pharmaceutical Compounding* 1999;3:10.
19. *International Journal of Pharmaceutical Compounding* 1999;3:48.
20. *International Journal of Pharmaceutical Compounding* 1999;3:294.
21. *International Journal of Pharmaceutical Compounding* 1999;3:304.
22. *International Journal of Pharmaceutical Compounding* 1999;3:81.
23. *International Journal of Pharmaceutical Compounding* 1998;2:56.
24. *International Journal of Pharmaceutical Compounding* 1999;3:401.
25. *International Journal of Pharmaceutical Compounding* 1998;2:277.
26. *International Journal of Pharmaceutical Compounding* 1997;1:106.
27. *International Journal of Pharmaceutical Compounding* 1997;1:175.
28. *International Journal of Pharmaceutical Compounding* 1998;2:151.
29. *International Journal of Pharmaceutical Compounding* 1998;2:206.
30. Winiarski AP, Infeld MH, Tscherne R, et al. Preparation and stability of extemporaneous oral liquid formulations of oseltamivir using commercially available capsules. *Journal of the American Pharmacist's Association* 2007;47:747–755.

18

Selected Calculations Involving Veterinary Pharmaceuticals

Objectives

Upon successful completion of this chapter, the student will be able to:

- Demonstrate an understanding of the spectrum of medications used in the care and treatment of animals.
- Define the *extralabel* use of drugs in veterinary medicine.
- Describe guidelines for the compounding of veterinary pharmaceuticals.
- Perform pharmaceutical calculations, including dosing calculations, relevant to veterinary pharmaceuticals.

Veterinary medicine, like human medicine, uses pharmaceuticals of various dosage forms and strengths in the diagnosis, prevention, treatment, and cure of disease and illness. Animals suffer from many of the same diseases and illnesses affecting humans, such as anemias, cardiovascular disease, infectious disease, and cancer.[1-2] Thus, many of the medications used in human medicine also apply in veterinary medicine.

Diseases that are unique to a specific species of animal require medications developed for that purpose. Veterinary drugs gain approval for specific uses in an intended animal species through the Center for Veterinary Medicine (CVM) of the Food and Drug Administration (FDA).[3-4] In addition to the use of veterinary drugs for FDA-approved uses, veterinarians also are permitted to prescribe both human- and animal-approved drugs for *extralabel* uses in animals—that is, for uses *not* specified in the approved labeling, so long as the drug is used within the context of a "veterinarian-client-patient relationship."[5-6] This permits greater flexibility for using a wide range of approved drugs in animal care.

The dosage forms used in veterinary medicine are like those used in human medicine—for example, tablets (as chewable tablets), capsules, oral liquids, injections, eye drops, and topical applications. However, specialized drug delivery devices commonly are used to administer the dosage forms. This includes esophageal syringes, drench guns, and oral tubes designed to deliver medication directly into an animal's stomach; pole-mounted syringes and projectile delivery systems, which allow injections to be administered from a safe distance; mastitis syringes, for inserting a drug formulation directly into the mammary gland; and others.[7]

The most obvious and striking difference between veterinary medicine and human medicine is the nature of the patient. Whereas humans *do* differ from one another in many respects, the differences are relatively minor compared with the wide-ranging differences among veterinary patients.

The various species of animals differ quite dramatically in size, structure, physical appearance, physiologic and biochemical characteristics, and in many other respects, including intelligence, temperament, and natural habitat.[8-10] There are at least 24,000 species of fish, 9,000 species of birds, 4,000 kinds of mammals, and 40,000 species of vertebrates.[10] Thus, the range of veterinary patient varies widely from birds, fish, and small domestic pets to various farm animals, the thoroughbred horse, and the exotic animal species of the jungle or zoological park.

Today's veterinarian specializes not only in small- and large-animal medicine, but also in various subspecialties, such as avian medicine, wildlife disease, *zoonoses* (animal diseases that can be transmitted to humans), and others. Community pharmacists, as well as those who practice in veterinary clinics and hospitals, fill the prescription orders of veterinarians.

Of special importance in animal medicine is the calculation of dosage based on an animal's weight, since this is such an important variable among animals. Consider this contrast: a pet cockatiel may weigh less than 100 grams, a kitten several pounds, a race horse 1,000 pounds, and an elephant 12,000 pounds or more. Even among pet dogs, the range is dramatic, from the small "toy" dogs—the Chihuahua that may weigh 2 pounds—to one of the heaviest dogs, the Saint Bernard that may weigh up to 180 pounds. In some instances, an animal's body surface area (BSA) is the factor used in determining drug dosage (Table 18.1). Species variation is another important consideration, as each species presents unique physiologic and pharmacokinetic characteristics. This includes *blood serum chemistry* values for animals that differ species to species.

TABLE 18.1 WEIGHT TO BODY SURFACE AREA CONVERSION FOR DOGS AND CATS

BODY SURFACE AREA (BSA) IN SQUARE METERS = K × (BODY WT IN GRAMS$^{2/3}$) × 10^{-4}
K = CONSTANT (10.1 FOR DOGS AND 10.0 FOR CATS)

DOGS				CATS	
BODY WT (kg)	BSA (m^2)	BODY WT (kg)	BSA (m^2)	BODY WT (kg)	BSA (m^2)
0.5	0.06	26	0.88	0.5	0.06
1	0.10	27	0.90	1	0.10
2	0.15	28	0.92	1.5	0.12
3	0.20	29	0.94	2	0.15
4	0.25	30	0.96	2.5	0.17
5	0.29	31	0.99	3	0.20
6	0.33	32	1.01	3.5	0.22
7	0.36	33	1.03	4	0.24
8	0.40	34	1.05	4.5	0.26
9	0.43	35	1.07	5	0.28
10	0.46	36	1.09	5.5	0.29
11	0.49	37	1.11	6	0.31
12	0.52	38	1.13	6.5	0.33
13	0.55	39	1.15	7	0.34
14	0.58	40	1.17	7.5	0.36
15	0.60	41	1.19	8	0.38
16	0.63	42	1.21	8.5	0.39
17	0.66	43	1.23	9	0.41
18	0.69	44	1.25	9.5	0.42
19	0.71	45	1.26	10	0.44
20	0.74	46	1.28		
21	0.76	47	1.30		
22	0.78	48	1.32		
23	0.81	49	1.34		
24	0.83	50	1.36		
25	0.85				

Adapted, with permission, from Rosenthal RC. Chemotherapy. In: Ettinger SJ, Feldman EC, eds. *Textbook of Internal Medicine, Diseases of the Dog and Cat.* 4th Ed. Philadelphia: W.B. Saunders Company, 1995.

Special Considerations in Compounding Veterinary Pharmaceuticals

Compounded prescriptions for veterinary use have the same benefits and restrictions as do counterpart compounded prescriptions for human use. The primary benefit is the ability of a pharmacist to compound a preparation that meets the specific requirements of the patient in terms of strength or dose and/or dosage form, when a similar commercially prepared product is unavailable. In 2003, the FDA released a Compliance Policy Guide that restricted the use of bulk substances in pharmaceutical compounding.[11,12] The Medicinal Animal Drug Use Clarification Act of 1994 (AMDUCA) previously identified compounding as an extralabel use.[13] Together, these legal requirements limit pharmacists to the use of commercially available prefabricated dosage forms in compounding procedures Specific guidance for compounding for animal patients may be found in the cited references.[6,11–14] In essence, the following apply:

- a valid veterinarian-client patient relationship must exist;
- failure to treat may result in adverse consequences to the animal;
- the compounded prescription must meet standards of safety, effectiveness, and stability;
- no FDA-approved human or animal drug in desired dosage form and/or strength is commercially available;
- the compounded dosage form must be prepared from an FDA-approved commercially available human or animal drug;
- the product must be compounded by a licensed pharmacist upon order from a licensed veterinarian or by a veterinarian within the scope of professional practice;
- the scale of the compounding must be commensurate with the need of the individual client-patient;
- compounded products intended for food animals must address special concerns of food safety including the avoidance of remaining tissue residues of drug; and
- all relevant federal and state laws relating to the compounding of drugs for use in animals must be followed including the regulations of the state Board of Pharmacy having jurisdiction.

The doses and treatments used in the "Practice Problems" that follow were derived from the referenced sources.[15–21] The problems may be solved using the calculation techniques described in previous chapters. It should be noted that the prescription abbreviation sid, meaning "once a day," finds particular application in veterinary prescriptions.

CALCULATIONS CAPSULE

Veterinary Dosing

While most veterinary dosing parallels that for human dosing in the considerations of age, weight, pathological condition, concomitant therapy, and the diagnostic skill and experience of the prescriber, species variation is a special consideration in the treatment of animals. In addition, there is a unique equation for the determination of the body surface area (BSA) in dosage calculations for dogs and cats[15]:

$$BSA \ (m^2) = K \times (Body \ weight \ [grams])^{2/3} \times 10^{-4}$$

where K is the constant 10.1 for dogs and 10.0 for cats.

CASE IN POINT 18.1: A pharmacist received a prescription for the drug allopurinol for a pet parakeet in the treatment of gout. The veterinarian prescribed 0.5 mg to be administered by oral drops four times a day.

The pharmacist has 100-mg tablets and a dropper that has been calibrated to deliver 20 drops/mL. The pharmacist decides to crush a tablet, mix it with a sufficient quantity of water and make a suspension such that the pet's owner can conveniently administer the doses to the parakeet.

(a) How many milliliters of suspension should be prepared from the crushed 100-mg allopurinol tablet?

(b) How many drops should be administered to the parakeet per dose?

PRACTICE PROBLEMS

1. The drug pimobendan (VETMEDIN) is used in the treatment of CHF in dogs at a daily dose of 0.5 mg/kg. Scored, chewable tablets are commercially available containing 1.25 mg and 5 mg per tablet. Which of the following would best approximate the daily dose for a 16.5-lb. dog?
   (a) one-half 5-mg tablet
   (b) two 1.25-mg-tablets
   (c) two and a half 1.25-mg tablets
   (d) three 1.25-mg tablets

2. An aerosol spray containing 150 mg/120 mL of beclomethasone dipropionate in an alcohol/saline solution was used in treating a quarter horse suffering chronic obstructive pulmonary disease. If the oral dose was 2.5 mg of beclomethasone dipropionate, how many milliliters of spray were administered?

3. Canine Diarrhea Capsules[18]:

Neomycin Sulfate	1.44	g
Sulfaguanidine	14.8	g
Sulfadiazine	920	mg
Sulfamerazine	920	mg
Sulfathiazole	920	mg
Kaolin	30	g
Pectin	1	g

   M&Ft Caps #C

   (a) What is the weight, in grams, of the total content of each capsule; and (b) how many milligrams of total sulfa drugs are contained in each capsule?

4. Canine Eye Ulceration Drops[19]:

Acetylcysteine	720 mg
Gentamicin Sulfate	36 mg
Atropine Sulfate	36 mg
Sterile Water qs ad	15 mL

   (a) If gentamicin sulfate has 590 μg of gentamicin activity per milligram, calculate the milligrams of gentamicin activity per milliliter of solution, and (b) how many milliliters of a 1% stock solution of atropine sulfate could be used in compounding the formula?

5. Phenolated Glycerin Otic Solution for Animals[20]:

Phenol, crystals	3 g
Glycerin ad	100 mL

   (a) How many milliliters of liquefied phenol (90% w/w, sp gr 1.07) could be used in filling this order and (b) if glycerin has a specific gravity of 1.25, calculate the specific gravity of the mixture (to three decimal places).

6. A 0.12% solution of chlorhexidine gluconate may be used as an oral cleansing solution to clean pets' teeth. Calculate the quantity of a 2% concentrate required to prepare a pint of the diluted solution.

7. The dose of acetylcysteine to treat acetaminophen toxicity in dogs is 150 mg/kg initially followed by 50 mg/kg q4h for 17 additional doses. Calculate the total dose, in grams, administered to an 8-lb. dog.

8. If acetylcysteine is available in a solution containing 200 mg/mL, how many milliliters should be administered as the initial dose in Problem 7?

9. Albuterol sulfate is administered orally to horses for bronchospasm at a dose of 8 mcg/kg. Calculate the number of milliliters of an 0.083% solution of albuterol sulfate to administer to a 900-lb. horse.

10. A veterinarian writes a prescription for metronidazole, 20 mg/kg, for an 1100-lb. horse to be administered every 8 hours for 10 days. The pharmacist has 250-mg metronidazole tablets. How many tablets should be (a) administered per dose and (b) dispensed?[21]

11. What fraction of a 50-mg aspirin suppository should be administered as an antipyretic to a 5.5-lb. cat if the veterinary dose is 10 mg/kg?

12. The dose of methotrexate sodium for neoplastic disease in cats is 2.5 mg/m² po twice weekly. If a 2-kg cat is determined to have a BSA of 0.15 m², calculate the single dose.

13. Phenylbutazone, an anti-inflammatory agent, may be administered to horses by intravenous injection at an average dose of 1.5 g/450 kg for 5 consecutive days. The usual injection contains phenylbutazone 200 mg/mL.
    How many milliliters of injection would be required in treating a 990-lb. horse?

14. How many milliliters of a gentamicin injection, 100 mg/mL, should be administered to a 1250-lb. horse for a dose of 6.6 mg/kg?[21]

15. The maximum dose of doxorubicin in canine chemotherapy is 200 mg/m². Using Table 18.1, calculate the maximum dose for a dog weighing 20 kg.

16. Furosemide in the treatment of CHF in animals is used as a maintenance dose of 0.5 mg/kg sid. Calculate the dose for a 15-lb. dog.

17. Which strength tablets of enalapril maleate (ENACARD) would be most convenient to dispense in the treatment of an 11-lb. dog at a daily dose of 0.5 mg/kg?
    (a) 1-mg tablets
    (b) 2.5-mg tablets
    (c) 5-mg tablets
    (d) 10-mg tablets
    (e) 20-mg tablets

18. The dose of digoxin in dogs is 0.005 to 0.010 mg/kg po. Calculate the dosage range for a dog weighing 15 lb.

19. For large-breed dogs, the dose of digoxin is 0.22 mg/m². Using Table 18.1, calculate the dose for a dog weighing 22 kg.

20. For coccidiosis of sheep, sulfaquinoxaline may be added to drinking water to a concentration of 0.015%. How many milligrams of sulfaquinoxaline should be used per gallon of water?

21. A cockatiel may be given 6 mg of ketamine intramuscularly for anesthesia. Calculate the dose, on a mg/kg basis, for an 85-g cockatiel.

22. Horses may be administered diazepam as a sedative at a dose of up to 0.4 mg/kg intravenously. Calculate the dose, in milligrams, for a 900-lb. horse.

23. Some veterinarians treat seizures in dogs with potassium bromide, administering a loading dose of 90 mg/kg/day for 5 days concurrently with a maintenance dose of 30 mg/kg/day, the latter continued after the initial 5-day period. Calculate: (a) the daily dose (each day for days 1 to 5) for a 12-lb. dog; (b) the maintenance dose; (c), the quantity of potassium bromide needed to prepare one pint of a solution containing 250 mg of patassium bromide per milliliter; and (d), the number of milliliters of the solution needed to provide the maintenance dose.

24. A veterinarian is treating a 66-lb. dog for ascarids with fenbendazole, 50 mg/kg/day orally for 3 days. How many milliliters of a 10% w/v suspension of fenbendazole should the pharmacist dispense?[21]

25. Acetazolamide may be used as adjunct therapy for glaucoma in cats at a dose of 7 mg/kg. Acetazolamide is available in 125-mg tablets. If one tablet is crushed and mixed into 30 grams of cat food, what weight of the food would contain a dose of medication for an 11-lb. cat?

26. Baclofen tablets, prescribed for a dog's owner, were accidentally ingested by the 22-lb. dog who demonstrated clinical signs of toxicosis, that is, respiratory paralysis. It was estimated that the dog chewed and swallowed six 10-mg tablets. What was the dose consumed (a) on a mg/kg basis, and (b) if in treating the animal a veterinarian administered diazepam, 1 mg/kg intravenously, how many milliliters of a 5 mg/mL injection should have been used?[22]

ANSWERS TO "CASE IN POINT" AND PRACTICE PROBLEMS

Case in Point 18.1

(a) For the pet owner's convenience, the pharmacist arbitrarily decided that the 0.5-mg dose of allopurinol should be contained in each drop of the suspension. Working backward in the calculation:

$$\frac{0.5 \text{ mg}}{1 \text{ drop}} = \frac{x \text{ mg}}{20 \text{ drops}}; x = 10 \text{ mg}$$
allopurinol (in 20 drops or 1 mL)

then, $\dfrac{10 \text{ mg}}{1 \text{ mL}} = \dfrac{100 \text{ mg (tablet)}}{x \text{ mL}};$
$x = 10$ mL suspension, *answer*.

(b) 1 drop/dose (predetermined), *answer*.

Practice Problems

1. (d) Three 1.25 mg tablets pimobendan

2. 2 mL beclomethasone dipropionate spray

3. (a) 0.5 g
   (b) 175.6 or 176 mg sulfa drugs

4. (a) 1.42 mg/mL gentamicin activity
   (b) 3.6 mL atropine sulfate solution

5. (a) 3.12 mL liquefied phenol
   (b) 1.244

6. 28.4 mL chlorhexidine gluconate concentrate

7. 3.636 g acetylcysteine

8. 2.73 mL acetylcysteine solution

9. 3.94 mL albuterol sulfate solution

10. (a) 40 metronidazole tablets
    (b) 1200 metronidazole tablets

11. ½ aspirin suppository

12. 0.375 mg methotrexate sodium

13. 37.5 mL phenylbutazone injection

14. 37.5 mL gentamicin injection

15. 148 mg doxorubicin

16. 3.4 mg furosemide

17. (b) 2.5 mg enalapril maleate tablets

18. 0.034 to 0.068 mg digoxin

19. 0.17 mg digoxin

20. 567.75 or 568 mg sulfaquinoxaline

21. 70.6 mg/kg ketamine

22. 163.6 or 164 mg diazepam

23. (a) 655 mg
    (b) 164 mg

(c) 118.25 g potassium bromide

(d) 0.66 mL

24. 45 mL fenbendazole

25. 8.4 g food

26. (a) 6 mg/kg
    (b) 2 mL

REFERENCES

1. The Merck Veterinary Manual. 8th Ed. In: Aiello S, ed. Whitehouse Station, NJ: Merck & Co, 1998. Available at: http://www.merckvetmanual.com/mvm/index.jsp. Accessed January 10, 2005.
2. Plumb DC. *Veterinary Drug Handbook.* 3rd Ed. Ames, IA: Iowa State University Press, 1999.
3. Code of Federal Regulations, Title 21, Part 514, 2000.
4. Center for Veterinary Medicine. Available at: http://www.fda.gov/cvm/default.html. Accessed January 10, 2005.
5. Extralabel drug use in animals. Federal Register. 61:57731–57746; November 7, 1996.
6. Comyn G. Extralabel drug use in veterinary medicine. Available at: http://users.erols.com/nafv/extra.pdf. Accessed January 4, 2008.
7. Animal drug delivery systems. *International Journal of Pharmaceutical Compounding* 1997;1:229. Adapted from: Blodinger J. *Formulation of Veterinary Dosage Forms.* New York: Marcel Dekker, 1983.
8. Jordan DG. Compounding for animals—a bird's eye view. *International Journal of Pharmaceutical Compounding* 1997; 1:222–227.
9. Compounding for veterinary patients: pharmaceutical, biopharmaceutical, and physiologic considerations. *International Journal of Pharmaceutical Compounding* 1997;1:233–234.
10. *Concise Encyclopedia.* Buckinghamshire, GB: DK Publishing, 1999.
11. Lust E. Compounding for animal patients: contemporary issues. *Journal of the American Pharmacists Association* 2004; 44:375–386.
12. *Pharmacy Today* June 2004:43.
13. Animal medicinal drug use clarification act of 1994 (AMDUCA). Available at: http://www.fda.gov/cvm/amduca toc.htm. Accessed January 4, 2008.
14. http://www.avma.org/issues/drugs/compounding/veterinary_compounding.asp. Accessed January 4, 2008.
15. Rosenthal RC. Chemotherapy. In: Ettinger SJ, Feldman EC, eds. *Textbook of Internal Medicine, Diseases of the Dog and Cat.* 4th Ed. Philadelphia: W.B. Saunders, 1995.
16. Crabbe B. *The Comprehensive Guide to Equine Veterinary Medicine.* New York: Sterling Publishing Company, 2007.
17. Ford PR. A 12-year-old quarter horse gelding with chronic obstructive pulmonary disease. *International Journal of Pharmaceutical Compounding* 1997;1:242–243.
18. Holm D. *International Journal of Pharmaceutical Compounding* 1997;1:252.
19. Holm D. *International Journal of Pharmaceutical Compounding* 1997;1:253.
20. *International Journal of Pharmaceutical Compounding* 1997;1:260.
21. Lindell H. Athens, GA: College of Veterinary Medicine, University of Georgia, 2005.
22. Wismer T. Baclofen overdose in dogs. *Veterinary Medicine* 2004;99:406–410.

19

Selected Calculations Associated with Plant Extractives

Objectives

Upon successful completion of this chapter, the student will be able to:

- Differentiate between *extracts*, *fluidextracts*, and *tinctures* on the basis of active drug content.
- Perform calculations related to the concentration and dose of extracted botanicals.
- Perform calculations related to the concentration and dose of botanic dietary supplements.

Currently, the consuming public has renewed interest in the use of botanicals and dietary supplements. These products are widely available to consumers, and a variety of governmental agencies are trying to ensure their safety by setting appropriate quality standards.[1] The *United States Pharmacopeia—National Formulary* (USP/NF) includes official monographs, general tests, assays, and manufacturing practices for a number of botanicals and dietary supplements.[2] Included among the official monographs for botanicals are those for echinacea, feverfew, garlic, ginkgo, ginseng, goldenseal, hawthorn, Saint John's wort, saw palmetto, and valerian. Dosage forms may be prepared from the dried and pulverized plant parts (e.g., leaves) containing the desired components.

Other pharmaceutical preparations are made by the process of **extraction**—that is, by removing desired constituents from plant materials through the use of select solvents. The plant materials (termed **crude drugs**) include seeds, leaves, bark, or other plant parts that contain known or suspected **active therapeutic ingredients** (ATIs) or **active ingredients** (AIs), including alkaloids, glycosides, or other pharmacologically active complex organic molecules.

Two major processes are used for the extraction of active constituents from plant materials, namely *maceration* and *percolation*.

The term **maceration** comes from the Latin *macerare,* meaning "to soak." By this process, comminuted crude drug is placed in a suitable vessel and allowed to soak in a solvent or mixture of solvents (termed the **menstruum**) for a sufficient period to soften the botanic material and effect the extraction of the soluble constituents. The menstruum selected is based on the solubility characteristics of the desired constituents. Hydroalcoholic mixtures commonly are employed. The dissolved constituents are separated from the exhausted crude drug (termed the *marc*) by straining or filtration.

The term **percolation** is derived from the Latin *per,* meaning "through," and *colare,* meaning "to strain." By this process, comminuted crude drug is extracted of its soluble constituents by the slow passage of a menstruum through a column of the botanic material. The crude drug is carefully packed in an extraction apparatus (termed a **percolator**) and allowed to macerate for a prescribed period of time prior to percolation. Percolators are of various sizes and construction. Small-glass percolators, cone- or cylindrical-shaped, several inches in diameter, and about 12 inches in height, are available for laboratory use. In contrast, large stainless-steel percolators for industrial use may be six to eight feet in diameter and 12 to 18 feet in height. An orifice at the bottom of a percolator permits the convenient removal of the extractive (termed the ***percolate***).

By maceration or percolation, therapeutically active as well as inactive constituents (e.g., sugars) that are soluble in the menstruum are extracted. Thus, an extractive is a mixture of plant constituents.

The primary dosage forms of plant extractives are extracts, fluidextracts, and tinctures. Frequently, however, the active therapeutic ingredient(s) are separated from plant extractives by physicochemical methods and then chemically identified, purified, and used as single therapeutic agents in various dosage forms (e.g., tablets, capsules, elixirs, syrups). In some instances, synthetic replicas of the ATIs, or chemical congeners of them, are prepared and used in pharmaceutical products rather than the naturally occurring therapeutic agents.

Extracts, Fluidextracts, and Tinctures

Extracts are concentrated preparations of vegetable (or animal) drugs. Most extracts are prepared by percolation followed by the evaporation of all or nearly all the menstruum, yielding a powdered or ointment-like product of extracted drug in concentrated form. On a weight-for-weight basis, extracts commonly are two to six times as potent as the crude drug. In other words, 1 gram of extract may be equivalent in active constituents to 2 to 6 grams of the crude drug. Thus, an extract may be described as a "2×" (or other multiple) or as a "200%" (or other %) extract. Among the extracts in the USP/NF are: *Belladonna Extract, Cascara Sagrada Extract, Powdered Echinacea pallida Extract, Powdered Ginkgo Extract,* and *Powdered Asian Ginseng Extract*.[3]

Fluidextracts are liquid extractives of plant materials adjusted for drug content so that each milliliter of fluidextract is equivalent in constituents to 1 gram of the crude drug that it represents. Among the fluidextracts in the USP/NF are: *Cascara Sagrada Fluidextract, Garlic Fluidextract, Licorice Fluidextract,* and *Senna Fluidextract*.[3]

Tinctures are alcoholic or hydroalcoholic solutions prepared from plant materials. (Tinctures also may be prepared from chemical substances [e.g., iodine tincture].) Among the botanical tinctures in the USP/NF are: *Belladonna Tincture, Compound Cardamom Tincture, Opium Tincture, Sweet Orange Peel Tincture,* and *Tolu Balsam Tincture*.[3] Although there is no set strength for tinctures, those prepared from plant materials traditionally have used the following quantities of crude drug in the preparation of each 100 mL of tincture:

Potent drug (e.g., belladonna leaf)	10 g crude drug
Nonpotent drug (e.g., tolu balsam)	20 g crude drug
Fruit/Flavor (e.g., sweet orange peel)	50 g crude drug

The relative strengths of extracts, fluidextracts, and tinctures are depicted in Figure 19.1, which shows an example of the quantity of each that may be prepared from a quantity of crude drug. In terms of equivalency:

1 g =	1 mL =	0.25 g =	10 mL
crude drug	fluidextract	"400%" extract	"potent" tincture

Examples of calculations pertaining to plant extractives are as follows.

Example Calculations of Extracted Botanicals

If 1 mg of active ingredient (AI) is present in each gram of a crude drug, determine the concentration, in mg/g or mg/mL, of AI in the corresponding (a) fluidextract, (b) "400%" extract, and (c) potent tincture.

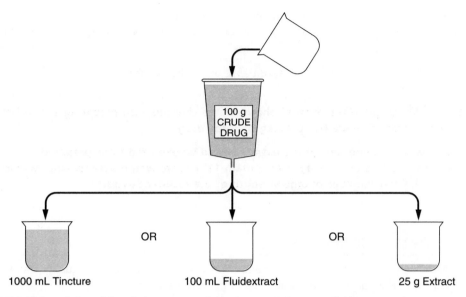

FIGURE 19.1 Depiction of the relative concentrations of a potent tincture, a fluidextract, and an extract using as the example a "10%" tincture and a "400%" extract (see text for further explanation).

(a) Since, by definition, 1 mL of fluidextract is equivalent in active ingredient to 1 g of crude drug, 1 mg of active ingredient would be present in 1 mL of fluidextract.

$$1 \text{ mg AI/mL, } answer.$$

(b) A "400%" extract represents, in each gram, 4 g of crude drug. Thus:

$$\frac{1 \text{ g crude drug}}{4 \text{ g crude drug}} = \frac{1 \text{ mg AI}}{x \text{ mg AI}}; \quad x = 4 \text{ mg AI/g crude drug, } answer.$$

(c) Since a "potent tincture" represents in each 100 mL, the AI from 10 g of crude drug, 0.1 g of crude drug would be needed to prepare 1 mL of tincture. Thus:

$$\frac{1 \text{ g crude drug}}{0.1 \text{ g crude drug}} = \frac{1 \text{ mg AI}}{x \text{ mg AI}}; \quad x = 0.1 \text{ mg AI/mL tincture, } answer.$$

If the dose of belladonna tincture is 0.6 mL, determine the equivalent corresponding dose of (a) belladonna leaf, (b) belladonna fluidextract, and (c) an extract (200%) of belladonna.

(a) Since a potent tincture contains in each 100 mL, the AI from 10 g of crude drug is:

$$\frac{100 \text{ mL tr.}}{0.6 \text{ mL tr.}} = \frac{10 \text{ g crude drug}}{x \text{ g crude drug}}; \quad x = 0.06 \text{ g, } answer.$$

(b) Since 1 mL of fluidextract contains the AI from 1 g of crude drug:

$$\frac{1 \text{ g crude drug}}{0.06 \text{ g crude drug}} = \frac{1 \text{ mL fluidextract}}{x \text{ mL fluidextract}}; \quad x = 0.06 \text{ mL fluidextract, } answer.$$

Or, since a fluidextract is 10 times as concentrated as a potent tincture, its dose would be $\frac{1}{10}$ that of a corresponding tincture:

$$\frac{1}{10} \text{ of } 0.6 \text{ mL} = 0.06 \text{ mL, } answer.$$

(c) Since a "400%" extract has four times the AI content as the crude drug, and since the dose of the crude drug as calculated above is 0.06 g, the dose of the extract would be ¼ of that dose:

$$0.06 \text{ g} \times ¼ = 0.015 \text{ g or } 15 \text{ mg}, \textit{answer.}$$

CASE IN POINT 19.1: An industrial pharmacist is charged with preparing a "400%" extract of cascara sagrada from 100 kg of crude drug.

(a) How many kilograms of the extract would be expected to be prepared?
(b) If the crude drug is assayed to contain 11% hydroxyanthracenes, what would be the expected percentage strength of the resultant extract?

Botanic Dietary Supplements

The official monographs (USP/NF) for botanic dietary supplements include quality standards for the content of their active constituents including, for example[2]:

Asian ginseng	NLT 0.2% ginsenoside Rg$_1$
	NLT 0.1% ginsenoside Rb$_1$
American ginseng	NLT 4% ginsenosides
Black cohosh	NLT 0.4% triterpene glycosides
Echinacea pallida	NLT 0.5% phenols (caftaric acid, chicoric acid, chlorogenic acid, and echinacoside)
Eleuthero	NLT 0.8% eleutheroside and eleutheroside E
Ginkgo	NLT 0.1% terpene lactones
Garlic	NLT 0.5% alliin
Goldenseal	NLT 2% hydrastine
	NLT 2.5% berberine
Red clover	NLT 0.5% isoflavones
Saint John's wort	NLT 0.3% hypericin extract
Valerian	NLT 0.8% valeric acid

The following are examples of calculations applicable to botanic dietary supplements.

Example Calculations of Botanic Supplements

A batch of garlic is determined to contain 10 mg of allicin in a 4-g sample. How many micrograms of allicin would be present in a 500-mg dose of garlic from this batch?

$$10 \text{ mg} = 10,000 \ \mu\text{g}$$
$$500 \text{ mg} = 0.5 \text{ g}$$
$$\frac{4 \text{ g}}{0.5 \text{ g}} = \frac{10,000 \ \mu\text{g}}{\text{x} \ \mu\text{g}}; \quad \text{x} = 1250 \ \mu\text{g}, \textit{answer.}$$

The herb feverfew, when standardized as a powdered leaf, contains 0.2 percent of the agent parthenolide. How many milligrams of parthenolide would be present in a capsule containing 125 mg of powdered feverfew?

$$125 \text{ mg} \times 0.2\% = 0.25 \text{ mg}, \textit{answer.}$$

PRACTICE PROBLEMS

1. How many milliliters of a fluidextract would be equivalent in active ingredient to the following?
   (a) 10 g of crude drug
   (b) 10 mL of a "potent" tincture
   (c) 10 g of a "300%" extract

2. How many milliliters of a "potent" tincture may be prepared from the following?
   (a) 10 mL of a fluidextract
   (b) 10 g of a "400%" extract
   (c) 10 g of a "2X" extract

3. Cascara sagrada (bark) USP contains 7% of hydroxyanthracene derivatives, whereas the cascara sagrada extract USP contains 11 grams of hydroxyanthracene derivatives in each 100 g. Calculate the "%" of the extract relative to the crude drug (e.g., "250%").

4. How many milliliters of a cascara sagrada fluidextract can be prepared from a pound of cascara sagrada bark?

5. Powdered opium USP contains 10.25% of anhydrous morphine. How many grams of powdered opium should be used to prepare 100 mL of opium tincture USP, which contains 10 mg/mL of anhydrous morphine?

6. If senna leaves contain 25 mg of sennosides per gram of leaves, how many milli-grams of sennosides would be contained in a formula for 1000 mL of a senna syrup that contains 250 mL of senna fluidex-tract?

7. SENOKOT Children's Syrup contains 8.8 mg of sennosides per teaspoonful. How many grams of a senna extract containing 75 mg of sennosides per gram should be used in preparing each 60 mL of syrup?

8. If ginkgo biloba contains 24% of ginkgo heterosides, and if 120 mg are taken daily in three divided doses, how many milli-grams of the ginkgo heterosides are con-tained in each of the divided doses?

9. If milk thistle is standardized to contain 70% of silymarin, how many milligrams of this substance are contained in a 200-mg dose of milk thistle?

10. If Saint John's wort is standardized to contain 0.3% of hypericin extract, how many milligrams of the extract would be taken daily when Saint John's wort is ad-ministered as a 300-mg capsule taken three times a day?

11. The herb valerian is administered as an extract containing 0.8% valeric acid. How many milligrams of valeric acid would be contained in each 300-mg dose of vale-rian extract?

ANSWERS TO "CASE IN POINT" AND PRACTICE PROBLEMS

Case in Point 19.1

By definition, a 400% extract represents four times the potency of the corresponding crude drug. Thus:

(a) 100 kg ÷ 4 = 25 kg extract, *and*

(b) 11% × 4 = 44% hydroxyanthracenes, *answers.*

Practice Problems

1. (a) 10 mL
   (b) 1 mL
   (c) 30 mL

2. (a) 100 mL
   (b) 400 mL
   (c) 200 mL

3. "157%" extract

4. 454 mL cascara sagrada fluidextract

5. 9.76 g powdered opium

6. 6250 mg sennosides

7. 1.41 g senna extract

8. 9.6 mg ginkgo heterosides

9. 140 mg silymarin

10. 2.7 mg hypericin

11. 2.4 mg valeric acid

REFERENCES

1. Grauds C. Dietary supplements: new rules ensure quality. *Pharmacy Today* 2007;13:25.
2. United States Pharmacopeia 31st Rev. National Formulary 26. Rockville, MD: United States Pharmacopeial Convention, 2008;1:907–1052.
3. United States Pharmacopeia 31st Rev. National Formulary 26. Rockville, MD: United States Pharmacopeial Convention, 2008; Volumes 1–3.

20

Calculation of Active Drug Moiety

Objectives

Upon successful completion of this chapter, the student will be able to:

- Calculate the percentage composition of a chemical compound.
- Calculate the active drug moiety portion of a chemical compound.
- Perform calculations using active drug moiety in compounding procedures.

A pharmacist must be able to calculate the pharmacologically active drug (chemical) moiety when present in salt, ester, hydrated, or complex chemical form. Such calculations are essential when quantitatively comparing products of the same drug moiety but differing in chemical form. The calculations are applied in compounding procedures in which a different form of a drug is used to satisfy formulation requirements while the quantity of the pharmacologically active drug moiety is maintained at the desired therapeutic dose or concentration.[1]

The *United States Pharmacopeia* (USP) points out that there are cases in which a dose is specified in terms of a cation (e.g., Li^+), an anion (e.g., F^-), or a molecule (e.g., theophylline in theophylline ethylenediamine), and the exact amount of the salt or chemical complex to use must be calculated.[1]

The calculations required involve application of atomic and molecular weights, as reviewed in the sections that follow. For reference, a list of atomic weights is presented on the inside back cover of the book.

Atomic and Molecular Weights

Most chemical problems involve the use of *atomic* or *combining weights* of the elements, and the validity of their solutions depends on the *Law of Definite Proportions*.

The **atomic weight** of an element is the ratio of the weight of its atom to the weight of an atom of another element taken as a standard. Long ago, hydrogen, with a weight taken as 1, was used as the standard. For many years, the weight of oxygen, taken as 16, proved a more convenient standard. In 1961, however, the International Union of Pure and Applied Chemistry (following similar action by the International Union of Pure and Applied Physics) released the most up-to-date table of atomic weights based on carbon, taking 12 as the relative nuclidic mass of the isotope ^{12}C. The rounded *approximate* atomic weights in the table given on the inside back cover of this book and those based on the long-familiar oxygen table are identical and continue to be sufficiently accurate for most chemical calculations likely to be encountered by pharmacists.

The **combining** or **equivalent weight of an element** is the weight of a given element that will combine with (or displace) 1-g atomic weight of hydrogen (or the equivalent weight of some other element). For example, when hydrogen and chlorine react to form HCl, 1.008 g of hydrogen reacts with 35.45 g of chlorine; therefore, the equivalent weight of chlorine is 35.45.

The *equivalent weight of a compound* is the weight of a given compound that is chemically equivalent to 1.008 g of hydrogen. Thus, 1 mol or 36.46 g of HCl contains 1.008 g of hydrogen, and this amount is displaceable by one equivalent weight of a metal; hence, its equivalent weight is 36.46. Also, 1 mol or 40.00 g of NaOH is capable of neutralizing 1.008 g of hydrogen; therefore, its equivalent weight is 40.00. One mol or 98.09 g of H_2SO_4, however, contains 2.016 g of hydrogen, which is displaceable by *two* equivalent weights of a metal; consequently, its equivalent weight is 98.08/2 or 49.04.

The Law of Definite Proportions states that elements invariably combine in the same proportion by weight to form a given compound.

Example Calculations of Atomic and Molecular Weights

Calculate the percentage composition of anhydrous dextrose, $C_6H_{12}O_6$.

$$
\begin{array}{llll}
C_6 & H_{12} & O_6 & \\
(6 \times 12.01) & + \quad (12 \times 1.008) & + \quad (6 \times 16.00) & = \\
72.06 & + \qquad 12.096 & + \qquad 96.00 & = 180.16
\end{array}
$$

$$\frac{180.16}{72.06} = \frac{100\,(\%)}{x\,(\%)}$$

$$x = 40.00\% \text{ of carbon, } and$$

$$\frac{180.16}{12.096} = \frac{100\,(\%)}{y\,(\%)}$$

$$y = 6.71\% \text{ of hydrogen, } and$$

$$\frac{180.16}{96.00} = \frac{100\,(\%)}{z\,(\%)}$$

$$z = 53.29\% \text{ of oxygen, } answers.$$

Check: $40.00\% + 6.71\% + 53.29\% = 100\%$

Calculate the percentage of lithium (Li) in lithium carbonate, Li_2CO_3.

Molecular weight of lithium carbonate = 74
Atomic weight of lithium = 7

$$\frac{74}{2 \times 7} = \frac{100\,(\%)}{x\,(\%)}$$

$$x = 18.9\%, \text{ } answer.$$

A ferrous sulfate elixir contains 220 mg of ferrous sulfate ($FeSO_4 \cdot 7H_2O$) per teaspoonful dose. How many milligrams of elemental iron are represented in the dose?

Molecular weight of $FeSO_4 \cdot 7H_2O$ = 278
Atomic weight of Fe = 56

$$\frac{278}{56} = \frac{220\,(mg)}{x\,(mg)}$$

$$x = 44.3 \text{ or } 44 \text{ mg, } answer.$$

How many milligrams of sodium fluoride will provide 500 μg of fluoride ion?

$$
\begin{array}{cc}
Na & F \\
23 + & 19 = 42
\end{array}
$$

$$\frac{19}{42} = \frac{500\,(\mu g)}{x\,(\mu g)}$$

$$x = 1105 \text{ } \mu g \text{ or } 1.1 \text{ mg, } answer.$$

Chemically Equivalent Quantities

Example Calculations of Chemically Equivalent Quantities

The formula for 1000 g of a cosmetic cream calls for 14.7 g of potassium carbonate (K_2CO_3 ·$1\frac{1}{2}H_2O$). How many grams of 85% potassium hydroxide (KOH) could be used to replace the potassium carbonate in formulating the cream?

	Molecular weights:	Equivalent weights:
$K_2CO_3 \cdot 1\frac{1}{2}H_2O$	165	82.5
KOH	56	56

$$\frac{82.5}{56} = \frac{14.7\ (g)}{x\ (g)}$$
$$x = 9.98\ g\ of\ 100\%\ KOH$$
$$and\ \frac{85\ (\%)}{100\ (\%)} = \frac{9.98\ (g)}{x\ (g)}$$
$$x = 11.74\ g\ of\ 85\%\ KOH,\ answer.$$

The formula for magnesium citrate oral solution calls for 27.4 g of anhydrous citric acid ($C_6H_8O_7$) in 350 mL of the product. How many grams of citric acid monohydrate ($C_6H_8O_7 \cdot H_2O$) may be used in place of the anhydrous salt?

Molecular weights:
$$C_6H_8O_7 \cdot H_2O = 210 \qquad C_6H_8O_7 = 192$$

$$\frac{192}{210} = \frac{27.4\ (g)}{x\ (g)}$$
$$x = 29.97\ or\ 30\ g,\ answer.$$

Active Drug Moiety Equivalence

In pharmacotherapeutics, it is the pharmacologically active moiety of a drug compound that is responsible for the therapeutic response. To accommodate such diverse factors as drug solubility, drug absorption, and formulation/dosage form considerations, an active drug moiety may be developed into a salt, ester, or other complex chemical form.

Prefabricated dosage forms that contain such chemical forms of a therapeutic entity frequently are labeled to indicate the product's drug composition, as for example, "each mL contains 1 mg of albuterol sulfate equivalent to 0.83 mg of albuterol."

TABLE 20.1 EXAMPLES OF ACTIVE DRUG MOIETY PORTION OF SOME DRUG COMPOUNDS

		MOLECULAR WEIGHT	
			ACTIVE DRUG MOIETY
DRUG	EMPIRICAL FORMULA	COMPOUND	(FREE BASE)
Cinacalcet HCl (SENSIPAR)	$C_{22}H_{22}F_3N \cdot HCl$	393.90	357.40
Escitalopram oxalate (LEXAPRO)	$C_{20}H_{21}FN_2O \cdot C_aH_2O_4$	414.40	336.38
Fluoxetine HCl (PROZAC)	$C_{17}H_{18}F_3NO \cdot HCl$	345.79	309.29
Metaproterenol sulfate (ALUPENT)	$(C_{11}H_{17}NO_3)_2 \cdot H_2SO_4$	520.59	211.26
Nelfinavir mesylate (VIRACEPT)	$C_{32}H_{45}N_3O_4S \cdot CH_4O_3S$	663.90	567.79
Rosiglitazone maleate (AVANDIA)	$C_{18}H_{19}N_3O_3S \cdot C_4H_4O_4$	473.52	357.44
Sumatriptan succinate (IMITREX)	$C_{14}H_{21}N_3O_2S \cdot C_4H_6O_4$	413.50	295.40

In contemporary practice, the pharmacist may need to calculate the active drug moiety in a given preparation and/or compare the content between products.

Calculations of Active Drug Moiety in Compounding Procedures

According to the USP, pharmacists must perform calculations to determine the exact quantities of ingredients needed to compound a medication order.[1] This may include the calculation of the precise quantity of the active moiety required, taking into account the molecular composition of the substance, its anhydrous equivalent if it is a chemical hydrate, and the possible effect of ambient humidity on the ingredient's gain or loss of water.

The USP provides the following formula to calculate the theoretical weight of an ingredient in a compounded preparation[1]:

$$W = ab/de$$

Where:

W = *amount of substance to be weighed*
a = *prescribed or calculated weight of active moiety*
b = *chemical or formula weight of the ingredient (a) including any water of hydration*
d = *decimal fraction of dry weight (from known moisture content)*
e = *formula weight of active drug moiety*

Example Calculations of Active Drug Moiety Equivalence

What is the percentage strength of methadone (m.w. 313) in a solution containing 10 mg of methadone hydrochloride (m.w. 349) in each milliliter?

$$\frac{10 \text{ mg methadone HCl} \times 313 \text{ g/mole}}{349 \text{ g/mole}} = 8.97 \text{ mg, methadone equivalent;}$$

and, since 8.97 mg $\cong$ 0.009 g;

$$\frac{1 \text{ mL}}{100 \text{ mL}} = \frac{0.009 \text{ g}}{x \text{ g}}; \quad x = 0.9 \text{ g/100 mL} = 0.9\%, \textit{answer.}$$

How many milligrams of aminophylline (theophylline ethylenediamine) USP should be weighed to obtain 250 mg of anhydrous theophylline? The molecular weight of aminophylline dihydrate is 456, and the container indicates the presence of 0.4% w/w adsorbed moisture. The molecular weight of theophylline is 180, with 2 molecules present in aminophylline. By applying the formula:

$$W = \frac{250 \text{ mg} \times 456 \text{ g/mole}}{0.994 \times 360 \text{ g/mole}} = 318.578 \text{ or } 319 \text{ mg, } \textit{answer.}$$

If a prescription calls for the preparation of 30 mL of a 1% solution of lidocaine (m.w. 234), but for the purposes of solubility the pharmacist used lidocaine hydrochloride (m.w. 288), how many milligrams of the latter should be used?

$$30 \text{ mL} \times 1\% \text{ w/v} = 0.3 \text{ g or } 300 \text{ mg (lidocaine required)}$$

$$W = \frac{300 \text{ mg} \times 288 \text{ g/mole}}{1 \times 234 \text{ g/mole}} = 369 \text{ mg, } \textit{answer.}$$

CALCULATIONS CAPSULE

Active Drug Moiety

To calculate the portion of a drug compound that is the active drug moiety, the following equation may be used:

$$\frac{Drug\ moiety\ (g/mole)}{Drug\ compound\ (g/mole)} = Drug\ moiety\ (fraction)$$

CASE IN POINT 20.1[2]: A pediatrician wishes to prescribe the drug metronidazole (m.w. 171) for a pediatric patient in the oral treatment of amebiasis. The patient is unable to swallow solid dosage forms, and an oral suspension of the drug would be extremely bitter. An alternative would be for the pharmacist to compound an oral suspension using metronidazole benzoate (m.w. 275), which has a low water solubility and thus little taste.

If the pediatric dosage range of metronidazole in the treatment of amebiasis is 35 to 50 mg/kg/day, calculate the dosage range of metronidazole benzoate.

PRACTICE PROBLEMS

1. Calculate the percentage composition of ether, $(C_2H_5)_2O$.

2. What is the percentage composition of dibasic sodium phosphate USP, $Na_2HPO_4 \cdot 7H_2O$?

3. What is the percentage composition of monobasic sodium phosphate USP, $NaH_2PO_4 \cdot H_2O$?

4. Calculate the percentage of water in dextrose, $C_6H_{12}O_6 \cdot H_2O$.

5. How many grams of water are represented in 2000 g of magnesium sulfate, $MgSO_4 \cdot 7H_2O$?

6. What is the percentage of calcium in calcium gluconate, $C_{12}H_{22}CaO_{14}$?

7. A commercially available tablet contains 0.2 g of $FeSO_4 \cdot 2H_2O$. How many milligrams of elemental iron are represented in a daily dose of three tablets?

8. A certain solution contains 110 mg of sodium fluoride, NaF, in each 1000 mL. How many milligrams of fluoride ion are represented in each 2 mL of the solution?

9. How many milliliters of a solution containing 0.275 mg of histamine acid phosphate (m.w. 307) per milliliter should be used in preparing 30 mL of a solution that is to contain the equivalent of 1:10,000 of histamine (m.w. 111)?

10. ℞   Sodium Fluoride   q.s
        Multiple Vitamin
            Drops   ad   60 mL
        (Five drops = 1 mg
            of fluoride ion)
        Sig. Five drops in
            orange juice daily.

    The dispensing dropper calibrates 20 drops/mL. How many milligrams of sodium fluoride should be used in preparing the prescription?

11. In preparing magnesium citrate oral solution, 2.5 g of potassium bicarbonate ($KHCO_3$) are needed to charge each bottle. If no potassium bicarbonate is available, how much sodium bicarbonate ($NaHCO_3$) should be used?

12. The formula for Albright's solution "M" calls for 8.84 g of anhydrous sodium carbonate (Na_2CO_3) per 1000 mL. How many grams of 95% sodium hydroxide (NaOH) should be used to replace the anhydrous sodium carbonate in preparing 5 liters of the solution?

13. Ferrous sulfate syrup contains 40 g of ferrous sulfate ($FeSO_4 \cdot 7H_2O$) per 1000 mL. How many milligrams of iron (Fe) are represented in the usual dose of 10 mL of the syrup?

14. How many grams of 42% (MgO equivalent) magnesium carbonate are required to prepare 14 liters of magnesium citrate oral solution so that 350 mL contain the equivalent of 6.0 g of MgO?

15. Five hundred grams of effervescent sodium phosphate contain 100 g of anhydrous dibasic sodium phosphate (Na_2HPO_4). How many grams of dibasic sodium phosphate USP ($Na_2HPO_4 \cdot 7H_2O$) are represented in each 10-g dose of effervescent sodium phosphate?

16. How many grams of epinephrine bitartrate (m.w. 333) should be used in preparing 500 mL of an ophthalmic solution containing the equivalent of 2% of epinephrine (m.w. 183)?

17. From the molecular weight (385.8) of ciprofloxacin hydrochloride, $C_{17}H_{18}FN_3O_3 \cdot HCl \cdot H_2O$, calculate the molecular weight of ciprofloxacin base.

18. If 600 mg of glucosamine hydrochloride is equivalent to 500 mg of glucosamine (m.w. 179.2), calculate the molecular weight of glucosamine hydrochloride.

19. How many milligrams of betamethasone dipropionate (m.w. 504) should be used to prepare a 50-g tube of ointment labeled to contain the equivalent of 0.5 mg of betamethasone (m.w. 392) base per gram?

20. Sertraline Hydrochloride Capsules[3]:

    ℞: Sertraline Hydrochloride
    (ZOLOFT tablets,
    100 mg)   3 tablets
    Silica Gel   6 g
    Calcium Citrate   4 g
    M.ft. caps no. 40
    Sig. Use as directed.

    Calculate the grams of calcium in the formula derived from calcium citrate, $C_{10}H_{10}Ca_3O_{14} \cdot 4H_2O$ (m.w. 570.5).

21. Iontophoresis Solution[4]:

    ℞: Dexamethasone
    Sodium Phosphate   200 mg
    Lidocaine Hydrochloride   1 g
    Sterile Water for
    Injection   ad   100 mL
    Sig. Use as directed.

    If the molecular weight of dexamethasone sodium phosphate is 516 and that of dexamethasone base is 392, calculate the milligrams of dexamethasone per milliliter of solution.

22. Fentanyl Inhalation[5]:

    ℞: Fentanyl Citrate   4.71 mg
    Sterile Sodium Chloride
    Inhalation   ad   60 mL
    Sig. Use as directed.

    Fentanyl citrate has a molecular weight of 528. Calculate the milligrams of the active drug moiety, fentanyl (m.w. 336), in the prescription.

23. A pediatric suspension of erythromycin ethylsuccinate (m.w. 862) contains the equivalent of 200 mg of erythromycin (m.w. 734) per 5-mL dose. Calculate the milligrams of erythromycin ethylsuccinate contained in 100 mL of the suspension.

24. A sterile ophthalmic suspension of BET-OPTIC S contains 0.25% of betaxolol base (m.w. 307), present as the hydrochloride salt (m.w. 344). Calculate the percentage of betaxolol hydrochloride in the suspension.

25. If the molecular weight of the HIV protease inhibitor nelfinavir is 568 and that of nelfinavir mesylate is 664, calculate the milligrams of the latter in each tablet labeled to contain the equivalent of 250 mg of nelfinavir.

26. An ophthalmic solution is labeled to contain the equivalent of 0.3% of ciprofloxacin base (m.w. 332). How many milligrams of ciprofloxacin hydrochloride (m.w. 386) may be used to prepare each 5 mL of the solution?

27. A product label for 324-mg tablets of quinidine gluconate (m.w. 520) states that 62.3% of the drug is present as quinidine base (m.w. 324). Calculate the milligrams of quinidine present in each tablet.

28. How many milligrams of morphine hydrochloride (m.w. 322) should be used to obtain 300 mg of morphine (m.w. 285) if the morphine hydrochloride is determined to contain 0.5% moisture?

ANSWERS TO "CASE IN POINT" AND PRACTICE PROBLEMS

Case in Point 20.1

$$\frac{171 \ (m.w.)}{275 \ (m.w.)} = \frac{35 \ mg/kg/day}{x},$$

$x = 56.29$ mg/kg/day, *and*

$$\frac{171 \ (m.w.)}{275 \ (m.w.)} = \frac{50 \ mg/kg/day}{x},$$

$x = 80.41$ mg/kg/day, *answers.*

Practice Problems

1. C: 64.81%
   H: 13.60%
   O: 21.59%

2. Na: 17.16%
   H: 5.60%
   P: 11.57%
   0: 65.67%

3. Na: 16.66%
   H: 2.92%
   P: 22.45%
   O: 57.97%

4. 9.1% water

5. 1024 g water

6. 9.3% calcium

7. 178.5 or 179 mg elemental iron

8. 0.1 mg fluoride ion

9. 30 mL

10. 530.5 or 531 mg sodium fluoride

11. 2.1 g sodium bicarbonate

12. 35.1 g sodium hydroxide

13. 80.5 mg iron

14. 571 g magnesium carbonate

15. 3.78 g dibasic sodium phosphate

16. 18.2 g epinephrine bitartrate

17. 331.3

18. 215

19. 32.1 mg betamethasone dipropionate

20. 0.842 g calcium

21. 1.52 mg dexamethasone

22. 2.99 or 3 mg fentanyl

23. 4697.5 or 4698 mg erythromycin ethylsuccinate

24. 0.28% betaxolol hydrochloride

25. 292.3 mg nelfinavir mesylate

26. 17.4 mg ciprofloxacin hydrochloride

27. 201.8 or 202 mg quinidine

28. 340.6 or 341 mg morphine hydrochloride

REFERENCES

1. United States Pharmacopeia 31st Rev. National Formulary 26. Rockville, MD: United States Pharmacopeial Convention, 2008;1:627–628.
2. Beach W. Athens, GA: College of Pharmacy, University of Georgia, 2005.
3. *International Journal of Pharmaceutical Compounding* 1998;2:443.
4. *International Journal of Pharmaceutical Compounding* 1997;1:410.
5. *International Journal of Pharmaceutical Compounding* 1998;2:153.

21

Selected Calculations Involving Radiopharmaceuticals

Objectives

Upon successful completion of this chapter, the student will be able to:

- Differentiate, quantitatively, between the standard units of radioactivity.
- Convert between the units of radioactivity.
- Perform half-life calculations.
- Perform activity and dose calculations for radiopharmaceuticals.

Radioisotopes

The atoms of a given element are not necessarily alike. In fact, certain elements actually consist of several components, called *isotopes*, that are chemically identical but physically may differ slightly in mass. Isotopes, then, may be defined as atoms that have the same nuclear charge, and hence the same atomic number, but different masses. The mass number physically characterizes a particular isotope.

Isotopes can be classified as stable and unstable. Stable isotopes never change unless affected by some outside force; unstable isotopes are distinguishable by radioactive transformations and hence are said to be radioactive. The radioactive isotopes of the elements are called *radioisotopes* or *radionuclides*. They can be divided into two types: naturally occurring and artificially produced radionuclides.

The use of naturally occurring radioisotopes in medicine dates back to early in the twentieth century, when radium was first introduced in radiologic practice. It was not until after 1946, however, that artificially produced radioisotopes were readily available to hospitals and to the medical profession. Since that time, radionuclides have become important tools in medical research, and selected radioisotopes have been recognized as extremely valuable diagnostic and therapeutic agents.

The branch of medicine that utilizes radioisotopes and radiation in the diagnosis and treatment of disease is *nuclear medicine*. Pharmacists who prepare radioactive pharmaceuticals or *radiopharmaceuticals* for use in patient care, practice *nuclear pharmacy* and are referred to as *nuclear pharmacists*.

The United States Pharmacopeia/National Formulary devotes a chapter to the compounding of radiopharmaceuticals for positron emission tomography (PET).[1] Radiopharmaceuticals administered for PET procedures typically incorporate radionuclides, which have very short half-lives, as technetium-99m, gallium-67, and thallium-201. The radioisotope used in about 80 percent of nuclear diagnostic procedures is Tc-99m (the *m* standing for metastable).[2] It has a half-life of about 6 hours.

The USP/NF outlines procedures for the: control of components, materials, and supplies; verification of compounding procedures; quality control and stability testing; sterilization and sterility assurance; and expiration dating.[1] Appropriate calculations, dilutions, and corrections for radioactive decay are performed by nuclear pharmacists when preparing products for dosage administration.[3]

A list of some radiopharmaceuticals official in the USP/NF is presented in Table 21.1.

TABLE 21.1 EXAMPLES OF SOME RADIOPHARMACEUTICALS OFFICIAL IN THE USP/NF[a]

Chromic Phosphate P 32 Suspension
Chromium Cr 51 Edetate Injection
Cyanocobalamin Co 57 Capsules
Fludeoxyglucose F 18 Injection
Flumazenil C 11 Injection
Fluorodopa F 18 Injection
Gallium Citrate Ga 67 Injection
Indium In 111 Chloride Solution
Indium In 111 Pentetate Injection
Iobenguane I 123 Injection
Iodinated I 131 Albumin Aggregated Injection
Iodinated I 125 Albumin Injection
Iodinated I 131 Albumin Injection
Iodohippurate Sodium I 123 Injection
Iodohippurate Sodium I 131 Injection
Iothalamate Sodium I 125 Injection
Mespiperone C 11 Injection
Methionine C 11 Injection
Rose Bengal Sodium I 131 Injection
Rubidium Chloride Rb 82 Injection
Sodium Acetate C 11 Injection
Sodium Chromate Cr 51 Injection
Sodium Fluoride F 18 Injection
Sodium Iodide I 123 Capsules
Sodium Iodide I 123 Solution
Technetium Tc 99m Albumin Aggregated Injection
Technetium Tc 99m Albumin Injection
Technetium Tc 99m Disofenin Injection
Technetium Tc 99m Etidronate Injection
Technetium Tc 99m Exametazine Injection
Technetium Tc 99m Gluceptate Injection
Technetium Tc 99m Lidofenin Injection
Technetium Tc 99m Mebrofenin Injection
Technetium Tc 99m Medronate Injection
Technetium Tc 99m Oxidronate Injection
Technetium Tc 99m Pentetate Injection
Technetium Tc 99m (Pyro- and Trimeta-) Phosphates Injection
Technetium Tc 99m Pyrophosphate Injection
Technetium Tc 99m Succimer Injection
Technetium Tc 99m Sulfur Colloid Injection
Thallous Chloride Tl 201 Injection
Urea C 14 Capsules
Xenon Xe 133 Injection

[a]United States Pharmacopeia 31st Rev. National Formulary 26. Rockville, MD: United States Pharmacopeial Convention, 2008; Volumes 2–3.

Radioactivity

The breakdown of an unstable isotope is characterized by radioactivity. In the process of radioactivity, an unstable isotope undergoes changes until a stable state is reached, and in the transformation, it emits energy in the form of radiation. This radiation may consist of *alpha particles, beta particles,* and *gamma rays.* The stable state is reached as a result of *radioactive decay,* which is characteristic of all types of radioactivity. Individual radioisotopes differ in the rate of radioactive decay, but in each case, a definite time is required for half the original atoms to decay. This time is called the **half-life** of the radioisotope. Each radioisotope, then, has a distinct half-life.

An illustration of the decay rate/half life of radioisotopes is shown in Figure 21.1 and a list of the half-lives of some commonly used radioisotopes is presented in Table 21.2.

The rate of decay is always a constant fraction of the total number of undecomposed atoms present. Mathematically, the rate of disintegration may be expressed as follows:

$$-\frac{dN}{dt} = \lambda N \qquad \text{(Equation 1)}$$

in which N is the number of undecomposed atoms at time t, and λ is the decay constant or the fraction disintegrating per unit of time.

The constant may be expressed in any unit of time, such as reciprocal seconds, minutes, or hours, among others. The numeric value of the decay constant will be 24 times as great when expressed in days, for example, as when expressed in hours. This equation may be integrated to give the expression of the *exponential decay law,* which may be written,

$$N = N_0 e^{-\lambda t} \qquad \text{(Equation 2)}$$

in which N is the number of atoms remaining at elapsed time t, N_0 is the number of atoms originally present (when t = 0), λ is the decay constant for the unit of time in terms of which the interval t is expressed, and e is the base of the natural logarithm 2.71828.

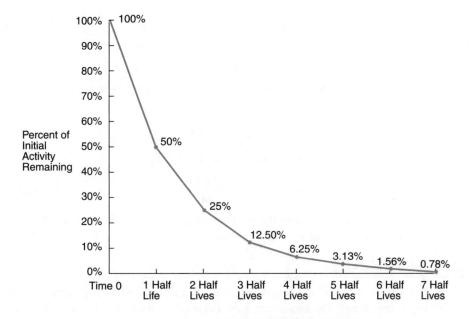

FIGURE 21.1 Illustration of the decay rate/half-life of radioisotopes. *(From U.S. Department of Health and Human Services: Radiation Event Medical Management. Available at: http://remm.nlm.gov/halflife.htm. Accessed January 7, 2008.)*

TABLE 21.2 HALF-LIVES OF SOME RADIOISOTOPES

RADIOISOTOPE	HALF-LIFE
^{198}Au	2.70 days
^{14}C	5,700 years
^{45}Ca	180 days
^{57}Co	270 days
^{60}Co	5.27 years
^{51}Cr	27.8 days
^{59}Fe	45.1 days
^{67}Ga	78.3 hours
^{203}Hg	46.6 days
^{123}I	13.2 hours
^{125}I	60 days
^{131}I	8.08 days
^{111}In	2.83 days
^{42}K	12.4 hours
^{81m}Kr	13.1 seconds
^{99}Mo	2.6 years
^{22}Na	2.6 years
^{24}Na	15.0 hours
^{32}P	14.3 days
^{35}S	87.2 days
^{75}Se	120 days
^{85}Sr	64 days
^{99m}Tc	6.03 hours
^{201}Tl	73.1 hours
^{133}Xe	5.24 days
^{169}Yb	32.0 days

Because the rate of decay can also be characterized by the half-life ($T_{1/2}$), the value of N in equation 2 at the end of a half period is $\frac{1}{2}N_0$. The equation then becomes,

$$\tfrac{1}{2}N_0 = N_0{}^{-\lambda T_{1/2}} \qquad \text{(Equation 3)}$$

Solving equation 3 by natural logarithms results in the following expression:

$$\ln \tfrac{1}{2} = -\lambda T_{1/2}$$

$$\text{or} \quad \lambda T_{1/2} = \ln 2$$

$$\text{then} \quad \lambda T_{1/2} = 2.303 \log 2$$

$$\text{and} \quad T_{1/2} = \frac{0.693}{\lambda} \qquad \text{(Equation 4)}$$

The half-life ($T_{1/2}$) is thus related to the disintegration constant λ by equation 4. Hence, if one value is known, the other can be readily calculated.

Units of Radioactivity

The quantity of activity of a radioisotope is expressed in absolute units (total number of atoms disintegrating per unit time). The basic unit is the *curie* (Ci), which is defined as that quantity of a radioisotope in which 3.7×10^{10} (37 billion) atoms disintegrate per second. The *millicurie* (mCi) is one thousandth of a curie, and the *microcurie* (μCi) is one millionth of a curie. The *nanocurie* (nCi), also known as the *millimicrocurie*, is one billionth of a curie (10^{-9} Ci).

TABLE 21.3 CONVERSION EQUIVALENTS

1 Ci =	3.7×10^{10} Bq = 3.7×10^4 MBq = 37×10^3 MBq
1 mCi =	37 MBq
1 μCi =	0.037 MBq
1 Bq =	2.7×10^{-11} Ci
1 MBq =	10^6 Bq = 2.7×10^{-5} Ci
=	$2.7 \ 10^{-2}$ mCi = 0.027 mCi
=	27 μCi

The International System (SI; see Chapter 2) unit for radioactivity is the **becquerel** (Bq), which is defined as 1 disintegration per second. Because the becquerel is so small, it is more convenient to use multiples of the unit, such as the **kilobecquerel** (kBq), which is equal to 10^3 disintegrations per second; the **megabecquerel** (MBq), which is equal to 10^6 disintegrations per second; and the **gigabecquerel** (GBq), which is equal to 10^9 disintegrations per second.

The *United States Pharmacopeia* has adopted the becquerel to eventually replace the long-familiar curie as a matter of international agreement. For the present, both units are used to label radioactivity, and the doses of many radiopharmaceuticals are expressed in megabecquerels as well as in millicuries and/or microcuries.

Table 21.3 provides equivalents for conversion from the curie (and its subunits) to the becquerel (and its multiples), and vice versa.

Example Calculations of Radioactivity Unit Conversion

A thallous chloride Tl 201 injection has a labeled activity of 550 microcuries (μCi). Express this activity in terms of megabecquerels.

$$550 \ \mu Ci = 0.55 \ mCi$$
$$1 \ mCi = 37 \ MBq$$

$$\frac{1 \ (mCi)}{0.55 \ (mCi)} = \frac{37 \ (MBq)}{x \ (MBq)}$$
$$x = 20.35 \ MBq, \ answer.$$

Sodium chromate Cr 51 injection is administered in a dose of 3.7 MBq for the determination of blood volume. Express this dose in terms of microcuries.

$$1 \ MBq = 0.027 \ mCi$$

$$\frac{1 \ (MBq)}{3.7 \ (MBq)} = \frac{0.027 \ (mCi)}{x \ (mCi)}$$
$$x = 0.1 \ mCi$$
$$= 100 \ \mu Ci, \ answer.$$

Other units that may be encountered in practice, but are not used in the calculations that follow, include the roentgen and the rad. The **roentgen** is the international unit of x-rays or gamma radiation. It is the quantity of x-rays or gamma radiation that produces, under standard conditions of temperature and pressure, ions carrying 1 electrostatic unit of electrical charge of either sign. The **rad** (acronym for "radiation absorbed dose") is a unit of measurement of the absorbed dose of ionizing radiation. It corresponds to an energy transfer of 100 ergs/g of any absorbing material (including tissues).

Example Calculations of Half-Life and Disintegration Constant

The disintegration constant of a radioisotope is 0.02496 day $^{-1}$. Calculate the half-life of the radioisotope.

$$T_{1/2} = \frac{0.693}{\lambda}$$

$$\text{Substituting, } T_{1/2} = \frac{0.693}{0.02496 \text{ day}^{-1}}$$

$$T_{1/2} = 27.76 \text{ or } 27.8 \text{ days, } answer.$$

The half-life of ^{198}Au is 2.70 days. Calculate its disintegration constant.

$$T_{1/2} = \frac{0.693}{\lambda}$$

$$\text{Substituting, } 2.70 \text{ days} = \frac{0.693}{\lambda}$$

$$\lambda = \frac{0.693}{2.70 \text{ days}} = 0.2567 \text{ day}^{-1}, answer.$$

The original quantity of a radioisotope is given as 500 μCi (18.5 MBq)/mL. If the quantity remaining after 16 days is 125 μCi (4.625 MBq)/mL, calculate (a) the disintegration constant and (b) the half-life of the radioisotope.

(a) Equation 2, written in logarithmic form, becomes

$$\ln \frac{N}{N_0} = -\lambda t$$

or

$$\lambda = \frac{2.303}{t} \log \frac{N_0}{N}$$

Substituting:

$$\lambda = \frac{2.303}{16} \log \frac{500}{125} \text{ or, } \frac{2.303}{16} \log \frac{18.5 \text{ (MBq)}}{4.625 \text{ (MBq)}}$$

$$\lambda = \frac{2.303}{16} (0.6021)$$

$$\lambda = 0.08666 \text{ day}^{-1}, answer.$$

(b) Equation 4 may now be used to calculate the half-life.

$$T_{1/2} = \frac{0.693}{\lambda}$$

$$\text{Substituting, } T_{1/2} = \frac{0.693}{0.08666 \text{ day}^{-1}} = 8.0 \text{ days, } answer.$$

CALCULATIONS CAPSULE

Half-Life

The half-life equation is:

$$T_{1/2} = \frac{0.693}{\lambda}$$

λ = Half-life coefficient or disintegration constant

Example Calculations of Remaining Activity Over Time

A sample of ^{131}I has an initial activity of 30 μCi (1.11 MBq). Its half-life is 8.08 days. Calculate its activity, in microcuries (megabecquerels), at the end of exactly 20 days.

$$\text{By substituting } \lambda = \frac{0.693}{T_{1/2}} \text{ and } e^{-0.693} = \tfrac{1}{2}$$

In Equation 2, the activity of a radioactive sample decreases with time according to the following expression:

$$N = N_0 \left(2^{-t/T_{1/2}} \right) = N_0 \left(\frac{1}{2^{t/T_{1/2}}} \right)$$

$$\text{Since} \quad t/T\tfrac{1}{2} = \frac{20}{8.08} = 2.475$$

$$\text{then} \quad N = 30 \left(\frac{1}{2^{2.475}} \right)$$

Solving by logarithms, log N = log 30 − log 2 (2.475)
$$= 1.4771 - 0.7450$$
$$\log N = 0.7321$$
$$N = 5.39 \text{ or } 5.4 \text{ μCi, } answer.$$

Or, using megabecquerel units:

$$N = 1.11 \left(\frac{1}{2^{2.475}} \right)$$

Solving by logarithms, log N = log 1.11 − log 2 (2.475)
$$= 0.0453 - 0.7450$$
$$\log N = -0.6997$$
$$N = 0.1997 \text{ or } 0.2 \text{ MBq, } answer.$$

A vial of sodium phosphate P 32 solution has a labeled activity of 500 μCi (18.5 MBq)/mL. How many milliliters of this solution should be administered exactly 10 days after the original assay to provide an activity of 250 Ci (9.25 MBq)? The half-life of ^{32}P is 14.3 days.

The activity exactly 10 days after the original assay is given by

$$N = N_0 \left(\frac{1}{2^{t/T_{1/2}}} \right)$$

$$\text{Since} \quad t/T_{1/2} = \frac{10}{14.3} = 0.6993$$

$$\text{then} \quad N = 500 \left(\frac{1}{2^{0.6993}} \right)$$

$$\log N = \log 500 - \log 2 \ (0.6993)$$
$$= 2.6990 - 0.2105$$
$$\log N = 2.4885$$
$$N = 308 \text{ μCi/mL, activity after radioactive decay}$$

$$\frac{308 \ (\mu Ci)}{250 \ (\mu Ci)} = \frac{1 \ (mL)}{x \ (mL)}$$
$$x = 0.81 \text{ mL, } answer.$$

Or, using megabecquerel units:

$$N = 18.5 \left(\frac{1}{2^{0.6993}} \right)$$

$$\log N = \log 18.5 - \log 2 \, (0.6993)$$
$$= 1.2672 - 0.2105$$
$$\log N = 1.0567$$
$$= 11.39 \text{ MBq/mL, activity after radioactive decay}$$

$$\frac{11.39 \text{ (MBq)}}{9.25 \text{ (MBq)}} = \frac{1 \text{ (mL)}}{x \text{ (mL)}}$$

$$x = 0.81 \text{ mL, } answer.$$

CASE IN POINT 21.1[4]: The Nuclear Pharmacy receives an order for a 25-mCi technetium Tc 99m MDP (bone scan dose) to be administered at 10:00 AM (1000 hours). The pharmacist has prepared an MDP bone kit with the concentration of 50 mCi/mL at 0600. What volume of the kit should be dispensed to provide the dose as ordered? The half-life of technetium Tc 99m is 6.03 hours.

PRACTICE PROBLEMS

1. Cyanocobalamin Co 57 capsules are administered in doses of 0.5 to 1.0 μCi in a test for pernicious anemia. Express this dosage range in terms of becquerel units.

2. If 1 mCi of radioactivity is equivalent to 37 MBq in activity, how many becquerels of radioactivity would be the equivalent of 1 Ci?

3. A gallium citrate Ga 67 injection has a labeled activity of 366 MBq. Express this activity in terms of millicuries.

4. If 1.85 MBq of radioactivity is equivalent to 50 μCi, how many millicuries would be represented in 7.4 MBq?

5. If 50 μCi of radioactivity is equivalent to 1.85 MBq of activity, how many megabecquerels of radioactivity would be the equivalent of 10 mCi?

6. Express an administered dose of 5 mCi sodium phosphate P 32 solution in terms of megabecquerels.

7. Calculate the half-life of a radioisotope that has a disintegration constant of 0.00456 day^{-1}.

8. Calculate the half-life of ^{203}Hg, which has a disintegration constant of 0.0149 day^{-1}.

9. Calculate the disintegration constant of ^{64}Cu, which has a half-life of 12.8 hours.

10. Calculate the disintegration constant of ^{35}S, which has a half-life of 87.2 days.

11. The original quantity of a radioisotope is given as 100 mCi (3700 MBq). If the quantity remaining after 6 days is 75 mCi (2775 MBq), calculate the disintegration constant and the half-life of the radioisotope.

12. A series of measurements on a sample of a radioisotope gave the following data:

Days	Counts per Minute
0	5600
4	2000

    Calculate the disintegration constant and the half-life of the radioisotope.

13. The original activity of a radioisotope is given as 10 mCi (370 MBq) per 10 mL. If the quantity remaining after exactly 15 days is 850 μCi (31.45 MBq)/mL, calculate the disintegration constant and the half-life of the radioisotope.

14. If the half-life of a radioisotope is 12 hours, what will be the activity after 4 days of a sample that has an original activity of 1 Ci (37,000 MBq)? Express the activity in terms of microcuries (megabecquerels).

15. Sodium iodide I 131 capsules have a labeled potency of 100 μCi (3.7 MBq). What will be their activity exactly 3 days after the stated assay date? The half-life of ^{131}I is 8.08 days.

16. A sodium chromate Cr 51 injection has a labeled activity of 50 mCi (1850 MBq) at 5:00 PM on April 19. Calculate its activity at 5:00 PM on May 1. The half-life of ^{51}Cr is 27.8 days.

17. Iodinated I 125 albumin injection contains 0.5 mCi (18.5 MBq) of radioactivity per milliliter. How many milliliters of the solution should be administered exactly 30 days after the original assay to provide an activity of 60 μCi (2.22 MBq)? The half-life of ^{125}I is 60 days.

18. An ytterbium Yb 169 pentetate injection has a labeled radioactivity of 5 mCi (185 MBq)/mL. How many milliliters of the injection should be administered 10 days after the original assay to provide an activity of 100 μCi (3.7 MBq)/kg of body weight for a person weighing 110 lb? The half-life of ^{169}Yb is 32.0 days.

19. A sodium pertechnetate Tc 99m injection has a labeled activity of 15 mCi (555

MBq)/mL. If the injection is administered 10 hours after the time of calibration, (a) what will be its activity, and (b) how many milliliters of the injection will be required to provide a dose of 15 mCi (555 MBq)? The half-life of ^{99m}Tc is 6.0 hours.

20. A sodium phosphate P 32 solution contains 1 mCi (37 MBq)/mL at the time of calibration. How many milliliters of the solution will provide an activity of 500 μCi (18.5 MBq) 1 week after the original assay? The half-life of ^{32}P is 14.3 days.

21.[4] An iodine I 131 capsule has been ordered for administration on Tuesday, November 11, at 12 noon. The requested dose is 25 mCi. If the patient is unable to make the appointment on November 11, what dose remains for a 12 noon appointment on Thursday, November 13? The half-life of iodine I 131 is 8 days.

22.[4] An order is received for a 100-mCi vial of technetium Tc 99m pertechnetate calibrated for 8:00 AM (0800 hours) to be used as a linearity source for dose calibrator testing at one of the nuclear medicine accounts. The pharmacy must prepare the dose for delivery at 0500. What activity should be dispensed at 0500 to deliver the desired activity? The half-life of technetium Tc 99m pertechnetate is 6.02 hours.

ANSWERS TO "CASE IN POINT" AND PRACTICE PROBLEMS

Case in Point 21.1

Solving first for the half-life coefficient, lambda (λ), for Tc 99m:

$\lambda = 0.693/T_{1/2}$
$\lambda = 0.693/6$ (hours)
$\lambda = 0.1155$ hours^{-1}

Since the stock solution was compounded to contain 50 mCi/mL at 0600, we can decay this concentration to the 1000 dosage time and solve as a proportion problem.

Using the decay formula: $A = A_0 e^{-\lambda t}$

A = Final activity
A_0 = Initial activity
t = Decay time
$A = 50\ e^{-(0.1155)4}$
$A = 50\ (0.63)$
$A = 31.5$ mCi/mL

Required dose = 25 mCi

Volume to dispense = 25mCi/31.5 mCi/mL
= 0.79 mL, *answer.*

Practice Problems

1. 18,500 to 37,000 Bq

2. 3.7×10^{10} Bq

3. 9.9 mCi

4. 0.2 mCi

5. 370 MBq

6. 185 MBq

7. 152 days

8. 46.5 days

9. 0.0541 hour^{-1}

10. 0.00795 hour^{-1}

11. $\lambda = 0.04794$ day^{-1}
    $T_{1/2} = 14.5$ days

12. $\lambda = 0.2574$ day^{-1}
    $T_{1/2} = 2.7$ days

13. $\lambda = 0.01084$ day^{-1}
    $T_{1/2} = 64$ days

14. 3907 μCi (144.5 MBq)

15. 77.3 μCi (2.86 MBq)

16. 37.1 mCi (1372.7 MBq)

17. 0.17 mL

18. 1.24 mL

19. (a) 4.7 mCi (174.8 MBq)
    (b) 3.2 mL

20. 0.7 mL

21. 21 mCi

22. 141.4 mCi

REFERENCES

1. Radiopharmaceuticals for positron emission tomography—compounding. United States Pharmacopeia 31st Rev. National Formulary 26. Rockville, MD: United States Pharmacopeial Convention, 2008;1:347–351.
2. The regulation and use of radioisotopes in today's world. U.S. Nuclear Regulatory Commission. Available at: http://www.nrc.gov. Accessed January 7, 2008.
3. Basmadjian N. Prescription preparation in a nuclear pharmacy: three case studies. *International Journal of Pharmaceutical Compounding* 1998;2:429–431.
4. Duke K. Athens, GA: College of Pharmacy, University of Georgia, 2005.

22

Selected Bioavailability and Pharmacokinetic Calculations

Objectives

Upon successful completion of this chapter, the student will be able to:

- Define the terms *bioavailability* and *pharmacokinetics*.
- Correctly interpret a time versus serum concentration plot.
- Perform basic calculations of bioavailability and bioequivalence.
- Perform basic calculations of elimination half-life and volume of distribution.

The availability to the biologic system of a drug substance formulated into a pharmaceutical product is integral to the goals of dosage form design and paramount to the effectiveness of the medication.

Before a drug substance can be absorbed by the biologic system, it must be released from its dosage form (e.g., tablet) or drug delivery system (e.g., transdermal patch) and dissolved in the physiologic fluids. Several factors play a role in a drug's biologic availability, including the physical and chemical characteristics of the drug itself, such as its particle size and solubility, and the features of the dosage form or delivery system, such as the nature of the formulative ingredients and the method of manufacture. The area of study that deals with the properties of drug substances and dosage forms that influence the release of the drug for biologic activity is termed **biopharmaceutics.** The term **bioavailability** refers to the *relative amount* of drug from an administered dosage form that enters the systemic circulation.

Pharmacokinetics is the study and characterization of the time course of the absorption, distribution, metabolism, and elimination (ADME) of drugs. **Drug absorption** is the process of uptake of the compound from the site of administration into the systemic circulation. **Drug distribution** refers to the transfer of the drug from the blood to extravascular fluids and tissues. **Drug metabolism** is the enzymatic or biochemical transformation of the drug substance to (usually less toxic) metabolic products, which may be eliminated more readily from the body. **Drug elimination** is the removal of the drug substance or its metabolites from the body, such as through the kidney (urine), intestines (feces), skin (sweat), saliva, and/or milk.

The relationship among the processes of absorption, distribution, metabolism, and elimination influences the therapeutic and toxicologic effects of drugs. The application of pharmacokinetic principles in the treatment of individual patients in optimizing drug therapy is referred to as *clinical pharmacokinetics.*

Drug Availability from Dosage Forms and Delivery Systems

The availability of a drug from a dosage form or delivery system is determined by measuring its dissolution characteristics *in vitro* (outside the biologic system) and/or its absorption patterns

343

in vivo (within the biologic system). Generally, data are collected that provide information on both *rate* and *extent* of drug dissolution and/or absorption. The data collected may be plotted on graph paper to depict concentration versus time curves for the drug's dissolution and/or absorption.

Plotting and Interpreting Drug Dissolution Data

Drug dissolution data are obtained in vitro for tablets or capsules using the USP Dissolution Test, which defines the apparatus and methods to be used.[1] The data obtained may be presented in tabular form and depicted graphically, as in the following example.

The following dissolution data were obtained from a 250-mg capsule of ampicillin. Plot the data on graph paper and determine the approximate percentage of ampicillin dissolved following 15, 30, and 45 minutes of the study.

Period (minutes)	Ampicillin Dissolved (mg)
5	12
10	30
20	75
40	120
60	150

Plotting the data:

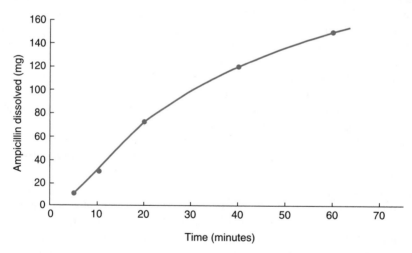

Determining the intercepts at 15, 30, and 45 minutes:

At 15 minutes, approximately 50 mg or 20% of the ampicillin,
At 30 minutes, approximately 100 mg or 40% of the ampicillin,
At 45 minutes, approximately 125 mg or 50% of the ampicillin, *answers.*

Example Calculations of Bioavailability and Bioequivalence

Amount of Drug Bioavailable from a Dosage Form

If drug dissolution or drug absorption studies demonstrate consistently that only a portion of a drug substance in a dosage form is "available" for biologic absorption, the drug's bioavailability factor (F), which represents the decimal percentage of a drug substance available, may be used to calculate bioavailability. The value of F may be zero, indicating no absorption, to a maximum of a value of 1, indicating complete absorption.

If the bioavailability factor (F) for a drug substance in a dosage form is 0.60, how many milligrams of drug would be available for absorption from a 100-mg tablet of the drug?

The bioavailability factor (F) indicates that only 60% of the drug present in the dosage form is available for absorption. Thus:

$$100 \text{ mg} \times 0.60 = 60 \text{ mg, } answer.$$

"Bioequivalent" Amounts of "Bioinequivalent" Dosage Forms

The bioavailability of a given drug substance may vary when in different dosage forms or in the same dosage form but from a different manufacturer. Thus, it may be desired to calculate the equivalent doses for two *bioinequivalent* products.

If the bioavailability (F) of digoxin in a 0.25-mg tablet is 0.60 compared to the bioavailability (F) of 0.75 in a digoxin elixir (0.05 mg/mL), calculate the dose of the elixir equivalent to the tablet.

First, calculate the amount of "bioavailable" digoxin in the tablet:

$$0.25 \text{ mg} \times 0.60 = 0.15 \text{ mg, bioavailable amount of digoxin in the tablet}$$

Next, calculate the amount of "bioavailable" digoxin per milliliter of the elixir:

$$0.05 \text{ mg} \times 0.75 = 0.0375 \text{ mg, bioavailable amount of digoxin per milliliter of the elixir}$$

Finally, determine the quantity of elixir that will provide 0.15 mg of "bioavailable" digoxin: By proportion:

$$\frac{0.0375 \text{ (mg)}}{0.15 \text{ (mg)}} = \frac{1 \text{ (mL)}}{\text{x (mL)}}$$

$$x = 4 \text{ mL, } answer.$$

Plotting and Interpreting a Blood-Drug–Concentration-Time Curve

Following the administration of a medication, if blood samples are drawn from the patient at specific time intervals and analyzed for drug content, the resulting data may be plotted on ordinary graph paper to prepare a blood-drug–concentration-time curve. The vertical axis of this type of plot characteristically presents the concentration of drug present in the blood (or serum or plasma) and the horizontal axis presents the times the samples were obtained after administration of the drug. When the drug is first administered (time zero), the blood concentration of the drug should also be zero. As an orally administered drug passes into the stomach and/or intestine, it is released from the dosage form, fully or partially dissolves, and is absorbed. As the sampling and analysis continue, the blood samples reveal increasing concentrations of drug, until the maximum (peak) concentration (C_{max}) is reached. Then the blood level of the drug decreases progressively and, if no additional dose is given, eventually falls back to zero.

For conventional dosage forms, such as tablets and capsules, the C_{max} will usually occur at only a single time point, referred to as T_{max}. The amount of drug is usually expressed in terms of its concentration in relation to a specific volume of blood, serum, or plasma. For example, the concentration may be expressed as g/100 mL, μg/mL, mg/dL, or mg% (mg/100 mL). The quantity of a dose administered and its bioavailability, dissolution, and absorption characteristics influence the blood level concentration for a drug substance. The rate or speed of drug absorption determines the T_{max}, the time of greatest blood drug concentration after administration; the faster the rate of absorption, the sooner the T_{max}.

In a blood-drug–concentration-time curve, the area under the curve (AUC) is considered representative of the *total* amount of drug absorbed into systemic circulation. The area under the curve may be measured mathematically, using a technique known as the trapezoidal rule. The procedure may be found in other texts and references.[2]

From the following data, plot a serum concentration-time curve and determine (a) the peak height concentration (C_{max}) and (b) the time of the peak height concentration (T_{max}).

Time Period (hours)	Serum Drug Concentration ($\mu g/mL$)
0.5	1.0
1.0	2.0
2.0	4.0
3.0	3.8
4.0	2.9
6.0	1.9
8.0	1.0
10.0	0.3
12.0	0.2

Plotting the data and interpretation of the curve:

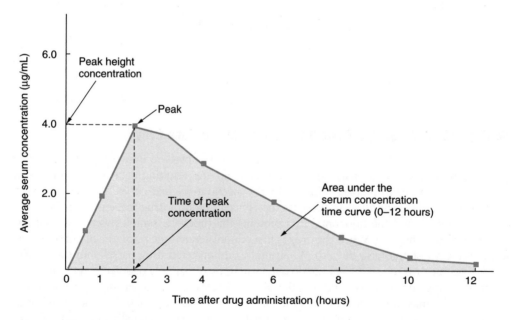

Determining the intercept for C_{max} and T_{max}:

$$C_{max} = 4.0 \ \mu g/mL$$
$$T_{max} = 2 \text{ hours, } answers.$$

Calculation of the bioavailability (F) of a drug may be determined by comparison of the AUC data for the particular dosage form against the intravenous form[3]:

$$F = \frac{AUC_{\text{dosage form}}}{AUC_{\text{intravenous}}}$$

It is recalled that the value F is the fraction of an administered dose that enters the systemic circulation. The intravenous route is the reference standard for comparison since the quantity of drug administered intravenously is considered to enter completely into the systemic circulation.[3]

If the AUC for an oral dose of a drug administered by tablet is 4.5 µg/mL and the intravenous dose is 11.2 µg/mL, calculate the bioavailability of the oral dose of the drug.[4]

$$F = \frac{AUC_{oral\ tablet}}{AUC_{IV}}$$

$$F = \frac{4.5\ \mu g/mL}{11.2\ \mu g/mL} = 0.4\ or\ 40\%,\ answer.$$

CASE IN POINT 22.1[4]**:** A hospitalized patient has been receiving ranitidine (ZANTAC) 50 mg by intravenous injection every 8 hours. After discharge, the patient's physician wishes to continue treatment with a bioequivalent dose of the oral liquid form of ranitidine. From the literature, the community pharmacist determines that the oral liquid is 50% bioavailable. The product is available in a concentration of 75 mg/5 mL, to be taken twice a day. How many milliliters of the oral liquid should be indicated per dose on the prescription label?

INTRODUCTORY CONCEPTS AND CALCULATIONS INVOLVED IN PHARMACOKINETICS

As defined previously, pharmacokinetics is the study and characterization of the time course of absorption, distribution, metabolism, and elimination of drugs. Many of the calculations involved in pharmacokinetics are complex and the subject of advanced textbooks devoted to this important field. The intention in the following discussion is to define and describe some of the more introductory concepts and calculations.

Example Calculations of Selected Pharmacokinetic Parameters

Plasma Concentration of Unbound Versus Bound Drugs

Once absorbed into the circulation, a portion of the total drug plasma concentration (C_T) is bound to plasma proteins (usually albumin), and a portion remains unbound, or free. It is the unbound drug (C_U) that is available for further transport to its site of action in the body. The fraction of unbound drug compared with bound drug (C_B) is primarily a function of the affinity of the drug molecules for binding to the plasma proteins and the concentration of the latter (some patients may have a reduced or elevated serum albumin concentration). Some drug molecules may be more than 90% bound to plasma proteins, whereas others may be bound only slightly. Any change in the degree of binding of a given drug substance can alter its distribution and elimination and thus its clinical effects.

The fraction of unbound drug in the plasma compared with the total plasma drug concentration, bound and unbound, is termed *alpha* (or α).

Thus,

$$\alpha = \frac{C_U}{C_U + C_B} = \frac{C_U}{C_T}$$

If one knows the value of α for a drug and the total plasma concentration (C_T), the concentration of free drug in the plasma may be determined by a rearranged equation:

$$C_U = \alpha \times (C_T)$$

If the alpha (α) value for the drug digoxin is 0.70, what would be the concentration of free drug in the plasma if the total plasma concentration of the drug were determined to be 0.7 ng/mL?

$$
\begin{aligned}
C_U \quad &= (0.70) \times (0.7 \text{ ng/mL}) \\
&= 0.49 \text{ ng/mL, } answer.
\end{aligned}
$$

Apparent Volume of Distribution of a Drug Substance

The apparent volume of distribution for a drug is not a "real" volume but rather a hypothetical volume of body fluid that would be required to dissolve the total amount of drug at the same concentration as that found in the blood. The volume of distribution is an indicator of the extent of a drug's distribution throughout the body fluids and tissues. The information is useful in understanding how the body processes and distributes a given drug substance. After a dose of a drug is administered intravenously, a change in the concentration of the drug in the blood means a corresponding change in the drug's concentration in another body fluid or tissue. This sequence allows an understanding of the pattern of the drug's distribution.

It may be useful in understanding the concept of volume of distribution to imagine a 100-mg amount of a drug substance dissolved in an undetermined volume of water. If the analysis of a sample of the resultant solution revealed a drug concentration of 20 mg per liter, it can be seen that the total volume of water in which the drug was dissolved equaled 5 liters; that is:

$$
\frac{20 \text{ (mg)}}{100 \text{ (mg)}} = \frac{1 \text{ (liter)}}{x \text{ (liters)}}
$$
$$
x = 5 \text{ liters}
$$

Different drugs administered in the same amount will show different volumes of distribution because of different distribution characteristics. For example, drugs that remain in the blood after intravenous administration because of drug binding to plasma proteins or to blood cells show high blood concentrations and low volumes of distribution. Conversely, drugs that exit the circulation rapidly and diffuse into other body fluids and tissues show low blood concentrations and high volumes of distribution.

If the volume of distribution in an adult is 5 liters, the drug is considered confined to the circulatory system, as it would be immediately after a rapid intravenous injection (IV bolus). If the volume of distribution is between 10 and 20 liters, or between 15% and 27% of the body weight, it is assumed that the drug has been distributed into the extracellular fluids; if it is between 25 and 30 liters, or between 35% and 42% of body weight, it is assumed that the drug has been distributed into the intracellular fluid; if it is about 40 liters, or 60% of the body weight, the assumption is that the drug has been distributed in the whole body fluid.[5] If the apparent volume of distribution actually exceeds the body weight, it is assumed that the drug is being stored in body fat, bound to body tissues, or is distributed in peripheral compartments.

The equation for determining the volume of distribution (Vd) is:

$$
Vd = \frac{D}{C_P}
$$

in which D is the total amount of drug in the body, and C_p is the drug's plasma concentration. The apparent volume of distribution may be expressed as a simple volume or as a percentage of body weight.

A patient received a single intravenous dose of 300 mg of a drug substance that produced an immediate blood concentration of 8.2 μg of drug per milliliter. Calculate the apparent volume of distribution.

$$Vd = \frac{D}{C_P}$$
$$= \frac{300 \text{ mg}}{8.2 \text{ μg/mL}} = \frac{300 \text{ mg}}{8.2 \text{ mg/L}}$$
$$= 36.6 \text{ L, } answer.$$

Total Amount of Drug Given Volume of Distribution and Plasma Concentration

Calculating the total amount of drug in a body, given the volume of distribution and the plasma drug concentration, involves the following.

Four hours following the intravenous administration of a drug, a patient weighing 70 kg was found to have a drug blood level concentration of 10 μg/mL. Assuming the apparent volume of distribution is 10% of body weight, calculate the total amount of drug present in body fluids 4 hours after the drug was administered.

$$Vd = \frac{D}{C_P} \quad D = (Vd) \times (C_p)$$
$$Vd = 10\% \text{ of } 70 \text{ kg} = 7 \text{ kg} = 7 \text{ L}$$
$$C_P = 10 \text{ μg/mL} = 10 \text{ mg/L}$$
$$7 \text{ L} = \frac{D}{10 \text{ mg/L}}$$
$$D = (7 \text{ L}) \times (10 \text{ mg/L})$$
$$= 70 \text{ mg, } answer$$

Elimination Half-Life and Elimination Rate Constant

The elimination phase of a drug from the body is reflected by a decline in the drug's plasma concentration. The *elimination half-life* ($t\frac{1}{2}$) is the time it takes for the plasma drug concentration (as well as the amount of drug in the body) to fall by one half. For example, if it takes 3 hours for the plasma concentration of a drug to fall from 6 to 3 mg/L, its half-life would be 3 hours. It would take the same period of time (3 hours) for the concentration to fall from 3 to 1.5 mg/L, or from 1.5 to 0.75 mg/L. Many drug substances follow first-order kinetics in their elimination from the body, meaning that the rate of drug elimination per unit of time is proportional to the amount present at that time. As demonstrated previously, the elimination half-life is independent of the amount of drug in the body, and the amount of drug eliminated is less in each succeeding half-life. After five elimination half-lives, it may be expected that virtually all of a drug (97%) originally present will have been eliminated. The student might wish to examine this point, starting with a 100-mg dose of a drug (after first half-life, 50 mg, etc.).

Blood level data from a drug may be plotted against time on regular graph paper to obtain an exponential curve, or it may be plotted on semilogarithmic graph paper to obtain a straight line. From the latter, the elimination half-life may be determined, as shown in the example that follows in this section.

The elimination rate constant (K_{el}) characterizes the elimination process and may simply be regarded as the *fractional rate of drug removal per unit time, expressed as a decimal fraction* (e.g., 0.01 min^{-1}, meaning 1% per minute). The elimination rate constant for a first-order process may be calculated using the equation:

$$K_{el} = \frac{0.693}{t_{1/2}}$$

The derivation of this equation is described for the exponential decay of radioisotopes (see Chapter 21).

A patient received 12 mg of a drug intravenously and blood samples were drawn and analyzed at specific time intervals, resulting in the following data. Plot the data on semilogarithmic graph paper and determine the elimination half-life of the drug.

Plasma Drug Level Concentration (μg/100 mL)	Time (hours)
26.5	1
17.5	2
11.5	3
7.6	4
5.0	5
3.3	6

Plotting the data:

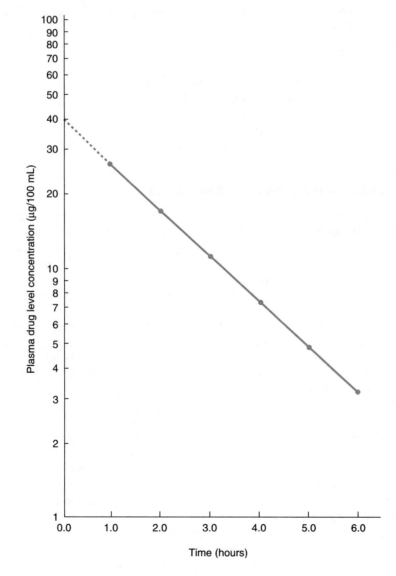

From the plotted data, the straight line may by extrapolated to time zero to determine the initial plasma drug concentration, which is found to be 40 μg/100 mL. The time it takes to reduce that level to one-half, or 20 μg/100 mL, is the elimination half-life. The 20 μg/100 mL concentration intersects the straight line at 1.7 hours.

Therefore, the elimination half-life is 1.7 hours, *answer.*

Note: The same answer may be obtained by selecting any plasma drug concentration (for example, 10 μg/100 mL), determining the time of that plasma level from the intercept, repeating the process for one-half of that drug level (5 μg/100 mL), and determining the elapsed time by subtraction to obtain the elimination half-life.

Calculate the elimination rate constant for a drug that has an elimination half-life of 50 minutes.

$$K_{el} = \frac{0.693}{t_{1/2}}$$
$$= \frac{0.693}{50 \text{ min}}$$
$$= 0.0139 \text{ min}^{-1}, \textit{answer.}$$

Additional related calculations, such as drug dosage based on creatinine clearance, may be found in Chapter 10.

CALCULATIONS CAPSULE

Selected Bioavailability and Pharmacokinetics

Bioavailability factor (F) for a dosage form:

$$F = \frac{AUC_{dosage\ form}}{AUC_{intravenous}}$$

Volume of distribution (Vd):

$$Vd = \frac{D}{C_P}$$

$$D = \text{total administered (IV) amount of drug}$$

$$C_P = \text{blood/plasma concentration of drug}$$

Elimination rate constant (K_{el}):

$$K_{el} = \frac{0.693}{t_{1/2}}$$

Calculations of Bioavailability and Bioequivalence

1. If the bioavailability factor (F) for a 100-mg tablet of a drug is 0.70 compared with the bioavailability factor of 1.0 for an injection of the same drug, how many milliliters of the injection containing 40 mg/mL would be considered bioequivalent to the tablet?

2. If 5 mL of an elixir containing 2 mg/mL of a drug is bioequivalent to a 15-mg tablet having a bioavailability factor of 0.60, what is the bioavailability factor (F) of the elixir?

3. If 500 mg of a drug are administered orally and 300 mg are absorbed into the circulation, calculate the bioavailability factor (F).

4.[4] A drug is 40% bioavailable by the oral route and 58% bioavailable by the transdermal route. If a patient is taking a 2.5-mg oral dose twice a day and is switched to the counterpart 2% ointment, how many grams of the ointment should be administered to provide the equivalent dose of the drug?

5.[4] A drug used to treat asthma is 55% bioavailable as 5-mg tablets. If a patient is switched to the inhalant form of the drug, which is 87% bioavailable, how many metered 500-μg sprays should the patient administer every 12 hours to receive an equivalent drug dose?

Calculations of Bound Drug, Elimination Half-Life, and Volume of Distribution

6.[4] If a 6-mg dose of a drug is administered intravenously and produces a blood concentration of 0.4 μg/mL, calculate its apparent volume of distribution.

7. If at equilibrium, two thirds of the amount of a drug substance in the blood is bound to protein, what would be the alpha (α) value of the drug?

8. The alpha (α) value for a drug in the blood is 0.90, equating to 0.55 ng/mL. What is the concentration of total drug in the blood?

9. A patient received an intravenous dose of 10 mg of a drug. A blood sample was drawn, and it contained 40 μg/100 mL. Calculate the apparent volume of distribution for the drug.

10. The volume of distribution for a drug was found to be 10 liters with a blood level concentration of 2 μg/mL. Calculate the total amount of drug present in the patient.

11. Calculate the elimination rate constant for a drug having an elimination half-life of 1.7 hours.

12. Plot the following data on semilogarithmic graph paper and determine (a) the elimination half-life of the drug and (b) the elimination rate constant.

Plasma Drug Concentration (μg/100 mL)	Time (hours)
8.5	0.5
6.8	1.0
5.4	1.5
4.0	2.0
3.2	2.5
2.5	3.0

13. What percentage of an originally administered intravenous dose of a drug remains in the body following three half-lives?

14. If the half-life of a drug is 4 hours, approximately what percentage of the drug administered would remain in the body 15 hours after administration?

15. If 100 mg of a drug are administered intravenously, and the resultant drug plasma concentration is determined to be 2.5 μg/mL, calculate the apparent volume of distribution.

16. If a dose of 1 g of a drug is administered intravenously to a patient and the drug plasma concentration is determined to be 65 μg/mL, calculate the apparent volume of distribution.

17. The volume of distribution for chlordiazepoxide has been determined to be 34 liters. Calculate the expected drug plasma concentration of the drug, in micrograms per deciliter, immediately after an intravenous dose of 5 mg.

18. In normal subjects, blood makes up about 7% of the body weight.
    (a) Calculate the approximate blood volume, in liters, for a man weighing 70 kg.
    (b) If the drug ZANTAC reached peak blood levels of about 500 ng/mL 2 to 3 hours after an oral dose, calculate the total amount of the drug, in milligrams, in the blood of the patient described in (a) when peak blood levels are achieved.

ANSWERS TO "CASE IN POINT" AND PRACTICE PROBLEMS

Case in Point 22.1

IV daily dose

$$= \frac{50 \text{ mg}}{1 \text{ dose}} \times \frac{3 \text{ doses}}{1 \text{ day}} = 150 \text{ mg/day}$$

F for the IV route = 1 or 100%

$$100\% \times 150 \text{ mg/day} = 50\% \times \text{Dose}_{oral}$$

$$\text{Dose}_{oral} = 300 \text{ mg/day}$$

$$\frac{300 \text{ mg}}{1 \text{ day}} \times \frac{1 \text{ day}}{2 \text{ doses}} = 150 \text{ mg/dose}$$

$$\frac{150 \text{ mg}}{1 \text{ dose}} \times \frac{5 \text{ mL}}{75 \text{ mg}} = 10 \text{ mL/dose, } \textit{answer.}$$

Practice Problems

1. 1.75 mL injection

2. 0.9

3. 0.6

4. 0.17 g ointment

5. 3.16 or 3 sprays

6. 15 L

7. 0.33

8. 0.61 mg/mL

9. 25 L

10. 20 mg

11. 0.408 hr^{-1}

12. graph

13. 12.5%

14. 7.43%

15. 40 L

16. 15.4 L

17. 14.7 μg/dL chlordiazepoxide

18. (a) 4.9 L
    (b) 2.45 mg ZANTAC

REFERENCES

1. Dissolution. United States Pharmacopeia 31st Rev. National Formulary 26. Rockville, MD: United States Pharmacopeial Convention, 2008;1:267–274

2. Gibaldi M. *Biopharmaceutics and Clinical Pharmacokinetics.* 4th ed. Philadelphia: Lea & Febiger, 1991:377.

3. Chereson R. Bioavailability, bioequivalence, and drug selection. Available at: http://www.pharmacyonline.creighton.edu/pha443/pdf/pkin08.pdf. Accessed September 25, 2008.

4. Prince SJ. In: Ansel HC, Prince SJ. *Pharmaceutical Calculations: The Pharmacist's Handbook.* Baltimore: Lippincott Williams & Wilkins, 2004:150–164.

5. Ritschel WA. *Handbook of Basic Pharmacokinetics.* 2nd ed. Hamilton, IL: Drug Intelligence Publications, 1982:219.

23

Selected Pharmacoeconomic Calculations

Objectives

Upon successful completion of this chapter, the student will be able to:

- Differentiate between the pharmacoeconomic methods: *cost-benefit analysis*, *cost-effectiveness analysis*, and *cost-minimization analysis* and perform example calculations of each.
- Perform cost-differential calculations between branded drug products and generic equivalents.
- Perform cost-differential calculations between dosage forms and routes of administration.
- Perform cost-differential calculations based on dosing regimens.
- Perform cost-differential calculations based on alternative treatment plans.
- Perform cost-differential calculations based on patient conversions.
- Calculate drug acquisition costs.
- Perform markup and selling price calculations.
- Perform calculations of prescription pricing methods.

The term ***pharmacoeconomics*** encompasses the economic aspects of drugs, from the costs associated with drug discovery and development to the costs of drug therapy analyzed against therapeutic outcomes. It includes many additional considerations, including drug product acquisition costs at the retail, institutional, and consumer levels; inventory, financial, and human resource management; cost/benefit relationships of drug therapy decisions, nondrug treatment alternatives, and health outcomes; factors associated with drug product selection and drug formulary decisions; the impact of proper drug utilization on incidence of hospitalization and length of stay; economic and health consequences of patient noncompliance, drug misuse, and adverse drug reactions; and the demographics of medication use by patients of various age groups, gender, and socioeconomic status, among other factors.

Pharmacoeconomics is the subject of much current research, with a broad array of information available in the primary literature and through various references and textbooks dedicated to the topic. The scope of this chapter necessarily is limited to the presentation of some introductory calculations, including general methods of pharmacoeconomic analysis, cost differentials related to drug product selection, patient conversions to alternative treatment plans, drug acquisition costs, and dispensing fees.

Pharmacoeconomic Methods of Analysis

There are a number of established methods of pharmacoeconomic analysis, including *cost-benefit analysis (CBA), cost-effectiveness analysis (CEA)*, and *cost-minimization analysis (CMA)*.[1-3]

355

Example Calculations for Pharmacoeconomic Methods of Analysis

Cost-Benefit Analysis (CBA)

Cost-benefit analysis involves identifying and measuring all the costs of providing a program or treatment and comparing those costs with the benefits that result. The analysis is expressed through a *benefit-to-cost ratio, that is:*

$$\text{Benefit-to-cost ratio} = \frac{\text{Benefits (\$)}}{\text{Costs (\$)}}$$

Obviously, if the data inserted in the ratio yield a number greater than 1, the benefits exceed the costs, and the program or treatment is considered beneficial.

Determine the benefit-to-cost ratio for a program in which the cost of pharmacist intervention was determined to be $12,000 and the benefits accrued to be $26,000.

$$\text{Benefit-to-cost ratio} = \frac{\$26,000}{\$12,000} = 2.167 \text{ or } 2.2, \textit{ answer.}$$

Cost-Effectiveness Analysis (CEA)

Cost-effectiveness analysis may be used to compare treatment alternatives with cost measured in dollars and treatment outcomes expressed in terms of the therapeutic objective (as the lowering of blood cholesterol). The results are expressed through a *cost-to-effectiveness (C/E) ratio, that is:*

$$\text{Cost-to-effectiveness ratio} = \frac{\text{Costs (\$)}}{\text{Therapeutic effect (in measurable units)}}$$

Determine the cost-effectiveness ratios for two 12-month treatments for the lowering of systolic blood pressure. Treatment A cost $1200 and lowered systolic blood pressure by an average of 5 mm of mercury. Treatment B cost $800 and lowered systolic blood pressure by an average of 8 mm of mercury.

$$\text{Treatment A: C/E ratio} = \frac{\$1200}{5 \text{ mm Hg}} = 240 \text{ (\$/mm Hg), } \textit{and}$$

$$\text{Treatment B: C/E ratio} = \frac{\$800}{8 \text{ mm Hg}} = 100 \text{ (\$/mm Hg), } \textit{answers.}$$

Cost-Minimization Analysis (CMA)

Cost-minimization analysis involves the comparison of two or more treatment alternatives, the outcomes of which are assumed or determined to be equivalent. The cost of each treatment alternative is expressed in dollars, and the costs are compared.

If cost minimization analyses demonstrate that two alternative treatments cost $1120 (treatment A) and $1450 (treatment B), respectively, calculate the cost benefit of treatment A compared with treatment B.

$$\$1450 - \$1120 = \$330, \textit{ answer.}$$

Cost Considerations of Drug and Drug Product Selection

Drug therapy and other means of treatment (e.g., surgery) are intended to serve the health care interests of the patient while being cost effective. In prescribing drug therapy, clinical as well as economic factors are important considerations in the selection of the drug substance and drug product. For example, if an expensive drug reduces morbidity and hospitalization time, it is considered both therapeutically advantageous and cost effective. If, however, a less expensive drug would provide therapeutic benefit comparable to the more expensive drug, the less costly drug is likely to be selected for use. Interventions by pharmacists in pharmaceutical care decisions have been shown to be cost effective and can enhance therapeutic outcomes.

In general, new drug entities and/or novel dosage forms that are protected by patents and are available from only a single source are more expensive than older, off-patent drugs available from multiple manufacturers or distributors. *Multisource pharmaceuticals* generally are lower priced because, unlike the innovator product, they do not bear the original research costs incurred in developing and bringing the new drug to market. Multisource pharmaceuticals generally are available to the pharmacist both as brand name and generic products and at a range of prices. For economic reasons, the prescribing physician, patient, health care institution, state or federally sponsored program, or other third-party payer may request or reimburse only for the dispensing of a generic product, when available.

It is common practice for drug use decision makers, such as drug formulary committees at hospitals, to establish a list of drugs approved for use and funding that balances therapeutic outcome and cost containment goals. Drug and drug product selection choices may be presented to prescribers on the basis of cost per day or cost per course of treatment.

Programs that are directed toward changing a patient's current drug, drug product, or route of drug administration often are referred to as ***conversion programs***.

Example Calculations Based on Drug or Drug Product Selection

Cost Differential Between Therapeutic Agents

Often there is a substantial cost differential between therapeutic agents within a therapeutic category. The cost differential may be based on the newness, innovation, patent status, and/or the cost of development or production of some members of the therapeutic class compared with others. In general, newer agents introduced into the marketplace are more expensive than older counterpart drugs. *Therapeutic interchange* programs, which allow for the substitution of one drug for another while maintaining comparable therapeutic benefit, can result in cost savings.

Calculate the cost differential between the thrombolytic agents streptokinase (250,000 IU; $96.41) and the biotechnology derived drug alteplase (50 mg; $1,100) if the total amount proposed to be administered to a patient is either 1,500,000 IU of streptokinase or 90 mg of alteplase.

Cost of streptokinase: $\dfrac{250,000 \text{ IU}}{1,500,000 \text{ IU}} = \dfrac{\$96.41}{x}$; $x = \$578.46$, *and*

Cost of alteplase: $\dfrac{50 \text{ mg}}{90 \text{ mg}} = \dfrac{\$1100}{x}$; $x = \$1980$, *and*

Cost differential: $\$1980 - \$578.46 = \$1401.54$, *answer.*

Cost Differential Between Branded Drug Products and Generic Equivalents

Drugs introduced to the marketplace as innovator, patented, and brand-name products often remain higher in price than generic equivalents, even after their patent protections expire. *Drug product selection* decisions may be made on this cost basis by health care providers, consumers, and insurance or health benefits managers.

The generic equivalent of a drug costs $12.40/100 tablets, whereas the innovator product costs $46.20/100 tablets. Calculate the drug cost differential for a 30-day supply if two tablets are taken daily.

Tablets required:	2 tablets (daily) $\times$ 30 (days) = 60 tablets
Cost of generic drug:	$\dfrac{100 \text{ tablets}}{60 \text{ tablets}} = \dfrac{\$12.40}{x}$; $x = \$7.44$, *and*
Cost of innovator drug:	$\dfrac{100 \text{ tablets}}{60 \text{ tablets}} = \dfrac{\$46.20}{x}$; x $27.72, *and*
Cost differential:	\$27.72 − \$7.44 = \$20.28, *answer*.

Cost Differential Between Dosage Forms and Routes of Administration

There is often a cost differential between dosage forms of the same therapeutic agent due to the costs of development or production. For instance, tablets are generally less expensive to develop and manufacture than are liquid forms, with injectable products and transdermal patches being among the most expensive. For patients receiving intravenous therapy, the associated costs are expanded greatly by the additional personnel and adjunctive materials and equipment needed to administer the medication. Many hospital cost containment programs encourage the conversion from parenteral medications to oral therapy as soon as feasible without compromising the desired therapeutic outcomes.

Verapamil 80-mg tablets are taken three times a day and cost \$7.52/100 tablets. Extended-release capsules containing 240 mg of verapamil are taken once daily and cost \$15.52/100 capsules. Calculate the treatment cost differential over a 30-day period.

80-mg tablets:	\$7.52 ÷ 100 (tablets) = \$0.0752 (per tablet) 3 tablets (per day) $\times$ 30 (days) = 90 tablets \$0.0752 $\times$ 90 (tablets) = \$6.768 or \$6.77, *and*
240-mg capsules:	\$15.52 ÷ 100 (capsules) = \$0.1552 (per capsule) 1 capsule (per day) $\times$ 30 (days) = 30 capsules \$0.01552 $\times$ 30 (capsules) = \$4.656 or \$4.66, *and*
Cost differential:	\$6.77 − \$4.66 = \$2.11, *answer*.

A hospitalized patient was switched from intravenous ciprofloxacin (400 mg q12h) to oral ciprofloxacin (500 mg q12h). Calculate the daily drug cost savings if the intravenous product cost is \$12.00 per 200 mg and the oral product cost is \$2.95 per 250-mg capsule.

Intravenous ciprofloxacin:	400 mg $\times$ 2 (times per day) = 800 mg 800 mg $\times$ \$12.00/200 mg = \$48.00, *and*
Oral ciprofloxacin:	500 mg $\times$ 2 (times per day) = 1000 mg 1000 mg $\times$ \$2.95/250 mg = \$11.80, *and*
Cost differential:	\$48.00 − \$11.80 = \$36.20, *answer*.

Cost Differential of Dosing Regimens

A dosing regimen for a specific drug may be changed to be more cost effective without affecting the desired therapeutic outcome.

A dosage interval adjustment was made in the intravenous administration of the drug ranitidine in a group of 23 hospitalized patients such that the number of doses per patient per treatment day was reduced from an average of 2.33 to 1.51 without sacrificing therapeutic outcomes. If the cost of each dose of ranitidine was \$4.02, calculate the daily cost savings to the hospital.

Reduction in doses per patient per day:	2.33–1.51 = 0.82 doses
Reduction in doses in patient group:	0.82 dose × 23 (patients) = 18.86 doses
Cost savings:	$4.02 × 18.86 (doses) = $75.8172 or $75.82, *answer.*

Cost Differential of Alternative Treatment Plans

Preventive medicine, drug therapy, surgery, radiation, and many other choices may be valid alternatives in maintaining health or in treating illness.

If the daily treatment of an ulcer patient with cimetidine prevents readmission to a hospital, calculate the potential savings over reoccurrence of hospitalization if the daily drug costs are $1.38 and the prior 5-day hospital bill was $4056.

Drug cost:	$1.38 × 5 (days) = $6.90
Potential savings:	$4056 − $6.90 = $4049.10, *answer.*

CASE IN POINT 23.1: A hospital's Pharmacy and Therapeutics Committee is determining the most economical of three drugs considered to be therapeutically equivalent. The least expensive drug, per patient treatment day, is to be added to the hospital's drug formulary.

  Drug A: 0.5 g/mL, 5-mL vial; dose, 1 mL q6h; cost, $16.50/vial
  Drug B: 1 g/mL, 10-mL vial; dose, 0.75 mL q8h; cost, $57.42/vial
  Drug C: 1.5 g/mL, 1-mL ampul; dose, 1 mL q12h; cost, $15.94/ampul

  Which drug is most economical, per patient treatment day, not taking into consideration any material or personnel costs?

Drug Acquisition Costs

Pharmacists purchase prescription and nonprescription drugs and other merchandise from wholesalers, distributors, and manufacturers. A pharmacy's actual acquisition cost (AAC) for a given product is the ***trade price***, or the basic list price to the pharmacy, less all discounts that are applied.

Discounts provided by suppliers may be based on quantity buying and/or payment of invoices within a specified period. In addition, for nonprescription products, discounts may be available for certain seasonal or other promotional products, bonuses in terms of free merchandise, and advertising and display allowances. These discounts provide the pharmacy with a means of increasing the gross profit on selected merchandise.

Example Calculation of Net Cost After Discount

The list price of an antihistamine elixir is $6.50 per pint, less 40%. What is the net cost per pint of the elixir?

List Price		Discount		Net Cost
100%	−	40%	=	60%
$6.50	×	0.60	=	$3.90, *answer.*

Example Calculations of Series Discounts

Several discounts may be allowed on promotional deals. For example, the list price on some merchandise may be subject to a trade discount of 33.5%, plus a quantity discount of 12% and a cash discount of 2% for prompt payment of the invoice. This chain of deductions, sometimes referred to as a *series discount*, may be converted to a single discount equivalent. In such cases, the discounts in the series cannot be figured by adding them; rather, the first discount is deducted from the list price and each successive discount is taken on the balance remaining after deduction of the preceding discount. The order in which the discounts in a series discount are taken is immaterial.

The list price of 12 bottles (100 count) of analgesic tablets is $36.00, less a trade discount of 33⅓%. If purchased in quantities of 12 dozens, an additional discount of 10% is allowed by the manufacturer, plus a 2% cash discount for payment of the invoice within 10 days of billing. Calculate the net cost of 144 bottles (100 count) of the analgesic tablets when purchased under the terms of the offer.

$$\text{List price of 12 (100 count)} = \$36.00$$
$$\text{List price of 144 (100 count)} = \$432.00$$

$$100\% - 33\tfrac{1}{3}\% = 66\tfrac{2}{3}\% \quad 100\% - 10\% = 90\% \quad 100\% - 2\% = 98\%$$
$$\$432.00 \times 66\tfrac{2}{3}\% = \$288.00, \text{ cost after } 33\tfrac{1}{3}\% \text{ is deducted}$$
$$\$288.00 \times 90\% = \$259.20, \text{ cost after } 10\% \text{ is deducted}$$
$$\$259.20 \times 98\% = \$254.02, \text{ net cost, } answer.$$

To compute a single discount equivalent to a series of discounts, subtract each discount in the series from 100% and multiply the net percentages. The product thus obtained is subtracted from 100% to give the single discount equivalent to the series of discounts.

A promotional deal provides a trade discount of 33.5%, an off invoice allowance of 12%, and a display allowance of 5%. Calculate the single discount equivalent to these deductions.

$$100\% - 33.5\% = 66.5\% \quad 100\% - 12\% = 88\% \quad 100\% - 5\% = 95\%$$
$$0.665 \times 0.88 \times 0.95 = 0.556 \text{ or } 55.6\% = \% \text{ to be paid}$$
$$\text{Discount} = 100\% - 55.6\% = 44.4\%, answer.$$

Markup

The term **markup**, sometimes used interchangeably with the term *margin of profit or gross profit*, refers to the difference between the cost of merchandise and its selling price. For example, if a pharmacist buys an article for $1.50 and sells it for $2.50, the markup (or gross profit) as a dollars-and-cents item is $1.00.

Markup percentage (percentage of gross profit) refers to the markup divided by the selling price. The expression of the markup percentage may be somewhat ambiguous because it may be based on either the cost or the selling price of merchandise. In modern retail practice, this percentage is invariably based on selling price, and in this context, the markup percentage is a percentage of the selling price. If, however, a pharmacist can, for convenience, base markup percentage on the cost of merchandise, the pharmacist must not overlook the fact that the markup on cost must yield the desired percentage of gross profit on the selling price.

Example Calculations of Selling Price Given Cost and Percentage of Gross Profit

The cost of 100 antacid tablets is $2.10. What should be the selling price per 100 tablets to yield a 66⅔% gross profit on the cost?

$$\begin{aligned}
\text{Cost} \times \% \text{ of gross profit} &= \text{Gross profit} \\
\$2.10 \times 66\tfrac{2}{3}\% &= \$1.40 \\
\text{Cost} + \text{Gross profit} &= \text{Selling price} \\
\$2.10 + \$1.40 &= \$3.50, \text{ answer.}
\end{aligned}$$

The cost of 100 antacid tablets is $2.10. What should be the selling price per 100 tablets to yield a 40% gross profit on the selling price?

$$\begin{aligned}
\text{Selling price} &= 100\% \\
\text{Selling price} - \text{Gross profit} &= \text{Cost} \\
100\% - 40\% &= 60\%
\end{aligned}$$

$$\frac{60\,(\%)}{100\,(\%)} = \frac{(\$)\,2.10}{(\$)\,x}$$
$$x = \$3.50, \text{ answer.}$$

Example Calculation of Cost Given Selling Price and Percent Gross Profit on Cost

A bottle of headache tablets is sold for $2.25, thereby yielding a gross profit of 60% on the cost. What was the cost of the bottle of tablets?

$$\begin{aligned}
\text{Cost} + \text{Gross profit} &= \text{Selling price} \\
x + 0.6x &= \$2.25 \\
1.6x &= \$2.25 \\
x &= \$1.40, \text{ answer.}
\end{aligned}$$

Example Calculation of Markup Percentage Based on Cost, Given Percent of Gross Profit on Selling Price

What should the markup percentage be on the cost of an item to yield a 40% gross profit on the selling price?

$$\begin{aligned}
\text{Selling price} &= 100\% \\
\text{Selling price} - \text{Gross profit} &= \text{Cost} \\
100\% - 40\% &= 60\%
\end{aligned}$$

$$\frac{\text{Cost as \% of selling price}}{\text{Selling price as \%}} = \frac{\text{Gross profit as \% of selling price}}{x\,(\%)}$$
$$x = \% \text{ gross profit on the cost}$$

$$\frac{60\,(\%)}{100\,(\%)} = \frac{40\,(\%)}{x\,(\%)}$$
$$x = 66\tfrac{2}{3}\%, \text{ answer.}$$

Prescription Pricing

Each pharmacy should have a uniform and consistently applied system of prescription pricing that ensures a fair return on investment and costs and enables the pharmacy to provide the needed services to the community.

Example Calculations of Prescription Pricing Methods

Although many methods of prescription pricing have been used over the years, the following are the most common[4]:

1. *Markup Percentage.* In this common method, the desired markup percentage is taken of the cost of the ingredients and *added to* the cost of the ingredients to obtain the prescription price. The markup percentage applied may vary depending on the cost of the ingredients, with a lower markup percentage generally used for prescription items of higher cost, and a higher markup percentage applied for prescription items of lower cost.

Cost of ingredients + (Cost of ingredients × % Markup) = Prescription price

If the cost of the quantity of a drug product to be dispensed is $4.00 and the pharmacist applies an 80% markup on cost, what would be the prescription price?

$$\$4.00 + (\$4.00 \times 80\%) = \$4.00 + \$3.20 = \$7.20, answer.$$

2. *Markup Percentage Plus a Minimum Professional Fee.* In this method, both a markup percentage and a minimum professional fee are added to the cost of the ingredients. The markup percentage in this method is usually lower than that used in the method just described. The minimum fee is established to recover the combined cost of the container, label, overhead, and professional services.

Cost of ingredients + (Cost of ingredients × % Markup) + Minimum professional fee = Prescription price

If the cost of the quantity of a drug product to be dispensed is $4.00 and the pharmacist applies a 40% markup on cost plus a professional fee of $2.25, what would be the prescription price?

$$\$4.00 + (\$4.00 \times 40\%) + \$2.25 = \$4.00 + \$1.60 + \$2.25 = \$7.85, answer.$$

3. *Professional Fee.* This method involves the addition of a specified professional fee to the cost of the ingredients used in filling a prescription. The professional fee includes all the dispensing costs and professional remuneration. A *true* professional fee is independent of the cost of the ingredients and thus does not vary from one prescription to another. Some pharmacists, however, use a *variable* or *sliding* professional fee method whereby the amount of the fee varies on the basis of the cost of the ingredients. By this method, the greater the cost of prescription ingredients, the greater the fee, the rationale being that the cost of inventory maintenance must be recovered in this manner.

A pharmacy may determine its professional fee by (1) averaging the amount previously charged, above the cost of ingredients, for prescriptions dispensed over a specified period; or (2) using a more exacting cost analysis method in which all costs attributed to the prescription department are divided by the prescription volume in determining the actual cost of filling a prescription, with the profit and desired fee then determined. Pharmacies that charge a professional fee commonly make adjustments for prescriptions requiring compounding to compensate for the extra time, materials, and equipment used.

Cost of ingredients + Professional fee = Prescription price

If the cost of the quantity of a drug product to be dispensed is $4.00 and the pharmacist applies a professional fee of $4.25, what would be the prescription price?

$$\$4.00 + \$4.25 = \$8.25, answer.$$

Example Calculations of Third-Party Reimbursement for Professional Services

Many governmental agencies, such as state human services departments, and many insurance companies have adopted the professional fee method for reimbursing pharmacists who fill prescriptions covered under their programs. Each third-party payer establishes the professional fee it will pay the pharmacists interested in participating in its program. In addition, because the actual acquisition cost of a given drug product may vary substantially among pharmacies, depending on the discounts received, most third-party payers use the *average wholesale price (AWP)* less an established percentage as the cost basis for the drug in reimbursement programs. The AWP is obtained from commercial listings. The reimbursed amount is calculated from a predetermined formula, such as "AWP less 10% plus $4.50 professional fee." Many third-party programs have a "copayment" provision, which requires the patient to pay a portion of the charge for each prescription filled.

If a third-party payer reimburses a pharmacy "AWP less 15%" plus a professional fee of $4.75, what would be the total reimbursement on a prescription calling for 24 capsules having an AWP of $25.00 per 100 capsules?

$$\text{AWP for 24 capsules} = \$6.00, \text{ less } 15\% = \$5.10$$
$$\$5.10 + \$4.75 = \$9.85, \textit{answer.}$$

If a pharmacy provider contract calls for a copayment of $2.00 to be paid directly to the pharmacy for each prescription the patient has filled, how much would the third party reimburse the pharmacy in the preceding example?

$$\$9.85 - \$2.00 = \$7.85, \textit{answer.}$$

A patient's individual or group health insurance coverage often provides reimbursement benefits only after a patient reaches a self-paid level (the stated "deductible" amount) of his or her health care expenses, after which the coverage may pay fully or partially for certain covered expenses.

A patient's health insurance covers 80% of prescription drug costs after a $200.00 deductible is reached. If after making payments of $184.00 toward the deductible amount, a patient pays a pharmacy $86.00 for a prescription, how much can the patient expect to be reimbursed by the insurance carrier?

$$\$200.00 - \$184.00 = \$16.00, \text{ remaining toward the deductible amount}$$
$$\$86.00 - \$16.00 = \$70.00, \text{ covered expense}$$
$$\$70.00 \times 80\% = \$56.00 \text{ reimbursement, } \textit{answer.}$$

PRACTICE PROBLEMS

Pharmacoeconomic Methods of Analysis Calculations

1. Using the ratio for cost-benefit analysis, determine the numerical result of a program in which pharmacist intervention costing $8875 resulted in benefits valued at $14,200.

2. Using the ratio for cost-effectiveness analysis, determine the numerical difference between two drug therapies for total serum cholesterol reduction in which treatment A, costing $55, lowered total cholesterol by 5 dg/100 mL of serum, and treatment B, costing $98, lowered total cholesterol by 7 dg/100 mL of serum.

Drug and Drug Product Selection and Utilization Calculations

3. An antianginal drug is available in a three-times-a-day tablet at $42.50/100 tablets, in a twice-a-day tablet at $64.00/100 tablets, and in a once-a-day tablet at $80.20/100 tablets. Which form would be most economical to a compliant patient and at what cost?

4. A physician inquires of a pharmacist regarding the most economical of the following antihypertensive therapies: drug A, 30-mg tablets taken q.i.d. costing $0.33/tablet; drug B, 10-mg tablets taken t.i.d. costing $0.20/tablet; or drug C, 2.5-mg tablets taken b.i.d, costing $0.38/tablet. Indicate the most economical drug and the drug cost for a 30-day supply.

5. A physician offers a patient the option of prescribing 30 scored ZOLOFT 100-mg tablets (for the patient to break in half with a dose of one-half tablet) or 60 tablets containing 50 mg of the drug. Calculate the cost differential and indicate the most economical option for the patient if the 100-mg tablets cost $192.76 per 100 tablets and the 50-mg tablets cost $187.34 per 100 tablets.

6. Calculate the daily drug cost differential between a dose of a drug administered q8h and costing $6.25/dose and a counterpart drug administered once daily and costing $26.50/dose.

7. If 100 tablets of an innovator drug cost $114.50 and 60 tablets of a generic equivalent cost $27.75, calculate the cost differential for a 30-day supply.

8. A pharmacist can purchase 5-mg tablets of a drug at (a) $16.21 for a bottle of 100 tablets, (b) $73.41 for a bottle of 500 tablets, or (c) $124.25 for a bottle of 1000 tablets. Calculate the drug costs for each of the package sizes to fill a prescription for 60 tablets.

9. A hospital pharmacy recommended parenteral cefazolin (dose: 0.5 g q8h; cost: $1.80/g) over parenteral cefoxitin (dose: 1 g q6h; cost: $6.48/g) to balance therapeutic outcomes with cost containment. Calculate the difference in drug cost between these two treatments per patient day.

10. An anti-AIDS compound is commonly taken at an adult daily dose of 600 mg, in two or more divided doses. If 300-mg tablets cost $265 per 60, calculate the drug cost per year.

11. The drug hydralazine may be administered intravenously when needed to control hypertension at 20-mg doses in D5W every 12 hours for 48 hours, after which the patient is converted to oral dosage, 10-mg tablets four times per day for 2 days, then 25-mg tablets four times per day for the next 5 days. If the 20-mg IV ampul costs $6.00; 10-mg tablets, $18.00/100 tablets; 25-mg tablets, $26.00/100 tablets; and D5W, $10.00 per bottle, calculate the *average daily* costs of intravenous and oral therapy.

12. A physician has a choice of prescribing the following ACE inhibitor drugs to treat hypertension, with the pharmacist's cost of each, per 100 tablets, given in parentheses: drug A, 10 mg ($63.00); drug B, 25 mg ($59.00); drug C, 5 mg ($84.00); and drug D, 10 mg ($70.00). Each drug is once-a-day dosing except for drug B tablets, which are taken twice a day. Calculate the 30-day medication cost for each drug.

13. The cost to a hospital of a drug is $16.97 per 10-mg vial. If the drug is administered by intermittent injection at 0.15 mg/kg/hr for 24 hours, calculate the daily cost of the drug used for a 70-kg patient.

14. If the drug in the preceding problem may be administered to the same patient by continuous infusion (rather than by intermittent injection) with a 0.1 mg/kg loading dose and subsequent doses of 0.05 mg/kg for the next 23 hours, calculate the daily cost of the drug by this route of administration.

15. The intravenous dosing schedules and costs of the following cephalosporin antimicrobial agents are: cefazolin, 1 g every 8 hours ($3.00); cefoxitin, 1 g every 6 hours ($6.24); and cefotan, 1 g every 24 hours ($31.39). Calculate the daily cost of each drug.

16. The drug diltiazem is available as follows: 60-mg tablets taken q.i.d. ($63.00/100 tablets); 120-mg sustained-release capsules taken b.i.d. ($110.00/100 capsules); and 240-mg sustained-release capsules taken once daily ($162.00/100 capsules). Calculate the cost per month of each dosage form.

Acquisition Cost, Markup, and Selling Price Calculations

17. Calculate the single discount equivalent to each of the following series of deductions:
    (a) Trade discount of 40%, a quantity discount of 5%, and a cash discount of 2%
    (b) Trade discount of 33⅓%, a 10% off invoice allowance, and a 6% display allowance
    (c) Trade discount of 30%, a display allowance of 5%, and a cash discount of 2%

18. If an ointment is listed at $5.40/lb., less 33⅓%, what is the net cost of 10 lb.?

19. A pain relief lotion is listed at $52.35 per dozen 6-oz bottles, less a discount of 33.5%. The manufacturer offers 2 bottles free with the purchase of 10 on a promotional deal. What is the net cost per bottle when the lotion is purchased on the deal?

20. A cough syrup is listed at $54.00 per gallon, less 40%. What is the net cost of 1 pint of the cough syrup?

21. A pharmacist receives a bill of goods amounting to $1200.00, less a 5% discount for quantity buying and a 2% cash discount for paying the invoice within 10 days. What is the net amount of the bill?

22. ℞   Glycerin   120
       Boric Acid Solution
       Witch Hazel   aa   ad   500
       Sig. Apply to affected areas.

Witch hazel is listed at $12.00 per gallon, less 34.5%. What is the net cost of the amount needed in filling the prescription?

23. Zinc oxide ointment in 1-oz tubes is purchased at $10.80 per 12 tubes. At what price per tube must it be sold to yield a gross profit of 66⅔% on the cost?

24. A topical antibacterial ointment is listed at $3.70 per tube, less 35%, and the manufacturer allows 6 tubes free with the purchase of 66 tubes.
    (a) What is the net cost per tube?
    (b) At what price per tube must the ointment be sold to yield a gross profit of 45% on the selling price?

25. Twelve bottles of 100 analgesic tablets cost $18.96 when bought on a promotional deal. If the tablets sell for $2.69 per 100, what percentage of gross profit is realized on the selling price?

26. At what price must a pharmacist mark an item that costs $2.60 so that the selling price can be reduced 25% for a special sale and still yield a gross profit of 35% on the cost price?

27. A prescription item costs a pharmacist $8.40. Using a markup of 50% on the cost, what would be the price of the dispensed prescription?

28. A prescription item costs a pharmacist $12.20. Using a markup of 25% on the cost plus a professional fee of $4.75, calculate the prescription price.

29. A pharmacist decided to determine a professional fee by calculating the average markup on a series of previously filled prescriptions. A sample of 100 prescriptions had a total cost to the pharmacist of $850 and a total prescription price of $1310. Calculate the average professional fee that could be used in prescription pricing.

30. A recent annual survey of pharmacies revealed the following:

    Number of ℞s filled: 45,097
    Number of refill ℞s: 18,595
    Number of third-party ℞s: 20,912
    ℞ dollar volume: $1,039,005
    Total (store) dollar volume:

$5,102,809
Using these data, calculate (a) the average
prescription price, (b) the percentage of
new prescriptions filled, (c) the percentage of third-party prescriptions, and (d)
the percentage of store volume attributed
to the prescriptions.

ANSWERS TO "CASE IN POINT" AND PRACTICE PROBLEMS

Case in Point 23.1

Drug A dose, in mL/day:
1 mL/dose × 4 doses/day = 4 mL/day

Cost/day:
$$\frac{5\ mL}{\$16.50} = \frac{4\ mL}{x}; x = \$13.20/day$$

Drug B dose, in mL/day:
0.75 mL/dose × 3 doses/day = 2.25 mL/day

Cost/day:
$$\frac{10\ mL}{\$57.42} = \frac{2.25}{x}; x = \$\ 12.92/day$$

Drug C dose, in mL/day:
1 mL/dose × 2 doses/day = 2 mL/day

Cost/day:
$$\frac{1\ mL}{\$15.94} = \frac{2\ mL}{x}; x = \$31.84/day$$

Therefore, drug B is the least expensive per
day, *answer.*

Practice Problems

1. 1.6

2. $3/dg

3. once-a-day tablet, $0.80/day

4. drug B, $18.00

5. $54.58, 100-mg tablets

6. $7.75

7. $20.47

8. (a) $9.73
   (b) $8.81
   (c) $7.46

9. $23.22

10. $3224.17

11. IV therapy, $32.00 per day, average
    oral therapy, $0.74 per day, average

12. drug A, $18.90
    drug B, $35.40
    drug C, $25.20
    drug D, $21.00

13. $427.64

14. $148.49

15. cefazolin, $9.00
    cefoxitin, $24.96
    cefotan, $31.39

16. 60-mg tablets, $75.60
    120-mg capsules, $66.00
    240-mg capsules, $48.60

17. (a) 44.1%
    (b) 43.6%
    (c) 34.8%

18. $36.00

19. $2.42

20. $4.05

21. $1117.20

22. 40 cents

23. $1.50

24. (a) $2.20
    (b) $4.00

25. 41.3%

26. $4.68

27. $12.60

28. $20.00

29. $4.60

30. (a) $23.04
    (b) 58.8%
    (c) 46.4%
    (d) 20.4%

REFERENCES

1. Sanchez LA. Pharmacoeconomic principles and methods: an introduction for hospital pharmacists. *Hospital Pharmacy* 1994;29:774–779.
2. Gurnee MC, Sylvestri MF, Ortmeier BG. Understanding the basic principles of pharmacoeconomics. *Managed Care Pharmacy Practice* 1995;2:34–42.
3. Draugalis JR, Bootman JL, Larson LN, et al. Pharmacoeconomics. *Current Concepts* 1989;1–32.
4. Ansel HC. The prescription. In: *Remington's Pharmaceutical Sciences.* 18th Ed. Easton, PA: Mack Publishing, 1990; 1828–1844.

APPENDICES

Common Systems of Measurement and Intersystem Conversion

The International System of Units (SI) is the *official* system for weights and measures as stated in the *United States Pharmacopeia—National Formulary*.[1] However, other so-called *common systems of measurement* are encountered in pharmacy and must be recognized and understood. The a*pothecaries' system of measurement* is the traditional system of pharmacy, and although it is now largely of historic significance, components of this system are occasionally found on prescriptions. The *avoirdupois system* is the common system of commerce, employed along with the SI in the United States. It is through this system that items are purchased and sold by the ounce and pound. This appendix defines these common systems, expresses their quantitative relationship to one another and to the SI, and provides the means for intersystem conversion. Conversion of temperature between the Fahrenheit and Celsius (or centigrade) scales, and alcohol conversion of proof strength are also included in this appendix.

Apothecaries' Fluid Measure

$$60 \text{ minims } (\mathfrak{m}) = 1 \text{ fluidrachm or fluidram } (f\mathfrak{z} \text{ or } \mathfrak{z})^a$$
$$8 \text{ fluidrachms } (480 \text{ minims}) = 1 \text{ fluidounce } (f\mathfrak{z} \text{ or } \mathfrak{z})^a$$
$$16 \text{ fluidounces} = 1 \text{ pint } (pt)$$
$$2 \text{ pints } (32 \text{ fluidounces}) = 1 \text{ quart } (qt)$$
$$4 \text{ quarts } (8 \text{ pints}) = 1 \text{ gallon } (gal)$$

This table may also be written:

gal	qt	pt	f$\mathfrak{z}$	f$\mathfrak{z}$	$\mathfrak{m}$
1	4	8	128	1024	61440
	1	2	32	256	15360
		1	16	128	7680
			1	8	480
				1	60

Apothecaries' Measure of Weight

$$20 \text{ grains } (gr) = 1 \text{ scruple } (\vartheta)$$
$$3 \text{ scruples } (60 \text{ grains}) = 1 \text{ drachm or dram } (\mathfrak{z})$$
$$8 \text{ drachms } (480 \text{ grains}) = 1 \text{ ounce } (\mathfrak{z})$$
$$12 \text{ ounces } (5760 \text{ grains}) = 1 \text{ pound } (\text{tb})$$

This table may also be written:

tb	$\mathfrak{z}$	$\mathfrak{z}$	ϑ	gr
1	12	96	288	5760
	1	8	24	480
		1	3	60
			1	20

---

a When it is clear that a liquid is to be measured, the *f* may be omitted in this symbol.

A typical set of Apothecaries' Weights consists of the following units:

$$\mathrm{\bar{3}ii} \quad \mathrm{\bar{3}i} \quad \mathrm{\bar{3}ss} \quad \mathrm{\Im ii} \quad \mathrm{\Im i} \quad \mathrm{\Im ss} \quad \Im\mathrm{ii} \quad \Im\mathrm{i} \quad \Im\mathrm{ss}$$

5-grain, 4-grain, 3-grain, 2-grain, 1-grain, ½-grain

Avoirdupois Measure of Weight

$$437\tfrac{1}{2} \text{ or } 437.5 \text{ grain (gr)} = 1 \text{ ounce (oz.)}$$
$$16 \text{ ounces (7000 grains)} = 1 \text{ pound (lb.)}$$

This table may also be written:

lb.	oz.	gr
1	16	7000
	1	437.5

Fundamental Operations and Calculations

Only one denomination has a value common to the apothecaries' and avoirdupois systems of measuring weight: the *grain*. The other denominations bearing the same name have different values.

Bulk or stock packages of powdered drugs and chemicals (and occasionally some liquids when they are sold by weight) are customarily provided to the pharmacist in avoirdupois units of weight by manufacturers and wholesalers. The pharmacist likewise sells bulk packages of nonprescription drug and chemical items by the avoirdupois system.

In contrast with the invariable use of *simple* quantities in the metric system, measurements in the common systems are recorded whenever possible in *compound quantities*, i.e., quantities expressed in two or more denominations. So, 20 f$\mathrm{\bar{3}}$ may be used during the process of calculating, but as a final result, it should be recorded as 1 pt 4 f$\mathrm{\bar{3}}$. The process of reducing a quantity to a compound quantity beginning with the highest possible denomination is called **simplification**. Decimal fractions may be used in calculation, but the subdivision of a minim or a grain in a final result is recorded as a *common fraction*.

In days gone by, when prescriptions were written in the apothecaries' system, the following format was used, with Roman numerals placed after the abbreviations or symbols for the denominations.

R	Codeine Sulfate	gr iv
	Ammonium Chloride	$\mathrm{3}$ iss
	Cherry Syrup ad	f$\mathrm{\bar{3}}$ iv
	Sig. $\mathrm{3i}$ as directed.	

Example Calculations in the Apothecaries' System

Usually, before a compound quantity can be used in a calculation, it must be expressed in terms of a single denomination. To do so, each denomination in the compound quantity must be reduced to the required denomination and the results added.

Reduce $\mathrm{\bar{3}ss}$ $\mathrm{3ii}$ $\Im i$ to grains.

$$\begin{aligned}
\mathrm{\bar{3}ss} &= \tfrac{1}{2} \times 480 \text{ gr} &= 240 \text{ gr} \\
\mathrm{3ii} &= 2 \times 60 \text{ gr} &= 120 \text{ gr} \\
\Im\mathrm{i} &= 1 \times 20 \text{ gr} &= \underline{\ 20 \text{ gr}} \\
& & 380 \text{ gr, } answer.
\end{aligned}$$

Reduce f℥iv f℈iiss to fluidrachms.

$$f℥iv = 4 \times 8 \, f℥ \quad = 32 \quad f℥$$
$$f℈iiss \quad\quad\quad = \underline{2\frac{1}{2} \, f℥}$$
$$34\frac{1}{2} \, f℥, \, answer.$$

Before being weighed, a given quantity should be expressed in denominations equal to the actual weights on hand. Before a volume is measured, a given quantity should be expressed in denominations represented by the calibrations on the graduate.

Change 165 grains to weighable apothecaries' units.

By selecting larger weight units to account for as many of the required grains as possible, beginning with the largest, we find that we may use the following weights:

℈ii, ℈ss, ℈ss, 5 gr, *answer.*

$$Check: ℈ii = 120 \, gr$$
$$℈ss = 30 \, gr$$
$$℈ss = 10 \, gr$$
$$5 \, gr = \underline{\quad 5 \, gr}$$
$$165 \, gr, \, total.$$

In enlarging a formula, we are to measure 90 f℥ of a liquid. Using two graduates, if necessary, in what denominations may we measure this quantity?

11 f℥ and 2 f℥, *answer.*

$$Check: 11 \, f℥ = 88 \, f℥$$
$$2 \, f℥ = \underline{\quad 2 \, f℥}$$
$$90 \, f℥, \quad total.$$

Addition or Subtraction

To add or subtract quantities in the common systems, reduce to a common denomination, add or subtract, and reduce the result (unless it is to be used in further calculations) to a compound quantity.

A formula contains ℈ii of ingredient A, ℥i of ingredient B, ℥iv of ingredient C, and gr viiss of ingredient D. Calculate the total weight of the ingredients.

$$℈ii = 2 \times 20 \, gr = \quad 40 \quad gr$$
$$℥i = 1 \times 60 \, gr = \quad 60 \quad gr$$
$$℥iv = 4 \times 60 \, gr = 240 \quad gr$$
$$gr \, viiss = \underline{\quad 7\frac{1}{2} \, gr}$$
$$347\frac{1}{2} \, gr = 5 \, ℥ \, 2 \, ℈ \, 7\frac{1}{2} \, gr, \, answer.$$

A pharmacist had 1 gallon of alcohol. At different times, he dispensed f℥iv, 2 pt, f℥viii, and f℥iv. What volume of alcohol was left?

$$f℥iv \quad\quad\quad\quad\quad = \quad 4 \quad f℥$$
$$2 \, pt = 2 \times 16 \, f℥ \quad = 32 \quad f℥$$
$$f℥viii \quad\quad\quad\quad\quad = \quad 8 \quad f℥$$
$$f℥iv \quad\quad\quad\quad\quad = \underline{\quad \frac{1}{2} \quad f℥}$$
$$44\frac{1}{2} \, f℥, \, total \, dispensed.$$

$$1 \, gal = 128 \quad f℥$$
$$- \underline{\quad 44\frac{1}{2} \, f℥}$$
$$83\frac{1}{2}f℥ = 5 \, pt \, 3 \, f℥ \, 4 \, f℥, \, answer.$$

Multiplication and Division

A *simple* quantity may be multiplied or divided by any *pure* number, such as *12 × 10 oz.* = *120 oz.* or *7 lb. 8 oz.*

If, however, *both* terms in division are derived from denominate numbers (as when we express one quantity as a fraction of another), they must be reduced to a *common* denomination before division.

A *compound* quantity is most easily multiplied or divided, and with least chance of careless error, if it is first reduced to a *simple* quantity: *2 × 8 ʒ̅ 6 ʒ = 2 × 70 ʒ = 140 ʒ or 17 ʒ̅ 4 ʒ.*

The *result* of multiplication should be (1) left as it is, if it is to be used in further calculations, (2) simplified, or (3) reduced to weighable or measurable denominations.

A prescription for 24 powders calls for gr ¼ of ingredient A, Өss of ingredient B, and gr v of ingredient C in each powder. How much of each ingredient should be used in compounding the prescription?

$$
\begin{aligned}
24 \times \text{gr } \tfrac{1}{4} &= 6 \text{ gr of ingredient A,} \\
24 \times \tfrac{1}{2}Ө &= 12 \text{ Ө, or 4 ʒ of ingredient B,} \\
24 \times \text{gr v} &= 120 \text{ gr, or 2 ʒ of ingredient C, } answers.
\end{aligned}
$$

How many 15-minim doses can be obtained from a mixture containing fʒ̅iii of one ingredient and fʒii of another?

$$
\begin{aligned}
\text{fʒ̅iii} &= 3 \times 480 \text{ ℳ} &= 1440 \text{ ℳ} \\
\text{fʒii} &= 2 \times 60 \text{ ℳ} &= \underline{120 \text{ ℳ}} \\
& & 1560 \text{ ℳ, } total. \\
\,^{1560}\!/_{15} \text{ doses} & &= 104 \text{ doses, } answer.
\end{aligned}
$$

Relationship Between Avoirdupois and Apothecaries' Weights

As noted previously, the *grain* is the same in both the avoirdupois and apothecaries' systems of weight, but other denominations with the same names are not equal.

To convert from either system to the other, first reduce the given quantity to grains in the one system, and then reduce to any desired denomination in the other system.

The custom of buying chemicals by avoirdupois weight and compounding prescriptions by apothecaries' weight leads to problems, many of which can be most conveniently solved by proportion.

Example Calculations Involving the Avoirdupois System

Convert ʒ̅ii ʒii to avoirdupois weight.

$$
\begin{aligned}
\text{ʒ̅ii} &= 2 \times 480 \text{ gr} &= 960 \text{ gr} \\
\text{ʒii} &= 2 \times 60 \text{ gr} &= \underline{120 \text{ gr}} \\
\text{Total:} & & 1080 \text{ gr}
\end{aligned}
$$

$$
1 \text{ oz} = 437.5 \text{ gr}
$$

$$
\frac{1080}{437.5} \text{ oz} = 2 \text{ oz, 205 gr, } answer.
$$

How many grains of a chemical are left in a 1-oz (avoir.) bottle after ʒvii are dispensed from it?

$$1 \text{ oz} = 1 \times 437.5 \text{ gr} \quad = 437.5 \text{ gr}$$
$$\text{ʒvii} = 7 \times 60 \text{ gr} \quad\quad = 420.0 \text{ gr}$$
$$\text{Difference:} \quad\quad\quad\quad\quad 17.5 \text{ gr, } answer.$$

If a drug costs $8.75 per oz (avoir.), what is the cost of 2 ʒ?

$$1 \text{ oz} = 437.5 \text{ gr, and } 2 \text{ ʒ} = 120 \text{ gr}$$
$$\frac{437.5 \text{ (gr)}}{120 \text{ (gr)}} = \frac{8.75 \text{ (\$)}}{\text{x (\$)}}$$
$$\text{x} = \$2.40, \; answer.$$

Intersystem Conversion

In pharmacy and medicine, the SI currently predominates in use over the common systems. Most prescriptions and medication orders are written in the SI, and labeling on prefabricated pharmaceutical products has drug strengths and dosages described in SI units. Manufacturing formulas are similarly expressed almost exclusively in SI units, replacing use of the common systems of measurement.

On occasion, however, it may be necessary to translate a weight or measurement from units of one system to units of another system. This translation is called **conversion**. The translation of a denomination of one system to that of another system requires a **conversion factor** or **conversion equivalent.**

Table A.1 presents both practical and precise conversion equivalents. In most pharmacy practice applications, the practical equivalents may be used. The precise equivalents show their derivation. *The practical equivalents should be memorized.*

Note that such equivalents may be used in two ways. For example, to convert a number of fluidounces to milliliters, *multiply by 29.57*; to convert a number of milliliters to fluidounces, *divide by 29.57.*

Some individuals prefer to set up a ratio of a known equivalent and solve conversion problems by proportion. For example, in determining the number of milliliters in 8 fluidounces, an equivalent relating *milliliters to fluidounces is selected* (1 fʒ = 29.57 mL) and the problem is solved by proportion as follows:

$$\frac{1 \text{ (fʒ)}}{8 \text{ (fʒ)}} = \frac{29.57 \text{ (mL)}}{\text{x (mL)}}$$
$$\text{x} = 236.56 \text{ mL, } \; answer.$$

In using the ratio and proportion method, the equivalent that contains both the units named in the problem is the best one to use. Sometimes, more than one equivalent may be appropriate. For instance, in converting grams to grains, or vice versa, the gram-to-grain relationship is found in the following basic equivalents, 1 g = 15.432 gr and 1 gr = 0.065 g, as well as in *derived equivalents,* such as 31.1 g = 480 gr and 28.35 g = 437.5 gr. It is best to use the basic equivalents when converting from one system to another and to select the equivalent that provides the answer most readily.

In response to the question, *must we round off results so as to contain no more significant figures than are contained in the conversion factor?*, the answer is *yes*. If we desire greater accuracy, we should use a more accurate conversion factor. But to the question, *If a formula includes the one-figure quantity 5 g, and we convert it to grains, must we round off the result to one significant figure?*, the answer is decidedly *no*. We should interpret the quantity given in a formula as expressing the precision we are expected to achieve in compounding—usually not less than three-figure

TABLE A.1 PRACTICAL AND PRECISE CONVERSION EQUIVALENTS

UNIT	PRACTICAL PHARMACY EQUIVALENT	PRECISE EQUIVALENT[a]	
Conversion Equivalents of Length			
1 m	39.37 in	39.37008	in
1 in	2.54 cm (exact)		
Conversion Equivalents of Volume			
1 mL	16.23 ℳ	16.23073	ℳ
1 ℳ	0.06 mL	0.06161152	mL
1 f℥	3.69 mL	3.696691	mL
1 f℥	29.57 mL	29.57353	mL
1 pt.	473 mL	473.1765	mL
1 gal. (U.S.)[b]	3785 mL	3785.412	mL
Conversion Equivalents of Weight			
1 g	15.432 gr	15.43236	gr
1 kg	2.20 lb (avoir.)	2.204623	lb (avoir.)
1 gr	0.065 g (65 mg)	0.06479891	g
1 oz. (avoir.)	28.35 g	28.349523125	g
1 ℥	31.1 g	31.1034768	g
1 lb (avoir.)	454 g	453.59237	g
1 lb (apoth.)	373 g	373.2417216	g
Other Useful Equivalents			
1 oz. (avoir.)	437.5 gr (exact)		
1 ℥	480 gr (exact)		
1 gal. (U.S.)	128 f℥ (exact)		

[a] Precise equivalents from the National Institute of Standards and Technology. Available at: http://ts.nist.gov/htdocs/200/2002/mpohome.htm. Accessed September 25, 2008.
[b] The U.S. gallon is specified because the British imperial gallon and other counterpart measures differ substantially, as follows: British imperial gallon, 4545 mL; pint, 568.25 mL; f℥, 28.412 mL; f℥, 3.55 mL; and ℳ, 0.059 mL. Note, however, that the SI is used in both the *United States Pharmacopeia* and the *British Pharmacopeia*.

accuracy. Hence, 5 g in a formula or prescription should be interpreted as meaning *5.00 g* or greater precision.

For prescriptions and all other problems stated in the apothecaries' or avoirdupois systems of measurement, it is recommended that all such quantities be converted to equivalent metric quantities before solving in the usual manner described in this text.

Conversion of Linear Quantities

Example Calculations of Linear Conversion

The fiber length of a sample of purified cotton is 6.35 mm. Express the length in inches.

$$6.35 \text{ mm} = 0.635 \text{ cm}$$
$$1 \text{ in} = 2.54 \text{ cm}$$

Solving by proportion:

$$\frac{1 \text{ (in)}}{x \text{ (in)}} = \frac{2.54 \text{ (cm)}}{0.635 \text{ (cm)}}$$
$$x = 0.250 \text{ in, or } \frac{1}{4} \text{ in, } answer.$$

Or, solving by dimensional analysis:

$$6.35 \text{ mm} \times \frac{1 \text{ cm}}{10 \text{ mm}} \times \frac{1 \text{ in}}{2.54 \text{ cm}} = 0.250 \text{ in}, \textit{answer.}$$

A medicinal plaster measures 4½ in. by 6½ in. What are its dimensions in centimeters?

Assuming three-figure precision in the measurement,

$$4\tfrac{1}{2} \text{ or } 4.50 \times 2.54 \text{ cm} \quad = 11.4 \text{ cm wide,}$$
$$6\tfrac{1}{2} \text{ or } 6.50 \times 2.54 \text{ cm} \quad = 16.5 \text{ cm long}, \textit{answers.}$$

Rulers are often calibrated in dual scale.

Conversion of Liquid Quantities

Example Calculations of Fluid Volume Conversions

Convert 0.4 mL to minims.

To achieve two-figure precision,

$$0.40 \times 16.23 \, \text{m} = 6.492 \text{ or } 6.5 \, \text{m}, \textit{answer.}$$

Or, solving by dimensional analysis:

$$0.4 \text{ mL} \times \frac{16.23 \, \text{m}}{1 \text{ mL}} = 6.492 \text{ or } 6.5 \, \text{m}, \textit{answer.}$$

Convert 2.5 L to fluidounces.

$$2.5 \text{ L} = 2500 \text{ mL}$$

Solving by proportion:

$$\frac{1 \, (\text{f}\text{z})}{x \, (\text{f}\text{z})} = \frac{29.57 \, (\text{mL})}{2500 \, (\text{mL})}$$
$$x = 84.5 \, \text{f}\text{z}, \quad \textit{answer.}$$

Or, solving by dimensional analysis:

$$2.5 \text{ L} \times \frac{1000 \text{ mL}}{1 \text{ L}} \times \frac{1 \, \text{f}\text{z}}{29.57 \text{ mL}} = 84.5 \, \text{f}\text{z}, \textit{answer.}$$

Convert 2½ pt. to milliliters.

$$2\tfrac{1}{2} \text{ pt.} = 2\tfrac{1}{2} \times 16 \, \text{f}\text{z} = 40 \, \text{f}\text{z}$$
$$40 \times 29.57 \text{ mL} = 1182.8 \text{ or } 1180 \text{ mL}, \textit{answer.}$$

Or, solving by dimensional analysis:

$$2\tfrac{1}{2} \text{ pt.} \times \frac{16\text{f}\text{z}}{1 \text{ pt}} \times \frac{29.57 \text{ mL}}{1 \, \text{f}\text{z}} = 1182.8 \text{ or } 1180 \text{ mL}, \textit{answer.}$$

Conversion of Weights

Example Calculations of Weight Conversion

Convert 12.5 g to grains.

$$12.5 \times 15.432 \text{ gr} = 192.9 \text{ or } 193 \text{ gr}, \textit{answer.}$$

Alternate solution (about 0.5% less accurate):

$$\frac{12.5}{0.065} \text{ gr } = 192.3 \text{ or } 192 \text{ gr, } answer.$$

Convert 5 mg to grains.

Solving by proportion:

$$\frac{1 \text{ (gr)}}{\text{x (gr)}} = \frac{65 \text{ (mg)}}{5 \text{ (mg)}}$$

$$\text{x} = \frac{5}{65} \text{ gr } = \frac{1}{13} \text{ gr, } answer.$$

Convert 15 kg to avoirdupois pounds.

Solving by proportion:

$$\frac{1 \text{ (kg)}}{15 \text{ (kg)}} = \frac{2.2 \text{ (lb.)}}{\text{x (lb.)}}$$

$$\text{x} = 33.0 \text{ lb., } answer.$$

Convert 6.2 gr to milligrams.

$$6.2 \times 65 \text{ mg } = 403 \text{ or } 400 \text{ mg, } answer.$$

Or, solving by dimensional analysis:

$$6.2 \text{ gr } \times \frac{1 \text{ g}}{15.432 \text{ gr}} \times \frac{1000 \text{ mg}}{1 \text{ g}} = 401.8 \text{ or } 400 \text{ mg, } answer.$$

Convert 176 avoirdupois pounds to kilograms.

$$\frac{176}{2.2} \text{ kg } = 80.0 \text{ kg, } answer.$$

Conversion of Temperatures

In 1709, the German scientist Gabriel Fahrenheit discovered that according to the scale he had marked on a thermometer, ice melted at 32° and water boiled at 212°, a difference of 180 degrees. In 1742, Anders Celsius, a Swedish astronomer, suggested the convenience of a thermometer with a scale having a difference of 100° between two fixed points, with 0° for the freezing point and 100° for the boiling point of water. Thus, the *Fahrenheit* and the *Celsius,* or *centigrade,* thermometers were established.

Because 100 degrees centigrade (°C) measures the same difference in temperature that is measured by 180 degrees Fahrenheit (°F), each degree centigrade is the equivalent of 1.8 or 9/5 the size of each degree Fahrenheit.

There are a number of different arithmetic methods for the conversion of temperatures from the centigrade scale to the Fahrenheit scale and vice versa, as described in an earlier edition of this text.[2] One of these methods, as used in the *United States Pharmacopeia* (USP), is described by the following equations. It should be noted that temperatures in the USP are expressed in degrees centigrade.[3]

$$°F = \frac{9}{5}°C + 32, \text{ and}$$

$$°C = \frac{5}{9} \times (°F - 32)$$

Example Calculations of Temperature Conversions

Convert 26°C to corresponding degrees Fahrenheit.

$$°F = \frac{9}{5}(26°C) + 32 = 78.8° \ F, \ answer.$$

Convert 98.6°F to corresponding degrees centigrade.

$$°C = \frac{5}{9} \times (98.6°F - 32) = 37°C, \ answer.$$

Clinical Aspects of Thermometry

The instrument used to measure body temperature is termed a *clinical* or *fever thermometer.* Traditional clinical thermometers include (1) the *oral thermometer,* slender in the design of stem and bulb reservoir; (2) the *rectal thermometer,* having a blunt, pear-shaped, thick-bulb reservoir for both safety and to ensure retention in the rectum; and (3) a *universal* or *security thermometer,* which is stubby in design, for both oral or rectal use. In addition, *oral electronic digital fever thermometers* and *infrared emission detection (IRED) ear thermometers* are widely used. The oral electronic digital fever thermometer works by the absorption of heat from the point of body contact. Heat causes the expansion and rise of mercury in the thermometer and the response of the thermocouple. The infrared emission detection (IRED) ear thermometer measures heat radiated from the tympanic membrane without actually touching the membrane.

A recent innovation is a thermometry system of *single-use disposable* clinical thermometers that reduce the risk of passing harmful micro-organisms between patients.[4] These disposable thermometers are commercially available in both nonsterile and sterile units. The thermometers use a dot sensor matrix consisting of temperature-sensitive indicating dots. Each dot changes color at a specific temperature relative to the melting point of the specific chemical mixture in the dot. Each dot changes color at a temperature of 0.2°F or 0.1°C higher than the preceding dot. Body temperature is read from a numerical temperature scale. Clinically accurate oral body temperatures are obtained in 60 seconds and axillary temperatures in 3 minutes.

Specialized thermometers include *basal thermometers* and *low-reading thermometers.* The *basal temperature* is the body's normal resting temperature, generally taken immediately on awakening in the morning. In women, body temperature normally rises slightly because of hormonal changes associated with ovulation. Basal thermometers, calibrated in tenths of a degree, are designed to measure these slight changes in temperature. When charted over the course of a month, these changes are useful in assessing optimal times for conception.

Low-reading thermometers are required in diagnosing hypothermia. The standard clinical thermometer reads from 34.4°C (94°F) to 42.2°C (108°F), which is not fully satisfactory for measuring hypothermia, which may involve body temperatures of 35°C (95°F) or lower. A low-reading thermometer registers temperatures between 28.9°C (84°F) and 42.2°C (108°F). Examples of various thermometers are shown in Figure A.1.

In the past, the *normal* body temperature for healthy adults was accepted to be 37°C (98.6°F) based on studies performed over a century ago.[6] The use of advanced electronic digital thermometers, however, has shown that normal adult temperature may vary widely between individuals (from 96.3°F to 99.9°F in one study).[7] Lowest body temperatures generally occur in the early morning and peak high temperatures in the late afternoon, with an average diurnal variation of approximately 0.9°F.

Pharmaceutical Aspects of Temperature

Temperature control is an important consideration in the manufacture, shipping, and storage of pharmaceutical products. Excessive temperature can result in chemical or physical instability of a therapeutic agent or its dosage form. For this reason, the labeling of pharmaceutical products

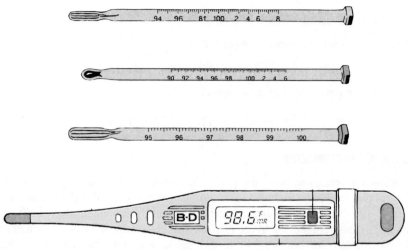

FIGURE A.1 Examples of various clinical thermometers. From top to bottom: oral fever thermometer; rectal thermometer; basal thermometer; oral digital fever thermometer. *(Courtesy of Becton Dickinson and Company.)*

contains information on the appropriate temperature range under which the product should be maintained. The *United States Pharmacopeia* provides the following definitions for the storage of pharmaceuticals.[5]

Freezer – between $-25°C$ and $-10°C$ ($-13°F$ and $14°F$)

Cold – not exceeding $8°C$ ($46°F$)

Refrigerator – between $2°C$ and $8°C$ ($36°F$ and $46°F$)

Cool – between $8°C$ and $15°C$ ($46°F$ and $59°F$)

Warm – between $30°C$ and $40°C$ ($86°F$ and $104°F$)

Excessive Heat – above $40°C$ ($104°F$)

Controlled Room Temperature – between $20°C$ and $25°C$ ($68°F$ and $77°F$)

Alcohol Proof Strength Conversions

Alcohol is commonly employed in the small- and large-scale manufacturing of pharmaceuticals. There are special terms associated with alcohol that require understanding for correct interpretation and conversion.

Proof spirit is an aqueous solution containing 50% v/v of **absolute alcohol** (100% v/v ethyl alcohol). Alcohols of other percentage strengths are said to be *above proof* or *below proof*, depending on whether they contain more or less than 50% v/v of absolute alcohol.

Proof strength is twice the percentage strength of alcohol and thus 50% v/v alcohol is 100 proof. In reverse then, alcohol that is 90 proof is equivalent to 45% v/v alcohol.

Alcohol for manufacturing use may be purchased by the **proof gallon.** A proof gallon is a gallon by measure of proof spirit; that is, a gallon of 100 proof or 50% v/v absolute alcohol.

Example Calculations Involving Proof Strength and Proof Gallons

To calculate the number of proof gallons contained in a given quantity of alcohol of specified strength, observe the following. Because a proof gallon has a percentage strength of 50% (v/v), the equivalent number of proof gallons may be calculated by the formula:

$$\text{Proof gallons} = \frac{\text{gallons} \times \text{Percentage strength of solution}}{50\ (\%)}$$

Because proof strength is twice percentage strength, the formula may be revised as follows:

$$\text{Proof gallons} = \frac{\text{gallons} \times \text{Proof strength of solution}}{100\ (\text{proof})}$$

How many proof gallons are contained in 5 gallons of 75% v/v alcohol?

First method:
1 proof gallon = 1 gallon of 50% v/v strength

$$\frac{5\ (\text{gallons}) \times 75\ (\%)}{50\ (\%)} = 7.5 \text{ proof gallons, } \textit{answer.}$$

Second method:
75% v/v = 150 proof

$$\frac{5\ (\text{gallons}) \times 150\ (\text{proof})}{100\ (\text{proof})} = 7.5 \text{ proof gallons, } \textit{answer.}$$

To calculate the number of gallons of alcohol of specified strength equivalent to a given number of proof gallons, observe the following.

$$\text{gallons} = \frac{\text{Proof gallons} \times 50\ (\%)}{\text{Percentage strength of solution}}$$

or,

$$\text{gallons} = \frac{\text{Proof gallons} \times 100\ (\text{proof})}{\text{Proof strength of solution}}$$

How many gallons of 20% v/v alcohol would be the equivalent of 20 proof gallons?

First method:
1 proof gallon = 1 wine gallon of 50% v/v strength

$$\frac{20\ (\text{proof gallons}) \times 50\ (\%)}{20\ (\%)} = 50 \text{ gallons, } \textit{answer.}$$

Second method:
20% v/v = 40 proof

$$\frac{20\ (\text{proof gallons}) \times 100\ (\text{proof})}{40\ (\text{proof})} = 50 \text{ gallons, } \textit{answer.}$$

To calculate the tax on a given quantity of alcohol of a specified strength, observe the following.

If the tax on alcohol is quoted at $13.50 per proof gallon, how much tax would be collected on 10 gallons of alcohol marked 190 proof?

$$\frac{10\ (\text{gallons}) \times 190\ (\text{proof})}{100\ (\text{proof})} = 19 \text{ proof gallons}$$
$$\$13.50 \times 19\ (\text{proof gallons}) = \$256.50, \textit{answer.}$$

Note: when specific equations, as those described above, are difficult to recall, it is always an option to perform calculations in a stepwise and logical fashion. Although a greater number of steps may be required, the outcome is worth the time.

For example, in the above-stated problem, *"How many proof gallons are contained in 5 gallons of 75% v/v alcohol?"* If one worked logically on the basis of the amount of absolute alcohol in 5 gallons of 75% v/v alcohol, the answer to the problem may be deduced as follows:

5 gallons × 75% v/v = 3.75 gallons of absolute alcohol (100% v/v)

then, it follows that:

3.75 gallons of absolute alcohol × 2 = 7.5 proof gallons, *answer.*

The student may wish to work the same problem in terms of milliliters (3785 mL/gallon) to arrive at the same answer.

PRACTICE PROBLEMS

Calculations of the Avoirdupois and Apothecaries' Systems

1. Reduce each of the following quantities to grains:
   (a) ʒii ϴiss.
   (b) ℥ii ʒiss.
   (c) ℥i ʒss ϴi.
   (d) ʒi ϴi gr x.

2. Reduce 1 pint, f℥ii to fluidrachms.

3. Reduce each of the following quantities to weighable apothecaries' denominations:
   (a) 158 gr
   (b) 175 gr
   (c) 210 gr
   (d) 75 gr
   (e) 96 gr

4. How many f℥ii-bottles of cough syrup can be obtained from 5 gallons of the cough syrup?

5. Low-dose aspirin tablets contain 1¼ grains of aspirin in each tablet. How many tablets can be prepared from 1 avoirdupois pound of aspirin?

6. How many ¼₀₀-gr tablets of nitroglycerin can a manufacturer prepare from a quantity of a trituration of nitroglycerin that contains ⅛ oz of the drug?

Intersystem Conversion Calculations

7. A brand of nitroglycerin transdermal patch measures 2.5 inches in diameter. Express this dimension in centimeters.

8. Urethral suppositories are traditionally prepared to the following lengths: 50 mm for females and 125 mm for males. Convert these dimensions to inches.

9. A pharmacist received a prescription calling for 30 capsules, each to contain ¹⁄₂₀₀ gr of nitroglycerin. How many 0.4-mg nitroglycerin tablets would supply the amount required?

10. If a physician prescribed 4 grams of aspirin to be taken by a patient daily, about how many 5-grain tablets should the patient take each day?

11. ℞   Codeine Sulfate   30 mg
        Acetaminophen   325 mg
        M. ft. cap. D.T.D. no. 24
        Sig. One capsule t.i.d. for pain.

    How many grains each of codeine sulfate and acetaminophen would be contained in the prescription?

12. If a child accidentally swallowed 2 fluidounces of FEOSOL Elixir, containing ⅔ gr of ferrous sulfate per 5 mL, how many milligrams of ferrous sulfate did the child ingest?

13. Sustained-release tablets of nitroglycerin contain the following amounts of drug: $\frac{1}{25}$ gr, $\frac{1}{10}$ gr, and $\frac{1}{50}$ gr. Express these quantities as milligrams.

14. A physician advises an adult patient to take a children's tablet (81 mg of aspirin per tablet) daily as a precaution against a heart attack. Instead, the patient decides to cut 5-gr aspirin tablets into dosage units. How many doses could be obtained from each 5-gr tablet?

15. A hematinic tablet contains 525 mg of ferrous sulfate, which is equivalent to 105 mg of elemental iron. How many grains each of ferrous sulfate and elemental iron would a patient receive from one tablet?

16. The usual dose of colchicine for an acute gout attack is $\frac{1}{120}$ gr every hour for 8 doses. How many milligrams of colchicine are represented in the usual dose?

17. If f$\mathfrak{Z}$i of a cough syrup contains 10 gr of sodium citrate, how many milligrams are contained in 5 mL?

18. A formula for a cough syrup contains $\frac{1}{8}$ gr of codeine phosphate per teaspoonful (5 mL). How many grams of codeine phosphate should be used in preparing 1 pint of the cough syrup?

19. A drug substance has been shown to be embryotoxic in rats at doses of 50 mg/kg/day. Express the dose on the basis of micrograms per pound per day.

20. Tetracycline has been shown to form a calcium complex in bone-forming tissue in infants given oral tetracycline in doses of 0.011 g/lb. of body weight every 6 hours. Express the dose in terms of milligrams per kilogram of body weight.

Temperature Conversions

21. Convert the following from centigrade to Fahrenheit:
    (a) 10°C
    (b) −30°C
    (c) 4°C
    (d) −173°C

22. Convert the following from Fahrenheit to centigrade:
    (a) 77°F
    (b) 240°F
    (c) 98.9°F
    (d) 227.1°F

23. A patient's rectal temperature reading is frequently 1°F higher than the oral temperature reading. Express this difference in degrees centigrade.

24. A woman charting her basal temperature finds that her body temperature on day 14 is 97.7°F and on day 18 is 98.6°F. Express this temperature range and the difference in degrees centigrade.

Proof Strength Conversions

25. If the tax on alcohol is $13.50 per proof gallon, how much tax must be paid on 5 gallons of alcohol, USP, which contains 94.9% v/v of pure alcohol?

26. On the first of the month, a hospital pharmacist had on hand a drum containing 54 gallons of 95% alcohol. During the month, the following amounts were used:
    • 10 gallons in the manufacture of bathing lotion
    • 20 gallons in the manufacture of medicated alcohol
    • 5 gallons in the manufacture of soap solution

    How many proof gallons of alcohol were on hand at the end of the month?

ANSWERS TO PRACTICE PROBLEMS

1. (a) 150 gr
   (b) 1050 gr
   (c) 530 gr
   (d) 90 gr

2. 144 f℈

3. (a) 23 1/23 8 gr, or 23 1℈ 1/2℈ 8 gr
   (b) 23 2℈ 1/2℈ 5 gr, or 23 1/23 1℈ 5 gr
   (c) 23 13 1℈ 1/2 ℈, or 33 1℈ 1/2℈
   (d) 13 1/2℈ 5 gr
   (e) 13 1/23 6 gr, or 13 1℈ 1/2℈ 6 gr

4. 320 tablets

5. 5600 tablets

6. 21,875 tablets

7. 6.35 cm

8. 1.97 in., 4.92 in.

9. 24.4 or 25 tablets

10. 12 tablets

11. 11 7/100 or 11.08 gr of codeine sulfate
    120 gr of acetaminophen

12. 512.55 mg

13. 2.6 mg (1/25 gr)
    6.5 mg (1/10 gr)
    1.3 mg (1/50 gr)

14. 4 doses

15. 8 7/100 or 8.08 gr of ferrous sulfate
    1 62/100 or 1 3/5 or 1.62 gr of elemental iron

16. 0.54 mg

17. 109.9 mg

18. 0.769 g

19. 22,727 μg/lb/day

20. 24.2 mg/kg

21. (a) 50°F
    (b) −22°F
    (c) 39.2°F
    (d) −279.4°F

22. (a) 25°C
    (b) 115.6°C
    (c) 37.2°C
    (d) 108.4°C

23. 0.56°C

24. 36.5° to 37°C
    0.5°C

25. $128.12

26. 361.1 proof gallons

REFERENCES

1. United States Pharmacopeia 31st Rev. National Formulary 26. Rockville, MD: United States Pharmacopeial Convention, 2008;1:13.
2. Ansel HC, Stoklosa MJ. *Pharmaceutical Calculations*. 11th Ed. Baltimore: Lippincott Williams & Wilkins, 2001; 299–304.
3. United States Pharmacopeia 31st Rev. National Formulary 26. Rockville, MD: United States Pharmacopeial Convention, 2008;1:8, 905–906.
4. http://www.3m.com/Product/information/Tempa-DOT-Thermometer.html. Accessed January 11, 2008.
5. The United States Pharmacopeia 31st Rev. National Formulary 26. Rockville, MD: The United States Pharmacopeial Convention, 2008;1:10.
6. Wunderlich CR, Sequin E. *Medical Thermometry and Human Temperature*. New York: William Wood, 1871.
7. Mackowiak PA, Wasserman SS, Levine MM. A critical appraisal of 98.6°F, the upper limit of the normal body temperature and other legacies of Carl Reinhold Wunderlich. *Journal of American Medical Association* 1992;268:1578.

Selected Graphical Methods $\quad$ B

The accurate and effective presentation and interpretation of data are important components of pharmacy and the biomedical sciences. Data obtained from laboratory research, through clinical investigations, and as a result of studies of drug utilization, health care statistics, demographics, and economics are prominently presented in the scientific and professional literature. These data provide the basis for further research and for professional judgment. Therefore, it is important for students in all health professions to become familiar with the various techniques of data presentation and interpretation.

In pharmacy, as in other sciences, the study of the influence of one variable on another is common. Curves, and the equations they represent, give a clear picture of tabulated data and the relationship between variables. Pharmacists are often called on to plot experimental data, interpret graphical material and equations, and manipulate the relationship between curves and their equations.

For simple first-degree equations, in which the variable contains no exponent greater than 1, a straight line will result when the two variables are plotted on rectangular graph paper (rectangular coordinates). Such pharmaceutical phenomena as the influence of temperature on solubility, decomposition of drug suspensions, influence of drug dose on pharmacologic response, and standard assay curves usually give straight-line relationships when plotted on rectangular graph paper.

Exponential or logarithmic relationships are common in pharmaceutical studies. Drug degradation in solution, chemical equilibria, and vapor pressure changes are some examples of exponential phenomena. If a logarithmic or exponential relationship occurs between the two variables, a straight line usually can be obtained by plotting the logarithm of one variable against the other variable or plotting the data on semilogarithmic graph paper.

Linear Relationships on Rectangular Graph Paper

Several straight lines and their corresponding equations on rectangular graph paper are presented in Figure B.1. The plotting of data on rectangular coordinates should be familiar to all students. The horizontal axis is called the X axis, and the magnitude of the independent variable is plotted along this horizontal scale. The other variable, the dependent variable, is measured along the vertical or Y axis. A point on any of the curves in Figure B.1 is defined by two coordinates. The x value, or abscissa, is the distance from the Y axis, and the y value, or ordinate, is the distance from the X axis. By convention, the x value is designated first and the y value second. For example, the point 1, 3 when substituted into the equation $y = -2x + 5$ gives $3 = -2 + 5$ and, as expected, satisfies the equation. The point 0, 4.5 satisfies the equation $y = 4.5$, whereas the point 2.5, 0 satisfies the equation $x = 2.5$ because both of these curves run parallel to the X or Y axis, respectively.

The fundamental algebraic equation that describes first-degree or straight-line equations is:

$$y = mx + b$$

in which m and b are constants. The constant m is the slope of the line. It is a ratio of a change in y with a corresponding change in x and is expressed as $m = \Delta y / \Delta x$. The constant b is the y intercept when $x = 0$ and can usually be determined by extrapolating the straight line to the Y axis.

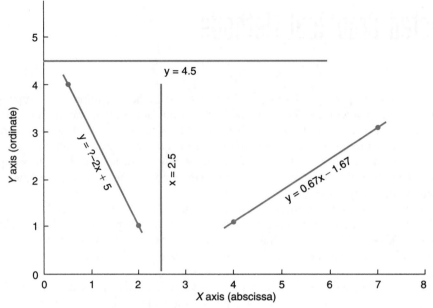

FIGURE B.1 Straight lines and their first-degree equations.

The most convenient equation for determining the equation for the straight line that passes through two given points is the two-point form of the straight line equation,

$$y - y_1 = \frac{y_2 - y_1}{x_2 - x_1} (x - x_1)$$

The results of measuring the ultraviolet absorbance (UV) of various concentrations of drug A and drug B in solutions are shown in Table B.1.

The data of Table B.1 are plotted in Figure B.2, and the results are two straight lines with positive slopes. By selecting two widely separated points (1, 0.1) and (5, 0.5) on the drug A curve and substituting the values into the two-point equation as follows,

$$y - 0.1 = \frac{0.5 - 0.1}{5 - 1} (x - 1)$$

the equation for the straight line becomes

TABLE B.1 DATA FOR ULTRAVIOLET ABSORBANCE OF VARIOUS CONCENTRATIONS OF DRUG

x DRUG CONCENTRATION (µg/mL)	y ABSORBANCE DRUG A	y ABSORBANCE DRUG B
1.0	0.10	0.195
2.0	0.20	0.33
3.0	0.30	0.465
4.0	0.40	0.60
5.0	0.50	—

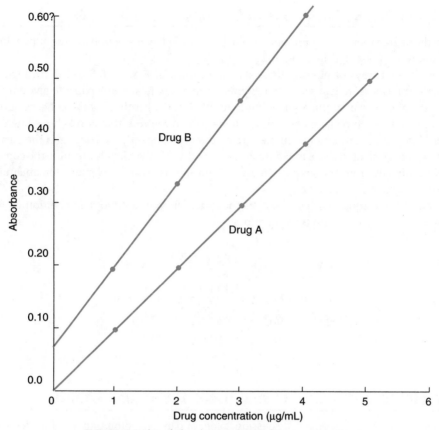

FIGURE B.2 Plot of absorbance against drug concentration.

$$y - 0.1 = \frac{0.4}{4.0}(x - 1)$$
$$y - 0.1 = 0.1(x - 1)$$
$$y - 0.1 = 0.1x - 0.1$$
$$y = 0.1x$$

Because the line passes through the origin, the constant b in the straight line equation is 0.

The equation of the line for drug B is obtained the same way, using the points (1, 0.195) and (4, 0.60) and substituting into the two-point equation to give:

$$y - 0.195 = \frac{0.6 - 0.195}{4 - 1}(x - 1)$$
$$y - 0.195 = \frac{0.405}{3}(x - 1)$$
$$y - 0.195 = 0.135x - 0.135$$
$$y = 0.135x + 0.06$$

This equation can now be used to calculate one variable given a value for the other. For example, what is the concentration of drug B in solution when the absorbance reading is 0.30? Substituting into the equation gives $0.30 = 0.135x + 0.06$ and solving for x gives 1.78 $\mu g/$ mL. The same value can also be determined directly from the curve in Figure B.2.

Linear Relationships on Semilogarithmic Graph Paper

Data for the degradation of an antibiotic in aqueous solution over a period of time at two different temperatures are presented in Table B.2.

Three different ways of plotting these data are shown in Figures B.3 to B.5. In Figure B.3, the experimental measurements are plotted directly on rectangular graph paper to give curvilinear lines typical of exponential phenomena. In Figure B.4, the logarithms of the concentrations are plotted against time on rectangular coordinate paper and the resulting curves are straight lines. In Figure B.5, the concentration values are plotted on semilogarithmic paper and the curves are straight lines equivalent to those in Figure B.4. Figure B.5 is convenient for reading the concentration values directly from the graph, whereas Figure B.4 is more convenient for obtaining the straight-line equation of each curve.

The straight-line equation that describes the degradation of antibiotic in solution at 40°C is determined by using the two-point equation:

$$\log y - \log y_1 = \frac{\log y_2 - \log y_1}{x_2 - x_1}(x - x_1)$$

$$\log y - 1.903 = \frac{1.152 - 1.903}{15 - 0}(x - 0)$$

$$\log y - 1.903 = 0.05x$$

$$\log y = -0.05x + 1.903$$

Other Methods of Data Presentation: Tables and Charts

As demonstrated in the preceding discussion, plots of data are commonly used to describe the relationships between two or more variables. Absolute data often are best presented by *tables,* which indicate the precise values. Others methods of data treatment, such as *histograms, bar charts, and circular* or *pie charts,* effectively illustrate trends represented by the data.[1,2]

Tables are a common and useful means of presenting established data, such as the table of atomic weights (inside back cover), as well as experimental research results, exemplified by Table B.3. When properly constructed with clear column headings, a table provides a quick and

TABLE B.2 DECREASE OF ANTIBIOTIC IN SOLUTION AT 30°C AND 40°C

| TIME (DAYS) | CONCENTRATION (mg/mL) (y) AND LOGARITHM OF CONCENTRATION (LOG y) | | | |
| | AT 30°C | | AT 40°C | |
x	y	LOG y	y	LOG y
0	80.0	1.903	80	1.903
2	72.1	1.858	63	1.799
3	69.0	1.839	56.2	1.750
5	62.0	1.792	44.8	1.651
10	49.0	1.690	25.2	1.401
15	38.5	1.586	14.2	1.152
20	30.5	1.480	—	—
25	24.0	1.380	—	—

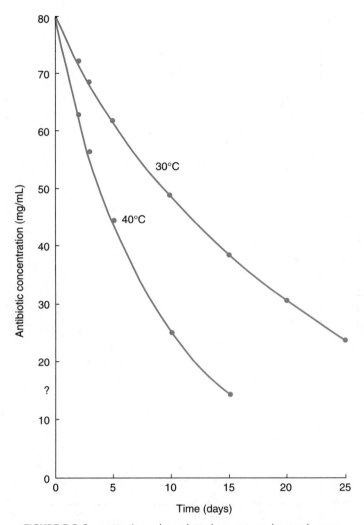

FIGURE B.3 Concentration values plotted on rectangular graph paper.

Figs. B.3–B.5 Show three different ways of plotting the concentration of antibiotic (*y*) as a function of time (*x*).

accurate means of finding the data item desired through right-angle vertical and horizontal locations; for example:

Using Table B.3, determine the C_{max} for subject 1 and the T_{max} for subject 7.
Following the horizontal for subject 1 to the "C_{max}" column, the figure is 2.1 ng/mL, *answer*.
Following the horizontal for subject 7 to the "T_{max}" column, the value is 6.0 hours, *answer*.

Bar graphs are familiar to most persons because they are used widely in professional and lay publications. Bar graphs contain a series of horizontal rectangles with the length of each bar reflecting the quantity of the (usually *different*) item it represents (Fig. B.6). Each bar may be subdivided to identify additional comparisons within the group represented.

In contrast to bar graphs, **column graphs** generally are used to compare the *same* item with bars arranged vertically. By joint-pairing columns (adjoining columns side by side) in the same grouping, two or more items may be compared.

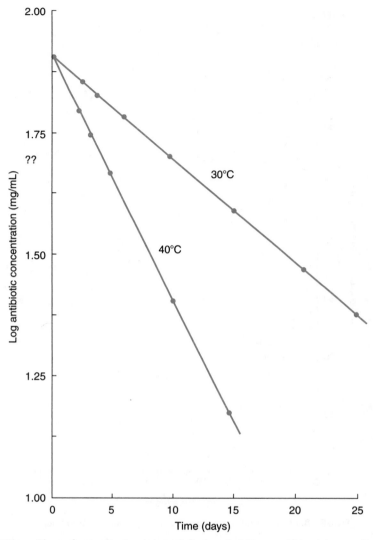

FIGURE B.4 Logarithms of concentration values plotted against time on rectangular coordinate paper.

A *histogram* is a type of graph that defines a frequency distribution.[1] In a histogram, the horizontal scale represents the characteristic or class intervals (as years) being measured, and the vertical scale indicates the corresponding frequency of occurrence (usually a percentage). Histograms are useful in displaying groups of data for the ease of their visual interpretation. In preparing histograms, the rectangles may be of equal or unequal widths, defining the magnitude of the class. When the rectangles are of equal width, the heights of the rectangles are proportional to the frequency—that is, twice the height, twice the frequency. If the rectangles are not of equal width, the heights must be accommodated accordingly (i.e., twice the width, half the height), and it is more difficult to visually interpret the histogram.

Circular charts or *pie charts* are prepared by subdividing a circle into sections by radial lines to indicate the portion of the whole represented by related items. Pie charts are common in the lay press and in scientific and professional literature and should be familiar to most students.

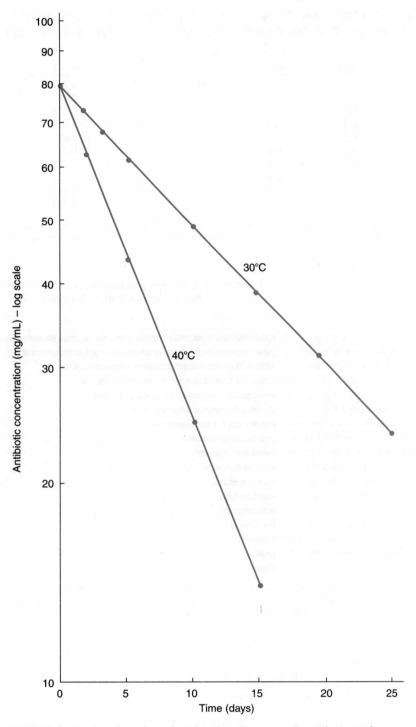

FIGURE B.5 Concentration values plotted against time on semilogarithmic graph paper.

TABLE B.3 NONCOMPARTMENTAL PHARMACOKINETIC PARAMETERS AFTER RECTAL ADMINISTRATION OF DROPERIDOL TO HEALTHY VOLUNTEERS

SUBJECT	C_{max} (ng/ml)	T_{max} (hr)	MAT (hr)	F (%)	K_a (hr^{-1})	AUC_{inf} (ng-hr/ml)
1	2.1	6.0	4.61	65	0.217	42
2	2.0	8.0	3.94	51	0.254	40
3	1.8	10.0	5.84	55	0.171	38
4	2.3	6.0	1.39	38	0.719	31
5	2.3	4.0	2.23	49	0.448	42
6	2.2	10.0	4.53	41	0.221	33
7	1.8	6.0	3.64	38	0.275	32
8	2.7	8.8	4.77	65	0.210	49
Mean	2.1	7.3	3.87	50	0.314	38
SD	0.3	2.3	1.44	11	0.184	6

From Gupta SK. Pharmacokinetics of droperidol in healthy volunteers following intravenous infusion and rectal administration from an osmotic drug delivery module. Pharmaceutical Research. 1992;9:694. With permission.

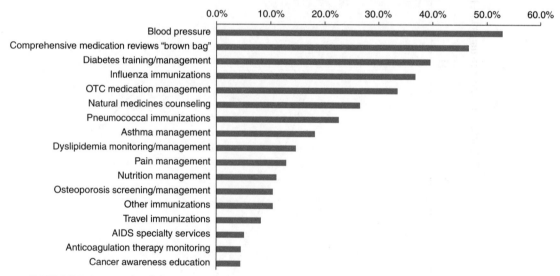

FIGURE B.6 An example of data presentation by bar graph. *(From Peacock G, Kidd R, Rahman A. Patient care services in independent community pharmacies: A descriptive report.* Journal of the American Pharmacists Association *2007;47:762–767. Copyright American Pharmacists Association (APhA). Reprinted by permission of APhA.)*

PRACTICE PROBLEMS

1. In Figure B.1, what is the y intercept for the equation $y = -2x + 5$? For $y = 0.67x - 1.67$?

2. On regular coordinate graph paper, plot the curves for the following equations.
   (a) $y = -4.0 \times 10^{-2}x + 1.5$
   (b) $y = 500x + 3$
   (c) $3y = 9x + 21$

3. A drug suspension containing 250 mg of drug per 5 mL was placed in a 50°C storage oven. Samples were removed periodically and assayed for drug content. The following results were obtained.

Time (days)	5	10	20	30	40	50
Drug Concentration (mg/5 mL)	232	213	175	133	102	65

   (a) Plot the data on rectangular coordinate paper.
   (b) Calculate the straight-line equation.
   (c) What is the concentration after 15 days?
   (d) The rate of decomposition K is equal to the slope of the curve. What is this rate of decomposition?

4. From Figure B.4, calculate the straight-line equation for the degradation of antibiotic solution at 30°C. How much antibiotic would be left in solution after 30 days?

5. An area of a wound was determined every 4 days by drawing the outline of the wound on a sterile sheet of transparent plastic. After applying an antibiotic cream on the initial day (0), the following results were obtained:

Time (days)	0	4	8	12	16	20
Area (cm^2)	60	46.5	36	28	21.5	16.7

   (a) Plot the data on regular coordinate graph paper.
   (b) Plot the data on semilogarithmic graph paper.
   (c) Plot the log area versus time on regular coordinate graph paper.
   (d) Calculate the straight-line equation.
   (e) How much time would elapse before the wound reduced to 50% of the original size? To 5 cm^2?
   (f) If the rate constant of this equation is defined as $k = 2.3\ m$, calculate k.

ANSWERS TO PRACTICE PROBLEMS

1. 5
   -1.67

2. graphs

3. (a) graph
   (b) $y = -3.7x + 250$
   (c) 194.5 mg/5 mL
   (d) -3.7 mg/5 mL/day or -0.74 mg/mL/day

4. log Conc $= -0.021$ time $+ 1.903$
   18.75 mg/mL

5. (a) graph
   (b) graph
   (c) graph
   (d) log $y = -0.028x + 1.78$
   (e) 10.83 or 11 days (50%)
       38.82 or 39 days (5 cm^2)
   (f) 0.064 day^{-1}

REFERENCES

1. Simmonds D, ed. *Charts and Graphs.* Lancaster, England: MTP Press, 1980.
2. Bolton S, Bon C. *Pharmaceutical Statistics: Practical and Clinical Applications.* 4th Ed. New York: Marcel Dekker, 2004.

Glossary of Pharmaceutical Dosage Forms and Drug Delivery Systems[a]

Aerosols

Pharmaceutical aerosols are products packaged under pressure that contain therapeutically active ingredients that are released as a fine mist, spray, or foam on actuation of the valve assembly. Some aerosol emissions are intended to be inhaled deep into the lungs (*inhalation aerosol*), whereas others are intended for topical application to the skin or to mucous membranes. Aerosols with metered valve assemblies permit a specific quantity of emission for dosage regulation.

Aromatic Waters

Aromatic waters are clear, saturated solutions of volatile oils or other aromatic substances in water. They are used orally, topically, or pharmaceutically for the characteristics of the aromatic material they contain.

Boluses

Boluses are large elongated tablets intended for administration to animals.

Capsules

Capsules are solid dosage forms in which one or more medicinal and/or inert substances are enclosed within small shells of gelatin. Capsule shells are produced in varying sizes, shapes, color, and hardness. *Hard-shell* capsules, which have two telescoping parts, are used in the manufacture of most commercial capsule products and in the extemporaneous filling of prescriptions. They are filled with powder mixtures or granules.

Soft-shell gelatin capsules are formed, filled, and sealed in a continuous process by specialized large-scale equipment. They may be filled with powders, semisolids, or liquids.

Capsules contain a specific quantity of fill, with the capsule size selected to accommodate that quantity. In addition to their medication content, capsules usually contain inert substances, such as fillers. When swallowed, the gelatin capsule shell is dissolved by gastrointestinal fluids, releasing the contents.

Delayed-release capsules are prepared in such a manner as to resist the release of the contents until the capsules have passed through the stomach and into the intestines.

Extended-release capsules are prepared in such a manner as to release the medication from the capsules over an extended period following ingestion.

Creams

Creams are semisolid preparations containing one or more drug substances dissolved or dispersed in a suitable base. Many creams are either oil-in-water emulsions or aqueous microcrystalline dispersions in a water-washable base. Compared to ointments, creams are easier to spread and

---

[a] Some portions of this Glossary have been abstracted from the *United States Pharmacopeia 31—National Formulary 26*. Copyright 2008, United States Pharmacopeial Convention, Inc. Permission granted.

remove. Creams are used for administering drugs to the skin and, to a lesser extent, to mucous membranes.

Drug Delivery Systems

Drug delivery systems are physical carriers used to deliver medications to site-specific areas. They include transdermal, ocular, and intrauterine systems.

Transdermal drug delivery systems support the passage of drug substances from the surface of the skin, through its various layers, and into the systemic circulation. These systems are sophisticated skin patches containing a drug formulation within a reservoir for the controlled delivery of drug.

Ocular drug delivery systems consist of drug-impregnated membranes that, when placed in the lower conjunctival sac, release medication over an extended period.

Intrauterine drug delivery systems consist of a drug-containing intrauterine device that releases medication over an extended period after insertion into the uterus.

Elixirs

Elixirs are sweetened, flavored, hydroalcoholic solutions intended for oral administration. They may be medicated or nonmedicated. Compared to syrups, elixirs are usually less sweet and less viscous because they contain a lesser amount of sugar. Because of their hydroalcoholic character, elixirs are better able than are syrups to maintain both water-soluble and alcohol-soluble components in solution.

Emulsions

An emulsion is a type of dispersal system in which one liquid is dispersed throughout another liquid in the form of fine droplets. The two liquids, generally an oil and water, are immiscible and constitute two phases that would separate into layers without the presence of a third agent, an *emulsifier* or *emulsifying agent*. The latter facilitates the emulsification process and provides physical stability to the system.

If oil is the internal phase, then the emulsion is termed an oil-in-water, or o/w, emulsion. If water is the internal phase, then the emulsion is termed a water-in-oil, or w/o, emulsion. The type of emulsion produced is largely determined by the emulsifying agent, with hydrophilic agents generally producing oil-in-water emulsions and lipophilic agents generally producing water-in-oil emulsions. Emulsifying agents may have both hydrophilic and lipophilic characteristics, hence the term hydrophilic-lipophilic balance (HLB).

Depending on their formulation, emulsions may be administered orally, topically, or by intravenous injection.

Extracts

Extracts are concentrated preparations of vegetable or animal drugs prepared by extracting the constituents from the natural source and drying the extractive to the desired pilular or powdered form.

Fluidextracts

Fluidextracts are liquid extractives of vegetable drugs generally prepared such that 1 mL represents the active constituents from 1 g of the vegetable drug.

Gels

Gels are semisolid systems consisting of either suspensions of small inorganic particles or large organic molecules interpenetrated by a liquid.

Implants or Pellets

Implants or pellets are small, sterile, solid dosage forms containing a concentrated drug for subcutaneous implantation in the body where they continuously release their medication over prolonged periods.

Inhalations

Inhalations are finely powdered drug substances, solutions, or suspensions of drug substances administered by the nasal or oral respiratory route for local or systemic effects. Special devices are used to facilitate their administration.

Injections

Injections are sterile preparations intended for parenteral administration by needle or pressure syringe. Drugs may be injected into most any vessel or tissue of the body, but the most common routes are intravenous (IV), intramuscular (IM), and subcutaneous (SC). Injections may be solutions or suspensions of a drug substance in an aqueous or nonaqueous vehicle. They may be small-volume injections, packaged in ampuls for single-dose administration, or vials for multiple-dose injections. Large-volume parenterals, containing 100 mL to 1 liter of fluid, are intended for the slow intravenous administration (or infusion) of medications and/or nutrients in the institutional or home care setting.

Irrigations

Irrigations are sterile solutions intended to bathe or flush open wounds or body cavities. They are not intended for injection.

Liniments

Liniments are alcoholic or oleaginous solutions, suspensions, or emulsions of medicinal agents intended for external application to the skin, generally by rubbing.

Lotions

Lotions are liquid preparations intended for external application to the skin. They are generally suspensions or emulsions of dispersed solid or liquid materials in an aqueous vehicle. Their fluidity allows rapid and uniform application over a wide skin surface. Lotions are intended to soften the skin and leave a thin coat of their components on the skin's surface as they dry.

Lozenges

Lozenges are solid preparations containing one or more medicinal agents in a flavored, sweetened base intended to dissolve or disintegrate slowly in the mouth, releasing medication generally for localized effects.

Magmas

Magmas are pharmaceutical suspensions of fine particles that, because of a high degree of physical attraction to the aqueous vehicle, form a gelatinous mixture. This characteristic maintains the uniformity and stability of the suspension. Magmas are administered orally.

Ointments

Ointments are semisolid preparations intended for topical application to the skin, eye, ear, or various mucous membranes. With some exceptions, ointments are applied for their local effects on the tissue membrane rather than for systemic effects. *Ophthalmic ointments* are sterile preparations intended for application to the eye.

Nonmedicated ointments serve as vehicles, or as *ointment bases*, in the preparation of medicated ointments. Because ointments are semisolid preparations, they are prepared and dispensed on a weight basis.

Pastes

Pastes are semisolid dosage forms that contain one or more drug substances intended for topical application to the skin. Generally, pastes contain a higher proportion of solid materials than do ointments and thus are more stiff, less greasy, and more absorptive of serous secretions.

Plasters

Plasters are solid or semisolid adhesive masses spread across a suitable backing material and intended for external application to a part of the body for protection or for the medicinal benefit of added agents.

Powders

Powders are dry mixtures of finely divided medicinal and nonmedicinal agents intended for internal or external use. Powders may be dispensed in bulk form, or they may be divided into single-dosage units and packaged in folded papers or unit-of-use envelopes.

Premixes

Premixes are mixtures of one or more drug substances with suitable vehicles intended for admixture to animal feedstuffs before administration. They are generally in powdered, pelletized, or granulated form.

Solutions

Solutions are liquid preparations that contain one or more chemical substances (*solutes*) dissolved in a solvent or mixture of solvents. The most common solvent used in pharmaceuticals is water; however, alcohol, glycerin, and propylene glycol also are widely used as solvents or cosolvents.

Depending upon their purpose, solutions are formulated and labeled for use by various routes, including oral, topical, ophthalmic, otic, nasal, rectal, urethral, and parenteral. The concentration of active ingredients in solutions varies widely depending on the nature of the therapeutic agent and its intended use. The concentration of a given solution may be expressed in molar strength, milliequivalent strength, percentage strength, ratio strength, milligrams per milliliter, or another expression describing the amount of active ingredient per unit of volume.

Spirits

Spirits are alcoholic or hydroalcoholic solutions of volatile substances. Depending on their contents, some spirits are used orally for medicinal purposes and others as flavoring agents.

Suppositories

Suppositories are solid dosage forms intended for insertion into body orifices. They are used rectally, vaginally, and, occasionally, urethrally. Suppositories are of various weights, sizes, and shapes, depending on their intended use. Various types of *suppository bases* are used as vehicles for the medication, including cocoa butter (theobroma oil), glycerinated gelatin, polyethylene glycols, hydrogenated vegetable oils, and fatty acid esters of polyethylene glycol. Depending on the base used, the suppository either softens, melts, or dissolves after insertion, releasing its medication for the intended local action or for absorption and systemic effects.

Suspensions

Suspensions are preparations containing finely divided, undissolved drug particles dispersed throughout a liquid vehicle. Because the drug particles are not dissolved, suspensions assume a degree of opacity depending on the concentration and size of the suspended particles. Because particles tend to settle when left standing, suspensions should be shaken to redistribute any settled particles before use to ensure uniform dosing. Depending on their formulation, suspensions are administered orally, by intramuscular injection, and topically to the eye.

Syrups

Syrups are concentrated aqueous solutions of a sugar or sugar substitute. Syrups may be medicated or nonmedicated. *Nonmedicated syrups* are used as vehicles for medicinal substances to be added later, either in the extemporaneous compounding of prescriptions or in the preparation

TABLE C.1 ROUTES OF DRUG ADMINISTRATION AND PRIMARY DOSAGE FORMS AND DRUG DELIVERY SYSTEMS

ROUTE	SITE	DOSAGE FORMS/DRUG DELIVERY SYSTEMS
Oral	Mouth	Tablets, capsules, oral solutions, drops, syrups, elixirs, suspensions, magmas, gels, powders, troches and lozenges (oral cavity)
Sublingual	Under the tongue	Tablets
Parenteral		Solutions, suspensions
Intravenous	Vein	
Intra-arterial	Artery	
Intracardiac	Heart	
Intraspinal/Intrathecal	Spine	
Intraosseous	Bone	
Intra-articular	Joint	
Intrasynovial	Joint fluid	
Intracutaneous/Intradermal/ Subcutaneous	Skin	
Intramuscular	Muscle	
Epicutaneous	Skin surface	Ointments, creams, pastes, plasters, powders, aerosols, lotions, transdermal patches, solutions (topical)
Conjunctival	Eye conjunctiva	Ointments
Intraocular	Eye	Solutions, suspensions
Intranasal	Nose	Solutions, ointments
Aural	Ear	Solutions and suspensions (drops)
Intrarespiratory	Lung	Solutions (aerosols)
Rectal	Rectum	Solutions, ointments, suppositories
Vaginal	Vagina	Solutions, ointments, emulsion foams, gels, tablets/inserts
Urethral	Urethra	Solutions and suppositories

of a formula for a medicated syrup. In addition to the sugar or sweetener, syrups also contain flavoring agents, colorants, cosolvents, and antimicrobial preservatives to prevent microbial growth. Syrups are administered orally for the therapeutic value of the medicinal agent(s).

Tablets

Tablets are solid dosage forms containing one or more medicinal substances. Most tablets also contain added pharmaceutical ingredients, as diluents, disintegrants, colorants, binders, solubilizers, and coatings. Tablets may be coated for appearance, for stability, to mask the taste of the medication, or to provide controlled drug release. Most tablets are manufactured on an industrial scale by compression, using highly sophisticated machinery. Punches and dies of various shapes and sizes enable the preparation of a wide variety of tablets of distinctive shapes, sizes, and surface markings.

Most tablets are intended to be swallowed whole. However, some are prepared to be chewable, others to be dissolved in the mouth (*buccal tablets*) or under the tongue (*sublingual tablets*), and still others to be dissolved in water before taking (*effervescent tablets*). Tablets are formulated to contain a specific quantity of medication. To enable flexibility in dosing, manufacturers commonly make available various tablet strengths of a given medication. Some tablets are scored, or grooved, to permit breaking into portions that the patient can take.

Tinctures

Tinctures are alcoholic or hydroalcoholic solutions of either pure chemical substances or of plant extractives. Most chemical tinctures are applied topically (e.g., iodine tincture). Plant extractives are used for their content of active pharmacologic agents.

Review Problems

A. Fundamental Systems and Methods of Pharmaceutical Calculations

Weighing Accuracy

1. What is the least amount that should be weighed on Class A prescription balances with the following ensitivity requirements (SRs) and maximum errors:
   (a) SR 5 mg; error NMT 5%
   (b) SR 6 mg; error NMT 5%
   (c) SR 7 mg; error NMT 4%

2. Calculate the percentage error in the following weighings:
   (a) 6 mg in 120 mg weighing
   (b) 10 mg in 115 mg weighing

3. ℞   Drug A   0.5 mg
       Lactose   300   mg
       M.ft. such caps # 12

   Using a torsion prescription balance with a sensitivity requirement of 6 mg, explain how to obtain the correct amount of drug A with an error not greater than 5%.

International System of Units and Intersystem Conversions

4. Perform the following equivalencies:
   (a) 5 mg/dL = _____ mcg/mL
   (b) 40 mg/kg = _____ mg/lb
   (c) 0.04 μg/μL = _____ mg/mL
   (d) 500 g = _____ kg
   (e) 12 f℥ = _____ mL
   (f) 1½pt. = _____ mL
   (g) 40°F = _____ °C

5. How many grams of levothyroxine sodium (SYNTHROID) would a manufacturing pharmacist need to manufacture a batch of 250,000 tablets, each containing 25 mcg of the drug?

6. A certain injectable solution contains 30 mg of a drug substance in 30 mL. How many milliliters of the solution would provide 100 μg of the drug substance?

7. How many grams of codeine phosphate are left in an original 5-g bottle after the amount required to prepare 100 capsules, each containing 15 mg of codeine phosphate, is used?

8. BONIVA (ibandronate sodium) tablets are available in 2.5-mg and 150-mg strengths. The 2.5-mg tablets are taken daily whereas the 150-mg tablets are taken once per month. Calculate the difference in the quantity of drug taken during a 30-day month.
   (a) 37.5 mg
   (b) 0.075 g
   (c) 137.5 mg
   (d) 0.15 g

9. Premature octuplets born in 1998 ranged in weight from the smallest, 10.3 ounces, to the largest, 1 pound 9.7 ounces. Convert these weights to grams.

10. If 240 mL of a cough syrup contain 0.6 g of diphenhydramine hydrochloride, which of the following strengths is correct?
    (a) 0.025 g/100 mL
    (b) 2500 mcg/mL
    (c) 0.74 g/fl oz
    (d) 1.25 mg/tsp

11. If 30 mL of an injection containing metoclopramide (REGLAN), 5 mg/mL, are used to prepare 50 mL of an intravenous infusion, calculate the concentration of metoclopramide, on a mg/mL basis, in the infusion.

12. The fatal dose of cocaine has been approximated at 1.2 g for a 150-lb. person. Express this effect on an mg/kg basis.

13. If a patient is determined to have 100 mg blood glucose/100 mL of blood, what is the equivalent concentration in terms of mg/dL?

14. Calculate the difference, in μg/mL, between two injections, each containing filgrastim (NEUPOGEN), one at 0.3 mg/0.5 mL and the other 480 μg/0.8 mL.

15. ASTELIN nasal spray contains 0.1% w/v of azelastine hydrochloride. A container is capable of delivering 200 metered sprays of 0.137 mL each. How much azelastine hydrochloride would be contained in each spray?
    (a) 137 mcg
    (b) 13.7 mg
    (c) 0.00137 g
    (d) 1.37 mg

16. Using the above problem data, how much nasal spray would be contained in the package?
    (a) 27.4 mL
    (b) 20 mL
    (c) 1 fl oz
    (d) 0.75 fl oz

17. LANTUS contains 100 international units of insulin glargine, equivalent to 3.6378 mg per milliliter of injection. How many milligrams of insulin glargine would be present in each 0.8 mL of injection?

Specific Gravity

18. Calculate the following specific gravities:
    (a) 120 mL weigh 112 g
    (b) 96 mL weigh 104 g
    (c) 5 L of a syrup weighing 6.565 kg

19. Calculate the following weights:
    (a) 400 mL with a specific gravity of 1.25
    (b) 1 pint with a specific gravity of 0.90

20. Calculate the following volumes:
    (a) 30 g with a specific gravity of 0.90
    (b) 1 oz with a specific gravity of 1.11

21. A saturated solution contains, in each 100 mL, 100 g of a substance. If the solubility of the substance is 1 g in 0.7 mL of water, what is the specific gravity of the saturated solution?
    (a) 0.7
    (b) 1.0
    (c) 1.43
    (d) 1.7

Percentage Strength and Ratio Strength Expressions of Concentration

22. Calculate the percentage strength of the following:
    (a) 1 mg in 1 g
    (b) 2 mcg in 50 mg
    (c) 0.25 g in 60 mL
    (d) 10 mg in 5 mL
    (e) 1:5000 w/v solution

23. Calculate the ratio strength of the following:
    (a) 1 mg in 1 g
    (b) 2 mcg in 50 mg
    (c) 0.0025% v/v

24. Filgrastim (NEUPOGEN) prefilled syringes contain 480 mcg of drug in 0.8 mL of injection. Calculate the percentage of filgrastim in the injection.

25. Ipratropium bromide (ATROVENT) inhalation solution contains 0.02% w/v of drug per 2.5 mL. Calculate the equivalent concentration.
    (a) 2 mg/mL
    (b) 1 mg/5 mL
    (c) 100 mcg/0.5 mL
    (d) 20 mg/2.5 mL

26. How many grams of active ingredient are present in a 60-g tube of a 0.005% w/w fluticasone propionate (CUTIVATE) ointment?

27. If a solution contains 157 μg of fentanyl citrate in each 100 mL, calculate its percentage concentration.

28. If 78 mL of a 20% w/v solution of the surfactant PLURONIC F 127 are used in preparing 100 mL of a product, calculate the percentage strength of the surfactant in the final product.

29. Mesalamine rectal suspension contains 4 g of mesalamine in each 60 mL of suspension. Calculate its percentage concentration.

30. If a 0.5-mL vial of levalbuterol hydrochloride (XOPENEX) contains the equivalent of 1.25 mg of levalbuterol, calculate its percentage concentration.

31. If 15 g of a 5% w/w acyclovir ointment are used in preparing 60 g of a compound ointment, calculate the resultant concentration of acyclovir in the final product.

32. If an ophthalmic solution contains 0.02% w/v of mitomycin, how many milligrams of the drug were used in preparing each 100 mL of solution?

33. ZYMAR Ophthalmic Drops contain 0.3% w/v gatifloxacin. How many micrograms of the drug would be administered per drop from a dropper delivering 20 drops/mL?

34. How many milligrams of moxifloxacin (VIGAMOX) would be contained in a 3-mL container of a 0.5% w/v solution of the drug?

35. TRAVATAN Ophthalmic Solution contains 0.004% w/v of the drug travoprost and 0.015% w/v of the preservative benzalkonium chloride. Calculate (a) the micrograms of each agent in a 2.5-mL container and (b) the ratio strength of the benzalkonium chloride.

36. Ipratropium bromide (ATROVENT) nasal spray packages contain 0.03% w/v drug in a 30-mL container and 0.06% w/v drug in a 15-mL container. Calculate the difference in the milligrams of drug present in the two packages.

37. If a solution of potassium permanganate is prepared by dissolving sixteen 0.2-g tablets in enough purified water to make 1600 mL, calculate (a) the percentage strength and (b) the ratio strength of the solution.

38. Calculate the percentage strength of misoprostol in the formula[1]:
    Misoprostol   400 µg
    Polyethylene Oxide   200 mg
    Hydroxypropyl Methylcellulose ad   15 g

39. The cancer chemotherapy drug doxorubicin is available as an injection (2 mg/mL), which is diluted in 250 mL of 0.9% sodium chloride injection for intravenous infusion. For a particular patient, a dose of 16 mg of drug is to be infused. The concentration of doxorubicin in the infusion is:
    (a) 6.2%
    (b) 6.4%
    (c) 0.0062%
    (d) 0.0064%

40. If the herb Saint John's wort contains 0.3% w/w of pharmacologically active constituent, how many milligrams of active constituent would 900 mg of the herb provide?

41. Insulin injection is preserved with 0.25% w/v of metacresol. (a) Express this concentration as a ratio strength, and (b) calculate the quantity, in milligrams, of metacresol in a 20-mL vial of the injection.

Milliequivalents, Millimoles, and Milliosmoles

42. Express a patient's cholesterol level of 175 mg/dL in terms of millimoles per liter.

43. How many milliosmoles of sodium chloride are represented in 1 liter of a 3% w/v hypertonic sodium chloride solution? Assume complete dissociation.

44. It is estimated that an adult with an average daily diet has a sodium chloride intake of 15 g per day. (a) How many milliequivalents of sodium and (b) how many millimoles of sodium chloride are represented in the daily salt intake?

45. What is the percentage concentration (w/v) of a solution containing 100 mEq of ammonium chloride per liter?

46. One liter of blood plasma contains 5 mEq of Ca^{++}. How many millimoles of calcium are represented in this concentration?

47. One hundred milliliters of blood plasma normally contains 3 mg of Mg^{++}. Express this concentration in milliequivalents per liter.

48. How many milliequivalents of potassium are in each 10 mL of a 5% w/v solution of potassium chloride?

49. Calculate the milliosmoles per liter of a sodium chloride solution containing 2.5 mEq of sodium chloride per milliliter.

Chemical and Physical Calculations

50. Calculate (a) the concentration of fentanyl (m.w. 336) on a μg/mL basis in a solution containing 0.007% w/v fentanyl citrate (m.w. 528) and (b) the milligrams of erythromycin ethylsuccinate (m.w. 862) needed to provide 400 mg of erythromycin base (m.w. 734).

51. Sodium phosphates oral solution contains, in each 100 mL, 18 g of dibasic sodium phosphate ($Na_2HPO_4A7H_2O$, m.w. 268) and 48 g of monobasic sodium phosphate ($NaH_2PO_4AH_2O$, m.w. 138). How many grams of dried dibasic sodium phosphate (Na_2PO_4, m.w. 142) and of anhydrous monobasic sodium phosphate (NaH_2PO_4, m.w. 120) should be used in preparing 1 gallon of the solution?

52. The dissociation constant of benzoic acid is 6.30×10^{-5}. Calculate its pK_a.

53. Calculate the pH of a buffer solution containing 0.8 mol of sodium acetate and 0.5 mol of acetic acid per liter. The pK_a value of acetic acid is 4.76.

54. What molar ratio of sodium acetate to acetic acid is required to prepare an acetate buffer solution with a pH of 5.0? The K_a value of acetic acid is 1.75×10^{-5}.

55. Calculate the molar ratio of dibasic sodium phosphate and monobasic sodium phosphate required to prepare a buffer system with a pH of 7.9. The pK_a value of monobasic sodium phosphate is 7.21.

56. What molar ratio of sodium borate to boric acid should be used in preparing a borate buffer with a pH of 8.8? The K_a value of boric acid is 6.4×10^{-10}.

57. Calculate the half-life (years) of ^{60}Co that has a disintegration constant of 0.01096 month^{-1}.

58. A sodium iodide I 131 solution has a labeled activity of 1 mCi/mL as of noon on November 17. How many milliliters of the solution should be administered at noon on December 1 to provide an activity of 250 μCi? The half-life of ^{131}I is 8.08 days.

59. Sodium phosphate P 32 solution is used intravenously in tumor localization in a dose range of 250 μCi to 1 mCi. Express this dose range of radioactivity in megabecquerel units.

60. A commercial product of thallous chloride Tl 291 contains 244.2 MBq of radioactivity. Express this radioactivity in terms of millicuries.

B. Prescriptions, Formulations, and Compounding Calculations

Interpreting Prescription Notations and Prescription Calculations

61. Interpret the following prescription and medication order notations:
    (a) tab ii stat; i q4h prn pain
    (b) cap i w/gl H_2O qd AM for CHD
    (c) Sig. ʒii qid
    (d) 20 mg/kg postop; rep q6h prn
    (e) 50,000 IU in 500 mL D5W IV drip over 8 h

62. Identify any errors in the calculations for each of the following prescriptions and, when incorrect, correct the arithmetic error:

 (a) ℞ Allopurinol   20 mg/mL
      Cherry Syrup   60 mL
      Methylcellulose Suspension ad   120 mL
      Sig. Take one teaspoonful daily in AM.

   Having no allopurinol powder, the pharmacist used eight 300-mg tablets of allopurinol in compounding this prescription.

 (b) ℞ Triamcinolone Acetonide Cream 0.1%
      Aquaphor Unibase aa   30 g
      M. ft. ungt.
      Sig. Apply to affected area on skin t.i.d.

   The pharmacist used 15 g of a 0.1% triamcinolone acetonide cream and 15g of Aquaphor Unibase in compounding this prescription.

 (c) ℞ Ephedrine Sulfate   0.4% w/v
      Benzocaine   1:1000 w/v
      Cocoa Butter ad   2 g
      M. ft. suppos. DTD no. 24
      Sig. Insert one rectal suppository each night at bedtime.

   In compounding this prescription, the pharmacist calculated for two extra suppositories to account for unavoidable loss in compounding (correct) and used a 10% w/w benzocaine ointment as the source of the benzocaine. Calculations then showed that 208 mg of ephedrine sulfate and 0.52 g of the benzocaine ointment would supply the proper amounts of these ingredients.

 (d) ℞ Epinephrine   1 % w/v
      Chlorobutanol   0.5% w/v
      Sodium Chloride, q.s.
      Sterile Water for Injection ad   15 mL
      Make isotonic sol.
      Sig. Two drops in each eye at h.s.

   The pharmacist calculated the need for 273 mg of epinephrine bitartrate (m.w. 333) to obtain the equivalent of epinephrine (m.w. 183), 75 mg of chlorobutanol, and 58 mg of sodium chloride to preparing this prescription.

 (e) ℞ Potassium Permanganate, q.s.
      Purified Water ad   500 mL
      M.ft. solution. 5 mL added to a quart of water equals a 1:8000 solution
      Sig. Add one teaspoonful to a quart of warm water and soak toe as directed.

   The pharmacist used 59 0.2-g tablets of potassium permanganate in compounding this prescription.

63. Identify and correct any errors in the corresponding prescriptions or labels for the following:

 (a) Patient: John Smith   Weight: 165 lb.
     Rx: ZITHROMAX
        Disp: caps # 16
     Sig: caps ii stat; cap i qAM with food × 4 days

     Label: Joan Smith
            ZITHROMAX
            Take 2 capsules to start, then take 1 capsule every morning for 4 days.

(b) Patient: Bob James   Weight 180 lb.
  Rx: Lisinopril 20 mg
     Disp: 30 tabs
  Sig: tab i s.i.d

  Label: Bob James
        Lisinopril 20 mg
        Sig: Take 1 tablet several times a day.

(c) Patient: Mary Jones   Weight 132 lb.
  Rx: LEUKERAN   0.1 mg/kg/day
     Disp: 2 mg tabs # 50
  Sig: Take _____ tablet(s) every day × 21 days

  Label: Mary Jones
        LEUKERAN 2 mg tablets
        Sig: Take 3 tablets daily for 21 days

(d) Patient: Sara Smith   Height, 5′2″; Weight 108 lb.
  Rx: Dexamethasone
     Dose @ 20 mg/m²/day
     Disp: 5-mg tablets
  Sig: take _____ tablets daily for treatment cycle on days 1,2,3,4,9,10,11

  Label: Sara Smith
        Dexamethasone 5-mg tablets
        Take 6 tablets daily for treatment cycle on days 1,2,3,4 and then on days 9, 10, and 11.

64. ℞   Cyanocobalamin   10 μg per mL
     Disp. 10-mL sterile vial.
     Sig. 1.5 mL every other week

(a) How many micrograms of cyanocobalamin will be administered over 12 weeks?
(b) How many milligrams of cyanocobalamin are in 10 mL of this preparation?

65. ℞   Clindamycin Phosphate   0.6 g
     Propylene Glycol   6   mL
     Purified Water   8   mL
     Isopropyl Alcohol ad   60   mL
     Sig. Apply b.i.d.

(a) How many capsules, each containing 150 mg of clindamycin phosphate, should be used in preparing the prescription?
(b) What is the percentage concentration of clindamycin phosphate in the prescription?

66. ℞   Codeine Sulfate   15 mg/tsp
     ROBITUSSIN ad   120 mL
     Sig. Two (2) teaspoonfuls q6h for cough.

  How many 30-mg tablets of codeine sulfate should be used in preparing the prescription?

67. ℞   Hydrocortisone   1.5%
     Neomycin Ointment
     Emulsion Base aa ad   30 g
     Sig. Apply.

  If the hydrocortisone is available in the form of 20-mg scored tablets, how many tablets should be used to obtain the hydrocortisone needed in preparing the prescription?

68. ℞   Penicillin G Potassium   10,000 units per mL
        Isotonic Sodium Chloride Solution ad   15 mL
        Sig. For the nose. Store in the refrigerator.

    Only soluble penicillin tablets, each containing 400,000 units of penicillin G potassium, are available. Explain how to obtain the penicillin G potassium needed to prepare the prescription.

69. ℞   Dextromethorphan   15 mg/5 mL
        Guaifenesin Syrup ad   240 mL
        Sig. 5 mL q4h p.r.n. cough.

    How many milligrams of dextromethorphan should be used in preparing the prescription?

70. ℞²   Noscapine   0.72 g
        Guaifenesin   4.8 g
        Alcohol   15   mL
        Cherry Syrup ad   120 mL
        Sig. 5 mL t.i.d. p.r.n. cough.

    How many milligrams each of noscapine and guaifenesin would be contained in each dose?

71. ℞²   Cisapride   1 mg/mL
        OraSweet   ad   120 mL

    (a) How many 10-mg tablets of cisapride may be used in compounding the prescription?
    (b) What is the percentage concentration of cisapride in the prescription?

72. A commercial vial contains 20 million units of penicillin. The label directions state that when 32.4 mL of sterile water for injection are added, an injection containing 500,000 units of penicillin per milliliter results. If a physician prescribes 1 million units of penicillin per milliliter, how many milliliters of sterile water for injection should be used to prepare the product?

73. A physician prescribes 1.6 million units of penicillin G potassium daily for 7 days. If 1 mg of penicillin G potassium is equal to 1595 penicillin G units, how many 250-mg tablets of penicillin G potassium should be dispensed for the prescribed dosage regimen?

74. Rabies vaccine contains 1.25 international units per 0.5 mL. The postexposure dose is 2.5 international units administered the day of the exposure and an additional 2.5 international units on days 3, 7, 14, and 28 after exposure. How many milliliters of vaccine are needed for the full course of treatment?
    (a) 2.5 mL
    (b) 5 mL
    (c) 4 mL
    (d) 12.5 mL

75. If a physician prescribed penicillin V potassium, 500 mg q.i.d. for 10 days, how many milliliters of a suspension containing 500 mg of penicillin V potassium per 5 mL should be dispensed?

Formula and Admixture Calculations

76. The following is a formula for a diltiazem hydrochloride topical gel[3]:

Diltiazem Hydrochloride	2 g
Propylene Glycol	10 mL
Hydroxyethylcellulose	2 g
Preserved Water qs ad	100 mL

    If the specific gravity of propylene glycol is 1.04, how many grams of this agent may be used in the formula?

77. The following is a formula for a clotrimazole and gentamicin sulfate otic liquid[2]:

Clotrimazole	1 g
Gentamicin Sulfate	300 mg
Polyethylene Glycol ad	100 mL

    If the product is to be administered by drop, calculate the amount of gentamicin sulfate present in two drops from a dropper service delivering 20 drops/mL.
    (a) 3 mg
    (b) 30 μg
    (c) 0.03 mg
    (d) 300 mcg

78. The following is a formula for a miconazole and tolnaftate topical liquid[2]:

Miconazole	2% w/v
Tolnaftate	1 g
Polyethylene Glycol 300 qs ad	100 mL

    How many grams each of (a) miconazole and (b) tolnaftate would be needed to prepare 1.5 L of the formulation?

79. The following is a formula for 30 antiemetic suppositories[4]:

Metoclopramide Hydrochloride	1.2 g
Haloperidol, powder	30 mg
Lorazepam	30 mg
Benztropine	30 mg
FATTIBASE	56 g

    If, in compounding the formula, 30 1-mg lorazepam tablets, each weighing 200 mg, and 15 benztropine 2-mg tablets, each weighing 180 mg, are used as the sources of the two components, how much would each suppository weigh?

80. The following is a formula for acyclovir and chlorhexidine gel[4]:

Acyclovir	1 g
Chlorhexidine Digluconate	200 mg
Hydroxypropyl Methylcellulose	300 mg
Propylene Glycol	1 mL
Preserved Water ad	10 g

    How many milliliters of a 20% w/v aqueous solution of chlorhexidine digluconate may be used in the formula?

81. The following is a formula for a dexamethasone topical cream:[4]

Dexamethasone	0.1% w/w
Hydrophilic Ointment	qs 100 g

    If dexamethasone sodium phosphate (m.w. 516.41) rather than dexamethasone (m.w. 392.47) were used to prepare the formula, how many milligrams would be required?

82. The following is a formula for one sertraline hydrochloride capsule[5]:
    Sertraline Hydrochloride   75 mg
    Silica Gel   0.15 g
    Calcium Citrate   0.1 g

    Calculate the quantities of each ingredient required to manufacture 100,000 such capsules.

83. The following is a formula for one verapamil hydrochloride suppository[4]:
    Verapamil Hydrochloride   40 mg
    Base:
    Polyethylene Glycol 1450   65% w/w
    Polyethylene Glycol 6000   28% w/w
    Purified Water   7% w/w

    Calculate the quantities of each ingredient required for the preparation of 48 suppositories, each with 2 g of base.

84. The following is a formula for an interferon ophthalmic solution[6]:
    Interferon alpha-2a   100 million units
    Ammonium Acetate   7.7 mg
    Benzyl Alcohol   100   mg
    Human Albumin   10   mg
    Sterile Water for Injection ad   10   mL

    Interferon alpha-2a is available in vials containing 18 million units or 66.7 μg in 3 mL of solution. Calculate (a) the milliliters of this solution required to prepare the prescription and (b) the number of micrograms and units of interferon alpha-2a in each 0.05 mL of the filled prescription.

85. Coal Tar   10 g
    Polysorbate 80   5 g
    Zinc Oxide Paste   985 g

    Calculate the quantity of each ingredient required to prepare 10 lb. of the ointment.

86. Menthol   0.2 g
    Hexachlorophene   0.1 g
    Glycerin   10   mL
    Isopropyl Alcohol   35   mL
    Purified Water ad   100   mL

    Calculate the quantity of each ingredient required to prepare 1 gallon of the lotion.

87. Set up a formula for 5 lb. of glycerogelatin containing 10 parts by weight of zinc oxide, 15 parts by weight of gelatin, 40 parts by weight of glycerin, and 35 parts by weight of water.

88. The following formula for glycerin suppositories is sufficient to prepare 50 suppositories. Calculate the amount of each ingredient needed to prepare 300 suppositories.
    Glycerin   91 g
    Sodium Stearate   9 g
    Purified Water   5 g

89. The formula for a potassium chloride elixir is as follows:
    Potassium Chloride   5 mEq/tsp
    Elixir Base   q.s.

    How many grams of potassium chloride are needed to prepare 5 gallons of the elixir?

90. A vitamin liquid contains, in each 0.5 mL, the following:

Thiamine Hydrochloride	1 mg
Riboflavin	400 μg
Ascorbic Acid	50 mg
Nicotinamide	2 mg

    Calculate the quantity, expressed in grams, of each ingredient in 30 mL of the liquid.

91. A formula for 200 g of an ointment contains 10 g of glycerin. How many milliliters of glycerin, with a specific gravity of 1.25, should be used in preparing 1 lb. of the ointment?

92. Furosemide injection contains 10 mg of furosemide in each milliliter, packaged in prefilled 2-mL syringes. Calculate the amount, in grams, of furosemide required to manufacture 4000 such syringes.

93. How many milliliters of a 2.5% w/v solution of a drug and how many milliliters of water are required to prepare 500 mL of a 0.3% w/v solution of the drug?

94.
Triethanolamine	100 g
Purified Water ad	100 mL

    Triethanolamine is a liquid with a specific gravity of 1.25. Calculate (a) the milliliters of triethanolamine needed to prepare the formula, (b) the percentage strength of triethanolamine in the formula on a v/v basis, and (c) the percentage strength of triethanolamine in the formula on a w/w basis (assume no contraction of volume on mixing the liquids).

95. How many fluidounces of a commercially available 17% w/v solution of benzalkonium chloride should be used to prepare 1 gallon of a 1:750 w/v solution?

96. How many grams of lidocaine should be added to 1 lb. of a 1% lidocaine w/w ointment to increase the strength to 2% w/w?

97. How many grams of benzethonium chloride and how many milliliters of 95% v/v alcohol should be used in preparing 1 gallon of a 1:1000 solution of benzethonium chloride in 70% v/v alcohol?

98. How many grams of talc should be added to 1 lb. of a powder containing 20 g of zinc undecylenate per 100 g to reduce the concentration of zinc undecylenate to 3% w/w?

99. How many milliliters of 36% w/w hydrochloric acid, with a specific gravity of 1.18, are required to prepare 5 gallons of 10% w/v hydrochloric acid?

100. A formula for an ophthalmic solution calls for 500 mL of a 0.02% w/v solution of benzalkonium chloride. How many milliliters of a 1:750 w/v solution should be used to obtain the amount of benzalkonium chloride needed in preparing the ophthalmic solution?

101. How many milliliters of each of two liquids with specific gravities of 0.950 and 0.875 should be used to prepare 12 liters of a liquid with a specific gravity of 0.925?

102. A medication order calls for triamcinolone acetonide suspension to be diluted with normal saline solution to provide 3 mg/mL of triamcinolone acetonide for injection into a lesion. If each 5 mL of the suspension contains 125 mg of triamcinolone acetonide, how many milliliters should be used to prepare 10 mL of the prescribed dilution?

103. If a dry powder mixture of the antibiotic amoxicillin is diluted with water to 80 mL by a pharmacist to prepare a prescription containing 125 mg of amoxicillin per 5 mL, (a) how many grams of amoxicillin are in the dry mixture, and (b) what is the percentage strength of amoxicillin in the prepared prescription?

104. If 3 mL of diluent are added to a vial containing 1 g of a drug for injection, resulting in a final volume of 3.4 mL, what is the concentration, in milligrams per milliliter, of the drug in the injectable solution?

105. A medication order calls for the addition of 25 mEq of sodium bicarbonate to a hyperalimentation formula. How many milliliters of an 8.4% w/v solution should be added to the hyperalimentation formula? (You have on hand a 50-mL ampul of 8.4% w/v sodium bicarbonate solution.)

106. How many grams of calcium chloride ($CaCl_2 \cdot 2H_2O$, m.w. 147) are required to prepare half a liter of a solution containing 5 mEq of calcium chloride per milliliter?

107. A hospital medication order calls for the addition of 20 mEq of sodium chloride to a liter of mannitol injection. How many milliliters of a 14.5% w/v sodium chloride additive solution should be used?

C. Dosage Calculations and Other Patient/Clinical Parameters

Dosage Calculations Based on Weight

108. The initial dose of a drug is 0.25 mg/kg of body weight. How many milligrams should be prescribed for a person weighing 154 lb.?

109. If a dosage table for a prefabricated drug product indicates the dose for a patient weighing 110 lb. is 0.4 mg/kg of body weight, taken three times a day for 10 days, how many 10-mg tablets of the product should be dispensed?

110. The child's dose of gentamicin for a urinary tract infection is 1 mg/kg administered every 8 hours for 10 days. What would be (a) the single dose and (b) the total dose for a 15-year-old child weighing 110 lb.?

111. The maintenance dose of oxtriphylline (CHOLEDYL) is 13.2 mg/kg/day or 800 mg, whichever is less, in q.i.d. dosing. How many 100-mg tablets of the drug should a 200-lb. patient take at each dosing interval?

112. A medication order calls for 6 μg/kg of body weight of pentagastrin to be administered subcutaneously to a patient weighing 154 lb. The source of the drug is an ampul containing 0.5 mg in each 2 mL of the solution. How many milliliters of the solution should be injected?

113. The rectal dose of sodium thiopental is 45 mg/kg of body weight. How many milliliters of a 10% w/v solution should be used for a person weighing 150 lb.?

114. How many capsules, each containing 250 mg of drug, are needed to provide 25 mg/kg per day for 1 week for a person weighing 175 lb.?

115. The dose of a drug is 50 mg/kg of body weight once daily for seven consecutive days. How many milliliters of a syrup containing 500 mg of drug per teaspoonful should be prescribed for a child weighing 66 lb.?

116. A physician prescribed 5 mg of a drug per kilogram of body weight once daily for a patient weighing 132 lb. How many 100-mg tablets of the drug are required for a dosage regimen of 2 weeks?

117. If the loading dose of kanamycin is 7 mg/kg of body weight, how many grams should be administered to a patient weighing 165 lb.?

118. A medication order calls for 0.1 mg/kg of albuterol sulfate to be administered to a 23-lb. child. The source of the drug is a solution containing 0.5 g of albuterol sulfate in 100 mL. How many milliliters of the solution should be used in filling the order?

119. If the recommended dose of gentamicin sulfate for a patient with normal kidney function is 3 mg/kg/day, divided into three equal doses given every 8 hours, how many milligrams should be administered per dose to a patient weighing 182 lb.?

120. Plasma protein fraction (PPF) is available as a 5% w/v solution. If the dose of the solution for a child is given as 5 mL/lb., how many grams of PPF should be administered to a child weighing 20 kg?

121. The loading dose of DILANTIN in children is 20 mg/kg administered at an infusion rate of 0.5 mg/kg/min.
    (a) What would be the dose for a child weighing 32 lb.?
    (b) Over what period should the dose be administered?

122. If two patients, each weighing 110 lb., were given the drug amikacin sulfate, one at a regimen of 7.5 mg/kg every 12 hours and the other at 5 mg/kg every 8 hours, what is the difference in the total quantity of drug administered over a 24-hour period?

123. The loading dose of theophylline for a child is 5 mg/kg of body weight. For each milligram per kilogram of theophylline administered, the serum theophylline concentration increases by approximately 2 μg/mL. (a) Calculate the loading dose for a child weighing 44 lb., and (b) determine the approximate serum theophylline concentration.

Dosage Calculations Based on Body Surface Area

124. Using the equation in Chapter 8 for the determination of body surface area (BSA), calculate the BSA for a patient 6 feet in height and weighing 185 lb.

125. The dose of a drug is 15 mg/m^2 b.i.d. for 1 week. How many milligrams of the drug would be required for a full course of therapy for a child 42 in tall and weighing 50 lb.?

126. The dose of methotrexate for meningeal leukemia in children is 12 mg/m^2 by the intrathecal route. Calculate the dose, in milligrams, for a child 28 in. tall and weighing 52 lb.

127. The usual pediatric dose of a drug is 300 mg/m^2. Using the nomogram in Chapter 8, calculate the dose for a child weighing 20 kg and measuring 90 cm in height.

128. If the dose of a drug is 17.5 mg/m^2/day, how many milligrams of the drug should be administered daily to a patient weighing 65 lb. and measuring 3 ft 6 in in height?

129. If the intravenous pediatric dose of dactinomycin is 2.5 mg/m^2/week, how many micrograms of the drug will a child having a BSA of 0.50 m^2 average per day of therapy?

130. The drug cyclophosphamide is administered for breast cancer at a daily dose of 100 mg/m^2 for up to 14 consecutive days. What would be the total quantity administered over the 2-week period for a patient measuring 5 ft 2 in in height and weighing 102 lb.?

131. The following is a 28-day cycle of a GC regimen for treating advanced non-small-cell lung cancer[7]:
    Gemcitabine 1,000 mg/m^2 IV, D-1, 8,15
    Cisplatin 100 mg/m^2 IV, D-1 *or* 2 *or* 15
    Calculate the total quantity each of gemcitabine and cisplatin administered over the course of a single cycle to a patient determined to have a BSA of 1.6 m^2.

132. The following drugs are administered for metastatic colon cancer over a 4-week period, with the cycle repeating every 6 weeks[8]:
Irinotecan 125 mg/m² IV, D-1, 8,15, 22
Fluorouracil 500 mg/m² IV, D-1, 8,15, 22
Leucovorin 20 mg/m² IV, D-1, 8, 15, 22

If irinotecan is available in an injection containing 20 mg/mL, and fluorouracil is available in an injection containing 50 mg/mL, how many milliliters of each of the two injections would be used during a treatment cycle for a patient determined to have a BSA of 1.7 m²?

133. Granulocyte macrophage colony stimulating factor (GM-CSF) is available as a lyophilized powder for injection in 250- and 500-µg vials. A dosage regimen is 250 µg/m²/day intravenously over a 4-hour period.[9]
     (a) What would be the daily dose for a patient with a BSA of 1.59 m²?
     (b) What would be the final drug concentration in µg/mL if the dose in (a) is diluted to 50 mL with 0.9% sodium chloride solution?
     (c) How many milligrams of human albumin should be added prior to diluting with the 0.9% w/v sodium chloride solution to achieve a concentration of 0.1% w/v human albumin in the 50-mL injection?
     (d) How many milliliters of 5% w/v human albumin can provide the required amount in (c)?

134. An anticancer drug is available in 30-mg vials costing $147 each. What would be the drug cost of administering 135 mg/m² once every 3 weeks during a 9-week period to a 1.9-m² patient?

135. From the information in Chapter 14, calculate the estimated daily water requirement for a healthy adult with a BSA of 1.75 m².

136. The pediatric dose of a drug may be determined on the basis of (a) 8 mg/kg of body weight or (b) a pediatric dose of 250 mg/m². Calculate the dose on each basis for a child weighing 44 lb. and measuring 36 in in height.

137. The pediatric dose of acyclovir for aplastic anemia is given as 15 mg/kg/day for 10 days. Using the nomogram in Chapter 8, give the corresponding dose on a mg/m² basis for a child measuring 55 cm in height and weighing 10 kg.

138. Using Table 18.1, calculate the dose of a drug for a cat weighing 6.6 lb. if the drug is administered at 2 mg/m².

Intravenous Infusions and Infusion Rate Calculations

139. From Table 13.3, determine the infusion delivery rate, in mL/hr, for a patient weighing 72.5 kg and scheduled to receive the drug at 9 mcg/kg/min.

140. A hospital pharmacy has available 2-mL prefilled syringes containing 80 mg of tobramycin and 1.5-mL prefilled syringes containing 60 mg of tobramycin. The syringes are calibrated in 0.25-mL units. Explain how you would prepare a medication order calling for 110 mg of tobramycin to be added to 100 mL of D5W for intravenous infusion.

141. Using prefilled tobramycin syringes as described in the preceding problem and with a minimum of waste, explain how you would prepare a medication order calling for three piggyback infusions, each containing 110 mg of tobramycin in 100 mL of D5W.

142. A liter of an intravenous solution of potassium chloride is to be administered over 5 hours, and the dropper in the venoclysis set calibrates 25 drops/mL. What is the required rate of flow in drops per minute?

143. A large-volume parenteral fluid contains 20 mg of a drug per liter. If the desired drug delivery rate is 1 mg per hour, and the venoclysis set calibrates 25 drops/mL, what should be the rate of flow in drops per minute?

144. A physician prescribes a 5-μg/kg/min IV drip of dopamine for a 175-lb. patient, and the pharmacist adds an ampul of dopamine (200 mg/5 mL) to a 250-mL bottle of D5W. What drip rate should be run, in drops per minute, using a minidrip set that delivers 60 drops/mL?

145. A medication order calls for 1 liter of a TPN solution to be administered over 6 hours. If the venoclysis set calibrates 20 drops/mL, at what rate of flow, in drops per minute, should the set be adjusted to administer the solution in the designated interval?

146. A medication order calls for 20 mEq of potassium chloride in 500 mL of D5W/0.45 NSS to be administered at the rate of 125 mL per hour. If the intravenous set is calibrated at 12 drops/mL, what should be the infusion rate in drops per minute?

147. The intravenous dose of ondansetron is three 0.15-mg/kg doses infused over 15 minutes.[10]
    (a) What would be the initial dose for a patient weighing 134 lb.?
    (b) If the dose is diluted to 50 mL with 5% dextrose, what flow rate, in mL/hr, would be needed to administer the dose over 15 minutes?
    (c) What flow rate, in drops/minute, would be needed using an infusion set that delivers 20 drops/mL?

148. A drug is administered intravenously at a loading dose of 50 μg/kg over 10 minutes, followed by continuous intravenous infusion of 0.375 μg/kg/minute.
    (a) How many micrograms of the drug would be administered to a 160-lb. patient in the first hour of therapy?
    (b) If the drug is available in 10-mL vials containing the drug in a concentration of 1 mg/mL, how many vials would be needed for 4 hours of therapy?

149. A certain hyperalimentation solution contains 600 mL of a 5% w/v protein hydrolysate, 400 mL of 50% w/v dextrose injection, 35 mL of a 20% w/v sterile potassium chloride solution, 100 mL of sodium chloride injection, and 10 mL of a 10% calcium gluconate injection. The solution is to be administered over 6 hours. If the dropper in the venoclysis set calibrates 20 drops/mL, at what rate, in drops per minute, should the flow be adjusted to administer the solution during the designated interval?

150. A solution prepared by dissolving 500,000 units of polymyxin B sulfate in 10 mL of water for injection is added to 250 mL of 5% dextrose injection. The infusion is to be administered over 2 hours. If the dropper in the venoclysis set calibrates 25 drops/mL, at what rate, in drops per minute, should the flow be adjusted to administer the total volume over the designated interval?

151. A physician orders an intravenous solution to contain 10,000 units of heparin in 1 liter of 5% w/v dextrose solution to be infused at such a rate that the patient will receive 500 units per hour. If the intravenous set delivers 10 drops/mL, how many drops per minute should be infused to deliver the desired dose?

152. A certain hyperalimentation solution measures 1 liter. If the solution is to be administered over 6 hours and the administration set is calibrated at 25 drops/mL, at what rate should the set be adjusted to administer the solution during the designated interval?

153. If, in the previous problem, the patient was to receive nitroglycerin at the rate of 5 μg per minute, at how many milliliters per hour should the infusion pump be set to deliver this dose?

154. If an infusion pump system is calibrated to deliver 15 microdrops per minute, equivalent to a delivery rate of 15 mL per hour, how many microdrops would be delivered per milliliter by the system?

155. A nitroglycerin concentrate solution contains 5 mg of nitroglycerin in each milliliter. A 10-mL ampul of the concentrate is added to 500 mL of D5W and infused into a patient at a flow rate of 3 microdrops per minute. If the infusion pump system delivers 60 microdrops/mL, how many micrograms of nitroglycerin would the patient receive in the first hour of therapy?

156. The drug alprostadil is administered to infants by intravenous infusion following dilution in dextrose injection. If one ampul, containing 500 μg of alprostadil, is added to the indicated volume of dextrose injection, complete the table by calculating (a) the approximate concentration of the resulting solutions and (b) the infusion rates needed to provide 0.1 μg/kg/min of alprostadil.

500 μg Added to mL of Dextrose Injection	Approximate Concentration of Resulting Solution (μg/mL)	Infusion Rate (mL/kg/min)
250	_____	_____
100	_____	_____
50	_____	_____
25	_____	_____

Body Mass Index and Nutrition Calculations

157. Using the Harris-Benedict equation in Chapter 14 and assuming no stress factor, calculate (a) the daily calories required and (b) the daily protein needed for a 69-year-old male who is 5 ft. 9 in. tall and weighs 165 lb.

158. Using the formula in Chapter 14, calculate the body mass index for a person 5 ft 4 in tall and weighing 140 lb.

159. How many food calories would be provided by a daily diet of 50 grams of fat, 600 grams of carbohydrate, and 120 grams of protein?

160. A hyperalimentation solution includes 500 mL of D5W. If each gram of dextrose supplies 3.4 kcal, how many kilocalories would the hyperalimentation solution provide?

Other Dosage and Clinical Calculations

161. Calculate the creatinine clearance for a 30-year-old male patient weighing 80 kg with a serum creatinine of 2 mg/dL.

162. If 150 mg of a drug are administered intravenously and the resultant drug plasma concentration is determined to be 30 μg/mL, calculate the apparent volume of distribution.

163. In a neonatal intensive care unit, a 7.4-mg loading dose of aminophylline was ordered for a premature infant. Instead, by a tragic and fatal error, 7.4 mL of a 250-mg/10 mL solution were administered.[11] How many milligrams of aminophylline were administered rather than the prescribed amount?

164. The epidural dose of morphine sulfate should not exceed 10 mg/24 hours. A pharmacist needs to set up a patient-controlled analgesia epidural infusion that allows a patient to self-administer a dose every 30 minutes.[10]
    (a) If a solution with a morphine sulfate concentration of 0.5 mg/mL is used, what would be the maximum volume administered per dose that would not exceed 10 mg/24 hours?
    (b) How many days would a 50-mL cassette of the 0.5-mg/mL solution last a patient who administers the maximum dose?

165. A study of vancomycin dosing in neonates shows that average peak serum vancomycin concentrations of 30 μg/mL are achieved following doses of 10 mg/kg of body weight. On this basis, what would be the expected serum concentration of the drug if a 2500-g child received 20 mg of vancomycin?

166. Captopril is prescribed for an 11-pound dog at a dose of 1 mg/kg. How many drops of a suspension containing 50 mg/mL should be administered if a dropper delivers 20 drops/mL?

D. Miscellaneous Calculations

167. From Figure 7.2, determine the duration (number of hours) that the serum concentration of a hypothetic drug is at or above its minimum effective concentration.

168. Cefuroxime axetil for oral suspension should be constituted at the time of dispensing and stored in a refrigerator for maximum stability. If stored at room temperature, however, the half-life of the drug is only 10 days. If the original concentration of the constituted suspension was 250 mg/5 mL, how much cefuroxime axetil will remain per 5 mL after storage at room temperature for 25 days?

169. A transdermal patch contains 24.3 mg of testosterone and releases the drug at a rate of 5 mg/24 hours. The patch is intended to be worn for 24 hours, then removed and replaced by a new patch.
    (a) How many milligrams of testosterone would be released from the patch in 2 hours?
    (b) What percentage of total drug would have been released on removal of the patch?
    (c) Assuming that all the drug would be released from the patch at a constant rate, how many hours would it take for the patch to be exhausted of drug?

170. The AUC for an oral dose of a drug is 4.5 μg/mL/hr and for an IV dose is 11.2 μg/mL/hr. What is the bioavailability of an oral dose of the drug?[12]

171. The half-life of warfarin is 1 to 2.5 days. What is the elimination rate constant?[12]

172. The elimination rate constant for a drug is 0.58 hour^{-1}. What is its half-life?[12]

173. The drug ranibizumab (LUCENTIS) is administered by intravitreal injection in treating age-related macular degeneration. The recommended dose is 0.5 mg once a month for the first four treatments then an injection once every 3 months. The 0.2-mL vial for injection contains ranibizumab, 10 mg/mL. How many milliliters of injection should be administered per dose?

174. The antineoplastic drug decitabine is supplied in single-dose vials containing 50 mg of dry powdered drug. Immediately prior to use, the drug is reconstituted with 10 mL of sterile water for injection and then further diluted with 0.9% sodium chloride injection to a final drug concentration of 0.1 to 1 mg/mL for intravenous infusion. For the latter concentration, what would be the final volume of the infusion fluid?
    (a) 40 mL
    (b) 50 mL
    (c) 490 mL
    (d) 500 mL

175. If, in problem 174, the dose is 15 mg/m^2 and a drug concentration of 0.1 mg/mL is to be administered by continuous intravenous infusion over a 3-hour period, what should be the flow rate in mL/min for a patient with a BSA of 1.85 m^2?

176. If, in problem 175, the drop set used delivered 15 drops/mL, what should be the flow rate in drops/minute?

177. If the chemotherapy drug vinblastine is prescribed for intravenous administration at a dose of 4 mg/m^2, to be administered on days 1, 8, 15, 22, 29, and 36, what would be the (a) total dose per cycle for a patient with a BSA of 1.65 m^2 and (b) what would be the total dose per cycle on a mg/m^2 basis for that patient?

178. The anticancer drug mephalan may be administered orally at a dose of 8 mg/m^2 on days 1, 2, 3, and 4 during a 4-week cycle, or, intravenously at a dose of 15 mg/m^2 on day 1 of a 4-week cycle. Calculate the difference in total dose between the regimens on a mg/m^2 basis.

179. The starting pediatric dose of valsartan (DIOVAN) is 1.3 mg/kg once daily to a maximum of 40 mg. On this basis, what would be the weight, in pounds, of a pediatric patient who received the maximum starting dose?

E. Physicians' Medication Orders

180. Medication Order: Sirolimus Oral Solution (RAPAMUNE), 1 mg/m^2/d
    Available: sirolimus, 1 mg/mL oral solution with oral syringe
    Question: mL daily dose, patient, BSA 1.25 m^2?

181. Medication Order: Cefixime, 8 mg/kg/d in two divided doses
    Available: cefixime oral suspension, 75 mL; cefixime, 200 mg/5 mL
    Question: mL dose, 36-lb. child?

182. Medication Order: Heparin, 15 units/kg/h
    Preparation: 25,000 heparin units in 500-mL normal saline solution
    Question: mL/h infusion rate, 187-lb. patient?

183. Medication Order: Zidovudine (RETROVIR) 160 mg/m^2 q8h
    Available: RETROVIR Syrup, 50 mg zidovudine/5 mL
    Question: dose, mL, 12-year-old child, BSA 1.46 m^2?

184. Medication Order: Bevacizumab (AVASTIN), 5 mg/kg
    Preparation: 16 mL vial (25 mg/mL), in sodium chloride injection to 100-mL
    Question (a): mL infusion, 135-lb. patient?
    Question (b): 30-minute infusion rate, mL/min?

185. Medication Order: Lidocaine, 2 mcg/kg/min
     Available: lidocaine, 1 g in 500 mL infusion
     Question: flow-rate, mL/hr, 142-lb. patient?

186. Medication Order: IV chlorothiazide sodium (IV SODIUM DIURIL), administer 500 mg
     Available: reconstituted solution, chlorothiazide sodium, 28 mg/mL
     Question: mL, dose?

187. Medication Order: D5W by infusion, 100 mL/hr
     Administration Set: 15 drops/mL
     Question: infusion rate, drops/minute?

188. Medication Order: Augmentin, 45 mg q12h
     Available: reconstituted oral suspension, 125 mg/5 mL
     Question: mL, dose?

189. Medication Order: 1.5% hydrocortisone cream, 30 g
     Available: 1% hydrocortisone cream and hydrocortisone powder
     Question: grams each of hydrocortisone cream and hydrocortisone powder to use?

Answers to Review Problems

1. (a) 100 mg
   (b) 120 mg
   (c) 175 mg

2. (a) 5%
   (b) 8.7%

3. LWQ = 120 mg
   0.5 mg × 12 (caps) = 6 mg drug A needed
   6 mg × 20 (factor) = 120 mg drug A
   weigh 120 mg drug A
   dilute with 2280 mg lactose
   weigh 120 mg of the 2400 mg mixture

4. (a) 50 mcg/mL
   (b) 18.2 mg/lb
   (c) 0.04 mg/mL
   (d) 0.5 kg
   (e) 354.84 mL
   (f) 709.5 mL
   (g) 4.44°C

5. 6.25 g levothyroxine sodium

6. 0.1 mL

7. 3.5 g codeine phosphate

8. (b) 0.075 g ibandronate sodium

9. 292.01 g, 728.59 g

10. (b) 2500 mcg/mL

11. 3 mg/mL metoclopramide

12. 17.6 mg/kg cocaine

13. 100 mg/dL

14. zero

15. (a) 137 mcg azelastine hydrochloride

16. (a) 27.4 mL

17. 2.9102 mg insulin glargine

18. (a) 0.93
    (b) 1.08
    (c) 1.31

19. (a) 500 g
    (b) 425.7 g

20. (a) 33.33 mL
    (b) 25.54 mL

21. (d) 1.7

22. (a) 0.1% w/w
    (b) 0.004 % w/w
    (c) 0.42% w/v
    (d) 0.2% w/v
    (e) 0.02% w/v

23. (a) 1:1000 w/w
    (b) 1:25,000 w/w
    (c) 1:40,000 v/v

24. 0.6% filgrastim

25. (b) 1 mg/5 mL ipratropium bromide

26. 0.003 g fluticasone propionate

27. 0.000157% w/v fentanyl citrate

28. 15.6% w/v PLURONIC F 127

29. 6.67% w/v mesalamine

30. 0.25% w/v levalbuterol hydrochloride

31. 1.25% w/w acyclovir

32. 20 mg mitomycin

33. 150 mcg gatifloxacin

34. 15 mg moxifloxacin

35. (a) 100 mcg travoprost
        375 mcg benzalkonium chloride
    (b) 1.6667 w/v benzalkonium chloride

36. zero

37. (a) 0.2% w/v potassium permanganate
    (b) 1:500 w/v potassium permanganate

38. 0.0027% w/v misoprostol

39. (c) 0.0062%

40. 2.7 mg active constituent

41. (a) 1:400 w/v metacresol
    (b) 50 mg metacresol

42. 4.52 mmol/L cholesterol

43. 1025.64 mOsmol sodium chloride

44. (a) 256.41 mEq sodium
    (b) 256.41 mOsmol sodium chloride

45. 0.54% w/v ammonium chloride

46. 2.5 mmol calcium

47. 2.47 mEq magnesium

48. 6.71 mEq potassium

49. 5000 mOsmol sodium chloride

50. (a) 44.5 μg/mL fentanyl
    (b) 469.75 mg erythromycin ethylsuccinate

51. 360.99 g dibasic sodium phosphate
    1579.83 g monobasic sodium phosphate

52. 4.2

53. 4.96

54. 1.7:1

55. 4.9:1

56. 0.4:1

57. 5.27 years

58. 0.83 mL sodium iodide I 131 solution

59. 9.25 to 37 MBq

60. 6.6 mCi

61. (a) Take 2 tablets to start, then 1 tablet every 4 hours as needed for pain.
    (b) Take 1 capsule with a glass of water every morning for congestive heart disease.
    (c) Take 2 teaspoonfuls 4 times a day.
    (d) Give 20 mg per kilogram postoperatively. Repeat every 6 hours if there is need.
    (e) 50,000 international units in 500 mL of dextrose 5% in water. Administer by intravenous drip over 8 hours.

62. (a) correct
    (b) incorrect; use 30 g of each
    (c) correct
    (d) incorrect quantity of sodium chloride; use 67.86 mg
    (e) correct

63. (a) patient's name incorrect on label; drug strength missing; "with food" missing on label; incorrect number of capsules prescribed
    (b) s.i.d. means "once a day"
    (c) insufficient number of tablets prescribed; 63 tablets needed
    (d) correct

64. (a) 90 mcg
    (b) 0.1 mg

65. (a) 4 capsules clindamycin phosphate
    (b) 1% w/v clindamycin phosphate

66. 12 tablets codeine sulfate

67. 22.5 tablets hydrocortisone

68. 3/8 tablet needed; dissolve 1 tablet in enough isotonic sodium chloride solution to make 8 mL, and use 3 mL of the solution

69. 720 mg dextromethorphan

70. 30 mg noscapine
    200 mg guaifenesin

71. (a) 12 tablets cisapride
    (b) 0.1% w/v

72. 12.4 mL sterile water for injection

73. 128 tablets

74. (b) 5 mL rabies vaccine

75. 200 mL penicillin V potassium suspension

76. 10.4 g propylene glycol

77. (d) 300 mcg gentamicin sulfate

78. (a) 30 g miconazole
    (b) 15 g tolnaftate

79. 2.198 or 2.2 g

80. 1 mL chlorhexidine digluconate solution

81. 131.58 mg dexamethasone sodium phosphate

82. 7.5 kg sertraline hydrochloride
    15 kg silica gel
    10 kg calcium citrate

83. 1.92 g verapamil hydrochloride
    62.4 g polyethylene glycol 1450
    26.88 g polyethylene glycol 6000
    6.72 g purified water

84. (a) 16.67 mL interferon solution
    (b) 1.85 μg and 500,000 Units interferon

85. 45.4 g coal tar
    22.7 g polysorbate 80
    4471.9 g zinc oxide paste

86. 7.57 g menthol
    3.785 g hexachlorophene
    378.5 mL glycerin
    1324 mL isopropyl alcohol
    ad 3785 with purified water

87. 227 g zinc oxide
    340.5 g gelatin
    908 g glycerin
    795 g water

88. 546 g glycerin
    54 g sodium stearate
    30 g purified water

89. 1409.91 g potassium chloride

90. 0.06 g thiamine hydrochloride
    0.024 g riboflavin
    3 g ascorbic acid
    0.12 g nicotinamide

91. 18.16 mL glycerin

92. 80 g furosemide

93. 60 mL drug solution
    440 mL water

94. (a) 80 mL triethanolamine
    (b) 80% v/v triethanolamine
    (c) 83.3% w/w triethanolamine

95. 1 fluidounce benzalkonium chloride solution

96. 4.633 g lidocaine

97. 3.785 g benzethonium chloride
    2788.95 mL alcohol

98. 2572.7 g talc

99. 4455 mL hydrochloric acid, 36% w/w

100. 75 mL benzalkonium chloride solution

101. 8000 mL (sp gr 0.95) and 4000 mL (sp gr 0.875)

102. 1.2 mL triamcinolone acetonide suspension

103. (a) 2 g amoxicillin
     (b) 2.5% w/v amoxicillin

104. 294.12 mg/mL

105. 25 mL sodium bicarbonate solution

106. 183.75 g calcium chloride

107. 8.07 mL sodium chloride solution

108. 17.5 mg

109. 60 tablets

110. (a) 50 mg gentamicin
     (b) 1500 mg gentamicin

111. 2 tablets oxtriphylline

112. 1.68 mL pentagastrin solution

113. 30.68 mL or 31 mL sodium thiopental

114. 56 capsules

115. 105 mL

116. 42 tablets

117. 0.525 g kanamycin

118. 0.21 mL albuterol sulfate solution

119. 82.73 mg gentamicin sulfate

120. 11 g PPF

121. (a) 290.9 mg or 291 mg DILANTIN
     (b) 40 minutes

122. zero

123. (a) 100 mg theophylline
     (b) 10 μg/mL theophylline

124. 2.067 or 2.07 m^2

125. 168 mg

126. 7.3 mg methotrexate

127. 201 mg

128. 15.58 mg

129. 178.6 μg dactinomycin

130. 2016 mg cyclophosphamide

131. 4800 mg gemcitabine
     160 mg cisplatin

132. 42.5 mL irinotecan injection
     68 mL fluorouracil injection

133. (a) 397.5 μg/day GM-CSF
     (b) 7.95 μg/mL GM-CSF
     (c) 50 mg human albumin
     (d) 1 mL human albumin (5%)

134. $3770.55

135. 2625 mL water

136. (a) 160 mg
     (b) 167.5 mg

137. 428.57 mg/m^2 acyclovir

138. 0.4 mg

139. 196 mL/hr

140. use all of a 2-mL (80 mg) syringe and 0.75 mL (30 mg) of a 1.5-mL syringe

141. use two 2-mL syringes (160 mg) and three 1.5-mL syringes (180 mg);
     bottle 1: one 2-mL syringe (80 mL) + 0.75 mL (30 mg) of one 1.5-mL syringe
     bottle 2: one 2-mL syringe (80 mg) + the remaining 0.75 mL (30 mg) used in bottle 1
     bottle 3: one full 1.5-mL syringe (60 mg) + 1.25 mL (50 mg) of another 1.5-mL syringe

142. 83.3 or 83 drops/min

143. 20.8 or 21 drops/min

144. 30.45 or 30 drops/min

145. 55.6 or 56 drops/min

146. 25 drops/min

147. (a) 9.136 or 9.14 mg ondansetron
     (b) 200 mL/hr
     (c) 66.7 or 67 drops/min

148. (a) 5000 µg
     (b) 1 vial

149. 63.6 or 64 drops/min

150. 54.2 or 54 drops/min

151. 8.3 or 8 drops/min

152. 69.44 or 69 drops/min

153. 3.06 mL/hr

154. 60 microdrops/mL

155. 294.12 µg nitroglycerin

156. (a) 2 µg/mL
         5 µg/mL
         10 µg/mL
         20 µg/mL
     (b) 0.05 mL/kg/min
         0.02 mL/kg/min
         0.01 mL/kg/min
         0.005 mL/kg/min

157. 1500.6 kcal
     56.25 g protein

158. 24.08 BMI

159. 3330 calories

160. 850 kcal

161. 61 mL/min

162. 5 L

163. 185 mg

164. (a) 0.417 or 0.42 mL
     (b) 2.5 days

165. 24 µg/mL

166. 2 drops

167. 8 hours

168. 44.19 mg/5 mL

169. (a) 0.42 mg
     (b) 20.6%
     (c) 116.64 hours

170. 0.4 or 40%

171. 0.69 day^{-1}

172. 1.19 hr

173. 0.05 mL ranibizumab injection

174. (b) 50 mL infusion fluid

175. 1.54 mL per minute

176. 23 drops per minute

177. (a) 39.6 mg vinblastine
     (b) 24 mg/m^2 vinblastine

178. 17 mg/m^2

179. 67.7 pounds

180. 1.25 mL sirolimus oral solution

181. 1.6 mL cefixime oral suspension

182. 25.5 mL/h

183. 23.4 mL zidovudine syrup

184. (a) 76.7 mL bevacizumab infusion
     (b) 2.6 mL/min

185. 3.87 mL/hr

186. 17.9 mL IV chlorothiazide sodium

187. 25 drops/minute D5W

188. 1.8 mL Augmentin oral suspension

189. hydrocortisone cream, 29.85 g and hydrocortisone powder, 0.15 g

REFERENCES

1. *International Journal of Pharmaceutical Compounding* 2000;4:212.
2. Allen LV Jr. Misoprostol 0.0027% mucoadhesive powder.
3. Paddock Laboratories. Compounding. Available at: http://www.paddocklabs.com/compounding.html. Accessed January 22, 2005.
4. *International Journal of Pharmaceutical Compounding* 2002;6:43.
5. Allen LV Jr. Diltiazem HCl 2% topical gel.
6. Allen LV Jr. *Allen's Compounded Formulations*. 2nd Ed. Washington, DC: American Pharmacists Association, 2004.
7. *International Journal of Pharmaceutical Compounding* 1998;2:443.
8. Allen LV Jr. Sertraline 7.5-mg capsules.
9. *International Journal of Pharmaceutical Compounding* 2000;4:380.
10. Allen LV Jr. Interferon ophthalmic solution.
11. Waddell JA, Solimando DA Jr. Gemcitabine and cisplatin (GC) regimen for advanced non-small-cell lung cancer. *Hospital Pharmacy* 2000;35:1169–1175.
12. Mayer MI, Solimando DA Jr, Waddell JA. Irinotecan, fluorouracil, and leucovorin for metastatic colorectal cancer. *Hospital Pharmacy* 2000;35:1274–1279.
13. Prince SJ. Calculations. *International Journal of Pharmaceutical Compounding* 2000;4:393.
14. Prince SJ. Calculations. *International Journal of Pharmaceutical Compounding* 2000;4:314.
15. Cohen MR, Pacetti S. Infant's death reinforces need for adequate check systems and ready-to-use medications forms. *Hospital Pharmacy* 1998;33:1306.
16. Prince SJ. In: Ansel HC, Prince SJ. *Pharmaceutical Calculations: The Pharmacist's Handbook*. Baltimore, MD: Lippincott Williams & Wilkins, 2004.

Index

Page numbers in *italic* denote figures; those followed by *t* denote tables.

TABLE OF ATOMIC WEIGHTS[a]

Name	Symbol	Atomic number	Atomic weight (accurate to 4 figures[b])	Approximate atomic weight
Actinium	Ac	89	*	227
Aluminum	Al	13	26.98	27
Americium	Am	95	*	243
Antimony	Sb	51	121.8	122
Argon	Ar	18	39.95	40
Arsenic	As	33	74.92	75
Astatine	At	85	*	210
Barium	Ba	56	137.3	137
Berkelium	Bk	97	*	247
Beryllium	Be	4	9.012	9
Bismuth	Bi	83	209.0	209
Bohrium	Bh	107	*	272
Boron	B	5	10.81	11
Bromine	Br	35	79.90	80
Cadmium	Cd	48	112.4	112
Calcium	Ca	20	40.08	40
Californium	Cf	98	*	251
Carbon	C	6	12.01	12
Cerium	Ce	58	140.1	140
Cesium	Cs	55	132.9	133
Chlorine	Cl	17	35.45	35
Chromium	Cr	24	52.00	52
Cobalt	Co	27	58.93	59
Copper	Cu	29	63.55	64
Curium	Cm	96	*	247
Darmstadtium	Ds	110	*	281
Dubnium	Db	105	*	268
Dysprosium	Dy	66	162.5	163
Einsteinium	Es	99	*	252
Erbium	Er	68	167.3	167
Europium	Eu	63	152.0	152
Fermium	Fm	100	*	257
Fluorine	F	9	19.00	19
Francium	Fr	87	*	223
Gadolinium	Gd	64	157.3	157
Gallium	Ga	31	69.72	70
Germanium	Ge	32	72.64	73
Gold	Au	79	197.0	197
Hafnium	Hf	72	178.5	179
Hassium	Hs	108	*	277
Helium	He	2	4.003	4
Holmium	Ho	67	164.9	165
Hydrogen	H	1	1.008	1
Indium	In	49	114.8	115
Iodine	I	53	126.9	127
Iridium	Ir	77	192.2	192
Iron	Fe	26	55.85	56
Krypton	Kr	36	83.80	84
Lanthanum	La	57	136.9	139
Lawrencium	Lr	103	*	260
Lead	Pb	82	207.2	207
Lithium	Li	3	6.941	7
Lutetium	Lu	71	175.0	175
Magnesium	Mg	12	24.31	24
Manganese	Mn	25	54.94	55
Meitnerium	Mt	109	*	276
Mendelevium	Md	101	*	258
Mercury	Hg	80	200.6	201
Molybdenum	Mo	42	95.94	96

[a] Table derived from Weiser ME. Pure and Applied Chemistry 2006; 78:2051–2066. Available at http://www.iupac.org/publications/pac/2006. Accessed October 4, 2008.
[b] When rounded off to 4-figure accuracy, these weights are practically identical to the similarly rounded-off weights in the older table based on oxygen = 16.0000.

Name	Symbol	Atomic number	Atomic weight (accurate to 4 figures[b])	Approximate atomic weight
Neodymium	Nd	60	144.2	144
Neon	Ne	10	20.18	20
Neptunium	Np	93	*	237
Nickel	Ni	28	58.69	59
Niobium	Nb	41	92.91	93
Nitrogen	N	7	14.01	14
Nobelium	No	102	*	259
Osmium	Os	76	190.2	190
Oxygen	O	8	16.00	16
Palladium	Pd	46	106.4	106
Phosphorus	P	15	30.97	31
Platinum	Pt	78	195.1	195
Plutonium	Pu	94	*	244
Polonium	Po	84	*	209
Potassium	K	19	39.10	39
Praseodymium	Pr	59	140.9	141
Promethium	Pm	61	*	145
Protactinium	Pa	91	231.0	231
Radium	Ra	88	226.0	226
Radon	Rn	86	*	222
Rhenium	Re	75	186.2	186
Rhodium	Rh	45	102.9	103
Roentgenium	Rg	111	*	280
Rubidium	Rb	37	85.47	85
Ruthenium	Ru	44	101.1	101
Rutherfordium	Rf	104	*	267
Samarium	Sm	62	150.4	150
Scandium	Sc	21	44.96	45
Seaborgium	Sg	106	*	271
Selenium	Se	34	78.96	79
Silicon	Si	14	28.09	28
Silver	Ag	47	107.9	108
Sodium	Na	11	22.99	23
Strontium	Sr	38	87.62	88
Sulfur	S	16	32.07	32
Tantalum	Ta	73	180.9	181
Technetium	Tc	43	*	98
Tellurium	Te	52	127.6	128
Terbium	Tb	65	158.9	159
Thallium	Tl	81	204.4	204
Thorium	Th	90	232.0	232
Thulium	Tm	69	168.9	169
Tin	Sn	50	118.7	119
Titanium	Ti	22	47.87	48
Tungsten	W	74	183.8	184
Unnilhexium	Unh	116	*	263
Unnilpentium	Unp	115	*	262
Unnilquadium	Unq	114	*	261
Ununbium	Uub	112	*	285
Ununoctium	Uuo	118	*	294
Ununtrium	Uut	113	*	284
Uranium	U	92	238.0	238
Vanadium	V	23	50.94	51
Xenon	Xe	54	131.3	131
Ytterbium	Yb	70	173.0	173
Yttrium	Y	39	88.91	89
Zinc	Zn	30	65.38	65
Zirconium	Zr	40	91.22	91

* The isotopic composition of natural or artificial radioactive elements usually varies in specific samples, depending upon their origin.